D0212133

THE ENCYCLOPEDIA OF
NORTH AMERICAN
INDIAN WARS,
1607–1890

THE ENCYCLOPEDIA OF NORTH AMERICAN INDIAN WARS 1607–1890

A Political, Social, and Military History

VOLUME III: DOCUMENTS

Dr. Spencer C. Tucker
Editor

James Arnold and Roberta Wiener
Editors, Documents Volume

Dr. Paul G. Pierpaoli Jr.
Associate Editor

Dr. David Coffey
Dr. Jim Piecuch
Assistant Editors

 ABC-CLIO

Santa Barbara, California   Denver, Colorado   Oxford, England

KALAMAZOO PUBLIC LIBRARY

Copyright © 2011 by ABC-CLIO, LLC

All rights reserved. No part of this publication may be reproduced, stored in a retrieval system, or transmitted, in any form or by any means, electronic, mechanical, photocopying, recording, or otherwise, except for the inclusion of brief quotations in a review, without prior permission in writing from the publisher.

Library of Congress Cataloging-in-Publication Data

The encyclopedia of North American Indian wars, 1607-1890 : a political, social, and military history / Spencer C. Tucker, editor ; James Arnold and Roberta Wiener, editors, documents volume ; Paul G. Pierpaoli, Jr., associate editor ; David Coffey, Jim Piecuch, assistant editors.
    p. cm.
  Includes bibliographical references and index.
  ISBN 978-1-85109-697-8 (hard back : alk. paper) -- ISBN 978-1-85109-603-9 (ebook)
  1. Indians of North America—Wars—Encyclopedias.   I. Tucker, Spencer, 1937–   II. Arnold, James R.   III. Wiener, Roberta, 1952–
  E81.E984   2011
  970.004'97003—dc23
                                                                                    2011027913

ISBN: 978-1-85109-697-8
EISBN: 978-1-85109-603-9

15 14 13 12 11   1 2 3 4 5

This book is also available on the World Wide Web as an eBook.
Visit www.abc-clio.com for details.

ABC-CLIO, LLC
130 Cremona Drive, P.O. Box 1911
Santa Barbara, California 93116-1911

This book is printed on acid-free paper ∞
Manufactured in the United States of America

Contents

List of Documents

Documents

1. Iroquois Constitution

Introduction

Probably dating back to the late 16th century, the Iroquois Constitution is attributed to the legendary leader Dekanawidah. Dekanawidah lived in what is now upstate New York from around 1550 to 1600, although his exact life dates remain obscure. Dekanawidah formed a confederation of several tribes in the region—including the Cayugas, Mohawks, Oneidas, Onondagas, and Senecas—all of which were subgroups of the Iroquois peoples. Sometimes referred to as the Five Nations, the Iroquois Confederation actually contained a varying number of tribes that frequently totaled more than five. After their defeat in the South in 1713, the Tuscaroras migrated north and joined the Iroquois Confederation, which then became known as the Six Nations. The confederation, which emerged as the strongest Native American group in North America at the time when European settlement began, controlled a huge expanse of territory across northern New York and Pennsylvania and featured the most sophisticated native government in North America. The Iroquois had long considered the French their enemies and thus allied themselves with the British. The Iroquois remained loyal to the British in the American Revolutionary War. Consequently, the American victory cost the Iroquois much of their territory and power. Authorities consider the Iroquois Constitution a remarkable statement of human rights, noting that some of its principles can be seen in the U.S. Constitution of 1787.

Primary Source

The Great Binding Law, Gayanashagowa

1. I am Dekanawidah and with the Five Nations' Confederate Lords I plant the Tree of Great Peace. I plant it in your territory, Adodarhoh, and the Onondaga Nation, in the territory of you who are Firekeepers.

I name the tree the Tree of the Great Long Leaves. Under the shade of this Tree of the Great Peace we spread the soft white feathery down of the globe thistle as seats for you, Adodarhoh, and your cousin Lords.

We place you upon those seats, spread soft with the feathery down of the globe thistle, there beneath the shade of the spreading branches of the Tree of Peace. There shall you sit and watch the Council Fire of the Confederacy of the Five Nations, and all the affairs of the Five Nations shall be transacted at this place before you, Adodarhoh, and your cousin Lords, by the Confederate Lords of the Five Nations.

2. Roots have spread out from the Tree of the Great Peace, one to the north, one to the east, one to the south and one to the west. The name of these roots is The Great White Roots and their nature is Peace and Strength.

If any man or any nation outside the Five Nations shall obey the laws of the Great Peace and make known their disposition to the Lords of the Confederacy, they may trace the Roots to the Tree and if their minds are clean and they are obedient and promise to obey the wishes of the Confederate Council, they shall be welcomed to take shelter beneath the Tree of the Long Leaves.

We place at the top of the Tree of the Long Leaves an Eagle who is able to see afar. If he sees in the distance any evil approaching or any danger threatening he will at once warn the people of the Confederacy.

3. To you Adodarhoh, the Onondaga cousin Lords, I and the other Confederate Lords have entrusted the caretaking and the watching of the Five Nation's Council Fire.

When there is any business to be transacted and the Confederate Council is not in session, a messenger shall be dispatched either to Adodarhoh, Hononwirehtonh or Skanawatih, Fire Keepers, or to their War Chiefs with a full statement of the case desired to be considered. Then shall Adodarhoh call his cousin (associate) Lords together and consider whether or not the case is of sufficient importance to demand the attention of the Confederate Council. If so, Adodarhoh shall dispatch messengers to summon all the Confederate Lords to assemble beneath the Tree of the Long Leaves.

When the Lords are assembled the Council Fire shall be kindled, but not with chestnut wood, and Adodarhoh shall formally open the Council.

Then shall Adodarhoh and his cousin Lords, the Fire Keepers, announce the subject for discussion.

The Smoke of the Confederate Council Fire shall ever ascend and pierce the sky so that other nations who may be allies may see the Council Fire of the Great Peace.

Adodarhoh and his cousin Lords are entrusted with the Keeping of the Council Fire.

4. You, Adodarhoh, and your thirteen cousin Lords, shall faithfully keep the space about the Council Fire clean and you shall allow neither dust nor dirt to accumulate. I lay a Long Wing before you as a broom. As a weapon against a crawling creature I lay a staff with you so that you may thrust it away from the Council Fire. If you fail to cast it out then call the rest of the United Lords to your aid.

5. The Council of the Mohawk shall be divided into three parties as follows: Tekarihoken, Ayonhwhathah and Shadekariwade are the first party; Sharenhowaneh, Deyoenhegwenh and Oghrenghrehgowah are the second party; and Dehennakrineh, Aghstawenserenthah and Shoskoharowaneh are the third party. The third party is to listen only to the discussion of the first and second parties and if an error is made or the proceeding is irregular they are to call attention to it, and when the case is right and properly decided by the two parties they shall confirm the decision of the two parties and refer the case to the Seneca Lords for their decision. When the Seneca Lords have decided in accord with the Mohawk Lords, the case or question shall be referred to the Cayuga and Oneida Lords on the opposite side of the house.

6. I, Dekanawidah, appoint the Mohawk Lords the heads and the leaders of the Five Nations Confederacy. The Mohawk Lords are the foundation of the Great Peace and it shall, therefore, be against the Great Binding Law to pass measures in the Confederate Council after the Mohawk Lords have protested against them.

No council of the Confederate Lords shall be legal unless all the Mohawk Lords are present.

7. Whenever the Confederate Lords shall assemble for the purpose of holding a council, the Onondaga Lords shall open it by expressing their gratitude to their cousin Lords and greeting them, and they shall make an address and offer thanks to the earth where men dwell, to the streams of water, the pools, the springs and the lakes, to the maize and the fruits, to the medicinal herbs and trees, to the forest trees for their usefulness, to the animals that serve as food and give their pelts for clothing, to the great winds and the lesser winds, to the Thunderers, to the Sun, the mighty warrior, to the moon, to the messengers of the Creator who reveal his wishes and to the Great Creator who dwells in the heavens above, who gives all the things useful to men, and who is the source and the ruler of health and life.

Then shall the Onondaga Lords declare the council open.

The council shall not sit after darkness has set in.

8. The Firekeepers shall formally open and close all councils of the Confederate Lords, and they shall pass upon all matters deliberated upon by the two sides and render their decision.

Every Onondaga Lord (or his deputy) must be present at every Confederate Council and must agree with the majority without unwarrantable dissent, so that a unanimous decision may be rendered.

If Adodarhoh or any of his cousin Lords are absent from a Confederate Council, any other Firekeeper may open and close the Council, but the Firekeepers present may not give any decisions, unless the matter is of small importance.

9. All the business of the Five Nations Confederate Council shall be conducted by the two combined bodies of Confederate Lords. First the question shall be passed upon by the Mohawk and Seneca Lords, then it shall be discussed and passed by the Oneida and Cayuga Lords. Their decisions shall then be referred to the Onondaga Lords, (Fire Keepers) for final judgement.

The same process shall obtain when a question is brought before the council by an individual or a War Chief.

10. In all cases the procedure must be as follows: when the Mohawk and Seneca Lords have unanimously agreed upon a question, they shall report their decision to the Cayuga and Oneida Lords who shall deliberate upon the question and report a unanimous decision to the Mohawk Lords. The Mohawk Lords will then report the standing of the case to the Firekeepers, who shall render a decision as they see fit in case of a disagreement by the two bodies, or confirm the decisions of the two bodies if they are identical. The Fire Keepers shall then report their decision to the Mohawk Lords who shall announce it to the open council.

11. If through any misunderstanding or obstinacy on the part of the Fire Keepers, they render a decision at variance with that of the Two Sides, the Two Sides shall reconsider the matter and if their

decisions are jointly the same as before they shall report to the Fire Keepers who are then compelled to confirm their joint decision.

12. When a case comes before the Onondaga Lords (Fire Keepers) for discussion and decision, Adodarho shall introduce the matter to his comrade Lords who shall then discuss it in their two bodies. Every Onondaga Lord except Hononwiretonh shall deliberate and he shall listen only. When a unanimous decision shall have been reached by the two bodies of Fire Keepers, Adodarho shall notify Hononwiretonh of the fact when he shall confirm it. He shall refuse to confirm a decision if it is not unanimously agreed upon by both sides of the Fire Keepers.

13. No Lord shall ask a question of the body of Confederate Lords when they are discussing a case, question or proposition. He may only deliberate in a low tone with the separate body of which he is a member.

14. When the Council of the Five Nation Lords shall convene they shall appoint a speaker for the day. He shall be a Lord of either the Mohawk, Onondaga or Seneca Nation.

The next day the Council shall appoint another speaker, but the first speaker may be reappointed if there is no objection, but a speaker's term shall not be regarded more than for the day.

15. No individual or foreign nation interested in a case, question or proposition shall have any voice in the Confederate Council except to answer a question put to him or them by the speaker for the Lords.

16. If the conditions which shall arise at any future time call for an addition to or change of this law, the case shall be carefully considered and if a new beam seems necessary or beneficial, the proposed change shall be voted upon and if adopted it shall be called "Added to the Rafters."

Rights, Duties and Qualifications of Lords

17. A bunch of a certain number of shell (wampum) strings each two spans in length shall be given to each of the female families in which the Lordship titles are vested. The right of bestowing the title shall be hereditary in the family of the females legally possessing the bunch of shell strings and the strings shall be the token that the females of the family have the proprietary right to the Lordship title for all time to come, subject to certain restrictions hereinafter mentioned.

18. If any Confederate Lord neglects or refuses to attend the Confederate Council, the other Lords of the Nation of which he is a member shall require their War Chief to request the female sponsors of the Lord so guilty of defection to demand his attendance of the Council. If he refuses, the women holding the title shall immediately select another candidate for the title.

No Lord shall be asked more than once to attend the Confederate Council.

19. If at any time it shall be manifest that a Confederate Lord has not in mind the welfare of the people or disobeys the rules of this Great Law, the men or women of the Confederacy, or both jointly, shall come to the Council and upbraid the erring Lord through his War Chief. If the complaint of the people through the War Chief is not heeded the first time it shall be uttered again and then if no attention is given a third complaint and warning shall be given. If the Lord is contumacious the matter shall go to the council of War Chiefs. The War Chiefs shall then divest the erring Lord of his title by order of the women in whom the titleship is vested. When the Lord is deposed the women shall notify the Confederate Lords through their War Chief, and the Confederate Lords shall sanction the act. The women will then select another of their sons as a candidate and the Lords shall elect him. Then shall the chosen one be installed by the Installation Ceremony.

When a Lord is to be deposed, his War Chief shall address him as follows:

"So you, _____, disregard and set at naught the warnings of your women relatives. So you fling the warnings over your shoulder to cast them behind you.

"Behold the brightness of the Sun and in the brightness of the Sun's light I depose you of your title and remove the sacred emblem of your Lordship title. I remove from your brow the deer's antlers, which was the emblem of your position and token of your nobility. I now depose you and return the antlers to the women whose heritage they are."

The War Chief shall now address the women of the deposed Lord and say:

"Mothers, as I have now deposed your Lord, I now return to you the emblem and the title of Lordship, therefore repossess them."

Again addressing himself to the deposed Lord he shall say:

"As I have now deposed and discharged you so you are now no longer Lord. You shall now go your way alone, the rest of the people of the Confederacy will not go with you, for we know not the kind of mind that possesses you. As the Creator has nothing to do with wrong so he will not come to rescue you from the precipice of destruction in which you have cast yourself. You shall never be restored to the position which you once occupied."

Then shall the War Chief address himself to the Lords of the Nation to which the deposed Lord belongs and say:

"Know you, my Lords, that I have taken the deer's antlers from the brow of _____, the emblem of his position and token of his greatness."

The Lords of the Confederacy shall then have no other alternative than to sanction the discharge of the offending Lord.

20. If a Lord of the Confederacy of the Five Nations should commit murder the other Lords of the Nation shall assemble at the place where the corpse lies and prepare to depose the criminal Lord. If it is impossible to meet at the scene of the crime the Lords shall discuss the matter at the next Council of their Nation and request their War Chief to depose the Lord guilty of crime, to "bury" his women relatives and to transfer the Lordship title to a sister family.

The War Chief shall address the Lord guilty of murder and say:

"So you, _____ (giving his name), did kill _____ (naming the slain man), with your own hands! You have committed a grave sin in the eyes of the Creator. Behold the bright light of the Sun, and in the brightness of the Sun's light I depose you of your title and remove the horns, the sacred emblems of your Lordship title. I remove from your brow the deer's antlers, which was the emblem of your position and token of your nobility. I now depose you and expel you and you shall depart at once from the territory of the Five Nations Confederacy and nevermore return again. We, the Five Nations Confederacy, moreover, bury your women relatives because the ancient Lordship title was never intended to have any union with bloodshed. Henceforth it shall not be their heritage. By the evil deed that you have done they have forfeited it forever."

The War Chief shall then hand the title to a sister family and he shall address it and say:

"Our mothers, _____, listen attentively while I address you on a solemn and important subject. I hereby transfer to you an ancient Lordship title for a great calamity has befallen it in the hands of the family of a former Lord. We trust that you, our mothers, will always guard it, and that you will warn your Lord always to be dutiful and to advise his people to ever live in love, peace and harmony that a great calamity may never happen again."

21. Certain physical defects in a Confederate Lord make him ineligible to sit in the Confederate Council. Such defects are infancy, idiocy, blindness, deafness, dumbness and impotency. When a Confederate Lord is restricted by any of these conditions, a deputy shall be appointed by his sponsors to act for him, but in case of extreme necessity the restricted Lord may exercise his rights.

22. If a Confederate Lord desires to resign his title he shall notify the Lords of the Nation of which he is a member of his intention. If his coactive Lords refuse to accept his resignation he may not resign his title.

A Lord in proposing to resign may recommend any proper candidate which recommendation shall be received by the Lords, but unless confirmed and nominated by the women who hold the title the candidate so named shall not be considered.

23. Any Lord of the Five Nations Confederacy may construct shell strings (or wampum belts) of any size or length as pledges or records of matters of national or international importance.

When it is necessary to dispatch a shell string by a War Chief or other messenger as the token of a summons, the messenger shall recite the contents of the string to the party to whom it is sent. That party shall repeat the message and return the shell string and if there has been a summons he shall make ready for the journey.

Any of the people of the Five Nations may use shells (or wampum) as the record of a pledge, contract or an agreement entered into and the same shall be binding as soon as shell strings shall have been exchanged by both parties.

24. The Lords of the Confederacy of the Five Nations shall be mentors of the people for all time. The thickness of their skin shall be seven spans—which is to say that they shall be proof against anger, offensive actions and criticism. Their hearts shall be full of peace and good will and their minds filled with a yearning for the welfare of the people of the Confederacy. With endless patience they shall carry out their duty and their firmness shall be tempered with a tenderness for their people. Neither anger nor fury shall find lodgment in their minds and all their words and actions shall be marked by calm deliberation.

25. If a Lord of the Confederacy should seek to establish any authority independent of the jurisdiction of the Confederacy of the Great Peace, which is the Five Nations, he shall be warned three times in open council, first by the women relatives, second by the men relatives and finally by the Lords of the Confederacy of the Nation to which he belongs. If the offending Lord is still obdurate he shall be dismissed by the War Chief of his nation for refusing to conform to the laws of the Great Peace. His nation shall then install the candidate nominated by the female name holders of his family.

26. It shall be the duty of all of the Five Nations Confederate Lords, from time to time as occasion demands, to act as mentors and spiritual guides of their people and remind them of their Creator's will and words. They shall say:

"Hearken, that peace may continue unto future days!

"Always listen to the words of the Great Creator, for he has spoken.

"United people, let not evil find lodging in your minds.

"For the Great Creator has spoken and the cause of Peace shall not become old.

"The cause of peace shall not die if you remember the Great Creator."

Every Confederate Lord shall speak words such as these to promote peace.

27. All Lords of the Five Nations Confederacy must be honest in all things. They must not idle or gossip, but be men possessing those honorable qualities that make true royaneh (nobility). It shall be a serious wrong for anyone to lead a Lord into trivial affairs, for the people must ever hold their Lords high in estimation out of respect to their honorable positions.

28. When a candidate Lord is to be installed he shall furnish four strings of shells (or wampum) one span in length bound together at one end. Such will constitute the evidence of his pledge to the Confederate Lords that he will live according to the constitution of the Great Peace and exercise justice in all affairs.

When the pledge is furnished the Speaker of the Council must hold the shell strings in his hand and address the opposite side of the Council Fire and he shall commence his address saying: "Now behold him. He has now become a Confederate Lord. See how splendid he looks." An address may then follow. At the end of it he shall send the bunch of shell strings to the opposite side and they shall be received as evidence of the pledge. Then shall the opposite side say:

"We now do crown you with the sacred emblem of the deer's antlers, the emblem of your Lordship. You shall now become a mentor of the people of the Five Nations. The thickness of your skin shall be seven spans—which is to say that you shall be proof against anger, offensive actions and criticism. Your heart shall be filled with peace and good will and your mind filled with a yearning for the welfare of the people of the Confederacy. With endless patience you shall carry out your duty and your firmness shall be tempered with tenderness for your people. Neither anger nor fury shall find lodgment in your mind and all your words and actions shall be marked with calm deliberation. In all of your deliberations in the Confederate Council, in your efforts at law making, in all your official acts, self-interest shall be cast into oblivion. Cast not over your shoulder behind you the warnings of the nephews and nieces should they chide you for any error or wrong you may do, but return to the way of the Great Law which is just and right. Look and listen for the welfare of the whole people and have always in view not only the present but also the coming generations, even those whose faces are yet beneath the surface of the ground—the unborn of the future Nation."

29. When a Lordship title is to be conferred, the candidate Lord shall furnish the cooked venison, the corn bread and the corn soup, together with other necessary things and the labor for the Conferring of Titles Festival.

30. The Lords of the Confederacy may confer the Lordship title upon a candidate whenever the Great Law is recited, if there be a candidate, for the Great Law speaks all the rules.

31. If a Lord of the Confederacy should become seriously ill and be thought near death, the women who are heirs of his title shall go to his house and lift his crown of deer antlers, the emblem of his Lordship, and place them at one side. If the Creator spares him and he rises from his bed of sickness he may rise with the antlers on his brow.

The following words shall be used to temporarily remove the antlers:

"Now our comrade Lord (or our relative Lord) the time has come when we must approach you in your illness. We remove for a time the deer's antlers from your brow, we remove the emblem of your Lordship title. The Great Law has decreed that no Lord should end his life with the antlers on his brow. We therefore lay them aside in the room. If the Creator spares you and you recover from your illness you shall rise from your bed with the antlers on your brow as before and you shall resume your duties as Lord of the Confederacy and you may labor again for the Confederate people."

32. If a Lord of the Confederacy should die while the Council of the Five Nations is in session the Council shall adjourn for ten days. No Confederate Council shall sit within ten days of the death of a Lord of the Confederacy.

If the Three Brothers (the Mohawk, the Onondaga and the Seneca) should lose one of their Lords by death, the Younger Brothers (the Oneida and the Cayuga) shall come to the surviving Lords of the Three Brothers on the tenth day and console them. If the Younger Brothers lose one of their Lords then the Three Brothers shall come to them and console them. And the consolation shall be the reading of the contents of the thirteen shell (wampum) strings of Ayonhwhathah. At the termination of this rite a successor shall be appointed, to be appointed by the women heirs of the Lordship title. If the women are not yet ready to place their nominee before the Lords the Speaker shall say, "Come let us go out." All shall leave the Council or the place of gathering. The installation shall then wait until such a time as the women are ready. The Speaker shall lead the way from the house by saying, "Let us depart to the edge of the woods and lie in waiting on our bellies."

When the women title holders shall have chosen one of their sons the Confederate Lords will assemble in two places, the Younger Brothers in one place and the Three Older Brothers in another. The Lords who are to console the mourning Lords shall choose one of their number to sing the Pacification Hymn as they journey to the sorrowing Lords. The singer shall lead the way and the Lords and the people shall follow. When they reach the sorrowing Lords they shall hail the candidate Lord and perform the rite of Conferring the Lordship Title.

33. When a Confederate Lord dies, the surviving relatives shall immediately dispatch a messenger, a member of another clan, to the Lords in another locality. When the runner comes within hailing distance of the locality he shall utter a sad wail, thus: "Kwa-ah, Kwa-ah, Kwa-ah!" The sound shall be repeated three times and then again and again at intervals as many times as the distance may require. When the runner arrives at the settlement the people shall assemble and one must ask him the nature of his sad message. He shall then say, "Let us consider." Then he shall tell them of the death of the Lord. He shall deliver to them a string of shells (wampum) and say "Here is the testimony, you have heard the message." He may then return home.

It now becomes the duty of the Lords of the locality to send runners to other localities and each locality shall send other messengers until all Lords are notified. Runners shall travel day and night.

34. If a Lord dies and there is no candidate qualified for the office in the family of the women title holders, the Lords of the Nation shall give the title into the hands of a sister family in the clan until such a time as the original family produces a candidate, when the title shall be restored to the rightful owners.

No Lordship title may be carried into the grave. The Lords of the Confederacy may dispossess a dead Lord of his title even at the grave.

Election of Pine Tree Chiefs

35. Should any man of the Nation assist with special ability or show great interest in the affairs of the Nation, if he proves himself wise, honest and worthy of confidence, the Confederate Lords may elect him to a seat with them and he may sit in the Confederate Council. He shall be proclaimed a 'Pine Tree sprung up for the Nation' and shall be installed as such at the next assembly for the installation of Lords. Should he ever do anything contrary to the rules of the Great Peace, he may not be deposed from office—no one shall cut him down—but thereafter everyone shall be deaf to his voice and his advice. Should he resign his seat and title no one shall prevent him. A Pine Tree chief has no authority to name a successor nor is his title hereditary.

Names, Duties and Rights of War Chiefs

36. The title names of the Chief Confederate Lords' War Chiefs shall be: Ayonwaehs, War Chief under Lord Takarihoken (Mohawk), Kahonwahdironh, War Chief under Lord Odatshedeh (Oneida), Ayendes, War Chief under Lord Adodarhoh (Onondaga), Wenenhs, War Chief under Lord Dekaenyonh (Cayuga), Shoneradowaneh, War Chief under Lord Skanyadariyo (Seneca).

The women heirs of each head Lord's title shall be the heirs of the War Chief's title of their respective Lord.

The War Chiefs shall be selected from the eligible sons of the female families holding the head Lordship titles.

37. There shall be one War Chief for each Nation and their duties shall be to carry messages for their Lords and to take up the arms of war in case of emergency. They shall not participate in the proceedings of the Confederate Council but shall watch its progress and in case of an erroneous action by a Lord they shall receive the complaints of the people and convey the warnings of the women to him. The people who wish to convey messages to the Lords in the Confederate Council shall do so through the War Chief of their Nation. It shall ever be his duty to lay the cases, questions and propositions of the people before the Confederate Council.

38. When a War Chief dies another shall be installed by the same rite as that by which a Lord is installed.

39. If a War Chief acts contrary to instructions or against the provisions of the Laws of the Great Peace, doing so in the capacity of his office, he shall be deposed by his women relatives and by his men relatives. Either the women or the men alone or jointly may act in such a case. The women title holders shall then choose another candidate.

40. When the Lords of the Confederacy take occasion to dispatch a messenger in behalf of the Confederate Council, they shall wrap up any matter they may send and instruct the messenger to remember his errand, to turn not aside but to proceed faithfully to his destination and deliver his message according to every instruction.

41. If a message borne by a runner is the warning of an invasion he shall whoop, "Kwa-ah, Kwa-ah," twice and repeat at short intervals; then again at a longer interval.

If a human being is found dead, the finder shall not touch the body but return home immediately shouting at short intervals, "Koo-weh!"

Clans and Consanguinity

42. Among the Five Nations and their posterity there shall be the following original clans: Great Name Bearer, Ancient Name Bearer, Great Bear, Ancient Bear, Turtle, Painted Turtle, Standing Rock, Large Plover, Deer, Pigeon Hawk, Eel, Ball, Opposite-Side-of-the-Hand, and Wild Potatoes. These clans distributed through their respective Nations, shall be the sole owners and holders of the soil of the country and in them is it vested as a birthright.

43. People of the Five Nations members of a certain clan shall recognize every other member of that clan, irrespective of the Nation, as relatives. Men and women, therefore, members of the same clan are forbidden to marry.

44. The lineal descent of the people of the Five Nations shall run in the female line. Women shall be considered the progenitors of the Nation. They shall own the land and the soil. Men and women shall follow the status of the mother.

45. The women heirs of the Confederated Lordship titles shall be called Royaneh (Noble) for all time to come.

46. The women of the Forty Eight (now fifty) Royaneh families shall be the heirs of the Authorized Names for all time to come.

When an infant of the Five Nations is given an Authorized Name at the Midwinter Festival or at the Ripe Corn Festival, one in the cousinhood of which the infant is a member shall be appointed a speaker. He shall then announce to the opposite cousinhood the names of the father and the mother of the child together with the clan of the mother. Then the speaker shall announce the child's name twice. The uncle of the child shall then take the child in his arms and walking up and down the room shall sing: "My head is firm, I am of the Confederacy." As he sings the opposite cousinhood shall respond by chanting, "Hyenh, Hyenh, Hyenh, Hyenh," until the song is ended.

47. If the female heirs of a Confederate Lord's title become extinct, the title right shall be given by the Lords of the Confederacy to the sister family whom they shall elect and that family shall hold the name and transmit it to their (female) heirs, but they shall not appoint any of their sons as a candidate for a title until all the eligible men of the former family shall have died or otherwise have become ineligible.

48. If all the heirs of a Lordship title become extinct, and all the families in the clan, then the title shall be given by the Lords of the Confederacy to the family in a sister clan whom they shall elect.

49. If any of the Royaneh women, heirs of a titleship, shall willfully withhold a Lordship or other title and refuse to bestow it, or if such heirs abandon, forsake or despise their heritage, then shall such women be deemed buried and their family extinct. The titleship shall then revert to a sister family or clan upon application and complaint. The Lords of the Confederacy shall elect the family or clan which shall in future hold the title.

50. The Royaneh women of the Confederacy heirs of the Lordship titles shall elect two women of their family as cooks for the Lord when the people shall assemble at his house for business or other purposes.

It is not good nor honorable for a Confederate Lord to allow his people whom he has called to go hungry.

51. When a Lord holds a conference in his home, his wife, if she wishes, may prepare the food for the Union Lords who assemble with him. This is an honorable right which she may exercise and an expression of her esteem.

52. The Royaneh women, heirs of the Lordship titles, shall, should it be necessary, correct and admonish the holders of their titles. Those only who attend the Council may do this and those who do not shall not object to what has been said nor strive to undo the action.

53. When the Royaneh women, holders of a Lordship title, select one of their sons as a candidate, they shall select one who is trustworthy, of good character, of honest disposition, one who manages his own affairs, supports his own family, if any, and who has proven a faithful man to his Nation.

54. When a Lordship title becomes vacant through death or other cause, the Royaneh women of the clan in which the title is hereditary shall hold a council and shall choose one from among their sons to fill the office made vacant. Such a candidate shall not be the father of any Confederate Lord. If the choice is unanimous the name is referred to the men relatives of the clan. If they should disapprove it shall be their duty to select a candidate from among their own number. If then the men and women are unable to decide which of the two candidates shall be named, then the matter shall be referred to the Confederate Lords in the Clan. They shall decide which candidate shall be named. If the men and the women agree to a candidate his name shall be referred to the sister clans for confirmation. If the sister clans confirm the choice, they shall refer their action to their Confederate Lords who shall ratify the choice and present it to their cousin Lords, and if the cousin Lords confirm the name then the candidate shall be installed by the proper ceremony for the conferring of Lordship titles.

Official Symbolism

55. A large bunch of shell strings, in the making of which the Five Nations Confederate Lords have equally contributed, shall symbolize the completeness of the union and certify the pledge of the nations represented by the Confederate Lords of the Mohawk, the Oneida, the Onondaga, the Cayuga and the Seneca, that all are united and formed into one body or union called the Union of the Great Law, which they have established.

A bunch of shell strings is to be the symbol of the council fire of the Five Nations Confederacy. And the Lord whom the council of Fire Keepers shall appoint to speak for them in opening the council shall hold the strands of shells in his hands when speaking. When he finishes speaking he shall deposit the strings on an elevated place (or pole) so that all the assembled Lords and the people may see it and know that the council is open and in progress.

When the council adjourns the Lord who has been appointed by his comrade Lords to close it shall take the strands of shells in his hands and address the assembled Lords. Thus will the council adjourn until such time and place as appointed by the council. Then shall the shell strings be placed in a place for safekeeping.

Every five years the Five Nations Confederate Lords and the people shall assemble together and shall ask one another if their minds are still in the same spirit of unity for the Great Binding Law and if any of the Five Nations shall not pledge continuance and steadfastness to the pledge of unity then the Great Binding Law shall dissolve.

56. Five strings of shell tied together as one shall represent the Five Nations. Each string shall represent one territory and the whole a completely united territory known as the Five Nations Confederate territory.

57. Five arrows shall be bound together very strong and each arrow shall represent one nation. As the five arrows are strongly bound

this shall symbolize the complete union of the nations. Thus are the Five Nations united completely and enfolded together, united into one head, one body and one mind. Therefore they shall labor, legislate and council together for the interest of future generations.

The Lords of the Confederacy shall eat together from one bowl the feast of cooked beaver's tail. While they are eating they are to use no sharp utensils for if they should they might accidentally cut one another and bloodshed would follow. All measures must be taken to prevent the spilling of blood in any way.

58. There are now the Five Nations Confederate Lords standing with joined hands in a circle. This signifies and provides that should any one of the Confederate Lords leave the council and this Confederacy his crown of deer's horns, the emblem of his Lordship title, together with his birthright, shall lodge on the arms of the Union Lords whose hands are so joined. He forfeits his title and the crown falls from his brow but it shall remain in the Confederacy.

A further meaning of this is that if any time any one of the Confederate Lords choose to submit to the law of a foreign people he is no longer in but out of the Confederacy, and persons of this class shall be called "They have alienated themselves." Likewise such persons who submit to laws of foreign nations shall forfeit all birthrights and claims on the Five Nations Confederacy and territory.

You, the Five Nations Confederate Lords, be firm so that if a tree falls on your joined arms it shall not separate or weaken your hold. So shall the strength of the union be preserved.

59. A bunch of wampum shells on strings, three spans of the hand in length, the upper half of the bunch being white and the lower half black, and formed from equal contributions of the men of the Five Nations, shall be a token that the men have combined themselves into one head, one body and one thought, and it shall also symbolize their ratification of the peace pact of the Confederacy, whereby the Lords of the Five Nations have established the Great Peace.

The white portion of the shell strings represent the women and the black portion the men. The black portion, furthermore, is a token of power and authority vested in the men of the Five Nations.

This string of wampum vests the people with the right to correct their erring Lords. In case a part or all the Lords pursue a course not vouched for by the people and heed not the third warning of their women relatives, then the matter shall be taken to the General Council of the women of the Five Nations. If the Lords notified and warned three times fail to heed, then the case falls into the hands of the men of the Five Nations. The War Chiefs shall then, by right of such power and authority, enter the open council to warn the Lord or Lords to return from the wrong course. If the Lords heed the warning they shall say, "we will reply tomorrow." If then an answer is returned in favor of justice and in accord with

this Great Law, then the Lords shall individually pledge themselves again by again furnishing the necessary shells for the pledge. Then shall the War Chief or Chiefs exhort the Lords urging them to be just and true.

Should it happen that the Lords refuse to heed the third warning, then two courses are open: either the men may decide in their council to depose the Lord or Lords or to club them to death with war clubs. Should they in their council decide to take the first course the War Chief shall address the Lord or Lords, saying: "Since you the Lords of the Five Nations have refused to return to the procedure of the Constitution, we now declare your seats vacant, we take off your horns, the token of your Lordship, and others shall be chosen and installed in your seats, therefore vacate your seats."

Should the men in their council adopt the second course, the War Chief shall order his men to enter the council, to take positions beside the Lords, sitting between them wherever possible. When this is accomplished the War Chief holding in his outstretched hand a bunch of black wampum strings shall say to the erring Lords: "So now, Lords of the Five United Nations, harken to these last words from your men. You have not heeded the warnings of the women relatives, you have not heeded the warnings of the General Council of women and you have not heeded the warnings of the men of the nations, all urging you to return to the right course of action. Since you are determined to resist and to withhold justice from your people there is only one course for us to adopt." At this point the War Chief shall let drop the bunch of black wampum and the men shall spring to their feet and club the erring Lords to death. Any erring Lord may submit before the War Chief lets fall the black wampum. Then his execution is withheld.

The black wampum here used symbolizes that the power to execute is buried but that it may be raised up again by the men. It is buried but when occasion arises they may pull it up and derive their power and authority to act as here described.

60. A broad dark belt of wampum of thirty-eight rows, having a white heart in the center, on either side of which are two white squares all connected with the heart by white rows of beads shall be the emblem of the unity of the Five Nations.

The first of the squares on the left represents the Mohawk nation and its territory; the second square on the left and the one near the heart, represents the Oneida nation and its territory; the white heart in the middle represents the Onondaga nation and its territory, and it also means that the heart of the Five Nations is single in its loyalty to the Great Peace, that the Great Peace is lodged in the heart (meaning the Onondaga Lords), and that the Council Fire is to burn there for the Five Nations, and further, it means that the authority is given to advance the cause of peace whereby hostile nations out of the Confederacy shall cease warfare; the white square to the right of the heart represents the Cayuga nation and its territory and the fourth and last white square represents the Seneca nation and its territory.

White shall here symbolize that no evil or jealous thoughts shall creep into the minds of the Lords while in Council under the Great Peace. White, the emblem of peace, love, charity and equity surrounds and guards the Five Nations.

61. Should a great calamity threaten the generations rising and living of the Five United Nations, then he who is able to climb to the top of the Tree of the Great Long Leaves may do so. When, then, he reaches the top of the tree he shall look about in all directions, and, should he see that evil things indeed are approaching, then he shall call to the people of the Five United Nations assembled beneath the Tree of the Great Long Leaves and say: "A calamity threatens your happiness."

Then shall the Lords convene in council and discuss the impending evil.

When all the truths relating to the trouble shall be fully known and found to be truths, then shall the people seek out a Tree of Ka-hon-ka-ah-go-nah, and when they shall find it they shall assemble their heads together and lodge for a time between its roots. Then, their labors being finished, they may hope for happiness for many days after.

62. When the Confederate Council of the Five Nations declares for a reading of the belts of shell calling to mind these laws, they shall provide for the reader a specially made mat woven of the fibers of wild hemp. The mat shall not be used again, for such formality is called the honoring of the importance of the law.

63. Should two sons of opposite sides of the council fire agree in a desire to hear the reciting of the laws of the Great Peace and so refresh their memories in the way ordained by the founder of the Confederacy, they shall notify Adodarho. He then shall consult with five of his coactive Lords and they in turn shall consult with their eight brethren. Then should they decide to accede to the request of the two sons from opposite sides of the Council Fire, Adodarho shall send messengers to notify the Chief Lords of each of the Five Nations. Then they shall dispatch their War Chiefs to notify their brother and cousin Lords of the meeting and its time and place.

When all have come and have assembled, Adodarhoh, in conjunction with his cousin Lords, shall appoint one Lord who shall repeat the laws of the Great Peace. Then shall they announce whom they have chosen to repeat the laws of the Great Peace to the two sons. Then shall the chosen one repeat the laws of the Great Peace.

64. At the ceremony of the installation of Lords if there is only one expert speaker and singer of the law and the Pacification Hymn to stand at the council fire, then when this speaker and singer has finished addressing one side of the fire he shall go to the opposite side and reply to his own speech and song. He shall thus act for both sides of the fire until the entire ceremony has been completed. Such a speaker and singer shall be termed the "Two Faced" because he speaks and sings for both sides of the fire.

65. I, Dekanawida, and the Union Lords, now uproot the tallest pine tree and into the cavity thereby made we cast all weapons of war. Into the depths of the earth, down into the deep underearth currents of water flowing to unknown regions we cast all the weapons of strife. We bury them from sight and we plant again the tree. Thus shall the Great Peace be established and hostilities shall no longer be known between the Five Nations but peace to the United People.

Laws of Adoption

66. The father of a child of great comeliness, learning, ability or specially loved because of some circumstance may, at the will of the child's clan, select a name from his own (the father's) clan and bestow it by ceremony, such as is provided. This naming shall be only temporary and shall be called, "A name hung about the neck."

67. Should any person, a member of the Five Nations' Confederacy, specially esteem a man or woman of another clan or of a foreign nation, he may choose a name and bestow it upon that person so esteemed. The naming shall be in accord with the ceremony of bestowing names. Such a name is only a temporary one and shall be called "A name hung about the neck." A short string of shells shall be delivered with the name as a record and a pledge.

68. Should any member of the Five Nations, a family or person belonging to a foreign nation submit a proposal for adoption into a clan of one of the Five Nations, he or they shall furnish a string of shells, a span in length, as a pledge to the clan into which he or they wish to be adopted. The Lords of the nation shall then consider the proposal and submit a decision.

69. Any member of the Five Nations who through esteem or other feeling wishes to adopt an individual, a family or number of families may offer adoption to him or them and if accepted the matter shall be brought to the attention of the Lords for confirmation and the Lords must confirm adoption.

70. When the adoption of anyone shall have been confirmed by the Lords of the Nation, the Lords shall address the people of their nation and say: "Now you of our nation, be informed that such a person, such a family or such families have ceased forever to bear their birth nation's name and have buried it in the depths of the earth. Henceforth let no one of our nation ever mention the original name or nation of their birth. To do so will be to hasten the end of our peace."

Laws of Emigration

71. When any person or family belonging to the Five Nations desires to abandon their birth nation and the territory of the Five Nations, they shall inform the Lords of their nation and the Confederate Council of the Five Nations shall take cognizance of it.

72. When any person or any of the people of the Five Nations emigrate and reside in a region distant from the territory of the Five Nations Confederacy, the Lords of the Five Nations at will may send a messenger carrying a broad belt of black shells and when the messenger arrives he shall call the people together or address them personally displaying the belt of shells and they shall know that this is an order for them to return to their original homes and to their council fires.

Rights of Foreign Nations

73. The soil of the earth from one end of the land to the other is the property of the people who inhabit it. By birthright the Ongwehonweh (Original beings) are the owners of the soil which they own and occupy and none other may hold it. The same law has been held from the oldest times.

The Great Creator has made us of the one blood and of the same soil he made us and as only different tongues constitute different nations he established different hunting grounds and territories and made boundary lines between them.

74. When any alien nation or individual is admitted into the Five Nations the admission shall be understood only to be a temporary one. Should the person or nation create loss, do wrong or cause suffering of any kind to endanger the peace of the Confederacy, the Confederate Lords shall order one of their war chiefs to reprimand him or them and if a similar offence is again committed the offending party or parties shall be expelled from the territory of the Five United Nations.

75. When a member of an alien nation comes to the territory of the Five Nations and seeks refuge and permanent residence, the Lords of the Nation to which he comes shall extend hospitality and make him a member of the nation. Then shall he be accorded equal rights and privileges in all matters except as after mentioned.

76. No body of alien people who have been adopted temporarily shall have a vote in the council of the Lords of the Confederacy, for only they who have been invested with Lordship titles may vote in the Council. Aliens have nothing by blood to make claim to a vote and should they have it, not knowing all the traditions of the Confederacy, might go against its Great Peace. In this manner the Great Peace would be endangered and perhaps be destroyed.

77. When the Lords of the Confederacy decide to admit a foreign nation and an adoption is made, the Lords shall inform the adopted nation that its admission is only temporary. They shall also say to the nation that it must never try to control, to interfere with or to injure the Five Nations nor disregard the Great Peace or any of its rules or customs. That in no way should they cause disturbance or injury. Then should the adopted nation disregard these injunctions, their adoption shall be annulled and they shall be expelled.

The expulsion shall be in the following manner: The council shall appoint one of their War Chiefs to convey the message of annulment and he shall say, "You (naming the nation) listen to me while I speak. I am here to inform you again of the will of the Five Nations' Council. It was clearly made known to you at a former time. Now the Lords of the Five Nations have decided to expel you and cast you out. We disown you now and annul your adoption. Therefore you must look for a path in which to go and lead away all your people. It was you, not we, who committed wrong and caused this sentence of annulment. So then go your way and depart from the territory of the Five Nations and from the Confederacy."

78. Whenever a foreign nation enters the Confederacy or accepts the Great Peace, the Five Nations and the foreign nation shall enter into an agreement and compact by which the foreign nation shall endeavor to persuade other nations to accept the Great Peace.

Rights and Powers of War

79. Skanawatih shall be vested with a double office, duty and with double authority. One-half of his being shall hold the Lordship title and the other half shall hold the title of War Chief. In the event of war he shall notify the five War Chiefs of the Confederacy and command them to prepare for war and have their men ready at the appointed time and place for engagement with the enemy of the Great Peace.

80. When the Confederate Council of the Five Nations has for its object the establishment of the Great Peace among the people of an outside nation and that nation refuses to accept the Great Peace, then by such refusal they bring a declaration of war upon themselves from the Five Nations. Then shall the Five Nations seek to establish the Great Peace by a conquest of the rebellious nation.

81. When the men of the Five Nations, now called forth to become warriors, are ready for battle with an obstinate opposing nation that has refused to accept the Great Peace, then one of the five War Chiefs shall be chosen by the warriors of the Five Nations to lead the army into battle. It shall be the duty of the War Chief so chosen to come before his warriors and address them. His aim shall be to impress upon them the necessity of good behavior and strict obedience to all the commands of the War Chiefs. He shall deliver an oration exhorting them with great zeal to be brave and courageous and never to be guilty of cowardice. At the conclusion of his oration he shall march forward and commence the War Song and he shall sing:

Now I am greatly surprised
And, therefore I shall use it—
The power of my War Song.
I am of the Five Nations
And I shall make supplication

To the Almighty Creator.
He has furnished this army.
My warriors shall be mighty
In the strength of the Creator.
Between him and my song they are
For it was he who gave the song
This war song that I sing!

82. When the warriors of the Five Nations are on an expedition against an enemy, the War Chief shall sing the War Song as he approaches the country of the enemy and not cease until his scouts have reported that the army is near the enemies' lines when the War Chief shall approach with great caution and prepare for the attack.

83. When peace shall have been established by the termination of the war against a foreign nation, then the War Chief shall cause all the weapons of war to be taken from the nation. Then shall the Great Peace be established and that nation shall observe all the rules of the Great Peace for all time to come.

84. Whenever a foreign nation is conquered or has by their own will accepted the Great Peace their own system of internal government may continue, but they must cease all warfare against other nations.

85. Whenever a war against a foreign nation is pushed until that nation is about exterminated because of its refusal to accept the Great Peace and if that nation shall by its obstinacy become exterminated, all their rights, property and territory shall become the property of the Five Nations.

86. Whenever a foreign nation is conquered and the survivors are brought into the territory of the Five Nations' Confederacy and placed under the Great Peace the two shall be known as the Conqueror and the Conquered. A symbolic relationship shall be devised and be placed in some symbolic position. The conquered nation shall have no voice in the councils of the Confederacy in the body of the Lords.

87. When the War of the Five Nations on a foreign rebellious nation is ended, peace shall be restored to that nation by a withdrawal of all their weapons of war by the War Chief of the Five Nations. When all the terms of peace shall have been agreed upon a state of friendship shall be established.

88. When the proposition to establish the Great Peace is made to a foreign nation it shall be done in mutual council. The foreign nation is to be persuaded by reason and urged to come into the Great Peace. If the Five Nations fail to obtain the consent of the nation at the first council a second council shall be held and upon a second failure a third council shall be held and this third council shall end the peaceful methods of persuasion. At the third council the War Chief of the Five nations shall address the Chief of the foreign nation and request him three times to accept the Great Peace. If refusal steadfastly follows the War Chief shall let the bunch of white lake shells drop from his outstretched hand to the ground and shall bound quickly forward and club the offending chief to death. War shall thereby be declared and the War Chief shall have his warriors at his back to meet any emergency. War must continue until the contest is won by the Five Nations.

89. When the Lords of the Five Nations propose to meet in conference with a foreign nation with proposals for an acceptance of the Great Peace, a large band of warriors shall conceal themselves in a secure place safe from the espionage of the foreign nation but as near at hand as possible. Two warriors shall accompany the Union Lord who carries the proposals and these warriors shall be especially cunning. Should the Lord be attacked, these warriors shall hasten back to the army of warriors with the news of the calamity which fell through the treachery of the foreign nation.

90. When the Five Nations' Council declares war any Lord of the Confederacy may enlist with the warriors by temporarily renouncing his sacred Lordship title which he holds through the election of his women relatives. The title then reverts to them and they may bestow it upon another temporarily until the war is over when the Lord, if living, may resume his title and seat in the Council.

91. A certain wampum belt of black beads shall be the emblem of the authority of the Five War Chiefs to take up the weapons of war and with their men to resist invasion. This shall be called a war in defense of the territory.

Treason or Secession of a Nation

92. If a nation, part of a nation, or more than one nation within the Five Nations should in any way endeavor to destroy the Great Peace by neglect or violating its laws and resolve to dissolve the Confederacy, such a nation or such nations shall be deemed guilty of treason and called enemies of the Confederacy and the Great Peace.

It shall then be the duty of the Lords of the Confederacy who remain faithful to resolve to warn the offending people. They shall be warned once and if a second warning is necessary they shall be driven from the territory of the Confederacy by the War Chiefs and his men.

Rights of the People of the Five Nations

93. Whenever a specially important matter or a great emergency is presented before the Confederate Council and the nature of the matter affects the entire body of the Five Nations, threatening their utter ruin, then the Lords of the Confederacy must submit

the matter to the decision of their people and the decision of the people shall affect the decision of the Confederate Council. This decision shall be a confirmation of the voice of the people.

94. The men of every clan of the Five Nations shall have a Council Fire ever burning in readiness for a council of the clan. When it seems necessary for a council to be held to discuss the welfare of the clans, then the men may gather about the fire. This council shall have the same rights as the council of the women.

95. The women of every clan of the Five Nations shall have a Council Fire ever burning in readiness for a council of the clan. When in their opinion it seems necessary for the interest of the people they shall hold a council and their decisions and recommendations shall be introduced before the Council of the Lords by the War Chief for its consideration.

96. All the Clan council fires of a nation or of the Five Nations may unite into one general council fire, or delegates from all the council fires may be appointed to unite in a general council for discussing the interests of the people. The people shall have the right to make appointments and to delegate their power to others of their number. When their council shall have come to a conclusion on any matter, their decision shall be reported to the Council of the Nation or to the Confederate Council (as the case may require) by the War Chief or the War Chiefs.

97. Before the real people united their nations, each nation had its council fires. Before the Great Peace their councils were held. The five Council Fires shall continue to burn as before and they are not quenched. The Lords of each nation in future shall settle their nation's affairs at this council fire governed always by the laws and rules of the council of the Confederacy and by the Great Peace.

98. If either a nephew or a niece see an irregularity in the performance of the functions of the Great Peace and its laws, in the Confederate Council or in the conferring of Lordship titles in an improper way, through their War Chief they may demand that such actions become subject to correction and that the matter conform to the ways prescribed by the laws of the Great Peace.

Religious Ceremonies Protected

99. The rites and festivals of each nation shall remain undisturbed and shall continue as before because they were given by the people of old times as useful and necessary for the good of men.

100. It shall be the duty of the Lords of each brotherhood to confer at the approach of the time of the Midwinter Thanksgiving and to notify their people of the approaching festival. They shall hold a council over the matter and arrange its details and begin the Thanksgiving five days after the moon of Dis-ko-nah is new. The people shall assemble at the appointed place and the nephews shall notify the people of the time and place. From the beginning to the end the Lords shall preside over the Thanksgiving and address the people from time to time.

101. It shall be the duty of the appointed managers of the Thanksgiving festivals to do all that is needed for carrying out the duties of the occasions.

The recognized festivals of Thanksgiving shall be the Midwinter Thanksgiving, the Maple or Sugar-making Thanksgiving, the Raspberry Thanksgiving, the Strawberry Thanksgiving, the Corn-planting Thanksgiving, the Corn Hoeing Thanksgiving, the Little Festival of Green Corn, the Great Festival of Ripe Corn and the complete Thanksgiving for the Harvest.

Each nation's festivals shall be held in their Long Houses.

102. When the Thanksgiving for the Green Corn comes the special managers, both the men and women, shall give it careful attention and do their duties properly.

103. When the Ripe Corn Thanksgiving is celebrated the Lords of the Nation must give it the same attention as they give to the Midwinter Thanksgiving.

104. Whenever any man proves himself by his good life and his knowledge of good things, naturally fitted as a teacher of good things, he shall be recognized by the Lords as a teacher of peace and religion and the people shall hear him.

The Installation Song

105. The song used in installing the new Lord of the Confederacy shall be sung by Adodarhoh and it shall be:

"Haii, haii Agwah wi-yoh
"   " A-kon-he-watha
"   " Ska-we-ye-se-go-wah
"   " Yon-gwa-wih
"   " Ya-kon-he-wa-tha

Haii, haii It is good indeed
"   " (That) a broom,—
"   " A great wing,
"   " It is given me
"   " For a sweeping instrument."

106. Whenever a person properly entitled desires to learn the Pacification Song he is privileged to do so but he must prepare a feast at which his teachers may sit with him and sing. The feast is provided that no misfortune may befall them for singing the song on an occasion when no chief is installed.

Protection of the House

107. A certain sign shall be known to all the people of the Five Nations which shall denote that the owner or occupant of a house is absent. A stick or pole in a slanting or leaning position shall indicate this and be the sign. Every person not entitled to enter the house by right of living within it upon seeing such a sign shall not approach the house either by day or by night but shall keep as far away as his business will permit.

Funeral Addresses

108. At the funeral of a Lord of the Confederacy, say: "Now we become reconciled as you start away. You were once a Lord of the Five Nations' Confederacy and the United People trusted you. Now we release you for it is true that it is no longer possible for us to walk about together on the earth. Now, therefore, we lay it (the body) here. Here we lay it away. Now then we say to you, 'Persevere onward to the place where the Creator dwells in peace. Let not the things of the earth hinder you. Let nothing that transpired while yet you lived hinder you. In hunting you once took delight; in the game of Lacrosse you once took delight and in the feasts and pleasant occasions your mind was amused, but now do not allow thoughts of these things to give you trouble. Let not your relatives hinder you and also let not your friends and associates trouble your mind. Regard none of these things.'

"Now then, in turn, you here present who were related to this man and you who were his friends and associates, behold the path that is yours also! Soon we ourselves will be left in that place. For this reason hold yourselves in restraint as you go from place to place. In your actions and in your conversation do no idle thing. Speak not idle talk neither gossip. Be careful of this and speak not and do not give way to evil behavior. One year is the time that you must abstain from unseemly levity but if you can not do this for ceremony, ten days is the time to regard these things for respect."

109. At the funeral of a War Chief, say: "Now we become reconciled as you start away. You were once a War Chief of the Five Nations' Confederacy and the United People trusted you as their guard from the enemy." (The remainder is the same as the address at the funeral of a Lord.)

110. At the funeral of a Warrior, say: "Now we become reconciled as you start away. Once you were a devoted provider and protector of your family and you were ever ready to take part in battles for the Five Nations' Confederacy. The United People trusted you." (The remainder is the same as the address at the funeral of a Lord.)

111. At the funeral of a young man, say: "Now we become reconciled as you start away. In the beginning of your career you are taken away and the flower of your life is withered away." (The remainder is the same as the address at the funeral of a Lord.)

112. At the funeral of a chief woman, say: "Now we become reconciled as you start away. You were once a chief woman in the Five Nations' Confederacy. You once were a mother of the nations. Now we release you for it is true that it is no longer possible for us to walk about together on the earth. Now, therefore, we lay it (the body) here. Here we lay it away. Now then we say to you, 'Persevere onward to the place where the Creator dwells in peace. Let not the things of the earth hinder you. Let nothing that transpired while you lived hinder you. Looking after your family was a sacred duty and you were faithful. You were one of the many joint heirs of the Lordship titles. Feastings were yours and you had pleasant occasions. . . .'" (The remainder is the same as the address at the funeral of a Lord.)

113. At the funeral of a woman of the people, say: "Now we become reconciled as you start away. You were once a woman in the flower of life and the bloom is now withered away. You once held a sacred position as a mother of the nation. (Etc.) Looking after your family was a sacred duty and you were faithful. Feastings. . . . (etc.)" (The remainder is the same as the address at the funeral of a Lord.)

114. At the funeral of an infant or young woman, say: "Now we become reconciled as you start away. You were a tender bud and gladdened our hearts for only a few days. Now the bloom has withered away. Let none of the things that transpired on earth hinder you. Let nothing that happened while you lived hinder you."

115. When an infant dies within three days, mourning shall continue only five days. Then shall you gather the little boys and girls at the house of mourning and at the funeral feast a speaker shall address the children and bid them be happy once more, though by a death, gloom has been cast over them. Then shall the black clouds roll away and the sky shall show blue once more. Then shall the children be again in sunshine.

116. When a dead person is brought to the burial place, the speaker on the opposite side of the Council Fire shall bid the bereaved family cheer their minds once again and rekindle their hearth fires in peace, to put their house in order and once again be in brightness for darkness has covered them. He shall say that the black clouds shall roll away and that the bright blue sky is visible once more. Therefore shall they be in peace in the sunshine again.

117. Three strings of shell one span in length shall be employed in addressing the assemblage at the burial of the dead. The speaker shall say: "Hearken you who are here, this body is to be covered. Assemble in this place again ten days hence for it is the decree of the Creator that mourning shall cease when ten days have expired. Then shall a feast be made."

Then at the expiration of ten days the speaker shall say: "Continue to listen you who are here. The ten days of mourning have expired and your minds must now be freed of sorrow as before the loss of a relative. The relatives have decided to make a little compensation to those who have assisted at the funeral. It is a mere expression of thanks. This is to the one who did the cooking while the body was lying in the house. Let her come forward and receive this gift and be dismissed from the task." In substance this shall be repeated for every one who assisted in any way until all have been remembered.

Source: Gerald Murphy, "The Great Binding Law, Gayanashagowa," Cleveland Free-Net—aa300, 1986–1999. Distributed by the Cybercasting Services Division of the National Public Telecomputing Network.

laws that the ground which before was neither good nor profitable for the one nor for the other, is now sufficient and fruitful enough for them both. But if the inhabitants of that land will not dwell with them, to be ordered by their laws, then they drive them out of those bounds which they have limited and appointed out for themselves. And if they resist and rebel, then they make war against them. For they count this the most just cause of war, when any people holdeth a piece of ground void and vacant to no good nor profitable use, keeping other from the use and possession of it, which notwithstanding by the law of nature ought thereof to be nourished and relieved.

Source: Sir Thomas More, *Utopia* (New York: A. L. Burt Co., n.d.), 246–247.

2. Sir Thomas More, *Utopia*, 1516 [Excerpt]

Introduction

Sir Thomas More (1478–1535) was a British philosopher and statesman. He was charged with treason and executed because he refused to recognize Henry VIII as head of the Church of England. The Catholic Church eventually declared More a saint. He wrote his 1516 novel *Utopia* in Latin. It was finally translated into English in 1551. With the publication of this novel, More coined the word "utopia" and produced the first widely known example of the Utopian literary genre. Some readers saw *Utopia* as a satirical commentary on the chaos of European society, while others claim that it was a true expression of More's beliefs. Whether news of Spanish ventures in the Americas influenced the work remains a matter of speculation. This excerpt from *Utopia* is the first-known public statement of the idea that civilized peoples are justified in seizing, by force if necessary, the seemingly "waste and unoccupied" land of indigenous peoples. The citizens of Utopia were instructed to first invite the original inhabitants to live with them under Utopian laws, and only drive them away if they refuse. Centuries later in his 1829 and 1830 messages to Congress, American president Andrew Jackson justified his Indian removal policy in nearly identical terms.

Primary Source

But if so be that the multitude throughout the whole island pass and exceed the due number, then they choose out of every city certain citizens and build up a town under their own laws in the next land where the inhabitants have much waste and unoccupied ground, receiving also of the inhabitants to them, if they will join and dwell with them. They, thus joining and dwelling together, do easily agree in one fashion of living, and that to the great wealth of both the peoples. For they so bring the matter about by their

3. The First Relation of Jacques Cartier, 1534

Introduction

Jacques Cartier was born in a French coastal town in 1491. A veteran of many North Atlantic fishing expeditions, Cartier received a commission from the king of France to sail to North America and build on Verrazano's successful voyage of 1524. Like earlier European explorers, Cartier was to seek the still hoped-for passage to Asia as well as search for gold, spices, and other valuable trade goods. Cartier set sail from France in April 1534. He explored the Gulf of Saint Lawrence and returned to France with two natives. The following year the king placed Cartier in command of another larger expedition. Returning to the Saint Lawrence and guided by the two natives, Cartier reached present-day Quebec and Montreal. His party spent a brutal winter at Quebec, and many died. When spring came, Cartier abducted several Iroquois chiefs and returned to France. This second voyage established the first French presence in Canada and made lasting enemies of the Iroquois. In 1541 the king, concerned about Spanish claims in the Americas, ordered another attempt to establish a permanent colony. After another brutal winter, Cartier again abandoned Quebec. France lost interest in the region until Samuel de Champlain returned decades later. Either Cartier or one of his men wrote this firsthand account.

Primary Source

How our men set up a great Crosse upon the poynt of the sayd Porte, and the Captaine of those wild men, after a long Oration, was by our Captain appeased, and contented that two of his Children should goe with him.

Upon the 25 of the moneth, wee caused a faire high Crosse to be made of the height of thirty foote, which was made in the presence of many of them, upon the point of the entrance of the sayd haven, in the middest whereof we hanged up a Shield with three Floure de Luces in it, and in the top was carved in the wood with Anticke letters this posie, Vive le Roy de France. Then before them all we set it upon the sayd point. They with great heed beheld both the making and setting of it up.

So soone as it was up, we altogether kneeled downe before them, with our hands toward Heaven, yeelding God thankes: and we made signes unto them, shewing them the Heavens, and that all our salvation dependeth onely on him which in them dwelleth: whereat they shewed a great admiration, looking first one at another, and then upon the Crosse. And after wee were returned to our ships, their Captaine clad with an old Beares skin, with three of his sonnes, and a brother of his with him, came unto us in one of their boates, but they came not so neere us as they were wont to doe: there he made a long Oration unto us, shewing us the crosse we had set up, and making a crosse with two fingers, then did he shew us all the Countrey about us, as if he would say that all was his, and that wee should not set up any crosse without his leave. His talke being ended, we shewed him an Axe, faining that we would give it him for his skin, to which he listned, for by little and little hee came neere our ships. One of our fellowes that was in our boate, tooke hold on theirs, and suddenly leapt into it, with two or three more, who enforced them to enter into our ships, whereat they were greatly astonished. But our Captain did straightwaies assure them, that they should have no harme, nor any injurie offred them at all, and entertained them very friendly, making them eate and drinke. Then did we shew them with signes, that the crosse was but onely set up to be as a light and leader which wayes to enter into the port, and that wee would shortly come againe, and bring good store of iron wares and other things, but that we would take two of his children with us, and afterward bring them to the sayd port againe: and so wee clothed two of them in shirts, and coloured coates, with red cappes, and put about every ones necke a copper chaine, whereat they were greatly contented: then gave they their old clothes to their fellowes that went backe againe, and we gave to each one of those three that went backe, a hatchet, and some knives, which made them very glad. After these were gone, and had told the newes unto their fellowes, in the afternoone there came to our ships six boates of them, with five or sixe men in every one, to take their farewels of those two we had detained to take with us, and brought them some fish, uttering many words which we did not understand, making signes that they would not remove the crosse we had set up.

How after we were departed from the sayd porte, following our voyage along the sayd coast, we went to discover the land lying Southeast, and Northwest.

The next day, being the 25 of the moneth, we had faire weather, and went from the said port: and being out of the river, we sailed Eastnortheast, for after the entrance into the said river, the land is environed about, and maketh a bay in maner of halfe a circle, where being in our ships, we might see all the coast sayling behind, which we came to seeke, the land lying Southeast and Northwest, the course of which was distant from the river about twentie leagues.

Source: Henry S. Burrage, ed., *Early English and French Voyages* (New York: Scribner, 1906), 24–26.

4. Accounts of Spanish Explorers in the Southeast, 1536 and 1540 [Excerpts]

Introduction

Between 1492 and the first Spanish landfall in the present-day United States, Spain had established a presence in the Caribbean and brutally conquered the Aztecs in Mexico. Impressed by the wealth won by Cortez in Mexico, Spaniards turned northward in search of precious metals. In 1528 Pánfilo de Narváez landed his expedition on Tampa Bay in Florida. Failing to find riches, the men were defeated by the Apalachees and fled to the coast. After Narvaez and others drowned in a shipwreck off Texas, the survivors became captives of the natives. Alvar Nuñez Cabezça de Vaca and three companions, who spent eight years among the Indians, were the only ones to eventually be returned to their countrymen, which occurred in 1536. In his account, Cabeza de Vaca repeated rumors of great wealth in the interior of North America, and this inspired other Spaniards to explore the region. In 1539 Hernando de Soto landed an expedition in Florida and cut a swath of pillage and destruction through the southeastern region, finally crossing the Mississippi River and entering the Great Plains. In 1540 Francisco Vasquez de Coronado entered the southwestern region from Mexico in search of the rumored cities of gold. He too killed and pillaged with abandon but failed to find the fabled riches. Participants in each of these expeditions left eyewitness accounts.

Primary Source

Account by Alvar Nuñez Cabeça de Vaca

Alvar Nuñez Cabeça de Vaca to Holy Roman Emperor Charles V of what befell the armament in the Indies whither Pánfilo de Narváez went for Governor from the year 1527 to 1537

SACRED CAESARIAN CATHOLIC MAJESTY:

Among the many who have held sway, I think no prince can be found whose service has been attended with the ardor and emulation shown for that of your Highness at this time. The inducement is evident and powerful: men do not pursue together the same career without motive, and strangers are observed to strive with those who are equally impelled by religion and loyalty.

Although ambition and love of action are common to all, as to the advantages that each may gain, there are great inequalities of fortune, the result not of conduct, but only accident, nor caused by the fault of anyone, but coming in the providence of God and solely by His will. Hence to one arises deeds more signal than he thought to achieve; to another the opposite in every way occurs, so that he can show no higher proof of purpose than his effort, and at times even this is so concealed that it cannot of itself appear.

As for me, I can say in undertaking the march I made on the main by the royal authority, I firmly trusted that my conduct and services would be as evident and distinguished as were those of my ancestors and that I should not have to speak in order to be reckoned among those who for diligence and fidelity in affairs your Majesty honors. Yet, as neither my counsel nor my constancy availed to gain aught for which we set out, agreeably to your interests, for our sins, no one of the many armaments that have gone into those parts has been permitted to find itself in straits great like ours, or come to an end alike forlorn and fatal. To me, one only duty remains, to present a relation of what was seen and heard in the ten years I wandered lost and in privation through many and remote lands. Not merely a statement of positions and distances, animals and vegetation, but of the diverse customs of the many and very barbarous people with whom I talked and dwelt, as well as all other matters I could hear of and discern, that in some way I may avail your Highness. My hope of going out from among those nations was always small, still my care and diligence were none the less to keep in particular remembrance everything, that if at any time God our Lord should will to bring me where I now am, it might testify to my exertion in the royal behalf.

As the narrative is in my opinion of no trivial value to those who in your name go to subdue those countries and bring them to a knowledge of the true faith and true Lord, and under the imperial dominion, I have written this with much exactness; and although in it may be read things very novel and for some persons difficult to believe, nevertheless they may without hesitation credit me as strictly faithful. Better than to exaggerate, I have lessened in all things, and it is sufficient to say the relation is offered to your Majesty for truth. I beg it may be received in the name of homage, since it is the most that one could bring who returned thence naked. . . .

Our arrival at Apalache

When we came in view of Apalachen, the Governor ordered that I should take nine cavalry with fifty infantry and enter the town. Accordingly the assessor and I assailed it; and having got in, we found only women and boys there, the men being absent; however these returned to its support, after a little time, while we were walking about, and began discharging arrows at us. They killed the horse of the assessor, and at last taking to flight, they left us.

We found a large quantity of maize fit for plucking, and much dry that was housed; also many deer-skins, and among them some mantelets of thread, small and poor, with which the women partially cover their persons. There were numerous mortars for cracking maize. The town consisted of forty small houses, made low, and set up in sheltered places because of the frequent storms. The material was thatch. They were surrounded by very dense woods, large groves and many bodies of fresh water, in which so many and so large trees are fallen, that they form obstructions rendering travel difficult and dangerous. . . .

Narrative of the Expedition of Hernando de Soto

How the Governor arrived at Palache, and was informed that there was much gold inland.

On the twenty-third day of September the Governor left Napetaca, and went to rest at a river, where two Indians brought him a deer from the cacique of Uzachil; and the next day, having passed through a large town called Hapaluya, he slept at Uzachil. He found no person there; for the inhabitants, informed of the deaths at Napetaca, dared not remain. In the town was found their food, much maize, beans, and pumpkins, on which the Christians lived. The maize is like coarse millet; the pumpkins are better and more savory than those of Spain.

Two captains having been sent in opposite directions, in quest of Indians, a hundred men and women were taken, one or two of whom were chosen out for the Governor, as was always customary for officers to do after successful inroads, dividing the others among themselves and companions. They were led off in chains, with collars about the neck, to carry luggage and grind corn, doing the labor proper to servants. Sometimes it happened that, going with them for wood or maize, they would kill the Christian, and flee, with the chain on, which others would file at night with a splinter of stone, in the place of iron, at which work, when caught, they were punished, as a warning to others, and that they might not do the like. The women and youths, when removed a hundred leagues from their country, no longer cared, and were taken along loose, doing the work, and in a very little time learning the Spanish language.

From Uzachil the Governor went towards Apalache, and at the end of two days' travel arrived at a town called Axille. After that, the Indians having no knowledge of the Christians, they were come upon unawares, the greater part escaping, nevertheless, because there were woods near town. The next day, the first of October, the

Governor took his departure in the morning, and ordered a bridge to be made over a river which he had to cross. The depth there, for a stone's throw, was over the head, and afterward the water came to the waist, for the distance of a crossbow-shot, where was a growth of tall and dense forest, into which the Indians came, to ascertain if they could assail the men at work and prevent a passage; but they were dispersed by the arrival of crossbowmen, and some timbers being thrown in, the men gained the opposite side and secured the way. On the fourth day of the week, Wednesday of St. Francis, the Governor crossed over and reached Uitachuco, a town subject to Apalache, where he slept. He found it burning, the Indians having set it on fire.

Thenceforward the country was well inhabited, producing much corn, the way leading by many habitations like villages. Sunday, the twenty-fifth of October, he arrived at the town of Uzela, and on Monday at Anhayca Apalache, where the lord of all that country and province resided. The camp-master, whose duty it is to divide and lodge the men, quartered them about the town, at the distance of half a league to a league apart. There were other towns which had much maize, pumpkins, beans, and dried plums of the country, whence were brought together at Anhayca Apalache what appeared to be sufficient provision for the winter. These *ameixas* are better than those of Spain, and come from trees that grow in the fields without being planted.

Informed that the sea was eight leagues distant, the Governor directly sent a captain thither, with cavalry and infantry, who found a town called Ochete, eight leagues on the way; and, coming to the coast, he saw where a great tree had been felled, the trunk split up into stakes, and with the limbs made into mangers. He found also the skulls of horses. With these discoveries he returned, and what was said of Narváez was believed to be certain, that he had there made boats, in which he left the country, and was lost in them at sea. Presently Juan de Añasco made ready to go to the port of Espiritu Santo, taking thirty cavalry, with orders from the Governor to Calderon, who had remained there, that he should abandon the town, and bring all the people to Apalache.

In Uzachill, and other towns on the way, Añasco found many people who had already become careless; still, to avoid detention, no captures were made, as it was not well to give the Indians sufficient time to come together. He went through the towns at night, stopping at a distance from the population for three or four hours, to rest, and at the end of ten days arrived at the port. He despatched two caravels to Cuba, in which he sent to Doña Ysabel twenty women brought by him from Ytara and Potano, near Cale; and, taking with him the foot-soldiers in the brigantines, from point to point along the coast by sea, he went towards Palache. Calderon with the cavalry, and some crossbowmen of foot, went by land. The Indians at several places beset him, and wounded some of the men. On his arrival, the Governor ordered planks and spikes to be taken to the coast for building a piragua, into which thirty men entered well armed from the bay, going to and coming from sea, waiting the arrival of the brigantines, and sometimes fighting with the natives, who went up and down the estuary in canoes. On Saturday, the twenty-ninth of November, in a high wind, an Indian passed through the sentries undiscovered, and set fire to the town, two portions of which, in consequence, were instantly consumed.

On Sunday, the twenty-eighth of December, Juan de Añasco arrived; and the Governor directed Francisco Maldonado, captain of infantry, to run the coast to the westward with fifty men, and look for an entrance; proposing to go himself in that direction by land on discoveries. The same day, eight men rode two leagues about the town in pursuit of Indians, who had become so bold that they would venture up within two crossbow-shots of the camp to kill our people. Two were discovered engaged in picking beans, and might have escaped, but a woman being present, the wife of one of them, they stood to fight. Before they could be killed, three horses were wounded, one of which died in a few days. Calderon going along the coast near by, the Indians came out against him from a wood, driving him from his course, and capturing from many of his company a part of their indispensable subsistence.

Three or four days having elapsed beyond the time set for the going and return of Maldonado, the Governor resolved that, should he not appear at the end of eight days, he would go thence and wait no longer; when the captain arrived, bringing with him an Indian from a Province called Ochus, sixty leagues from Apalache, and the news of having found a sheltered port with a good depth of water. The Governor was highly pleased, hoping to find a good country ahead; and he sent Maldonado to Havana for provisions, with which to meet him at that port of his discovery, to which he would himself come by land; but should he not reach there that summer, then he directed him to go back to Havana and return there the next season to await him, as he would make it his express object to march in quest of Ochus.

Francisco Maldonado went, and Juan de Guzman remained instead, captain of his infantry. Of the Indians taken in Napetuca, the treasurer, Juan Gaytan, brought a youth with him, who stated that he did not belong to that country, but to one afar in the direction of the sun's rising, from which he had been a long time absent visiting other lands; that its name was Yupaha, and was governed by a woman, the town she lived in being of astonishing size, and many neighboring lords her tributaries, some of whom gave her clothing, others gold in quantity. He showed how the metal was taken from the earth, melted, and refined, exactly as though he had seen it all done, or else the Devil had taught him how it was; so that they who knew aught of such matters declared it impossible that he could give that account without having been an eyewitness; and they who beheld the signs he made, credited all that was understood as certain. . . .

How the Indians rose upon the Governor, and what followed upon that rising.

The Governor, in view of the determination and furious answer of the cacique, thought to soothe him with soft words; to which he made no answer, but, with great haughtiness and contempt, withdrew to where Soto could not see nor speak to him. The Governor, that he might send word to the cacique for him to remain in the country at his will, and to be pleased to give him a guide, and persons to carry burdens, that he might see if he could pacify him with gentle words, called to a chief who was passing by. The Indian replied, loftily, that he would not listen to him. Baltasar de Gallegos, who was near, seized him by the cloak of marten-skins that he had on, drew it off over his head, and left it in his hands; whereupon, the Indians all beginning to rise, he gave him a stroke with a cutlass, that laid open his back, when they, with loud yells, came out of the houses, discharging their bows.

The Governor, discovering that if he remained there they could not escape, and if he should order his men, who were outside of the town, to come in, the horses might be killed by the Indians from the houses and great injury done, he ran out; but before he could get away he fell two or three times, and was helped to rise by those with him. He and they were all badly wounded: within the town five Christians were instantly killed. Coming forth, he called out to all his men to get farther off, because there was much harm doing from the palisade. The natives discovering that the Christians were retiring, and some, if not the greater number, at more than a walk, the Indians followed with great boldness, shooting at them, or striking down such as they could overtake. Those in chains having set down their burdens near the fence while the Christians were retiring, the people of Mauilla lifted the loads on to their backs, and, bringing them into the town, took off their irons, putting bows and arms in their hands, with which to fight. Thus did the foe come into possession of all the clothing, pearls, and whatsoever else the Christians had beside, which was what their Indians carried. Since the natives had been at peace as far as to that place, some of us, putting our arms in the luggage, had gone without any; and two, who were in the town, had their swords and halberds taken from them, and put to use.

The Governor, presently as he found himself in the field, called for a horse, and, with some followers, returned and lanced two or three of the Indians; the rest, going back into the town, shot arrows from the palisade. Those who would venture on their nimbleness came out a stone's throw from behind it, to fight, retiring from time to time, when they were set upon.

At the time of the affray there was a friar, a clergyman, a servant of the Governor, and a female slave in the town, who, having no time in which to get away, took to a house, and there remained until after the Indians became masters of the place. They closed the entrance with a lattice door; and there being a sword among them, which the servant had, he put himself behind the door, striking at the Indians that would have come in; while, on the other side, stood the friar and the priest, each with a club in hand, to strike down the first that should enter. The Indians, finding that they could not get in by the door, began to unroof the house: at this moment the cavalry were all arrived at Mauilla, with the infantry that had been on the march, when a difference of opinion arose as to whether the Indians should be attacked, in order to enter the town; for the result was held doubtful, but finally it was concluded to make the assault.

How the Governor set his men in order of battle and entered the town of Mauilla.

So soon as the advance and the rear of the force were come up, the Governor commanded that all the best armed should dismount, of which he made four squadrons of footmen. The Indians, observing how he was going on arranging his men, urged the cacique to leave, telling him, as was afterwards made known by some women who were taken in the town, that as he was but one man, and could fight but as one only, there being many chiefs present very skilful and experienced in matters of war, anyone of whom was able to command the rest, and as things in war were so subject to fortune, that it was never certain which side would overcome the other, they wished him to put his person in safety; for if they should conclude their lives there, on which they had resolved rather than surrender, he would remain to govern the land: but for all that they said, he did not wish to go, until, from being continually urged, with fifteen or twenty of his own people he went out of the town, taking with him a scarlet cloak and other articles of the Christians' clothing, being whatever he could carry and that seemed best to him.

The Governor, informed that the Indians were leaving the town, commanded the cavalry to surround it; and into each squadron of foot he put a soldier, with a brand, to set fire to the houses, that the Indians might have no shelter. His men being placed in full concert, he ordered an arquebuse to be shot off: at the signal the four squadrons, at their proper points, commenced a furious onset, and, both sides severely suffering, the Christians entered the town. The friar, the priest, and the rest who were with them in the house, were all saved, though at the cost of the lives of two brave and very able men who went thither to their rescue. The Indians fought with so great spirit that they many times drove our people back out of the town. The struggle lasted so long that many Christians, weary and very thirsty, went to drink at a pond near by, tinged with the blood of the killed, and returned to the combat. The Governor, witnessing this, with those who followed him in the returning charge of the footmen, entered the town on horseback, which gave opportunity to fire the dwellings; then breaking in upon the Indians and beating them down, they fled out of the place, the cavalry and infantry driving them back through the gates, where, losing the hope of escape, they fought valiantly; and the Christians getting among them with cutlasses, they found themselves met on all sides by their strokes, when many, dashing headlong into the flaming houses, were smothered, and, heaped one upon another, burned to death.

They who perished there were in all two thousand five hundred, a few more or less: of the Christians there fell eighteen, among whom was Don Carlos, brother-in-law of the Governor; one Juan de Gamez, a nephew; Men. Rodriguez, a Portuguese; and Juan Vazquez, of Villanueva de Barcarota, men of condition and courage; the rest were infantry. Of the living, one hundred and fifty Christians had received seven hundred wounds from the arrow; and God was pleased that they should be healed in little time of very dangerous injuries. Twelve horses died, and seventy were hurt. The clothing the Christians carried with them, the ornaments for saying mass, and the pearls, were all burned there; they having set the fire themselves, because they considered the loss less than the injury they might receive of the Indians from within the houses, where they had brought the things together.

The Governor learning in Mauilla that Francisco Maldonado was waiting for him in the port of Ochuse, six days' travel distant, he caused Juan Ortiz to keep the news secret, that he might not be interrupted in his purpose; because the pearls he wished to send to Cuba for show, that their fame might raise the desire of coming to Florida, had been lost, and he feared that, hearing of him without seeing either gold or silver, or other thing of value from that land, it would come to have such reputation that no one would be found to go there when men should be wanted: so he determined to send no news of himself until he should have discovered a rich country. . . .

How the Governor set out from Mauilla to go to Chicaça, and what befell him.

From the time the Governor arrived in Florida until he went from Mauilla, there died one hundred and two Christians, some of sickness, others by the hand of the Indians. Because of the wounded, he stopped in that place twenty-eight days, all the time remaining out in the fields. The country was a rich soil, and well inhabited: some towns were very large, and were picketed about. The people were numerous everywhere, the dwellings standing a crossbow-shot or two apart.

On Sunday, the eighteenth of November the sick being found to be getting on well, the Governor left Mauilla, taking with him a supply of maize for two days. He marched five days through a wilderness, arriving in a province called Pafallaya, at the town Taliepataua; and thence he went to another, named Cabusto, near which was a large river, whence the Indians on the farther bank shouted to the Christians that they would kill them should they come over

there. He ordered the building of a piragua within the town, that the natives might have no knowledge of it; which being finished in four days, and ready, he directed it to be taken on sleds half a league up stream, and in the morning thirty men entered it, well armed. The Indians discovering what was going on, they who were nearest went to oppose the landing, and did the best they could; but the Christians drawing near, and the piragua being about to reach the shore, they fled into some cane-brakes. The men on horses went up the river to secure a landing place, to which the Governor passed over, with the others that remained. Some of the towns were well stored with maize and beans.

Thence towards Chicaça the Governor marched five days through a desert, and arrived at a river, on the farther side of which were Indians, who wished to arrest his passage.

In two days another piragua was made, and when ready he sent an Indian in it to the cacique, to say, that if he wished his friendship he should quietly wait for him; but they killed the messenger before his eyes, and with loud yells departed. He crossed the river the seventeenth of December, and arrived the same day at Chicaça, a small town of twenty houses. There the people underwent severe cold, for it was already winter, and snow fell: the greater number were then lying in the fields, it being before they had time to put up habitations. The land was thickly inhabited, the people living about over it as they do in Mauilla; and as it was fertile, the greater part being under cultivation, there was plenty of maize. So much grain was brought together as was needed for getting through with the season.

Some Indians were taken, among whom was one the cacique greatly esteemed. The Governor sent an Indian to the cacique to say, that he desired to see him and have his friendship. He came, and offered him the services of his person, territories, and subjects: he said that he would cause two chiefs to visit him in peace. In a few days he returned with them, they bringing their Indians. They presented the Governor one hundred and fifty rabbits, with clothing of the country, such as shawls and skins. The name of the one was Alimamu, of the other Nicalasa. . . .

Account of the Expedition to Cibola, 1540, by Pedro de Castañeda, of Najera

To me it seems very certain, my very noble lord, that it is a worthy ambition for great men to desire to know and wish to preserve for posterity correct information concerning the things that have happened in distant parts, about which little is known. I do not blame those inquisitive persons who, perchance with good intentions, have many times troubled me not a little with their requests that I clear up for them some doubts which they have had about different things that have been commonly related concerning the events and occurrences that took place during the expedition to

Cibola, or the New Land, which the good viceroy—may he be with God in His glory—Don Antonio de Mendoza, ordered and arranged, and on which he sent Francisco Vásquez de Coronado as captain-general. In truth, they have reason for wishing to know the truth, because most people very often make things of which they have heard, and about which they have perchance no knowledge, appear either greater or less than they are. They make nothing of those things that amount to something, and those that do not they make so remarkable that they appear to be something impossible to believe. This may very well have been caused by the fact that, as that country was not permanently occupied, there has not been anyone who was willing to spend his time in writing about its peculiarities, because all knowledge was lost of that which it was not the pleasure of God—He alone knows the reason—that they should enjoy. In truth, he who wishes to employ himself thus in writing out the things that happened on the expedition, and the things that were seen in those lands, and the ceremonies and customs of the natives, will have matter enough to test his judgment, and I believe that the result can not fail to be an account which, describing only the truth, will be so remarkable that it will seem incredible.

And besides, I think that the twenty years and more since that expedition took place have been the cause of some stories which are related. For example, some make it an uninhabitable country, others have it bordering on Florida, and still others on Greater India, which does not appear to be a slight difference. They are unable to give any basis upon which to found their statements. There are those who tell about some very peculiar animals, who are contradicted by others who were on the expedition, declaring that there was nothing of the sort seen. Others differ as to the limits of the provinces and even in regard to the ceremonies and customs, attributing what pertains to one people to others. All this has had a large part, my very noble lord, in making me wish to give now, although somewhat late, a short general account for all those who pride themselves on this noble curiosity, and to save myself the time taken up by these solicitations. Things enough will certainly be found here which are hard to believe. All or the most of these were seen with my own eyes, and the rest is from reliable information obtained by inquiry of the natives themselves. Understanding as I do that this little work would be nothing in itself, lacking authority, unless it were favored and protected by a person whose authority would protect it from the boldness of those who, without reverence, give their murmuring tongues liberty, and knowing as I do how great are the obligations under which I have always been, and am, to your grace, I humbly beg to submit this little work to your protection. May it be received as from a faithful retainer and servant. It will be divided into three parts, that it may be better understood. The first will tell of the discovery and the armament or army that was made ready, and of the whole journey, with the captains who were there; the second, of the villages and provinces which were found, and their limits,

and ceremonies and customs, the animals, fruits, and vegetation, and in what parts of the country these are; the third, of the return of the army and the reasons for abandoning the country, although these were insufficient, because this is the best place there is for discoveries—the marrow of the land in these western parts, as will be seen. And after this has been made plain, some remarkable things which were seen will be described at the end, and the way by which one might more easily return to discover that better land which we did not see, since it would be no small advantage to enter the country through the land which the Marquis of the Valley, Don Fernando Cortes, went in search of under the Western star, and which cost him no small sea armament. May it please our Lord to so favor me that with my slight knowledge and small abilities I may be able by relating the truth to make my little work pleasing to the learned and wise readers, when it has been accepted by your grace. For my intention is not to gain the fame of a good composer or rhetorician, but I desire to give a faithful account and to do this slight service to your grace, who will, I hope, receive it as from a faithful servant and soldier, who took part in it. Although not in a polished style, I write that which happened—that which I heard, experienced, saw, and did.

I always notice, and it is a fact, that for the most part when we have something valuable in our hands, and deal with it without hindrance, We do not value or prize it so highly as if we understood how much we should miss it after we had lost it, and the longer we continue to have it the less we value it; but after We have lost it and miss the advantages of it, we have a great pain in the heart, and we are all the time imagining and trying to find ways and means by which to get it back again. It seems to me that this has happened to all or most of those who went on the expedition which, in the year of our Savior Jesus Christ 1540, Francisco Vásquez Coronado led in search of the Seven Cities. Granted that they did not find the riches of which they had been told, they found a place in which to search for them and the beginning of a good country to settle in, so as to go on farther from there. Since they came back from the country which they conquered and abandoned, time has given them a chance to understand the direction and locality in which they were, and the borders of the good country they had in their hands, and their hearts weep for having lost so favorable an opportunity. Just as men see more at the bullfight when they are upon the seats than when they are around in the ring, now when they know and understand the direction and situation in which they were, and see, indeed, that they can not enjoy it nor recover it, now when it is too late they enjoy telling about what they saw, and even of what they realize that they lost, especially those who are now as poor as when they went there. They have never ceased their labors and have spent their time to no advantage. I say this because I have known several of those who came back from there who amuse themselves now by talking of how it would be to go back and proceed to recover that which is lost, while others enjoy trying to find the reason why it was discovered at all. And now I will proceed to relate all that happened from the beginning.

In the year 1530 Nuño de Guzman, who was President of New Spain, had in his possession an Indian, a native of the valley or valleys of Oxitipar, who was called Tejo by the Spaniards. This Indian said he was the son of a trader who was dead, but that when he was a little boy his father had gone into the back country with fine feathers to trade for ornaments, and that when he came back he brought a large amount of gold and silver, of which there is a good deal in that country. He went with him once or twice, and saw some very large villages, which he compared to Mexico and its environs. He had seen seven very large towns which had streets of silver workers. It took forty days to go there from his country, through a wilderness in which nothing grew, except some very small plants about a span high. The way they went was up through the country between the two seas, following the northern direction. Acting on this information, Nuño de Guzman got together nearly 400 Spaniards and 20,000 friendly Indians of New Spain, and, as he happened to be in Mexico, he crossed Tarasca, which is in the province of Michoacan, so as to get into the region which the Indian said was to be crossed toward the North Sea, in this way getting to the country which they were looking for, which was already named "The Seven Cities." He thought, from the forty days of which Tejo had spoken, that it would be found to be about 200 leagues, and that they would easily be able to cross the country. Omitting several things that occurred on this journey, as soon as they had reached the province of Culiacan, where his government ended, and where the New Kingdom of Galicia is now, they tried to cross the country, but found the difficulties very great, because the mountain chains which are near that sea are so rough that it was impossible, after great labor, to find a passageway in that region. His whole army had to stay in the district of Culiacan for so long on this account that some rich men who were with him, who had possessions in Mexico, changed their minds, and every day became more anxious to return. Besides this, Nuño de Guzman received word that the Marquis of the Valley, Don Fernando Cortes, had come from Spain with his new title, and with great favors and estates, and as Nuño de Guzman had been a great rival of his at the time he was president, and had done much damage to his property and to that of his friends, he feared that Don Fernando Cortes would want to pay him back in the same way, or worse. So he decided to establish the town of Culiacan there and to go back with the other men, without doing anything more. After his return from this expedition, he founded Xalisco, where the city of Compostela is situated, and Tonala, which is called Guadalaxara, and now this is the New Kingdom of Galicia. The guide they had, who was called Tejo, died about this time, and thus the name of these Seven Cities and the search for them remain until now, since they have not been discovered. . . .

Source: Frederick W. Hodge, ed., *Spanish Explorers in the Southern United States, 1528–1543* (New York: Scribner, 1907), 12–287.

5. Juan Rogel, Account of the Massacre of Spanish Jesuits in Chesapeake Bay, August 28, 1572

Introduction

Like the other European powers, Spain hoped to find a seagoing passage to Asia. The Chesapeake Bay (called Bahia de Santa Maria by the Spanish) appeared to be a promising direction in which to search. The Spanish explorer Juan Menendez Marques promoted the establishment of a Jesuit mission on the bay. During his visit Menendez exchanged a Spanish youth for an Indian one. In 1570 eight Jesuits from Florida, accompanied by the Indian youth, built a mission on the York River. The Indian youth returned to his people and reportedly turned against the Spanish. The Jesuits expected the Powhatans to give them food, which was in short supply. Instead the Spanish demand led the Indians to attack and kill them in 1571. The Indians also attacked a Spanish supply ship that arrived after the massacre. Yet another Spanish expedition attacked the Powhatans and rescued the Spanish youth. A Jesuit who accompanied the rescue expedition wrote this letter to his superior. He describes the recovery of the Spanish youth, Alonso, and relates Alonso's account of how the Jesuits died. The Jesuit also suggests that a well-armed Spanish settlement would keep a new mission safe. However, Spain made no further attempts to settle the Chesapeake Bay.

Primary Source

Our Most Reverend Father in Christ,

At the end of last June, I wrote to Your Paternity from Havana, telling how, under an order of holy obedience, I made ready to make this journey in search of Ours who had come to these parts. Although I had written from there that at the end of the trip I had to go to the Isles of Azores, because the Governor Pedro Menendez was obliged to take the ship, in which I had come here, for the trip to Spain; nevertheless, when he reached San Agustin, he changed his plans. He decided to make this trip in person at the head of his fleet, and on completing the trip, to give me a ship in which I might go back to the island of Cuba. Thus, on July 30, we left San Agustin for this purpose, and after staying at Santa Elena for five days, we arrived at the Bay of the Mother of God. With me are Brother Juan de la Carrera and Francisco de Villareal and the small store of supplies we had on Santa Elena. After this we will all go to Havana to await the order of Father Provincial since Father Sedeño would order me to do that.

Reaching this bay, the Governor immediately ordered us to search for Alonso, the boy who came with Father Baptista. He had not died, according to what we heard from one of the Indians of this region, who was captured by the pilot on his second trip. This

Indian has been brought along in chains. Anchoring the fleet in a port of this bay, the Governor sent an armed *fragatilla* with 30 soldiers to a fresh-water stream where Ours disembarked when they came here. This place is 20 leagues from this port. It seemed best to me to take the bound native in company to be our spokesman. The order of the Governor was to take the uncle of Don Luis, a principal chief of that region, as well as some leading Indians. On taking them, we were to ask them to give us the boy and we would let them go. Everything happened in excellent fashion, for within an hour after our arrival, he took the chief with five of the leaders and eight other Indians.

This was the method of capture. After we had anchored in the middle of the narrow stream, Indians soon appeared on the bank and some entered the boat. To these the Spaniards gave gift and made some exchanges. When they left the boat very contentedly, others arrived. With a third group came the chief and his leaders; one of them wore as a decoration or trinket a silver paten that Ours had brought. At once the Spaniards seized them and forced them down into the boat, and dressing the ship, passed to the mouth of the stream 3 leagues away by oar. On the way, the soldiers killed some Indians who were trying to shoot arrows at us and had wounded a soldier.

At the mouth of the river, which was very wide, we anchored again an arquebus shot away from the shore. Canoes of Indians came in peace, and they said that the boy was in the hands of a leading chief who lived two days' journey from there, near this port. They asked that we give them time to send for him and bring him. This we did, and we gave them trinkets to give the chief who held the boy and we stayed there waiting for him. It seems that as soon as the chief learned of the capture of the others and about the fleet and the imminent death of the Indians, he sought to curry favor with the Governor. For he did not want to let the boy be brought to our ship, but he sent him to this port with two Indians. It is a marvelous thing in how short a time the Governor learned what was happening there from the mouth of the boy.

When the Indians did not bring the boy, we fought off an ambush of many canoes loaded with archers ready to attack the vessel. First, there came two large canoes filled with Indians who were so concealed that no one was seen except the two who steered and they pretended they brought us oysters. Before they got aboard the watchman discovered them. We made ready and the others retreated. At my request, the steersmen were not fired upon, for we were still not certain whether it was an ambush or whether they came in peace. When the time was up and the boy did not come we waited for a night and further into midday and finally we set sail with our captives. By way of farewell, the pilot steered the ship towards land with the excuse that he wanted to speak to them, and then he ordered a blast from the arquebuses into the group of Indians who were standing crowded together on the shore. I believe many of them were killed and this was done without any knowledge of mine until it happened. Then we returned to this port.

Now I will relate to Your Paternity how Ours who were here suffered death, as this boy tells it. After they arrived there, Don Luis abandoned them, since he did not sleep in their hut more than two nights nor stay in the village where the Fathers made their settlement for more than five days. Finally he was living with his brothers a journey of a day and a half away. Father Master Baptista sent a message by a novice Brother on two occasions to the renegade. Don Luis would never come, and Ours stayed therein a great distress, for they had no one by whom they could make themselves understood to the Indians. They were without means of support, and no one could buy grain from them. They got along as best they could, going to other villages to barter maize with copper and tin, until the beginning of February. The boy says that each day Father Baptista caused prayers to be said for Don Luis, saying that the devil held him in great deception. As he had twice sent for him and he had not come, he decided to send Father Quirós and Brother Gabriel de Solis and Brother Juan Baptista to the village of the chief near where Don Luis was staying. Thus they could take Don Luis along with them and barter for maize on the way back. On the Sunday after the feast of the Purification, Don Luis came to the three Jesuits who were returning with other Indians. He sent an arrow through the heart of Father Quirós and then murdered the rest who had come to speak with him. Immediately Don Luis went on to the village where the Fathers were, and with great quiet and dissimulation, at the head of a large group of Indians, he killed the five who waited there. Don Luis himself was the first to draw blood with one of those hatchets which were brought along for trading with the Indians; then he finished the killing of Father Master Baptista with his axe, and his companions finished off the others. This boy says that when he saw them killing the Fathers and Brothers, he sought to go among the Indians as they inflicted the wounds so that they might kill him too. For it seemed better to him to die with Christians than live alone with Indians. A brother of Don Luis took him by the arm and did not let him go. This happened five or six days after the death of the others. This boy then told Don Luis to bury them since he had killed them, and at least in their burial, he was kind to them.

The boy stayed in the same hut for 15 days. Because of the famine in the land, Don Luis told him that they should go and seek grain. Alonso came in this way with him to the chief where he remained. The chief told the boy to stay and he would treat him well and hold him as a son. This he did. Finally Don Luis distributed the clothes of the Fathers among himself and his two brothers who shared in the murders. The boy took nothing but the relics and beads of Father Baptista which he kept till now and handed over to us. After this Don Luis went away very anxious to get hold of the boy to kill him, so that there would be no one to give details of what happened to Ours, but because of this fear of the chief with whom the boy was staying, he gave up the idea.

When he had learned the truth, the Governor acted in this fashion. He told the captured chief that he must bring in Don Luis and his two brothers for punishment, and if he did not do this, the Governor would punish all those captured. Since three had been killed in that chief's lands, he could not escape blame for the murders. The chief promised that he would bring them within five days. We are waiting for this time to elapse, and I am not sure whether the Governor will send us on our trip to the island of Cuba before the time is up. He will report to Spain, God willing, whatever action he will have taken. The country remains very frightened from the chastisement the Governor inflicted, for previously they were free to kill any Spaniard who made no resistance. After seeing the opposite of what the Fathers were, they tremble. This chastisement has become famous throughout the land, and if this further one is done, it will be all the more famous.

I have noticed something about this region. There are more people here than in any of the other lands I have seen so far along the coast explored. It seemed to me that the natives are more settled than in other regions I have been and I am confident that should Spaniards settle here, provided they would frighten the natives that threaten harm, we could preach the Holy Gospel more easily than elsewhere. We are keeping this boy with us. He is very fluent in the language and had almost forgotten his Spanish. After he was freed from his captivity, we asked him if he wished to be with us, or go with his father who is also here. He said that he wanted to be with us only. In order to make sure that he retains the language and does not forget it, I am debating whether to bring along with me an Indian boy, who has come along with Alonso, leaving his parent and home to be with him. Thus he might train in the language, unless, meanwhile, Your Paternity or Father Provincial order otherwise.

For my part, I can say to Your Paternity that if it is judged in Our Lord that this enterprise ought to be begun, and if you desire that the task should fall to me, I would consider myself most fortunate. I fear that there will be the same difficulty among these people in making conversions, as has been found in the places where we have been. If there is to be some fruit here, it will have to be by wearing them away like water on a rock. I believe there are fewer inconveniences and difficulties than in regions where I have already stayed. First, because the country is so cold, there will be no reason for long absences away from their huts in winter. Also it appears to me that there are more tribes and more natives in this region than in others where I have dwelt.

When this boy was with Don Luis, following the death of the others, Don Luis left the vestments and books and everything else locked up in chests. On returning, they took up their share of spoils. He said that a brother of Don Luis is going around clothed in the Mass vestment and altar cloths. The captured chief told me that Don Luis gave the silver chalice to an important chief in the interior. The paten was given to one of those Indians we captured, while the other images were thrown away. Among other things there was a large crucifix in a chest; some Indians told this boy that they do not dare approach that chest since three Indians who wanted to see what was in it, fell down dead on the spot. So they keep it closed and protected. About the books, Alonso said that after pulling off the clasps, the Indians tore them all up and threw them away.

If I should learn any other details, whether those sent out by the Governor bring in Don Luis and his companions, I will write them from Havana to Your paternity, when, in Our Lord's pleasure, we arrive there.

As I can not think of anything else to write, I close. I commend myself to the holy sacrifices and prayers of Your Paternity and of the Fathers and Brothers of the Company. God Our Lord Grant Your Paternity His Holy Spirit for all success in fulfilling His Divine Will.

From the Bay of the Mother of God in Florida, August 28, 1572.

Your Paternity's unworthy son and servant in Our Lord,

[signed] Juan Rogel

Source: David B. Quinn, ed., *New American World: A Documentary History of North America to 1612,* Vol. 2 (New York: Arno, 1979).

6. Pedro Menéndez de Avilés, Letters to the King of Spain regarding the Indians of Florida, 1572 and 1573

Introduction

Between 1492 and the first Spanish landfall in the present-day United States, Spain had established a presence in the Caribbean and brutally conquered the Aztecs in Mexico. Spanish contact with native peoples invariably resulted in decimation of the natives by violence and disease. The Spaniards turned northward to explore for precious metals. Pánfilo de Narváez landed his expedition on Tampa Bay, Florida, in 1528. The Apalachees defeated the Spanish and forced them to flee. In 1539 Hernando de Soto landed an expedition in Florida and cut a swath of pillage and destruction through the southeastern region. In 1565 the king of Spain sent an expedition, commanded by Pedro Menéndez de Avilés, to establish a base at Saint Augustine. A French expedition had arrived on Florida's coast a year earlier and built Fort Caroline. After wiping out the French and executing their leader, Menéndez turned his attention to the Indians, many of whom remained intractably hostile to the Spanish. In 1572 he wrote a letter to King Philip II recommending that the hostile natives be exterminated or captured and sold into slavery. The king apparently did not grant the desired permission, so Menéndez presented his arguments more forcefully in 1573. However, Philip II ordered that the Spanish focus on converting Native Americans to Christianity rather than conquering or destroying them.

Primary Source

1572

The Adelantado, Pedro Menéndez, says that it is seven years since he went upon the conquest and settlement of Florida from these parts, and he has tried and is trying his utmost that the Indians may be taught and very well treated, and no trouble or vexations be caused them, in order that they may listen to the religious, and render obedience to your Majesty, with the more love and willingness; but all the Indians, from the river of Mosquitos, at the beginning of the Bahama Channel, as far as Los Martires, and returning up to the bay of Tocobaga (although great gifts and demonstrations of friendship have been made them, and many were brought to Havana and taken back to their lands, and gave allegiance to your Majesty)—have broken the peace many times, slaying many Christians, and they have been forgiven. And yet withal this is of no use, nor has it been, for they have been accustomed since the Indies have been discovered to kill all the people from the ships which are, the most of them, lost in this district; and although concerning this I have told the caciques of that land they should not do it, and that if they slew them I would make war upon them, killing them and making slaves of those I captured alive—and they promised me not to do it—they do not keep their word, nor have they wished to comply. I have made peace with them three times, and three times they have broken it, and when they saw they could kill Christians safely, they did it, as it happened after this in Tocobaga, when they treacherously slew twenty soldiers. At Los Martires, about twenty months ago, they killed eight Spaniards from a boat which was going from Florida to Havana; and in Giga, which is in that same Bahama Channel, when an English corsair had seized a vessel wherein came thirty persons, and they, under a deceptive peace were preparing the boat so that it would have more available space, that they might go therein to Havana, the Indians killed them all, except one woman with two little girls, and one little boy, and one man whom they left for dead, and he lived, for afterward I had him removed and taken to Havana. Two other ships, which were going from New Spain to Santo Domingo to take on sugar and hides, were lost by reason of a storm off Cape Canaveral, at the end of the Bahama Channel; and as the crews were journeying to the fort of San Agustin, thirty leagues thence, the Indians slew most of them, when they had gone half the distance, and they kept others alive to use as slaves, whom I afterward ransomed; others took refuge at the fort of San Agustin. About

thirteen months ago, when I sailed from Florida with two frigates to go to Havana, and thence in search of corsairs, I was wrecked at Cape Canaveral because of a storm which came upon me, and the other boat was lost fifteen leagues farther on in the Bahama Channel, in a river they call Ays, because the cacique is so called. Seeing the opportunity, he killed nineteen persons who were on board the frigate, without leaving one, and I, by miracle, reached the fort of San Agustin with seventeen persons I was taking. Three times the Indians gave the order to attack me, and the way I escaped from them was by ingenuity and arousing fear in them, telling them that behind me many Spaniards were coming who would slay them if they found them; that they should seek safety in the forest. The first year I set out on the conquest, I ransomed from among the Indians thirty-two persons, men and women, who had been slaves of the caciques and Indians for fifteen, eighteen and twenty years. There were some who had been numbered among two hundred and thirty Spaniards, men and women together, from wrecked ships, and each year the Indians sacrificed seventeen or eighteen in the feasts they hold, and they used the heads in their balls and ceremonies. They are so bloodthirsty in this because they consider it a great glory and victory for them and that the other caciques of the interior may hold a high opinion of them and they may triumph, saying that they live on the seashore and are the masters of the Christians and hold them as slaves. They follow this custom because they consider it the pious and natural order of things, without observing amity, or hope that later on they may observe it in the service of God Our Lord and of your Majesty. It is needful that this should be remedied by permitting that war be made upon them with all rigor, a war of fire and blood, and that those taken alive shall be sold as slaves, removing them from the country and taking them to the neighboring islands, Cuba, Santo Domingo, Puerto Rico. So that in this manner, besides the service rendered to God Our Lord and to your Majesty, this district where war must be made on such people, because it is the most full of danger and where many ships are lost coming from the Indies to these kingdoms, will remain clear and unobstructed. It is very poor land, subject to inundation, and the Indians cannot sustain themselves except on roots and shellfish. And if this be done, no Indian will be living therein, and if any vessel shall be wrecked, the people can easily go in safety to the fort of San Agustin and take refuge there; and this will arouse fear, and be a great example among the friendly Indians, so that they may observe and fulfil the amity they establish; wherefore, etc.

1573

The Adelantado, Pedro Menéndez, says that through the reports he has presented, it will be found that God Our Lord and your Majesty will be well served in giving up as slaves the Indians of the Cabeca de los Martires and the Bahama Channel, from Ays to Tocobaga, which is in the provinces of Florida; for all of them, since the Indies were discovered, have killed many Christians, under the pledge of peace and friendship they made to the captains-general who have gone there by order of your Majesty. And although, since he has gone about pacifying them, he has exerted his utmost ability with them, fearing God and your Majesty, trying to do all the good he could among them to preserve the friendship they established with him after having rendered obedience to your Majesty, and to pass over without coming to an open breach, many cases of Christians slain by them; and giving them to understand that he did this because he loved them and that if he wished to harm them he could safely do so, whereby they might be killed and made captive; and they knew this to be truth, without their being able to help it—it was not enough. On the contrary, they have continued in their evil ways, killing Christians under the peace pledge, exulting in victory over the inland caciques, their enemies; telling them that the Spaniards are their slaves, and that for this reason the inland caciques must obey them; these caciques of the coast being infamous people, Sodomites, sacrificers to the devil of many souls, in their ancient ceremonies; wherefore it would greatly serve God Our Lord and your Majesty if these same were dead, or given as slaves. Being informed of all this by the aforesaid reports, your majesty replies to the last petition presented concerning this matter, on the seventeenth of this month, that at present there is no occasion for giving up the Indians as slaves; and because the injury from delay may be irreparable, and Our Lord and your Majesty may be very ill-served thereby:

He beseeches your Majesty to be pleased to command that all the reports which he has given on this be examined, and that if expedient, what he has petitioned be decreed; for he knows that Our Lord will be well served thereby. It may appear that he will be better served if such Indians of that said district are not allowed to be sold or given as slaves, excepting the islands of Hispaniola, San Juan and Cuba for a period of twelve years, the buyers of them obligating themselves to teach them, and endeavor that they become Christians and be saved; and that before they land they shall be declared before the royal officials of your Majesty's Exchequer, in order that there may be no trickery so that, instead of the Indians of Florida, they might want to make slaves of others who are not from there; and if your Majesty should decree neither the one nor the other, he fears that the Indies of Florida will be depopulated of the Spaniards who are settled there. Because they are the key to all the Indies, as the treasure that comes therefrom must pass through that Bahama Channel; and because even though your Majesty may spend much from your Royal Exchequer, you will not be able to bring them to the point where they now are; besides the risk there is of Lutherans settling there, on account of the many Indian friends they have in those provinces—he entreats your Majesty to order that it all be examined, and, if there be reason, that what he has begged for be decreed; and if not, this is the last he asks, since thereby God Our Lord and your Majesty and the profit of your Royal Exchequer will be so greatly served; and it is for the general good of all the Indies and those who navigate therein. And

since he is occupied in your Majesty's service in these parts and the states of Flanders, let it not at any time be held to be his fault and charge if the settlers should depart from that land, because of the notable injuries they receive from the said Indians.

Source: Jeannette M. Thurber Connor, *Colonial Records of Spanish Florida: Letters and Reports of Governors and Secular Persons* (Deland: Florida State Historical Society, 1925).

7. Royal Ordinances for the Discovery, the Population, and the Pacification of the Indies, July 13, 1573

Introduction

Beginning in 1492, Spain established a presence in the Caribbean, brutally conquered the Aztecs in Mexico, and turned their attention to exploiting North America. By 1536, Spanish explorers had heard rumors of fabulous cities of gold in the interior of the continent. Spanish ventures in the New World, though licensed by the king, were privately financed and were expected to make a profit. Thus, conquistadors were primarily seeking their personal fortunes and would stop at nothing to find riches. Typical of these was Hernando de Soto, who in 1539 landed an expedition in Florida and cut a swath of pillage and destruction through the southeastern region. Some of the men accompanying these expeditions of conquest began to express misgivings about their treatment of the native peoples, but these were in the minority. As late as 1573, for example, Pedro Menéndez de Avilés, governor of Florida, was recommending to King Philip II of Spain that the natives be exterminated or captured and sold into slavery. In 1573, however, Philip II issued a set of ordinances from which talk of conquest was absent. Instead, he emphasized "pacification" and conversion of the natives to Christianity, expressed concern for their welfare, and gave explicit instructions for earning their friendship and cooperation.

Primary Source

Don Felipe, by the Grace of God, King of Castilla . . . let it be known: That in order that the discoveries and new settlements and pacification of the land and provinces that are to be discovered, settled, and pacified in the Indies be done with greater facility and in accordance with the service to God Our Lord, and for the welfare of the natives, among other things, we have prepared the following ordinances:

1. No person, regardless of state or condition, should, on his own authority make a new discovery by sea or land, or enter a new settlement or hamlet in areas already discovered. If he were found without our license and approval or by those who had our power

to give it, he would face a death penalty and loss of all his possessions to our coffers. And, we order to all our viceroys, audiencias, and governors and other justices of the Indies, that they give no license to make new discoveries without previous consultation with us and only after having obtained our permission; but we do consent that in areas already discovered, they can give license to build towns as necessary, adhering to the order that in so doing they must keep to the laws of February regarding settlements in discovered lands, then they should send us a description.

2. Those who are in charge of governing the Indies, whether spiritually or temporally, should inform themselves diligently whether within their districts, including lands and provinces bordering them, there is something to be discovered and pacified, of the wealth and quality, of the peoples and nations who inhabit there; but do this without sending to them war personnel nor persons who can cause scandal. They [the governors] should inform themselves by the best means available; and likewise, they should obtain information on the persons who are best suited to carry out discoveries—and with those who are best fit for this purpose, they [the governors] should confer and make arrangements, offering them the honors and advantages that justly, without injury to the natives, can be given them—and—before carrying out what has been arranged or has been learned, give narratives to the viceroy and the audiencias and also send them to the Council, which, after looking at the case, will issue a license to proceed with the discovery, which should be carried out in the following order:

3. Having made, within the confines of the province, a discovery by land, pacified it, subjected it to our obedience, find an appropriate site to be settled by Spaniards—and if not [arrange] for the vassal Indians so they be secure.

4. If the boundaries of the settlement are populated, utilising commerce and ransom, go with vassal Indians and interpreters to discover those lands, and with churchmen and Spaniards, carrying offerings and ransoms and peace, try to learn about the place, the contents and quality of the land, the nation(s) to which the people there belong, who governs them, and carefully take note of all you can learn and understand, and always send these narratives to the Governor so that they reach the Council [Consejo de Indias].

5. Look carefully at the places and ports where it might be possible to build Spanish settlements without damage to the Indian population.

[…]

41. Do not select sites for towns in maritime locations because of the danger that exists of pirates and because they are not very healthy, and because in these [locations] there are less people able to work and cultivate the land, nor is it possible to instill in them these habits. Unless the site is in an area where there are good and principal harbors, among these, select for settlement only those that are necessary for the entry of commerce and for the defense of the land.

[…]

136. If the natives should resolve to take a defensive position toward the [new] settlement, they should be made aware of how we intend to settle, not to do damage to them nor take away their lands, but instead to gain their friendship and teach them how to live civilly, and also to teach them to know our God so they learn His law through which they will be saved. This will be done by religious, clerics, and other persons designated for this purpose by the governor and through good interpreters, taking care by the best means available that the town settlement is carried out peacefully and with their consent, but if they [the natives] still do not want to concur after having been summoned repeatedly by various means, the settlers should build their own town without taking what belongs to the Indians and without doing them more harm than it were necessary for the protection of the town in order that the settlers are not disturbed.

137. While the town is being completed, the settlers should try, inasmuch as this is possible, to avoid communication and traffic with the Indians, or going to their towns, or amusing themselves or spilling themselves on the ground [sensual pleasures?]; nor allow the Indians to enter within the confines of the town until it is built and its defenses ready and houses built so that when the Indians see them they will be struck with admiration and will understand that the Spaniards are there to settle permanently and not temporarily. They [the Spaniards] should be so feared that they [the Indians] will not dare offend them, but they will respect them and desire their friendship. At the beginning of the building of a town, the governor shall name one person who will occupy himself with the sowing and cultivation of the land, planting wheat and vegetables so that the settlers can be assisted in their maintenance. The cattle that they brought shall be put out to pasture in a safe area where they will not damage cultivated land nor Indian property, and so that the aforesaid cattle and its offspring may be of service, help, and sustenance to the town.

138. Having completed the erection of the town and the buildings within it, and not before this is done, the governor and settlers, with great care and holy zeal, should try to bring peace into the fraternity of the Holy Church and bring on to our obedience all the natives of the province and its counties, by the best means they know or can understand, and in the following manner:

139. Obtain information of the diversity of nations, languages, sects, and prejudices of the natives within the province, and about the lords they may pledge allegiance to, and by means of commerce and exchange, [the Spaniards] should try to establish friendship with them [the Indians], showing great love and caressing them and also giving them things in barter that will attract their interest, and not showing greediness for their things. [The Spaniards]

should establish friendship and alliances with the principal lords and other influential persons who would be most useful in the pacification of the land.

140. Having made peace and alliance with [the Indians' lords] and with their republics, make careful efforts so that they get together, and then [our] preachers, with utmost solemnity, should communicate and begin to persuade them that they should desire to understand matters pertaining to the holy Catholic faith. Then shall begin our teaching [efforts]—with great providence and discretion, and in the order stipulated in the first book of the holy Catholic faith—utilizing the mildest approach so as to entice the Indians to want to learn about it. Thus you will not start by reprimanding their vices or their idolatry, nor taking away their women nor their idols, because they should not be scandalized or develop an enmity against the Christian doctrine. Instead, they should be taught first, and after they have been instructed, they should be persuaded that on their own will they should abandon all that runs contrary to our holy Catholic faith and evangelical doctrine.

[. . .]

148. The Spaniards to whom the Indians are entrusted [*encomendados*], should seek with great care that these Indians be settled into towns, and that, within these, churches be built so that the Indians can be instructed into Christian doctrine and live in good order. Because we order you see to it that these Ordinances, as presented above, be incorporated, complied with, and executed, and that you make what in them is contained be complied with and executed, and never take action or move against them, nor consent that others take action or move against either their content or form, under penalty of our Lord.

Dated in the Woods of Segovia, the thirteenth of July, in the year fifteen hundred and seventy-three, I the King; the Licendiado Otalaza; the Licendiado Diego Gasca de Alazar; the Licenciado Gamboa, the Doctor Gomez de Santillán.

Source: Alex I. Mundigo and Dora P. Crouch, "The City Planning Ordinances of the Laws of the Indies Revisited," *Town Planning Review* 48(3) (1977): 247–268.

8. John White, Account of the Fifth Voyage to Virginia at Roanoke Island, 1593

Introduction

Under charter from Queen Elizabeth, Walter Raleigh sponsored five expeditions to North America: in 1584, 1585, 1587, 1588, and 1590. The first expedition returned to England in September 1584

with glowing reports of the North Carolina coast, a temperate land of plenty inhabited by welcoming natives. The land was named Virginia, to honor the virgin queen. The second expedition, in 1585, left a garrison under command of Ralph Lane on Roanoke Island. The men built Fort Raleigh, which was to serve as a base from which to raid Spanish shipping. Having arrived with insufficient food and too late to plant crops, they fell to fighting with the Indians. The expedition soon abandoned the fort, but future settlers paid the price for Lane's treatment of the Indians. John White, known for his firsthand paintings of the Indians of the North Carolina coast, came to Roanoke Island in 1587 as governor of a new colony of 117 men, women, and children. His granddaughter, Virginia Dare, was the first European child born in North America. This colony also arrived too late for planting and faced starvation. White sailed for England to organize a relief mission, but political events conspired to delay his return to Roanoke Island until 1590. He found the colony ruined and deserted. He wrote this report shortly before his death in 1593, knowing that he would never learn the fate of the lost colonists. Some historians speculate that the native people either killed, enslaved, or adopted the colonists into their villages.

Primary Source

The Admirals boat first passed the breach, but not without some danger of sinking, for we had a sea brake into our boat which filled us halfe full of water, but by the will of God and carefull styrage of Captaine Cooke we came safe ashore, saving onely that our furniture, victuals, match and powder were much wet and spoyled. For at this time the winde blue at Northeast and direct into the harbour so great a gale, that the Sea brake extremely on the barre, and the tide went very forcibly at the entrance. By that time our Admirals boat was halled ashore, and most of our things taken out to dry, Captaine Spicer came to the entrance of the breach with his mast standing up, and was halfe passed over, but by the rash and undiscreet styrage of Ralph Skinner his Masters mate, a very dangerous Sea brake into their boate and overset them quite, the men kept the boat some in it, and some hanging on it, but the next sea set the boat on ground, where it beat so, that some of them were forced to let goe their hold, hoping to wade ashore: but the Sea still beat them downe, so that they could neither stand nor swimme, and the boat twise or thrise was turned the keele upward, whereon Captaine Spicer and Skinner hung untill they sunke, and were seene no more. But foure that could swimme a litle kept themselves in deeper water and were saved by Captaine Cookes meanes, who so soone as he saw their oversetting, stripped himselfe, and foure other that could swimme very well, and with all haste possible rowed unto them, and saved foure. There were 11 in all and 7 of the chiefest were drowned, whose names were Edward Spicer, Ralph Skinner, Edward Kelly, Thomas Bevis, Hance the Surgion, Edward Kelborne, Robert Coleman. This mischance did so much discomfort the saylers, that they were all of one mind not to goe any further to seeke the planters. But in the end by the commandement and perswasion of me and Captaine Cooke, they prepared the boates: and seeing the Captaine and me so resolute, they seemed much more willing. Our boates and all things fitted againe, we put off from Hatorask, being the number of 19 persons in both boates: but before we could get to the place where our planters were left, it was so exceeding darke, that we overshot the place a quarter of a mile: there we espied towards the North end of the Island the light of a great fire thorow the woods, to which we presently rowed: when wee came right over against it, we let fall our Grapnel neere the shore and sounded with a trumpet a Call, and afterwardes many familiar English tunes of Songs, and called to them friendly; but we had no answere, we therefore landed at day-breake, and comming to the fire, we found the grasse and sundry rotten trees burning about the place. From hence we went thorow the woods to that part of the Iland directly over against Dasamongwepeuk, and from thence we returned by the water side, round about the North point of the Iland, untill we came to the place where I left our Colony in the yeere 1586. In all this way we saw in the sand the print of the Salvages feet of 2 or 3 sorts troaden the night, and as we entred up the sandy banke upon a tree, in the very browe thereof were curiously carved these faire Romane letters C R O: which letters presently we knew to signifie the place, where I should find the planters seated, according to a secret token agreed upon betweene them and me at my last departure from them, which was, that in any wayes they should not faile to write or carve on the trees or posts of the dores the name of the place where they should be seated; for at my comming away they were prepared to remove from Roanoak 50 miles into the maine. Therefore at my departure from them in An. 1587 I willed them, that if they should happen to be distressed in any of those places, that then they should carve over the letters or name, a Crosse † in this forme, but we found no such signe of distresse. And having well considered of this, we passed toward the place where they were left in sundry houses, but we found the houses taken downe, and the place very strongly enclosed with a high palisado of great trees, with cortynes and flankers very Fortlike, and one of the chiefe trees or postes at the right side of the entrance had the barke taken off, and 5 foote from the ground in fayre Capitall letters was graven CROATOAN without any crosse or signe of distresse; this done, we entred into the palisado, where we found many barres of iron, two pigges of Lead, foure yron fowlers, Iron sacker-shotte, and such like heavie thinges, throwen here and there, almost over-grown with grasse and weedes. From thence wee went along by the water side, towards the poynt of the Creeke to see if we could find any of their botes or Pinnisse, but we could perceive no signe of them, nor any of the last Falkons and small Ordinance which were left with them, at my departure from them. At our returne from the Creeke, some of our Saylers meeting us, told us that they had found where divers chests had bene hidden, and long sithence digged up againe and broken up, and much of the goods in them spoyled and scattered about, but nothing left, of such things as the Savages knew any use of, undefaced. Presently Captaine Cooke and I went to the place, which was in the ende of an olde trench, made two yeeres past by Captaine Amadas: wheere wee found five Chests, that had

bene carefully hidden of the Planters, and of the same chests three were my owne, and about the place many of my things spoyled and broken, and my bookes torne from the covers, the frames of some of my pictures and Mappes rotten and spoyled with rayne, and my armour almost eaten through with rust; this could bee no other but the deede of the Savages our enemies at Dasamongwepeuk, who had watched the departure of our men to Croatoan; and as soone as they were departed digged up every place where they suspected any thing to be buried: but although it much grieved me to see such spoyle of my goods, yet on the other side I greatly joyed that I had safely found a certaine token of their safe being at Croatoan, which is the place where Manteo was borne, and the Savages of the Iland our friends.

Source: Henry S. Burrage, ed., *Early English and French Voyages* (New York: Scribner, 1906), 303–323.

9. Pedro Fernandez de Chocas, Account of the Guale Uprising, October 4, 1597

Introduction

Between 1492 and the first Spanish landfall in the present-day United States, Spain had established a presence in the Caribbean and brutally conquered the Aztecs in Mexico. Spanish contact with native peoples invariably resulted in decimation of the natives by violence and disease. The Spaniards turned northward to explore for precious metals, mounting expeditions in 1528, 1539, and 1540. By 1565 they had established a base at St. Augustine. The governor of Florida wrote to his king recommending that the hostile natives be exterminated or captured and sold into slavery. Philip II instead ordered that the Spanish focus on converting Native Americans to Christianity rather than conquering them. During the 1590s, Franciscan friars began establishing missions in the regions surrounding St. Augustine. They used a combination of gifts, trade goods, destruction of native idols, and punishment to win converts. Epidemics of European diseases caused many Indians to seek—in vain—divine protection from the friars' religion. In 1597 the Guale region, along the coast of present-day Georgia, erupted into violence against the Spanish missions. This report describes how the uprising began with the killing of five friars and the capture of a sixth. The governor of Florida avenged the deaths by destroying Guale villages and enslaving the captives.

Primary Source

Fray Pedro Fernandez de Chocas to Gonzalo Mendez de Canzo

Let Him through whose virtues hell is rendered powerless, give me strength to endure the hardships which confront us at each moment. To-day Saturday, in the morning, twenty-three canoes filled with Indians from all the land and province of Guale appeared to this river of Puturiba; they were going to Guale. After the men of the two of the canoes had disembarked at the village of San Pedro, the principal village of this province, and shot arrows at the Indian who came out of his house when the dogs made a noise and barked, their presence was immediately made known through the whole village from the cries of the wounded man, who is not dead yet. Don Juan and his Indians went in two canoes after the two canoes of the enemy, who drew over to the other side of the river, and landed, leaving in the canoes everything they were carrying. Our Christian Indians went in pursuit of them into the forest until they overtook one, and according to the custom of Indians, they slew him and took his scalp, although his hair was short, as he was a Christian. I censured this, for if they had bound him, as I had told them to do, the cause and reason of the war could have been learned from him. Another canoe was also found adrift, and leaving it at the landing-place, the enemy fled into the forest without the men of this village being able to overtake them. The rest went to Bejesse, which is beyond this island; and there, through an *arequi*, my fiscal, spoke with the Cacique of Asao and censured him, and he went to his district and begged him to land. He would not do so; rather did he shamelessly show the hat of the Father Vicar of Asao, Fray Francisco de Berascula, saying: "See, hero, [what belonged] to that Father. Come, you others, and bring him *tortas*." He also showed the arquebue with which the said father used to call for a canoe by the streams he had to pass when he went to visit his villages. And [the cacique] said, in a loud voice, that there no longer was any Christianity since Our Lord had permitted this, and the enemy of our Catholic faith had ordained it thus, for the condemnation of so many souls. It is much to be deplored that with the said Father they killed the Father of Guale, Fray Miguel de Aunon; him of Tolomato, Fray Pedro de Corpa; him of Tupiqui, Fray Blas Rodriguez; him of Talapuz, Fray Francisco de Avila, priests all of them; and that they had only kept alive as a prisoner and slave the Father, Fray Antonio de Badajoz, a lay-brother; and they took him to Tulufina with all the martyred religious, as is proved to be the truth by all the spoils which are taken away from them here: cowls and shreds of garments which the Indians divided among themselves. For that is what they did with such inhumanity to the most innocent Lamb [of all]. How they must have felt, Senor General, those little lambs, on receiving martyrdom all alone as they were! The thought of this so moves me that I cannot go on farther. I envy them the crowns of glory which they bear before us; and I await in this desert, by saintly obedience, that which Our Lord in His mercy may have in store for me; for the enemy Indians are already threatening those of this land, telling them to wander away from it and go to Timucua, because there they will not be warred upon again. The number of all the Indians who came might have been upwards of four hundred. May that religious whom they say they have spared from death and are keeping in Tulufina be favored by the one only God; and may they give decent burial to the bodies of

the blessed dead; and may it be possible that the dead are not so many. There may be peril in any delay in assistance, although it is not my purpose that they be avenged by fire and sword; rather should the remedy be gentleness and forbearance, as is your Honor's custom and intent, for they should be taken and treated like children. But I beg in mercy that the religious who have been saved may be visited, and taken from the hands of their foes; and if this cannot be shortly provided for our defence, and for the assistance of these Christian natives, it would be well to send six or more veteran soldiers, who could be divided meantime between Bezesi, here and San Pedro, doing the duty of sentinels with the Indians, if they can content themselves with *tortas, gacha,* and fish whenever there is any for here there is nothing else; and even this could not be furnished unless it be for a short time. But they, being honorable men, God will not fail them, for the love of Whom we subject ourselves to these perils; and may He inspire your Honor for the good task, and defend us from our enemies. From Puturiba, the fourth day of October, 1597. The altar-furnishings I used when I said mass in this mission, which his Majesty gave us with the corporal cloths, and a silver chalice from the convent which I had borrowed, were left in Tolomato when I made the journey to the mountains in safety [to Tama?], glory be to God. If it be right, may another be supplied me from his Majesty's funds. Well does your Honor see how necessary this is for my consolation and that of the Indians, and the good and benefit of the souls of purgatory, which has its part in the sacrifice. I supplicate your Honor to provide [in these matters], since therein God our Lord will be served, etc.

[signed] Fray Pedro Fernandez de Chocas

> **Source:** Jeannette M. Thurber Connor, *Colonial Records of Spanish Florida: Letters and Reports of Governors and Secular Persons* (Deland: Florida State Historical Society, 1925).

10. Don Juan de Oñate, Letter from New Mexico, March 1599

Introduction

Spanish ventures in the New World, though licensed by the king, were privately financed and were expected to make a profit. In 1573 King Philip II of Spain ordered that Spanish conquistadors focus on pacifying and converting Native Americans to Christianity rather than conquering them. The order to pacify rather than conquer made it more difficult for investors to realize a profit. Don Juan de Oñate was named to pacify and colonize New Mexico, a land of scarce resources populated by pueblo-dwelling natives. Oñate entered New Mexico in 1598 with several hundred colonists, including soldiers and Franciscan friars. His soldiers rampaged through the country plundering the natives. In January 1599 the inhabitants of Acoma Pueblo revolted and killed about a dozen

Spaniards. Oñate ordered massive retaliation. His forces killed 800 men, women, and children and enslaved and mutilated hundreds of captives. His letter, written shortly after the massacre, gives lip service to pacification and only briefly mentions events at Acoma. Oñate then led several futile expeditions in search of fabled riches. His colonists, failing to find wealth in New Mexico, eventually returned to old Mexico and complained of his conduct. The royal governor of Mexico recalled and prosecuted Oñate. The Spanish founded a permanent settlement at Santa Fe, New Mexico, in 1610.

Primary Source

From Rio de Nombre de Dios I last wrote to you, Illustrious Sir, giving you an account of my departure, and of the discovery of a wagon road to the Rio del Norte, and of my certain hopes of the successful outcome of my journey, which hopes God has been pleased to grant, may He be forever praised; for greatly to His advantage and that of his royal Majesty, they have acquired a possession so good that none other of his Majesty in these Indies excels it, judging it solely by what I have seen, by things told of in reliable reports, and by things almost a matter of experience, from having been seen by people in my camp and known by me at present.

This does not include the vastness of the settlements or the riches of the West which the natives praise, or the certainty of pearls promised by the South Sea from the many shells containing them possessed by these Indians, or the many settlements called the seven caves, which the Indians report at the head of this river, which is the Rio del Norte; but includes only the provinces which I have seen and traversed, the people of this eastern country, the Apaches, the nation of the Cocoyes, and many others which are daily being discovered in this district and neighborhood, as I shall specify in this letter. I wish to begin by giving your Lordship an account of it, because it is the first since I left New Spain.

I departed, Illustrious Sir, from Rio de Nombre de Dios on the sixteenth of March, with the great multitude of wagons, women, and children, which your Lordship very well knows, freed from all my opponents, but with a multitude of evil predictions conforming to their desires and not to the goodness of God. His Majesty was pleased to accede to my desires, and to take pity on my great hardships, afflictions, and expenses, bringing me to these provinces of New Mexico with all his Majesty's army enjoying perfect health.

Although I reached these provinces on the twenty-eighth day of May (going ahead with as many as sixty soldiers to pacify the land and free it from traitors, if in it there should be any, seizing Humana and his followers, to obtain full information, by seeing with my own eyes, regarding the location and nature of the land, and regarding the nature and customs of the people, so as to order what might be best for the army, which I left about twenty-two leagues from the first pueblos, after having crossed the Rio del Norte, at which river I took possession, in the name of his Majesty, of all these kingdoms and pueblos which I discovered before departing from it with scouts), the army did not overtake me at the place where I established it and where I now have it established, in this province of the Teguas, until the nineteenth day of August of the past year. During that time I travelled through settlements sixty-one leagues in extent toward the north, and thirty-five in width from east to west. All this district is filled with pueblos, large and small, very continuous and close together.

At the end of August I began to prepare the people of my camp for the severe winter with which both the Indians and the nature of the land threatened me; and the devil, who has ever tried to make good his great loss occasioned by our coming, plotted, as is his wont, exciting a rebellion among more than forty-five soldiers and captains, who under pretext of not finding immediately whole plates of silver lying on the ground, and offended because I would not permit them to maltreat these natives, either in their persons or in their goods, became disgusted with the country, or to be more exact, with me, and endeavored to form a gang in order to flee to that New Spain, as they proclaimed, although judging from what has since come to light their intention was directed more to stealing slaves and clothing and to other acts of effrontery not permitted. I arrested two captains and a soldier, who they said were guilty, in order to garrote them on this charge, but ascertaining that their guilt was not so great, and on account of my situation and of the importunate pleadings of the religious and of the entire army, I was forced to forego the punishment and let bygones be bygones.

Although by the middle of September I succeeded in completely calming and pacifying my camp, from this great conflagration a spark was bound to remain hidden underneath the ashes of the dissembling countenances of four of the soldiers of the said coterie. These fled from me at that time, stealing from me part of the horses, thereby violating not only one but many proclamations which, regarding this matter and others, I had posted for the good of the land in the name of his Majesty.

Since they had violated his royal orders, it appeared to me that they should not go unpunished; therefore I immediately sent post-haste the captain and procurator-general Gaspar Perez de Villagran and the captain of artillery Geronimo Marques, with an express order to follow and overtake them and give them due punishment. They left in the middle of September, as I have said, thinking that they would overtake them at once, but their journey was prolonged more than they or I had anticipated, with the result to two of the offenders which your Lordship already knows from the letter which they tell me they wrote from Sancta Barbara. The other two who fled from them will have received the same at your Lordship's hands, as is just.

I awaited their return and the outcome for some days, during which time I sent my *sargento mayor* to find and utilize the buffalo to the east, where he found an infinite multitude of them, and had the experience which he set forth in a special report. Both he and the others were so long delayed that, in order to lose no time, at the beginning of October, this first church having been founded, wherein the first mass was celebrated on the 8th of September, and the religious having been distributed in various provinces and *doctrinas,* I went in person to the province of Abo and to that of the Xumanas and to the large and famous salines of this country, which must be about twenty leagues east of here.

From there I crossed over to the west through the province of Puaray to discover the South Sea, so that I might be able to report to your Lordship. When Captain Villagran arrived I took him for this purpose.

What more in good time it was possible to accomplish through human efforts is in substance what I shall set forth in the following chapter. For this purpose it shall be day by day, and event by event, especially regarding the death of my nephew and *maese de campo,* who, as my rear-guard, was following me to the South Sea. His process, along with many other papers, I am sending to your Lordship. To despatch them earlier has been impossible. I have, then, discovered and seen up to the present the following provinces:

The province of the Piguis, which is the one encountered in coming from that New Spain; the province of the Xumanas; the province of the Cheguas, which we Spaniards call Puaray; the province of the Cheres; the province of the Trias; the province of the Emmes; the province of the Teguas; the province of the Picuries; the province of the Taos; the province of the Peccos; the province of Abbo and the salines; the province of Juni; and the province of Mohoce.

These last two are somewhat apart from the rest, towards the west, and are the places where we recently discovered the rich mines, as is attested by the papers which your Lordship will see there. I could not work or improve these mines because of the death of my *maese de campo,* Joan de Zaldivar, and of the rectification of the results of it, which I completed at the end of last month. Nor could I complete my journey to the South Sea, which was the purpose with which I went to the said provinces, leaving my camp in this province of the Teguas, whence I am now writing.

There must be in this province and in the others abovementioned, to make a conservative estimate, seventy thousand Indians, settled after our custom, house adjoining house, with square plazas. They have no streets, and in the pueblos, which contain many plazas or wards, one goes from one plaza to the other through alleys. They are of two and three stories, of an *estado* and a half or an *estado* and a third each, which latter is not so common; and some houses are of four, five, six, and seven stories. Even whole pueblos

dress in very highly colored cotton *mantas,* white or black, and some of thread-very good clothes. Others wear buffalo hides, of which there is a great abundance. They have most excellent wool, of whose value I am sending a small example.

It is a land abounding in flesh of buffalo, goats with hideous horns, and turkeys; and in Mohoce there is game of all kinds. There are many wild and ferocious beasts, lions, bears, wolves, tigers, *penicas,* ferrets, porcupines, and other animals, whose hides they tan and use. Towards the west there are bees and very white honey, of which I am sending a sample. Besides, there are vegetables, a great abundance of the best and greatest salines in the world, and a very great many kinds of very rich ores, as I stated above. Some discovered near here do not appear so, although we have hardly begun to see anything of the much there is to be seen. There are very fine grape vines, rivers, forests of many oaks, and some cork trees, fruits, melons, grapes, watermelons, Castilian plums, *capuli,* pine-nuts, acorns, ground-nuts, and *coralejo,* which is a delicious fruit, and other wild fruits. There are many and very good fish in this Rio del Norte, and in others. From the ores here are made all the colors which we use, and they are very fine.

The people are in general very comely; their color is like those of that land, and they are much like them in manner and dress, in their grinding, in their food, dancing, singing, and many other things, except in their languages, which are many, and different from those there. Their religion consists in worshipping idols, of which they have many; and in their temples, after their own manner, they worship them with fire, painted reeds, feathers, and universal offering of almost everything they get, such as small animals, birds, vegetables, etc. In their government they are free, for although they have some petty captains, they obey them badly and in very few things.

We have seen other nations such as the Querechos, or herdsmen, who live in tents of tanned hides, among the buffalo. The Apaches, of whom we have also seen some, are innumerable, and although I heard that they lived in rancherias, a few days ago I ascertained that they live like these in pueblos, one of which, eighteen leagues from here, contains fifteen plazas. They are a people whom I have compelled to render obedience to His Majesty, although not by means of legal instruments like the rest of the provinces. This has caused me much labor, diligence, and care, long journeys, with arms on the shoulders, and not a little watching and circumspection; indeed, because my *maese de campo* was not as cautious as he should have been, they killed him with twelve companions in a great pueblo and fortress called Acoma, which must contain about three thousand Indians. As punishment for its crime and its treason against his Majesty, to whom it had already rendered submission by a public instrument, and as a warning to the rest, I razed and burned it completely, in the way in which your Lordship will see by the process of this cause. All these provinces, pueblos, and peoples, I have seen with my own eyes.

There is another nation, that of the Cocoyes, an innumerable people with huts and agriculture. Of this nation and of the large settlements at the source of the Rio del Norte and of those to the northwest and west and towards the South Sea, I have numberless reports, and pearls of remarkable size from the said sea, and assurance that there is an infinite number of them on the coast of this country. And as to the east, a person in my camp, an Indian who speaks Spanish and is one of those who came with Humana, has been in the pueblo of the said herdsmen. It is nine continuous leagues in length and two in width, with streets and houses consisting of huts. It is situated in the midst of the multitude of buffalo, which are so numerous that my *sargento mayor,* who hunted them and brought back their hides, meat, tallow, and suet, asserts that in one herd alone he saw more than there are of our cattle in the combined three ranches of Rodrigo del Rio, Salvago, and Jeronimo Lopez, which are famed in those regions.

I should never cease were I to recount individually all of the many things which occur to me. I can only say that with God's help I shall see them all, and give new worlds, new, peaceful, and grand, to his Majesty, greater than the good Marquis gave to him, although he did so much, if you, Illustrious Sir, will give to me the aid, the protection, and the help which I expect from such a hand. And although I confess that I am crushed at having been so out of favor when I left that country, and although a soul frightened by disfavor usually loses hope and despairs of success, it is nevertheless true that I never have and never shall lose hope of receiving many and very great favors at the hand of your Lordship, especially in matters of such importance to his Majesty. And in order that you, Illustrious Sir, may be inclined to render them to me, I beg that you take note of the great increase which the royal crown and the rents of his Majesty have and will have in this land, with so many and such a variety of things, each one of which promises very great treasures. I shall only note these four, omitting the rest as being well known and common:

First, the great wealth which the mines have begun to reveal and the great number of them in this land, whence proceed the royal fifths and profits. Second, the certainty of the proximity of the South Sea, whose trade with Piru, New Spain, and China is not to be depreciated, for it will give birth in time to advantageous and continuous duties, because of its close proximity, particularly to China and to that land. And what I emphasize in this matter as worthy of esteem is the traffic in pearls, reports of which are so certain, as I have stated, and of which we have had ocular experience from the shells. Third, the increase of vassals and tributes, which will increase not only the rents, but his renown and dominion as well, if it be possible that for our king these can increase. Fourth, the wealth of the abundant salines, and of the mountains of brimstone, of which there is a greater quantity than in any other

province. Salt is the universal article of traffic of all these barbarians and their regular food, for they even eat or suck it alone as we do sugar. These four things appear as if dedicated solely to his Majesty. I will not mention the founding of so many republics, the many offices, their quittances, vacancies, provisions, etc., the wealth of the wool and hides of buffalo, and many other things, clearly and well known, or, judging from the general nature of the land, the certainty of wines and oils.

In view, then, Illustrious Sir, of things of such honor, profit, and value, and of the great prudence, magnanimity, and nobility of your Lordship, who in all matters is bound to prosper me and overcome the ill fortune of my disgrace, I humbly beg and supplicate, since it is of such importance to the service of God and of his Majesty, that the greatest aid possible be sent to me, both for settling and pacifying, your Lordship giving your favor, mind, zeal, and life for the conservation, progress, and increase of this land, through the preaching of the holy gospel and the founding of this republic, giving liberty and favor to all, opening wide the door to them, and, if it should be necessary, even ordering them to come to serve their king in so honorable and profitable a matter, in a land so abundant and of such great beginnings of riches. I call them beginnings, for although we have seen much, we have not yet made a beginning in comparison with what there is to see and enjoy. And if the number should exceed five hundred men, they all would be needed, especially married men, who are the solid rock on which new republics are permanently founded; and noble people, of whom there is such a surplus there. Particularly do I beg your Lordship to give a license to my daughter Mariquita, for whom I am sending, and to those of my relatives who may wish so honorably to end their lives.

For my part, I have sunk my ships and have furnished an example to all as to how they ought to spend their wealth and their lives and those of their children and relatives in the service of their king and lord, on whose account and in whose name I beg your Lordship to order sent to me six small cannon and some powder, all of which will always be at the service of his Majesty, as is this and everything else. Although on such occasions the necessities increase, and although under such circumstances as those in which I now find myself others are wont to exaggerate, I prefer to suffer from lack of necessities rather than to be a burden to his Majesty or to your Lordship, feeling assured that I shall provide them for many poor people who may look to me if your Lordship will grant the favor, which I ask, of sending them to me.

To make this request of you, illustrious Sir, I am sending the best qualified persons whom I have in my camp, for it is but reasonable that such should go on an errand of such importance to the service of God and his Majesty, in which they risk their health and life, looking lightly upon the great hardships which they must suffer and have suffered. Father Fray Alonso Martinez, apostolic commissary of these provinces of New Mexico, is the most meritorious person with whom I have had any dealings, and of the kind needed by such great kingdoms for their spiritual government. Concerning this I am writing to his Majesty, and I shall be greatly favored if your Lordship will do the same. I believe your Lordship is under a loving obligation to do this, both because the said Father Commissary is your client as well as because of the authority of his person and of the merits of his worthy life, of which I am sending to his Majesty a special report, which your Lordship will see if you desire, and to which I refer. In his company goes my cousin, Father Fray Cristobal de Salazar, concerning whom testimony can be given by his prelate, for in order not to appear an interested witness in my own cause I refrain from saying what I could say with much reason and truth. For all spiritual matters I refer you to the said fathers, whom I beg your Lordship to credit in every respect as you would credit me in person. I say but little to your Lordship as to your crediting them as true priests of my father Saint Francis. With such as these may your Lordship swell these your kingdoms, for there is plenty for them to do.

For temporal matters go such honorable persons as Captain and Procurator-general Gaspar Perez de Villagran, captain of the guard, Marcos Farfan de los Godos, and Captain Joan Pinero, to whom I refer you, as also to the many papers which they carry. In them your Lordship will find authentic information regarding all that you may desire to learn of this country of yours.

I remain as faithful to you, Illustrious Sir, as those who most protest. Your interests will always be mine, for the assurance and confidence which my faithfulness gives me is an evidence that in past undertakings I have found in your Lordship true help and love; for although when I left I did not deserve to receive the cedula from my king dated April 2, I shall deserve to receive it now that I know that I have served him so well.

And in order to satisfy his royal conscience and for the safety of the creatures who were preserved at Acoma, I send them to your Lordship with the holy purpose which the Father Commissary will explain, for I know it is so great a service to God that I consider very well employed the work and expense which I have spent in the matter. And I do not expect a lesser reward for your Lordship on account of the prayers of those few days. Honor it, Illustrious Sir, for it redounds to the service of God. May He prosper and exalt you to greater offices. In His divine service, which is the highest and greatest I can name, I again beg for the aid requested, much, good, and speedy—priests as well as settlers and soldiers.

Source: Herbert Eugene Bolton, ed., *Spanish Exploration in the Southwest, 1542–1706*, Vol. 17 (New York: Scribner, 1916), 212–222.

11. Powhatan, Remarks to John Smith, 1609 [Excerpts]

Introduction

Captain John Smith (1580–1631) was part of the first expedition to colonize Virginia in 1607. Smith spent much of his time in Virginia exploring the countryside, forging a relationship with the native peoples, and mapping the coastal waterways. The native peoples consisted of the Algonquian inhabitants of some 30 villages who accepted the leadership of their chieftain, Powhatan. Ongoing power struggles propelled Captain Smith to the presidency of the colony after the first two presidents were discredited. Unlike the previous leaders, Smith imposed discipline and forced the settlers to work for the survival of the colony. Nevertheless, they faced months of starvation, and many fell ill and died. Smith maintained a tenuous peace with Powhatan, who provided the colony with food and thus saved it from complete failure. Smith left Virginia in 1609 and returned home to recuperate from an injury. He wrote an account of his adventures in which he described the colonists' early relations with Powhatan and his people. In the remarks reproduced here, Powhatan explains to Smith his suspicions regarding the colonists and his desire for peace. Powhatan was succeeded at his death in 1618 by his brother Opechancanough, who was far less tolerant of the colonists and ordered the devastating Massacre of 1622 in which one-third of the white population died at the hands of Indians.

Primary Source

Captain Smith, some doubt I have of your coming hither . . . for many do inform me, your coming is not for trade, but to invade my people and possess my Country. . . . I am now grown old, and must soon die; and the succession must descend, in order, to my brothers, Opitchapan, Opekankanough, and Catataugh, and then to my two sisters, and their two daughters. I wish their experience was equal to mine; and that your love to us might not be less than ours to you. Why should you take by force that from us which you can have by love? Why should you destroy us, who have provided you with food? What can you get by war? We can hide our provisions, and fly into the woods; and then you must consequently famish by wronging your friends. What is the cause of your jealousy? You see us unarmed, and willing to supply your wants, if you will come in a friendly manner, and not with swords and guns, as to invade an enemy. I am not so simple, as not to know it is better to eat good meat, lie well, and sleep quietly with my women and children; to laugh and be merry with the English; and, being their friend, to have copper, hatchets, and whatever else I want, than to fly from all, to lie cold in the woods, feed upon acorns, roots, and such trash, and to be so hunted, that I cannot rest, eat, or sleep. In such circumstances, my men must watch, and if a twig should break, all would cry out, "Here comes Capt. Smith": and so, in this miserable manner, to end my miserable life; and, Capt. Smith, this might be soon your fate too, through your rashness and unadvisedness. I, therefore, exhort you to peaceable councils; and, above all, I insist that the guns and swords, the cause of all our jealousy and uneasiness, be removed and sent away.

Source: Samuel Drake, *Biography and History of the Indians of North America,* 11th ed. (Boston, 1841), 353.

12. John Smith, Letter to Queen Anne about Pocahontas, 1616

Introduction

John Smith was the only English witness to his legendary first encounter with Pocahontas, the 11-year-old daughter of Powhatan, the powerful leader of a confederation of native villages surrounding Jamestown. Smith left the colony frequently to explore and trade with the Indians. On one such journey a group of Indians captured him and killed his companions. According to Smith, his captors were about to execute him when Pocahontas threw herself down next to him and pleaded for his life. Powhatan spared his life, called him a friend and, a few days later, released him. Whether or not the events took place exactly as Smith described them, Pocahontas became a frequent visitor to Jamestown after Smith's release. At Jamestown, Pocahontas learned to speak English, converted to Christianity, and was renamed Rebecca. Her 1614 wedding to the Englishman John Rolfe brought about a period of peace between the colonists and Pocahontas's people. The couple and their infant son visited England in 1616, where Pocahontas met King James I. Before the Rolfes could return to Virginia, Pocahontas fell ill and died in 1617 at the age of 21. Her young son, Thomas Rolfe, grew up to found a long line of Virginians. Smith wrote this letter to Queen Anne (wife of King James I) asking the royal family to treat Pocahontas well in gratitude for all she had done for the Jamestown colonists. The letter also contains Smith's first account of his rescue by Pocahontas.

Primary Source

To the most high and virtuous Princesse Queene Anne of Great Brittanie.

Most admired Queene,

The love I beare my God, my King and Countrie, hath so oft emboldened mee in the worst of extreme dangers, that now honestie doth constraine mee presume thus farre beyond my selfe, to present your Majestie this short discourse: if ingratitude be a deadly poyson to all honest vertues, I must bee guiltie of that crime if I should omit any meanes to bee thankfull. So it is,

That some ten yeeres agoe being in Virginia, and taken prisoner by the power of *Powhatan* their chiefe King, I received from this great Salvage exceeding great courtesie, especially from his sonne *Nantaquaus,* the most manliest, comeliest, boldest spirit, I ever saw in a Salvage, and his sister Pocahontas, the Kings most deare and wel-beloved daughter, being but a childe of twelve or thirteene yeeres of age, whose compassionate pitifull heart, of my desperate estate, gave me much cause to respect her: I being the first Christian this proud King and his grim attendants ever saw: and thus inthralled in their barbarous power, I cannot say I felt the least occasion of want that was in the power of those my mortall foes to prevent, notwithstanding al their threats. After some six weeks fatting amongst those Salvage Courtiers, at the minute of my execution, she hazarded the beating out of her owne braines to save mine, and not onely that, but so prevailed with her father, that I was safely conducted to James towne, where I found about eight and thirtie miserable poore and sicke creatures, to keepe possession of all those large territories of Virginia, such was the weaknesse of this poore common-wealth, as had the Salvages not fed us, we directly had starved.

And this reliefe, most gracious Queene, was commonly brought us by this Lady *Pocahontas,* notwithstanding all these passages when inconstant Fortune turned our peace to warre, this tender Virgin would still not spare to dare to visit us, and by her our jarres have beene oft appeased, and our wants still supplied; were it the policie of her father thus to imploy her, or the ordinance of God thus to make her his instrument, or her extraordinarie affection to our Nation, I know not: but of this I am sure; when her father with the utmost of his policie and power, sought to surprize mee, having but eighteen with mee, the darke night could not affright her from comming through the irksome woods, and with watered eies gave me intelligence, with her best advice to escape his furie; which had hee knowne, hee had surely slaine her. James towne with her wild traine she as freely frequented, as he fathers habitation; and during the time of two or three yeeres, she next under God, was still the instrument to preserve this Colonie from death, famine and utter confusion, which if in those times had once beene dissolved, Virginia might have line as it was at our first arrivall to this day. Since then, the businesse having beene turned and varied by many accidents from that I left it at: it is most certaine, after a long and troublesome warre after my departure, betwixt her father and our Colonie, all which time shee was not heard of, about two yeeres after she her selfe was taken prisoner, being so detained neere two yeeres longer, the Colonie by that meanes was relieved, peace concluded, and at last rejecting her barbarous condition, was married to an *English* Gentleman, with whom at this present she is in England; the first Christian ever of that Nation, the first *Virginian* ever spake *English,* or had a childe in marriage by an *Englishman,* a matter surely, if my meaning bee truly considered and well understood, worthy a Princes understanding.

Thus most gracious Lady, I have related to your Majestie, what at your best leasure our approved Histories will account you at large, and done in the time of your Majesties life, and however this might bee presented you from a more worthy pen, it cannot come from a more honest heart, as yet I never begged anything of the state, or any, and it is my want of abilitie and her exceeding desert, your birth, meanes and authoritie, her birth, virtue, want and simplicite, doth make mee thus bold, humbly to beseech your Majestie to take this knowledge of her, though it be from one so unworthy to be the reporter, as my selfe, her husbands estate not being able to make her fit to attend your Majestie: the most and least I can doe, is to tell you this, because none so oft hath tried it as my selfe, and the rather being of so great a spirit, how ever he stature: if she should not be well received, seeing this Kingdome may rightly have a Kingdome by her meanes; her present love to us and Christianitie, might turne to such scorne and furie, as to divert all this good to the worst of evill, where finding so great a Queene should doe her some honour more than she can imagine, for being so kinde to your servants and subjects, would so ravish her with content, as endeare her dearest bloud to effect that, your Majestie and all the Kings honest subjects more earnestly desire: And so I humbly kisse your gracious hands.

Being about this time preparing to set saile for New-England, I could not stay to doe her that service I desired, and she well deserved; but hearing she was at *Branford* with divers of my friends, I went to see her: After a modest salutation, without any word, she turned about, obscured her face, as not seeming well contented; and in that humour her husband, with divers others, we all left her two or three houres, repenting my selfe to have writ she could speake *English*. But not long after, she began to talke, and remembred mee well what courtesies she had done: saying, You did promise *Powhatan* what was yours should bee his, and he the like to you; you called him father being in his land a stranger, and by the same reason so must I doe you: which though I would have excused, I durst not allow of that title, because she was a Kings daughter; with a well set countenance she said, Were you not afraid to come into my fathers Countrie, and caused feare in him and all his people (but mee) and feare you here I should call you father; I tell you then I will, and you shall call mee childe, and so I will bee for ever and ever your Countrieman. They did tell us alwaies you were dead, and I knew no other till I came to *Plimoth;* yet *Powhatan* did command Uttamatomakkin to seeke you, and know the truth, because your Countriemen will lie much.

This Salvage, one of *Powhatans* Councell, being amongst them held an understanding fellow; the King purposely sent him, as they say, to number the people here, and informe him well what wee were and our state. Arriving at *Plimoth,* according to his directions, he got a long sticke, whereon by notches hee did thinke to have kept the number of all the men hee could see, but

he was quickly wearie of that taske: Comming to *London,* where by chance I met him, having renewed our acquaintance, where many were desirous to heare and see his behaviour, hee told me *Powhatan* did bid him to finde me out, to shew shim our God, the King, Queene, and Prince, I so much had told them of: Concerning God, I told him the best I could, the King I heard he had seene, and the rest hee should see when he would; he denied ever to have seene the King, till by circumstances he was satisfied he had: Then he replyed very sadly, You gave *Powhatan* a white Dog, which *Powhatan* fed as himselfe, but your King gave me nothing, and I am better than your white Dog.

The small time I staid in *London,* divers Courtiers and others, my acquaintances, hath gone with mee to see her, that generally concluded, they did thinke God had a great hand in her conversion, and they have seene many *English* Ladies worse favoured, proportioned and behavioured, and as since I have heard, it pleased both the King and Queenes Majestie honourably to esteeme her, accompanied with the honourable Lady the Lady *De la Ware,* and that honourable Lord her husband, and divers other persons of good qualities, both publikely at the maskes and otherwise, to her great satisfaction and content, which doubtlesse she would have deserved, had she lived to arrive in *Virginia.*

Source: John Smith, *The Generall Historie of Virginia, New-England, and the Summer Isles with the Names of the Adventurers, Planters, and Governours from Their First Beginning* (London: Printed by I. D. and I. H. for Michael Sparkes, 1624), 121–122.

13. Massasoit Peace Treaty, 1621

Introduction

The Wampanoag chief Massasoit was the first Indian leader to deal with the New England colonists shortly after the Pilgrims' arrival at Plymouth, Massachusetts, in late 1620. At the Pilgrims' request, Massasoit agreed to this treaty in March 1621. After the separatist Pilgrims founded the colony, a mix of Puritans and non-Puritans from England founded settlements along the New England coast. By 1635 about 2,000 immigrants were arriving each year, most of them Puritans. The newcomers settled all along the coast from Maine to Long Island. The English and the Wampanoags worked hard to maintain peace throughout Massasoit's life, despite bitter conflicts between Indians and colonists in other parts of New England, such as the Pequot War of 1637 in Connecticut. Massasoit died in 1662 and was succeeded by his son Metacom, known to the English as King Philip. Metacom led an Indian coalition in a war to resist English expansion. Called King Philip's War (1675–1676), this hugely destructive conflict pushed the colonists back from the frontier and came close to driving them from New England. At the cost of 1 in 16 fighting men, the colonists prevailed and crushed all Indian resistance.

Primary Source

1. That neither he nor any of his should injure or do hurt to any of our people.

2. And if any of his did hurt to any of ours, he should send the offender, that we might punish him.

3. That if any of our tools were taken away when our people were at work, he should cause them to be restored; and if ours did any harm to any of his, we would do the like to them.

4. If any did unjustly war against him, we would aid him; if any did war against us, he should aid us.

5. He should send to his neighbor confederates, to certify them of this, that they might not wrong us, but might be likewise comprised in the conditions of peace.

6. That when their men came to us, they should leave their bows and arrows behind them, as we should do our pieces when we came to them.

Lastly, that doing thus, King James would esteem of him as his friend and ally.

Source: William Bradford, *History of the Plymouth Plantation* (Boston: Little, Brown, 1856), 94.

14. John Smith, Account of the Massacre of 1622 in Virginia, 1624

Introduction

Captain John Smith (1580–1631) was part of the first expedition to colonize Virginia in 1607. The son of a tenant farmer, he became a professional soldier. Smith spent much of his time in Virginia exploring the countryside, forging a relationship with the native peoples, and mapping the coastal waterways. The native peoples consisted of the Algonquian inhabitants of some 30 villages who accepted the leadership of their chieftain, Powhatan. After a period as president of the struggling colony, Smith left Virginia in 1609 and returned home to recuperate from an injury. He returned to North America in 1614 and mapped the coast of New England. After his final return to England, Smith wrote an account of his adventures as well as a general history of the colony in Virginia. Here he recounts the coordinated surprise attacks of March 22, 1622, and the resulting massacre of 347 men, women, and children, more than one-third of Virginia's English population. The deaths of Pocahontas in 1617 and Powhatan the following year doomed the fragile peace between their people and the colonists. Powhatan's half brother Opechancanough planned the operation to drive the English from his land. The colony survived and launched a brutal all-out war of extermination.

Primary Source

The massacre upon the two and twentieth of March.

The Prologue to this Tragedy, is supposed was occasioned by Nemattanow, otherwise called Jack of the Feather, because hee commonly was most strangely adorned with them; and for his courage and policy, was accounted amongst the Salvages their chiefe Captaine, and immortall from any hurt could bee done him by the English. This Captaine comming to one Morgans house, knowing he had many commodities that hee desired, perswaded Morgan to goe with him to Pamaunke to trucke, but the Salvage murdered him by the way; and after two or three daies returned againe to Morgans house, where he found two youths his Servants, who asked for their Master: Jack replied directly he was dead; the Boyes suspecting as it was, by seeing him weare his Cap, would have had him to Master Thorp: But Jack so moved their patience, they shot him, so he fell to the ground, put him in a Boat to have him before the Governor, then seven or eight miles from them. But by the way Jack finding the pangs of death upon him, desired of the Boyes two things; the one was, that they would not make it knowne hee was slaine with a bullet; the other, to bury him amongst the English. At the losse of this Salvage Opechankanough much grieved and repined, with great threats of revenge; but the English returned him such terrible answers, that he cunningly dissembled his intent, with the greatest signes he could of love and peace, yet within fourteene daies after he acted what followeth.

Sir Francis Wyat at his arrival was advertised, he found the Countrey setled in such a firme peace, as most men there thought sure and unviolable, not onely in regard of their promises, but of a necessitie. The poore weake Salvages being every way bettered by us, and safely sheltred and defended, whereby wee might freely follow our businesse: and such was the conceit of this conceited peace, as that there was seldome or never a sword, and seldomer a peece, except for a Deere or Fowle, by which assurances the most plantations were placed straglingly and scatteringly, as a choice veine of rich ground invited them, and further from neighbours the better. Their houses generally open to the Salvages, who were alwaies friendly fed at their tables, and lodged in their bedchambers, which made the way plaine to effect their intents, and the conversion of the Salvages as they supposed.

Having occasion to send to Opechankanough about the middle of March, hee used the Messenger well, and told him he held the peace so firme, the sky should fall or he dissolved it; yet such was the treachery of those people, when they had contrived our destruction, even but two daies before the massacre, they guided our men with much kindnesse thorow the woods, and one Browne that lived among them to learne the language, they sent home to his Master; yea, they borrowed our Boats to transport themselves over the River, to consult on the devillish murder that insued, and of our utter extirpation, which God of his mercy (by the meanes of one of themselves converted to Christianitie) prevented, and as well on the Friday morning that fatall day, being the two and twentieth of March, as also in the evening before as at other times they came unarmed into our houses, with Deere, Turkies, Fish, Fruits, and other provisions to sell us, yea in some places sat downe at breakfast with our people, whom immediately with their owne tooles they slew most barbarously, not sparing either age or sex, man woman or childe, so sudden in their execution, that few or none discerned the weapon or blow that brought them to destruction: In which manner also they slew many of our people at severall works in the fields, well knowing in what places and quarters each of our men were, in regard of their familiaritie with us, for the effecting that great master-peece of worke their conversion; and by this meanes fell that fatall morning under the bloudy and barbarous hands of that perfidious and inhumane people, three hundred forty seven men, women and children, most by their owne weapons, and not being content with their lives, they fell againe upon the dead bodies, making as well as they could a fresh murder, defacing, dragging, and mangling their dead carkases into many peeces, and carying some parts away in derision, with base and brutish triumph.

Neither yet did these beasts spare those amongst the rest well knowne unto them, from whom they had daily received many benefits, but spightfully also massacred them without any remorse or pitie; being in this more fell then Lions and Dragons, as Histories record, which have preserved their Benefactors; such is the force of good deeds, though done to cruell beasts, to take humanitie upon them, but these miscreants put on a more unnaturall brutishnesse then beasts, as by those instances may appeare.

That worthy religious Gentleman Master George Thorp, Deputie to the College lands, sometimes one of his Majesties Pensioners, and in command one of the principall in Virginia; did so truly affect their conversion, that whosoever under him did them the least displeasure, were punished severely. He thought nothing too deare for them, he never denied them any thing, in so much that when they complained that our Mastives did feare them, he to content them in all things, caused some of them to be killed in their presence, to the great displeasure of the owners, and would have had all the rest guelt to make them the milder, might he have had his will. The King dwelling but in a Cottage, he built him a faire house after the English fashion, in which he tooke such pleasure, especially in the locke and key, which he so admired, as locking and unlocking his doore a hundred times a day, he thought no device in the world comparable to it.

Thus insinuating himselfe into this Kings favour for his religious purpose, he conferred oft with him about Religion, as many other in this former Discourse had done, and this Pagan confessed to him as he did to them, our God was better then theirs, and seemed to be much pleased with that Discourse, and of his company, and to requite all those courtesies; yet this viperous brood did, as the sequell shewed, not onely murder him, but with such spight and scorne abused his dead corps as is unfitting to be heard with civill eares. One thing I cannot omit, that when this good Gentleman upon his fatall houre, was warned by his man, who perceiving some treachery intended by those hell-hounds, to looke to himselfe, and withall ran away for feare he should be apprehended, and so saved his owne life; yet his Master out of his good meaning was so void of suspition and full of confidence, they had slaine him, or he could or would beleeve they would hurt him. Captaine Nathaniel Powell one of the first Planters, a valiant Souldier, and not any in the Countrey better knowne amongst them; yet such was the error of an over-conceited power and prosperitie, and their simplicities, they not onely slew him and his family, but butcher-like hagled their bodies, and cut off his head, to expresse their uttermost height of cruelty. Another of the old company of Captaine Smith, called Nathaniel Causie, being cruelly wounded, and the Salvages about him, with an axe did cleave one of their heads, whereby the rest fled and he escaped: for they hurt not any that did either fight or stand upon their guard. In one place where there was but two men that had warning of it, they defended the house against 60. or more that assaulted it. Master Baldwin at Warraskoyack, his wife being so wounded, she lay for dead, yet by his oft discharging of his peece, saved her, his house, himselfe, and divers others. At the same time they came to one Master Harisons house, neere halfe a mile from Baldwines, where was Master Thomas Hamer with six men, and eighteene or nineteene women and children. Here the Salvages with many presents and faire perswasions, fained they came for Captaine Ralfe Hamer to go to their King, then hunting in the woods, presently they sent to him, but he not comming as they expected, set fire of a Tobacco-house, and then came to tell them in the dwelling house of it to quench it; all the men ran towards it, but Master Hamer not suspecting any thing, whom the Salvages pursued, shot them full of arrowes, then beat out their braines. Hamer having finished a letter hee was a writing, followed after to see what was the matter, but quickly they shot an arrow in his back, which caused him returne and barricado up the doores, whereupon the Salvages set fire on the house. Harisons Boy finding his Masters peece loaded, discharged it at randome, at which bare report the Salvages all fled, Baldwin still discharging his peece, and Master Hamer with two and twentie persons thereby got to his house, leaving their owne burning. In like manner, they had fired Lieutenant Basse his house, with all the rest there about, slaine the people, and so left that Plantation.

Captaine Hamer all this while not knowing any thing, comming to his Brother that had sent for him to go hunt with the King, meeting the Salvages chasing some, yet escaped, retired to his new house then a building, from whence he came; there onely with spades, axes, and brickbats, he defended himselfe and his Company till the Salvages departed. Not long after, the Master from the ship had sent six Musketiers, with which he recovered their Merchants store-house, where he armed ten more, and so with thirtie more unarmed workmen, found his Brother and the rest at Baldwins: Now seeing all they had was burnt and consumed, they repaired to James Towne with their best expedition; yet not far from Martins hundred, where seventy three were slaine, was a little house and a small family, that heard not of any of this till two daies after.

All those, and many others whom they have as maliciously murdered, sought the good of those poore brutes, that thus despising Gods mercies, must needs now as miscreants be corrected by Justice: to which leaving them, I will knit together the thred of this discourse. At the time of the massacre, there were three or foure ships in James River, and one in the next, and daily more to come in, as there did within foureteene daies after, one of which they indevoured to have surprised: yet were the hearts of the English ever stupid, and averted from beleeving any thing might weaken their hopes, to win them by kinde usage to Christianitie. But divers write from thence, that Almighty God hath his great worke in this Tragedy, and will thereout draw honor and glory to his name, and a more flourishing estate and safetie to themselves, and with more speed to convert the Salvage children to himselfe, since he so miraculously hath preserved the English; there being yet, God be praised, eleven parts of twelve remaining, whose carelesse neglect of their owne safeties, seemes to have beene the greatest cause of their destructions: yet you see, God by a converted Salvage that disclosed the plot, saved the rest, and the Pinnace then in Pamaunkes River, whereof (say they) though our sinnes made us unworthy of so glorious a conversion, yet his infinite wisdome can neverthelesse bring it to passe, and in good time, by such meanes as we thinke most unlikely: for in the delivery of them that survive, no mans particular carefulnesse saved one person, but the meere goodnesse of God himselfe, freely and miraculously preserving whom he pleased.

The Letters of Master George Sands, a worthy Gentleman, and many others besides them returned, brought us this unwelcome newes, that hath beene heard at large in publike Court, that the Indians and they lived as one Nation, yet by a generall combination in one day plotted to subvert the whole Colony, and at one instant, though our severall Plantations were one hundred and fortie miles up on River on both sides.

But for the better understanding of all things, you must remember these wilde naked natives live not in great numbers together, but dispersed, commonly in thirtie, fortie, fiftie, or sixtie in a company. Some places have two hundred, few places more, but many lesse; yet they had all warning given them one from another in all their habitations, though farre asunder, to meet at the day and houre appointed for our destruction at al our several Plantations; some directed to one place, some to another, all to be done at the time appointed, which they did accordingly: Some entring their houses under colour of trading, so tooke their advantage; others drawing us abroad under faire pretences, and the rest suddenly falling upon those that were at their labours.

Six of the counsell suffered under this treason, and the slaughter had beene universall, if God had not put it into the heart of an Indian, who lying in the house of one Pace, was urged by another Indian his Brother, that lay with him the night before to kill Pace, as he should doe Perry which was his friend, being so commanded from their King; telling him also how the next day the execution should be finished: Perrys Indian presently arose and reveales it to Pace, that used him as his sonne; and thus them that escaped was saved by this one converted Infidell. And though three hundred fortie seven were slaine, yet thousands of ours were by the meanes of this alone thus preserved, for which Gods name be praised for ever and ever.

Pace upon this, securing his house, before day rowed to James Towne, and told the Governor of it, whereby they were prevented, and at such other Plantations as possibly intelligence could be given: and where they saw us upon our guard, at the sight of a peece they ranne away; but the rest were most slaine, their houses burnt, such Armes and Munition as they found they tooke away, and some cattell also they destroied. Since wee finde Opechankanough the last yeare had practised with a King on the Easterne shore, to furnish him with a kind of poison, which onely growes in his Country to poison us. But of this bloudy acte never griefe and shame possessed any people more then themselves, to be thus butchered by so naked and cowardly a people, who dare not stand the presenting of a staffe in manner of a peece, nor an uncharged peece in the hands of a woman. (But I must tell those Authors, though some might be thus cowardly, there were many of them had better spirits.)

Thus have you heard the particulars of this massacre, which in those respects some say will be good for the Plantation, because now we have just cause to destroy them by all meanes possible: but I thinke it had beene much better it had never happened, for they have given us an hundred times as just occasions long agoe to subject them, (and I wonder I can heare of none but Master Stockam and Master Whitaker of my opinion). Moreover, where before we were troubled in cleering the ground of great Timber, which was to them of small use: now we may take their owne plaine fields and Habitations, which are the pleasantest places in the Countrey. Besides, the Deere, Turkies, and other Beasts and Fowles will exceedingly increase if we beat the Salvages out of the Countrey, for at all times of the yeare they never spare Male nor Female, old nor young, egges nor birds, fat nor leane, in season or out of season with them, all is one. The like they did in our Swine and Goats, for they have used to kill eight in tenne more then we, or else the wood would most plentifully abound with victuall; besides it is more easie to civilize them by conquest then faire meanes; for the one may be made at once, but their civilizing will require a long time and much industry. The manner how to suppresse them is so often related and approved, I omit it here: And you have twenty examples of the Spaniards how they got the West-Indies, and forced the treacherous and rebellious Infidel's to doe all manner of drudgery worke and slavery for them, themselves living like Souldiers upon the fruits of their labours. This will make us more circumspect, and be an example to posteritie: (But I say, this might as well have beene put in practise sixteene yeares agoe as now.)

Thus upon this Anvill shall wee now beat our selves an Armour of proofe hereafter to defend us against such incursions, and ever hereafter make us more circumspect: but to helpe to repaire this losse, besides his Majesties bounty in Armes, he gave the Company out of the Tower, and divers other Honorable persons have renewed their adventures, we must not omit the Honorable Citie of London, to whose endless paraise wee may speake it, are now settling forward one hundred persons, and divers others at their owne costs are a repairing, and all good men doe thinke never the worse of the businesse for all these disasters.

What growing state was there ever in the world which had not the like? Rome grew by oppression, and rose upon the backe of her enemies: and the Spaniards have had many of those counterbuffes; more than we. Columbus, upon his returne from the West Indies into Spaine, having left his people with the Indies, in peace and promise of good usage amongst them, at his returne backe found not one of them living, but all treacherously slaine by the Salvages. After this againe, when the Spanish Colonies were increased to great numbers, the Indians from whom the Spaniards for trucking stuffe used to have all their corne, generally conspired together to plant no more at all, intending thereby to famish them; themselves living in the meane time upon Cassava, a root to make bread, onely then knowne to themselves. This plot of theirs by the Spaniards oversight, that foolishly depended upon strangers for their bread, tooke such effect, and brought them to such misery by the rage of famine, that they spared no uncleane nor loathsome beast, no not the poisonous and hideous Serpents, but eat them up also, devouring one death to save them from another; and by this meanes their whole Colony well-neere surfeted, sickned and died miserably, and when they had againe recovered this losse, by their incontinency an infinite number of them died on the Indian disease, we call the French Pox, which at first being a strange and an unknowne malady, was deadly upon whomsoever it lighted: then had they a little flea called Nigua, which got betweene the skinne and the flesh before they were aware, and there bred and multiplied, making swellings and putrifactions, to the decay and losse of many of their bodily members.

Againe, divers times they were neere undone by their ambition, faction, and malice of the Commanders. Columbus, to whom they were also much beholden, was sent with his Brother in chaines into Spaine; and some other great Commanders killed and murdered one another. Pizzaro was killed by Almagros sonne, and him Vasco beheaded, which Vasco was taken by Blasco, and Blasco was likewise taken by Pizzaros Brother: And thus by their covetous and spightfull quarrels, they were ever shaking the maine pillars of their Commonweale. These and many more mischiefes and calamities hapned them, more then ever did to us, and at one time being even at the last gaspe, had two ships not arrived with supplies as they did, they were so disheartned, they were a leaving the Countrey: yet we see for all those miseries they have attained to their ends at last, as is manifest to all the world, both with honour, power, and wealth: and whereas before few could be hired to goe to inhabit there, now with great sute they must obtaine it; but where there was no honesty, nor equity, nor sanctitie, nor veritie, nor pietie, nor good civilitie in such a Countrey, certainly there can bee no stabilitie.

Therefore let us not be discouraged, but rather animated by those conclusions, seeing we are so well assured of the goodnesse and commodities may bee had in Virginia, nor is it to be much doubted there is any want of Mines of most sorts, no not of the richest, as is well knowne to some yet living that can make it manifest when time shall serve: and yet to thinke that gold and silver Mines are in a country otherwise most rich and fruitfull, or the greatest wealth in a Plantation, is but a popular error, as is that opinion likewise, that the gold and silver is now the greatest wealth of the West Indies at this present. True it is indeed, that in the first conquest the Spaniards got great and mighty store of treasure from the Natives, which they in long space had heaped together, and in those times the Indians shewed them entire and rich Mines, which now by the relations of them that have beene there, are exceedingly wasted, so that now the charge of getting those Metals is growne excessive, besides the consuming the lives of many by their pestilent smoke and vapours in digging and refining them, so that all things considered, the cleere gaines of those metals, the Kings part defraied, to the Adventurers is but small, and nothing neere so much as vulgarly is imagined; and were it not for other rich Commodities there that inrich them, those of the Contraction house were never able to subsist by the Mines onely; for the greatest part of their Commodities are partly naturall, and partly transported from other parts of the world, and planted in the West Indies, as in their mighty wealth of Sugarcanes, being first transported from the Canaries; and in Ginger and other things brought out of the East-Indies, in their Cochanele, Indicos, Cotton, and their infinite store of Hides, Quick-silver, Allum, Woad, Brasill woods, Dies, Paints, Tobacco, Gums, Balmes, Oiles, Medicinals and Perfumes, Sassaparilla, and many other physic all drugs: These are the meanes whereby they raise that mighty charge of drawing out their gold and silver to the great and cleare revenue of their King. Now seeing the most of those commodities, or as usefull, may be had in Virginia by the same meanes, as I have formerly said; let us with all speed take the priority of time, where also may be had the priority of place, in chusing the best seats of the Country, which now by vanquishing the salvages, is like to offer a more faire and ample choice of fruitfull habitations, then hitherto our gentlenesse and faire comportments could attaine unto.

The numbers that were slaine in those severall Plantations.

At Captaine Berkleys Plantation, himselfe and 21. others, seated at the Falling-Crick, 66. miles from James City.	22
2 Master Thomas Sheffelds Plantation, some three miles from the Falling-Crick, himselfe and 12. others.	13
3 At Henrico Iland, about two miles from Sheffelds Plantation.	6
4 Slaine of the College people, two miles from Henrico.	17
5 At Charles City, and of Captaine Smiths men.	5
6 At the next adjoyning Plantation.	8
7 At William Farrars house.	10
8 At Berkley hundred, five miles from Charles City, Master Thorp and	10
9 At Westover, a mile from Berkley.	2
10 At Master John Wests Plantation.	2
11 At Captaine Nathaniel Wests Plantation.	2
12 At Lieutenant Gibs his Plantation.	12
13 At Richard Owens house, himselfe and	6
14 At Master Owen Macars house, himselfe and	3
15. At Martins hundred, seven miles from James City.	73
16 At another place.	7
17 At Edward Bennets Plantation.	50
18 At Master Waters his house, himselfe and	4
19 At Apamatucks River, at Master Peirce his Plantation, five miles from the College.	4
20 At Master Macocks Divident, Captaine Samuel Macock, and	4
21 At Flowerdieu hundred, Sir George Yearleys Plantation.	6
22 On the other side opposite to it.	7
23 At Master Swinhows house, himselfe and	7
24 At Master William Bickars house, himselfe and	4
25 At Weanock, of Sir George Yearleys people.	21
26 At Powel Brooke, Captaine Nathaniel Powel, and	12
27 At Southhampton hundred.	5
28 At Martin Brandons hundred.	7
29 At Captaine Henry Spilmans house.	2
30 At Ensigne Spences house.	5
31 At Master Thomas Peirce his house by Mulbery Ile, himselfe and	4
The whole number	347

Source: Smith, John. *The General Historie of Virginia, New England, and the Summer Iles* (Richmond: Franklin, Press, 1819), Vol. II, 65–76.

15. John Martin, "The Manner Howe to Bringe the Indians into Subjection," December 15, 1622

Introduction

On March 22, 1622, coordinated surprise Indian attacks on the English settlements of Virginia resulted in the massacre of 347 men, women, and children, more than one-third of Virginia's English population. The deaths of Pocahontas in 1617 and Powhatan the following year had doomed the fragile peace between their people and the colonists. Powhatan's half brother Opechancanough began planning the operation to drive the English from his land. The colony survived and launched a brutal all-out war of extermination. The colonists burned the Indians' villages and crops and even went so far as to poison Indian peace negotiators. Some nine months after the opening of the war, colonist John Martin wrote this proposal suggesting how to subdue and conquer the Indians without exterminating them. Among his suggestions were burn their villages, destroy their stored food, patrol the rivers to prevent them from fishing and trading, and seize their trade goods, thus making them dependent on the colonists for their survival. He also argued that the Indians should not be exterminated because they were needed as laborers, and their presence would provide a buffer between the colonists and wild animals.

Primary Source

The manner howe to bring in the Indians into subjection wthout makinge an utter exterpation of them together wth the reasons.

First By disablinge the mayne bodie of the Enemye from haveinge the Sinnewes of all expedicons. As namely by Corne and all manner of victualls of anye worth.

This is to be acted two manner of wayes.

First by keepeinge them from setting Corne at home and fishinge.

Secondly by keepeinge them from their accustomed tradinge for Corne.

This first course I assure myselfe if they take it wthout the other, will make a tedious Warr.

For The first it is p'formed by haveinge some 200 Souldiers on foote, Contynuallie harrowinge and burneinge all their Townes in wynter, and spoileinge their weares. By this meanes o' people seacurely may followe their worke. And yet not to be negligent in keepeinge watch.

For The seacond there must provided some 10 Shallopps, that in May, June, Julye and August may scoure the Baye and keepe the Rivers yt are belonginge to Opichankanoe.

By this ariseth two happie ende.

First the assured takeinge of great purchases in skynnes and Prisoners.

Seacondly in keepinge them from tradinge for Corne on the Easterne shore and from ye Southward from whence they have five tymes more then they sett them selves.

This Course being taken they have noe meanes, but must yield to obedience, or flye to borderinge Neighbors who neither will receive them Nor indeede are able, for they have but groune Cleared for their owne use.

At the North west end of his dominions the Monecans are their enymies, On the Norther most side the Patomecks and other nations are their enemies.

The keepinge of them from tradeinge wth the Easterne shore p'duceth two worthie effecte to or exceedinge profit.

First or assurance of Corne att all, tymes.

Seacondly the ventinge of much, Cloth.

My Aunchiant & servante have seene in trade at one tyme 40 greate Canowes laden wth these commodities.

For the Certentye of Corne it is best knowne to my selfe for yt by sendinge, & discoueringe those places, First I have not onely reaped the benefitt, but all the whole Collonye since; whoe had perished had it not bene discouered before Sr George Yardley came in by my Aunchient Thomas Savage & servantt, besides necessitie hath made those Savages more industrious then any other Indians in or Baye, wch followeth to appeare in this seacond p'fitt.

For the assured ventinge of Cloth it followeth Consequently two wayes.

First by Varringe them of trade for skinns they haveinge none them selves.

Seacondly by the necessite of haveinge clothinge wch by us shall & may be tendered att all Convenyent tymes.

Reasons why it is not fittinge utterlye to make an exterpation of the Savages yett.

My reasons are grounded two foulde.

First uppon holy writt and my owne experience.

Seacondly other necessarie uses and p'fitte that maye retorne by the same.

Holy writt sayeth That god would not yt the Children of Israell though they were of farr greater numbrs., then wee are yet in many ages like to be, and came into a Countrie where weare walled townes, not to utterly distroy the heathen, least the woode and wilde beaste should over runn them.

My owne observacon hath bene such as assureth me yt if the Indians inhabitt not amongst us under obedience And as they have ever kept downe ye woode and slayne the wolves, beares, and other beaste, (wch are in greate numbr.) we shalbe more opressed in short tyme by their absence, then in their hveing by us both for or owne securitie as allso for or Cattle.

They by experience willing and able are to worke in the heate of ye day wch or sexe are not.

Seacondly when as by ye meanes before spoken of, they shalbe brought into subjection and shalbe made to deliver hostriges for theire obediance, there is no doubt by gods grace but of the saveinge of many of their soules And then beinge natives are apter for worke then yet or English are, knowinge howe to attayne great quantitie of silke, hempe, and flax, and most exquisite in the dressinge thereof For or uses fitt for guides uppon discou'ye into other Countries adiacent to ours, fitt to rowe in Gallies & friggetts and many other pregnant uses too tedious to sett downe.

Nowe for avoydinge future daynger in or Collonye that may growe Two especiall er vocable lawes are to be made uppon seaveare penallties.

First ye none of what ranke soeuer doe ever trinke or trade wth in the late prcinct of Opichankanoe nor any borderinge neighbors that ayded him in this last disaster.

Seacondly for or owne people to sett & sowe a sufficient proporcon of corne for their owne uses, and yearely to lay upp into a granary a p:porcon for wch if they have noe use for them selves the next yeare then to be sould and every man to have his dewe payd him.

My reason for the first is yt by this meanes the Savages shalbe frustrated of all meanes of buyinge any manner of victualls, and clothinge, but what they shall have from us for their labor and industrie As alsoe beinge disabled from hireinge anye Auxiliaries if at any tyme they would rebell.

The infinate trade they have had in this 4 years of securitie enabled Opichankanoe to hyer many auxiliaries wch in former tymes I knowe for want hereof Pohatan was never able to act the like.

For the seacond howe benifitiall the settinge and sowinge of Corne and layinge upp thereof for store, will luculently appeare by their nowe endureinge want being disturbed by theis Savages at this tyme, And likewise other unexpected accidente may happen both by forrayne and domesticke enymies hereafter.

Two Storehowses or Granaries to be erected and placed for this purpose fittest for salftie, and then for Convenience wch I Will leave to demonstrate to yor [honor] untill you Come to the Mapp of the Countrie As alsoe a neare passage to the Southward River and where the most necessarie places are for fortificadon against a forren Enemye.

Jho. Martin.

Source: Susan Myra Kingsbury, ed., *The Records of the Virginia Company of London* (Washington, DC: U.S. Government Printing Office, 1933), 704–706.

16. David Pietersz DeVries, Account of the Swanendael Massacre, 1632 [Excerpt]

Introduction

In 1629 a group of Dutch investors bought land from the Lenni Lenape (Delaware) Indians and built a trading post called Swanendael on the coast of Delaware. In 1631 David DeVries sailed from Amsterdam and set down a number of men and their supplies. The following year a Lenni Lenape man removed the metal coat of arms from its stake outside the Dutch trading post. The Dutch, seeing this as the theft of an important symbol of authority, vigorously protested. The resulting series of misunderstandings culminated in the slaughter of the traders by Indians. News of the massacre made its way via New Netherland to the Netherlands before the next planned expedition sailed. The investors abandoned their plan to send more settlers and recast the voyage as a whaling expedition. When the vessels arrived in December 1632, DeVries found the house burned down and the skeletons of 32 men and their animals. DeVries saw no point in trying to find the perpetrators and take revenge, so he made peace with the Indians and reestablished trade. The investors lost interest in Swanendael and sold the land to the Dutch West India Company by 1635. The existence of Swanendael and its episodic occupation by the Dutch during the period 1631–1633 permitted the Dutch to retain title to the area when challenged by the English of Maryland.

Primary Source

Journal by David Piertersz De Vries, 1632

[. . .]

The 2d, weighed anchor, with my yacht and the Englishman, of London, who had the Portuguese prisoners, whom he was to carry to Porto Rico. He left his barge behind, to follow him with some goods to St. Martin. We arrived in the evening at the anchorage before St. Martin, where we found the whole fleet there still which we had left there. I asked the captains of the flutes why they had not followed me when I weighed anchor. They answered that they thanked me for the offer which I had made them, but they had determined to remain by each other, and expected that they would be ready together, and the *Gelderland* would go with them.

The 4th, the Englishman, expecting his boat from St. Christopher, knew not what it meant that it staid so long, as it should have followed us at noon. This Englishman wished much to sail with me to the latitude of Porto Rico, which I must pass.

The 5th of this month, took my leave at the fort of our governor and the captains, and weighed anchor with my yacht also; having a fair sail set, I could not wait longer for the Englishman's boat. We understood afterwards that this boat was placed in great distress; that it was driven to the leeward by a strong wind, and being in want of provisions and water, the men cast lots whom they should first kill for the others to eat for food; having at length felled one, they fed themselves therewith, till they finally reached the island of Saba, where they subsisted on what they found there, and were afterwards recovered in great distress, but he who was eaten up for their subsistence was gone.

The 14th, in the thirty-second degree of latitude, the Bermudas to the east of us, encountered a severe storm from the northwest, and it was sheer luck that we managed to take in our sails; all around the waters swirled as if it were an hurricane; it blew so, that standing beside each other we could not understand each other. I feared when I saw the yacht, that it would finally capsize, so dreadful was it to see so small a yacht, of ten lasts, save itself from such a storm. This storm continued until the 18th, but towards the last the wind veered entirely west.

The 1st of December, threw the lead, in the thirty-ninth degree of latitude, in fifty-seven fathoms, sandy bottom; found out afterwards that we were then fourteen or fifteen leagues from the shore. This is a fiat coast. Wind westerly.

The 2d, threw the lead in fourteen fathoms, sandy bottom, and smelt the land, which gave a sweet perfume, as the wind came from the northwest, which blew off land, and caused these sweet odors. This comes from the Indians setting fire, at this time of year, to the woods and thickets, in order to hunt; and the land is full of sweet-smelling herbs, as sassafras, which has a sweet smell. When the wind blows out of the northwest, and the smoke is driven to sea, it happens that the land is smelt before it is seen. The land can be seen when in from thirteen to fourteen fathoms. Sand-hills are seen from the thirty-fourth to the fortieth degree, and the hills rise up full of pine-trees, which would serve as masts for ships.

The 3d of the same month, saw the mouth of the South Bay, or South River, and anchored on sandy ground at ten fathoms; because it blew hard from the northwest, which is from the shore, and as we could not, in consequence of the hard wind, sail in the bay, we remained at anchor.

The 5th, the wind southwest, we weighed anchor, and sailed into the South Bay, and in the afternoon lay, with our yacht, in four fathoms water, and saw immediately a whale near the ship. Thought this would be royal work—the whales so numerous—and the land so fine for cultivation.

The 6th, we went with the boat into the river, well armed, in order to see if we could speak with any Indians, but coming by our house, which was destroyed, found it well beset with palisades in place of breastworks, but it was almost burnt up. Found lying here and there the skulls and bones of our people whom they had killed, and the heads of the horses and cows which they had brought with them, but perceived no Indians and, without having accomplished anything, returned on board, and let the gunner fire a shot in order to see if we could find any trace of them the next day.

The 7th, in the morning, we thought we saw some smoke near our destroyed house; we landed opposite the house, on the other side of the river, where there is a beach with some dunes. Coming to the beach, looked across the river towards the house where we had been the day before, and where we thought in the morning we had seen signs of smoke, but saw nothing. I had a cousin of mine with me from Rotterdam, named Heyndrick de Liefde, and as a flock of gulls was flying over our heads, I told him to shoot at it, as he had a fowling-piece with him, and he shot one on the wing, and brought it down. With it came a shout from two or three Indians, who were lying in the brush on the other side of the river by the destroyed house. We called to them to come over to us. They answered that we must come into the river with our boat. We promised to do so in the morning, as the water was then low, and that we would then talk with them, and we went back to the ship. Going aboard, we resolved to sail in the river with the yacht, as otherwise in an open boat we might be in danger of their arrows.

The 8th of December, we sailed into the river before our destroyed house, well on our guard. The Indians came to the edge of the shore, near the yacht, but dared not come in. At length, one ventured to come aboard the yacht, whom we presented with a cloth dress, and told him we desired to make peace. Then immediately more came running aboard, expecting to obtain a dress also, whom we presented with some trinkets, and told the one to whom we had given the cloth garment, that we had given it to him because he had most confidence in us—that he was the first one who came in the yacht, and should they come the next day with their chief called Sakimas, we would then make a firm peace, which they call *rancontyn marenit*. An Indian remained on board of the yacht at night, whom we asked why they had slain our people, and how it happened. He then showed us the place where our people had set up a column, to which was fastened a piece of tin, whereon the arms of Holland were painted. One of their chiefs took this off for the purpose of making tobacco-pipes, not knowing that he was doing amiss. Those in command at the house made such an ado about it, that the Indians, not knowing how it was, went away and slew the chief who had done it, and brought a token of the dead to the house to those in command, who told them that they wished they had not done it, that they should have brought him to them, as they wished to have forbidden him to do the like again. They then went away, and the friends of the murdered chief incited their friends—as they are a people like the Italians, who are very revengeful—to set about the work of vengeance. Observing our people out of the house, each one at his work, that there was not more than one inside, who was lying sick, and a large mastiff, who was chained—had he been loose they would not have dared to approach the house—and the man who had command, standing near the house, three of the bravest Indians, who were to do the deed, bringing a lot of beaver-skins with them to exchange, asked to enter the house. The man in charge went in with them to make the barter; which being done, he went down from the loft where the stores lay, and in descending the stairs, one of the Indians seized an axe, and cleft the head of our agent who was in charge so that he fell down dead. They also relieved the sick man of life; and shot into the dog, who was chained fast, and whom they most feared, twenty-five arrows before they could despatch him. They then proceeded towards the rest of the men, who were at their work, and going among them with pretensions of friendship, struck them down. Thus was our young colony destroyed, causing us serious loss.

The 9th, the Indians came to us with their chiefs, and sitting in a ring, made peace. Gave them some presents of duffels, bullets, hatchets, and various Nuremberg trinkets. They promised to make a present to us, as they had been out a-hunting. They then departed again with great joy of us, that we had not remembered what they had done to us....

Source: Albert Cook Myers, ed., *Narratives of Early Pennsylvania, West New Jersey, and Delaware* (New York: Scribner, 1912), 14–17.

17. Lion Gardiner, Account of the Pequot Wars, 1660

Introduction

The Pequots, who were the most powerful Indians in Connecticut and were feared by the other native peoples, had moved into the area during the late 1500s, occupying land that had belonged to rival Indians. By the year 1600 at least 2,000 Pequots lived along the Connecticut coast and the border with Rhode Island. The other major tribe in Connecticut was the Mohegans, whose sachem, Uncas, remained loyal to the English for more than four decades. A group of English businessmen received a patent to occupy Connecticut. In 1635 they hired an English military engineer, Lion Gardiner, to supervise construction of settlements and defenses in Connecticut. Gardiner sailed to New England, where he designed and built a fort at Saybrook and laid out a town. From 1636 he lived there as commander of the fort for the duration of his four-year contract. Fearing for his family and the other settlers under his protection, Gardiner tried to dissuade New England authorities from their plan to go to war against the Pequots. When the New Englanders launched their attack from his fort, the settlers could no longer venture safely outside its walls. Gardiner later recounted what his men suffered at the hands of the Pequots as well as his initial unwillingness to trust Uncas.

Primary Source

In the year 1635, I, Lion Gardiner, engineer and master of works of fortification in the legers of the Prince of Orange, in the Low Countries, through the persuasion of Mr. John Davenport, Mr. Hugh Peters with some other well-affected Englishmen of Rotterdam, I made an agreement with the forenamed Mr. Peters for $100 per annum, for four years, to serve the company of patentees, namely, the Lord Say, the Lord Brooks [Brooke], Sir Arthur Hazilrig [Haslerigge], Sir Mathew Bonnington [Boynton], Sir Richard Saltingstone [Saltonstall], Esquire [George] Fenwick, and the rest of their company. I was to serve them only in the drawing, ordering and making of a city, towns or forts of defence.

And so I came from Holland to London, and from thence to New England, where I was appointed to attend such orders as Mr. John Winthrop, Esquire, as the present Governor of Conectecott, was to appoint, whether at Pequit [Pequot] river, or Conectecott, and that we should choose a place both for the convenience of a good harbour, and also for capableness and fitness for fortification.

But I landing at Boston the latter end of November, the afore said Mr. Winthrop had sent before one Lieut. Gibbons, Sergeant Willard, with some carpenters, to take possession of the river's mouth, where they began to build houses against the spring; we expecting, according to promise, that there would have come from England

to us 300 able men, whereof 200 should attend fortification, 50 to till the ground, and 50 to build houses.

But our great expectation at the river's mouth came only to two men, viz. Mr. Fenwick, and his man, who came with Mr. Hugh Peters, and Mr. Oldham and Thomas Stanton, bringing with them some otter-skin coats, and beaver, and skeins of wampum, which the Pequits [Pequots] had sent for a present, because the English had required those Pequits that had killed a Virginean [Virginian], one Capt. Stone, with his barks' crew, in Conectecott river, for they said they would have their lives and not their presents; then I answered, "seeing you will take Mr. Winthrop to the Bay to see his wife, newly brought to bed of her first child, and though you say he shall return, yet I know if you make war with these Pequits, he will not come hither again, for I know you will keep yourselves safe, as you think, in the Bay, but myself, with these few, you will leave at the stake to be roasted, or for hunger to be starved, for Indian corn is now 12s. per bushel, and we have but three acres planted, and if they will not make war for a Virginian and expose us to the Indians, whose mercies are cruelties, they, I say, love the Virginians better than us: for, have they stayed these four or five years, and will they begin now, we being so few in the river, and have scarce holes to put our heads in?"

—I pray ask the magistrates in the Bay if they have forgot what I said to them when they returned from Salem? For Mr. Winthrop, Mr. Haines, Mr. Dudley, Mr. Ludlow, Mr. Humfry, Mr. Belingam [Bellingham], Mr. Coddington, and Mr. Nowell;—these entreated me to go with Mr. Humfry and Mr. Peters to view the country, to see how fit it was for fortification. And I told them that nature had done more than half the work already, and I thought no foreign potent enemy would do them any hurt, but one that was near. They asked me who that was, and I said it was Capt. Hunger that threatened them most, for, said I, "war is like a three-footed stool, want one foot and down comes all; and these feet are men, victuals, and munition, therefore, seeing in peace you are like to be famished, what will or can be done if war? Therefore I think," said I, "it will be best only to fight against Capt. Hunger, and let fortification alone awhile; and if need hereafter require it, I can come to do you any service:" and they all liked my saying well.—

Entreat them to rest awhile, till we get more strength here about us, and that we hear where the seat of war will be, may approve of it, and provide for it, for I had but twenty-four in all, men, women, and boys and girls, and not food for them for two months, unless we saved our corn-field, which could not possibly be if they came to war, for it is two miles from our home.

Mr. Winthrop, Mr. Fenwick, and Mr. Peters promised me that they would do their utmost endeavour to persuade the Bay-men to desist from war a year or two, till we could be better provided for it; and then the Pequit Sachem was sent for, and the present returned, but full sore against my will.

So they three returned to Boston, and two or three days after came an Indian from Pequit, whose name was Cocommithus, who had lived at Plimoth, and could speak good English; he desired that Mr. Steven [Stephen] Winthrop go to Pequit with an §100 worth of trucking cloth and all other trading ware, for they knew that we had a great cargo of goods of Mr. Pincheon's, and Mr. Steven Winthrop had the disposing of it. And he said that if he would come he might put off all his goods, and the Pequit Sachem would give him two horses that had been there a great while. So I sent the shallop with Mr. Steven Winthrop, Sergeant Tille [Tilly], whom we called afterward Sergeant Kettle, because he put the kettle on his head and Thomas Hurlbut and three men more, charging them that they should ride in the middle of the river, and not go ashore until they had done all their trade, and that Mr. Steven Winthrop should stand in the hold of the boat, having their guns by them, and swords by their sides, the other four to be, two in the fore cuddie, and two in aft, being armed in like manner, that so they out of the loop-holes might clear the boat, if they were by the Pequits assaulted; and that they should let but one canoe come aboard at once, with no more but four Indians in her, and when she had traded then another; and that they should lie no longer there than one day, and at night to go out of the river; and if they brought the two horses, to take them in a clear piece of land at the mouth of the river, two of them to go ashore to help the horses in, and the rest to stand ready with their guns in their hands, if need were, to defend them from the Pequits, for I durst not trust them. So they went and found but little trade, and they having forgotten what I charged them, Thomas Hurlbut and one more went ashore to boil the kettle, and Thomas Hurlbut stepping into the Sachem's wigwam, not far from the shore, enquiring for the horses, the Indians went out of the wigwam, and Wincumbone, his mother's sister, was then the great Pequit Sachem's wife, who made signs to him that he should be gone, for they would cut off his head; which, when he perceived, he drew his sword and ran to the others, and got aboard, and immediately came abundance of Indians to the waterside and called them to come ashore, but they immediately set sail and came home, and this caused me to keep watch and ward, for I saw they plotted our destruction.

And suddenly after came Capt. Endecott, Capt. Turner, and Capt. Undrill [Underhill], with a company of soldiers, well fitted, to Seabrook, and made that place their rendezvous or seat of war, and that to my great grief, for, said I, "you come hither to raise these wasps about my ears, and then you will take wing and flee away;" but when I had seen their commission I wondered, and made many allegations against the manner of it, but go they did to Pequit, and as they came without acquainting any of us in the river with it, so they went against our will, for I knew that I should

loose our corn-field; then I entreated them to hear what I would say to them, which was this: "sirs, seeing you will go, I pray you, if you don't load your barks with Pequits, load them with corn, for that is now gathered with them, and dry, ready to put into their barns, and both you and we have need of it, and I will send my shallop and hire this Dutchman's boat, there present, to go with you, and if you cannot attain your end of the Pequits, yet you may load your barks with corn, which will be welcome to Boston and to me:" But they said they had no bags to load them with, then said I, "here is three dozen of new bags, you shall have thirty of them, and my shallop to carry them, and six of them my men shall use themselves, for I will with the Dutchmen send twelve men well provided;" and I desired them to divide the men into three parts, viz. two parts to stand without the corn, and to defend the other one-third part, that carried the corn to the water-side, till they have loaded what they can. And the men there in arms, when the rest are aboard, shall in order go aboard, the rest that are aboard shall with their arms clear the shore, if the Pequits do assault them in the rear, and then, when the General shall display his colours, all to set sail together. To this motion they all agreed, and I put the three dozen of bags aboard my shallop, and away they went, and demanded the Pequit Sachem to come into parley. But it was returned for answer, that he was from home, but within three hours he would come; and so from three to six, and thence to nine, there came none. But the Indians came without arms to our men, in great numbers, and they talked with my men, whom they knew; but in the end, at a word given, they all on a sudden ran away from our men, as they stood in rank and file, and not an Indian more was to be seen: and all this while before, they carried all their stuff away, and thus was that great parley ended. Then they displayed their colorus, and beat their drums, burnt some wigwams and some heaps of corn, and my men carried as much aboard as they could, but the army went aboard, leaving my men ashore, which ought to have marched aboard first. But they all set sail, and my men were pursued by the Indians, and they hurt some of the Indians, two of them came home wounded. The Bay-men killed not a man, save that one Kichomiquim, and Indian Sachem of the Bay, killed a Pequit; and thus began the war between the Indians and us in these parts.

So my men being come home, and having brought a pretty quantity of corn with them, they informed me, both Dutch and English, of all passages. I was glad of the corn.

After this I immediately took men and went to our corn-field, to gather our corn, appointing others to come about with the shallop and fetch it, and left five lusty men in the strong-house, with long guns, which house I had built for the defence of the corn. Now these men not regarding the charge I had given them, three of them went a mile from the house a fowling; and having loaded themselves with fowl they returned. But the Pequits let them pass first, till they had loaded themselves, but at their return they arose out of their ambush, and shot them all three; one of them escaped through the corn, shot through the leg, the other two they tormented. Then the next day I sent the shallop to fetch the five men, and the rest of the corn that was broken down, and they found but three, as is above said, and when they had gotten that they left the rest; and as soon as they had gone a little way from shore they saw the house on fire.

Now so soon as the boat came home, and brought us this bad news, old Mr. Mitchell was very urgent with me to lend him the boat to fetch hay home from the Six-mile Island, but I told him they were too few men, for his four men could but carry the hay aboard, and one must stand in the boat to defend them, and they must have two more at the foot of the rock, with their guns, to keep the Indians from running down upon them. And in the first place, before they carry any of the cocks of hay, to scour the meadow with their three dogs,—to march all abreast from the lower end up to the rock, and if they found the meadow clear, then to load their hay; but his was also neglected, for they all went ashore and fell to carrying off their hay, and the Indians presently rose out of the long grass, and killed three, and took the brother of Mr. Mitchell, who is the minister of Cambridge, and roasted him alive; and so they served a shallop of his, coming down the river in the Spring, having two men, one whereof they killed at Six-mile island, the other came down drowned to us ashore at our doors, with an arrow shot into his eye through his head.

In the 22d of February [1636–37], I went out with ten men and three dogs, half a mile from the house, to burn the weeds, leaves and reeds, upon the neck of land, because we had felled twenty timber-trees, which we were to roll to the water-side to bring home, every man carrying a length of match with brimstone-matches with him to kindle the fire withal, but when we came to the small of the Neck, the weeds burning, I having before this set two sentinels on the small of the Neck, I called to the men that were burning the reeds to come away, but they would not until they had burnt up the rest of their matches. Presently there starts up four Indians out of the fiery reeds, but ran away, I calling to the rest of our men to come away out of the marsh. Then Robert Chapman and Thomas Hurlbut, being sentinels, called to me, saying there came a number of Indians out of the other side of the marsh. Then I went to stop them, that they should not get the wood-land; but Thomas Hurlbut cried out to me that some of the men did not follow me, for Thomas Rumble and Arthur Branch threw down their two guns and ran away; then the Indians shot two of them that were in the reeds, and sought to get between us and home, but durst not come before us, but kept us in a half-moon, we retreating and exchanging many a shot, so that Thomas Hurlbut was shot almost through the thigh, John Spencer in the back, into his kidneys, myself into the thigh, two more were shot dead. But in our retreat I keep Hurlbut and Spencer still before us, we defending ourselves with our naked swords, or else they

had taken us all alive. So that the two sore wounded men, by our slow retreat, got home with their guns, when our two sound men ran away and left their guns behind them. But when I saw the cowards that left us, I resolved to let them draw lots which of them should be hanged, for the articles did hang up in the hall for them to read, and they knew they had been published long before. But at the intercession of old Mr. Mitchell, Mr. Higgisson [John Higginson, chaplain], and Mr. [Thomas] Pell [surgeon], I did forbear.

Within a few days after, when I had cured myself of my wound, I went out with eight men to get some fowl for our relief, and found the guns that were thrown away, and the body of one man shot through, the arrow going in at the right side, the head sticking fast, half through a rib on the left side, which I took out and cleansed it, and presumed to send to the Bay, because they had said that the arrows of the Indians were of no force.

Anthony Dike, master of a bark, having his bark at Rhode Island in the winter, was sent by Mr. [Henry] Vane, then Governor. Anthony came to Rhode Island by land, and from thence he came with his bark to me with a letter, wherein was desired that I should consider and prescribe the best way I could to quell these Pequits, which I also did, and with my letter sent the man's rib as a token.

A few days after came Thomas Stanton down the river, and staying for a wind, while he was there came a troop of Indians within musket shot, laying themselves and their arms down behind a little rising hill and two great trees; which I perceiving, called the carpenter whom I had shewed how to charge and level a gun, and that he should put two cartridges of musket bullets into two sackers guns that lay about; and we leveled them against the place, and I told him that he must look towards me, and when he saw me wave my hat above my head he should give fire to both the guns; then presently came three Indians, creeping out and calling to us to speak with us: and I was glad that Thomas Stanton was there, and I sent six men down by the Garden Pales to look that none should come under the hill behind us; and having placed the rest in places convenient closely, Thomas and I with my sword, pistol and carbine, went ten or twelve poles without the gate to parley with them. And when the six men came to the Garden Pales, at the corner, they found a great number of Indians creeping behind the fort, or betwixt us and home, but they ran away. Now I had said to Thomas Stanton, whatsoever they say to you, tell me first, for we will not answer them directly to anything, for I know not the mind of the rest of the English. So they came forth, calling us nearer to them, and we them nearer to us. But I would not let Thomas go any further than the great stump of a tree, and I stood by him; then they asked who we were, and he answered, "Thomas and Lieutenant." But they said he lied, for I was shot with many arrows; and so I was, but my buff coat preserved me, only one hurt me. But when I spake to them they knew my voice, for one of them had dwelt three months with us, but ran away when the Bay-men came first. Then they asked us if we would fight with Niantecut Indians, for they were our friends and came to trade with us. We said we knew not the Indians one from another, and therefore would trade with none. Then they said, have you fought enough? We said we knew not yet. Then they asked if we did use to kill women and children? We said that they should see that hereafter. So they were silent a small space, and then they said, We are Pequits, and have killed Englishmen, and can kill them as mosquetoes, and we will go to Conectecott and kill men, women, and children, and we will take away the horses, cows and hogs. When Thomas Stanton had told me this, he prayed me to shoot that rogue, for, said he, he hath an Englishman's coat on, and saith that he hath killed three, and these other four have their cloathes on their backs. I said, "no, it is not the manner of a parley, but have patience and I shall fit them ere they go." "Nay, now or never," said he; so when he could get no other answer but this last, I bid him tell them that they should not go to Conectecott, for if they did kill all the men, and take all the rest as they said, it would do them no good, but hurt, for Englishwomen are lazy, and can't do their work; horses and cows will spoil your corn-fields, and the hogs their clam-banks, and so undo them; then I pointed to our great house, and bid them tell them there lay twenty pieces of trucking cloth, of Mr. Pincheon's, with hoes, hatchets, and all manner of trade, they were better fight still with us, and so get all that, and then go up the river after they had killed all us. Having heard this, they were mad as dogs, and ran away; then when they came to the place from whence they came, I waved my hat about my head, and the two great guns went off, so that there was a great hubbub amongst them.

Then two days after came down Capt. Mason, and Sergeant Seely, with five men more, to see how it was with us; and whilst they were there, came down a Dutch boat, telling us the Indians had killed fourteen English, for by that boat I had sent up letters to Conectecott, what I heard, and what I thought, and how to prevent that threatened danger, and received back again rather a scoff, than nay thanks for my care and pains. But as I wrote, so it fell out to my great grief and theirs, for the next, or second day after, as major Mason well knows, came down a great many canoes, going down the creek beyond the marsh, before the fort, many of them having white shirts; then I commanded the carpenter whom I had shewed to level great guns, to put in two round shot in the two sackers, and we leveled them at a certain place, and I stood to bid him give fire, when I thought the canoe would meet the bullet, and one of them took off the nose of a great canoe wherein the two maids were, that were taken by the Indians, whom I redeemed and clothed, for the Dutchmen, whom I sent to fetch them, brought them away almost naked from Pequit, they putting on their own linen jackets to cover their nakedness; and though the redemption cost me ten pounds, I am yet to have thanks for my care and charge about them; these things are known to Major Mason.

Then came from the Bay Mr. Tille [John Tilly], with a permit to go up to Harford [Hartford], and coming ashore he saw a paper nailed up over the gate, whereon was written that no boat or bark should pass the fort, but that they come to an anchor first, that I might see whether they were armed and manned sufficiently, and they were not to land any where after they passed the fort till they came to Wethersfield; and this I did because Mr. Michell had lost a shallop before coming down from Wethersfield, with three men well armed. This Mr. Tille gave me ill language for my presumption, as he called it, with other expressions too long here to write. When he had done I bid him go to his warehouse, which he had built before I came, to fetch his goods from thence, for I would watch no longer over it. So he, knowing nothing, went and found his house burnt, and one of Mr. Plum's with others, and he told me to my face that I had caused it to be done; but Mr. Higgisson, Mr. Pell, Mr. Thomas Hurlbut and John Green can witness that the same day that our house was burnt at Cornfield-point I went with Mr. Higgisson, Mr. Pell, and four men more, broke open a door and took a note of all that was in the house and gave it to Mr. Higgisson to keep, and so brought all the goods to our house, and delivered it all to them again when they came for it, without any penny of charge. Now the very next day after I had taken the goods out, before the sun was quite down, and we all together in the great hall, all them houses were on fire in one instant. The Indians ran away, but I would not follow them. Now when Mr. Tille had received all his goods, I said unto him, I thought I had deserved for my honest care both for their bodies and goods of those that passed by here, at the least better language, and am resolved to order such malepert persons as you are; there I wish you and also charge you to observe that which you have read at the gate, 'tis my duty to God, my masters, and my love I bear to you all which is the ground of this, had you but eyes to see it; but you will not till you feel it. So he went up the river, and when he came down again to his place which I call Tille's folly, now called Tille's point, in our sight in despite, having a fair wind he came to an anchor, and with one man more went ashore, discharged his gun, and the Indians fell upon him, and he killed the other, and carried him alive over the river in our sight, before my shallop could come to them; for immediately I sent seven men to fetch the Pink down, or else it had been taken and three men more. So they brought her down, and I sent Mr. Higgisson and Mr. Pell aboard to take an invoice of all that was in the vessel, that nothing might be lost.

Two days after came to me, as I had written to Sir Henerie Vane, then governor of the Bay, I say came to me Capt. Undrill [Underhill], with twenty lusty men, well armed, to stay with me two months, or 'till something should be done about the Pequits. He came at the charge of my masters.

Soon after came down from Hartford Maj. Mason, Lieut. Seely, accompanied with Mr. Stone and eight Englishmen, and eighty Indians, with a commission from Mr. Ludlow and Mr. Steel, and some others; these came to go fight with the Pequits. But when Capt. Undrill and I had seen their commission, we both said they were not fitted for such a design, and we said to Maj. Mason, we wondered he would venture himself, being no better fitted; and he said the Magistrates could not or would not send better: then we said that none of our men should go with them, neither should they go unless we, that were bred soldiers from our youth, could see some likelihood to do better than the Bay-men with their strong commission last year.

Then I asked them how they durst trust the Mohegin Indians, who had but that year come from the Pequits. They said they would trust them, for they could not well go without them for want of guides. Yea, said I, but I will try them before a man of ours shall go with you or them; and I called for Uncas and said unto him, "you say you will help Maj. Mason, but I will first see it, therefore spend you not twenty men to the Bass river, for there went yester-night six Indians in a canoe thither; fetch them now dead or alive, and then you shall go with Maj. Mason, else not." So he sent his men who killed four, brought one a traitor to us alive, whose name was Kiswas, and one ran away. And I gave him fifteen yards of trading cloth on my own charge, to give unto his men according to their desert. And having staid there five or six days before we could agree, at last we old soldiers agreed about the way and act, and took twenty insufficient men from the eighty that came from Harford and sent them up again in a shallop, and Capt. Undrill with twenty of the lustiest of our men went in their room, and I furnished them with such things as they wanted, and sent Mr. Pell, the surgeon with them; and the Lord God blessed their design and way, so that they returned with victory to the glory of God, and honour of our nation, having slain three hundred, burnt their fort, and taken many prisoners.

Then came to me an Indian called Wequash, and I by Mr. Higgis-sion inquired of him, how many of the Pequits were yet alive that had helped to kill Englishmen; and he declared them to Mr. Hig-gisson, and he writ them down, as may appear by his own hand here enclosed, and I did as therein is written.

Then three days after the fight came Waiandance, next brother to the old Sachem of Long Island, and having been recommended to me by Maj. Gibbons, he came to know if we were angry with all Indians. I answered "no, but only with such as had killed Eng-lishmen." He asked me whether they that lived upon Long-Island might come to trade with us? I said "no, nor we with them, for if I should send my boat to trade for corn, and you have Pequits with you, and if my boat should come to some creek by reason of bad weather, they might kill my men, and I shall think that you of Long-Island have done it, and so we may kill all you for the Pequits; but if you will kill all the Pequits that come to you, and send me their heads, then I will give to you as to Weakwash [Wequash], and you shall have trade with us." Then, said he, I will

go to my brother, for he is the great Sachem of Long-Island, and if we may have peace and trade with you, we will give you tribute as we did the Pequits. Then I said, "If you have any Indians that have killed English, you must bring their heads also." He answered not any one, and said that Gibbons, my brother would have told you if it had been so; so he went away and did as I had said, and sent me five heads, three and four heads, for which I paid them that brought them as I had promised.

Then came Capt. Stoton [Stoughton] with an army of 300 men, from the Bay, to kill the Pequits; but they were fled beyond New Haven to a swamp. I sent Wequash after them, who went by night to spy them out, and the army followed him, and found them at the great swamp, who killed some and took others, and the rest fled to the Mowhakues with their Sachem. Then the Mohaws cut off his head and sent it to Harford, for then they all feared us, but now it is otherwise, for they say to our faces that our Commissioner's meeting once a year, and speak a great deal, or write a letter, and other's all for they dare not fight. But before they went to the Great Swamp they sent Thomas Stanton over to Long Island and Shelter island, to find Pequits there, but there was none, for Sachem Wai-andance, that was at Plimoth when the commissioners were there, and set there last, I say, that they durst not come there; and he and his men went with the English to the Swamp, and thus the Pequits were quelled at that time.

But there was like to be a great broil between Miantenomie [Mian-tonomoh] and Unchus [Uncas] who should have the rest of the Pequits, but we mediated between them and pacified them; also Unchus challenged the Narraganset Sachem out to a single com-bat, but he would not fight without all his men; but they were paci-fied, thought the grudge remained still, as it doth appear.

Thus far I had written in a book, that all men and posterity might know how and why so many honest men had their blood shed, yea, and some flayed alive, others cut in pieces, and some roasted alive, only because Kichamokin, a Bay Indian killed one Pequit; and thus far of the Pequit war, which was but a comedy in comparison of the tragedies which hath been here threatened since, and may yet come, if God do not open the eyes, ears, and hearts of some that I think are willfully deaf and blind, and think because there is no change that the vision fails, and put the evil threatened-day far off, for say they, we are to twenty to one to what we were then, and none dare meddle with us. Oh! wo be to the pride and security which hath been the ruin of many nations, as woful experience has proved.

But I wonder, and so doth many more with me, that the Bay doth not better revenge the murdering of Mr. Oldham, an honest man of their own, seeing they were at such cost for a Virginian. The Narraganset's there were at Block-Island killed him, and had $50 of gold of his, for I saw it when he had five pieces of me, and put it up into a clout and tied it up altogether, when he went away from me to Block-Island; but the Narragansets had it and punched holes into it, and put it about their necks for jewels; and afterwards I saw the Dutch have some of it, which they had of the Narraganset at a small rate.

And now I find that to be true which our friend Waiandance told me many years ago, that was this; seeing that all the plots of the Narraganset were always discovered, he said they would let us alone till they had destroyed Uncas, and him, and then they, with the Mowaukes and Mowhaukes and the Indians beyond the Dutch, and all the Northern and Eastern Indians would easily destroy us, man and mother's son. This have I informed the Governors of these parts, but all in vain, for I see they have done as those of Wethersfield, not regarding till they were impelled to it by blood; and thus we may be sure of the fattest of the flock are like to go first, if not altogether, and then it will be too late to read. Jer. XXV.—for drink we shall if the Lord be not the more meriful to us for our extreme pride and base security, which cannot but stink before the Lord; and we may expect this, that if there should be war again between England and Holland, our friends at the Dutch and our Dutch Englishmen would prove as true to us now, as they were when the fleet came out of England; but no more of that, a word to the wise is enough.

Source: Curtiss C. Gardiner, ed., *Lion Gardiner and His Descendants* (St. Louis: A. Whipple, 1890), 8–19.

18. Treaty of Hartford, 1638

Introduction

The New England colonists decided on a war against the Pequots, who stood in the way of their expansion. The Pequots, who were the most powerful Indians in Connecticut and were feared by the other native peoples, had moved into the area during the late 1500s, occupying land that had belonged to rival Indians. By the year 1600 at least 2,000 Pequots lived along the Connecticut coast and the border with Rhode Island. An English war party from Massachusetts raided and looted Pequot villages, and the Pequots attacked the English fort at Saybrook and settlers at Wethersfield. In May 1637 forces from Connecticut, joined by the Massachusetts Bay and Plymouth colonies along with the Narragansetts and the Mohegans, slaughtered more than 400 inhabitants of the main Pequot village. The Treaty of Hartford, signed on September 21, 1638, in Hartford, Connecticut, officially ended the war. The Pequots had been virtually extinguished as a tribe during the conflict, and this treaty provided that any surviving Pequots would be sold into slavery to either the Narragansetts or the Mohegans. The treaty is remarkable because it grants to the English colonists the right to mediate any disagreements between the Indians of southern New England.

Primary Source

Articles between the English in Connecticut and Indian Sachems

A Covenant and Agreement between the English Inhabiting the Jurisdiction of the River of Connecticut of the one part, and Miantinomy the chief Sachem of the Narragansetts in the behalf of himself and the other Sachems there; and Poquim or Uncas the chief Sachim of the Indians called the Mohegans in the behalf of himself and the Sachims under him, as Followeth, at Hartford the 21st of September, 1638.

Imp'r. There is peace and a Familiarity made between the said Miantinome and Narragansett Indians and the said Poquim and Mohegan Indians, and all former Injuryes and wrongs offered to each other Remitted and Burryed and never to be renued any more from henceforth.

2. It is agreed if there fall out Injuryes and wrongs for fuetur to be done or committed Each to other or their men, they shall not presently Revenge it But they are to appeal to the English and they are to decide the same, and the determination of the English to stand And they are each to do as is by the English sett down and if the one or the other shall Refuse to do, it shall be lawfull for the English to Compel him and to side and take part if they see cause, against the obstinate or Refusing party.

3. It is agreed and a conclusion of peace and friendship made between the said Miantinome and said Narragansetts and the said Poquim and the said Mohegans as long as they carry themselves orderly and give no just cause of offence and that they nor either of them do shelter any that may be Enemyes to the English that shall or formerly have had hand in murdering or killing any English man or woman or consented thereunto, They or either of them shall as soon as they can either bring the chief Sachem of our late enemies the Peaquots that had the chief hand in killing the English, to the said English, or take off their heads, As also for those murderers that are now agreed upon amongst us that are living they shall as soon as they can possibly take off their heads, if they may be in their custody or Else whensoever they or any of them shall come Amongst them or to their wigwams or any where if they can by any means come by them.

4. And whereas there be or is reported for to be by the said Narragansetts and Mohegans 200 Peaquots living that are men besides squawes and papooses. The English do give unto Miantinome and the Narragansetts to make up the number of Eighty with the Eleven they have already, and to Poquime his number, and that after they the Peaquots shall be divided as above said, shall no more be called Peaquots but Narragansetts and Mohegans and as their men and either of them are to pay for every Sanop one fathom of wampome peage and for every youth half so much—and for every Sanop papoose one hand to be paid at Killing time of Corn at Connecticut yearly and shall not suffer them for to live in the country that was formerly theirs but is now the Englishes

by conquest neither shall the Narragansetts nor Mohegans possess any part of the Peaquot country without leave from the English. And it is always expected that the English Captives are forthwith to be delivered to the English, such as belong to the Connecticut to the Sachems there, And such as belong to the Massachusetts; the said agreements are to be kept invoylably by the parties above said and if any make breach of them the other two may joyn and make warr upon such as shall break the same, unless satisfaction be made being Reasonably Required.

The Mark of Miantinomy,
The Marks of Poquim alias Uncas.
John Haines,
Roger Ludlow,
Edward Hopkins.

> **Source:** E. B. O'Callaghan, ed., *Laws and Ordinances of New Netherland, 1638–1674* (Albany, NY: Weed, Parsons, 1808), 215–217.

19. Account of Governor Kieft's War, 1643 [Excerpt]

Introduction

The Dutch West India Company established New Netherland in 1624 and eventually controlled territory extending from the Connecticut River to the Delaware River. At first the Dutch took great care to avoid conflict with the Indians. The Dutch purchased all the land on which they settled and refused to be drawn into the rivalry between the Algonquian and Iroquoian peoples. As the town of New Amsterdam grew, the colonists and the Algonquians came into increasing conflict. These accounts describe two massacres of Indian villages ordered by Director General Willem Kieft. David de Vries, president of the ruling council, decried Kieft's action in ordering the February 25, 1643, massacre of some 80 defenseless Algonquians. The anonymous account is clearly from the perspective of a Kieft opponent and recounts the 1644 massacre of some 700 Indians. Kieft hired New England officer John Underhill of Pequot War fame to command this operation. Both massacres spared neither women nor children. This period of war ended with at least 1,000 Indians slaughtered and numerous colonial farms and settlements burned to the ground. Between 1655 and 1664, New Netherland, under Director General Peter Stuyvesant, went to war against the Algonquians three more times.

Primary Source

[...]

The 24th of February, sitting at a table with the Governor, he began to state his intentions, that he had a mind to *wipe the mouths* of the savages; that he had been dining at the house of Jan Claesz. Damne,

where Maryn Adrianensz. And Jan Claesz. Damen, together with Jacob Planek, had presented a petition to him to begin this work. I answered him that they were not wise to request this; that such work could not be done without the approbation of the *Twelve Men;* that it could not take place without my assent, who was one of the Twelve Men; that moreover I was the first patroon, and no one else hitherto had risked there so many thousands, and also his person, as I was the first to come from Holland or Zeeland to plan a colony; and that he should consider what profit he could derive from this business, as he well knew that on account of trifling with the Indians we had lost our colony in the South River at Swanendael, in the Hoere-kil, with thirty-two men, who were murdered in the year 1630; and that in the year 1640, that cause of my people being murdered on Staten Island was a difficulty which he had brought on with the Raritaen Indians, where his soldiers had for some trifling thing killed some savages, and brought the brother of the chief a prisoner to the Mannates, who was ransomed there, as I have before more particularly related. But it appeared that my speaking was of no avail. He had, with his co-murderers, determined to commit the murder, deeming it a Roman deed, and to do it without warning the inhabitants in the open lands, that each one might take care of himself against the retaliation of the savages, for he could not kill all the Indians. When I had expressed all these things in full, sitting at the table, and the meal was over, he told me he wished me to go to the large hall, which he had been lately adding to his house. Coming to it, there stood all his soldiers ready to cross the river to Pavonia to commit the murder. Then spoke I again to Governor Willem Kieft: "Let this work alone; you wish to break the mouths of the Indians, but you will also murder our own nation, for there are none of the settlers in the open country who are aware of it. My own dwelling, my people, cattle, corn, and tobacco will be lost." He answered me, assuring me that there would be no danger; that some soldiers should go to my house to protect it. But that was not done. So was this business begun between the 25th and 26th of February in the year 1643. I remained that night at the Governor's, sitting up. I went and sat by the kitchen fire, when about midnight I heard a great shrieking, and I ran to the ramparts of the fort, and looked over to Pavonia. Saw nothing but firing, and heard the shrieks of the savages murdered in their sleep. I returned again to the house by the fire. Having sat there awhile, there came an Indian with his squaw, whom I knew well, and who lived about an hour's walk from my house, and told me that they two had fled in a small skiff, which they had taken from the shore at Pavonia; that the Indians from Fort Orange had surprised them; and that they had come to conceal themselves in the fort. I told them that they must go away immediately; that this was no time for them to come to the fort to conceal themselves; that they who had killed their people at Pavonia were not Indians, but the Swannekens, as they call the Dutch, had done it. They then asked me how they should get out of the forts. I took them to the door, and there was no sentry there, and so they betook themselves to the woods. When it was day the soldiers returned to the fort, having massacred or murdered eighty Indians, and considering they had done a deed of Roman valor, in murdering so many in their sleep; where infants were torn from the mother's breasts, and hacked to pieces in the presence of the parents, and the pieces thrown into the fire and in the water, and other sucklings, being bound to small boards, were cut, stuck, and pierced, and miserably massacred in a manner to move a heart of stone. Some were thrown into the river, and when the fathers and mothers endeavored to save them, the soldiers would not let them come on land but made both parents and children drown—children from five to six years of age, and also some old and decrepit persons. Those who fled from the onslaught, and concealed themselves in the neighboring sedge, and when it was morning, came out to beg a piece of bread, and to be permitted to warm themselves, were murdered in cold blood and tossed into the fire or the water. Some came to our people in the country with their hands, some with their legs cut off, and some holding their entrails in their arms, and others had such horrible cuts and gashes, that worse than they were could never happen. And these poor simple creatures, as also many of our own people, did not know any better than they had been attacked by a part of other Indians—the Maquas. After this exploit, the soldiers were rewarded for their services, and Director Kieft thanked them by taking them by the hand and congratulating them. At another place, on the same night, on Corler's Hook near Corler's plantation, forty Indians were in the same manner attacked in their sleep, and massacred there in the same manner. Did the Duke of Alva in the Netherlands ever do anything more cruel? This is indeed a disgrace to our nation, who have so generous a governor in our Fatherland as the Prince of Orange, who has always endeavored in his wars to spill as little blood as possible. As soon as the savages understood that the Swannekens had so treated them, all the men whom they could surprise on the farm-lands, they killed; but we have never heard that they have ever permitted women or children to be killed. They burned all the houses, farms, barns, grain, haystacks, and destroyed everything they could get hold of. So there was an open destructive war begun. They also burnt my farm, cattle, corn, bar, tobacco-house, and all the tobacco. My people saved themselves in the house where I alone lived, which was made with embrasures, through which they defended themselves. Whilst my people were in alarm the savage whom I had aided to escape from the fort in the night came there, and told the other Indians that I was a good chief, that I had helped him out of the fort, and the killing of the Indians took place contrary to my wish. Then they all cried out together to my people that they would not shoot them; that if they had not destroyed my cattle they would not do it, nor burn my house; that they would let my little brewery stand, though they wished to get the copper kettle, in order to make darts for their arrows; but hearing now that it had been done contrary to my wish, they all went away, and left my house unbesieged. When now the Indians had destroyed so many farms and men in revenge for their people, I went to Governor Willem Kieft, and asked him if it was not as I had said it

would be, that he would only effect the spilling of Christian blood. Who would not compensate us for our losses? But he gave me no answer. He said he wondered that no Indians came to the fort. I told him that I did not wonder at it; "why should the Indians come here where you have so treated them?"

[…]

Source: J. Franklin Jameson, ed., *Narratives of New Netherland* (New York: Scribner, 1909), 226–229.

20. Virginia Peace Treaty with the Indians, October 5, 1646

Introduction

The native peoples of Virginia, ruled by Powhatan's half brother Opechancanough, had attacked the colonists in 1622. By killing more than 300 Virginia settlers, the Powhatans brought about their own destruction. On April 17, 1644, the now old and ailing Opechancanough, angered by continuing encroachments on Indian land, launched a last all-out attack on the English. He sent his warriors against frontier settlers, killing more than 400 English men, women, and children. However, by 1644 the colony had grown to a population of nearly 10,000, so the death toll of Opechancanough's last attack did not have as great an effect as that of his earlier massacre. In fact, the colonists now outnumbered the Indians. Exposure to European diseases and long years of warfare had reduced the Indian population of Virginia to barely half of what it had been when the first Englishmen arrived. In 1646 the English finally captured Opechancanough, but before he could be transported to England for trial an English hothead murdered him at Jamestown. This treaty with Opechancanough's successor, Necotowance, ended the war with Powhatan's people and severely curtailed their territory and freedom of movement. They had to pay an annual tribute and could be shot on sight for trespassing on English territory.

Primary Source

ACT I.

Art. 1. *Be it enacted by this Grand Assembly,* that the articles of peace foll: between the inhabitants of this colony, and Necotowance King of the Indians bee duely & inviolably observed upon the penaltie within mentioned as followeth:

Imp. That Necotowance do acknowledge to hold his kingdome from the King's Ma'tie of England, and that his successors be appointed or confirmed by the King's Governours from time to time, And on the other side, This Assembly on the behalfe of this collony, doth, undertake to protect him or them against any rebells or other enemies whatsoever, and as an acknowledgment and tribute for such protection, the said Necotowance and his successors are to pay unto the King's Govern'r. the number of twenty beaver skins att the goeing away of Geese yearely.

Art. 2. That it shall be free for the said Necotowance and his people, to inhabit and hunt on the northside of Yorke River, without any interruption from the English. *Provided* that if hereafter, It shall be thought fitt by the Governor and council to permitt any English to inhabitt from Poropotanke downewards, that first Necotowance be acquainted therewith.

Art. 3. That Necotowance and his people leave free that tract of land betweene Yorke river and James river, from the falls of both the rivers to Kequotan, to the English to inhabitt on, and that neither he the said Necotowance nor any Indians do repaire to or make any abode upon the said tract of land, upon paine of death, and it shall be lawfull for any person to kill any such Indian, And in case any such Indian or Indians being seen upon the said tract of land shall make an escape, That the said Necotowance shall upon demand deliver the said Indian or Indians to the Englishmen, upon knowledge had of him or them, unless such Indian or Indians be sent upon a message from the said Necotowance.

And to the intent to avoid all injury to such a messenger, and that no ignorance may be pretended to such as shall offer any outrage, *It is thought fitt and herby enacted,* That the badge worne by a messenger, or, in case there shall be more than one, by one of the company, be a coate of striped stuffe which is to be left by the messenger from time to time so often as he shall returne at the places appointed for coming in.

Art. 4 *And it is further enacted,* That in case any English shall repaire contrary to the articles agreed upon, to the said north side of Yorke river, such persons so offending, being lawfully convicted, be adjudged as felons; *Provided* that this article shall not extend to such persons who by stresse of weather are forced upon the said land, *Provided alsoe* and it is agreed by the said Necotowance, that it may be lawfull for any Englishman to goe over to the said north side haveing occasion to fall timber trees or cut sedge, soe as the said persons have warr't for theyre soe doeing under the hand of the Gov. *Provided also* notwitstandinge any thing in this act to the contrary, That it shall bee free and lawfull for any English whatsoever between this present day and the first of March next to kill and bring away what cattle or hoggs that they can by any meanes kill or take upon the said north side of the said river.

Art. 5. *And it is further enacted* that neither for the said Necotowance nor any of his people, do frequent come in to hunt or make any abode nearer the English plantations then the lymits of Yapin the black water, and from the head of the black water upon a straite line to the old Monakin Towne, upon such paine and penaltie as aforesaid.

Art. 6. *And it is further ordered enacted* that if any English do entertain any Indian or Indians or doe conceale any Indian or Indians that shall come within the said limits, such persons being lawfully convicted thereof shall suffer death as in the case of felony, without benefit of clergy, excepted such as shall be authorized thereto by virtue of this act.

Art. 7. *And it is further enacted* that the said Necotowance and his people upon all occasions of messages to the Gov'r. for trade, doe repaire unto the ffort Royall only on the north side, at which place they are to receive the aforesaid badges, which shall shew them to be messengers, and therefore to be freed from all injury in their passage to the Governor, upon payne of death to any person or persons whatsoever that shall kill them, the badge being worn by one of the company, And in case of any other affront, the offence to be punished according to the quality thereof, and the trade admitted as aforesaid to the said Necotowance and his people with the commander of the said ffort only on the north side.

Art. 8. *And it is further thought fitt and enacted,* that upon any occasion of message to the Gov'r. or trade, The said Necotowance and his people the Indians doe repair to fforte Henery *alias* Appamattucke fforte, or to the house of Capt. John ffloud, and to no other place or places of the south side of the river, at which places the aforesaid badges of striped stuffe are to be and remaine.

Art. 9. *And it is further thought fitt and enacted,* That Necotowance doe with all convenience bring in the English prisoners, And all such negroes and guns which are yet remaining either in the possession of himselfe or any Indians, and that there deliver upon demand such Indian servants as have been taken prisoners and shall hereafter run away, In case such Indian or Indians shall be found within the limits of his dominions; provided that such Indian or Indians be under the age of twelve years at theire running away.

Art. 10. *And it is further enacted & consented,* That such Indian children as shall or will freely and voluntarily come in and live with the English, may remain without breach of the articles of peace provided they be not above twelve years old.

Art. 11. *And it is further thought fitt and enacted* That the several commanders of the fforts and places as aforesaid unto which the said Indians as aforesaid are admitted to repaire, In case of trade or Message doe forthwith provide the said coats in manner striped as aforesaid.

Source: William Waller Henning, *The Statutes at Large; Being A Collection of All the Laws of Virginia from . . . 1619,* Vol. 1 (New York: R&W&G Barton, 1823), 323–326.

21. Exclusion of Jews from Military Service in New Amsterdam, 1655

Introduction

Like the home country, New Netherland tolerated people of various religions, although the Dutch Reformed Church enjoyed official favor. The authorities believed that welcoming all sorts of people was good for the colony and good for business. As a result, Jews and Protestants from other European countries such as Belgium and France settled in New Netherland. New Englanders fleeing the religious intolerance of the Puritans also found a haven in New Netherland. However, these minorities did not receive all the privileges of full citizenship. Under Director General Petrus Stuyvesant, New Netherland went to war with the native Algonquians three times between 1655 and 1664. The Algonquians lost most of their land around New Amsterdam, but potential settlers feared moving there because of the nearly constant fighting. In 1655 a number of Jews living in New Amsterdam volunteered to join the city militia. New Amsterdam's council rejected them on the grounds that the other militiamen would object to their presence. However, the council ruled that Jewish men must pay for their "exemption" from service. The city could ill afford this exercise in prejudice. Only days later the outnumbered militia struggled to repulse an Indian attack.

Primary Source

The captains and officers of the trainbands of this city, having asked the director general and Council whether the Jewish people who reside in this city should also train and mount guard with the citizens' bands, this was taken in consideration and deliberated upon. First, the disgust and unwillingness of these trainbands to be fellow soldiers with the aforesaid nation and to be on guard with them in the same guardhouse, and, on the other side, that the said nation was not admitted or counted among the citizens, as regards trainbands or common citizens' guards, neither in the illustrious city of Amsterdam nor (to our knowledge) in any city in Netherland. But in order that the said nation may honestly be taxed for their freedom in that respect, it is directed by the director general and Council, to prevent further discontent, that the aforesaid nation shall, according to the usages of the renowned city of Amsterdam, remain exempt from the general training and guard duty, on condition that each male person over sixteen and under sixty years contribute for the aforesaid freedom toward the relief of the general municipal taxes sixty-five stivers (one stiver equals two cents) every month. And the military council of the citizens is hereby authorized and charged to carry this into effect until our further orders, and to collect, pursuant of the above, the aforesaid contribution once in every month, and, in case of refusal, to collect it by legal process. Thus done in Council at Fort Amsterdam.

Source: E. B. O'Callaghan, ed., *Laws and Ordinances of New Netherland, 1638–1674* (Albany, NY: Weed, Parsons, 1808), 191–192.

22. John Eliot, Account of New England Indians' Conversion to Christianity, ca. 1671

Introduction

As increasing numbers of English colonists came to Massachusetts, white settlements grew up around native villages. Most of the Puritan colonists wanted to drive off or kill the Indians. Beginning in the 1640s, Reverend John Eliot and fellow missionaries strove to convert the Indians to Christianity as well as to the English way of life. Eliot wrote this fictitious dialogue to illustrate the Indians' spiritual concerns to other missionaries working to convert them. With funding from a missionary society in England, Eliot produced a native-language translation of the Bible and trained native teachers and missionaries. By 1675, more than 1,500 Indians had converted and lived in 14 so-called praying villages. When King Philip's War broke out in 1675, the Christian Indians were caught between their two worlds and suffered sorely for their loyalty to the English. Some colonists accused the Indians of being spies, while other colonists simply slaughtered Indians because they made an easy target. Both to protect the Indians from the English and to keep the Indians from aiding their own people, Massachusetts authorities placed them on two islands in Boston Harbor. There they died by the hundred of exposure and starvation. The shot that killed King Philip and ended the war was fired by a Christian Indian.

Primary Source

Kinsman: I had rather that my actions of love should testifie how welcome you are, and how glad I am of this your kinde visitation, then that I should say it in a multitude of words. But in one word, You are very welcome to my hearts; and I account it among the best of the joyes of this day, that I see your face, and enjoy your company in my habitation.

Kinswoman: It is an addition to the joyes of this day, to see the face of my loving Kinsman: and I wish you had come a little earlier, that you might have taken part with us in the joyes of this day, wherein we have had all the delights that could be desired, in our merry meeting, and Dancing.

And I pray Cousin how doth your Wife, my loving Kinswoman, is she yet living? and is she not weary of your new way of praying to God? And what pleasure have you in those ways?

Piumbukhou: My wife doth remember her love to you, she is in good health of body, and her Soul is in a good condition, she is entered into the light of the knowledge of God, and of Christ; she is entered into the narrow way of heavenly joyes, and she doth greatly desire that you would turn from these ways of darkness in which you so much delight, and come taste and see how good the Lord is.

And whereas you wish I had come sooner, to have shared with you in your delights of this day; Alas, they are no delights, but griefs to me, to see that you do still delight in them. I am like a man that have tasted of sweet Wine and Honey, which have so altered the taste of my mouth, that I abhor to taste of your sinful and foolish pleasures, as the mouth doth abhor to taste the most filthy and stinking dung, the most sour grapes, or most bitter gall. Our joyes in the knowledge of God, and of Jesus Christ, which we are taught in the Book of God, and feel in our heart, is sweeter to our soul, than honey is unto the mouth and taste.

Kinswoman: We have all the delights that the flesh and blood of man can devise and delight in, and we taste and feel the delights of them, and would you make us believe that you have found out new joyes and delights, in comparison of which all our delights do stink like dung? Would you make us believe that we have neither eyes to see, nor ears to hear, nor mouthes to taste? Ha, ha, he! I appeal to the sense and sight and feeling of the Company present, whether this be so.

All. You say very true. Ha, ha, he!

Piumbukhou: Hearken to me, my friends, and see if I do not give a clear answer unto this seeming difficulty. Your dogs take as much delight in these Meetings, and the same kindes of delight as you do. They delight in each others company; they provoke each other to lust, and enjoy the pleasures of lust as you do; they eat and play and sleep as you do; what joys have you more than dogs have? to delight the body of flesh and blood.

But all mankinde have an higher and better part than the body, we have a Soul, and that Soul shall never die. Our soul is to converse with God, and to converse in such things as do concern God, and Heaven, and an eternal estate, either in happiness with God, if we walk with him and serve him in this life, or in misery and torment with the Devil, if we serve him in this life. The service of God doth consist in virtue, and wisdom, and delights of the soul, which will reach to heaven, and abide forever.

But the service of the Devil is in committing sins of the flesh, which defile both body and soul, and reach to Hell, and will turn all to fire and flame to torment your souls and bodies in all eternity.

Now consider, all your pleasures and delights are such as defile you with sin, and will turn to flame, to burn and torment you; they provoke God to wrath, who hath created the prison of hell to torment you, and the more you have took pleasure in sin, the greater are your offences against God, and the greater shall be your torments.

But we that pray to God repent of our old sins, and by faith in Christ we seek for, and find a pardon for what is past, and grace and strength to reform for time to come. So that our joyes are Soul-joyes in godliness, and virtue, and hope of glory in another world when we die.

Your joyes are bodily, fleshly, such as dogs have, and will all turn to flames in hell to torment you.

Kinsman. If these things be so, we had need to cease laughing, and fall to weeping, and see if we can draw water from our mournful eyes to quench these tormenting flames. My heart trembles to hear these things: I never heard so much before, nor have I any thing to say to the contrary, but that these things may be so. But how shall I know that you say true? Our forefathers were (many of them) wise men, and we have wise men now living, they all delight in these our Delights: they have taught us nothing about our Soul, and God, and Heaven, and Hell, and joy and torment in the life to come. Are you wiser than our fathers? May not we rather think that English men have invented these stories to amaze us and fear us out of our old customs, and bring us to stand in awe of them, that they might wipe us of our lands, and drive us into corners, to seek new ways of living, and new places too? And be beholding to them for that which is our own, and was ours, before we knew them.

All. You say right.

Piumbukhou: The Book of God is no invention of Englishmen. It is the holy law of God himself, which was given unto man by God, before Englishmen had any knowledge of God; and all the knowledge which they have, they have it out of the Book of God: and this Book is given to us as well as to them, and it is as free for us to search the Scriptures as for them. So that we have our instruction from a higher hand, then the hand of man. It is the great Lord God of Heaven and Earth, who teacheth us these great things of which we speak. Yet this is also true, that we have great cause to be thankful to the English, and to thank God for them, for they had a good Country of their own, but by ships sailing into these parts of the world, they heard of us, and of our country, and of our nakedness, ignorance of God, and wild condition; God put it into their hearts to desire to come hither, and teach us the good knowledge of God; and their King gave them leave so to do, and in our country to have their liberty to serve God according to the word of God. And being come hither, we gave them leave freely to live among us. They have purchased of us a great part of those lands which they possess; they love us, they do us right, and no wrong willingly; if any do us wrong, it is without the consent of their Rulers, and upon our Complaints our wrongs are righted. They are (many of them, especially the Ruling part) good men, and desire to do us good. God put it into the heart of one of their ministers (as you all know) to teach us the knowledge of God, by the word of God, and hath translated the holy Book of God into our Language, so that we can perfectly know the mind and counsel of God; and out of this book have I learned all that I say unto you, and therefore you need no more doubt of the truth of it, then you have cause to doubt that the Heaven is over our head, the Sun shineth, the earth is under our feet, we walk and live upon it, and breathe in the air; for as we see with our eyes these things to be so, so we read with our own eyes these things which I speak of, to be written in God's own Book, and we feel the truth thereof in our own hearts.

Kinswoman. Cousin, you have wearied your legs this day with a long journey to come and visit us, and you weary your tongue with long discourses. I am willing to comfort and refresh you with a short supper.

All. Ha, ha, he. Though short, if sweet, that has good favor to a man that is weary. Ha, ha, he.

Kinswoman. You make long and learned discourses to us which we do not well understand. I think our best answer is to stop your mouth, and fill your belly with a good supper, and when your belly is full you will be content to take rest yourself, and give us leave to be at rest from these gastering and heart-trembling discourses. We are well as we are, and desire not to be troubled with these new wise sayings.

Source: Colin G. Calloway, ed., *The World Turned Upside Down: Indian Voices from Early America* (Boston: St. Martin's, 1994).

23. John Gerrard, An Account of the Attack on the Susquehannock Stronghold, 1675

Introduction

The Susquehannocks lived along the Susquehanna River in present-day New York, Pennsylvania, and Maryland. Maryland first declared war on the Susquehannocks in 1642. Ten years later the Susquehannocks made peace with Maryland and gave the colony large tracts of land. The Susquehannocks had suffered huge losses in their ongoing war with the Iroquois and could no longer fight two wars at once. The peace endured for more than 20 years. In 1674 the Maryland government ordered the Susquehannocks, who were even more weakened by decades of warfare, to move to a settlement on the banks of the Potomac River. The next year an argument ended in the murder of a Virginian and some 20 Susquehannocks. Fearing reprisals, more than 1,000 Virginia and Maryland militia surrounded the Susquehannock town. Militiamen murdered 5 Susquehannock chiefs. In this report, a Virginia militiaman attributes the killing to Marylanders. The Susquehannocks fled to southern Virginia and then took revenge by attacking and killing settlers on the frontiers of both colonies. The Susquehannocks remained at war with the English for another 15 years, until the Susquehannocks were reduced to scattered remnants. The Maryland assembly tried and convicted the militia commander for the murders, but he was not punished.

Primary Source

A narrative of the transactions of the Susquehannock Fort. Soe fare as I know concerning the Killing of the five Indians Assoone as our Virginia forces were landed in Maryland wee found five susquehannock Indians, under a guard and inquireing the reason of theire restraint, where [i.e., were] answered they endeavoured an escape and thereof were secured till our comeing in order to a treaty wee informing the Marylanders our businesse was first to treat and require satisfaction for the murder perpetrated before wee declared ourselves open enimies and proceeded to hostile actions[.] Lt. Col. John Washington and Major Isaac Allerton upon this information thought it convenient to have them stronger guarded and themselves alsoe dureing the treaty which being donne and Col. Washington and Major Alerton accordingly treating there first demand was Satisfaction for the murder and spoyles committed on Virginia Shore Major Tilghman in the interim remaining silent: after long debate [word illegible] therein made by Col. Washington and Major Alerton the Indians disowned all that was Aledged to them and imputed it all to [the] senacas[.] Col Washington and Major Alerton urged that severall Cannoes loaded with beefe and pork had bin carried into theire fort alleadging that theire enimyes would not be soe kinde as to supply them with provisions and farther that some of their men had a little before been taken on Virginia side who had the Cloathes of such as had bin a little before murdered, upon there backes which made it appeare that they had bin the murderers: for these reasons Major Alerton and Col. Washington demanded Satisfaction or else they must proceed against them as enimyes and storme there fort and accordingly commanded the interpreter to bid them defiance[.] dureing the time of their Treaty Major [Thomas] Trewman came and asked the Gentlemen wheather they had finished[,] saying when you have donne I will Say something to them: And when col. Washington and Major Alerton had ended there treatie he went and commanded his interpreter John shanks to ask them how theire Indians came to be buried at [Hutsons?] and after a little further discourse caused them to be bound and told them he would Carry them to the place and show them theire owne Indians where they lay dead: Major Alerton asked him what he did intend to doe with them afterwards[.] Major Trewman answered he thought they deserved the like to which Major Alerton replyed I doe not think soe[.] noe sooner was this discourse ended between Major Allerton and Major Trewman than the Marylanders carried away those five Indians and before they had got five hundred yards distance from the place of this discourse and treaty spoken of[,] the Marylanders killed them and further saith not

John Gerrard

Sworne before us by virtue of an order to us from the right Honorable the Governor

Nicholas Spencer   June the 13th 1677 recorded
Richard Lee

Source: Warren M. Billings, ed., *The Old Dominion in the Seventeenth Century: A Documentary History of Virginia, 1606–1689* (Chapel Hill: University of North Carolina Press, 1975).

24. Nathaniel Saltonstall, Accounts of King Philip's War, 1675–1676 [Excerpts]

Introduction

These excerpts from a series of letters, sent to London by Boston merchant Nathaniel Saltonstall, recount episodes in King Philip's War (1675–1676). The Wampanoag Indians had lived in peace with the English ever since 1620, when their leader, Massasoit, had made a treaty of friendship with the Pilgrims. By the time of Massasoit's death in 1662, thousands of English colonists were arriving in New England every year. His son and successor, Metacom, called King Philip by the English, organized an Indian confederacy to resist English expansion. A June 1675 attack on a village in Plymouth Colony set off the hugely destructive war. The United Colonies of New England joined forces against the Narragansetts, Pocumtucs, Nipmucs and Wampanoags. The Indians destroyed numerous Massachusetts villages, making life on the frontier intolerable for the colonists. In December 1675 Plymouth governor Josiah Winslow led his militia into Rhode Island to attack the Narragansetts. Winslow found the Narragansetts camped on high ground in the middle of a vast swamp. The battle inflicted 240 English casualties and more than 900 Narragansett casualties. The war crushed Indian resistance but utterly destroyed parts of New England and killed 1 out of 16 English fighting men. The first excerpt demonstrates how the English treated their Indian allies. The second excerpt describes the Great Swamp Fight.

Primary Source

[. . .]

This Unkus, and all his Subjects professing Christianity, are called Praying Indians. In the first Week in August, the Authority of Boston sent an Express to him, to require him to come in and Surrender himself, Men, and Arms, to the English; Whereupon, he sent along with the Messenger his three Sons, and about Sixty of his Men, with his Arms, to be thus disposed of, viz. His two youngest sons, (about thirty Years old) to remain as Hostages (as now they do at Cambridg) and his Eldest Son to go Captain of the Men as Assistants to the English against the Heathens, which accordingly they did. And the English not thinking themselves yet secure enough, because they cannot know a Heathen from a Christian by his Visage, nor Apparel: The Authority of Boston, at a Council held there the 30th of August, Published this following Order.

At a Council held in Boston, August 30, 1675.

The Council judging it of absolute Necessity for the Security of the English, and the Indians that are in Amity with us, that they be Restrained their usual commerce with the English, and Hunting in the Woods, during the Time of Hostility with those that are our Enemies.

Do Order, that all those Indians that are desirous to Approve themselves Faithful to the English, be Confined to their several Plantations under-written, until the council shall take further Order; and that they so order the setting of their Wigwams, that they may stand Compact in some one Part of their Plantations respectively, where it may be best for their own Provision and Defence. And that none of them do presume to Travel above one Mile from the Center of such their Dwelling, unless in Company with some English, or in their Service near their Dwellings; and excepting for gathering and fetching in their Corn with one Englishman, on peril of being taken as our Enemies, or their Abettors: And in Case that any of them shall be taken without the Limits abovesaid, except as abovesaid, and do lose their Lives, or be otherwise damnified, by English or Indians; The Council do hereby Declare, that they shall account themselves wholly Innocent, and their Blood or other Dammage (by them sustained) will be upon their own Heads. Also it shall not be lawful for any Indians that are in Amity with us, to entertain any strange Indians, or receive any of our Enemies Plunder, but shall from Time to Time make Discovery thereof to some English, that shall be Appointed for that End to sojourn among them, on Penalty of being reputed our Enemies, and of being liable to be proceeded against as such.

Also, whereas it is the Manner of the Heathen that are now in Hostility with us, contrary to the Practice of all Civil nations, to Execute their bloody Insolencies by Stealth, and Sculking in small Parties, declining all open Decision of their Controversie, either by Treaty or by the Sword.

The Council do therefore Order, That after the Publication of the Provision aforesaid, It shall be lawful for any Person, whether English or Indian, that shall find any Indians Travelling or Sculking in any of our Towns or Woods, contrary to the Limits above-named, to command them under their Guard and Examination, or to Kill and destroy them as they best may or can. The Council hereby declaring, That it will be most acceptable to them that none be Killed or Wounded that are Willing to surrender themselves into Custody.

The Places of the Indians Residencies are, Natick, Punquapaog, Nashoba, Wamesit, and Hassanemesit: And if there be any that belong to any other Plantations, they are to Repair to some one of these.

By the Council

EDWARD RAWSON, *Secr.*

[...]

In the Afternoon of that Saturday, some of the Souldiers accidently espied an Indian alone, whom they took and carried to the General, who upon his Refusal to answer to those Questions demanded, was ordered to be Hanged forthwith; Whereupon the Indian to save his Life, told them where the whole Body of the Indians were together, as well King Philip, and all other confederate Sagamores and Sachems with their whole Retinue, as also the whole body of the Narragansets, being joined all in a body in November, about 4500 Indian Men, besides Wives and Children: Whereupon, keeping this Indian for their Guide, they having Provisions with them, marched all Night, the Indians being then 16 Miles distant from them, and that Night there fell a very hard Snow two or three Foot deep, and withal an extream hard Frost, so that some of our Men were frozen in their Hands and Feet, and thereby disabled for Service. The next Day, about Noon, they come to a large Swamp, which by Reasons of the Frost all the Night before, they were capable of going over (which else they could not have done). They forthwith in one Body entered the said Swamp, and in the Midst thereof was a Piece of firm Land, of about three or four Acres of Ground, whereon the Indians had built a Kind of Fort, being palisado'd round, and within that a Clay Wall, as also felled down Abundance of Trees to Lay quite round the said Fort, but they had not quite finished the said Work. The General placed Capt. Moseley in the Front, to enter the Fort, and the Rest of the Companies were placed according to discretion. In their march they met with three Indians sent out as Scouts, whom they shot dead at Sight thereof: as soon as ever the Indians saw our Army coming, they shot as fast as ever they could, and so our men did the like. Before our men could come up to take Possession of the Fort, the Indians had shot three Bullets through Capt. Davenport, whereupon he bled extreamly, and immediately called for his Lieutenant, Mr. Edward Ting, and committed the Charge of the Company to him, and desire him to take care of his Gun, and deliver it according to Order, and immediately died in the Place; his Company were extreamly grieved at his Death, in Regard he was so courteous to them; for he being Commander of that Company, belonging to Cambridge and Watertown etc. was

a Stranger to most of them; and at the same Time that he came to take Possession of his Company, he made a very civil Speech to them, and also gave them free Liberty to choose their Serjeants themselves, which pleased them very well, and accordingly did so; and it is very probable the Indians might think that Capt. Davenport was the General, because he had a very good Buff Suit on at that Time, and therefore might shoot at him. In a short Time our Forces entered the fort, Captain Moseley being in the Front, the Indians knowing him very well, many directed their shot to him, as he afterwards told the General that he believed he saw 50 aim at him: As soon as he and they had entred the Fort, he espied a Heap of above 50 Indians lay dead in a Corner, which the Indians had gathered together; as soon as ever our Men had entred the Fort, the Indians fled, our Men killed many of them, as also of their Wives and Children, amongst which an Indian Black-Smith (the only Man amongst them that fitted their Guns and Arrow-heads;) and amongst many other Houses burnt his, as also demolished his Forge, and carried away his tools; they fought with the Indians, and pursued them so long as was advantageous to them; then the General gave Order to sound a Retreat, which was done according to Order. The Retreat was no sooner beaten, and the Souldiers were in a Marching Posture, before they were got all out of the Fort, a thousand fresh Indians set on our Men, but in an Hour's Time the Indians were forced to Retreat and Flie. Our Men as near as they can judge, may have killed about 600 Indian Men, besides Women and Children. Many more Indians were killed which we could have no Account of, by Reason that they would carry away as many dead Indians as they could. Our Men before they had been set on by the fresh Indians, had set fire to most of the Wigwams in and about the Fort (which were near 1000 in all,) how many were burnt down they could not tell positively, only thus; That they marched above three Miles from the Fort by the Light of the Fires.

Source: Charles H. Lincoln, ed., *Narratives of the Indian Wars* (New York: Scribner, 1913), 32–33, 57–59.

25. Mary Rowlandson, *Narrative of the Captivity and Restoration,* 1682

Introduction

At sunrise on February 10, 1676, Narragansett Indians attacked and destroyed Lancaster, Massachusetts. The attackers killed 12 men, women, and children and took 24 captives. Among those taken were Mary Rowlandson, wife of the town's Puritan minister, and her 3 children. Her wounded 6-year-old daughter died nine days after their capture. The Indians took Mrs. Rowlandson with them as they moved their village from place to place, covering some 150 miles. Rowlandson and her surviving 2 children, a girl age 10 and a boy age 14, were sold to separate owners among the Indians. Mrs. Rowlandson, taking strength from her religious faith, used her wits to survive. She met King Philip himself and sewed some clothing for his son, for which he paid her. Others then gave her food in return for sewing. Some Indians in the village treated her with kindness, while others treated her with cruelty. After 11 weeks of captivity among the Indians, Rowlandson was ransomed and released on May 3, 1676. Several months passed before her children were freed. Rowlandson wrote *Narrative of the Captivity and Restoration,* which was published in Boston in 1682. The first of its kind, the book sold well, and stories of captivity among the Indians became a popular form of American literature. This excerpt recounts the day of the attack.

Primary Source

On the tenth of February 1675, Came the Indians with great numbers upon Lancaster: Their first coming was about Sun-rising; hearing the noise of some guns, we looked out; several Houses were burning, and the smoke ascending to Heaven. There were five persons taken in one house, the Father, and the Mother and a sucking Child, they knockt on the head; the other two they took and carried away alive. Their were two others, who being out of their Garison upon some occasion were set upon; one was knockt on the head, the other escaped: Another their was who running along was shot and wounded, and fell down; he begged of them his life promising them Money (as they told) but they would not hearken to him but knockt him in head, and stript him naked, and split open his Bowels. Another seeing many of the Indians about his Barn, ventured and went out, but was quickly shot down. There were three others belonging to the same Garison who were killed; the Indians getting up upon the roof of the Barn, had advantage to shoot down upon them over their Fortification. Thus these murderous wretches went on, burning and destroying before them.

At length they came and beset our house, and quickly it was the dolefullest day that ever min eyes saw. The House stood upon the edg of a hill; some of the Indians got behind the hill, others into the Barn, and others behind any thing that could shelter them; from all which places they shot against the House, so that the Bullets seemed to fly like hail; and quickly they wounded one man among us, then another, and then a third. About two hours (according to my observation, in that amazing time) they had been about the house before they prevailed to fire it (which they did with Flax and Hemp, which they brought out of the Barn, and there being no defence about the House, only two flankers at two opposite corners and one of them not finished) they fired it once and one ventured out and quenched it, but they quickly fired it again, and that took. Now is the dreadfull hour come, that I have often heard of (in time of War, as it was the case of others) but now mine eyes see it. Some in our house were fighting for their lives, others wallowing in their blood, the House on fire over our heads, and the bloody Heathen ready to knock us on the head, if we stirred out. Now might we hear Mothers and Children crying out for themselves,

and one another, Lord, What shall we do? Then I took my Children (and one of my sisters, hers) to go forth and leave the house: but as soon as we came to the dore and appeared, the Indians shot so thick that the bullets rattled against the House, as if one had taken an handful of stones and threw them, so that we were fain to give back. We had six stout dogs belonging to our Garrison, but none of them would stir, though another time, if any Indian had come to the door, they were ready to fly upon him and tear him down. The Lord hereby would make us the more to acknowledge his hand, and to see that our help is always in him. But out we must go, the fire increasing, and coming along behind us, roaring, and the Indians gaping before us with their Guns, Spears and Hatchets to devour us. No sooner were we out of the House, but my Brother in Law (being before wounded, in defending the house, in or near the throat) fell down dead, wherat the Indians scornfully shouted, and hallowed, and were presently upon him, stripping off his cloaths, the bullets flying thick, one went through my side, and the same (as would seem) through the bowels and hand of my dear Child in my arms. One of my elder sisters Children, named William, had then his Leg broken, which the Indians perceiving, they knockt him on head. Thus were we butchered by those merciless Heathen standing amazed, with the blood running down to our heels. My eldest Sister being yet in the House, and seeing those woful sights, the Infidels haling Mothers one way, and children another, and some wallowing in their blood: and her eldest Son telling her that her son William was dead, and my self was wounded, she said, And, Lord, let me dy with them, which was no sooner said, but she was struck with a Bullet and fell down dead over the threshold. I hope she is reaping the fruit of her good labours, being faithfull to the service of God in her place. In her younger years she lay under much trouble upon spiritual accounts, till it pleased God to make that precious Scripture take hold of her heart, 2 Cor 12.9: *and he said unto me, my Grace is sufficient for thee.* More then twenty years after I have heard her tell how sweet and comfortable that place was to her. But to return: The Indians laid hold of us, pulling me one way, and the Children another and said, Come go along with us: I told them they would kill me: they answered, If I were willing to go along with them, they would not hurt me.

Oh the dolefull sight that now was to behold at this House, *Come, behold the works of the Lord, what disolations he has made in the Earth.* Of thirty seven persons who were in this one House, none escaped either present death, or a bitter captivity, save only one, who might say as he, Job 1.15, *And I only am escaped alone to tell the News.* There were twelve killed, some shot, some stab'd with their Spears, some knock'd down with their hatchets. When we are in prosperity, Oh the little that we think of dreadfull sights, and to see our dear Friends, and Relations ly bleeding out their heart-blood upon the ground. There was one who was chopt into the head with a hatchet, and stript naked, and yet was crawling up and down. It is a solemn sight to see so many Christians lying in their blood, some here, and some there, like a company of Sheep torn by Wolves, All of them stript naked by a company of hell-hounds, roaring, singing, ranting and insulting, as if they would have torn our very hearts out; yet, the Lord by his Almighty power preserved a number of us from death, for there were twenty-four of us taken alive and carried Captive.

I had often before this said, that if the Indians should come, I should chuse rather to be killed by them then taken alive but when it came to the tryal my mind changed; their glittering weapons so daunted my spirit, that I chose rather to go along with those (as I may say) ravenous Beasts, then that moment to end my dayes; and that I may the better declare what happened to me during that grievous Captivity, I shall particularly speak of the severall Removes we had up and down the Wilderness.

The first Remove.

Now away we must go with those Barbarous Creatures, with our bodies wounded and bleeding, and our hearts no less than our bodies. About a mile we went that night, up upon a hill within sight of the Town, where they intended to lodge. There was hard by a vacant house (deserted by the English before, for fear of the Indians). I asked them whither I might no lodge in the house that night to which they answered, what will you love English men still? This was the dolefullest night that ever my eyes saw. Oh the roaring, and singing and dancing, and yelling of those black creatures in the night, which made the place a lively resemblance of hell.

Source: Charles H. Lincoln, ed., *Narratives of the Indian Wars* (New York: Scribner, 1913), 118–121.

26. Nathaniel Bacon, "Declaration in the Name of the People of Virginia," July 30, 1676

Introduction

William Berkeley governed Virginia from 1642 to 1652 and again from 1660 to 1677. His administration favored the interests of the wealthy upper class. He imposed heavy taxes on struggling farmers while paying himself a high salary and granted the best land to his favorites, forcing former indentured servants to wrest land from the Indians on the western frontier. Nathaniel Bacon, an upper-class 29-year-old distantly related to the governor, had served on Virginia's council. Bacon took up the cause of the struggling frontier dwellers and led an attack on the Indians. Berkeley opposed the expedition and accused Bacon of treason. Berkeley's declaration was an attempt to rally support. Bacon and his men then occupied Jamestown, forcing the governor to flee, and burned the capital to the ground. Bacon's declaration contains a list of grievances against the governor, accusing him of favoritism, corruption, and treachery. The rebellion came to a halt when Bacon suddenly fell ill and died in October 1676. After Bacon's death, the governor returned to the capital and hanged 23 of Bacon's rebels, seizing their property for his friends. King Charles II recalled the governor to London to explain his actions, but Berkeley died shortly after his arrival. Berkeley's successor signed the Treaty of Middle Plantation in 1677, ending the warfare between Indians and frontier settlers. Bacon's Rebellion eventually led to reform in Virginia, including a reduction in taxes and the availability of land for freed servants.

Primary Source

1. For having, upon specious pretenses of public works, raised great unjust taxes upon the commonalty for the advancement of private favorites and other sinister ends, but no visible effects in any measure adequate; for not having, during this long time of his government, in any measure advanced this hopeful colony either by fortifications, towns, or trade.

2. For having abused and rendered contemptible the magistrates of justice by advancing to places of judicature scandalous and ignorant favorites.

3. For having wronged his Majesty's prerogative and interest by assuming monopoly of the beaver trade and for having in it unjust gain betrayed and sold his Majesty's country and the lives of his loyal subjects to the barbarous heathen.

4. For having protected, favored, and emboldened the Indians against his Majesty's loyal subjects, never contriving, requiring, or appointing any due or proper means of satisfaction for their many invasions, robberies, and murders committed upon us.

5. For having, when the army of English was just upon the track of those Indians, who now in all places burn, spoil, murder and when we might with ease have destroyed them who then were in open hostility, for then having expressly countermanded and sent back our army by passing his word for the peaceable demeanor of the said Indians, who immediately prosecuted their evil intentions, committing horrid murders and robberies in all places, being protected by the said engagement and word past of him the said Sir William Berkeley, having ruined and laid desolate a great part of his Majesty's country, and have now drawn themselves into such obscure and remote places and are by their success so emboldened and confirmed by their confederacy so strengthened that the cries of blood are in all places, and the terror and consternation of the people so great, are now become not only difficult but a very formidable enemy who might at first with ease have been destroyed.

6. And lately, when, upon the loud outcries of blood, the assembly had, with all care, raised and framed an army for the preventing of further mischief and safeguard of this his Majesty's colony.

7. For having, with only the privacy of some few favorites without acquainting the people, only by the alteration of a figure, forged a commission, by we know not what hand, not only without but even against the consent of the people, for the raising and

effecting civil war and destruction, which being happily and without bloodshed prevented; for having the second time attempted the same, thereby calling down our forces from the defense of the frontiers and most weakly exposed places.

8. For the prevention of civil mischief and ruin amongst ourselves while the barbarous enemy in all places did invade, murder, and spoil us, his Majesty's most faithful subjects.

Of this and the aforesaid articles we accuse Sir William Berkeley as guilty of each and every one of the same, and as one who has traitorously attempted, violated, and injured his Majesty's interest here by a loss of a great part of this his colony and many of his faithful loyal subjects by him betrayed and in a barbarous and shameful manner exposed to the incursions and murder of the heathen. And we do further declare these the ensuing persons in this list to have been his wicked and pernicious councilors, confederates, aiders, and assisters against the commonalty in these our civil commotions.

Sir Henry Chichley   William Claiburne, Jr.
Lt. Col. Christopher Wormeley   Thomas Hawkins
Phillip Ludwell   William Sherwood
Robt. Beverley   John Page Clerke
Ri. Lee   John Clauffe Clerke
Thomas Ballard   John West
William Cole   Hubert Farrell
Richard Whitacre   Thomas Reade
Nicholas Spencer   Math. Kempe
Joseph Bridger

And we do further demand that the said Sir William Berkeley with all the persons in this list be forthwith delivered up or surrender themselves within four days after the notice hereof, or otherwise we declare as follows.

That in whatsoever place, house, or ship, any of the said persons shall reside, be hid, or protected, we declare the owners, masters, or inhabitants of the said places to be confederates and traitors to the people and the estates of them is also of all the aforesaid persons to be confiscated. And this we, the commons of Virginia, do declare, desiring a firm union amongst ourselves that we may jointly and with one accord defend ourselves against the common enemy. And let not the faults of the guilty be the reproach of the innocent, or the faults or crimes of the oppressors divide and separate us who have suffered by their oppressions.

These are, therefore, in his Majesty's name, to command you forthwith to seize the persons abovementioned as traitors to the King and country and them to bring to Middle Plantation and there to secure them until further order, and, in case of opposition, if you want any further assistance you are forthwith to demand it in the name of the people in all the counties of Virginia.

Source: *Collections of the Massachusetts Historical Society,* 4th Ser., Vol. 9 (Boston: Massachusetts Historical Society, 1871), 184–187.

27. Antonio de Otermin, Report on the Pueblo Uprising in New Mexico, 1680 [Excerpts]

Introduction

Don Juan de Oñate led the Spanish expedition to colonize New Mexico, a land of scarce resources populated by pueblo-dwelling natives. In 1598 he entered the territory with several hundred colonists. His soldiers rampaged through the country plundering the natives. In January 1599 Oñate brutally suppressed a revolt by Acoma Pueblo, killing 800 men, women, and children and enslaving hundreds of captives. Oñate then led several futile expeditions in search of fabled riches. Oñate's colonists gave up and returned to old Mexico, complaining of Oñate's conduct, so the governor recalled and prosecuted him. Not until 1610 did the Spanish establish a permanent settlement in New Mexico, at Santa Fe. As the colony expanded, the Spanish tried to convert the Indians to Christianity and suppress native religious practices. Although not as brutal as Oñate and his men, they earned the natives' resentment. The Spaniards were shocked in 1680 when even their converts rose up against them in a surprise attack on multiple settlements. The Pueblos killed some 400 Spaniards, burning their towns and churches. The attack drove the Spanish from New Mexico, and they did not return until 1692.

Primary Source

The time has come when, with tears in my eyes and deep sorrow in my heart, I commence to give an account of the lamentable tragedy, such as has never before happened in the world, which has occurred in this miserable kingdom and holy custodia. His divine Majesty having thus permitted it because of my grievous sins. . . .

. . . I received information that a plot for a general uprising of the Christian Indians was being formed and was spreading rapidly. This was wholly contrary to the existing peace and tranquility in this miserable kingdom, not only among the Spaniards and natives, but even on the part of the heathen enemy, for it had been a long time since they had done us any considerable damage. It was my misfortune that I learned of it on the eve of the day set for the beginning of the said uprising, and though I immediately, at that instant, notified the lieutenant-general on the lower river and all the other *alcaldes mayores*—so that they could take every care and precaution against whatever might occur, and so that they could make every effort to guard and protect the religious ministers and the temples—the cunning and cleverness of the rebels was such, and so great, that my efforts were of little avail. . . .

On Tuesday, the thirteenth of the said month [August 13, 1680] at about nine o'clock in the morning, there came in sight of us in the suburb of Analco, in the cultivated field of the hermitage of

San Miguel, and on the other side of the river from the villa, all the Indians of the Tanos and Pecos nations and the Queres of San Marcos, armed and giving war whoops. . . .

With this, seeing after a short time that they not only did not cease the pillage but were advancing toward the villa with shamelessness and mockery, I ordered all the soldiers to go out and attack them until they succeeded in dislodging them from the place. Advancing for this purpose, they joined battle, killing some at the first encounter. Finding themselves repulsed, they took shelter and fortified themselves in the said hermitage and the houses of the Mexicans, from which they defended themselves a part of the day with the firearms they had and with arrows. . . . Many of the rebels remained dead and wounded, and our men retired to the *casas reales* with one soldier killed and the *maese de campo,* Francisco Gómez, and some fourteen or fifteen soldiers wounded, to attend them and entrench and fortify ourselves as best we could.

[. . .]

On the next Friday, the nations of the Taos, Pecuríes, Jemez, and Queres having assembled during the past night, when dawn came more than 2,500 Indians fell upon us in the villa, fortifying and intrenching themselves in all its houses and at the entrances of all the streets, and cutting off our water, which comes through the *arroyo* and the irrigation canal in front of the *casas reales.* They burned the holy temple and many houses in the villa. . . .

On the next day, Saturday, they began at dawn to press us harder and more closely with gunshots, arrows, and stones, saying to us that now we should not escape them, and that, besides their own numbers, they were expecting help from the Apaches whom they had already summoned. They fatigued us greatly on this day, because all was fighting, and above all we suffered from thirst, as we were already oppressed by it. At nightfall, because of the evident peril in which we found ourselves by their gaining the two stations where the cannon were mounted, which we had at the doors of the *casas reales,* aimed at the entrances of the streets, in order to bring them inside it was necessary to assemble all the forces that I had with me, because we realized that this was their [the Indians'] intention. Instantly all the said Indian rebels began a chant of victory and raised war whoops, burning all the houses of the villa, and they kept us in this position the entire night, which I assure your reverence was the most horrible that could be thought of or imagined, because the whole villa was a torch and everywhere were war chants and shouts. What grieved us most were the dreadful flames from the church and the scoffing and ridicule which the wretched and miserable Indian rebels made of the sacred things, intoning the *alabado* and the other prayers of the church with jeers.

Finding myself in this state, with the church and the villa burned, and with the few horses, sheep, goats, and cattle which we had

without feed or water for so long that many had already died, and the rest were about to do so, and with such a multitude of people, most of them children and women, so that our numbers in all came to about a thousand persons, perishing with thirst—for we had nothing to drink during these two days except what had been kept in some jars and pitchers that were in the *casas reales*—surrounded by such a wailing of women and children, with confusion everywhere, I determined to take the resolution of going out in the morning to fight with the enemy until dying or conquering. Considering that the best strength and armor were prayers to appease the Divine wrath, though on the preceding days the poor women had made them with such fervor, that night I charged them to do so increasingly, and told the father guardian and the other two religious to say mass for us at dawn, and exhort all alike to repentance for their sins and to conformance with the Divine will, and to absolve us from guilt and punishment. These things being done, all of us who could mounted our horses, and the rest on foot with their arquebuses, and some Indians who were in our service with their bows and arrows, and in the best order possible we directed our course toward the house of the *maese de campo,* Francisco Xavier, which was the place where there were the most people and where they had been most active and boldest. On coming out of the entrance to the street it was seen that there was a great number of Indians. They were attacked in force, and though they resisted the first charge bravely, finally they were put to flight, many of them being overtaken and killed. Then turning at once upon those who were in the streets leading to the convent, they also were put to flight with little resistance. . . . The deaths of both parties in this and the other encounters exceeded three hundred Indians.

Finding myself a little relieved by this miraculous event, though I had lost much blood from two arrow wounds which I had received in the face and from a remarkable gunshot wound in the chest on the day before, I immediately had water given to the cattle, the horses, and the people. . . .

Source: Charles Wilson Hackett, *Historical Documents Relating to New Mexico, Nueva Vizcaya, and the Approaches Thereto, to 1773,* Vol. 3 (Washington, DC: Carnegie Institution, 1937).

28. Count Frontenac, Report on War with the Iroquois, November 2, 1681 [Excerpts]

Introduction

The French and the Iroquois had a long history of hostility dating back to the 1530s, when Jacques Cartier abducted several Iroquois chiefs. During the late 1500s, the five Iroquois nations formed a confederation that featured the most sophisticated native government in North America. The existence of New France began with Samuel de Champlain's founding of a settlement at Quebec in 1608. In 1609 Champlain perpetuated French-Iroquois enmity when he attacked the Iroquois on the shore of present-day Lake Champlain. Over the ensuing decades, the Iroquois acquired firearms from Dutch traders and grew more powerful and numerous, extending their influence far beyond their home territory. Iroquois country lay between English New York and New France, and the Iroquois allied themselves with the English. New France and the Iroquois fought a brutal war during the 1650s and 1660s. The Comte de Frontenac served as governor of New France from 1672 to 1682 and again from 1689 to 1698. In this letter he asks the king for a greater military presence to deter the Iroquois from renewing hostilities against New France. However, war resumed in 1683 and continued until 1698. During this period England and France also went to war against one another.

Primary Source

Frontenac to the King
November 2, 1681

. . . I have resolved to invite them (the Iroquois) to come next summer to Fort Frontenac to explain their conduct to me.

They have, Sire, become so insolent since this expedition against the Illinois, although they are of no consideration, and they are being so much strengthened in these sentiments in order to induce them to carry on the war, in the belief it will embarrass the explorations of Sieur de la Salle, that it is to be feared that they will push their boldness still further and that, after having seen that we give no support to our allies, will attribute it to a weakness which will give birth to the desire to come to attack us.

[. . .]

I pray you very humbly, to consider that for ten years I alone have kept these Indians in a spirit of obedience, of quiet, and of peace, by a little skill and tact—it is difficult, when one is deprived of everything, to do more, or to anticipate things which could easily be prevented if one had a little help; to consider that the Indians are becoming inured to all I can say to them to hold them in allegiance; and that all these journeys which they see me make almost every year to Fort Frontenac, no longer give them the same cause of amazement as they did at the beginning.

[. . .]

Five or six hundred regular soldiers would soon dispel all these various ideas and it would be necessary only to show them and to march them through their lakes, without any other hostile act, to ensure peace for ten years.

Source: Richard A. Preston, *Royal Fort Frontenac* (Toronto: Champlain Society for the Government of Ontario, University of Toronto Press, 1958). Used with permission.

29. Diego de Vargas, Accounts of the Spanish Reconquest of New Mexico, October 12, 1692

Introduction

Spanish ventures in the New World, though licensed by the king, were privately financed and expected to make a profit. Don Juan de Oñate led the first but failed Spanish expedition to colonize New Mexico, a land of scarce resources populated by pueblo-dwelling natives. In 1598 he entered the territory with several hundred colonists. After plundering the natives and brutally suppressing a revolt by Acoma Pueblo, he led several futile expeditions in search of fabled riches. The colonists gave up and returned to old Mexico. Not until 1610 did the Spanish establish a permanent settlement in New Mexico, at Santa Fe. As the colony expanded, the Spanish tried to convert the Indians to Christianity and suppress native religious practices. Although not as brutal as Oñate and his men, they earned the natives' resentment. The Spaniards were shocked in 1680 when even their converts rose up against them in a surprise attack on multiple settlements. The attack drove the Spanish from New Mexico, and they did not return until 1692, under the leadership of Diego de Vargas. In his letter of October 12, 1692, de Vargas reports his success and emphasizes that he undertook the expedition at his own expense. In his journal, he describes the military details of the successful raid to recapture Santa Fe.

Primary Source

Letter from Diego de Vargas to Ignacio López de Zárate
October 12, 1692

Son and dear sir,

I have written to Your Lordship on every occasion offered by the mail dispatched to Mexico City. I have apprised you of my progress in this government and of the fortunate results, which are to the satisfaction of the most excellent lord viceroy, the Conde de Galve, and the ministers of the Junta of the Royal Treasury.

I have no doubt that they will inform his majesty of these results in his Royal and Supreme Council of the Indies and of the present success, because it is such a triumph and glory to God and king. I decided to conquer and restore at my own expense this villa of Santa Fe, capital of the kingdom of New Mexico. It seemed appropriate to me to write, though briefly, to the king our lord. Because

I was appointed by his majesty, it would not be good to neglect to inform his Royal and Supreme Council of the Indies of this victory. I therefore give him the news of this conquest, of the pueblos and districts I have restored to his royal crown, and the number of people baptized. During the twelve years since the Indians of this kingdom rose up and separated themselves from Our Holy Faith, they have been living as apostates in their idolatry.

Finally, I want Your Lordship to be aware of how important this news will be to his majesty. In 1681, the Rev. Father fray Francisco de Ayeta (who resides at the Convento Grande in Mexico City), procurator general of the Holy Gospel Province of Our Father St. Francis for the entire kingdom of New Spain, left for Santa Fe in the governor's company. At that time, the most excellent lord Conde de Paredes, Marques de la Laguna, was governing the kingdom of New Spain. He gave Father Ayeta 95,000 pesos for this conquest. I could wish for no better chronicler of this important undertaking than this father, who came in that capacity. As I have said, he came with the then governor, but they did not succeed. They returned in despair after having restored to the faith only 385 people from the pueblo of Isleta, at such a high cost.

Though it was considered a desperate situation, with divine favor and at my own expense, I have now achieved the unexpected. As I write, I am dispatching a courier to the most excellent lord viceroy, the Conde de Galve, from this villa. I have just arrived from the pueblos and nations of the interior as far as the Taos, the most distant.

I am writing this father, although briefly, so that he will be informed of everything and because he will rejoice. I shall send the copy of the military proceedings of the conquest by the flota so that his majesty will be informed in the royal council. Now, don Toribio de la Huerta need not weary himself in this conquest. His majesty can only reward him for his wish, favoring him with the title of marques of this kingdom and the many other grants he was seeking. He even received on account an ayuda de costa. This is not meant to reproach his majesty for anything, but only to advise Your Lordship on this point. By the flota (if God Our Lord gives me life), I shall send the copy of the proceeding to date and whatever else I do here in the service of God and king.

Please do me the favor of inquiring whether by this packet boat the most excellent lord viceroy and the lords of the royal junta report to his majesty about what I am relating in this letter. It will be easy for Your Lordship to find out in the office of the Secretary of the Indies. Please advise me with all care of the particulars they may tell you and of the report on my services. Once I know with certainty what they tell Your Lordship, I can consider my possibilities for advancement. I long to see letters from Your Lordship and my beloved children. I have remitted to my son, Juan Manuel, two

drafts, each in the amount of 400 pesos of 8 reales, free of conveyance charge and placed on deposit in Madrid. I trust that my correspondent, Capt. don Luis Saenz de Tagle, knight of the Order of Alcantara and silver merchant in Mexico City, will have issued these drafts on don Enrique de la Rosa, with whom he has business dealings in Cadiz.

I shall redouble my effort (Our Lord giving me life), undertaking to remit part of the dowry to Your Lordship by the flota. No reason or cause other than paying what is due you could keep me exiled here. Be assured, therefore, that I shall not fail you, but serve you with the earnestness of a friend and father-in-law who esteems you. I have no doubt that you will be very considerate in your duties to my beloved daughter, Isabel, and my grandchildren. I imagine that by now you will have had more children. To everyone, I give my blessing and ask Your Lordship to embrace them in my name as I would like to personally. I hope that His Divine Majesty will grant me this wish. May He keep Your Lordship many happy years.

Will Your Lordship please hand deliver my letters to the lord Marques de Villanueva, your brother and my friend, and to my children. Please send to Torrelaguna the packet from this villa of Santa Fe, capital of the kingdom of New Mexico, newly restored to and conquered for the royal crown. 12 October 1692.

He who esteems and loves you as father and friend kisses Your Lordship's hand,

Don Diego de Vargas Zapata Lujan Ponce de Leon [rubrica]

To lord don Ignacio López de Zárate, my son-in-law

After having written this, it occurred to me that to save time, it would be good to ask his majesty for the favor when the report comes from the lord viceroy and the royal junta. Your Lordship will please have this letter presented and advise me, taking it upon yourself to reply. The letter is unsealed so that Your Lordship can read it and understand my just petition.

Journal of Diego de Vargas

I left there, arrived at, and surrounded the next pueblo. Entering its plaza, I examined the pueblo and found it very strong with high walls and abandoned dwellings and cuarteles. It is about 3 leagues away, rather more than less. So that the entrada and discovery of the abandoned pueblo may be of record, I signed it with the captain of the presidio, the alferez, and my secretary of government and war.

Don Diego de Vargas Zapata Luján Ponce de León
   Roque Madrid

Juan de Dios Lucero de Godoy

Before me, Alfonso Rael de Aguilar, secretary of government and war

Arrival of the sargento mayor and artillery captain with the provisions and horses

Immediately after, on the same day, month, and year, at about ten in the morning, the sargento mayor and artillery captain arrived at this pueblo of Santo Domingo. I had sent two soldiers to him to give him the information that I was at this pueblo, so that he might not go on to Cochiti. In compliance, they arrived with the provisions, horses, and men under his command.

Information they give about the Indians of San Felipe

He gave me the information that, as they were going along the road, they found the Indians from the pueblo of San Felipe who formerly lived down by the riverbank living on the mesas. As soon as they descried the Spaniards from the mesas, they all left their houses.

Information about having seen Indians of the pueblo of San Felipe, who fled as soon as they saw our men

Sgto. mayor don Fernando de Chaves and Capt. Antonio Jorge were in the escort and had advanced ahead of it on point. They stated that they saw an Indian in the distance and called him, signaling him to come to them. They stated that the Indian came on horseback. They told him that he and all the people of his pueblo should come down, that we were coming neither to make war on them nor to harm them. The Indian answered them in Castilian that they did not want war but peace with the Spaniards. Because the Tewas and Tanos, who all speak the same language, were making war against them and causing much damage, they celebrated the coming of the Spaniards and would help them and go kill the Tewas. The Indians told them they should wait in the pueblo and they would go call the people who were fleeing. The Spaniards replied that he had come down at just the right moment. In fulfillment of my order, these declarants carried out the one I had given the sargento mayor, and under it followed the march. They do not know if he returned or not. They saw that the Indians were taking their sheep, goats, and other animals that were in the cañada when they left, fleeing their pueblo. When they spoke with the Indian, they also saw a little corral with sheep and goats. The escort neither harmed the Indians nor entered the pueblo to sack it, which might frighten them. Instead, they did not follow them, though they could have easily run roughshod over them, plundering, and taking the livestock. They harmed neither their persons, property, nor milpas. So that it may be of record that they persevered and persisted in their flight and that their proposition about peace between us is fraudulent, I signed it with the sargento mayor and Capt. Antonio Jorge, with

the witnesses of these proceedings, the captain of the presidio, the alferez, and my secretary of government and war.

Don Diego de Vargas Zapata Luján Ponce de León

Roque Madrid

Cristobal de Tapia

Don Fernando de Chaves

Antonio Jorge

Juan de Dios Lucero de Godoy

Before me, Alfonso Rael de Aguilar, secretary of government and war

Departure from the pueblo of Santo Domingo for the dawn raid at the villa of Sante Fe

On that day, 11 September, the Indian Esteban came. In accord with the information above, I had sent him to the lomas and mesas of the pueblo of San Felipe. The Indian saw that there was no one in either place. So as not to delay myself with a matter that can be attended to on the return trip, if God Our Lord sees fit, I, the governor and captain general, ordered all the men to prepare to leave to march to the villa of Sante Fe. When we were all together at about five o'clock in the afternoon, I left the pueblo with the camp.

To the villa of Sante Fe

Less than a league away, we found the road and a cuesta composed of malpais, so eroded by continuous rain and the passage of time that it could not be crossed. It was necessary to clear the way by hand and move the two small wagons, gun carriages with the bronze cannon, and large stone mortar by brute strength. This forced a halt at a place called Las Bocas, with the camp arriving after vespers. Because the road was so difficult and filled with gullies, we had to spend the night at a campsite on the plain surrounded by mountains. The distance of that march was 3 leagues. So that it may be of record, I signed it with the captain of the presidio, the alferez, and my secretary of government and war.

Don Diego de Vargas Zapata Luján Ponce de León

Roque Madrid

Juan de Dios Lucero de Godoy

Before me, Alfonso Rael de Aguilar, secretary of government and war

The march continues to the pueblo of Cieneguilla

Today, Friday, 12 September of the current year, I, the governor and captain general, arrived at this pueblo called Cieneguilla, which I reconnoitered and found abandoned. Since the road seemed to have moved, because it was bad for 3 leagues, eroded and filled with gullies by the continuous rains, I halted with the camp, waiting for sunset. At that time, I advised and ordered the men-at-arms to be prepared for the entrada. Once they were ready, I left with the camp.

Words the governor and captain general speaks to the men-at-arms of the camp

On a plain, before vespers, I told them all that, as loyal vassals of his majesty, they should carry out their duties and attend to the fast approaching enterprise and battle at hand, which were such important obligations. As Catholics, it was our responsibility to defend our holy faith and, as vassals of his majesty, the reputation of his arms. Among other things, I told them that although we had so few men for the enterprise, I was confident of their sense of duty. Because of the respect they owed me, I trusted they would carry it out for me and I would achieve the triumph I wished for the honor and service of both majesties.

Traveling until about eleven o'clock at night, I called a halt at the end of the treeless plain on the bank of an arroyo called Arroyo Seco, although at the time there was water in it. I stopped with the camp to await the appropriate hour, which I told the captain of the presidio, other leaders, and war officials, would be three o'clock in the morning, based on their knowledge of the position of the stars. So that it may be of record, I signed it with the captain of the presidio, the alferez, and my secretary of government and war.

Don Diego de Vargas Zapata Luján Ponce de León
    Roque Madrid
    Juan de Dios Lucero de Godoy
    Before me, Alfonso Rael de Aguilar, secretary of government and war

Entrada to the villa of Sante Fe

Today, Saturday, 13 September of the current year, 1692, at about two in the morning, the captain of the presidio, in compliance with my order, ordered the men-at-arms to mount up with their weapons. He reported to me, the governor and captain general, that they had mounted their horses a little after three when the whole camp was ready to follow me. As a result, I mounted up, and having gone along the camino real, came upon a tumbledown hacienda, which the captain of the presidio said was his. I halted there to pass the time while the camp gathered, since it was spread out and the bosque thick.

Once we were all together, I continued the march. On a llano, I stopped again so that the men might gather, because it was a dark night. While there, I asked one of the reverend apostolic missionary fathers to grant absolution to me, as well as the men of the camp who requested it. Once it was given and received, we again

marched toward the bajada from the vega and open country where they said the villa would be, a quarter-league away. At that place, I again halted to collect the men-at-arms.

Order the governor and captain general gives his camp within sight of the villa of Sante Fe

Once they were all together, I told them that my order was that, after entering the plaza of the villa in sight of and near the fortress of the apostate, rebel, treacherous traitors, and their pueblo, the whole camp was to say five times, "Praise be the blessed sacrament of the altar." No one was to begin the battle, neither the men-at-arms nor the Indian allies, who are to be told this by the interpreters, although most of them and their captains speak and understand our language. The signal I would give to all to begin the battle and start the war with all force and courage was for me to unsheathe the sword I carried.

Having given the order, I continued the march, going in close formation. After a short distance, I found myself in the villa's milpas, which surround its plaza, and we gave praise to the Lord. Having done so, the people of the villa immediately came out onto the ramparts of the fortress, occupying them from end to end with all sorts of people, men, women, boys and girls, and children. As dawn was breaking, their forms could be distinguished, and "Praise be the holy sacrament" was repeated to them. The interpreters, Sgt. Juan Ruiz de Cáceres, Pedro Hidalgo, Sebastián de Monroy Mondragán, and Pedro de Tapia, spoke to them in their languages, Tewa and Tano, which are one and the same.

They replied that they believed we were not Spaniards, but Pecos and Apache liars. I, the governor and captain general, repeated the alabado to them, ordering the interpreters to say it. Having said it to them, they replied that if we were Spaniards, why were we not shooting? and that I should shoot an harquebus into the air. I replied to this that I was a Catholic and they should calm themselves. As the sun came up, it would grow lighter, and they would see the image of the Blessed Virgin carried on the standard.

To the Blessed Virgin

They replied, doubting this, saying that the bugle should be sounded to see with certainty that we were Spaniards. At this, I then ordered not only that the bugle be sounded, but also the war drum, ordering the squadron to pass the word that no one should get excited or begin the war. I also ordered each squad and the captain of the presidio to take the comers and positions of the fortress, seeing whether there were more gates than the one I, the governor and captain general, was laying siege to. They did so, and I remained with a squad made up of the leaders, the six citizens who had followed me, and the interpreters.

They are in a fighting mood and reply that they have to kill all the Spaniards

Having sounded the instruments of war, they replied that they were ready to fight for five days, they had to kill us all, we must not flee as we had the first time, and they had to take everyone's life. At the same time, they began a furious shouting that must have lasted more than an hour.

Shouting for one hour

With the interpreters and the men-at-arms, I saw at the same time the growing number of people hurriedly going about filling in the gaps in the ramparts, newly fortifying them with many round stones, large stones from the metates, and objects to take the offensive against our men and kill them as they advanced, if they could not breach the walls because of their height. This was done with considerable risk and danger to our lives, because of the massive, connected nature of the walls. The Indians were safe from anyone killing them. In the interim, while they were shouting and screaming, some of their leaders stood up, shouting many shameful things in their language, which the interpreters, including the sergeant of the company and the others, told me. I ordered him to tell them to calm themselves and be assured that I was not coming to do them any harm whatsoever. To this, they replied that we should not let the horses eat from the milpas. I said to them that the milpas were safe and would not be damaged. I had so ordered and had men and soldiers guarding them.

After sunrise, I approached about twenty paces closer with the interpreter, my secretary of government and war, and the captain of the presidio, telling them that I had come, sent from Spain by his majesty, the king, our lord, to pardon them and so that they might again be Christians, as they had been, and the devil would not lead them astray. This was so they might be assured of my truthfulness, given that they knew the Virgin, our Lady, whose image was on the standard, as witness to the truth I was telling them so that they might believe and be assured of my good intentions. I ordered the royal alferez to show them the image of the Virgin, as I myself took it in my hand, showing it and saying to them that they had but to look at her and recognize her to be our Lady the Queen and the Blessed Virgin and that on the other side of the royal standard were the arms of the king, our lord, so that they might know he sent me. The soldiers had come under my command by his order, and I was his governor and captain general, as I was theirs. They should not doubt what I was telling them, but see I was telling them the truth. I pitied them because they believed in the devil, who deceived them, and not in God Our Lord, and they should see that they were Christians like us.

They replied to this that if it was true I was the new governor, I should take off my morion so they could see my face clearly. At that, I asked my arms bearer for my hat, and, with it, I took off my morion. I went closer so that they might see and clearly recognize me, even taking the kerchief from my head. They said that when the Spaniards were in the kingdom, they had made peace with the Apaches and later gone out and killed them. They said I would do the same with them, to which I replied that the Apaches were not Christians but traitors who, while at peace, came in to better assure their thefts and killings, as they had done when the Spaniards lived in the land. They themselves came out of their homes to defend and guard their lives and those of their wives and children in them. What they had of clothing and horses, the Apaches took away with them. Even with the care the Spaniards had taken, in the pueblos where no soldiers lived or served, the Apaches succeeded in killing and robbing them, carrying off their property and their wives and children for slaves.

So that they might believe that peace was sure and I would pardon them in the name of his majesty, the king, our lord, I would offer as a witness the image of the Blessed Virgin on the royal standard, which I again showed them, taking it anew in my hand. Bracing myself in the stirrups, I effectively made the gestures necessary because of their disbelief. Taking the rosary from my pocket, I showed them a holy cross of Jerusalem I had placed on it, telling them that I took as my witnesses the holy cross and the Virgin, our most holy Lady, whose image I carried on the royal standard they were looking at. I would pardon them in his majesty's name, and they should believe me and come down and shake hands with me. I also brought the three fathers so that they might absolve them of the great sin they had committed of having left our holy faith.

They replied to this that although they believed what the governor and the fathers told them was true, they had had to work very hard, having been ordered to build the churches and homes of the Spaniards, and they were whipped if they did not do what they were told. The Spaniards and citizens had done this, and they indicated and named Javier, Quintana, and Diego López, asking whether they had come with us. I said they had not, and I did not know whether they were already dead. They could be assured that they would no longer come here.

One of the Indians, who I later found out was named Antonio and had been given the surname Balsas, was very fluent in Spanish and was on top of the big rampart above the gate. He spoke for everyone, who, with their lances, heavy spears, bows, arrows, and large lances, also occupied some other ramparts. Whenever the men-at-arms made any movement, the Indians quickly became excited, thinking war was about to break out.

The rest of the camp and provisions arrive
   Nota bene

At this time, the rest of the men of the camp and the provisions arrived. I ordered them to halt on the llano beyond the milpas and within sight of the fortress, about a musket shot away, and that the bronze stone mortar and the cannon should also be placed with the camp. It should be garrisoned with the squad of cavalry, muleteers, and some allies, all together, and no one was to move without my order.

The governor orders his camp quartered away from the milpas

Antonio Balsas spoke for the traitorous, rebel Indians, using as an excuse for their uprising that the devil was at work in their thoughts. Finally, he stated that the guilty had already died and the living were not at all guilty and most of them had been young men then. I replied that they could all be assured that I had already told them I was pardoning them in his majesty's name. I repeated this, with the Blessed Virgin and the holy cross I was showing them as my witnesses, and that I was telling them the truth.

At this, one of the Indians came out through the gate with his lance, leather shield, bow, and arrows, as if to say they were unafraid and were there. I replied to him that he should calm himself, approach me, and shake my hand. He responded in a different way, until as a result of what those above said to him in his language, he went back in, having first said that two of the three fathers who came should follow. Father fray Cristóbal Barroso and Father fray Francisco Corvera dismounted and wanted to enter, at which I, the governor and captain general, seeing that they were already below the rampart and Father fray Cristóbal was hurrying to enter, said to them, "Your reverences, stop!" shouting and calling them to return. I so ordered and requested, and the fathers, with much courtesy and care, obeyed me. I told them it was not the time for them to do such a thing, since the Indians were seen to be so rebellious and possessed by the devil. Once inside, they could kill them, and there would be no way to save their lives, with which we would all risk losing ours.

Warriors from neighboring pueblos came toward the flanks and corners

At that time, the squads on both flanks and corners spotted many men on horses and foot coming from the neighboring pueblos. Without a doubt, they would have rushed us from behind. When I arrived, an Indian, or someone in the milpas or torreones, had gone to warn the pueblos. Their men came, as I say, as fast as possible on foot and horseback with their weapons, most of them with lances on long shafts. According to what I later asked them, they have an Indian blacksmith who makes the lances for them. I ordered the captain of the presidio to leave the siege operations with a squad and, without going far, intercept those men and prevent them from passing. The other squad was to do the same on the other side, while I remained holding the position and siege of the fortress with the men from the third squad and the allies distributed among several positions.

The captain carried out my order, as did the leader of the second squad. The rebels, who were paying close attention to everything going on, sensed that we might keep them from being aided and so raised a great uproar from their ramparts, saying over and over that their men were on the way and that we would see. I replied to them that I did not fear them though they were all together, but pitied them because they did not believe in my good intentions. I had already told them that the devil was deceiving them. If I had wanted to kill them, I would not have said the alabado, but, as soon as I arrived, without making a sound or awakening them with the alabado, I would have made sure they were dead. I would not have allowed time for the men coming to their aid to find them alive. To favor them, as they may judge for themselves, I have not ordered them killed, because I only wish for them to become Christians again. I come to pardon them, as I have told them. They were rebellious and did not heed my kind words, but stubbornly persisted in securing themselves in their fortifications, bringing many round stones, painting themselves red, and making gestures and demonstrations so as to bring on war.

Seeing that they had many small reservoirs in front of the fortress near the gate, but noticing that since they had no water in them they had conduits going inside, I, the governor and captain general, ordered four men from my squad to go immediately to higher ground to divert and cut off the water from the ditch that was used in the fortress.

He cut off their water by diverting it

They did so, taking Indian allies and tools at my order to carry it out, as was done. The besieged rebels were saddened and greatly regretted it, asking why, if we had come in peace and as friends, we were depriving them of water. I answered them that, as far as I was concerned, peace was certain. So that they might see it was so, they should come down from the ramparts and come out to give me the peace. They were defiant and repeated that the fathers should come inside, and that afterward they would begin to come out. The fathers also said they all wanted to go in.

He restrains the fathers, who do not enter because they may be killed

Father fray Miguel Muñiz asked me for permission to do that, but I thanked him and said, "Father, it is not time for your reverence and the other fathers to enter, because the rebels are treacherous and can commit an atrocity against your reverences and even kill you. It is wrong for me to place you at such risk or consent to your going in."

Seeing that it was about eleven o'clock in the morning, and that they were persevering in new demonstrations, some coming out and others entering, I decided neither to risk anything else nor waste time, since I had for my part justly carried out the actions of a loyal Catholic vassal of his majesty by requesting his vassals to render proper obedience and vassalage to him, our holy faith, and Divine Majesty. In addition, I had forty men in the plaza and surrounding positions, with others guarding the entrances. The Indian allies able to take up arms were involved in the siege and numbered some fifty to sixty, since the rest were at the camp guarding the horses and supplies. Thus, I said through the interpreters that I was going to advise them once more of the peace I had required of them in his majesty's name. I was going again to wait for the peace without harming them, pardoning them all. I was reassuring them of it with our Lady, the Blessed Virgin, and the holy cross as my witnesses.

The governor and captain general requires and gives the period of one hour to give the peace and render obedience

I was giving them a period of one hour in which to decide and determine to render their obedience and give the peace. If they did not, I would consume and destroy them by fire and sword, holding nothing back. Thus, I make known, require, and give them the period of one hour, so that afterward they may not complain about their misery.

They replied in the desperate terms that are of record that I should do whatever I wanted. I ordered all the camp and the reverend fathers to come with me to the camp for breakfast and to arrange for the men-at-arms to do so at the same time. I carried that out, sending chocolate and biscuit to everyone. I ordered them to set out and take supplies of bullets and powder and the artillery captain to take the large, bronze stone mortar and the cannon down to the plaza, loaded to my satisfaction.

The governor's preparations for the decision to start fighting, because the period of one hour had passed

When we were about to go to the plaza to begin the war, since about two hours had been spent sending refreshments and breakfast to the squads at their posts, and changing the horses for me and my escort, the sergeant and other soldiers arrived, bringing two Indians on horseback and one on foot, with their weapons, arrows, lances, and leather shields.

Two Indians arrived from the pueblos of Tesuque, Santa Clara, and San Lázaro

I received them with kindness, and they told me they were from the pueblos of Tesuque, Santa Clara, and San Lázaro. Having word of my arrival, they were coming in response to the call from the rebellious, besieged traitors in the villa. They were all coming because they had learned of my arrival. They had been advised about it by some Indians from the villa who had gone to a dance at Santa Clara Pueblo.

I replied to them that I had not come for the reason they thought, to kill them, rob them, and carry off their women and children, but to pardon them so they might again become Christians. That was why the king, our lord, had sent me and why I had brought the fathers along with me. They should tell all the people of their pueblos to be calm and not leave them, because they were safe. So that they might believe me, I showed them the image of our Lady, the Blessed Virgin, which was on the royal standard, using it and the holy cross as witnesses to my truthfulness and good intentions.

The Indian chief Domingo, a Tewa, also arrives

After this, another soldier arrived, accompanied by a prominent Indian, their chief, who said his name was Domingo of the Tewa nation. I treated him with kindness and said the same things to him that I had said to the other three, adding in their presence that I had come to change neither their governors nor their captains, but to keep the ones they had since they were pleased with them. I had to leave them, because I had only come, and the king had only sent me, so that they might render him obedience as his vassals, which they were. I had come to pardon them so they might again be Christians. Thus, I ordered him to tell everyone, assuming that the people of the villa were subject to him and he should enter it to tell and counsel them. I would wait in the plaza for him to come out, since the period of one hour I had given them to come out of the fortress and render their obedience had already passed. If not, I was going to destroy the villa and fortress once and for all. For that reason, I was ordering that the large harquebuses, whose small wagons were being drawn by mules, be brought up, as he could see.

I told him many other things very gently and with all kindness, and the Indian responded warmly. I saw he had a heart that could be reduced. From this, I was certain that I could successfully convey my good intentions to the rebels through him. To better assure them, he was going, having already spoken with me. I had given him the explanation that would at last convince them to believe. It then occurred to me to take him at my side and enter the besieged plaza.

Having arrived there, I told him, with the rebels who remained on their ramparts hearing me, "Tell them, your children, who clearly understand what I have told them and what I have also told and ordered you to tell them. I must carry out my decision, based on their reply, because it is already late. The day will not end before what remains to be done is settled. This is why you have already seen that I have ordered the large harquebuses to be brought up." Then, their captain, Domingo, went in to speak to them.

Nota bene

He found them as rebellious as I had, and they paid little attention to him, remaining on the ramparts, not abandoning them.

They spoke to him from there and defied him, neither accepting nor being assured about my proposal. During this time, the artillery captain entered with the cannon, the large stone mortar, and the wagoners. I ordered the pieces set in position and adjusted so that their operation and charges would be effective. The men aimed at the ramparts, so that at the same time, they could be free to mine the facade of the fort and pack the blastholes with the two small cases of gunpowder I had prepared to blast open breaches. We could then advance from all sides, and the few men who make up my camp could make the assault in greater safety. Their number was insufficient to assault an open pueblo, much less a walled and fortified place like the present one. Nevertheless, bravery and eagerness moved them. I received from each equally the enthusiasm and joy with which they heeded not the risk and danger to their lives, but their love as vassals of his majesty and Catholics. Thus, they made no complaint about the risk resulting from our lack of security because we had already been seen.

The ramparts are abandoned, with only a few rebels remaining

Squads of them continued to come from everywhere on foot and horseback, with weapons at the ready. We had already seen that a large squad of from forty to fifty Indians had taken the mesa at the right-hand corner of the fort. It was necessary to send two squads to stop them. I remained at the siege operations in the plaza with the rest of the men, in order to quell the rebels' pride. As soon as they saw the cannon and stone mortar, they immediately abandoned the ramparts. I saw only a few loopholes occupied by the rebel Indians.

At this time, the Indian Domingo came to me, the governor and captain general. He told me very sadly that he had already told his people how good peace would be for them, reminding them of what had happened at Zia Pueblo. They should not be fools, but believe me. If they did not, he was tired of talking to them and responding to everything. They might want to die, but neither he nor the people of his pueblo did. He saw they were not obeying him, so he came out, taking his leave of them and told me he could not do anything with them. This is what he said to me and for his part, there was nothing more he could do.

They return to the ramparts

The Indians returned to their ramparts, occupying them in safety when they saw me at the siege operations in their plaza, speaking with their captain. I, the governor and captain general, went to the interpreters again, also ordering my royal alferez and secretary of government and war to come. Nearby and in front of the gate of the ramparts, speaking loudly, I again exhorted, persuaded, and warned them, saying it was now necessary for them to reply to me with their decision about whether they wanted to become Christians again, rendering the obedience and submission owed to our holy faith and to the king, our lord. I ordered them to come down and render obedience to the Divine and human majesties, reassuring them of a pardon, with our Lady, the Blessed Virgin, as my witness. I showed them her image on the royal standard, as I had so many times before. I showed it to them again and said they should give me their reply immediately. One person should speak for them all and they should not all speak at once, so that I might decide on peace or war. They replied that they would give me the peace if I returned to my camp with all the men, removed the large harquebuses, and came back with all the men unarmed. In that way, when we returned without our weapons to the plaza, they would come out to give me peace.

I replied that I was neither afraid of them nor humbled as they were, confined, besieged, without water, and subject to my burning them out and killing them all, which I could have done in the time that had passed since I arrived. Domingo repeated what he had said to them, and the fathers spoke to them through interpreters from the plaza below their ramparts.

Nota bene

Two unarmed Indians came out to give me the peace. I received them, shaking their hands, and, dismounting, embraced them. At that time, the reverend father, fray Francisco Corvera, entered the patio of the fortress, followed by the captain of the presidio, and then by the reverend father, Miguel Muñiz, who emerged on the ramparts. The Indians, although frightened, began to come out to give me the peace, which I gave them all, with all my love. I dismounted and embraced them, shook their hands, and spoke words of tenderness and love, so that they might be reassured about my good intentions and greeting. In that way, they might make the others who had not come down understand, although some women, young and old, did come down.

When the plaza was empty, since they had immediately returned to the fortress, the captain of the presidio came to inform me and ask whether the squads should allow the people who had been detained to enter, as well as those who, as is of record, were again seen on the mesa. I replied to the captain that he and the squad that had been with me should come with me. I also ordered my secretary of government and war to accompany me.

When I arrived at the mesa, I found a large squad of Indians from the villa on foot and horseback who had gone to the dance at Santa Clara Pueblo. I also found the captain of that pueblo with most of his people. Drawing near to them, I said, "Praise be the blessed sacrament." Through the interpreters, I welcomed them and gave them the peace in the manner referred to. I embraced them and shook their hands after they had dismounted and laid their weapons aside. I told them to order the people of their pueblo not to leave their houses, because they were safe there, and that they could continue living there as they always had with the same governor and captains, if they were pleased with them. I also told them that the only thing his majesty, the king, our lord, who was their lord and lord of all the land, wanted was for them to be Christians again and not idolaters.

With that they were satisfied, and I took my leave of them. I returned to the plaza, ordering the captain of the fortress and all the rebels to wear crosses around their necks and set up a large cross in the middle of the patio of their house. Since it was after four or five o'clock in the afternoon, I withdrew with the fathers to eat, leaving the men distributed around the plaza and sides of the fortress. I also left the order that, unless they had a new one from me, they should not let any Indians enter the fortress. Re-forming with them, they could strengthen themselves and lay an ambush, which they could secure from outside, and attack the camp or horses. We could fear that some calamity might occur from this. In spite of peace, we should not leave our fear aside, but be diligent and vigilant, by dint of the sense of duty as good soldiers and his majesty's loyal vassals.

At the camp, seeing some Indians coming and going, I thought to put some trust in fortune, because God Our Lord had seen fit to provide a successful beginning. To better assure them that I did not fear them, and of the peace I had given and they had received, and the pardon I had granted them in his majesty's name, I decided to command and order as I did. I ordered the captain of the presidio to go to the plaza and gather the men-at-arms he had left at the siege operations and have them come by virtue of my order. I also ordered the artillery captain to move the cannon and large, bronze stone mortar, taking the mules to transport them. This was all carried out in the manner referred to. So that the entrada and what occurred during it; how the siege that was laid against the fortress in the plaza of the villa was raised; the questions, answers, and reports; and everything that has been referred to may be of record, as it is of record to the letter, so that its truth may be of record for all time, I signed it with the military leaders, war officials, citizens who knew how, and my secretary of government and war, on the said day ut supra.

Don Diego de Vargas Zapata Luján Ponce de León
   Cristóbal de Tapia
   Roque Madrid
   Francisco Lucero de Godoy
   José Gallegos
   Don Fernando de Chaves
   Antonio Jorge
   Alonso García
   Pedro Hidalgo
   Diego Arias de Quirís
   Juan López Holguín
   Diego Zervín

Before me, Alfonso Rael de Aguilar, secretary of government and war

Order the governor and captain general gives to his men-at-arms after having raised the siege laid in the plaza of the villa of Sante Fe against the fortress and walled pueblo

On 13 September 1692, the captain of the presidio, by virtue of my order, gathered the men-at-arms with whom I had laid siege and cordoned off the plaza and in it the fortress of the villa of Sante Fe. The artillery captain brought the bronze cannon and large stone mortar and set them on their carriages at a place that faces the villa about a musket shot away. I, the governor and captain general, designated it as the plaza de armas for as long as I am present in this area, as it is convenient for holding audience to listen to and receive the rebel nations of the surrounding pueblos and provinces of this district and kingdom in peace.

They have heard of my arrival from the Indians gathered today at this outpost, who have spoken to me, and been received in peace. Through these eyewitnesses, I have assured the others that they should come to see me, in safety and without fear. I shall listen to and pardon them in his majesty's name, reassuring them in every way.

Because they are treacherous Indians and so accustomed to their apostasy and freedom, they can join with others, so that, rebel and allied, they may commit some outrage. We are so few, with the sierras so near and the montes surrounding us, that for our defense and safety, I ordered that tonight the horses and mules should have two squads on guard and not be allowed to wander, but be kept together, though there may be little pasture. The other two squads are to change horses immediately, leaving them saddled and bridled, and keep their weapons at the ready, so that if there is a surprise attack, everything will be battle ready to make war on the enemy. All the men of this camp are to keep, fulfill, and carry out this order. So that they may be informed about it, I order the captain and the alferez to notify them. So that it may be of record, they signed it with me, the governor and captain general, and my secretary of government and war.

Don Diego de Vargas Zapata Luján Ponce de León
   Roque Madrid
   Juan de Dios Lucero de Godoy
   Before me, Alfonso Rael de Aguilar, secretary of government and war

The governor and captain general goes to examine the fortress and see whether the holy cross is in place

Today, Sunday, 14 of the present month of the current year, the Day of the Exaltation of the Holy Cross, I, the governor and captain general, spent the night with the vigilance required and the men-at-arms on guard duty. They told me that many people had come and gone from the fortress all night long and it would be risky to enter in my finery, as I had dressed, without weapons. Nevertheless, I told them I was going to be present at the absolution the reverend missionary fathers were going to grant the rebel, apostate Indians and that no one should fire without my order. They should remain on horseback in the plaza of the villa with only the leaders, their captain, and the citizens entering with me and the missionary fathers.

In this manner, I left, marching from the plaza de armas toward the fortress. When the alferez arrived with the royal standard, I ordered him to enter with me, the fathers, and the men-at-arms indicated. Once inside, I found a cross slightly shorter than a man's height set up on the patio. Within view of the Indians, I knelt on one knee and kissed the cross.

There were only eight or ten Indians on the patio because they were so afraid and suspicious. They said the men who had come with me should not come in, because the women were afraid and crying, and the boys and girls were frightened. I did this to please them and so that they might not think I was afraid of them. They were standing on the drawbar they used to close the gate. Once assured in this manner, they began to come down from their houses, which are high and have pole ladders. They put the ladders in place to come down, and when they go up, they raise them and put them in their houses, remaining safe there as though walled in, since no one can come in.

Source: John L. Kessell, ed., *Remote beyond Compare* (Albuquerque: University of New Mexico Press, 1989).

30. Cotton Mather, *Decennium Lutuosum,* 1699 [Excerpt]

Introduction

The leading Puritan minister in colonial New England, Reverend Cotton Mather (1663–1728) distinguished himself as a theologian, a scholar, an author, a public speaker, and a popular leader. Descended from the prominent Puritans John Cotton and Increase Mather, Cotton Mather graduated from Harvard at the age of 15. He wrote more than 400 pamphlets and books. The sheer volume of his work influenced his contemporaries and provides a substantial source for understanding the historical events of his time. His

1699 book *Decennium Luctuosum,* a history of King William's War (1689–1697) in New England, was part of his more general religious history of New England. King William's War, in which England and the Netherlands were allied against France, was called the War of the Grand Alliance or the Nine-Years' War in Europe. During the war, French and Indian fighters from Canada launched devastating attacks against New England frontier towns. In this excerpt, Mather gives vent to his loathing of Quakers and criticizes a Quaker author for blaming the war on the Puritans' unjust dealings with the Indians. Massachusetts had long been an inhospitable place for Quakers, most notably when authorities executed several Quakers in 1660.

Primary Source

[. . .]

Quakers Encountered.

For the present then, we have done with the Indians: But while the Indians have been thus molesting us, we have suffered Molestations of another sort, from another sort of Enemies, which may with very good Reason be cast into the same History with them. If the Indians have chosen to prey upon the Frontiers, and Out-Skirts, of the Province, the Quakers have chosen the very same Frontiers, and Out-Skirts, for their more spiritual Assaults; and finding little Success elsewhere, they have been Labouring incessantly, and sometimes not unsuccessfully, to Enchant and Poison the Souls of poor people, in the very places, where the Bodies and Estates of the people have presently after been devoured by the Salvages. But that which makes it the more agreeable, to allow the Quakers an Article in our History of the Indians, is, That a certain silly Scribbler, the very First-born of Nonsensicality, (and a First-born too, that one might Salute as the Martyr Polycarp once did the wicked Marcion,) One Tom Maule, at this Time living in Salem, hath exposed unto the Publick a Volumn of Nonsensical Blasphemies and Heresies, wherein he sets himself to Defend the Indians in their Bloody villanies, and Revile the Countrey for Defending it self against them. And that the Venom of this Pamphlet might be Improved unto the Height of slanderous Wickedness, there hath been since added unto it, in another Pamphlet, a parcel of Ingredients compounded, for mischief, as if by the Art of Apothecary. None but he whom the Jews in their Talmuds call Ben-tamalion could have inspired such a Slanderer! Have the Quakers ever yet Censured this their Author, for holding-forth in his *Alcoran* That the Devil, Sin, Death, and Hell, are but Nothing, they are but a Non-Entity: And, That all men who have a body of Sin remaining in them are Witches? I have cause to believe, they never did! Nor that they ever advised him to pull in his Horns, from goring the sides of New-England, with such passages as those, in the same horrible Pamphlet: "God hath well Rewarded the Inhabitants of New-England, for their Unrighteous Dealings, towards the Native Indians, whom now the Lord hath suffered to Reward the Inhabitants, with a double measure of Blood, by Fire and Sword, etc." And those Unrighteous Dealings he Explains to be the Killing of the Indians, (or Murdering of them) by the Old Planters of these colonies in their First Settlement. Thus are the Ashes of our Fathers vilely staled upon, by one, who perhaps would not stick at the Villany of doing as much upon their Baptism it self. I must tell you, Friends, that if you don't publickly give forth a Testimony to Defie Tom Maule, and his Works, it will be thought by some, who it may be don't wish you so well as I do, that you own this Bloody Stuff: which, doubtless you'l not be so ill advised as to do. But, certainly, if the good people of New-England now make it not a proverb for a lyar of the first Magnitude, he is as very a liar as Tom Maule, they will deprive their Language of one Significant Expression, which now offers it self unto them.

[…]

Source: Charles H. Lincoln, ed., *Narratives of the Indian Wars, 1675–1699* (New York: Scribner, 1913), 277–279.

31. James Moore, Letters regarding the English Attack on Spanish Florida, 1704

Introduction

From 1701 to 1714, the English and the Dutch fought France and Spain in the War of the Spanish Succession. Known as Queen Anne's War in America, the war gave rise to battles in Canada, New England, South Carolina, and Florida. A series of campaigns involving the Spanish and English and their Indian allies began in 1702. In Charles Town, South Carolina, Governor James Moore advocated a preemptive strike at the Spanish in St. Augustine, some 250 miles distant. In September 1702 Moore led a combined force of more than 1,000 colonial militia and Indians in a failed campaign against St. Augustine. The Spanish in turn attacked Charles Town, but their expedition also failed. In 1704, having stepped down as governor, Moore mounted a second expedition against Spanish Florida at his own expense. His 1,000-man army marched overland through Georgia and into northern Florida, burning Spanish missions and communities of Indians who were loyal to the Spanish, and captured more than 1,000 Indians to be sold into slavery. Moore's campaign ultimately destroyed three-fourths of the Indian population in Spanish territory. In these letters, Moore reports on his success and asserts that his actions have made Carolina secure from Spanish attack.

Primary Source

Colonel Moore's Letter to Sir Nathaniel Johnson, April 16, 1704

May it please Your honour,

To accept of this short Narrative of what I, with the Army under my Command, have been doing since my departure from the Ockmulgee, which was on the 19th of December. On the 14th of January at the sun rising we came to a Town, a strong and almost regular Fort, called Aiavalla [Ayubale]: At our first approach the Indians in it fired, and shot Arrows at us briskly, from which we hid and Sheltered Ourselves under the Side of a great Mud Walled House, til we could take a View of the Fort, and consider of the best way of assaulting it, which we concluded to be by breaking open the Church doors, which were a part of the Fort, with Axes.

I no sooner proposed this, but my Men readily undertook it, run up to it briskly (the Enemy at the same time shooting at them), were beaten off, without effecting it, and 14 white men wounded. Two hours after that we thought fit to attempt burning the church, which we did, three or four Indians assisting us in it we burnt it. The Indians in it obstinately defended themselves and killed us two men, viz., Francis Plowden and Thomas Dale. After we were within their Fort a Fryar, the only [white] within it, came forth and begged mercy: In this we took 26 men alive and 58 women and children, the Indians took about as many more of each sort. The Fryar told us we killed in the two storms 24 men.

The next morning the Captain of St. Lewis's Fort with 23 Whites and 400 Indians came to fight us, which we did, beat him, and took eight of his men prisoners. And as the Indians (which say they did it) tell us, killed 5 or 6 whites. We have a particular account of 168 Indian men killed and taken in this fight and flight. The Apalatchee Indians say the lost 200, which we have reason to believe the least. In this fight Captain John Berringer, fighting bravely in the head of our men, was killed at my foot. Captain Fox died of a wound given him on our first storming of the fort.

Two days after I sent to the King of the Attachookas [Ivitachuco] (who with 130 men was in his strong and well-made Fort) to come to me to make this peace with me, he did it, and compounded for it with his church plate and led horses leaded with provision. After this I marched thro' two towns, which have all strong Forts and defenses against small armies, they all submitted and surrendered their Forts to me without conditions. I have now in my company all the whole people of three towns, and the greatest part of four more; we have totally destroyed all the people of two town[s], so that we have left in Apalatchee but that one town which compounded with me, part of St. Lewis's and the people of one town which run away altogether, their town, church, and fort, we have burnt. The people of St. Lewis's which remain, come unto me every night. I expect, and have advice, that the town which compounded with me, are coming after me. The waiting for these people make any marches slow; for I am willing to bring away free, as many Indians as I can, this being the address of the commons to order it so. This will make my mens part of plunder (which otherwise might have been $100 per man) but small, but I hope with your Honour's assistance, to find a way to gratify them for their bold and stout actions, and their great loss of blood. I never saw, or heard, of a stouter or braver thing done than the storming of the fort; it hath regained the reputation we seemed to have lost under the conduct of Captain Mackie, the Indians having now a mighty value for the whites.

Apalatchee is now reduced to that feeble, and low condition, that it neither can supply St. Augustine with provisions, or disturb, damage or frighten our Indians living between us and Apalatchee, and the French. In short, we have made Carolina as safe as the conquest of Apalatchee can make it.

If I had not had so many men wounded in our first attempt, I had assaulted St. Lewis's fort, in which is now but 28 or 30 men, and 20 of these came thence from Pensacola to buy provisions the first night after I took the first Fort.

On Sunday the 23rd of this month I came out of Apalatchee settlement, and am now about 30 miles in my way home, but do not expect to reach it til about the middle of March, notwithstanding my horses will not be able to carry me [to the] Cherokee nations.

I have had a dirty, tedious and uneasy journey, and tho I have no reason to fear any harm from the enemy, thro the difference between the Whites and the Indians, between Indian and Indian, bad way and false alarms, do still labour under the hourly uneasinesses. The number of free Apalatchee Indians, which are not under my protection, bound with me to Carolina, are 300; the Indians under my command killed and took prisoners in the plantations, whilst we stormed the Fort, as many Indians as we and they took and killed in the Fort.

I am &
    Ja. Moore

Extract of Colonel Moore's Letter to the Lords Proprietors, April 16, 1704

I will not trouble Your Lordships with a relation of the many hazards and difficulties I underwent in my expedition against Apalatchee, but beg leave to let you know what I have done there.

By my own interest and at my own charge I raised 50 whites, all the Government thought fit to spare out of the settlement at that time; with them and 1000 Indians, which by my own interest I raised to follow me, I went to Apalatchee: The first place I came to was the strongest Fort in Apalatchee, which after nine hours I took, and in it 200 persons alive, and killed 20 men in the engagement. I had killed 3 whites and 4 Indians; of the last there were but 15 ever came within shot of the fort. The next morning the Captain of the fort of St. Lewis and Governor of the Province of Apalatchee, with all the force of Whites and Indians he could raise in the province came and gave me battle in the field; after half an hour's fight we routed them and in the fight and flight killed six Spaniards, one of which was a Fryar; took the Captain and Governor and Adjutant General and Seven men Spaniards prisoners, and killed and took 200 Indian men. In this fight my Captain was killed and 11 of my Indians. I lay in the field of battle four days, some of my wounded men not being in a condition to march, or to be carried any way in this time[.] The next strongest Fort was surrendered to me upon conditions. On the 5th day I marched to two more Forts, both which were delivered up to me, without conditions, and the men, women and children of the whole town, which were in it, prisoners at discretion. In one of these Forts I lodged one night; the next day I marched to two more Forts, both [of] which with the people that were in them were delivered to me without conditions, as were the two other Forts. In one of these I lay two nights, here I offered freedom of persons and goods, to as many Kings, as with all the people under their government would go along with me, and live under and subject themselves to our Government. On these terms four Kings and all their people, came away with me, and part of the people of four more Kings; which I have planted among our Indians, and put them out of a capacity of returning back again alone[.] In this expedition I brought away 300 men, and 1000 women and children, have killed, and taken as slaves 325 men, and have taken slaves 4000 women and children; tho I did not make slave, or put to death one man, woman or child but what were taken in the fight, or in the fort I took by storm. All which I have done with the loss of 4 whites and 15 Indians, and without one penny charge to the publick. Before this expedition we were more afraid of the Spaniards of Apalatchee and their Indians in conjunction with the French of Mississippi, and their Indians doing us harm by land, than of any forces of the enemy by sea. This has wholly disabled them from attempting anything against us by land, the whole strength of Apalatchee not exceeding 300 Indians and 24 Whites, who cannot now (as I have seated our Indians) come at me that way, must they March thro 300 Indian men our friends, which were before this conquest of Apalatchee (for fear of the Spaniards and their Indians) every day moving to the Northway of us.

That colony of the French which is situated on the River Mississippi, are not the French we have reason to fear; they have seated another colony on a river call Coosa six days journey nearer us than Mississippi, and not above 50 miles from us than Apalatchee. These French and Their Indians (if suffered to live where they are now) will be no less a dangerous enemy to us in peace than in war, it being much easier for them to cut off our settlements from this place, than it is for the Canada Indians to cut off the inland towns in New England.

Source: Lyman Horace Weeks and Edwin M. Bacon, eds., *An Historical Digest of the Provincial Press,* Vol. 1 (Boston: Society for Americana, 1911), 64–65.

32. Robert Beverley, Report on the Indians of Virginia, 1705

Introduction

When the first English settlers came to Virginia in 1607, its native peoples consisted of the Algonquian inhabitants of some 30 villages who accepted the leadership of the chieftain, Powhatan. The 1614 wedding of Powhatan's daughter Pocahontas to the Englishman John Rolfe brought about a brief period of peace. By 1622, Powhatan's successor and half brother Opechancanough laid plans to drive the English from his land. The resulting massacre of more than a third of Virginia's English population spurred the survivors to launch a brutal reprisal. In 1644 Opechancanough launched another attack on the English. His warriors killed more than 400 frontier settlers. However, the colony had grown to a population of nearly 10,000, while exposure to European diseases and long years of warfare had reduced the Indian population of Virginia to barely half of what it had been when the first Englishmen arrived. In 1646 a treaty with Opechancanough's successor ended the war. The native peoples' territory and freedom of movement were severely restricted. A later frontier war ended in 1677 with a treaty that imposed even greater restrictions. This 1705 history written by a prominent Virginian provides the inevitable end of the story: "The Indians of Virginia are almost wasted."

Primary Source

The *Indians* of *Virginia* are almost wasted, but such Towns, or People as retain their Names, and live in Bodies, are hereunder set down; All which together can't raise five hundred fighting men. They live poorly, and much in fear of the Neighbouring *Indians.* Each Town, by the Articles of Peace in 1677. pays 3 *Indian* Arrows for their Land, and 20 Beaver Skins for protection every year.

In *Accomack* are 8 Towns, *viz.*

Matomkin is much decreased of late by the Small Pox, that was carried thither.

Gingoteque. The few remains of this Town are joyn'd with a Nation of the *Maryland Indians.*

Kiequotank, is reduc'd to very few Men.

Matchopungo, has a small number yet living.

Occahanock, has a small number yet living.

Pungoteque. Govern'd by a Queen, but a small Nation.

Oanancock, has but four or five Families.

Chiconessex, has very few, who just keep the name.

Nanduye. A Seat of the Empress. Not above 20 Families, but she hath all the Nations of this Shore under Tribute.

In *Northampton. Gangascoe,* which is almost as numerous as all the foregoing Nations put together.

In *Prince George. Wyanoke,* is almost wasted, and now gone to live among other *Indians.*

In *Charles City. Appamattox.* These Live in Collonel *Byrd's* Pasture, not being above seven Families.

In *Surry. Nottawayes,* which are about a hundred Bow-men, of late a thriving and increasing People.

By *Nansamond. Menheering,* has about thirty Bow men, who keep at a stand.

Nansamond. About thirty Bow-men: They have increased much of late.

In *King Williams County,* 2. *Pamunkie,* has about forty Bow-men, who decrease.

Chickahomonie, which had about sixteen Bow-men, but lately increas'd.

In *Essex. Rappahannock,* is reduc'd to a few Families, and live scatter'd upon the *English* Seats.

In *Richmond. Port-Tabago,* has [a]bout five Bow-men, but Wasting.

In *Northumberland. Wiccocomoco,* has but three men living, which yet keep up their Kingdom, and retain their Fashion; they live by themselves, separate from all other *Indians,* and from the *English.*

Thus I have given a succinct account of the *Indians;* happy, I think, in their simple State of Nature, and in their enjoyment of Plenty, without the Curse of Labour. They have on several accounts reason to lament the arrival of the *Europeans,* by whose means they seem to have lost their Felicity, as well as their Innocence. The *English* have taken away great part of their Country, and consequently made every thing less plenty amongst them. They have introduc'd Drunkenness and Luxury amongst them, which have multiply'd their Wants, and put them upon desiring a thousand things, they never dreamt of before. I have been the more concise in my account of this harmless people, because I have inserted several Figures, which I hope have both supplied the defect of Words, and render'd the Descriptions more clear. I shall in the next place proceed to treat of *Virginia,* as it is now improv'd, (I should rather say alter'd,) by the *English* and of its present Constitution and Settlement.

The End of the Third Book.

Source: Robert Beverley, *The History and Present State of Virginia,* Pt. 3 (London: Printed for R. Parker, 1705), 62–64.

33. John Williams, *The Redeemed Captive Returning to Zion,* 1707 [Excerpt]

Introduction

From 1701 to 1714, the English and the Dutch fought France and Spain in the War of the Spanish Succession. Known as Queen Anne's War in America, the war gave rise to battles in Canada, New England, South Carolina, and Florida. John Williams, a Harvard-educated Puritan minister in Massachusetts, was among the captives taken in a French and Indian raid on Deerfield in February 1704. The attackers killed Williams's two youngest sons and marched the captives, including his five other children, into Canada. The forced march killed Mrs. Williams. Williams himself gained his freedom late in 1706 after nearly three years of captivity. He participated as a chaplain in a later campaign of the war. Four of the Williams children, who had been scattered among several Indian villages, eventually returned home. One daughter, Eunice, six years old at the time of her capture, spent the remainder of her long life living as an Indian. She became the subject of a 1995 book, *The Unredeemed Captive.* Warfare between the French and the English in North America involved not only a fight for territory but also a fight for souls. This excerpt details the variety of ways in which the French captors tried to force Catholicism on their captives.

Primary Source

[. . .]

After another days travel, we came to a river where the ice was thawed; we made a canoe of elmbark in one day, and arrived on a Saturday near noon, at Chamblee, a small village, where is a garrison and fort of French soldiers.

[At Chamblee]

This village is about fifteen miles from Montreal. The French were very kind to me. A gentleman of the place took me into his house, and to his table; and lodged me at night on a good feather-bed. The inhabitants and officers were very obliging to me, the little time I staid with them, and promised to write a letter to the governor in chief, to inform him of my passing down the river. Here I saw a girl taken from our town, and a young man, who informed me that the greatest part of the captives were come in, and that two of my children were at Montreal; that many of the captives had been in three weeks before my arrival. Mercy in the midst of judgment! As we passed along the river towards Sorel, we went into a house, where was an English woman of our town, who had been left among the French in order to her conveyance to the Indian fort. The French were very kind to her, and to myself, and gave us the best provision they had; and she embarked with us, to go down to St. Francois fort. When we came down to the first inhabited house at Sorel, a French woman came to the river side, and desired us to go into her house; and when we were entered she compassioned our state, and told us, she had in the last war been a captive among the Indians, and therefore was not a little sensible of our difficulties. She gave the Indians something to eat in the chimney corner, and spread a cloth on the table for us with napkins; which gave such offence to the Indians, that they hasted away, and would not call in at the fort. But wherever we entered into houses, the French were very courteous. When we came to St. Francois river, we found some difficulty by reason of the ice; and entering into a Frenchman's house, he gave us a loaf of bread, and some fish to carry away with us; but we passed down the river till night, and there seven of us supped on the fish called bull-head or pout, and did not eat it up, the fish was so very large.

The next morning we met with such a great quantity of ice, that we were forced to leave our canoe, and travel on land. We went to a French officer's house, who took us into a private room, out of the sight of the Indians, and treated us very courteously. That night we arrived at the fort called St. Francois; where we found several poor children, who had been taken from the eastward in the summer before; a sight very affecting, they being in habit very much like Indians, and in manners very much symbolizing with them. At this fort lived two jesuits, one of which was made superior of the jesuits at Quebec. One of the jesuits met me at the fort gate, and asked me to go into the church, and give God thanks for preserving my life. I told him I would do that in some other place. When the bell rang for evening prayers, he that took me, bid me go; but I refused. The jesuit came to our wigwam, and prayed a short prayer, and invited me to sup with them, and justified the Indians in what they did against us; rehearsing some things done by major Walden, above thirty years ago; and how justly God retaliated them in the last war, and inveighed against us for beginning this war with the Indians: And said, we had before the last winter, and in the winter, been very barbarous and cruel, in burning and killing Indians. I told them, that the Indians, in a very perfidious manner, had committed murders on many of our inhabitants, after the signing articles of peace: And as to what they spake of cruelties, they were undoubtedly falsehoods, for I well knew the English were not approvers of any inhumanity or barbarity towards enemies. They said, an Englishman had killed one of St. Casteen's relations, who occasioned this war; for, say they, the nations, in a general counsel, had concluded not to engage in the war, on any side, till they themselves were first molested, and then all of them, as one, would engage against them that began a war with them; and that upon the killing of Casteen's kinsman, a post was dispatched to Canada, to advertise the Macquas, and Indians, that the English had begun a war: On which they gathered up their forces, and that the French joined with them, to come down on the eastern parts; and that when they came near New England, several of the eastern Indians told them of the peace made with the English, and the satisfaction given them from the English for that murder. But the Macquas told them, it was now too late; for they were sent for, and were now come, and would fall on them, if without their consent they made a peace with the English. Said also, that a letter was shown them, sent from the governour of Port-Royal, which, he said, was taken in an English ship, being a letter from the queen of England to our governour, writing how she approved his designs to ensnare and deceitfully to seize on the Indians; so that being enraged from that letter, and being forced, as it were, they began the present war. I told them the letter was a lie, forged by the French.

The next morning the bell rang for mass: My master bid me go to church: I refused: He threatened me, and went away in a rage. At noon, the jesuits sent for me to dine with them; for I eat at their table all the time I was at the fort. And after dinner, they told me, the Indians would not allow of any of their captives staying in their wigwams, whilst they were at church; and were resolved by force and violence to bring us all to church, if we would not go without. I told them it was highly unreasonable so to impose upon those who were of a contrary religion; and to force us to be present at such service, as we abhorred, was nothing becoming christianity. They replied, they were savages, and would not hearken to reason, but would have their wills: Said also, if they were in New-England themselves, they would go into their churches, to see their ways of worship. I answered, the case was far different, for there was nothing (themselves being judges) as to matter or manner of worship, but what was according to the word of God, in our churches; and therefore it could not be an offence to any man's conscience. But among them, there were idolatrous superstitions in worship. To which I answered, That I was not to do evil that good might come on it; and that forcing in matters of religion was hateful. They answered, The Indians were resolved to have it so, and they could not pacify them without my coming; and they would engage they should offer no force or violence to cause any compliance with their ceremonies.

The next mass, my master bid me go to church: I objected; he arose, and forcibly pulled me by the head and shoulders out of the wigwam to the church, which was near the door. So I went in, and sat down behind the door; and there saw a great confusion, instead of any gospel order; for one of the jesuits was at the altar, saying mass in a tongue unknown to the savages; and the other, between the altar and the door, saying and singing prayers among the Indians at the same time; and many others were at the same time saying over their pater nosters, and Ave Mary, by tale from their chapelit, or beads on a string. At our going out, we smiled at their devotion so managed; which was offensive to them; for they said we made a derision of their worship. When I was here, a certain savages died; one of the jesuits told me she was a very holy woman, who had not committed one sin in twelve years. After a day or two, the Jesuits asked me what I thought of their way, now I saw it? I told them, I thought Christ said of it as Mark vii. 7,8,9. *Howbeit, in vain do they worship me, teaching for doctrines the commandments of men. For laying aside the commandment of God, ye hold the tradition of men, as the washing of pots and cups; and many other such like things ye do. And he said unto them, Full well ye reject the commandment of God, that ye may keep your own tradition.* They told me, they were not the commandments of men, but apostolical tradition, of equal authority with the holy scriptures: And that after my death, I should bewail my not praying to the Virgin Mary; and that I should find the want of her intercession for me with her son; judging me to hell for asserting the scriptures to be a perfect rule of faith: And said, I abounded in my own sense, entertaining explications contrary to the sense of the pope, regularly fitting with a general council, explaining scripture, and making articles of faith. I told them, it was my comfort that Christ was to be my judge, and not they, at the great day; and as for their censuring and judging me, I was not moved with it.

One day, a certain savage, taken prisoner in Philip's war, who had lived at Mr. Buckley's at Weathersfield, called Ruth, who could speak English very well, who had been often at my house, but was now proselyted to the Romish faith, came into the wigwam, and with her an English maid, who was taken the last war, who was dressed up in Indian apparel, unable to speak one word of English, who said she could neither tell her own name, or the name of the place from whence she was taken. These two talked in the Indian dialect with my master a long time; after which, my master bade me cross myself; I told him I would not; he commanded me several times, and I as often refused. Ruth said, Mr. Williams, you know the scripture, and therefore act against your own light; for you know the scripture faith, *servants obey your masters;* he is your master, and you his servant. I told her she was ignorant, and knew not the meaning of the scripture, telling her, I was not to disobey the great God to obey any master, and that I was ready to suffer for God, if called thereto: On which she talked to my master; I suppose she interpreted what I said. My master took hold of my hand to force me to cross myself; but I struggled with him, and would not suffer him to guide my hand; upon this, he pulled off a crucifix from his own neck, and bade me kiss it; but I refused once and again; he told me he would dash out my brains with his hatchet if I refused. I told him I should sooner choose death than to sin against God. Then he ran and catched up his hatchet, and acted as though he would have dashed out my brains. Seeing I was not moved, he threw down his hatchet, saying he would first bite off all my nails if I still refused. I gave him my hand, and told him I was ready to suffer; he set his teeth in my thumb nail, and gave a gripe with his teeth, and then said, *no good minister, no love God, as bad as the devil;* and so left off. I have reason to bless God, who strengthened me to withstand. By this he was so discouraged as never more to meddle with me about my religion. I asked leave of the jesuits to pray with those English of our town who were with me; but they absolutely refused to give us any permission to pray one with another, and did what they could to prevent our having any discourse together.

After a few days, the governour de Vaudreuil, governour in chief, sent down two men with letters to the jesuits, desiring them to order my being sent up to him to Montreal; upon which, one of the jesuits went with my two masters, and took me along with them, as also two more of Deerfield, a man, and his daughter about seven years of age. When we came to the lake, the wind was tempestuous, and contray to us, so that they were afraid to go over; they landed and kindled a fire, and said they would wait a while to see whether the wind would fall or change. I went aside from the company, among the trees, and spread our case, with the temptations of it, before God, and pleaded that he would order the season so, that we might not go back again, but be furthered on our voyage, that I might have opportunity to see my children and neighbours, and converse with them, and know their state. When I returned, the wind was more boisterous; and then a second time, and the wind was more fierce. I reflected upon myself for my unquietness, and the want of a resigned will to the will of God. And a third time went and bewailed before God my anxious cares, and the tumultuous working of my own heart, begged a will fully resigned to the will of God, and thought that by the grace of God I was brought

to say *amen* to whatever God should determine. Upon my return to the company, the wind was yet high: The jesuit and my master said, Come, we will go back again to the fort, for there is no likelihood of proceeding in our voyage, for very frequently such a wind continues three days, sometimes six. After it continued so many hours, I said to them, The will of the Lord be done; and the canoe was put again into the river, and we embarked. No sooner had my master put me into the canoe, and put off the shore, but the wind fell; and coming into the middle of the river, they said, We may go over the lake well enough: And so we did. I promised, if God gave me opportunity, I would stir up others to glorify God in a continued persevering, committing their straits of heart to him. He is a prayer-hearing God, and the stormy winds obey him. After we passed over the lake, the French, wherever we came, were very compassionate to us.

[At Montreal]

When I came to Montreal, which was eight weeks after my captivity, the governour de Vaudreuil redeemed me out of the hands of the Indians, gave me good clothing, took me to his table, gave me the use of a very good chamber, and was in all respects, relating to my outward man, courteous and charitable to admiration. At my first entering into his house, he sent for my two children, who were in the city, that I might see them; and promised to do what he could to get all my children and neighbours out of the hands of the savages. My change of diet, after the difficulties of my journeys, caused an alteration in my body: I was physicked, blooded, and very tenderly taken care of in my sickness.

Source: John Williams, *Redeemed Captive Returning to Zion,* 6th ed. (Boston: Printed by Samuel Hall, 1795).

34. Christoph von Graffenried, Account of the Tuscarora Attack in North Carolina, 1711

Introduction

In 1710 the Swiss baron Christoph von Graffenried established the town of New Bern, North Carolina, with some 400 new inhabitants. This proved to be the last straw for the Tuscaroras, who had long resented unfair treatment by white traders. In September 1711 the Tuscaroras captured Graffenried, the English naturalist John Lawson, and two slaves while they were exploring along the Neuse River. The Tuscaroras executed Lawson but spared the other captives out of sympathy with black slaves and possibly in the mistaken belief that Graffenried was the colonial governor.

The Indians revealed to Graffenried their plans to attack the colonists, but Graffenried could not escape to raise the alarm. At dawn on September 22, 1711, the Tuscaroras mounted a surprise attack on the farms around New Bern, killing some 130 colonists. In this excerpt Graffenried describes these events as he observed them during his captivity. With help from South Carolina forces and Yamasee warriors, the colonists inflicted a decisive defeat on the Tuscaroras in 1713. Most of the Tuscaroras then migrated to New York and joined the Iroquois Confederacy. The Yamasees rose against the colonists of South Carolina in 1715 and killed several hundred. An alliance with the Cherokees proved crucial to the colonists' victory.

Primary Source

They let my negro loose also, but I never saw him again. Poor Lawson remaining in the same place could easily guess that it was all over and no mercy for him. He took his leave of me striving to see me in his danger; and I, not daring to speak with him or give him the least consolation, indicated my sympathy by some signs which I gave him.

A little while after this, the man who had spoken for me in the council led me to his hut, where I was to remain quietly until further orders, and in this interval the unfortunate Lawson was executed; with what sort of death I really do not know. To be sure I had heard before from several savages that the threat had been made that he was to have his throat cut with a razor which was found in his sack. The smaller negro, who was left alive, also testified to this; but some say he was hanged; others that he was burned. The savages keep it very secret how he was killed. May God have pity on his soul.

The day after the execution of Surveyor General Lawson the chief men of the village came to me with the report that they had it in mind to make war on North Carolina. Especially did they wish to surprise the people of Pamtego, Neuse, and Trent Rivers, and Core Sound. So that for good reasons they could not let me go until they were through with this expedition. What was I to do? I had to have patience, for none of my reasons helped. A hard thing about it was that I had to hear such sad news and yet could not help nor let these poor people know the least thing of it. It is true, they promised that Caduca, which is the old name of the little city of New Bern, should receive no harm; but the people of the colony should come down into the little city, otherwise they could not promise much for the damage. These were good words, but how was I to let the poor people know? Since no savage would take the warning to them, I had to leave this also to the Most High. There were about five hundred fighting men collected together, partly Tuscaroras, although the principal villages of this nation were not involved with them. The other Indians, the Marmuskits, those of Bay River, Weetock, Pamtego, Neuse, and Core began this massacring and plundering at the same time. Divided into

small platoons these barbarians plundered and massacred the poor people at Pamtego, Neuse, and Trent. A few days after, these murderers came back loaded with their booty. Oh what a sad sight to see this and the poor women and children captives. My heart almost broke. To be sure I could speak with them, but very guardedly. The first came from Pamtego, the others from Neuse and Trent. The very same Indian with whom I lodged brought a young boy with him, one of my tenants, and many garments and house utensils that I recognized. Oh how it went through my heart like a knife thrust, in the fear that my colony was all gone, and especially when I asked the little fellow what had happened and taken place. Weeping bitterly he told me that his father, mother, brother, yes, the whole family had been massacred by the very same Indian above mentioned. With all this I dared not act in any way as though I felt it. For about six weeks I had to remain a prisoner in this disagreeable place, Catechna, before I could go home. In what danger, terror, disgrace, and vexation is easily to be thought.

All sorts of things happened in this time. Once I was in great perplexity. The men folks were all on this massacring expedition, the women all somewhat distant to get cherries, others to dig sweet potatoes, a species of yellow roots, very good and pleasant. And so I found myself entirely alone that same day in the village. A struggle arose in me whether I should get away from there and go home or not. I studied long over it, considered it best to call upon my God for help in this doubt, so that he would put it into my mind what I should do in such critical circumstance. After I had made my prayer, examined and treated the matter pro et contra, I finally considered the better way would be to stay; comforting myself with this that He who had saved me from the first extreme peril would still help me further. Again, if any Indian met or saw me I should be a dead man, for there would be no hope of mercy. In addition they would be so embittered that before I could get home, since I did not know the way, everything would be plundered, burned, and murdered. Experience proved afterwards that I chose the better way.

After these heathens had made their barbarous expedition they came home and rested for a time. Then I watched the opportunity and when I found the chiefs of the village in good humor I asked whether I might not soon go home. To bring them to a favorable disposition I proposed to make a separate peace with them, promised at the same time each chief of the ten villages a cloth coat, something in addition for my ransom; to the king, two flasks of powder, five hundred bullets, two bottles of rum, a brandy made of sugar. But the Indians wanted to have much more, such as guns, more powder, and lead or bullets; but I told them this was contraband, that is, ware which was forbidden to offer for sale under penalty of hanging; that I would, at least, have to be neutral and help neither one side not the other: Otherwise there would nothing come of our peace. They accepted these and other reasons, and so we made an agreement as your Highness will see in the enclosed article of the treaty.

But although we made our treaty, still these suspicious fellows did not want to let me go without more secure and certain guarantee.

Source: Christoph von Graffenried, *Christoph von Graffenried's Account of the Founding of New Bern,* edited by Vincent H. Todd (Raleigh: Edwards & Broughton Printing, State Printers, 1920), 270–271.

35. Antoine le Page du Pratz, Quoting the Reply of the Stung Serpent, 1723

Introduction

The Frenchman René-Robert Cavelier, Sieur de La Salle, explored a vast North American territory encompassing the Mississippi River Valley in 1682. Two wars intervened before King Louis XIV of France could spare the resources to annex and colonize the land, called Louisiana and bounded by Carolina, New Mexico, and the Gulf of Mexico. In 1712 as Queen Anne's War (also called the War of the Spanish Succession) drew to a close, Louis XIV granted a French merchant a patent to establish trade relations and settlements in Louisiana. The first Frenchmen received a warm welcome from the Natchez Indians of southern Mississippi. The French built a fort, but the fort's commandant mistreated the Indians. The Natchezes came to realize that they were materially worse off than they had been before French colonization, and their resentment grew over the course of several years. They planned an attack to eject the French from their country. On November 29, 1729, the Natchezes mounted a coordinated attack and killed at least 200 Frenchmen. When news of the attack reached New Orleans, French vengeance was swift. Within a year they had destroyed the Natchezes as a people. This 1723 account, in which a French settler—the historian and naturalist Antoine le Page du Pratz—quotes a Natchez chief, provides early evidence of the building Natchez resentment of the French presence.

Primary Source

"Why," continued he, with an air of displeasure, "did the French come into our country? We did not go to seek them: they asked for land of us, because their country was too little for all the men that were in it. We told them they might take land where they pleased, there was enough for them and for us; that it was good the same sun should enlighten us both, and that we would walk as friends in the same path; and that we would give them of our provisions, assist them to build, and to labour in their fields. We have done so; is not this true? What occasion then had we for Frenchmen? Before they came, did we not live better than we do, seeing we deprive

ourselves of a part of our corn, our game, and fish, to give a part to them? In what respect, then, had we occasion for them? Was it for their guns? The bows and arrows which we used, were sufficient to make us live well. Was it for their white, blue, and red blankets? We can do well enough with buffalo skins, which are warmer; our women wrought feather-blankets for the winter, and mulberry-mantles for the summer; which indeed were not so beautiful; but our women were more laborious and less vain than they are now. In fine, before the arrival of the French, we lived like men who can be satisfied with what they have; whereas at this day we are like slaves, who are not suffered to do as they please."

Source: Le Page du Pratz, *The History of Louisiana or of the Western Parts of Virginia and Carolina* (London: Printed for T. Becket, 1774).

36. The Walking Purchase, August 25, 1737

Introduction

William Penn's three sons inherited the proprietorship of Pennsylvania. Thomas Penn came to Pennsylvania in 1732 hoping to restore his family's fortunes by selling land to the growing population of new settlers. First he had to purchase land from the Indians, but he did not share his father's sense of fairness toward the native peoples. Helped by James Logan, their late father's secretary, the Penn brothers plotted the infamous Walking Purchase. Having been pushed off their ancestral land in Delaware and New Jersey, the Lenni Lenape (Delaware) Indians lived in the upper Delaware and Lehigh River Valleys of eastern Pennsylvania. On August 25, 1737, the Delawares succumbed to pressure and ratified an alleged 1686 deed—probably fake—that gave the Penns all the land that a man could walk in a day and a half. On September 18, 1737, the Penns' three hired runners traversed paths that had been cleared in advance, and the Delaware witnesses could not keep up. Forced to relinquish a huge tract of land, the Delawares made a formal complaint to colonial officials but to no avail. A future generation of Delawares avenged themselves on frontier settlers during the French and Indian War (1754–1763).

Primary Source

We, Teesshakomen, alias Tisheekunk, and Tootamis alias Nutimus, two of the Sachem's or Chiefs of the Delaware Indians, having, almost three Years ago, at Durham, begun a treaty with our honourable Brethren John and Thomas Penn, and from thence another Meeting was appointed to be at Pensbury, the next Spring Following, to which We repaired with Lappawinzoe and Several others of the Delaware Indians, At which Treaty Several Deeds were produced and Shewed to us by our said Bretheren, concerning

Several Tracts of Land which our Forefathers had, more than fifty Years ago, Bargained and Sold unto our good Friend and Brother William Penn, the Father of the said John and Thomas Penn, and in particular one Deed from Mayhkeerickkishsho, Sayhoppy and Taughhaughsey, the Chiefs or Kings of the Northern Indians on Delaware, who, for large Quantities of Goods delivered by the Agents of William Penn, to those Indian Chiefs, did Bargain and Sell unto the said William Penn, All those Tract or Tracts of Land lying and being in the Province of Pennsylvania, Beginning upon a line formerly laid out from a Corner Spruce Tree by the River Delaware, about Makeerickkitton, and from thence running along the ledge or foot of the Mountains, West North West to a corner white Oak marked with the Letter P, Standing by the Indian Path that Leadeth to an Indian town called Playwickey, and from thence extending Westward to Neshameney Creek, from which said line the said Tract or Tracts therebyi Granted, doth extend itself back into the Woods as far as a Man can goe in one day and a helf, and bounded on the Westerly side with the Creek called Neshameny, or the most Westerly branch thereof, So far as the said Branch doth extend, and from thence by line to the utmost extent of the said one day and a half's Journey, and from thence to the afore-said River Delaware, and from thence down the Several Courses of the said River to the first mentioned Spruce tree. And all this did likewise appear to be true by William Biles and Joseph Wood, who upon their Affirmations, did solemnly declare that they well remembered the Treaty held between the Agents of William Penn and those Indians. But some of our Old Men being then Absent, We requested of our Brethren John Penn and Thomas Penn, that We might have more time to Consult with our People concerning the same, which request being granted us, We have, after more than two Years since the Treaty at Pensbury, now come to Phila-delphia, together with our chief Sachems Monochyhickan, and several of our Old Men, and upon a further Treaty held upon the same Subject, We Do Acknowledge Ourselves and every of Us, to be fully satisfyed that the above described Tract or Tracts of Land were truly Granted and Sold by the said Mayhkeericckkishsho, Sayhoppy, and Taughhaughsey, unto the said William Penn and his heirs, And for a further Confirmation thereof, We, the said Monockyhickan, Lappawinzoe, Tisheekunk, and Nutimus, Do, for ourselves and all other the Delaware Indians, fully, clearly and Absolutely Remise, Release, and forever Quit claim unto the said John Penn, Thomas Penn, and Richard Penn, All our Right Title, Interest, and pretentions whatsoever of, in, or to the said Tract or Tracts of Land, and every Part and Parcel thereof, So that neither We, or any of us, or our Children, shall or may at any time hereaf-ter, have Challenge, Claim, or Demand any Right, Title or Interest, or any pretentions whatsoever of, in, or to the said Tract or Tracts of Land, or any Part thereof, but of and from the same shall be excluded, and forever Debarred. And We do hereby further Agree, that the extent of the said Tract or Tracts of Land shall be forthwith Walked, Travelled, or gone over by proper Persons to be appointed for that Purpose, According to the direction of the aforesaid Deed.

In Witness whereof, We have hereunto set our hands and Seals, at Philadelphia, the Twenty-fifth day of the Month called August, in the Year, According to the English account, one thousand Seven hundred and thirty-seven.

MANAWKYHICKON, his X mark
LAPPAWINZOE, his X mark
TEESHACOMIN, his X mark
NOOTIMUS, his X mark

The above Deed being read and explained to all the Indians at this Treaty, the following Persons, on behalf of themselves and all the other Indians now present, have agreed to Sign or put their Names to the same as Witnesses, in Token of their free and full consent to what the above named Monochyhickan, Llappawinzoe, Tish-eekunk, and Nutimus, have signed and Sealed.

Sealed, Subscribed and Delivered, Tameckapa, his X mark,
In the presence of us, Oochqueahgtoe, his X mark,

James Logan,	Wayshaghinichon, his X mark,
A. Hamilton,	Nectotaylemet, his X mark,
Rd. Assheton,	Taarlichigh, his X mark,
James Steel,	Neeshalinicka, his X mark,
Thomas Griffitt,	Neepaheeiloman, alias Jo Tunum, his X mark,
William Allen,	Ayshaataghoe, alias Cornelius, his X mark,
Thomas Freame,	Aysolickon, his X mark
John Georges,	Chichagheway, his X mark
James Hamilton,	John Hans, his X mark
Edward Shippen,	Shawtagh, his X mark
Wm. Logan,	
James Letort,	
Robt. Charles,	
James Steel, Jun.,	
James Steel	
Bearefoot Brunson, Interpreter.	

Source: The Walking Purchase, Pennsylvania Archives, First Series, Vol. 1, pp. 541–543. http://www.docheritage.state.pa.us/documents/walkingpurchaseprint.htm.

37. Six Nations, Meeting with Colonial Officials at Albany, August 19, 1746

Introduction

The Iroquois, who had considered the French to be their enemies since French explorers had attacked them in the early 1600s, maintained a strong alliance with the English and cooperated with them in controlling the movements of other Indians in Iroquois territory. Iroquois land in northern New York and Pennsylvania served as a buffer between Canada and the British colonies. The European war called the War of the Austrian Succession (1740–1748) spilled over into North America when France entered the war against Great Britain. This became King George's War (1744–1748), fought in America between France and Great Britain. In 1744 warriors and sachems of the Iroquois Six Nations met colonial officials in Lancaster, Pennsylvania, and reaffirmed their alliance with the English. During a meeting in Albany, New York, two years later, New York officials urged the Iroquois to join them in a major operation against Canada. In his attempt to sway the Iroquois, the speaker cited French and Indian attacks on the English frontier, the necessity of avenging one's ancestors, and the opportunity to attain glory.

Primary Source

The King your Father, having been informed of the unmanly Murders committed on the Frontiers of New-England, and of this Province, is resolved to subdue the Country of Canada, and thereby put an End to all the mischievous Designs of the French in these Parts. And for this purpose, he has ordered his Governors of Virginia, Maryland, Pennsylvania, and New-Jersey, to join their Forces to the Forces of this Province, to attack Canada by Land: They are all now upon their march, and you will soon see them here.

At the same Time the Forces of the Massachusets-Bay, Connecticut, Rhode-Island, and New-Hampshire, are to go in Ships to Cape-Breton, and there join with his Majesty's Ships of War, and a great Army of experienc'd Soldiers from Great-Britain.

Many Ships of War are already arrived there, and some thousand of Soldiers; many more Ships and Soldiers are following; and I expect every Hour to hear of their Arrival; after which the Attack upon Canada will be made on all Sides, both by Sea and Land.

You may perceive the King has ordered a Strength sufficient to subdue Canada; but at the same Time, the King your Father expects and orders you his Children, to join with your whole Force in this Enterprize; and thereby gives the Six Nations a glorious Opportunity of establishing their Fame and Renown over all the Indian Nations in America, in the Conquest of your inveterate Enemies the French; who, however they may dissemble and profess Friendship, can never forget the Slaughter which your Fathers made of them; and for that purpose, caress those Nations who have always been your inveterate Enemies, and who desire nothing so much as to see the Name of the Six Nations become obliterate, and forgot for ever.

[Gave a Belt.]

Brethren, The French, on all Occasions, shew, that they act against your Brethren the English, like Men that know they dare not look them in the Face in Day-Light; and therefore, like Thieves, steal upon poor People, who do not expect them, in the Night, and consequently are not prepared for them: Your Brethren in their Revenge have acted like Men of Courage; they do not attack poor Farmers at their Labour, but boldly attempted the Reduction of Louisburg, the strongest Town the French had in America, in the fortifying of which they had spent above twenty Years: It was surrounded with strong Walls and Forts, in which they had planted their largest Cannon in every Place, where they thought the English could come near them; notwithstanding of all these Precautions and Advantages, they were forced to submit to the English Valour.

You must have heard from your Fathers, and I doubt not several of your old Men still remember what the French did at Onondaga; how they surprized your Countrymen at Cadarackui; how they invaded the Senekas, and what Mischiefs they did to the Mohawks; how many of your Countrymen suffered by the Fire at Montreal. Before they entered upon these cruel and mischievous Designs, they sent Priests among you to delude you, and lull you asleep, while they were preparing to knock you on the Head; and I hear they are attempting to do the same now.

[Gave a Belt.]

I need not put you in mind what Revenge your Fathers took for these Injuries, when they put all the Island of Montreal, and a great Part of Canada, to Fire and Sword; can you think that the French forget this? No, they have the Ax privately in their Hands against you, and use these deceitful Arts, by which only they have been able to gain Advantage over you, that by your trusting to them, they may at some time or other, at one Blow, remove from the Face of the Earth, the Remembrance of a People that have so often put them to Shame and Flight.

If your Fathers could now rise out of their Graves, how would their Hearts leap with Joy to see this Day; when so glorious an Opportunity is put into their Hands to revenge all the Injuries their Country has received from the French, and be never more exposed to their Treachery and Deceit.

I make no doubt you are the true Sons of such renowned and brave Ancestors, animated with the same Spirit for your Country's Glory, and in Revenge of the Injuries your Fathers received, uncapable of being deluded by the flattering Speeches of them, who always have been, and always must be, in their Hearts, your Enemies, and who desire nothing more, than the Destruction of your Nations.

I therefore invite you, Brethren, by this Belt, to join with us, and to share with us, in the Honour of the Conquest of our and your deceitful Enemies; and that you not only join all the Force of the Six Nations with us, but likewise invite all the Nations depending on you, to take a Share in this glorious Enterprize: And I will furnish your fighting Men with Arms, Ammunition, Cloathing,

Provisions, and every Thing necessary for the War; and in their Absence, take Care of their Wives and Children.

Source: Cadwallader Colden, *The History of the Five Indian Nations of Canada; Which Are Dependent on the Province of New York, and Are a Barrier between the English and the French in That Part of the World* (New York: Allerton Book Co., 1904), 230–233.

38. Robert Dinwiddie, Instructions to George Washington regarding the French in the Ohio Country, October 30, 1753

Introduction

During the 1740s, the French and English vied openly for control of trade and territory in the interior of North America. Traders from Virginia and Pennsylvania crossed the Allegheny mountains into the Ohio River Valley to conduct trade with the western Indians. French traders entered the same territory from Canada and the Mississippi River Valley. In 1752 Frenchmen led a troop of Indians in a brutal attack on an English trading post in the Ohio Country. The following year the French began building forts in the western part of present-day Pennsylvania. In these orders, Virginia governor Robert Dinwiddie, who was speculating in Ohio land, instructs a 21-year-old militia officer, George Washington, to lead an expedition into the Ohio Country to confront the French. Washington was to inform them that they were trespassing on Virginia property and gather intelligence on the placement of French forts and the strength of their garrisons. Washington set out from Williamsburg in October 1753 and returned in January 1754 to report that the French had no intention of leaving Ohio voluntarily. Trained as a surveyor, Washington produced a good map of the Ohio Country. Dinwiddie continued to send Virginia militia into the Ohio Valley, and in July 1754 Washington and his men fought the first American battle of the French and Indian War (1754–1763).

Primary Source

[Williamsburg, October 30, 1753]

Whereas I have receiv'd Information of a Body of French Forces being assembled in an hostile Manner on the River Ohio, intending by force of Arms to erect certain Forts on the said River, within this Territory & contrary to the Peace & Dignity of our Sovereign the King of Great Britain.

These are therefore to require & direct You the said George Washington Esqr. forthwith to repair to the Logstown on the said River Ohio; & having there inform'd YourSelf where the said French Forces have posted themselves, thereupon to proceed to such Place: & being there arriv'd to present Your credentials, together with my Letter to the chief commanding Officer, &, in the Name of His Britanic Majesty, to demand an Answer from him hereto.

On Your Arrival at the Logstown, You are to address Yourself to the Half King, to Monacatoocha & other the Sachems of the Six Nations; acquainting them with Your Orders to visit & deliver my Letter to the French commanding Officer; & desiring the said Chiefs to appoint You a sufficient Number of their Warriors to be Your Safeguard, as near the French as You may desire, & to wait Your further Direction.

You are diligently to enquire into the Numbers & Force of the French on the Ohio, & the adjacent Country; how they are like to be assisted from Canada; & what are the Difficulties & Conveniencies of that Communication, & the Time requir'd for it.

You are to take Care to be truly inform'd what Forts the French have erected, & where; How they are Garrison'd & appointed, & what is their Distance from each other, & from Logstown: And from the best Intelligence You can procure, You are to learn what gave Occasion to this Expedition of the French. How they are like to be supported, & what their Pretentions are.

When the French commandant has given You the requir'd & necessary Dispatches, you are to desire of him that, agreeable to the Law of nations, he wou'd grant You a proper Guard, to protect you as far on Your Return, as You may judge for Your Safety, against any stragling Indians or Hunters that may be ignorant of Yr Character & molest You.

Wishing You good Success in Yr Negotiations & a safe & speedy return I am Sr Yr hble Servt.

Source: "Dinwiddie's Instructions to Washington in 1773." *The National Magazine: A Monthly Journal of American History*, Vol. 10, no. 1 (1889): 114–115.

39. George Washington, Report to Robert Dinwiddie of General Edward Braddock's Defeat in Ohio Country, July 18, 1755

Introduction

During the 1740s, the French and English competition for control of the Ohio River Valley built inexorably toward war. In 1752

Frenchmen led a troop of Indians in a brutal attack on an English trading post in the Ohio Country. The following year the French began building forts in the western part of present-day Pennsylvania. Governor Robert Dinwiddie of Virginia first sent 21-year-old militia officer George Washington at the head of an expedition into the Ohio Country in 1753. Washington led another expedition into the Ohio Valley in 1754 and was defeated by a large French force at Fort Necessity in the first American battle of the French and Indian War (1754–1763). In response to the battle, Great Britain sent General Edward Braddock and some 1,000 troops to Virginia. Joined by Washington and colonial militiamen, Braddock's army marched toward the Ohio Valley. On July 9, 1755, French and Indian troops ambushed the British and colonial troops, inflicting an overwhelming defeat. Washington was instrumental in saving the survivors by taking command of the retreat. In this letter, Washington reports details of the engagement to Governor Dinwiddie. The British defeat left frontier settlers open to Indian raids. Colonel Washington spent the ensuing years commanding a militia regiment in defense of the Virginia frontier.

Primary Source

Fort Cumberland, July 18, 1755.

Honbl. Sir: As I am favour'd with an oppertunity, I shou'd think myself inexcusable was I to omit giv'g you some acct. of our late Engagem't with the French on the Monongahela the 9th. Inst.

We continued our March from Fort Cumberland to Frazier's (which is within 7 Miles of Duquisne) with't meet'g with any extraordinary event, hav'g only a stragler or two picked up by the French Indians. When we came to this place, we were attack'd (very unexpectedly I must own) by abt. 300 French and Ind'ns; Our numbers consisted of abt. 1300 well arm'd Men, chiefly Regular's, who were immediately struck with such a deadly Panick, that nothing but confusion and disobedience of order's prevail'd amongst them: The Officer's in gen'l behav'd with incomparable bravery, for which they greatly suffer'd, there being near 60 kill'd and wound'd. A large proportion, out of the number we had! The Virginian Companies behav'd like Men and died like Soldiers; for I believe out of the 3 Companys that were there that day, scarce 30 were left alive: Captn. Peyrouny and all his Officer's, down to a Corporal, were kill'd; Captn. Polson shar'd almost as hard a Fate, for only one of his Escap'd: In short the dastardly behaviour of the English Soldier's expos'd all those who were inclin'd to do their duty to almost certain Death; and at length, in despight of every effort to the contrary, broke and run as Sheep before the Hounds, leav'g the Artillery, Ammunition, Provisions, and, every individual thing we had with us a prey to the Enemy; and when we endeavour'd to rally them in hopes of regaining our invaluable loss, it was with as much success as if we had attempted to have stop'd the wild Bears of the Mountains.

The Genl. was wounded behind in the shoulder, and into the Breast, of w'ch he died three days after; his two Aids de Camp were both wounded, but are in a fair way of Recovery; Colo. Burton and Sir Jno. St. Clair are also wounded, and I hope will get over it; Sir Peter Halket, with many other brave Officers were kill'd in the Field. I luckily escap'd with't a wound tho' I had four Bullets through my Coat and two Horses shot under me. It is suppose that we left 300 or more dead in the Field; about that number we brought of wounded; and it is imagin'd (I believe with great justice too) that two thirds of both received their shott from our own cowardly English Soldier's who gather'd themselves into a body contrary to orders 10 or 12 deep, wou'd then level, Fire and shoot down the Men before them.

I tremble at the consequences that this defeat may have upon our back settlers, who I suppose will all leave their habitations unless there are proper measures taken for their security.

Colo. Dunbar, who commands at present, intends so soon as his Men are recruited at this place, to continue his March to Phila. into Winter Quarters: so that there will be no Men left here unless it is the poor remains of the Virginia Troops, who survive and will be too small to guard our Frontiers. As Captn. Orme is writg. to your honour I doubt not but he will give you a circumstantial acct. of all things, which will make it needless for me to add more than that I am, etc.

Source: "George Washington to Robert Dinwiddie, July 18, 1755," George Washington Papers at the Library of Congress, 1741–1799: Series 4, General Correspondence, 1697–1799, Images 242–244. Congress, http://memory.loc.gov/ammem/gwhtml/gwhome.html.

40. James Smith, *An Account of the Remarkable Occurrences in the Life and Travels of Col. James Smith*, 1799 [Excerpts]

Introduction

Virginia militiaman George Washington, leading a 1754 expedition into the Ohio Country, was defeated by a large French force at Fort Necessity in the first American battle of the French and Indian War (1754–1763). In response to the battle, Great Britain sent General Edward Braddock and some 1,000 troops to Virginia. Joined by George Washington and colonial militiamen, Braddock's army marched toward the Ohio Valley. On July 9, 1755, French and Indian troops ambushed the British and colonial troops, inflicting an overwhelming defeat. News of this defeat reached a Pennsylvania militiaman held captive at Fort Duquesne on the Ohio River in western Pennsylvania 10 miles distant from the battle. Colonel James Smith, 18 years old, had been captured by Indians in May 1755 while building a road for the expected arrival of Braddock's army. Held for a time at the French fort, Smith saw the Indians assemble to attack Braddock's army on the morning of July 9. Later he saw them return in triumph brandishing bloody scalps and plunder. The Indians also returned with a few prisoners, whom they burned to death within view of the fort. Smith was later taken to an Indian town. He escaped and returned home in 1759. He fought on the American side during the Revolutionary War. This account is from Smith's autobiography, published in 1799.

Primary Source

[. . .]

Shortly after this, on the 9th day of July, 1755, in the morning, I heard a great stir in the fort. As I could then walk with a staff in my hand, I went out of the door, which was just by the wall of the fort, and stood upon the wall and viewed the Indians in a huddle before the gate, where were barrels of powder, bullets, flints &c. and every one taking what suited; I saw the Indians also march off in rank, intire—likewise the French Canadians, and some regulars, after viewing the Indians and French in different positions, I computed them to be about four hundred, and wondered that they attempted to go out against Braddock with so small a party. I was then in high hopes that I would soon see them flying before the British troops, and that general Braddock would take the fort and rescue me.

I remained anxious to know the event of this day; and in the afternoon, I again observed a great noise and commotion in the fort, and though at that time I could not understand French, yet I found that it was the voice of Joy and triumph, and feared that they had received what I called bad news.

I had observed some of the old country soldiers speak Dutch, as I spoke Dutch I went to one of them, and asked him what was the news? He told me that a runner had just arrived, who said that Braddock would certainly be defeated; that the Indians and French had surrounded him, and were concealed behind trees and in gullies, and kept a constant fire upon the English, and that they saw the English falling in heaps, and if they did not take the river which was the only gap, and make their escape, there would not be one man left alive before sundown. Some time after this I heard a number of scalp halloos, and saw a company of Indians and French coming in. I observed they had a great many bloody scalps, grenadiers' caps, British canteens, bayonets, &c. with them. They brought the news that Braddock was defeated. After that, another company came in which appeared to be about one hundred, and chiefly Indians, and it seemed to me that almost every one of this

company was carrying scalps; after this came another company with a number of wagon-horses, and also a great many scalps. Those that were coming in, and those that had arrived, kept a constant firing of small arms, and also the great guns in the fort, which were accompanied with the most hideous shouts and yells from all quarters; so that it appeared to me as if the infernal regions had broke loose.

About sundown I beheld a small party coming in with about a dozen prisoners, stripped naked, with their hands tied behind their backs, and their faces and part of their bodies blacked—these prisoners they burned to death on the bank of Allegheny river opposite to the fort. I stood on the fort wall until I beheld them begin to burn one of these men; they had him tied to a stake, and kept touching him with firebrands, red-hot irons, &c. and he screaming in a most doleful manner,—the Indians in the mean time yelling like infernal spirits. As this scene appeared too shocking for me to behold, I retired to my lodging both sore and sorry.

[. . .]

The morning after the battle I saw Braddock's artillery brought into the fort, the same day I also saw several Indians in British officer's dress, with sash, half moon, laced hats, &c. which the British then wore.

[. . .]

Source: James Smith, *An Account of the Remarkable Occurrences in the Life and Travels of Col. James Smith* . . . (Lexington, KY: Printed by John Bradford, 1799), 10–13.

41. Mary Jemison as Told to James Seaver, *The Life of Mary Jemison*, 1755 [Excerpt]

Introduction

As the British colonies expanded westward, they pushed the native peoples before them. White settlers on the western frontier bore the brunt of the Indians' anger at the loss of their land. In deadly raids, Indians burned cabins, killed settlers, and plundered their household goods. Such raids grew more frequent after the outbreak of the French and Indian War (1754–1763). In 1755, six Seneca Indians and four Frenchmen attacked the home of Mary Jemison in western Pennsylvania and took her family captive. The Senecas were members of the Iroquois Confederacy, but unlike most Iroquois, some of them supported the French in the war.

The Indians selected Mary, then 12 years old, and another child for adoption into the tribe and murdered the others. It was the custom of the Indians to adopt selected captives as a way of restoring their population. The Indians trekked with the children to the French-held Fort Duquesne (at present-day Pittsburgh, Pennsylvania), where Mary was given to two Seneca women, taken to their village, and formally adopted. She eventually adjusted to her new life, married a Delaware Indian, and bore a number of children. She lived to the age of 90 and in her old age told her story to an American, who published the book that contained this account of her capture. The book captured the public imagination and went through may editions.

Primary Source

My education had received as much attention from my parents, as their situation in a new country would admit of. I had been at school some, where I learned to read in a book that was about half as large as a Bible; and in the Bible I had read a little. I had also learned the Catechism, which I used frequently to repeat to my parents, and every night, before I went to bed, I was obliged to stand up before my mother and repeat some words that I suppose was a prayer.

My reading, Catechism and prayers, I have long since forgotten; though for a number of the first years that I lived with the Indians, I repeated the prayers as often as I had an opportunity. After the revolutionary war, I remembered the names of some of the letters when I saw them; but have never read a word since I was taken prisoner. It is but a few years since a Missionary kindly gave me a bible, which I am very fond of hearing my neighbors read to me, and should be pleased to learn to read it myself; but my sight has been for a number of years, so dim that I have not been able to distinguish one letter from another.

As I before observed, I got home with the horse very early in the morning, where I found a man that lived in our neighborhood, and his sister-in-law who had three children, one son and two daughters. I soon learned that they had come there to live a short time; but for what purpose I cannot say. The woman's husband, however, was at that time in Washington's army, fighting for his country; and as her brother-in-law had a house she had lived with him in his absence. Their names I have forgotten.

Immediately after I got home, the man took the horse to go to his house after a bag of grain, and took his gun in his hand for the purpose of killing game, if he should chance to see any. Our family, as usual, was busily employed about their common business. Father was shaving an axe-helve at the side of the house; mother was making preparations for breakfast; my two oldest brothers were at work near the barn; and the little ones, with myself, and the woman and her three children, were in the house.

Breakfast was not yet ready, when we were alarmed by the discharge of a number of guns, that seemed to be near. Mother and the women before mentioned, almost fainted at the report, and every one trembled with fear. On opening the door, the man and horse lay dead near the house, having just been shot by the Indians.

I was afterwards informed, that the Indians discovered him at his own house with his gun, and pursued him to father's, where they shot him as I have related. They first secured my father, and then rushed into the house, and without the least resistance made prisoners of my mother, Robert, Matthew, Betsey, the woman and her three children, and myself, and then commenced plundering.

My two brothers, Thomas and John, being at the barn, escaped and went to Virginia, where my grandfather Erwin then lived, as I was informed by a Mr. Fields, who was at my house about the close of the revolutionary war.

The party that took us consisted of six Indians and four Frenchmen, who immediately commenced plundering, as I just observed, and took what they considered most valuable; consisting principally of bread, meal and meat. Having taken as much provision as they could carry, they set out with their prisoners in great haste, for fear of detection, and soon entered the woods. On our march that day, an Indian went behind us with a whip, with which he frequently lashed the children to make them keep up. In this manner we travelled till dark without a mouthful of food or a drop of water; although we had not eaten since the night before. Whenever the little children cried for water, the Indians would make them drink urine or go thirsty. At night they encamped in the woods without fire and without shelter, where we were watched with the greatest vigilance. Extremely fatigued, and very hungry, we were compelled to lie upon the ground supperless and without a drop of water to satisfy the cravings of our appetites. As in the day time, so the little ones were made to drink urine in the night if they cried for water. Fatigue alone brought us a little sleep for the refreshment of our weary limbs; and at the dawn of the day we were again started on our march in the same order that we had proceeded on the day before. About sunrise we were halted, and the Indians gave us a full breakfast of provision that they had brought from my father's house. Each of us being very hungry, partook of this bounty of the Indians, except father, who was so much overcome with his situation—so much exhausted by anxiety and grief, that silent despair seemed fastened upon his countenance, and he could not be prevailed upon to refresh his sinking nature by the use of a morsel of food. Our repast being finished, we again resumed our march, and before noon passed a small fort that I heard my father say was called Fort Canagojigge.

That was the only time that I heard him speak from the time we were taken till we were finally separated the following night.

Toward evening we arrived at the border of a dark and dismal swamp, which was covered with small hemlocks, or some other evergreen, and other bushes, into which we were conducted; and having gone a short distance we stopped to encamp for the night.

Here we had some bread and meat for supper: but the dreariness of our situation, together with the uncertainty under which we all labored, as to our future destiny, almost deprived us of the sense of hunger, and destroyed our relish for food.

Mother, from the time we were taken, had manifest a great degree of fortitude, and encouraged us to support our troubles without complaining; and by her conversation seemed to make the distance and time shorter, and the way more smooth. But father lost all his ambition in the beginning of our trouble, and continued apparently lost to every care—absorbed in melancholy. Here, as before, she insisted on the necessity of our eating; and we obeyed her, but it was done with heavy hearts.

As soon as I had finished my supper, an Indian took off my shoes and stocking and put a pair of moccasins on my feet, which my mother observed; and believing that they would spare my life, even if they should destroy the other captives, addressed me as near as I can remember in the following words:—

"My dear little Mary, I fear that the time has arrived when we must be parted forever. Your life, my child, I think will be spared; but we shall probably be tomahawked here in this lonesome place by the Indians. O! how can I part with you my darling? What will become of my sweet little Mary? Oh! How can I think of your being continued in captivity without a hope of your being rescued? O that death had snatched you from my embraces in your infancy; the pain of parting then would have been pleasing to what it now is; and I should have seen the end of your troubles!—Alas, my dear! My heart bleeds at the thoughts of what awaits you; but, if you leave us, remember my child your own name, and the name of your father and mother. Be careful and not forget your English tongue. If you shall have an opportunity to get away from the Indians, don't try to escape; for if you do they will find and destroy you. Don't forget, my little daughter, the prayers that I have learned you—say them often; be a good child, and God will bless you. May God bless you my child, and make you comfortable and happy."

During this time, the Indians stripped the shoes and stocking from the little boy that belonged to the woman who was taken with us, and put moccasins on his feet, as they had done before on mine. I was crying. An Indian took the little boy and myself by the hand, to lead us off from the company, when my mother exclaimed, "Don't cry Mary—don't cry my child. God will bless you! Farewell—farewell!"

The Indian led us some distance into the bushes, or woods, and there lay down with us to spend the night. The recollection of parting with my tender mother kept me awake, while the tears constantly flowed from my eyes. A number of times in the night the little boy begged of me earnestly to run away with him and get clear of the Indians; but remembering the advice I had so lately received, and knowing the dangers to which we should be exposed, in travelling without a path and without a guide, through a wilderness unknown to us, I told him that I would not go, and persuaded him to lie still till morning.

Early the next morning the Indians and Frenchmen that we had left the night before, came to us; but our friends were left behind. It is impossible for any one to form a correct idea of what my feelings were at the sight of those savages, whom I supposed had murdered my parents and brothers, sister, and friend, and left them in the swamp to be devoured by wild beasts! But what could I do? A poor little defenceless girl; without the power or means of escaping; without a home to go to, even if I could be liberated; without a knowledge of the direction or distance to my former place of residence; and without a living friend to whom to fly for protection, I felt a kind of horror, anxiety, and dread, that, to me, seemed insupportable. I durst not cry—I durst not complain; and to inquire of them the fate of my friends (even if I could have mustered resolution) was beyond my ability, as I could not speak their language, nor they understand mine. My only relief was in silent stifled sobs.

My suspicions as to the fate of my parents proved too true; for soon after I left them they were killed and scalped, together with Robert, Matthew, Betsey, and the woman and her two children, and mangled in the most shocking manner.

Having given the little boy and myself some bread and meat for breakfast, they led us on as fast as we could travel, and one of them went behind and with a long staff, picked up all the grass and weeds that we trailed down by going over them. By taking the precaution they avoided detection; for each weed was so nicely placed in its natural position that no one would have suspected that we had passed that way. It is the custom of Indians when scouting, or on private expeditions, to step carefully and where no impression of their feet can be left—shunning wet or muddy ground. They seldom take hold of a bush or limb, and never break one; and by observing those precautions and that of setting up the weeds and grass which they necessarily lop, they completely elude the sagacity of their pursuers, and escape that punishment which they are conscious they merit from the hand of justice.

After a hard day's march we encamped in a thicket, where the Indians made a shelter of boughs, and then built a good fire to warm and dry out benumbed limbs and clothing; for it had rained some through the day. Here we were again fed as before. When the Indians had finished their supper they took from their baggage a number of scalps and went about preparing them for the market, or to keep without spoiling, by straining them over small hoops which they prepared for that purpose, and then drying and scraping them by the fire. Having put the scalps, yet wet and bloody, upon the hoops, and stretched them to their full extent, they held them to the fire till they were partly dried and then with their knives commenced scraping off the flesh; and in that way they continued to work, alternately drying and scraping them, till they were dry and clean. That being done they combed the hair in the neatest manner, and then painted it and the edges of the scalps yet on the hoops, red. Those scalps I knew at the time must have been taken from our family by the color of the hair. My mother's hair was red; and I could easily distinguish my father's and the children's from each other. That sight was most appaling; yet, I was obliged to endure it without complaining.

In the course of the night they made me to understand that they should not have killed the family if the whites had not pursued them.

Mr. Fields, whom I have before mentioned, informed me that at the time we were taken, he lived in the vicinity of my father; and that on hearing of our captivity, the whole neighborhood turned out in pursuit of the enemy, and to deliver us if possible: but that their efforts were unavailing. They however pursued us to the dark swamp, where they found my father, his family and companions, stripped and mangled in the most inhuman manner: That from thence the march of the cruel monsters could not be traced in any direction; and that they returned to their homes with the melancholy tiding of our misfortunes, supposing that we had all shared in the massacre.

The next morning we went on; the Indian going behind us and setting up the weeds as on the day before. At night we encamped on the ground in the open air, without a shelter or fire.

In the morning we again set out early, and travelled as on the two former days, though the weather was extremely uncomfortable, from the continual falling of rain and snow.

At night the snow fell fast, and the Indians built a shelter of boughs, and a fire, where we rested tolerably dry through that and the two succeeding nights.

When we stopped, and before the fire was kindled, I was so much fatigued from running, and so far benumbed by the wet and cold, that I expected that I must fail and die before I could get warm and comfortable. The fire, however, soon restored the circulation, and after I had taken my supper I felt so that I rested well through the night.

On account of the storm, we were two days at that place. On one of those days, a party consisting of six Indians who had been to the frontier settlements, came to where we were, and brought with them one prisoner, a young white man who was very tired and dejected. His name I have forgotten.

Misery certainly loves company. I was extremely glad to see him, though I knew from his appearance, that his situation was as deplorable as mine, and that he could afford me no kind of assistance. In the afternoon the Indians killed a deer, which they dressed, and then roasted it whole; which made them a full meal. We were each allowed a share of their venison, and some bread, so that we made a good meal also.

Having spent three nights and two days at that place, and the storm having ceased, early in the morning the whole company, consisting of twelve Indians, four Frenchmen, the young man, the little boy and myself, moved on at a moderate pace without an Indian behind us to deceive our pursuers.

In the afternoon we came in sight of Fort Pitt (as it is now called), where we were halted while the Indians performed some customs upon their prisoners which they deemed necessary. That fort was then occupied by the French and Indians, and was called Fort Du Quesne. It stood at the junction of the Monongahela, which is said to signify, in some of the Indian languages, the Falling-in-Banks, and the Alleghany rivers, where the Ohio river begins to take its name. The word O-hi-o, signifies bloody.

At the place where we halted, the Indians combed the hair of the young man, the boy and myself, and then painted our faces and hair red, in the finest Indian style. We were then conducted into the fort, where we received a little bread and were then shut up and left to tarry alone through the night.

[. . .]

Source: James Everett Seaver, *A Narrative of the Life of Mary Jemison: The White Woman of the Genesee* (New York: American Scenic and Historic Preservation Society, 1918), 39–51.

42. Edmond Atkin, Report to the Lords Commissioners for Trade and Plantation, 1755 [Excerpts]

Introduction

The French traders of Louisiana and the British traders of South Carolina competed with one another for the loyalty of the Indians who lived between the two colonies. Edmond Atkin, a South Carolina trader and politician, offered the British Board of Trade his advice—in the form of a report, excerpted here—on how to manage relations with the major Indian tribes of the southern colonies. As war broke out with France, British authorities saw the wisdom of appointing Atkin superintendent of Indian affairs. Like a number of South Carolina colonists of earlier generations, he believed that the best defense against French or Spanish incursions was a strong community of Indians who were loyal to the British and lived in a buffer zone between the British and the other powers. Atkin argued that the Indians were honorable and that fair treatment would secure their friendship. He offered examples from previous wars, demonstrating correctly that only the most oppressive and unethical treatment caused Indians to attack European colonists. At the outbreak of the French and Indian War (1754–1763), the Creeks and Chickasaws were staunch allies of the British. However, Braddock's defeat left the western frontier open to deadly raids by enemy tribes. In 1757 South Carolina asked for help defending the frontier against French and Indian attacks.

Primary Source

[...]

The Importance of Indians is now generally known and understood, a Doubt remains not, that the prosperity of our Colonies on the Continent, will stand or fall with our Interest and favour among them. While they are our Friends, they are the Cheapest and strongest Barrier for the Protection of our Settlements; when Enemies, they are capable by ravaging in their method of War, in spite of all we can do, to render those Possessions almost useless. Of this the French are so sensible, as well as of our Natural Advantages beyond their own, that they have employed all their Art, not only to embroil us with our Indians, and to Set at work clandestinely some of their own to scalp our People even in times of Peace, but to destroy and utterly extirpate those Nations whose Affections they could not gain, by setting one against another, and themselves assisting to do it. The same

Reason should certainly make it our Policy, to support and preserve them.

[...]

No people in the World understand and pursue their true National Interest, better than the Indians. How sanguinary soever they are towards their Enemies, from a misguided Passion of Heroism, and a love of their country; yet they are otherways truly humane, hospitable, and equitable. And how fraudulent soever they have been reputed, from the Appearance of their military Actions, in which according to their method of War, Glory cannot be acquired without Cunning & Stratagem; Yet in their publick Treaties no People on earth are more open, explicit, and Direct. Nor are they excelled by any in the observance of them. Witness in particular the Treaties of the five Nations with the Government of New York; in which there hath been no Breach yet on their Part, since 1609 at first under the Dutch, and since 1664 under the English. And so patient are the Indians in general under the abuses of our Traders, that so numerous as the occasions have been for Complaint, I have never known an Instance in my time of a Complaint made, from either of the Nations in alliance with So. Carolina, against any particular Trader by name, with a view of punishing him by Removal. When they intended it, they have been easily pacified & prevented. It were easy to make appear, with respect to (I believe I may say) all Ruptures of Consequence between the Indians & the white People, and the Massacres that ensued, which have created such a Horror of the former, That the latter were first the Aggressors; the Indians being driven thereto under Oppressions and Abuses, and to vindicate their Natural Rights. The early and long Series of Calamities and Distreses which Virginia Struggled under with them in its Infancy, was owing, (tho' no Historian hath made the Observation) to Sr. Richd Grenville's burning an Indian Town and Destroying their Corn in 1585, after a very hospitable Reception, in revenge for a Silver Cup stolen by an Indian, who did not know the difference of Value between that and a horn Spoon; which could not but shock their natural Ideas of Equity—The great Massacre committed by the Yamasee Indians in So Carolina in 1715 was owing to the continued Oppressions and ill Usage they received from a publick Agent; of which they often Complained in vain; being such that their King told a Person from whom I had it, they could bear them no longer. But they were so unwilling to come to that Extremity, and there was so little Treachery in the Execution of it, that they declared beforehand not only their Intention, but named the very day, which was treated with Slight, till it was too late—The great Massacre committed by the Natchez Indians upon the French on the Mississippi River in 1729 was certainly owing to the Obstruction which the French gave to their Trading with the English. Le Pere Charlevoix owns, that M. de Chepar, who commanded the Post in that Nation was a little embroiled with them, without telling the Reason. But he could not conceal, that they were hurried into striking the Blow sooner than the day appointed, upon hearing that 120 Horses loaded with English Goods were enter'd into their Country—The Blow also which was struck upon the French by the Chactaw Indians in 1746 was owing to the French not permitting them to have a free Trade with the English, when that Nation was almost Naked, and the French themselves were unable to supply them with Necessaries. The policy of the Indians is Simple and Plain. Tis confined to the Securing their personal Safety, a Supply of Wants, and fair Usage. As we are the best able to supply all their wants, and on the easiest terms, they know it to be their true Interest to stick close to us, provided we shew an equal Regard also with the French, to their Safety and good usage. We have nothing therefore left to do, the Ballance being in our own hands, but, with the continuance of the same Trade as we now carry on with them, to Build Forts (not by Surprize, and against their will, as the French do but) for their sakes as well as our own, in such Nations as are or shall be desirous of it; To practice therein the same little ingratiating Arts as the French do; and above all, to begin with building Forts in their hearts, that is, *to put the Trade and Traders first under a good Regulation;* after which we may build Forts wherever we please.

[...]

As to the Character and Disposition of the Creeks; They are the most refined and Political Indians, being very Speculative, Sensible, Discreet, Sober, well Governed by their Head Men; and withal by no means wanting Bravery. The Lower Creeks indeed fall short of the upper in some part of this Character; being far less Sober, and therefore not so orderly. Which is occasioned by the great Quantities of Spirituous Liquors, carried by the Augusta Rum Traders to them being the nearest—The Policy of the Creeks leads them to live in Peace with all their Neighbours; but above all to preserve a good Understanding with all white People, English, French, and Spaniards; with each of whom they have Intercourse. This last principle is frequently inculcated by some of the Chiefs in their Harrangues, from the motives of their National Safety and Interest, while they take part against neither, but are Courted by them Severally, and receive Presents from each. The same Principle was enforced by the dying charge of the Old Emperor Brim to his Son Malatchi, the Present Chief of the lower Nation, "never to suffer the Blood of any White Men to be spilt on his Ground." The Conduct of the Creeks comformable to those Principles (which was eminent during the last War) hath rendered them of Superior Weight among the Southern Nations, as holding the Ballance between their European Neighbours, and esteemed or feared by the rest of the red People—Not withstanding the general Disposition of the Creeks to live in Peace with the Neighbouring Nations, they are often at War with the Cherokees, tho' the upper do not always take part with the Lower therein; as on the other hand, the upper Cherokees do not always take part with the lower. These two being the most numerous (the Chactaws excepted), are the contending Nations of the South. The Creeks have an old Grudge against the Cherokees, for joining the Carolina Army in the Indian War in 1715, and falling on them unexpectedly. The repeated losses they have sustained on each side since, have so imbittered their Minds, that it hath been found a very difficult matter to reconcile them. So that the Peace made between them from time to time, hath been of [no] long Duration, but soon followed by a Rupture. This under the present state of our Affairs among the Indians, hath been attended with lucky Consequences to Carolina, as it hath been the means of Disconcerting the Intrigues of the French. But whenever those affairs shall assume such a Change, that we may be intirely secure of both these Nations, it will then become a Point of great Moment, by any means possible to reconcile them effectually. The

Creeks do also sometimes go against the Floridans, against whom they were incited heretofore by the Carolina Government; who after the Conquest of Apalatchee having destroyed some whole Tribes (the Timooquas and Tacoboggas next to St. Augustine and St. Marks), encouraged the Creeks to War upon those Indians, for the sake of making Slaves of them. By which means until the breaking out of the Indian War, a Slave Trade only was promoted in Florida; which drove those Indians to the extreme Parts of the Cape among the bays, leaving the finest part of their Country uninhabited; as it remains to this Day—The Creeks in general are well affected to the English, for the sake of our Goods, much better than to the Spaniards or the French. The Lower Creeks are not quite so well Affected to us, as the Upper. This hath been much admired at, considering that the latter have a French Fort among them. But the real Reason is, that the abuses, disorderly Practices, and Evil Example of the Rum Dealers & other unlicensed Traders that frequent the lower Creeks, have produced in them a Contemptible Opinion of us; as the same Reasons have done among the Lower Cherokees.

[...]

The Chicasaw Nation is situated further West, about Seven hundred and Eighty Miles from Charles Town; about 80 or 90 Miles to the Eastward of the Mississippi, & less South of the great Cherokee River, at the head of the River Chactawhatchee; which taking its Rise from the same Ridge of Mountains as the Rivers in the upper Creek Country do, discharges itself also into the Bay and harbour of Mobile. This therefore (with the Permission of the Chicasaws) may be another way of Communication from thence with the Ohio and Illinois. These Indians live in 7 Towns, having each a Pallisade Fort with a Ditch, in an open rich Champain Plaine about ten Miles in Circumference, accessible only on one side, being almost surrounded by Swamps in a circular manner, about a Mile from any running Creek, and about 30 Miles from a place called the French Landing on the Chactawhatchee; which is as far as that River is Navigable with Boats.

[...]

The Chicasaws are of all Indians the most Manly in their Persons, Sentiments, and Actions; being of large gracefull figure, open Countenance and Manners, and generous Principles; Vigorous, Active, Intrepid, and Sharp in appearance even to Fierceness; expert Horsemen (having perhaps the finest breed of Horses in No. America); by much the best Hunters; and without Exception (by the acknowledgment of all Europeans as well as Indians that know them, who respect them as such) the best Warriors. Even their Women handle Arms, and face an Enemy like Men. They first put a stop formerly to the Spanish Conquests under Ferdinand de Soto. They are the only Indians that ever came voluntarily to a general Engagement with Europeans in open

Ground; as they did with the French in 1736; when after repelling an Attack made upon one of their Towns by some chosen old regular Troops, under excellent Officers, Superior in Number, and assisted by three times as many Indians, they engaged them in an open Plain; and having totally defeated them, pursued them with great Slaughter a considerable Distance. In a Subsequent & more formidable Invasion in 1739 by three times their number of French Troops, and as many Indians also, the Chicasaws went to meet them; and having obliged them to entrench themselves they even ventured (a thing before unheard of) to attack them in their Trenches which they entered & after making great Havock, put the rest all to Flight. In 1742 they defeated intirely a double Invasion made at the same time from different Quarters, to wit, by 2000 Chactaws, headed by only 10 French Men from N. Orleans or Mobile, and 500 Troops besides Indians from Canada, of which last, few ever returned. And in 1753 the last year they repelled another attempt made upon them. All those Invasions were undertaken by the French, professedly in order to extirpate the Chicasaw Nation. Yet such is the magnanimity of those Indians, that under those Circumstances they never asked the Assistance of any of their Neighbours; being aided only by the Presents of ammunition which they have received occasionally from the South Carolina Government; and being advised, in regard to their future Safety, to remove and live nearer to their Friends, they resolved never to leave their Country, declaring in their way of Expression, that they would go again into the same Ground they came out of. But for their better Defence and Security against any Surprize, they built a Pallisade Fort in each of their Towns and made a Ditch round it; and did ask for some Swivel Guns from us, tho' indeed they did not obtain them.

[. . .]

Source: Wilbur R. Jacobs, ed., *Indians of the Southern Colonial Frontier* (Columbia: University of South Carolina Press, 1954).

43. Chickasaw Headmen, Speech to the Governor of South Carolina, April 5, 1756

Introduction

The French traders of Louisiana and the British traders of South Carolina competed with one another for the loyalty of the Indians who lived between the two colonies. British colonists of the Carolinas believed that the best defense against French or Spanish incursions was a strong community of Indians who were loyal to the British and lived in a buffer zone between the British and the other powers. At the outbreak of the French and Indian War (1754–1763), the Creeks and Chickasaws were staunch allies of the British. The Chickasaws had been at war with the French and the French-allied Choctaws almost continuously since the mid-1600s. The French had tried in 1702 to reconcile the enemies and win them both over to the French side. Before 20 years had passed, the French changed course and encouraged the stronger Choctaws to exterminate the Chickasaws. As a result, the Chickasaw population had fallen to the point where they could field barely 400 fighting men. Nevertheless, they remained loyal to the British. This appeal by the headmen of the Chickasaws to the governor of South Carolina details their tenuous situation. They were suffering from poverty and hunger because they could not spare the men and ammunition to hunt for game. Therefore, they begged the governor to send reinforcements and firearms.

Primary Source

From the Headmen and Warriours of the Chekesaws Nation to the King of Carolina and his Beloved Men, This is to let you know we are daily cut oft by our Enemies the French and their Indians who seems to be resolved to drive us from this Land. Therefore we beg of you, our best Friends, to send back our People that are living in other Nations in order to enable us to keep our Lands from the French and their Indians. We hope you will think on us in our Poverty as we have not had the Liberty of Hunting these 3 Years but have had enough to do to defend our Lands and prevent our Women and Children from being Slaves to the French. Our Traders that come here are not willing to trust us Gun Powder and Bulletts to hunt and defend ourselves from our Enemies, neither are we able to buy from them. Many of our Women are without Flaps and many of our young Men without Guns which renders them uncapable of making any Defence against such a powerful Enemy. We are very thankful to you for your last Presents without which it would not have been possible for us to keep Possession of this Land. We have not forgotten all your old good Talks, they are stil fresh in our Minds and we shall always look upon the English as our best Friends and will always endeavour to hinder the French from incroaching on our Lands either to build Forts or make any other Improvments. We will never give up this Land but with the Loss of our Lives. We look upon your Enemies as ours and your Friends as our Friends. The Day shall never come while Sun shines and Water runs that we will join any other Nation but the English. We hope you will stil take Pity on us and give us a Supply of Powder and Bullets and Guns &c. to enable us to outlive our Enemies and revive a dying Friend. We have had no less than four Armies against us this Winter and have lost 20 of our Warriors and many of our Wives and Children carried off alive, our Towns sett on Fire in the Night and burnt down, many of our Houses &c. destroyed our Blanketts &c. We were out a hunting at the Time where we was all attacked by the Back Enemy at our Hunting Camp where we lost several of our Warriors, Women and Children so that we were obliged to leave our Hunting Camps and return to our Nation. Our Traders can tell you all this is true, if you think we tell Lies. We have told you the greatest of our Wants and are in hopes you will not forget us and leave us to be cutt off by our Enemies. Pray send all our People that lives amongst you to our Nation for we think they must be troublesome to you and would be of great Service to us for we are now reduced to small a Number we can hardly spare Men to guard our Traders to and from our Nation. We have no more to say at Present but hope you will pity us for we are very poor.

Tuska Chickamobbey	Pia Mattaha
Pia Hagego	Tanna Puskemingo
Tiske Omastabey	War King
Mucklassau Mingo	Pia Haggo
Mingo Opya	Funne Mingo Mas Habey

Source: William L. McDowell, ed., *Documents Relating to Indian Affairs, 1754–1765* (Columbia: University of South Carolina Department of Archives and History, 1970).

44. Robert Rogers, Journal Account on the Destruction of St. Francis, September 1759 [Excerpt]

Introduction

Rogers' Rangers was the name given to the units of British rangers raised by Major Robert Rogers (1731–1795). A New Hampshire–born frontiersman, Rogers recruited and trained the ranger units that operated behind enemy lines during the French and Indian War (1754–1763). He commanded one of the units and served in New York, the Great Lakes region, and Canada. New York was a major battleground in this war. Because few roads existed at this time, the combatants maneuvered by canoes and bateaux along lakes and rivers. French and Indian invasion forces traveled from Canada into New York on Lake Champlain, Lake George, and the Hudson River. Between 1755 and 1760, battles took place along this corridor as well as along the Mohawk River and the shores of Lake Ontario. These excerpts from Rogers's journal include his secret orders, from General Jeffrey Amherst, to destroy the Abenaki Indian village at St. Francis as well as his report to the general on the results of the predawn surprise attack. St. Francis in Quebec served as a base for Indian attacks into New England. While noting that the Indians had killed many women and children, Amherst ordered Rogers to refrain from doing the same. In fact, Rogers's men killed mostly women and children as they fled the burning village. Rogers claimed to have killed 200, but the actual number was closer to 30. Rogers joined the British forces during the American Revolutionary War.

Primary Source

* "You are this night to set out with the detachment as ordered yesterday, viz. of 200 men, which you will take under your command, and proceed to Misisquey Bay, from whence you will march and attack the enemy's settlements on the south-side of the river St. Lawrence, in such a manner as you shall judge most effectual to disgrace the enemy, and for the success and honour of his Majesty's arms.

"Remember the barbarities that have been committed by the enemy's Indian scoundrels on every occasion, where they had an opportunity of shewing their infamous cruelties on the King's subjects, which they have done without mercy. Take your revenge, but don't forget that tho' those villains have dastardly and promiscuously murdered the women and children of all ages, it is my orders that no women or children are killed or hurt.

"When you have executed your intended service, you will return with your detachment to camp, or to join me wherever the army may be.

Yours, &c.

* That this expedition might be carried on with the utmost secresy after the plan of it was concerted the day before my march, it was put into public orders, that I was to march a different way, at the same time I had private instructions to proceed directly to St. Francis.—*Note by the Author.*

Camp at Crown Point,
Jeff Amherst
Sept. 13, 1759.

To Major Rogers.

In pursuance of the above orders, I set out the same evening with a detachment; and as to the particulars of my proceedings, and the great difficulties we met with in effecting our design, the reader is referred to the letter I wrote to General Amherst upon my return, and the remarks following it.

Copy of my letter to the General upon my return from St. Francis.

"SIR,

"The twenty-second day after my departure from Crown Point, I came in sight of the Indian town St. Francis in the evening, which I discovered from a tree that I climbed, at about three miles distance. Here I halted my party, which now consisted of 142 men, officers included, being reduced to that number by the unhappy accident which befel Capt. Williams*, and several since tiring, whom I was obliged to send back. At eight o'clock this evening I left the detachment, and took with me Lieut. Turner, and Ensign Avery, and went to reconnoitre the town, which I did to my satisfaction, and I found the Indians in a high frolic or dance. I returned to my party at two o'clock, and at three marched it to within five hundred yards of the town, where I lightened the men of their packs, and formed them for the attack.

"At half an hour before sun-rise I surprised the town when they were all fast asleep, on the right, left, and center, which was done with so much alacrity by both the officers and men, that the enemy had not time to recover themselves, or take arms for their own defence, till they were chiefly destroyed, except some few of them who took to the water. About forty of my people pursued them, who destroyed such as attempted to make their escape that way, and sunk both them and their boats. A little after sun-rise I set fire to all their houses, except three, in which there was corn, that I reserved for the use of the party.

"The fire consumed many of the Indians who had concealed themselves in the cellars and lofts of their houses. About seven o'clock in the morning the affair was completely over, in which time we had killed at least two hundred Indians, and taken twenty of their women and children prisoners,* fifteen of whom I let go their own way, and five I brought with me, viz. two Indian boys, and three Indian girls."

[. . .]

This nation of Indians was notoriously attached to the French, and had for near a century past harrassed the frontiers of New England, killing people of all ages and sexes in a most barbarous manner, at a time when they did not in the least expect them; and to my own knowledge, in six years' time, carried into captivity, and killed, on the before mentioned frontiers, 400 persons. We found in the town hanging on poles over their doors, &c., about 600 scalps, mostly English.

* Capt. Williams of the Royal Regiment was, the fifth day of our march accidentally burnt with gun-powder, and several men hurt, which, together with some sick, returned back to Crown Point, to the number of forty, under tbe care of Capt. Williams, who returned with great reluctance.—*Note by the Author.*

Source: Robert Rogers, *Journals of Major Robert Rogers* (Albany, NY: Joel Munsell's Sons, 1883), 140–142, 147.

45. James Glen, Account of the Role of Indians in the Rivalry Involving France, Spain, and England, 1761

Introduction

James Glen, governor of South Carolina, understood the importance of colonial relations with the neighboring Indians during and after the French and Indian War (1754–1763) as well as the importance of trade in maintaining good relations. In this excerpt he reports on the continuing rivalry between the French traders remaining in Louisiana and the English traders of the southern colonies in attempting to secure the loyalty of the Cherokees, Choctaws, Chickasaws, Creeks, and Catawbas. Glen identifies the Choctaws as longtime allies of the French and asserts that they have switched their loyalty to the English. He also reports on how the number of fighting men among the Chickasaws, who had been at war with the French and the Choctaws almost continuously since the mid-1600s, has been depleted. The French had tried to win the Chickasaws over to the French side but then had changed course and encouraged the Choctaws to exterminate them. Glen describes a major purchase of land from the Cherokees, who had ceded it as a condition of peace after having fought against the English during the war.

Primary Source

The Situation, Strength, and Connections of the several Nations of Neighbouring Indians; the Hostilities they have committed on British Subjects, at the Instigation of the French, and lately upon those Instigators themselves; some Particulars relating to the French Forts, Forces and Proceedings in Louisiana and Mississippi.

The concerns of this Country are so closely connected and interwoven with Indian Affairs, and not only a great branch of our trade, but even the Safety of this Province, do so much depend upon our continuing in Friendship with the Indians, that I thought it highly necessary to gain all the knowledge I could of them; and I hope that the accounts which I have from time to time transmitted of Indian affairs will shew, that I am pretty well acquainted with the subject.

However I think it expedient upon the present Occasion to give a general Account of the several Tribes and Nations of Indians with whom the Inhabitants of this Province are or may be connected in Interest: which is the more necessary as all we have to apprehend from the French in this part of the world, will much more depend upon the Indians than upon any Strength of their own; for that is so inconsiderable in itself, and so far distant from us that without Indian Assistance, it cannot if exerted, do us much harm.

There are among our Settlements several small Tribes of Indians, consisting only of some few families each: but those Tribes of Indians which we, on account of their being numerous and having lands of their own, call Nations are all of them situated on the Western Side of this Province, and at various distances as I have already mentioned.

The Catawbaw Nation of Indians hath about Three hundred Fighting Men; brave fellows as any on the Continent of America and our firm friends; their Country is about two hundred miles from Charles-Town.

The Cherokees live at the distance of about Three hundred miles from Charles-Town, though indeed their hunting grounds stretch much nearer to us. They have about Three thousand Gun men, and are in Alliance with this Government.

I lately made a considerable purchase from that Indian Nation, of some of those hunting grounds, which are now become the property of the British Crown, at the Charge of this Province: I had the deeds of conveyance formally executed in their own Country, by their head men, in the name of the whole people, and with their universal approbation and good will.

They inhabit a Tract of Country about Two hundred miles in Extent, and form a good barrier, which is naturally strengthened by a Country hilly and mountainous, but said to be interspersed with pleasant and fruitful vallies, and watered by many limpid and wholsome Brooks and rivulets, which run among the Hills, and give those real pleasures which we in the lower Lands have only in imagination.

The Creek Indians are situated about Five hundred miles from Charles-Town; their number of fighting men is about two thousand five hundred, and they are in Friendship with us.

The Chickesaws live at the distance of near Eight hundred miles from Charles-Town: they have bravely stood their ground against the repeated attacks of the French and their Indians: but are now reduced to Two or Three hundred men.

The Chactaw Nation of Indians is situated at a somewhat greater distance from us, and have till within this year or two been in the Interest of the French, by whom they were reckoned to be the most numerous of any nation of Indians in America, and said to consist of many Thousand Men.

The people of most experience in the affairs of this Country, have always dreaded a French war; from an apprehension that an Indian war would be the consequence of it; for which reasons, I have ever since the first breaking out of the war with France, redoubled my Attention to Indian Affairs: and I hope, not without Success.

For notwithstanding all the intrigues of the French, they have not been able to get the least footing among our Nations of Indians; as very plainly appears by those Nations still continuing to give fresh proofs of their attachment to us: and I have had the happiness to bring over and fix the Friendship of the Chactaw Nation of Indians in the British Interest.

This powerful Engine, which the French for many years past, played against us and our Indians, even in times of Peace, is now happily turned against themselves, and I believe they feel the force of it.

For according to last accounts, which I have received from thence, by the Captain of a Sloop that touched at Mobile about two months ago, the Chactaw Indians had driven into the Town of Mobile all the French Planters who were settled either upon the river bearing the same name or in the Neighbouring Country, and there kept them in a manner besieged, so that a few of the French

who ventured out of the Town to hunt up Cattle were immediately scalped.

Monsieur Vaudreuille the Governor of Louisiana was then in Mobile endeavoring to support his people, and trying to recover the friendship of those Indians. At the same time there were some head men with about Twenty of their People in Charles-Town.

I have been the fuller in my Relation of this matter, because I humbly conceive it to be a very delicate Affair, for these Chactaw Indians, have formerly and even so lately as I have been in this Province, at the instigation of the French and assisted and headed by them, in time of Peace, murdered our Traders in their Way to the Chickesaw Indians, and Robbed them of their goods: but I hope the French Governors will never have it in their power to charge us with such unfair Practises.

I shall be particularly cautious of doing any thing inconsistent with the peace so lately concluded: but I think it incumbent on me to say, that it will be impossible to retain those Indians, or any other, in his Majesty's interest unless we continue to trade with them.

And since war and hunting are the business of the lives, both Arms and Ammunition as well as Cloaths other necessaries, are the goods for which there is the greatest demand among them, I therefore hope to receive instructions in this particular, as a rule of my conduct.

There are a pretty many Indians among the Kays, about the cape of Florida, who might be easily secured to the British Interest: but as they have little communication with any others on the main Land, and have not any goods to trade for, they could not be of any advantage either in peace or war.

There are also a few Yamasees, about twenty men near St. Augustine: and these are all the Indians in this part of the world that are in the Interest of the Crown of Spain.

The French have the Friendship of some few of the Creek Indians, such as inhabit near the Holbama Fort: and some of the Chactaw Indians have not as yet declared against them: They have also some tribes upon Mississippi River, and Ouabash, and in other parts: but most of these and all other Indians whatsoever, inhabit above a Thousand miles from Charles-Town; and yet it may be proper to give attention even to what happens among those who are so far from us; for to an Indian, a thousand miles is as one mile their Provisions being in the Woods, and they are never out of the way: they are slow, saying the Sun will rise again to-morrow, but they are steddy.

We have little intercourse with the French; but unless there have been alterations lately, the Accounts I have formerly sent may be relied on, there are not above six hundred men (Soldiers) in what they call Louisiana, and those thinly spread over a widely extended Country: some at New Orleans some at Mobile, and some as far up as the Ilinois.

They had a Fort at the Mouth of the Mississippi river called the Balise, but they found it was not of any service, and therefore they have built another farther up, where it commands the passage: their Forts Holbama, Chactawhatche, Notche, Notchitosh, and another on Ouabash are all inconsiderable stockaded Forts, garrisoned by 40 and some by only 20 men each. If ever the French settlements on the Missippi grow great, they may have pernicious effects upon South Carolina, because they produce the same sorts of Commodities as are produced there, viz., Rice and Indigo: but hitherto, the only Inconvenience that I know of, is, their attempting to withdraw our Indians from us, and attacking those who are most attached to our interest.

I beg Leave to assure you that I shall never do any thing inconsistent with that good faith which is the basis of all his Majesty's Measures, but it is easy for me at present to divert the French in their own way, and to find them business for double the number of men they have in that Country.

However, this, and even the Tranquility of South Carolina will depend upon preserving our Interest with the Indians, which it will be very difficult to do, unless the presents are continued to them, and those Forts built which I have formerly proposed, or at least, one of them, and that to be in the Country of the Cherokees. . . .

Source: Plowden Charles Jennett Weston, ed., *Documents Connected with the History of South Carolina* (London: South Carolina Historical Society, 1856), 94–98.

46. Henry Timberlake, *The Memoirs of Lieut. Henry Timberlake,* 1765 [Excerpts]

Introduction

Decades of British-Cherokee trade and friendship came to an end as British settlers moved westward and encroached on Cherokee land. In 1758 the Cherokees switched to the French side in the French and Indian War (1754–1763) and began raiding frontier settlers. British troops fought a series of battles with the Cherokees. Both sides committed atrocities and slaughtered prisoners. After the French and Indian War ended, the Cherokees could no longer obtain ammunition from the French. In 1761 a force of Scottish Highlanders destroyed some 15 Cherokee towns and their food supplies. The Cherokees, facing starvation, came to a British fort and sued for peace. Colonel Adam Stephen forged an agreement with them on November 19, 1761. Henry Timberlake, a soldier serving under Stephen, volunteered to conduct the Cherokee delegation home to finalize the articles of peace. In 1762 at their request, Timberlake then accompanied three Cherokee chiefs to London to meet the king. In his memoirs, excerpted here, Timberlake describes the peace-making ceremony and provides translations of Chief Ostenaco's speech and a Cherokee war song.

The treaty gave the Cherokees land in the mountains of the western Carolinas and eastern Tennessee. White settlers disregarded the treaty and soon began occupying the Cherokees' remaining territory.

Primary Source

After smoaking and talking some time, I delivered a letter from Colonel Stephen, and another from Captain M'Neil, with some presents from each, which were gratefully accepted by Ostenaco and his consort. He gave me a general invitation to his house, while I resided in the country; and my companions found no difficulty in getting the same entertainment, among an hospitable, tho' savage people, who always pay a great regard to any one taken notice of by their chiefs.

Some days after, the headmen of each town were assembled in the town-house of Chote, the metropolis of the country, to hear the articles of peace read, whither the interpreter and I accompanied Ostenaco.

The town-house, in which are transacted all public business and diversions, is raised with wood, and covered over with earth, and has all the appearance of a small mountain at a little distance. It is built in the form of a sugar loaf, and large enough to contain 500 persons, but extremely dark, having, besides the door, which is so narrow that but one at a time can pass, and that after much winding and turning, but one small aperture to let the smoak out, which is so ill contrived, that most of it settles in the roof of the house. Within it has the appearance of an ancient amphitheatre, the seats being raised one above another, leaving an area in the middle, in the center of which stands the fire; the seats of the head warriors are nearest it.

They all seemed highly satisfied with the articles. The peace-pipe was smoaked, and Ostenaco made an harangue to the following effect:

"The bloody tommahawke, so long lifted against our brethren the English, must now be buried deep, deep in the ground, never to be raised again; and whoever shall act contrary to any of these articles, must expect a punishment equal to his offence. Should a strict observance of them be neglected, a war must necessarily follow, and a second peace may not be so easily obtained. I therefore once more recommend to you, to take particular care of your behaviour towards the English, whom we must now look upon as ourselves; they have the French and Spaniards to fight, and we enough of our own colour, without medling with either nation. I desire likewise, that the white warrior, who has ventured himself here with us, may be well used and respected by all, wherever he goes amongst us."

[. . .]

A Translation of the War-Song

WHERE'ER the earth's enlighten'd by the sun,
Moon shines by night, grass grows, or waters run,
Be't known that we are going, like men, afar,
In hostile fields to wage destructive war;
Like men we go, to meet our country's foes,
Who, woman-like, shall fly our dreaded blows;
Yes, as a woman, who beholds a snake,
In gaudy horror, glisten thro' the brake,
Starts trembling back, and stares with wild surprize,
Or pale thro' fear, unconscious, panting, flies.

Just so these foes, more tim'rous than the hind,
Shall leave their arms and only cloaths behind;
Pinch'd by each blast, by ev'ry thicket torn,
Run back to their own nation, now its scorn:
Or in the winter, when the barren wood
Denies their gnawing entrails nature's food,
Let them sit down, from friends and country far,
And wish, with tears, they ne'er had come to war.

We'll leave our clubs, dew'd with their country show'rs,
And, if they dare to bring them back to our's,
Their painted scalps shall be a step to fame,
And grace our won and glorious country's name.
Or if we warriors spare the yielding foe,
Torments at home the wretch must undergo.
But when we go, who knows which shall return,
When growing dangers rise with each new morn?
Farewel, ye little ones, yet tender wives,
For you alone we would conserve our lives!
But cease to mourn, 'tis unavailing pain,
If not fore-doom'd, we soon shall meet again.
But, O ye friends! In case your comrades fall,
Think that on you our deaths for vengeance call;
With uprais'd tommahawkes pursue our blood,
And stain, with hostile streams, the conscious wood,
That pointing enemies may never tell
The boasted place where we, their victims, fell.

Source: Henry Timberlake, *The Memoirs of Lieut. Henry Timberlake, (Who Accompanied the Three Cherokee Indians to England in the Year 1762)* . . . (London: Printed for the Author, 1765), 31–33, 56–58.

47. Treaty of Paris, 1763

Introduction

The French and Indian War (1754–1763), known as the Seven Years' War in Europe, began in America in 1754. Active British-French combat in North America ended with the French surrender of Canada in 1760, although frontier battles with Indians continued in the South. However, a state of war between Britain and France persisted until 1763. Signed on February 10, 1763, by representatives from Great Britain, France, and Spain, the Treaty of Paris formally ended the conflict. The British emerged from the war victorious and, with substantial help from their American colonists, swept the French from the North American continent. Spain lost Cuba and Florida to Britain but, in a secret treaty with France in 1762, received the territory of Louisiana west of the Mississippi River. Britain also gained colonial possessions in Africa and the West Indies, establishing Britain as the world's leading imperial power. The territorial claims established by this treaty endured for less than 20 years. France was destined to return to North America as an American ally during the American Revolutionary War (1775–1783). Great Britain, in losing the Revolutionary War, ultimately lost control of the vast territory west of the Allegheny Mountains. In 1800 France reacquired the Louisiana Territory from Spain and sold it to the United States three years later. Those Indians who chose to remain loyal to the losing side in these European conflicts suffered for their error at the hands of the victors.

Primary Source

The definitive Treaty of Peace and Friendship between his Britannick Majesty, *the* Most Christian King, *and the* King *of* Spain. *Concluded at* Paris *the 10th day of* February, 1763. To *which the* King *of* Portugal *acceded on the same day.* (Printed from the Copy.)

In the Name of the Most Holy and Undivided Trinity, Father, Son, and Holy Ghost. So be it.

Be it known to all those whom it shall, or may, in any manner, belong,

It has pleased the Most High to diffuse the spirit of union and concord among the Princes, whose divisions had spread troubles in the four parts of the world, and to inspire them with the inclination to cause the comforts of peace to succeed to the misfortunes of a long and bloody war, which having arisen between England and France during the reign of the Most Serene and Most Potent Prince, George the Second, by the grace of God, King of Great Britain, of glorious memory, continued under the reign of the Most Serene and Most Potent Prince, George the Third, his successor, and, in its progress, communicated itself to Spain and Portugal: Consequently, the Most Serene and Most Potent Prince, George the Third, by the grace of God, King of Great Britain, France, and Ireland, Duke of Brunswick and Lunenbourg, Arch Treasurer and Elector of the Holy Roman Empire; the Most Serene and Most Potent Prince, Lewis the Fifteenth, by the grace of God, Most Christian King; and the Most Serene and Most Potent Prince, Charles the Third, by the grace of God, King of Spain and of the Indies, after having laid the foundations of peace in the preliminaries signed at Fontainebleau the third of November last; and the Most Serene and Most Potent Prince, Don

Joseph the First, by the grace of God, King of Portugal and of the Algarves, after having acceded thereto, determined to compleat, without delay, this great and important work. For this purpose, the high contracting parties have named and appointed their respective Ambassadors Extraordinary and Ministers Plenipotentiary, viz. his Sacred Majesty the King of Great Britain, the Most Illustrious and Most Excellent Lord, John Duke and Earl of Bedford, Marquis of Tavistock, &c. his Minister of State, Lieutenant General of his Armies, Keeper of his Privy Seal, Knight of the Most Noble Order of the Garter, and his Ambassador Extraordinary and Minister Plenipotentiary to his Most Christian Majesty; his Sacred Majesty the Most Christian King, the Most Illustrious and Most Excellent Lord, Cæsar Gabriel de Choiseul, Duke of Praslin, Peer of France, Knight of his Orders, Lieutenant General of his Armies and of the province of Britanny, Counsellor of all his Counsils, and Minister and Secretary of State, and of his Commands and Finances: his Sacred Majesty the Catholick King, the Most Illustrious and Most Excellent Lord, Don Jerome Grimaldi, Marquis de Grimaldi, Knight of the Most Christian King's Orders, Gentleman of his Catholick Majesty's Bedchamber in Employment, and his Ambassador Extraordinary to his Most Christian Majesty; his Sacred Majesty the Most Faithful King, the Most Illustrious and Most Excellent Lord, Martin de Mello and Castro, Knight professed of the Order of Christ, of his Most Faithful Majesty's Council, and his Ambassador and Minister Plenipotentiary to his Most Christian Majesty.

Who, after having duly communicated to each other their full powers, in good form, copies whereof are transcribed at the end of the present treaty of peace, have agreed upon the articles, the tenor of which is as follows:

Article I. There shall be a Christian, universal, and perpetual peace, as well by sea as by land, and a sincere and constant friendship shall be re established between their Britannick, Most Christian, Catholick, and Most Faithful Majesties, and between their heirs and successors, kingdoms, dominions, provinces, countries, subjects, and vassals, of what quality or condition soever they be, without exception of places or of persons: So that the high contracting parties shall give the greatest attention to maintain between themselves and their said dominions and subjects this reciprocal friendship and correspondence, without permitting, on either side, any kind of hostilities, by sea or by land, to be committed from henceforth, for any cause, or under any pretence whatsoever, and every thing shall be carefully avoided which might hereafter prejudice the union happily re-established, applying themselves, on the contrary, on every occasion, to procure for each other whatever may contribute to their mutual glory, interests, and advantages, without giving any assistance or protection, directly or indirectly, to those who would cause any prejudice to either of the high contracting parties: there shall be a general oblivion of every thing that may have been done or

committed before or since the commencement of the war which is just ended.

II. The treaties of Westphalia of 1648; those of Madrid between the Crowns of Great Britain and Spain of 1661, and 1670; the treaties of peace of Nimeguen of 1678, and 1679; of Ryswick of 1697; those of peace and of commerce of Utrecht of 1713; that of Baden of 1714; the treaty of the triple alliance of the Hague of 1717; that of the quadruple alliance of London of 1178; the treaty of peace of Vienna of 1738; the definitive treaty of Aix la Chapelle of 1748; and that of Madrid, between the Crowns of Great Britain and Spain of 1750: as well as the treaties between the Crowns of Spain and Portugal of the 13th of February, 1668; of the 6th of February, 1715; and of the 12th of February, 1761; and that of the 11th of April, 1713, between France and Portugal with the guaranties of Great Britain, serve as a basis and foundation to the peace, and to the present treaty: and for this purpose they are all renewed and confirmed in the best form, as well as all the general, which subsisted between the high contracting parties before the war, as if they were inserted here word for word, so that they are to be exactly observed, for the future, in their whole tenor, and religiously executed on all sides, in all their points, which shall not be derogated from by the present treaty, notwithstanding all that may have been stipulated to the contrary by any of the high contracting parties: and all the said parties declare, that they will not suffer any privilege, favour, or indulgence to subsist, contrary to the treaties above confirmed, except what shall have been agreed and stipulated by the present treaty.

III. All the prisoners made, on all sides, as well by land as by sea, and the hostages carried away or given during the war, and to this day, shall be restored, without ransom, six weeks, at least, to be computed from the day of the exchange of the ratification of the present treaty, each crown respectively paying the advances which shall have been made for the subsistance and maintenance of their prisoners by the Sovereign of the country where they shall have been detained, according to the attested receipts and estimates and other authentic vouchers which shall be furnished on one side and the other. And securities shall be reciprocally given for the payment of the debts which the prisoners shall have contracted in the countries where they have been detained until their entire liberty. And all the ships of war and merchant vessels Which shall have been taken since the expiration of the terms agreed upon for the cessation of hostilities by sea shall likewise be restored, *bonâ fide*, with all their crews and cargoes: and the execution of this article shall be proceeded upon immediately after the exchange of the ratifications of this treaty.

IV. His Most Christian Majesty renounces all pretensions which he has heretofore formed or might have formed to Nova Scotia or Acadia in all its parts, and guaranties the whole of it, and with all its dependencies, to the King of Great Britain: Moreover, his Most Christian Majesty cedes and guaranties to his said Britannick Majesty, in full right, Canada, with all its dependencies, as well as the island of Cape Breton, and all the other islands and coasts in the gulph and river of St. Lawrence, and in general, every thing that depends on the said countries, lands, islands, and coasts, with the sovereignty, property, possession, and all rights acquired by treaty, or otherwise, which the Most Christian King and the Crown of France have had till now over the said countries, lands, islands, places, coasts, and their inhabitants, so that the Most Christian King cedes and makes over the whole to the said King, and to the Crown of Great Britain, and that in the most ample manner and form, without restriction, and without any liberty to depart from the said cession and guaranty under any pretence, or to disturb Great Britain in the possessions above mentioned. His Britannick Majesty, on his side, agrees to grant the liberty of the Catholick religion to the inhabitants of Canada: he will, in consequence, give the most precise and most effectual orders, that his new Roman Catholic subjects may profess the worship of their religion according to the rites of the Romish church, as far as the laws of Great Britain permit. His Britannick Majesty farther agrees, that the French inhabitants, or others who had been subjects of the Most Christian King in Canada, may retire with all safety and freedom wherever they shall think proper, and may sell their estates, provided it be to the subjects of his Britannick Majesty, and bring away their effects as well as their persons, without being restrained in their emigration, under any pretence whatsoever, except that of debts or of criminal prosecutions: The term limited for this emigration shall be fixed to the space of eighteen months, to be computed from the day of the exchange of the ratification of the present treaty.

V. The subjects of France shall have the liberty of fishing and drying on a part of the coasts of the island of Newfoundland, such as it is specified in the XIIIth article of the treaty of Utrecht; which article is renewed and confirmed by the present treaty, (except what relates to the island of Cape Breton, as well as to the other islands and coasts in the mouth and in the gulph of St. Lawrence:) And his Britannick Majesty consents to leave to the subjects of the Most Christian King the liberty of fishing in the gulph of St. Lawrence, on condition that the subjects of France do not exercise the said fishery but at the distance of three leagues from all the coasts belonging to Great Britain, as well those of the continent as those of the islands situated in the said gulph of St. Lawrence. And as to what relates to the fishery on the coasts of the island of Cape Breton, out of the said gulph, the subjects of the Most Christian King shall not be permitted to exercise the said fishery but at the distance of fifteen leagues from the coasts of the island of Cape Breton; and the fishery on the coasts of Nova Scotia or Acadia, and every where else out of the said gulph, shall remain on the foot of former treaties.

VI. The King of Great Britain cedes the islands of St. Pierre and Macquelon, in full right, to his Most Christian Majesty, to serve as a shelter to the French fishermen; and his said Most Christian Majesty engages not to fortify the said islands; to erect no buildings upon them but merely for the conveniency of the fishery; and to keep upon them a guard of fifty men only for the police.

VII. In order to re-establish peace on solid and durable foundations, and to remove for ever all subject of dispute with regard to the limits of the British and French territories on the continent of America; it is agreed, that, for the future, the confines between the dominions of his Britannick Majesty and those of his Most Christian Majesty, in that part of the world, shall be fixed irrevocably by a line drawn along the middle of the River Mississippi, from its source to the river Iberville, and from thence, by a line drawn along the middle of this river, and the lakes Maurepas and Pontchartrain to the sea; and for this purpose, the Most Christian King cedes in full right, and guaranties to his Britannick Majesty the river and port of the Mobile, and every thing which he possesses, or ought to possess, on the left side of the river Mississippi, except the town of New Orleans and the island in which it is situated, which shall remain to France, provided that the navigation of the river Mississippi shall be equally free, as well to the subjects of Great Britain as to those of France, in its whole breadth and length, from its source to the sea, and expressly that part which is between the said island of New Orleans and the right bank of that river, as well as the passage both in and out of its mouth: It is farther stipulated, that the vessels belonging to the subjects of either nation shall not be stopped, visited, or subjected to the payment of any duty whatsoever. The stipulations inserted in the IVth article, in favour of the inhabitants of Canada shall also take place with regard to the inhabitants of the countries ceded by this article.

VIII. The King of Great Britain shall restore to France the islands of Guadeloupe, of Mariegalante, of Desirade, of Martinico, and of Belleisle; and the fortresses of these islands shall be restored in the same condition they were in when they were conquered by the British arms, provided that his Britannick Majesty's subjects, who shall have settled in the said islands, or those who shall have any commercial affairs to settle there or in other places restored to France by the present treaty, shall have liberty to sell their lands and their estates, to settle their affairs, to recover their debts, and to bring away their effects as well as their persons, on board vessels, which they shall be permitted to send to the said islands and other places restored as above, and which shall serve for this use only, without being restrained on account of their religion, or under any other pretence whatsoever, except that of debts or of criminal prosecutions: and for this purpose, the term of eighteen months is allowed to his Britannick Majesty's subjects, to be computed from the day of the exchange of the ratifications of the present treaty; but, as the liberty granted to his Britannick Majesty's subjects, to bring away their persons and their effects, in vessels of their nation, may be liable to abuses if precautions were not taken to prevent them; it has been expressly agreed between his Britannick Majesty and his Most Christian Majesty, that the number of English vessels which have leave to go to the said islands and places restored to France, shall be limited, as well as the number of tons of each one; that they shall go in ballast; shall set sail at a fixed time; and shall make one voyage only; all the effects belonging to the English being to be embarked at the same time. It has been farther agreed, that his Most Christian Majesty shall cause the necessary passports to be given to the said vessels; that, for the greater security, it shall be allowed to place two French clerks or guards in each of the said vessels, which shall be visited in the landing places and ports of the said islands and places restored to France, and that the merchandize which shall be found therein shall be confiscated.

IX. The Most Christian King cedes and guaranties to his Britannick Majesty, in full right, the islands of Grenada, and the Grenadines, with the same stipulations in favour of the inhabitants of this colony, inserted in the IVth article for those of Canada: And the partition of the islands called neutral, is agreed and fixed, so that those of St. Vincent, Dominico, and Tobago, shall remain in full right to Great Britain, and that of St. Lucia shall be delivered to France, to enjoy the same likewise in full right, and the high contracting parties guaranty the partition so stipulated.

X. His Britannick Majesty shall restore to France the island of Goree in the condition it was in when conquered: and his Most Christian Majesty cedes, in full right, and guaranties to the King of Great Britain the river Senegal, with the forts and factories of St. Lewis, Podor, and Galam, and with all the rights and dependencies of the said river Senegal.

XI. In the East Indies Great Britain shall restore to France, in the condition they are now in, the different factories which that Crown possessed, as well as on the coast of Coromandel and Orixa as on that of Malabar, as also in Bengal, at the beginning of the year 1749. And his Most Christian Majesty renounces all pretension to the acquisitions which he has made on the coast of Coromandel and Orixa since the said beginning of the year 1749. His Most Christian Majesty shall restore, on his side, all that he may have conquered from Great Britain in the East Indies during the present war; and will expressly cause Nattal and Tapanoully, in the island of Sumatra, to be restored; he engages farther, not to erect fortifications, or to keep troops in any part of the dominions of the Subah of Bengal. And in order to preserve future peace on the coast of Coromandel and Orixa, the English and French shall acknowledge Mahomet Ally Khan for lawful Nabob of the Carnatick, and Salabat Jing for lawful Subah of the Decan; and both parties shall renounce all demands and pretensions of satisfaction with which they might charge each other, or their Indian allies, for the depredations or pillage committed on the one side or on the other during the war.

XII. The island of Minorca shall be restored to his Britannick Majesty, as well as Fort St. Philip, in the same condition they were in when conquered by the arms of the Most Christian King; and with the artillery which was there when the said island and the said fort were taken.

XIII. The town and port of Dunkirk shall be put into the state fixed by the last treaty of Aix la Chapelle, and by former treaties. The Cunette shall be destroyed immediately after the exchange of the ratifications of the present treaty, as well as the forts and batteries which defend the entrance on the side of the sea; and provision shall be made at the same time for the wholesomeness of the air, and for the health of the inhabitants, by some other means, to the satisfaction of the King of Great Britain.

XIV. France shall restore all the countries belonging to the Electorate of Hanover, to the Landgrave of Hesse, to the Duke of Brunswick, and to the Count of La Lippe Buckebourg, which are or shall be occupied by his Most Christian Majesty's arms: the fortresses of these different countries shall be restored in the same condition they were in when conquered by the French arms; and the pieces of artillery, which shall have been carried elsewhere, shall be replaced by the same number, of the same bore, weight and metal.

XV. In case the stipulations contained in the XIIIth article of the preliminaries should not be compleated at the time of the signature of the present treaty, as well with regard to the evacuations to be made by the armies of France of the fortresses of Cleves, Wezel, Guelders, and of all the countries belonging to the King of Prussia, as with regard to the evacuations to be made by the British and French armies of the countries which they occupy in Westphalia, Lower Saxony, on the Lower Rhine, the Upper Rhine, and in all the empire; and to the retreat of the troops into the dominions of their respective Sovereigns: their Britannick and Most Christian Majesties promise to proceed, *bonâ fide,* with all the dispatch the case will permit of to the said evacuations, the entire completion whereof they stipulate before the 15th of March next, or sooner if it can be done; and their Britannick and Most Christian Majesties farther engage and promise to each other, not to furnish any succours of any kind to their respective allies who shall continue engaged in the war in Germany.

XVI. The decision of the prizes made in time of peace by the subjects of Great Britain, on the Spaniards, shall be referred to the Courts of Justice of the Admiralty of Great Britain, conformably to the rules established among all nations, so that the validity of the said prizes, between the British and Spanish nations, shall be decided and judged, according to the law of nations, and according to treaties, in the Courts of Justice of the nation who shall have made the capture.

XVII. His Britannick Majesty shall cause to be demolished all the fortifications which his subjects shall have erected in the bay of Honduras, and other places of the territory of Spain in that part of the world, four months after the ratification of the present treaty; and his Catholick Majesty shall not permit his Britannick Majesty's subjects, or their workmen, to be disturbed or molested under any pretence whatsoever in the said places, in their occupation of cutting, loading, and carrying away log-wood; and for this purpose, they may build, without hindrance, and occupy, without interruption, the houses and magazines necessary for them, for their families, and for their effects; and his Catholick Majesty assures to them, by this article, the full enjoyment of those advantages and powers on the Spanish coasts and territories, as above stipulated, immediately after the ratification of the present treaty.

XVIII. His Catholick Majesty desists, as well for himself as for his successors, from all pretension which he may have formed in favour of the Guipuscoans, and other his subjects, to the right of fishing in the neighbourhood of the island of Newfoundland.

XIX. The King of Great Britain shall restore to Spain all the territory which he has conquered in the island of Cuba, with the fortress of the Havannah; and this fortress, as well as all the other fortresses of the said island, shall be restored in the same condition they were in when conquered by his Britannick Majesty's arms, provided that his Britannick Majesty's subjects who shall have settled in the said island, restored to Spain by the present treaty, or those who shall have any commercial affairs to settle there, shall have liberty to sell their lands and their estates, to settle their affairs, recover their debts, and to bring away their effects, as well as their persons, on board vessels which they shall be permitted to send to the said island restored as above, and which shall serve for that use only, without being restrained on account of their religion, or under any other pretence whatsoever, except that of debts or of criminal prosecutions: And for this purpose, the term of eighteen months is allowed to his Britannick Majesty's subjects, to be computed from the day of the exchange of the ratifications of the present treaty: but as the liberty granted to his Britannick Majesty's subjects, to bring away their persons and their effects, in vessels of their nation, may be liable to abuses if precautions were not taken to prevent them; it has been expressly agreed between his Britannick Majesty and his Catholick Majesty, that the number of English vessels which shall have leave to go to the said island restored to Spain shall be limited, as well as the number of tons of each one; that they shall go in ballast; shall set sail at a fixed time; and shall make one voyage only; all the effects belonging to the English being to be embarked at the same time: it has been farther agreed, that his

Catholick Majesty shall cause the necessary passports to be given to the said vessels; that for the greater security, it shall be allowed to place two Spanish clerks or guards in each of the said vessels, which shall be visited in the landing places and ports of the said island restored to Spain, and that the merchandize which shall be found therein shall be confiscated.

XX. In consequence of the restitution stipulated in the preceding article, his Catholick Majesty cedes and guaranties, in full right, to his Britannick Majesty, Florida, with Fort St. Augustin, and the Bay of Pensacola, as well as all that Spain possesses on the continent of North America, to the East or to the South East of the river Mississippi. And, in general, every thing that depends on the said countries and lands, with the sovereignty, property, possession, and all rights, acquired by treaties or otherwise, which the Catholick King and the Crown of Spain have had till now over the said countries, lands, places, and their inhabitants; so that the Catholick King cedes and makes over the whole to the said King and to the Crown of Great Britain, and that in the most ample manner and form. His Britannick Majesty agrees, on his side, to grant to the inhabitants of the countries above ceded, the liberty of the Catholick religion; he will, consequently, give the most express and the most effectual orders that his new Roman Catholic subjects may profess the worship of their religion according to the rites of the Romish church, as far as the laws of Great Britain permit. His Britannick Majesty farther agrees, that the Spanish inhabitants, or others who had been subjects of the Catholick King in the said countries, may retire, with all safety and freedom, wherever they think proper; and may sell their estates, provided it be to his Britannick Majesty's subjects, and bring away their effects, as well as their persons.

Without being restrained in their emigration, under any pretence whatsoever, except that of debts, or of criminal prosecutions: the term limited for this emigration being fixed to the space of eighteen months, to be computed from the day of the exchange of the ratifications of the present treaty. It is moreover stipulated, that his Catholick Majesty shall have power to cause all the effects that may belong to him, to be brought away, whether it be artillery or other things.

XXI. The French and Spanish troops shall evacuate all the territories, lands, towns, places, and castles, of his Most faithful Majesty in Europe, without any reserve, which shall have been conquered by the armies of France and Spain, and shall restore them in the same condition they were in when conquered, with the same artillery and ammunition, which were found there: And with regard to the Portuguese Colonies in America, Africa, or in the East Indies, if any change shall have happened there, all things shall be restored on the same footing they were in, and conformably to the preceding treaties which subsisted between the Courts of France, Spain, and Portugal, before the present war.

XXII. All the papers, letters, documents, and archives, which were found in the countries, territories, towns and places that are restored, and those belonging to the countries ceded, shall be, respectively and *bonâ fide,* delivered, or furnished at the same time, if possible, that possession is taken, or, at latest, four months after the exchange of the ratifications of the present treaty, in whatever places the said papers or documents may be found.

XXIII. All the countries and territories, which may have been conquered, in whatsoever part of the world, by the arms of their Britannick and Most Faithful Majesties, as well as by those of their Most Christian and Catholick Majesties, which are not included in the present treaty, either under the title of cessions, or under the title of restitutions, shall be restored without difficulty, and without requiring any compensations.

XXIV. As it is necessary to assign a fixed epoch for the restitutions and the evacuations, to be made by each of the high contracting parties, it is agreed, that the British and French troops shall compleat, before the 15th of March next, all that shall remain to be executed of the XIIth and XIIIth articles of the preliminaries, signed the 3d day of November last, with regard to the evacuation to be made in the Empire, or elsewhere. The island of Belleisle shall be evacuated six weeks after the exchange of the ratifications of the present treaty, or sooner if it can be done. Guadeloupe, Desirade, Mariegalante Martinico, and St. Lucia, three months after the exchange of the ratifications of the present treaty, or sooner if it can be done. Great Britain shall likewise, at the end of three months after the exchange of the ratifications of the present treaty, or sooner if it can be done, enter into possession of the river and port of the Mobile, and of all that is to form the limits of the territory of Great Britain, on the side of the river Mississippi, as they are specified in the VIIth article. The island of Goree shall be evacuated by Great Britain, three months after the exchange of the ratifications of the present treaty; and the island of Minorca by France, at the same epoch, or sooner if it can be done: And according to the conditions of the VIth article, France shall likewise enter into possession of the islands of St Peter, and of Miquelon, at the end of three months after the exchange of the ratifications of the present treaty. The Factories in the East Indies shall be restored six months after the exchange of the ratifications of the present treaty, or sooner if it can be done. The fortress of the Havannah, with all that has been conquered in the island of Cuba, shall be restored three months after the exchange of the ratifications of the present treaty, or sooner if it can be done: And, at the same time, Great Britain shall enter into possession of the country ceded by Spain according to the XXth article. All the places and countries of his most Faithful Majesty, in Europe, shall be restored immediately after the exchange of the ratification of the present treaty: And the Portuguese colonies, which may have been conquered, shall be restored in the space of three months in the West Indies, and of six months in the East Indies, after the exchange of the ratifications of

the present treaty, or sooner if it can be done. All the fortresses, the restitution whereof is stipulated above, shall be restored with the artillery and ammunition, which were found there at the time of the conquest. In consequence whereof, the necessary orders shall be sent by each of the high contracting parties, with reciprocal passports for the ships that shall carry them, immediately after the exchange of the ratifications of the present treaty.

XXV. His Britannick Majesty, as Elector of Brunswick Lunenbourg, as well for himself as for his heirs and successors, and all the dominions and possessions of his said Majesty in Germany, are included and guarantied by the present treaty of peace.

XXVI. Their sacred Britannick, Most Christian, Catholick, and Most Faithful Majesties, promise to observe sincerely and *bonâ fide,* all the articles contained and settled in the present treaty; and they will not suffer the same to be infringed, directly or indirectly, by their respective subjects; and the said high contracting parties, generally and reciprocally, guaranty to each other all the stipulations of the present treaty.

XXVII. The solemn ratifications of the present treaty, expedited in good and due form, shall be exchanged in this city of Paris, between the high contracting parties, in the space of a month, or sooner if possible, to be computed from the day of the signature of the present treaty.

In witness whereof, we the underwritten their Ambassadors Extraordinary, and Ministers Plenipotentiary, have signed with our hand, in their name, and in virtue of our full powers, have signed the present definitive treaty, and have caused the seal of our arms to be put thereto. Done at Paris the tenth day of February, 1763.

Bedford, C.P.S. *Choiseul, Duc de Praslin. El Marq. de Grimaldi.*
   (L.S.) (L.S.) (L.S.)

Separate Articles

I. Some of the titles made use of by the contracting powers, either in the full powers, and other acts, during the course of the negociation, or in the preamble of the present treaty, not being generally acknowledged; it has been agreed, that no prejudice shall ever result therefrom to any of the said contracting parties, and that the titles, taken or omitted on either side, on occasion of the said negociation, and of the present treaty, shall not be cited or quoted as a precedent.

II. It has been agreed and determined, that the French language made use of in all the copies of the present treaty, shall not become an example which may be alledged, or made a precedent of, or prejudice, in any manner, any of the contracting powers; and that they shall conform themselves, for the future, to what has been observed, and ought to be observed, with regard to, and on the part of powers, who are used, and have a right, to give and to receive copies of like treaties in another language than French; the present treaty having still the same force and effect, as if the aforesaid custom had been therein observed.

III. Though the King of Portugal has not signed the present definitive treaty, their Britannick, Most Christian, and Catholick Majesties, acknowledge, nevertheless, that his Most Faithful Majesty is formally included therein as a contracting party, and as if he had expressly signed the said treaty: Consequently, their Britannick, Most Christian, and Catholick Majesties, respectively and conjointly, promise to his Most Faithful Majesty, in the most express and most binding manner, the execution of all and every the clauses, contained in the said treaty, on his act of accession.

The present Separate Articles shall have the same force as if they were inserted in the treaty.

In witness whereof, We the under-written Ambassadors Extraordinary, and Ministers Plenipotentiary of their Britannick, Most Christian and Catholick Majesties, have signed the present separate Articles, and have caused the seal of our arms to be put thereto.

Done at Paris, the 10th of February, 1763.

Bedford, C.P.S. *Choiseul, Duc de Praslin. El Marq. de Grimaldi.*
(L.S.) (L.S.) (L.S.)
His Britannick Majesty's full Power.

George R.

GEORGE the Third, by the grace of God, King of Great Britain, France and Ireland, Defender of the Faith, Duke of Brunswick and Lunenbourg, Arch-Treasurer, and Prince Elector of the Holy Roman Empire, &c. To all and singular to whom these presents shall come, greeting. Whereas, in order to perfect the peace between Us and our good Brother the Most Faithful King, on the one part, and our good Brothers the Most Christian and Catholick Kings, on the other, which has been happily begun by the Preliminary Articles already signed at Fontainebleau the third of this month; and to bring the same to the desired end, We have thought proper to invest some fit person with full authority, on our part; Know ye, that We, having most entire confidence in the fidelity, judgment, skill, and ability in managing affairs of the greatest consequence, of our right trusty, and right entirely beloved Cousin and Counsellor, John Duke and Earl of Bedford, Marquis of Tavistock, Baron Russel of Cheneys, Baron Russel of Thornhaugh, and Baron Howland of Streatham, Lieutenant-general of our forces, Keeper of our Privy Seal, Lieutenant and Custos Rotulorum of the counties of Bedford and Devon, Knight of our most noble order of the Garter, and our Ambassador Extraordinary and Plenipotentiary to our good Brother the Most Christian King, have nominated,

made, constituted and appointed, as by these presents, we do nominate, make, constitute, and appoint him, our true, certain, and undoubted Minister, Commissary, Deputy, Procurator and Plenipotentiary, giving to him all and all manner of power, faculty and authority, as well as our general and special command (yet so as that the general do not derogate from the special, or on the contrary) for Us and in our name, to meet and confer, as well singly and separately, as jointly, and in a body, with the Ambassadors, Commissaries, Deputies, and Plenipotentiaries of the Princes, whom it may concern, vested with sufficient power and authority for that purpose, and with them to agree upon, treat, consult and conclude, concerning the re-establishing, as soon as may be, a firm and lasting peace, and sincere friendship and concord; and whatever shall be so agreed and concluded, for Us and in our name, to sign, and to make a treaty or treaties, on what shall have been so agreed and concluded, and to transact every thing else that may belong to the happy completion of the aforesaid work, in as ample a manner and form, and with the same force and effect, as We ourselves, if we were present, could do and perform; engaging and promising, on our royal word, that We will approve, ratify and accept, in the best manner, whatever shall happen to be transacted and concluded by our said Plenipotentiary, and that We will never suffer any person to infringe or act contrary to the same, either in the whole or in part. In witness and confirmation whereof We have caused our great Seal of Great Britain to be affixed to these presents, signed with our royal hand. Given at our Palace at St. James's, the 12th day of November, 1762, in the third year of our reign.

His Most Christian Majesty's Full Power.

LEWIS, by the grace of God, King of France and Navarre, To all who shall see these presents, Greeting. Whereas the Preliminaries, signed at Fontainebleau the third of November of the last year, laid the foundation of the peace re-established between us and our most dear and most beloved good Brother and Cousin the King of Spain, on the one part, and our most dear and most beloved good Brother the King of Great Britain, and our most dear and most beloved good Brother and Cousin the King of Portugal on the other, We have had nothing more at heart since that happy epoch, than to consolidate and strengthen in the most lasting manner, so salutary and so important a work, by a solemn and definitive treaty between Us and the said powers. For these causes, and other good considerations, Us thereunto moving, We, trusting entirely in the capacity and experience, zeal and fidelity for our service, of our most dear and well-beloved Cousin, Cæsar Gabriel de Choiseul, Duke of Praslin, Peer of France, Knight of our Orders, Lieutenant General of our Forces and of the province of Britany, Counsellor in all our Councils, Minister and Secretary of State, and of our Commands and Finances, We have named, appointed, and deputed him, and by these presents, signed with our hand, do name, appoint, and depute him our Minister Plenipotentiary, giving him full and absolute power to act in that quality, and to confer, negotiate, treat and agree jointly with the Minister Plenipotentiary of our most dear and most beloved good Brother the King of Great Britain, the Minister Plenipotentiary of our most dear and most beloved good Brother and Cousin the King of Spain and the Minister Plenipotentiary of our most dear and most beloved good Brother and Cousin the King of Portugal, vested with full powers, in good form, to agree, conclude and sign such articles, conditions, conventions, declarations, definitive treaty, accessions, and other acts whatsoever, that he shall judge proper for securing and strengthening the great work of peace, the whole with the same latitude and authority that We ourselves might do, if We were there in person, even though there should be something which might require a more special order than what is contained in these presents, promising on the faith and word of a King, to approve, keep firm and stable for ever, to fulfil and execute punctually, all that our said Cousin, the Duke of Praslin, shall have stipulated, promised and signed, in virtue of the present full power, without ever acting contrary thereto, or permitting any thing contrary thereto, for any cause, or under any pretence whatsoever, as also to cause our letters of ratification to be expedited in good form, and to cause them to be delivered, in order to be exchanged within the time that shall be agreed upon. For such is our pleasure. In witness whereof, we have caused our Seal to be put to these presents. Given at Versailles the 7th day of the month of February, in the year of Grace 1763, and of our reign the forty-eighth. Signed Lewis, and on the fold, by the King, the Duke of Choiseul. Sealed with the great Seal of yellow Wax.

His Catholick Majesty's full Power.

DON CARLOS, by the grace of God, King of Castille, of Leon, of Arragon, of the two Sicilies, of Jerusalem, of Navarre, of Granada, of Toledo, of Valencia, of Galicia, of Majorca, of Seville, of Sardinia, of Cordova, of Corsica, of Murcia, of Jaen, of the Algarves, of Algecira, of Gibraltar, of the Canary Islands, of the East and West Indies, Islands and Continent, of the Ocean, Arch Duke of Austria, Duke of Burgundy, of Brabant and Milan, Count of Hapsburg, of Flanders, of Tirol and Barcelona, Lord of Biscay and of Molino, &c. Whereas preliminaries of a solid and lasting peace between this Crown, and that of France on the one part, and that of England and Portugal on the other, were concluded and signed in the Royal Residence of Fontainbleau, the 3rd of November of the present year, and the respective ratifications thereof exchanged on the 22d of the same month, by Ministers authorised for that purpose, wherein it is promised, that a definitive treaty should be forthwith entered upon, having established and regulated the chief points upon which it is to turn: and whereas in the same manner as I granted to you, Don Jerome Grimaldi, Marquis de Grimaldi, Knight of the Order of the Holy Ghost, Gentleman of my Bed-chamber with employment, and my Ambassador Extraordinary to the Most Christian King, my full power to treat, adjust, and sign the before-mentioned preliminaries, it is necessary to grant the same to you, or to some other, to

treat, adjust, and sign the promised definitive treaty of peace as aforesaid: therefore, as you the said Don Jerome Grimaldi, Marquis de Grimaldi, are at the convenient place, and as I have every day fresh motives, from your approved fidelity and zeal, capacity and prudence, to entrust to you this, and other-like concerns of my Crown, I have appointed you my Minister Plenipotentiary, and granted to you my full power, to the end, that, in my name, and representing my person, you may treat, regulate, settle, and sign the said definitive treaty of peace between my Crown and that of France on the one part, that of England and that of Portugal on the other, with the Ministers who shall be equally and specially authorised by their respective Sovereigns for the same purpose; acknowledging, as I do from this time acknowledge, as accepted and ratified, whatever you shall so treat, conclude, and sign; promising, on my Royal Word, that I will observe and fulfil the same, will cause it to be observed and fulfilled, as if it had been treated, concluded, and signed by myself. In witness whereof, I have caused these presents to be dispatched, signed by my hand, sealed with my privy seal, and countersigned by my under-written Counsellor of State, and first Secretary for the department of State and of War. Buen Retiro, the 10th day of December, 1762.

Source: National Archives.

48. Proclamation of the Line of Settlement, October 7, 1763

Introduction

The end of the French and Indian War (1754–1763) in North America led to the replacement of French traders with British colonists on the western frontier. The French traders had treated the Indians with a measure of respect, while the British angered the Indians with their arrogant behavior. In addition, British colonists defied their government's treaties by crossing the mountains to settle on the Indian lands of the Ohio Valley. Pontiac's Rebellion broke out in 1763 as western Indians tried to drive the British traders and settlers back east. In an attempt to address the causes of the rebellion, the Board of Trade in London issued this October 1763 proclamation, which forbade colonists from settling on land west of a line running along the crest of the Appalachian Mountains and also ordered existing settlers to return east. The proclamation angered both land-hungry settlers and influential land speculators (including George Washington) who had bought large tracts of Ohio Valley land. The governments of several colonies had claimed jurisdiction all the way to the Pacific Ocean and now faced the loss of a huge territory. Settlers and speculators alike ignored the proclamation line. Over the course of several years, British authorities negotiated new Indian treaties and shifted the line of settlement inexorably westward.

Primary Source

Whereas We have taken into Our Royal Consideration the extensive and valuable Acquisitions in America, secured to our Crown by the late *Definitive Treaty of Peace,* concluded at Paris the 10th Day of February last; and being desirous that all Our loving Subjects, as well of our Kingdom as of our Colonies in America, may avail themselves with all convenient Speed, of the great Benefits and Advantages which must accrue therefrom to their Commerce, Manufactures, and Navigation, We have thought fit, with the Advice of our Privy Council, to issue this our Royal Proclamation, hereby to publish and declare to all our loving Subjects, that we have, with the Advice of our Said Privy Council, granted our Letters Patent, under our Great Seal of Great Britain, to erect, within the Countries and Islands ceded and confirmed to Us by the said Treaty, Four distinct and separate Governments, styled and called by the names of Quebec, East Florida, West Florida and Grenada, and limited and bounded as follows, viz.

First—The Government of Quebec bounded on the Labrador Coast by the River St. John, and from thence by a Line drawn from the Head of that River through the Lake St. John, to the South end of the Lake Nipissim; from whence the said Line, crossing the River St. Lawrence, and the Lake Champlain, in 45 Degrees of North Latitude, passes along the High Lands which divide the Rivers that empty themselves into the said River St. Lawrence from those which fall into the Sea; and also along the North Coast of the Baye des Chaleurs, and the Coast of the Gulph of St. Lawrence to Cape Rosieres, and from thence crossing the Mouth of the River St. Lawrence by the West End of the Island of Anticosti, terminates at the aforesaid River of St. John.

Secondly—The Government of East Florida, bounded to the Westward by the Gulph of Mexico and the Apalachicola River; to the Northward by a Line drawn from that part of the said River where the Chatahouchee and Flint Rivers meet, to the source of St. Mary's River, and by the course of the said River to the Atlantic Ocean; and to the Eastward and Southward by the Atlantic Ocean and the Gulph of Florida, including all Islands within Six Leagues of the Sea Coast.

Thirdly—The Government of West Florida, bounded to the Southward by the Gulph of Mexico, including all Islands within Six Leagues of the Coast, from the River Apalachicola to Lake Pontchartrain; to the Westward by the said Lake, the Lake Maurepas, and the River Mississippi; to the Northward by a Line drawn due East from that part of the River Mississippi which lies in 31 Degrees North Latitude, to the River Apalachicola or Chatahouchee; and to the Eastward by the said River.

Fourthly—The Government of Grenada, comprehending the Island of that name, together with the Grenadines, and the Islands of Dominico, St. Vincent's and Tobago. And to the end that the open and free Fishery of our Subjects may be extended to and carried on upon the Coast of Labrador, and the adjacent Islands. We have thought fit, with the advice of our said Privy Council to put all that Coast, from the River St. John's to Hudson's Streights, together with the Islands of Anticosti and Madelaine, and all other smaller Islands lying upon the said Coast, under the care and Inspection of our Governor of Newfoundland.

We have also, with the advice of our Privy Council, thought fit to annex the Islands of St. John's and Cape Breton, or Isle Royale, with the lesser Islands adjacent thereto, to our Government of Nova Scotia.

We have also, with the advice of our Privy Council aforesaid, annexed to our Province of Georgia all the Lands lying between the Rivers Alatamaha and St. Mary's.

And whereas it will greatly contribute to the speedy settling of our said new Governments, that our loving Subjects should be informed of our Paternal care, for the security of the Liberties and Properties of those who are and shall become Inhabitants thereof, We have thought fit to publish and declare, by this Our Proclamation, that We have, in the Letters Patent under our Great Seal of Great Britain, by which the said Governments are constituted, given express Power and Direction to our Governors of our Said Colonies respectively, that so soon as the state and circumstances of the said Colonies will admit thereof, they shall, with the Advice and Consent of the Members of our Council, summon and call General Assemblies within the said Governments respectively, in such Manner and Form as is used and directed in those Colonies and Provinces in America which are under our immediate Government. And We have also given Power to the said Governors, with the consent of our Said Councils, and the Representatives of the People so to be summoned as aforesaid, to make, constitute, and ordain Laws, Statutes, and Ordinances for the Public Peace, Welfare, and good Government of our said Colonies, and of the People and Inhabitants thereof, as near as may be agreeable to the Laws of England, and under such Regulations and Restrictions as are used in other Colonies; and in the mean Time, and until such Assemblies can be called as aforesaid, all Persons Inhabiting in or resorting to our Said Colonies may confide in our Royal Protection for the Enjoyment of the Benefit of the Laws of our Realm of England; for which Purpose We have given Power under our Great Seal to the Governors of our said Colonies respectively to erect and constitute, with the Advice of our said Councils respectively, Courts of Judicature and public Justice within our Said Colonies for hearing and determining all Causes, as well Criminal as Civil, according to Law and Equity, and as near as may be agreeable to the Laws of England, with Liberty to all Persons who may think themselves aggrieved by the Sentences of such Courts, in all Civil Cases, to appeal, under the usual Limitations and Restrictions, to Us in our Privy Council.

We have also thought fit, with the advice of our Privy Council as aforesaid, to give unto the Governors and Councils of our said Three new Colonies, upon the Continent full Power and Authority to settle and agree with the Inhabitants of our said new Colonies or with any other Persons who shall resort thereto, for such Lands. Tenements and Hereditaments, as are now or hereafter shall be in our Power to dispose of; and them to grant to any such Person or Persons upon such Terms, and under such moderate Quit-Rents, Services and Acknowledgments, as have been appointed and settled in our other Colonies, and under such other Conditions as shall appear to us to be necessary and expedient for the Advantage of the Grantees, and the Improvement and settlement of our said Colonies.

And Whereas, We are desirous, upon all occasions, to testify our Royal Sense and Approbation of the Conduct and bravery of the Officers and Soldiers of our Armies, and to reward the same, We do hereby command and impower our Governors of our said Three new Colonies, and all other our Governors of our several Provinces on the Continent of North America, to grant without Fee or Reward, to such reduced Officers as have served in North America during the late War, and to such Private Soldiers as have been or shall be disbanded in America, and are actually residing there, and shall personally apply for the same, the following Quantities of Lands, subject, at the Expiration of Ten Years, to the same Quit-Rents as other Lands are subject to in the Province within which they are granted, as also subject to the same Conditions of Cultivation and Improvement; viz.

To every Person having the Rank of a Field Officer—5,000 Acres.
    To every Captain—3,000 Acres.
    To every Subaltern or Staff Officer—2,000 Acres.
    To every Non-Commission Officer—200 Acres.
    To every Private Man—50 Acres.

We do likewise authorize and require the Governors and Commanders in Chief of all our said Colonies upon the Continent of North America to grant the like Quantities of Land, and upon the same conditions, to such reduced Officers of our Navy of like Rank as served on board our Ships of War in North America at the times of the Reduction of Louisbourg and Quebec in the late War, and who shall personally apply to our respective Governors for such Grants.

And whereas it is just and reasonable, and essential to our Interest, and the Security of our Colonies, that the several Nations or Tribes of Indians with whom We are connected, and who live under our Protection, should not be molested or disturbed in the Possession of such Parts of Our Dominions and Territories as, not having been ceded to or purchased by Us, are reserved to them, or any of them, as their Hunting Grounds.—We do therefore, with the Advice of our Privy Council, declare it to be our Royal Will and Pleasure, that no Governor or Commander in Chief in any of our

Colonies of Quebec, East Florida, or West Florida, do presume, upon any Pretence whatever, to grant Warrants of Survey, or pass any Patents for Lands beyond the Bounds of their respective Governments, as described in their Commissions: as also that no Governor or Commander in Chief in any of our other Colonies or Plantations in America do presume for the present, and until our further Pleasure be known, to grant Warrants of Survey, or pass Patents for any Lands beyond the Heads or Sources of any of the Rivers which fall into the Atlantic Ocean from the West and North West, or upon any Lands whatever, which, not having been ceded to or purchased by Us as aforesaid, are reserved to the said Indians, or any of them.

And We do further declare it to be Our Royal Will and Pleasure, for the present as aforesaid, to reserve under our Sovereignty, Protection, and Dominion, for the use of the said Indians, all the Lands and Territories not included within the Limits of Our said Three new Governments, or within the Limits of the Territory granted to the Hudson's Bay Company, as also all the Lands and Territories lying to the Westward of the Sources of the Rivers which fall into the Sea from the West and North West as aforesaid.

And We do hereby strictly forbid, on Pain of our Displeasure, all our loving Subjects from making any Purchases or Settlements whatever, or taking Possession of any of the Lands above reserved, without our especial leave and Licence for that Purpose first obtained.

And, We do further strictly enjoin and require all Persons whatever who have either wilfully or inadvertently seated themselves upon any Lands within the Countries above described, or upon any other Lands which, not having been ceded to or purchased by Us, are still reserved to the said Indians as aforesaid, forthwith to remove themselves from such Settlements.

And whereas great Frauds and Abuses have been committed in purchasing Lands of the Indians, to the great Prejudice of our Interests, and to the great Dissatisfaction of the said Indians: In order, therefore, to prevent such Irregularities for the future, and to the end that the Indians may be convinced of our Justice and determined Resolution to remove all reasonable Cause of Discontent, We do, with the Advice of our Privy Council strictly enjoin and require, that no private Person do presume to make any purchase from the said Indians of any Lands reserved to the said Indians, within those parts of our Colonies where, We have thought proper to allow Settlement: but that, if at any Time any of the Said Indians should be inclined to dispose of the said Lands, the same shall be Purchased only for Us, in our Name, at some public Meeting or Assembly of the said Indians, to be held for that Purpose by the Governor or Commander in Chief of our Colony respectively within which they shall lie: and in case they shall lie within the limits of any Proprietary Government, they shall be purchased only for the Use and in the name of such Proprietaries, conformable to such Directions and Instructions as We or they shall think proper to give for that Purpose: And we do, by the Advice of our Privy Council, declare and enjoin, that the Trade with the said Indians shall be free and open to all our Subjects whatever, provided that every Person who may incline to Trade with the said Indians do take out a Licence for carrying on such Trade from the Governor or Commander in Chief of any of our Colonies respectively where such Person shall reside, and also give Security to observe such Regulations as We shall at any Time think fit, by ourselves or by our Commissaries to be appointed for this Purpose, to direct and appoint for the Benefit of the said Trade:

And we do hereby authorize, enjoin, and require the Governors and Commanders in Chief of all our Colonies respectively, as well those under Our immediate Government as those under the Government and Direction of Proprietaries, to grant such Licences without Fee or Reward, taking especial Care to insert therein a Condition, that such Licence shall be void, and the Security forfeited in case the Person to whom the same is granted shall refuse or neglect to observe such Regulations as We shall think proper to prescribe as aforesaid.

And we do further expressly conjoin and require all Officers whatever, as well Military as those Employed in the Management and Direction of Indian Affairs, within the Territories reserved as aforesaid for the use of the said Indians, to seize and apprehend all Persons whatever, who standing charged with Treason, Misprisions of Treason, Murders, or other Felonies or Misdemeanors, shall fly from Justice and take Refuge in the said Territory, and to send them under a proper guard to the Colony where the Crime was committed, of which they stand accused, in order to take their Trial for the same.

Given at our Court at St. James's the 7th Day of October 1763, in the Third Year of our Reign.

GOD SAVE THE KING

Source: William MacDonald, ed., *Documentary Source Book of American History, 1606–1898* (New York: Macmillan, 1913), 113–116.

49. William Johnson, Report on the Iroquois Confederacy, November 13, 1763 [Excerpt]

Introduction

Sir William Johnson (1715–1774), superintendent of Indian affairs in British North America from 1756 to 1774, possessed a keen awareness of the importance of Native Americans to the British as they fought the French for control of North America. The Iroquois trusted Johnson, who treated them fairly and respectfully. In fact, Johnson lived among the Mohawks, was considered a sachem (chief), and had taken as his wife a member of the Mohawk elite. Johnson secured Iroquois allegiance during King George's War (1744–1748). Later, with Indian assistance, he led a successful campaign against the French in New York in 1755 and was knighted for his victory. Johnson's ability to gain Iroquois loyalty for the British had far-reaching effects in the conflict with the French because few Indians were willing to go against the Iroquois Confederacy. He sent a report, an excerpt of which appears below, to the Board of Trade in London in the autumn of 1763 stressing the strength of the Iroquois Confederacy, which controlled a vast territory throughout the Mid-Atlantic region and the Midwest. Johnson believed that if the British would befriend the Iroquois and supply them with weapons, the Iroquois would stymie French aggression in North America. In 1763 Johnson also obtained Iroquois assistance in putting down Pontiac's Rebellion.

Primary Source

[. . .]

As Original proprietors, this Confederacy claim the Country of their residence, South of Lake Ontario to the great Ridge of the Blew Mountains, with all the Western part of the province of New York towards Hudsons River, west of the Caats Kill, thence to Lake Champlain, and from Regioghne a Rock at the East side of said lake to Osswegatche or La Gattell on the River St. Lawrence (having long ceded their claim North of said line in favour of the Canada Indians as Hunting ground) thence up the River St. Lawrence and along the South side of Lake Ontario to Niagara.

In right of conquest, they claim all the Country (comprehending the Ohio) along the great Ridge of Blew Mountains at the back of Virginia, thence to the head of the Kentucke River, and down the same to the Ohio above the Rifts, thence Northerly to the South end of Lake Michigan, then along the eastern shore of said lake to Missillimackinac, thence easterly across the North end of Lake Huron to the great Ottwawa River, (including the Chippawea or Mississagey Country) and down the said River to the Island of Montreal.—However, these more distant claims being possessed by many powerful Nations, the Inhabitants have long began to render themselves independent by the assistance of the French, and the great decrease of the Six Nations; but their claim to the Ohio, and thence to the Lakes is not in the least disputed by the Shawanese Delawares ettc, who never transacted any Sales of Land or other matters without their consent, and who sent Deputys to the grand Council at Onondaga on all important occasions.

On my coming to the management of Indian Affairs in 1746, when the Indians refused to meet or treat with our Governours, the Indian interest was from our former neglect in so visible a State of decline, that it was conjectured by many, they would entirely abandon us; in this scituation, it was with the utmost difficulty that I was enabled to prevent their falling off, but by proper measures and personal interest, I was happy enough, not only to keep them in our interest but also to employ many parties of them against the Enemy, who greatly harassed them. On my further appointment by General Braddock (for which I never received any salary) I then acquainted them that I feared, the utmost I could do would be to preserve a neutrality, which alone would be of great consequence, and for this my opinion, I had sufficient reason, as the Indians had from the year 1749 to 1754, been continually complaining of neglect, and remonstrating against the growing power of the French, and repeatedly requesting our assistance, on which they would dispossess them notwithstanding their Interest with the western Indians whom they had at an immense expence, and by the artful insinuations of Jesuits and other proper Emissaries brought over to them, and which in the declining state of the Six Nations, were too formidable Enemies alone to cope with.

[. . .]

Source: John Romeyn Brodhead, *Documents Relative to the Colonial History of the State of New York,* Vol. 7 (Albany, NY: Weed, Parsons, 1856), 573.

50. Pontiac, Speech to the French, May 5, 1763

Introduction

The end of the French and Indian War (1754–1763) in North America greatly reduced the French presence in the Old Northwest, and British traders replaced French traders on the frontier. The French traders had treated the Indians with a measure of respect, while the British angered the Indians with their arrogant behavior. In addition, the British built a number of permanent frontier forts, and British colonists defied their own government by crossing the mountains to settle on the Indian lands of the Ohio Valley. For these reasons, many of the Indians in the Old Northwest preferred the French and wanted to see them restored to their former territory. Pontiac's Rebellion—named after a chief of the Ottawas—broke out in the spring of 1763 as western Indians tried to drive the British traders and settlers back east. In a meeting with some of the Frenchmen remaining in the region, Pontiac spoke of how his fight was not just for his own people but also for the benefit of the French. Calling himself a Frenchman, Pontiac asked only for provisions, understanding that the French had signed a treaty and could no longer take up arms against the British.

Primary Source

My brothers, we have never had in view to do you any evil. We have never intended that any should be done you. But amongst my young men there are, as amongst you, some who, in spite of all precautions which we take, always do evil. Besides, it is not only for my revenge that I make war upon the English, it is for you, my brothers, as for us. When the English, in their councils, which we have held with them, have insulted us, they have also insulted you, without your knowing anything about it, and as I know, and all our brothers know, the English have taken from you all means of avenging yourselves, by disarming you and making you write on a paper, which they have sent to their country, which they could not make us do; therefore, I will avenge you equally with us, and I swear annihilation as long as any of them shall remain on our land. Besides, you do not know all the reasons which oblige me to act as I do. I have told you only that which regards you. You will know the rest in time. I know well that I pass amongst many of my brothers for a fool, but you will see in the future if I am such as is said, and if I am wrong. I also know well that there are amongst you, my brothers, some who take the part of the English, to make war against us, and that only pains me on their account. I know them well, and when our father shall have come, I will name them and point them out to him, and they will see whether they or we shall be the most content in the future.

I doubt not, my brothers, that this war tries you, on account of the movements of our brothers, who all the time go and come to your houses. I am sorry for it but do not believe, my brothers, that I instigate the wrong which is done to you, and for proof that I do not wish it, remember the war of the Foxes, and the manner in which I have behaved in your interest. It is now seventeen years that the Sauteux and Ottawas of Michelimakinak and all the nations of the north have come with the Sacs and Foxes to annihilate you. Who has defended you? Was it not I and my people? When Mekinak, great chief of all the nations, said in his council that he would carry to his village the head of your commander, and eat his heart and drink his blood, have I not taken up your interest by going to his camp and telling him, if he wanted to kill the French, he must commence with me and my people? Have I not helped you to defeat them and drive them away? When or how came that? Would you, my brothers, believe that I to-day would turn my arms against you? No, my brothers, I am the same French Pondiak who lent you his hand seventeen years ago. I am a Frenchman, and I want to die a Frenchman! And I repeat to you they are both your interests and mine which I revenge. Let me go on. I don't ask your assistance, because I know you cannot give it. I only ask of you provisions for me and all my people. If, however, you would like to aid me, I would not refuse you. You would cause me pleasure, and you would sooner be out of trouble. For I warrant you, when the English shall be driven from here or killed, we shall all retire to our villages according to our custom, and await the arrival of our father, the Frenchman. These, you see, my brothers, are my sentiments. Rest assured, my brothers, I will watch that no more wrong shall be done to you by my people, nor by other Indians. What I ask of you is that our women be allowed to plant our corn on the fallows of your lands. We shall be obliged to you for that.

Source: *Report of the Pioneer and Historical Society of the State of Michigan,* Vol. 8 (Lansing, MI: Thorpe and Godfrey, 1886), 300–301.

51. William Trent, Account of the Siege of Fort Pitt, June 1763

Introduction

The end of the French and Indian War (1754–1763) in North America led to British traders replacing French traders on the western frontier. In addition, the British built a number of permanent frontier forts, and British colonists defied their government's treaties by crossing the mountains to settle on the Indian lands of the Ohio Valley. Pontiac's Rebellion—named after a chief of the Ottawas—broke out in the spring of 1763 as western Indians tried to drive the British traders and settlers back east. The tribes of the Northwest Territory killed or captured some 2,000 frontier settlers and attacked the major frontier forts, among them Fort Pitt (at the site of Pittsburgh, Pennsylvania). Fort Pitt remained under siege during the summer months of 1763 until relief came in August. To meet the crisis, the fort's commander placed Indian trader and former soldier William Trent in command of a newly raised company of militia. Trent kept a journal throughout the siege. Most notable in this excerpt is evidence of early biological warfare. Confronted with a delegation of Indians pretending friendship, Trent reports that he gave them a special gift for their chief: blankets and a handkerchief that had belonged to smallpox patients.

Primary Source

June 16th Four Shawnesse appeared on the opposite side of the Ohio and desired that Mr. McKee would go over and speak to them. . . .

June 17th The same Indians came and called again and desired Mr. McKee would come over, he refused; they then recommend it to him to set off for the Inhabitants in the Night, or to come over to them and they would take care of him at their Towns till the War was over, they acquainted him all Nations had taken up the Hatchett against us, and that they intended to attack this Post with a great Body in a few days; that Venango and all the other Posts that way were already cut off, that they were afraid to refuse taking up the Hatchet against us as so many Nations had done it before it came to them. . . .

18th The Enemy set fire to another House up the Ohio. . . .

19th Two Indians crep along the Bank of the Mono[ngahela towards the] Centinel who was posted on the Bank of the River and [FIRED AT HIM.] Soon after a number of Indians were seen at the Head of the [FIELDS] taking of some Horses, and the Garrison was turning out one Stuart a Soldiers Gun went of by accident and mortaly wounded him of which he dyed the next day. . . .

22nd Between 9 and 10 o'Clock in the Morning a smoke was seen rising on the Back of Grants Hill where the Indians had made a fire and about 2 o'Clock several of them appeared in the Spelts field moving of the Horses and Cattle. About 5 o'Clock one James Thompson who it was supposed was gone after a Horse was killed and scalped in sight of the Fort on this a great number of Inds appeared on each River and on Grants Hill shooting down the Cattle and Horses. A Shell was thron amongst a number of them from a Hauwitz [howitzer] which burst just as it fell among them. About an Hour after they fired on the Fort from Grant's Hill and the other side of the Ohio, a shot from the opposite side of the Ohio wounded a Man in the Mongehele Bastion. About 7 o'Clock three Indians were seen about 150 yards from the Fort on the Monongehela Bank. Mr. McKee and two others fired on them and killed one of them. . . .

24th The Turtles Heart a principal Warrior of the Delawares and Mamaltee a Chief came within a small distance of the Fort Mr. McKee went out to them and they made a Speech letting us know that all our [POSTS] as Ligonier was destroyed, that great numbers of Indians [were coming and] that out of regard to us, they had prevailed on 6 Nations [not to] attack us but give us time to go down the Country and they desired we would set of immediately. The Commanding Officer thanked them, let them know that we had everything we wanted, that we could defend it against all the Indians in the Woods, that we had three large Armys marching to Chastise those Indians that had struck us, told them to take care of their Women and Children, but not to tell any other Natives, they said they would go and speak to their Chiefs and come and tell us what they said, they returned and said they would hold fast of the Chain of friendship. Out of our regard to them we gave them two Blankets and an Handkerchief out of the Small Pox Hospital. I hope it will have the desired effect. They then told us that Ligonier had been attacked, but that the Enemy were beat off.

The 25th A Shawnese Indian came across the River and Spoke to Mr McKee and told him that two days ago Sixty Miles off, he left a large Body of Indians on their march for this place to attack it and the Delawares that were here were going to join them. . . .

The 26th Six o'Clock in the Morning Ensn Price with five men came in from Le Beauff [Fort Le Boef, now Waterford] and gave the following Account of his miraculous escape from that place and while they were Bringing him across the River seven Ind[ians showed them] selves on Grants Hill.

Early in the morning of the 18th instant five Indians [came to] his Post and asked for some Tobacco and provisions, which he gave to them. Soon after they went off about 30 men came down the Road leading to Prisque Isle, laid their Arms down a small distance off, came and asked liberty to come in and said they were going to War against the Cherokees, wou'd stay with him that night and that they purposed to pass by Fort Pitt in order to speak with Mr. Croghan; Mr Price suspecting their design had all his people under Arms and wou'd not suffer them to go in, upon this the Indians took up their Arms and got to the back of an Out store where they picked out the Stones it was underpinn'd with and got into it, then they began to roll out the Barrels of Provisions and shoot fired Arrows into the top of the Blockhouse which was put out several times, this continued till sometime in the night when Mr. Price finding it impossible to defend the place any longer or prevent its being consumed took the advantage of the Night, got all his people out of a window and made off without being observed, but unfortunately lost six of his men and a woman who he supposes fell into the hands of the Enemy, sometime after he left the Blockhouse the Indians began to fire it, when he came to Venangoe found it in Ashes, kept the Road all the way here and saw the bones of several people who had been killed going Exp[ress.] they were Six Nation Indians who attacked him. . . . 6 o'Clock in the Afternoon a S[oldier arrived] who made his escape from Presqu' Isle and says that on the 19th inst. that Post was attacked by 250 Indians which continued for two days, and that the Indians had made holes in the Bank and fired through, that the Officer (Mr. Christy) Capitulated, that the Indians were to give them 6 days Provisions and escort them safe to this Post. It was the Ottawas, Chipawas, Wyandotts and Senecas that took the Post, that after they had delivered the Indians their Arms, while the Indians were engaged in carrying out the Provisions and other Stores, he being at some distance hearing a Woman scream he imagined they were beginning to Tomhawk the Garrison he made his escape, that another Soldier likewise attempted to make his escape but fears he did not get off, that the Indians had fired the Roof of the Block House a great many times before they Capitulated and that they as often put it out, he further says that the Schooner was in sight and kep there sounding with their Boat to try if they could get in to their Assistance but that there was not Water enough, that the Indians told them they had destroyed 800 Barrels of Provisions at the Store House where the Schooner was to load and that he believes the Schooner had no Provisions on board. Nine o'Clock at Night two Expresses were sent of to the General by way of Fort Cumberland on the other side of Monongehela with these Accounts

> Source: Excerpt from *The Journal of William Trent*, by William Trent, from "Fort Pitt Holds Out: from *Pen Pictures of Early Western Penn-sylvania*, edited by John W. Harpster, copyright 1938. Reprinted by permission of the University of Pittsburgh Press.

52. Henry Bouquet, Reports on the Relief of Fort Pitt, August 28, 1763

Introduction

The end of the French and Indian War (1754–1763) in North America led to the replacement of French traders with British traders on the western frontier. In addition, the British built a number of permanent frontier forts, and British colonists defied their government's treaties by crossing the mountains to settle on the Indian lands of the Ohio Valley. Pontiac's Rebellion—named after a chief of the Ottawas—broke out in the spring of 1763 as western Indians tried to drive the British traders and settlers back east. The tribes of the Northwest Territory killed or captured some 2,000 frontier settlers and attacked the major frontier forts, among them Fort Pitt (at the site of Pittsburgh, Pennsylvania). Fort Pitt remained under siege during the summer months of 1763 until relief came in August. At least 400 Delawares, Shawnees, Wyandots, and Mingoes surrounded the fort. Colonel Henry Bouquet reports here that he led some 460 men on a march that departed Carlisle, Pennsylvania, on July 28 and arrived at Fort Pitt on August 5. A 12-hour battle ensued outside the fort. By the time they routed the Indians, 50 of Bouquet's men were killed and another 60 wounded. Bouquet and his troops continued to move westward and stayed on campaign until the rebellion was subdued.

Primary Source

Colonel Henry Bouquet to Major Henry Gladwin, August 28, 1763

Dear Sir

I had Last Night the very great Pleasure to receive Your Letter of the 28th July, by Your Express Andrew, who Says he was detan'd by Sicknes at Sandusky Your Letters for the General are forwarded.

A Mohawk having reported to Sir Wm Johnson that De Troite was taken, I could not help being uneasy tho' Long acquainted with Indian Lies.

It was a great Sattisfaction to me to Know from Your Self that You have been able to defend that post, with so few Men, against that Multitude, what was Known below of Your firm and prudent Conduct from the beginning of the Insurrection, had obtain'd the Generals approbation, and does You the greatest honor.

The Loss of all our Detain'd posts, is no more than could be expected from their Defenseless State; But Capt. Cambells Death affects me Sensibly.

I pity the unfortunate who remain Yet in the Power of the Barbarians, as every Step we take to rescue them, may and will probably hasten their Death.

Your Express says that after he left the De Troite, two Wiandots told him that the Detachment of 300 Men from Niagara had Joyn'd You with provisions. This will give You some ease till more Effectual reinforcements can be sent.

You Know that You are to have the Command of all the Troops destin'd for De Troite and to retake possession of the Country now fallen into the hands of the Enemy: To that Effect the General collects all the Troops that can be spar'd at Niagara and Presque Isle. The remains of the 42d. and 77th Were order'd to Joyn You this way when we had Intelligence that Venang had been Surpris'd Lt. Gordon and all his unfortunate Garrison Masacred; Le Beuf abandonn'd, and Presque Isle Surrender'd to my unspeakable astonishment, as I Knew the Strengt of that Block house, which would have been reliev'd from Niagara.

Fort Pitt was attack'd and invested by all the Delawar's and part of the Shavanese, Wiandots, and Mingoes, to the Number of 400 by their Account, but much more Considerable as we found afterwards, besides their Women and Children which they had brought here to Carry the plunder to their Towns, not doubting to take the Peace. Fort Burd on the Mononghehela, Bushy Run, and Stony Creek, were abandon'd for want of Men.

Ligoneer a post of great consequence to us was defended with a handful of Men by Lieut. Blane, and Capt. Ecuyer baffled all their Efforts here. [There] The fort was open on three Sides; The Floods having undermin'd the Sodwork, the rampart had tumbled in ye Ditch.

He Pallessadoed, and Frais'd the whole, rais'd a parapet all round, and in a short time with a small Garrison, he has made it impregnable for Savages. Besides their attacks on the Forts, they Kept parties on the Communication and interrupted all Expresses, while others falling upon the Fronteer Settlements Spread terror and desolation through the whole Country.

Things being in that Situation I receiv'd Orders to March with the above Troops, the only force the General could collect at that time for the relief of this Fort which was in great want of provisions, The Little Flouer they had being damag'd: In that pressing danger the provinces refus'd to give us the Least assistance; having form'd a Convoy. I march'd from Carlisle the 18th of July with about 460 Rank & File, being the remains of the 42d. & 77th Regts. Many of them convalesants. I Left 30 Men at Bedford and as many at Ligoneer, where I arriv'd on the 2d. Instant, Having no Intelligence of the enemy I determin'd to Leave the Waggons at that post, and to proceed with 400 Horses Loaded with Flour, to be Less incumber'd in case of an action.

I Left Ligoneer the 4th. And on the 5th. Instant at One O'Clock P.M. after marching 117 Miles we were Suddenly attack'd by all the Savages collected about Fort Pitt: I shall not enter into the Detail of that obstinate Action which Lasted till Night, and beginning Early on the 6th Continued till One O'Clock when at Last we routed them. They were pursued about two Miles and so well dispersed that we have not seen one since, as we were excessively distress'd by the total want of Water, we March'd immideately to the Nearest Spring without inquiring into the Loss of the enemy, who must have Suffer'd greatly by their repeated and bold Attacks in which they were constantly repuls'd; Our Loss is very Considerable.

Kill'd	50
Wounded	60
In all	110

After delivering our Convoy here Part of the Troops were embark'd and sent down the River to Cutt off the Shavanese the rest went back to Ligoneer, and brought our Waggons on the 22d. The great fatigues of Long Marches, and of being always under Arms has Occasion'd great Sickness, which with the Loss in the Action, puts it out of my power to Send You the remains of the two Regiments ordered to joyn You by Presque Isle, till I receive a reinforcement; This gives me great uneasiness, as I Know that they are much Wanted. But You may be assur'd that we shall do every thing in the Power of Men, to assist You. I am to remain here my self ready to go down the River with a Strong Body, which is to be ordered up for that Service.

As I have no means to procure Intelligence from Presque Isle, I am oblig'd to Send Your Express that Way, and at his return I will dispatch him by Sandusky, with what News I may then have receiv'd: and a Duplicate of this.

It is very agreeable to me to hear that our Officers with You, have been so happy as to obtain Your Approbation of their Services, and I am much obliged to You for the honor You have done them.

I inclose the Latest papers we have: Two of our Battalions are reduc'd. I know nothing Certain of the number of Corps remaining.

I am
Dear Sir
Your most obedient & Humble Servant

Colonel Henry Bouquet to Lieutenant James MacDonald, August 28, 1763

Sir

I had Last Night by the Indian Andrew Your Letter of the 29th. July with it's Enclosur's, for which I am much oblig'd to You. The other Letter of the 14th is not yet come to hand.

The Loss of our good and worthy Friend Captain Campbell affects me Extremely. He had treated those infamous Barbarians with so much Generosity and Benevolence, that I flatter'd myself they would have Spar'd his Life: but they must be rank'd with the Panthers of their Forests, and treated in the same Way.

I am much Concern'd of such of our Officers and Men who have had the Misfortune to fall in their hands, If we cannot rescue them, we shall at Least revenge their Death, upon the perfidious Wretches in whose power they now are.

We have on our March to the relief of this Fort, which was closely beset, defeated in the Woods a Large Body of Savages Compos'd of part of the Wiandots, Shavanese, Mingos and all the Delawar's, who are recon'd and thinck them selfs the best Warriors in the Woods; Indeed they fought with the greatest bravery and resolution for two days, that the Action Lasted, on the 5th and 6th Instant; They are now all dispers'd, and we have not Seen any since; The Highlands. Are the bravest men I ever Saw, and their behaviour in that obstinate affair does them the highest honor.

In all 50 Kill'd, and 60 Wounded

I wish the same Success, with a Less considerable Loss, may attend the other bodies of Troops employ'd against those Villains. They may fight this way but never with the same Spirit and confidence. We expect a Reinforcement to push this Luky plow and forward some Troops to Your assistance.

Major Gladwin expresses his Sattisfaction of the Services of the Officers with him in a manner very honorable to them, and which gives me very great pleasure.

I'll write You a duplicate by Sandusky. I beg my Compliments to our Friends, all is well here.

I am very Sincer'ly Sir
    Your most Obedient humble Servt.

Governor James Hamilton to Colonel Henry Bouquet, August 29, 1763

Sir/

I received with the greatest pleasure your letter of the 11 instant, and most sincerely congratulate you, as well on your Victory and triumph over the Indians, as on your having fully accomplish'd the purpose of your expedition, by the relief of Fort Pitt.

—very important services both, and of the utmost consequence to these Colonies! And which, I am in hopes, will appear so considerable in the eyes of Our Superiors, as to entitle the Conductor to some valuable work of their approbation.

Source: Henry Bouquet, *The Papers of Col. Henry Bouquet*, Ser. 21649, Pt. II (Harrisburg: Department of Public Instruction, Pennsylvania Historical Commission, 1942).

53. Pontiac, Letter Addressed to the Commander of Detroit, October 30, 1763

Introduction

The end of the French and Indian War (1754–1763) in North America led to British traders replacing French traders on the western frontier. In addition, the British built a number of permanent frontier forts, and British colonists defied their government's treaties by crossing the mountains to settle on the Indian lands of the Ohio Valley. Pontiac's Rebellion—named after a chief of the Ottawas—broke out in the spring of 1763 as western Indians tried to drive the British traders and settlers back east. The tribes of the Northwest Territory killed or captured some 2,000 frontier settlers and attacked the major frontier forts. The Indians succeeded in taking all but Fort Pitt, Fort Niagara, and Fort Detroit. The British held out at Detroit for five months against the siege mounted by Pontiac himself and the Ottawas. Running low on ammunition, Pontiac made a peace overture in this letter (the original was in French) to the British commander of the fort. Despite the name given to the uprising by the British, Pontiac did not command the other tribes and villages. The rebellion died down gradually over the course of the next two years, finally ending in 1766 after the many native combatants made peace one village at a time.

Primary Source

Detroit, Nov. 1, 1763

Copy of the Letter addressed to the Commander of Detroit by Pontiac, the 30th of October, 1763.

My Brother:

The word which my Father sent me to make peace, I have accepted; all my young men have buried their hatchets: I think that you will forget all the evil things which have occurred for some time past.

Likewise, I shall forget what you may have done to me, in order to think nothing but good. I, the Saulteurs, the Hurons, we will come to speak when you ask us. Give us a reply. I am sending this council to you in order that you may see it. If you are as good as I, you will send me a reply. I wish you good day.

Signed,

Pontiac

Source: Henry Bouquet, *The Papers of Col. Henry Bouquet*, Ser. 21649, Pt. II (Harrisburg: Department of Public Instruction, Pennsylvania Historical Commission, 1942).

54. Benjamin Franklin, Narrative of the Paxton Boys Massacre, 1764 [Excerpts]

Introduction

At the end of the French and Indian War (1754–1763) in North America, the British built a number of permanent frontier forts, and British colonists defied their government's treaties by crossing the mountains to settle on the Indian lands of the Ohio Valley. Pontiac's Rebellion—named after a chief of the Ottawas—broke out in the spring of 1763 as western Indians tried to drive the British traders and settlers back east. The settlers on the western frontier bore the brunt of the uprising as Indians killed or captured some 2,000 of them. Many of Pennsylvania's frontier dwellers believed that the pacifist-controlled colonial legislature, governing from the safety and comfort of Philadelphia, was not doing enough to protect them. In December 1763 some 50 Pennsylvania frontiersmen, members of a gang called the Paxton Boys, set upon the village of Conestoga, where 22 peaceable friendly Indians lived. The gang murdered 20 inhabitants, including children, and then moved on to Lancaster and killed another 14 Indians who had taken refuge there. In 1764 about 600 Paxton Boys marched to Philadelphia to present their grievances and demand legislative action to protect the frontier. The killings aroused widespread disgust, as expressed in this essay by Benjamin Franklin.

Primary Source

These Indians were the remains of a tribe of the Six Nations, settled at Conestogo, and thence called Conestogo Indians. On the first arrival of the English in Pennsylvania, messengers from this tribe came to welcome them, with presents of venison, corn, and skins; and the whole tribe entered into a treaty of friendship with the first proprietor, William Penn, which was to last "as long as the sun should shine, or the waters run in the rivers."

This treaty has been since frequently renewed, and the chain brightened, as they express it, from time to time. It has never been violated, on their part or ours, till now. As their lands by degrees were mostly purchased, and the settlements of the white people began to surround them, the proprietor assigned them lands on the manor of Conestogo, which they might not part with; there they have lived many years in friendship with their white neighbours, who loved them for their peaceable inoffensive behaviour.

It has always been observed that Indians settled in the neighbourhood of white people do not increase, but diminish continually. This tribe accordingly went on diminishing, till there remained in their town on the manor but twenty persons, viz.: seven men, five women, and eight children, boys and girls.

Of these, Shehaes was a very old man, having assisted at the second treaty held with them, by Mr. Penn, in 1701, and ever since continued a faithful and affectionate friend to the English. He is said to have been an exceeding good man, considering his education, being naturally of a most kind, benevolent temper.

Peggy was Shehaes's daughter; she worked for her aged father, continuing to live with him, though married, and attended him with filial duty and tenderness.

John was another good old man; his son Harry helped to support him.

George and Will Soc were two brothers, both young men.

John Smith, a valuable young man of the Cayuga nation, who became acquainted with Peggy, Shehaes's daughter, some few years since, married, and settled in that family. They had one child, about three years old.

Betty, a harmless old woman; and her son Peter, a likely young lad.

Sally, whose Indian name was Wyanjoy, a woman much esteemed by all that knew her, for her prudent and good behaviour in some very trying situations of life. She was a truly good and amiable woman, had no children of her own; but, a distant relation dying, she had taken a child of that relation's, to bring up as her own, and performed towards it all the duties of an affectionate parent.

The reader will observe that many of the names are English. It is common with the Indians, that have an affection for the English, to give themselves and their children the names of such English persons as they particularly esteem.

This little society continued the custom they had begun, when more numerous, of addressing every new governor, and every descendant of the first proprietor, welcoming him to the province, assuring him of their fidelity, and praying a continuance of that favor and protection they had hitherto experienced. They had accordingly sent up an address of this kind to our present governor, on his arrival; but the same was scarce delivered when the unfortunate catastrophe happened, which we are about to relate.

On Wednesday, the 14th of December, 1763, fifty-seven men from some of our frontier townships, who had projected the destruction of this little commonwealth, came, all well mounted, and armed with fire-locks, hangers, and hatchets, having travelled through the country in the night, to Conestogo manor. There they surrounded the small village of Indian huts, and just at break of day broke into them all at once. Only three men, two women, and a young boy were found at home, the rest being out among the neighbouring white people, some to sell the baskets, brooms, and bowls they manufactured, and others on other occasions. These poor defenceless creatures were immediately fired upon, stabbed, and hatcheted to death! The good Shehaes, among the rest, cut to pieces in his bed. All of them were scalped and otherwise horribly mangled. Then their huts were set on fire, and most of them burnt down. Then the troop, pleased with their own conduct and bravery, but enraged that any of the poor Indians had escaped the massacre, rode off, and in small parties, by different roads, went home.

The universal concern of the neighbouring white people, on hearing of this event, and the lamentations of the younger Indians, when they returned and saw the desolation, and the butchered, half-burnt bodies of their murdered parents and other relations, cannot well be expressed.

The magistrates of Lancaster sent out to collect the remaining Indians, brought them into the town for their better security against any farther attempt; and, it is said, condoled with them on the misfortune that had happened, took them by the hand, comforted, and promised them protection. They were all put into the workhouse, a strong building, as the place of greatest safety.

When the shocking news arrived in town, a proclamation was issued by the governor, in the following terms, viz.:

Whereas I have received information that on Wednesday, the fourteenth day of this month, a number of people, armed and mounted on horseback, unlawfully assembled together, and went to the Indian town in the Conestogo manor, in Lancaster county, and without the least reason or provocation, in cool blood, barbarously killed six of the Indians settled there, and burnt and destroyed all their houses and effects; and whereas so cruel and inhuman an act, committed in the heart of this province on the said Indians, who have lived peaceably and inoffensively among us during all our late troubles, and for

many years before, and were justly considered as under the protection of this government and its laws, calls loudly for the vigorous exertion of the civil authority, to detect the offenders, and bring them to condign punishment; I have, therefore, by and with the advice and consent of the council, thought fit to issue this proclamation, and do hereby strictly charge and enjoin all judges, justices, sheriffs, constables, officers, civil and military, and all other his Majesty's liege subjects within this province, to make diligent search and inquiry after the authors and perpetrators of the said crime, their abettors and accomplices, and to use all possible means to apprehend and secure them in some of the public gaols of this province, that they may be brought to their trials, and be proceeded against according to law.

And whereas a number of other Indians, who lately lived on or near the frontiers of this province, being willing and desirous to preserve and continue the ancient friendship, which heretofore subsisted between them and the good people of this province, have, at their own earnest request, been removed from their habitations, and brought into the county of Philadelphia, and seated for the present, for their better security, on the Province Island, and in other places in the neighborhood of the city of Philadelphia, where provision is made for them at the public expense; I do, therefore, hereby strictly forbid all persons whatsoever, to molest or injure any of the said Indians, as they will answer the contrary at their peril.

Given under my hand, and the great seal of the said province, at Philadelphia, the twenty-second day of December, *anno Domini,* one thousand seven hundred and sixty-three, and in the fourth year of his Majesty's reign.

John Penn
By his Honor's command,
Joseph Shippen, Jr., Secretary.
God save the King

Notwithstanding this proclamation, those cruel men again assembled themselves, and, hearing that the remaining fourteen Indians were in the workhouse at Lancaster, they suddenly appeared in that town, on the 27th of December. Fifty of them, armed as before, dismounting, went directly to the workhouse, and by violence broke open the door, and entered with the utmost fury in their countenances. When the poor wretches saw they had no protection nigh, nor could possibly escape, and being without the least weapon for defence, they divided into their little families, the children clinging to the parents; they fell on their knees, protested their innocence, declared their love to the English; and that in their whole lives they had never done them injury; and in this posture they all received the hatchet! Men, women, and little children were every one inhumanly murdered in cold blood!

The barbarous men who committed the atrocious fact, in defiance of government, of all laws human and divine, and to the eternal disgrace of their country and color, then mounted their horses, huzzaed in triumph, as if they had gained a victory, and rode off *unmolested!*

The bodies of the murdered were then brought out and exposed in the street, till a hole could be made in the earth to receive and cover them.

But the wickedness cannot be covered; the guilt will lie on the whole land, till justice is done on the murderers. The blood of the innocent will cry to Heaven for vengeance.

It is said that Shehaes being before told, that it was to be feared some English might come from the frontier into the country, and murder him and his people, he replied: "It is impossible; there are Indians, indeed, in the woods, who would kill me and mine, if they could get at us, for my friendship to the English; but the English will wrap me in their matchcoat, and secure me from all danger." How unfortunately was he mistaken!

Another proclamation has been issued, offering a great reward for apprehending the murderers, in the following terms, viz.:

Whereas on the twenty-second day of December last, I issued a proclamation for the apprehending and bringing to justice a number of persons, who, in violation of the public faith, and in defiance of all law, had inhumanly killed six of the Indians, who had lived in Conestogo manor, for the course of many years, peaceably and inoffensively, under the protection of this government, on lands assigned to them for their habitation; notwithstanding which, I have received information, that on the twenty-seventh of the same month, a large party of armed men again assembled and met together in a riotous and tumultuous manner, in the county of Lancaster, and proceeded to the town of Lancaster, where they violently broke open the workhouse, and butchered and put to death fourteen of the said Conestogo Indians, men, women, and children, who had been taken under the immediate care and protection of the magistrates of the said county, and lodged for their better security in the said workhouse, till they should be more effectually provided for by order of the government; and whereas common justice loudly demands, and the laws of the land (upon the preservation of which not only the liberty and security of every individual, but the being of the government itself depends) require, that the above offenders should be brought to condign punishment: I have, therefore, by and with the advice of the council, published this proclamation, and do hereby strictly charge and command all judges, justices, sheriffs, constables, officers, civil and military, and all other his Majesty's faithful and liege subjects within this province, to make diligent search and inquiries after the authors and perpetrators of the said last-mentioned offence, their abettors and accomplices, and that they use all possible means to apprehend and secure them in some of the public gaols [jails] of this province, to be dealt with according to law.

And I do hereby further promise and engage, that any person or persons who shall apprehend and secure, or cause to be apprehended and secured, any three of the ringleaders of the said party, and prosecute them to conviction, shall have and receive for each the public reward of two hundred pounds; and any accomplice, not concerned in the immediate shedding the blood of the said Indians, who shall make discovery of any or either of the said ringleaders, and apprehend and prosecute them to conviction, shall, over and above the said reward, have all the weight and influence of the government, for obtaining his Majesty's pardon for his offence.

Given under my hand, and the great seal of the said province, at Philadelphia, the second day of January, in the fourth year of his Majesty's reign, and in the year of our Lord one thousand seven hundred and sixty-four.

John Penn
By his Honor's command,
Joseph Shippen, Jr., Secretary.
God save the King

These proclamations have as yet produced no discovery, the murderers having given out such threatenings against those that disapprove their proceedings, that the whole country seems to be in terror, and no one dare speak what he knows; even the letters from thence are unsigned in which any dislike is expressed of the rioters.

There are some (I am ashamed to hear it) who would extenuate the enormous wickedness of these actions by saying: "The inhabitants of the frontiers are exasperated with the murder of their relations by the enemy Indians in the present war." It is possible; but though this might justify their going out into the woods to seek for those enemies and avenge upon them those murders, it can never justify their turning into the heart of the country to murder their friends.

If an Indian injures me, does it follow that I may revenge that injury on all Indians? It is well known that Indians are of different tribes, nations, and languages as well as the white people. In Europe, if the French, who are white people, should injure the Dutch, are they to revenge it on the English, because they too are white people? The only crime of these poor wretches seems to have been that they had a reddish-brown skin and black hair, and some people of that sort, it seems, had murdered some of our relations. If it be right to kill men for such a reason, then should any man with a freckled face and red hair kill a wife or child of mine, it would be right for me to revenge it by killing all the freckled, red-haired men, women, and children I could afterwards anywhere meet with.

But it seems these people think they have a better justification; nothing less than the Word of God. With the Scriptures in their hand and mouths they can set at nought that express demand, *Thou shalt do no murder,* and justify their wickedness by the command given Joshua to destroy the heathen. Horrid perversion of Scripture and of religion! To father the worst of crimes on the God of peace and love! Even the Jews, to whom that particular commission was directed, spared the Gibeonites on account of their faith once given. The faith of this government has been frequently given to those Indians; but that did not avail them with people who despise government.

We pretend to be Christians, and from the superior light we enjoy ought to exceed heathens, Turks, Saracens, Moors, Negroes, and Indians in the knowledge and practice of what is right. I will endeavour to show, by a few examples from books and history, the sense those people have had of such actions.

[...]

Unhappy people! to have lived in such times, and by such neighbours. We have seen that they would have been safer among the ancient heathens, with whom the rites of hospitality were sacred. They would have been considered as guests of the public, and the religion of the country would have operated in their favor. But our frontier people call themselves Christians! They would have been safer, if they had submitted to the Turks; forever since Mahomet's reproof to Khaled, even the cruel Turks never kill prisoners in cold blood. These were not even prisoners. But what is the example of Turks to Scripture Christians? They would have been safer, though they had been taken in actual war against the Saracens, if they had once drank water with them. These were not taken in war against us, and have drunk with us, and we with them, for fourscore years. But shall we compare Saracens to Christians?

They would have been safer among the Moors in Spain, though they had been murderers of sons; if faith had once been pledged to them, and a promise of protection given. But these have had the faith of the English given to them many times by the government, and, in reliance on that faith, they lived among us, and gave us the opportunity of murdering them. However, what was honorable in Moors, may not be a rule to us; for we are Christians! They would have been safer, it seems, among Popish Spaniards, even if enemies, and delivered into their hands by a tempest. These were not enemies; they were born among us, and yet we have killed them all. But shall we imitate idolatrous Papists, we that are enlightened Protestants? They would even have been safer among the Negroes

of Africa, where at least one manly soul would have been found, with sense, spirit, and humanity enough, to stand in their defence. But shall white men and Christians act like a Pagan Negro? In short, it appears, that they would have been safe in any part of the known world, except in the neighborhood of the Christian white savages of Peckstang and Donegall!

O, ye unhappy perpetrators of this horrid wickedness! reflect a moment on the mischief ye have done, the disgrace ye have brought on your country, on your religion and your Bible, on your families and children. Think on the destruction of your captivated countryfolks (now among the wild Indians) which probably may follow, in resentment of your barbarity! Think on the wrath of the United Five Nations, hitherto our friends, but now, provoked by your murdering one of their tribes, in danger of becoming our bitter enemies. Think of the mild and good government you have so audaciously insulted; the laws of your king, your country, and your God, that you have broken; the infamous death that hangs over your heads; for justice, though slow, will come at last. All good people everywhere detest your actions. You have imbrued your hands in innocent blood; how will you make them clean? The dying shrieks and groans of the murdered will often sound in your ears. Their spectres will sometimes attend you, and affright even your innocent children. Fly where you will, your consciences will go with you.

Source: John Bigelow, *The Works of Benjamin Franklin,* Vol. 4 (New York: Putnam, 1904), 54–75.

55. Paxton Boys Declaration, 1764

Introduction

Pontiac's Rebellion—named for a chief of the Ottawas—broke out in the spring of 1763 as western Indians tried to eject the British traders and settlers who had flooded into their territory at the close of the French and Indian War (1754–1763). The settlers on the western frontier bore the brunt of the uprising as Indians killed or captured some 2,000 of them. Many of Pennsylvania's frontier dwellers believed that the pacifist-controlled colonial legislature, governing from the safety and comfort of Philadelphia, was not doing enough to protect them. In December 1763 some 50 Pennsylvania frontiersmen, members of a gang called the Paxton Boys, set upon the village of Conestoga, where 22 peaceable friendly Indians lived. The gang murdered 20 inhabitants, including children, and then moved on to Lancaster and killed another 14 Indians who had taken refuge there. The murder of these innocents aroused widespread disgust. In 1764 about 600 Paxton Boys marched to Philadelphia to present their grievances, excerpted here, and demand legislative action to protect the frontier. Like the frontier dwellers of several other colonies, Pennsylvania's westerners believed that eastern politicians ignored their interests. The assembly eventually approved some expenditures for frontier defense.

Primary Source

To the Honourable John Penn, Esquire, Governor of the Province of *Pennsylvania*, and of the Counties of *New-Castle, Kent* and *Sussex*, on *Delaware*; and to the Representative of the Free-Men of said Province, in Assembly met.

We Mathew Smith, and James Gibson, in behalf of ourselves, and his Majesty's faithful and loyal subjects, the Inhabitants of the Frontier counties of *Lancaster, York*, Cumberland, *Berks*, and *Northampton*, humbly beg Leave to remonstrate, and to lay before you, the following Grievances, which we submit to your Wisdom for Redress.

1st. We apprehend, that as Free-Men and *English* subjects, we have an indisputable Title to the same Privileges and Immunities with his Majesty's other Subjects, who reside in the interior counties of *Philadelphia, Chester* and *Bucks*, and therefore ought not to be excluded from an equal Share with them in the very important privilege of Legislation. Nevertheless, contrary to the Proprietors Charter, and the acknowledged principles of common Justice and Equity, our five Counties are restrained from electing more than ten Representative, *viz.* four for *Lancaster,* Two for *York,* Two for *Cumberland,* and One for *Berks,* and One for *Northampton;* while the Three Counties (and City) of *Philadelphia, Chester,* and *Bucks,* elect Twenty-six; this we humbly conceive is oppressive, unequal and unjust, the Cause of many of our Grievances, and an infringement of our natural Privileges of Freedom and Equality, wherefore we humbly pray, that we may be no longer deprived of an equal Number with the Three aforesaid Counties, to represent us in Assembly.

2dly. We understand that a Bill is now before the House of Assembly, wherein it is Provided, that such Persons as shall be charged with killing any *Indians* in *Lancaster* County, shall not be tried in the county where the Fact was committed, but in the Counties of *Philadelphia, Chester,* or *Bucks*. This is manifestly to deprive *British* Subjects of their known Privileges, to cast an eternal Reproach upon whole Counties, as if they were unfit to serve their Country in the Quality of Jury-Men, and to contradict the well known Laws of the *British* Nation; in a point whereon Life, Liberty, and Security essentially depend: Namely, that of being tried by their Equals in the Neighbourhood where their own, their Accusers, and the Witnesses Character and Credit, with the Circumstances of the Fact are best known, and instead thereof, putting their Lives in the Hands of Strangers, who may as justly be suspected of Partiality to, as the Frontier Counties can be of Prejudices against *Indians;* and this too in favour of *Indians* only, against his Majesty's faithful and loyal Subjects. Besides it is well known that the Design of it is to comprehend a Fact committed before such a Law was thought of.

And if such Practices were tolerated, no man could be secure in his most invaluable Interests. We are also informed to our great Surprize, that this Bill has actually received the Assent of a Majority of the House, which we are perswaded could not have been the Case, had our Frontier Counties been equally represented in Assembly: However, we hope, that the Legislator of this Province will never enact a Law of so dangerous a tendency, or take away from his Majesty's good Subjects, a Privilege so long esteemed sacred by *English Men*.

3dly. During the late and present Indian Wars, the Frontiers of this province have been repeatedly attacked and ravaged by Skulking parties of the *Indians,* who have with the most savage Cruelty, murdered Men, Women and Children, without distinction; and have reduced near a Thousand Families to the most extream Distress. It grieves us to the very Heart, to see such of our Frontier Inhabitants as have escaped from savage Fury, with the loss of their Parents, their Children, their Husbands, Wives, or Relatives, left destitute by the Public, and exposed to the most cruel Poverty and Wretchedness; while upward of One Hundred and Twenty of the Savages, who are with great Reason suspected of being guilty of these horrid Barbarities, under the Mask of Friendship, have procured themselves to be taken under the Protection of the Government, with a view to elude the Fury of the brave Relatives of the Murdered; and are now maintained at the public Expence: Some of these *Indians* now in the Barracks of *Philadelphia,* are confessedly a part of the *Wyalusing Indians,* which Tribe is now at War with us; and the others are the *Moravian Indians,* who living amongst us under the Cloak of Friendship, carried on a Correspondence with our known Enemies on the *Great-Island.* We cannot but observe with Sorrow and Indignation, that some Persons in this Province are at pains to extenuate the barbarous Cruelties practiced by these savages on our Murdered Brethren and Relatives, which are shocking to human Nature, and must pierce every Heart but those of the hardened Perpetrators or their Abettors. Nor is it less Distressing to hear others pleading, that altho' the *Wyalusing* Tribe is at War with us; yet that part of it which is under the Protection of the Government may be friendly to the *English,* and Innocent. In what Nation under the Sun was it every the Custom, that when a neighbouring Nation took up Arms, not an individual of the nation should be touched, but only the Persons that offered Hostilities? Who ever proclaimed War with a part of a nation, and not with the Whole? Had these *Indians* disapproved of the Perfidy of their Tribe, and been willing to cultivate and preserve Friendship with us, why did they not give Notice of the War before it happened, as it is known to be the Result of long Deliberations, and a preconcerted Combination amongst them? Why did they not leave their Tribe immediately, and come amongst us before there was ground to suspect them, or War as actually waged with the Tribe? No, they stayed amongst them, were privy to their Murders and Ravages, until we had destroyed their Provisions, and when they could no longer subsist at Home, they came, not as Deserters, but as Friends, to be maintained thro' the Winter, that they may be able to scalp and butcher us in the Spring.

AND as to the *Moravian Indians,* there are strong grounds, at least to suspect their Friendship, as it is known that they carried on a Correspondence with our Enemies, on the *Great Island.* We killed three *Indians* going from *Bethelem* to the *Great-Island,* with Blankets, Ammunition and Provision; which is an undeniable proof, that, the *Moravian Indians* were in confederacy with our open Enemies. And we cannot but be filled with Indignation, to hear this Action of ours, painted in the most odious and detestable colours, as if we had inhumanly murdered our Guides, who preserved us from perishing in the Woods; when we only killed three of our known enemies, who attempted to shoot us when we surprised them. And besides all this, we understand that one of these very *Indians* is proved by the Oath of *Stenton's* Widow to be the very Person that murdered her Husband. How then comes it to pass, that he alone of all the *Moravian Indians* should join with the Enemy to murder that Family? Or can it be supposed that any Enemy *Indians* contrary to their known custom of making War, should penetrate into the Heart of a settled Country, to burn, plunder and murder the Inhabitants, and not molest any Houses on their Return, or ever be seen or heard of? Or how can we account for it that no Ravages have been committed in *Northampton* County since the Removal of the *Moravian Indians,* when the *Great Cove* has been struck since? These things put it beyond doubt with us, that the *Indians* now at *Philadelphia,* are His Majesty's perfidious Enemies, and therefore to protect and maintain them at the public Expence, while our suffering Brethren on the Frontiers are almost destitute of the Necessaries of Life and are neglected by the Public, is sufficient to make us mad with Rage, and tempt us to do what nothing but the most violent Necessity can vindicate. We humbly and earnestly pray therefore that these Enemies of his Majesty may be removed as soon as possible out of the Province.

4thly. We humbly conceive that it is contrary to the maxims of good policy and extreamly dangerous to our Frontiers, to suffer any *Indians* of what Tribe soever, to live within the inhabited Parts of this Province, while we are engaged in an Indian War; as Experience has taught us that they are all Perfidious, and their claim to Freedom and Independency puts it in their Power to act as spies, to entertain and give Intelligence to our Enemies, and to furnish them with Provisions and warlike Stores. To this fatal Intercourse between our pretended Friends and open Enemies we must ascribe the greatest Part of the Ravages and Murders that have been committed in the Course of this and the last Indian War. We therefore pray that this Greivance be taken under consideration and remedied.

5th. We cannot help lamenting that no Provision has been hitherto made, that such of our Frontier Inhabitants as have been wounded in defence of the Province, their Lives and Liberties, may be taken care of and cured of their Wounds at the public Expence. We therefore pray that this Grievance may be redressed.

6thly. In the late *Indian* War this Province, with others of his Majesty's Colonies gave rewards for *Indian* Scalps, to encourage the seeking them in their own country, as the most likely Means of destroying or reducing them to reason. But no such Encouragement has been given in this War, which has damped the Spirits of many brave Men, who are willing to venture their Lives in Parties against the Enemy. We therefore pray that public Rewards may be proposed for *Indian* Scalps, which may be adequate to the Dangers attending Enterprises of this Nature.

7th. We daily lament that Numbers of our nearest and dearest Relatives are still in captivity amongst the savage Heathen, to be trained up in al their Ignorance and Barbarity, or be tortured to death with all the Contrivances of Indian cruelty, for attempting to make their Escape from Bondage. We see they pay no regard to the many solemn Promises which they have made to restore our Friends, who are in Bondage amongst them; we therefore earnestly pray that no Trade may hereafter be permitted to be carried on with them, until our Brethren and Relatives are brought home to us.

8th. WE complain that a certain Society of People in this Province in the late *Indian* War and at several Treaties held by the Kings Representatives, openly loaded the *Indians* with Presents and that . . . a Leader of the said Society, in defiance of all Government not only abetted our Indian Enemies, but kept up a private Intelligence with them, and publickly received from them a Belt of Wampum, as if he had been our Governor or authorized by the King to treat with his Enemies. By this Means the *Indians* have been taught to dispise us as a weak and disunited People and from this fatal Source have arose many of our Calamities under which we groan. We humbly pray therefore this Grievance may be redressed and that no private subject be hereafter permitted to treat with or carry on a correspondence with our Enemies.

9thly. We cannot but observe with sorrow that Fort *Augusta* which has been very expensive to this Province, has afforded us but little assistance, during this or the last War. The Men that were stationed at that Place neither helped our distressed Inhabitants to save their Crops, nor did they attack our enemies in their Towns, or patrole on our Frontiers. We humbly request, that proper Measures may be taken to make that Garrison more serviceable to us in our Distress, if it can be done.

N.B. We are far from intending any Reflection against the Commanding Officer stationed at *Augusta,* as we presume his conduct was always directed by those from whom he received his Orders.

SIGNED on Behalf of ourselves, and by Appointment of a Great Number of the Frontier Inhabitants.

MATTHEW SMITH.
  JAMES GIBSON.

February 13th, 1764

Source: Matthew Smith, *A Declaration and Remonstrance of the Distressed and Bleeding Frontier Inhabitants of the Province of Pennsylvania* (Philadelphia: Printed by William Bradford, 1764).

56. Treaty of Fort Stanwix, November 5, 1768 [Excerpts]

Introduction

After the French and Indian War (1754–1763), British colonists streamed into the Indian lands of the Ohio Valley. Pontiac's Rebellion broke out in 1763 as western Indians tried to drive the British back east. In an attempt to address the causes of the rebellion, the British Board of Trade issued the October 1763 proclamation forbidding colonists from settling west of a line running along the crest of the Appalachian Mountains. Settlers ignored the proclamation line, so the king ordered Sir William Johnson, superintendent of Indian affairs, to negotiate with the Iroquois Confederacy and set a new boundary between British and Indian territory. Negotiations took place at Fort Stanwix, in the heart of Iroquois country. The Iroquois, who held Johnson in great esteem, agreed to cede their claims to land south of a line running from Fort Stanwix to Fort Pitt and then along the southern bank of the Ohio River to the mouth of the Tennessee River. However, the tribes that actually lived in this territory denied that the Iroquois had the authority to make the treaty. Colonists who moved into the territory soon fell victim to a new round of Indian raids. A second and more famous Treaty of Fort Stanwix, signed in 1784, formally ended hostilities between the United States and the Iroquois Confederacy, which had sided with the British during the American Revolutionary War (1775–1783).

Primary Source

Proceedings at a Treaty held by Sir William Johnson Baronet with the Six Nations, Shawanese, Delawares, Senecas of Ohio and other dependant Tribes, at Fort Stanwix in the months of October & November 1768, for the settlement of a Boundary Line between the Colonies and Indians, pursuant to His Majesty's orders

The Time appointed for the Indians to meet at Fort Stanwix being the 20th of Septr Sr Wm Johnson arrived there on the 19th accompanied by the Governor of New Jersey and several other Gentlemen, with 20 Boats loaded with the Goods intended for the Present to be made by the Cession of Lands to the King. The Commissioners from Virginia were already there, and on the 21st arrived Lieutt Govr Penn with Commrs from Pensilvania & several other gentlemen, The same day Messrs Wharton & Trent of Pensylvania delivered in an account of the Traders losses in 1763, together with their Powers of Attorney for obtaining a retribution in Lands, pursuant to an article of the Treaty of Peace in 1765

Several Indians came in & informed Sir Wm Johnson that those of Susquehanna were near at hand, and gave him sundry intelligences

On the 29th some Delawares arrived from Muskingham who left the Shawanees at Fort Pitt on their way to Fort Stanwix

30th The Bounds between the Mohawks and Stockbridge Indians were adjusted to mutual Satisfaction, and the latter returned home

At the beginning of October, there were 800 Indians assembled & continued coming in dayly till after the Treaty was opened. The upper Nations still remaining behind thro' evil Reports, and Belts sent amongst them. Sir William dispatched Messengers to hasten them and held several Congresses with those on the spot, antecedent to the Treaty, for adjusting differences and preparing them to enter heartily upon business on the arrival of the rest

On the 15th of Octr Govr Penn urged by the Affairs of his Province set off for Philadelphia leaving behind him as Commissioners Messrs Peters & Tilghman.

By the 22d there were 2200 Indians collected and several large Parties coming in the next day, amongst whom were all the cheifs of the upper Nations, Sir William prepared to open the Congress on the 24th

[. . .]

Then Sir William addressed the Govr of New Jersey & the Commissioners

Gentlemen

Agreeable to His Matys intentions signified to me by the secretary of State and for the satisfaction of the several Nations here assembled I take the liberty to recommend it strongly to your several Provinces to enact the most effectual Laws for the due observance of this Line & the preventing all future intrusions, as the expectations thereof and the reliance the Indians have on your Justice from the Assurances I gave them on that head have proved great inducements to the settlement of the Line now established between the Colonies and them

To this the Governors & Commissioners answered that nothing should be wanting on their parts to the obtaining such security for the Boundary as was deemed necessary on their return to their respective Colonies

Then Sir William at the desire of the Gentlemen Commissioners from Pensylvania acquainted the Indians, that they the Commissioners had a present ready to the amount of 500 Dollars to give in full satisfaction of the Conostoga Lands, which by the death of that People became vested in the Proprietaries—That they freely gave this sum as a farther Proof of the regard of that Province for them and of their concern for the unhappy fate of the Conostogas. Then Sir William told the Indians, that as the proprietaries did not know whether they would chuse money or Goods for the addition of Land to Pensylvania they were then unprovided, but that Sir William Johnson would be answerable for the speedy payment of the purchase, & would propose to them either to receive it in money to be sent on the Comrs return or in goods speedy as possible or to wait till the next spring by which time they could have goods better & more for the same money from England which was submitted to their determination

As it grew late Sir William dismissed the Indians till the next day when they were to subscribe to the Deed of Cession & receive the consideration

At night the cheifs came to Sir William told him that they had considered the proposals made by the Commissioners of Pensylvania, & preferred the receiving the purchase in Cash, as the speediest payment which was agreed to & security given that the same should be paid in Six Weeks

Novr 5th

The Present being placed in public view around the Buildings within the Fort early this morning the whole assembled in the Area, to subscribe to the Deed & receive the consideration

At a Congress with the several Nations Saturday Nov 5

PRESENT—as before.

The Speaker after repeating what Sir had said to them on the first Belt at the last Congress said

Brother

We thank you for what you have said & we are hopeful that you will observe your engagements as we mean to do on our parts; but as this will in a great measure depend upon the Colonies, We now desire their Representatives here present to do every thing for preserving those engagemts and keeping their people in good order

A Belt.

Then repeating what was said on the second Belt, said

Brother

We thank you for the advice you have given us not to listen to evil reports or lies.

Brother

We approve of your caution and shall observe it, and we shall from time to time give us the the earliest intelligence of any such Reports & from whence they come

A Belt.

Then in answer to Govr Francklin's Speech

Brother

We are glad to see that Governor Francklin is so well pleased with our having bestowed one of our own names upon him & are well pleased [to] hear you promise that he will always be ready to do us justice. We hope that all future Governors will act the same part. We acknowledge that several of our Nations now present were witnesses to the transaction at Easton & therefore acquit that Province of any demand and we have only to desire of him to follow your example in his future Conduct towards us, which will sufficiently recommend him and his people to our esteem

A Belt

Brother

The advice you gave us yesterday to continue firm and united and to live together as formerly we think it very salutary and intended for our Good. We are therefore intended to follow your advice shall lodge your Belt at our Fire place at Onondaga to the end that all our confederacy may have recourse to it & act accordingly

The Deed to His Majesty, that to the Proprietors of Pensylvania, with that to the Traders being then laid on the Table were executed in the presence of the Govr Commissioners, & the rest of the Gentlemen

After which the Cheifs of each Nation received the Cash which was piled on a Table for that purpose and then proceeded to divide the Goods amongst their People which occupied the remainder of that day

P M The Governor & Commissioners took leave and returned to their respive Provinces and that night Sir William took leave of the Cheifs recommending it to them to remember what had been then transacted & cautioning them against committing any Disorders at their Departure but to pack up their Goods & return home in peace & Good Order

Sunday Nov 6th

The Indians began to decamp & Sir William sett off on his return for Johnston Hall where he arrived on the ninth of that Month

A True Copy examined by
    G JOHNSON Deputy Agent as Secretary.

Deed Determining the Boundary Line between the Whites and the Indians

To all to whom, These presents shall come or may concern. We the Sachems & Cheifs of the Six confederate Nations, and of the Shawanese, Delawares, Mingoes of Ohio and other Dependant Tribes on behalf of our selves and of the rest of our Several Nations the Cheifs & Warriors of whom are now here convened by Sir William Johnson Baronet His Majestys Superintendant of our affairs send GREETING.

WHEREAS His Majesty was graciously pleased to propose to us in the year one thousand seven hundred and sixty five that a Boundary Line should be fixed between the English & us to ascertain & establish our Limitts and prevent those intrusions & encroachments of which we had so long and loudly complained and to put a stop to the many fraudulent advantages which had been so often taken of us in Land affairs which Boundary appearing to us a wise and good measure we did then agree to a part of a Line and promised to settle the whole finally when soever Sir William Johnson should be fully empowered to treat with us for that purpose

AND WHEREAS His said Majesty has at length given Sir William Johnson orders to compleat the said Boundary Line between the Provinces and Indians in conformity to which orders Sir William Johnson has convened the Cheifs & Warriors of our respective Nations who are the true and absolute Proprietors of the Lands in question and who are here now to a very considerable Number.

AND WHEREAS many uneasinesses and doubts have arisen amongst us which have given rise to an apprehension that the Line may not be strictly observed on the part of the English in which case matters may be worse than before which apprehension together with the dependant state of some of our Tribes and other circumstances which retarded the Settlement and became the subject of some Debate Sir William Johnson has at length so far satisfied us upon as to induce us to come to an agreement concerning the Line which is now brought to a conclusion the whole being fully explained to us in a large Assembly of our People before Sir William Johnson and in the presence of His Excellency the

Governor of New Jersey the Commissioners from the Provinces of Virginia and Pensilvania and sundry other Gentlemen by which Line so agreed upon a considerable Tract of Country along several Provinces is by us ceded to His said Majesty which we are induced to and do hereby ratify & confirm to His said Majesty from the expectation and confidence we place in His royal Goodness that he will graciously comply with our humble requests as the same are expressed in the speech of the several Nations addressed to His Majesty through Sir William Johnson on Tuesday the first of the Present Month of November wherein we have declared our expectation of the continuance of His Majestys Favour and our desire that our ancient Engagements be observed and our affairs attended to by the officer who has the management thereof enabling him to discharge all these matters properly for our Interest. That the Lands occupied by the Mohocks around their villages as well as by any other Nation affected by this our Cession may effectually remain to them and to their Posterity and that any engagements regarding Property which they may now be under may be prosecuted and our present Grants deemed valid on our parts with the several other humble requests contained in our said Speech

AND WHEREAS at the settling of the said Line it appeared that the Line described by His Majestys order was not extended to the Northward of Oswegy or to the Southward of Great Kanhawa river We have agreed to and continued the Line to the Northward on a supposition that it was omitted by reason of our not having come to any determination concerning its course at the Congress held in one thousand seven hundred and sixty five and in as much as the Line to the Northward became the most necessary of any for preventing encroachments at our very Towns & Residences We have given the Line more favorably to Pensylvania for the reasons & considerations mentioned in the Treaty, we have likewise continued it South to Cherokee River because the same is and we do declare it to be our true Bounds with the Southern Indians and that we have an undoubted right to the Country as far South as that River which makes our Cession to His Majesty much more advantageous than that proposed,

Now THEREFORE KNOW YE that we the Sachems and Cheifs aforementioned Native Indians and Proprietors of the Lands herein after described for and in behalf of ourselves and the whole of our Confederacy for the considerations herein before mentioned and also for and in consideration of a valuable Present of the several articles in use amongst Indians which together with a large sums of money amounts in the whole to the sum of Ten thousand four Hundred and Sixty pounds seven shillings and three pence sterling to us now delivered and paid by Sir William Johnson Baronet His Majestys sole Agent and superintendant of Indian affairs for the Northern department of America in the Name and on behalf of our Soverreign Lord George the third by the Grace of God of Great Britain France and Ireland King Defender of the Faith the receipt whereof we do hereby acknowledge WE the said Indians HAVE for us and our Heirs and Successors granted bargained sold released and confirmed and by these presents DO Grant bargain sell release and confirm unto our said Sovereign Lord King George the third, ALL that Tract of Land situate in North America at the Back of the British Settlements bounded by a Line which we have now agreed upon and do hereby establish as the Boundary between us and the British Colonies in America beginning at the Mouth of Cherokee or Hogohege River where it emptys into the River Ohio and running from thence upwards along the South side of said River to Kittaning which is above Fort Pitt from thence by a direct Line to the nearest Fork of the west branch of Susquehanna thence through the Allegany Mountains along the South side of the said West Branch untill it comes opposite to the mouth of a Creek callek Tiadaghton thence across the West Branch and along the South Side of that Creek and along the North Side of Burnetts Hills to a Creek called Awandae thence down the same to the East Branch of Susquehanna and across the same and up the East side of that River to Oswegy from thence East to Delawar River and up that River to opposite where Tianaderha falls into Susquehanna thence to Tianaderha and up the West side of its West Branch to the head thereof and thence by a direct Line to Canada Creek where it emptys into the wood Creek at the West of the Carrying Place beyond Fort Stanwix and extending Eastward from every part of the said Line as far as the Lands formerly purchased so as to comprehend the whole of the Lands between the said Line and the purchased Lands or settlements, except what is within the Province of Pensilvania, together with all the Hereditaments and Appurtenances to the same belonging or appertaining in the fullest & most ample manner and all the Estate Right Title Interest Property Possession Benefit claim and Demand either in Law or Equity of each & every of us of in or to the same or any part thereof TO HAVE AND TO HOLD the whole Lands and Premises hereby granted bargained sold released and confirmed as aforesaid with the Hereditaments and appurtenances thereunto belonging under the reservations made in the Treaty unto our said Sovereign Lord King George the third his Heirs & Successors to and for his and their own proper use and behoof for ever

In WITNESS whereof We the Cheifs of the Confederacy have hereunto set our marks and Seals at FORT STANWIX the fifth day of November one Thousand seven hundred and sixty eight in the ninth year of His Majestys Reign

for the Mohocks
    TYORHANSERE als ABRAHAM

for the Oneidas
    CANAGHQUIESON

for the Tuscaroras
    SEQUARUSERA

for the Onondagas
    OTSINOGHIYATA als BUNT

for the Cayugas
    TEGAAIA

for the Senecas
    GUASTRAX

Sealed and delivered and the consideration paid in the presence of

Wm Franklin Governor of New Jersey
    Fre. Smyth Cheif Justice of New Jersey
    Thomas Walker Commissioner for Virginia

Of the Council of Pensylvania
    Richard Peters
    James Tilghman

The above Deed was executed in my presence at Fort Stanwix the day and year above Written

W JOHNSON

Source: E. B. O'Callaghan, ed., *Documents Relative to the Colonial History of the State of New York,* Vol. 8 (Albany, NY: Weed, Parsons, 1857), 111–137.

57. Decharihoga, Speech to Sir William Johnson, July 11, 1774 [Excerpt]

Introduction

Six Native American tribes of the Iroquois language group—the Cayugas, Mohawks, Oneidas, Onondagas, Senecas, and Tuscaroras—formed a confederation known as the Iroquois Confederacy that controlled a huge expanse of territory across northern New York and Pennsylvania. Sir William Johnson, superintendent of Indian affairs in British North America from 1756 to 1774, lived among the Mohawks for several years. Johnson was considered a sachem, or major leader, and had taken as his wife a member of the Mohawk elite. The tribes of the Six Nations trusted Johnson, who treated them fairly and respectfully. During the French and Indian War (1754–1763), Johnson's ability to recruit the Iroquois to the British side had been invaluable. In 1774 Johnson, although extremely ill, called a meeting to hear the Indians' complaints of unfair treatment at the hands of British colonists. The complaint shown here details the offenses of a white trader who had been cheating the Indians out of their land. Johnson died suddenly during the proceedings. After his burial the hearings resumed, and

Johnson's successor, Guy Johnson (possibly his nephew), gave assurances that the matter would be pursued. Guy Johnson later succeeded in recruiting four of the six Iroquois nations to the British side of the American Revolutionary War (1775–1783). Only the Oneidas and Tuscaroras were loyal to the American side.

Primary Source

Brother:

It is with Pain I am under the necessity of Complaining again against that old Rogue, the old Disturber of our village, George Klock. You are long acquainted with his Artifices, and evil Conduct, and you have often assured us you had applied for Redress, but whatever is the Reason, we never yet Obtained any Satisfaction, and we begin to be doubtful whether the English will afford it to us, for which reason we are driven to the necessity of mentioning our Grievances to you in the Presence of the whole Confederacy, that they who know our Rank, may espouse our Cause, as it is their Duty to do, and convince the English that we have friends, and deserve Attention.

Brother—I will not take up your time with telling you, & your Brothers here present, the many Artifices he has made use of to Cheat us of our Lands, and to create Divisions among ourselves. I shall only mention his last Actions. This evil Spirit, last Winter by his Cunning, seduced one of our foolish young fellows to Steal away with him to England, where he exposed him for a shew, and Cheated him out of his Money. Klock has since Stolen home like a Rogue as he went out, and when we had notice of it, and applied to him to sign the Release, (which all the rest did) of the Lands which he Stole, he appointed a time for it, but when we came to his House, and brought a Justice of Peace to be present, he refused Admittance to him & us, and has since ran away, and propagated a Story that some of us threatened his Life. It is true, Brother, that the man he Cheated went and took some of his own Money, and probably, some of our young fellows after his own evil Example, might have used angry Threats to induce him to sign the Release, but we disavow it, as we do all his falsehoods, and are ready to wait for Justice. It has been often promised, but never afforded us. We beg that the great Men who manage the White People, may obtain Justice for us, and cause him to sign the Deed, and let us alone,—And if we thought this would still be done, we would willingly wait awhile patiently, otherwise, we cannot answer for the Consequences.

To which Sir William Johnson answd.

That they need not have mentioned this Matter to their Confederacy, who had no business with it,—that he would again lay the Matter before Government, and use all his endeavors for their satisfaction,—that they Should patiently wait without attempting any act of Violence, which wou'd be highly Resented, and that he

was Authorised to tell them that Klock's Conduct was disagreeable to the King.

When Sir William's immediate Deputy Col. Guy Johnson reasumed the affairs of the Congress after the Interment of Sr. Wm the Conajohares reminded him of their Speech concerning Klock, and were answered with Assurances that the same Should be laid before Government.

Taken from the Records

G. Johnson
  Super Intend't of Ind'n. Affairs

Source: E. B. O'Callaghan, *The Documentary History of the State of New-York* (Albany, NY: Weed, Parsons, 1850–1851), 582.

58. Accounts of Lord Dunmore's War, 1774 [Excerpts]

Introduction

John Murray, Lord Dunmore, was appointed royal governor of Virginia in 1771. Loyal to the British Crown, he punished the House of Burgesses for its rebellious activities by disbanding it in 1773 and again in 1774. During the same period, Indians had been attacking colonists living on the western frontier, and white frontiersmen retaliated. The Shawnees formally went to war and stepped up the pace and severity of their raids against settlers. Dunmore mustered the militia and in September 1774 led 2,000 men into the Ohio Valley. A major battle took place at Point Pleasant, at the mouth of the Kanawha River, on October 10, and Colonel Andrew Lewis and 1,000 militiamen defeated an equal number of Shawnees before Dunmore's force arrived. Dunmore then concluded a peace with Shawnee chief Cornstalk. In these excerpts, a militia officer describes the battle, and Dunmore recounts the peace negotiations. The parties agreed on the Ohio River as the dividing line between white and Indian territory. At the outbreak of the American Revolutionary War (1775–1783), Dunmore raised loyalist regiments and prepared to hold Virginia for the Crown. The rebels forced him to leave Virginia in July 1776.

Primary Source

Fleming's Account of the Battle of Point Pleasant

Colonel Fleming to His Wife

MY Dear Nancy—I take this Opportunity to write you that you may be convinced I am yet amongst the living on Munday last, we were Alarmed by some from Camp that had been pursued by

Indians. On the News being confirmed 150 from Augusta line & as many from the Botetourt, were ordered out. We marched in two Colums Colo. Ch: Lewis led the Augusta, I was at the head of the Botetourt line we had not march[ed] above three quarters of a mile before the Right line or Augusta line was Attack'd & in a second of time the Botetourt line likewise. The fire became general & very heavy. Colo. C. Lewis Receivd a mortal wound. I receivd three balls two through my left Arm, & one in my left breast, but I praise the Almighty, I did not fall and had strength with Assistance to reach my tent where I heard C[ol.] C. Lewis was just come in after I was dresd I went to see him. Colo. Lewis who as we did not expect a general engagement was in Camp behaved with the greatest Conduct & prudence and by timely & opportunely supporting the lines secured under God both the Victory & prevented the Enemy Attempts to break into Camp it was a hard fought Battle, lasted from 7 in the Morning to an hour by sun. The Indians were computed at 1000. but for a perticular Acct I must referr you to another time. I Bless God my wounds are in a good way. If it please God to spare me I propose coming in to the Inhabitants the first Opportunity. I am my Dear Nancy Yours &

WM FLEMING

OCTOBER 13, 1774

RICHD Wilson & Smith are both well Attend me Closely & will Return with me God willing

————————

Colonel William Fleming to William Bowyer

DEAR WILL—Agreeable to my Last from Belmont, I set out on Monday Aug. 21st and without any thing Remarkable Reached this place. Ye 6th Inst. where we continued without Interruption till Monday the 10th. when about Sunrise we had intelligence of a Man being kild & several closely pursued, by a large party or parties of Indians. Colo A: Lewis ordered 300 Men from the two Lines of Augusta & Botetourt Forces to go in Quest of the Enemy, little Imagining as we afterwards found it to be the Case that we were to engage the whole United Force of the Enemy Ohio Indians. We Marched from Camp in two lines. Colo. Charles Lewis led the Right line. I led the left. About ¾ of a mile from Camp, the Indians began the Attack on the right & in a Second of time the Left line was Attacked. I must refer you to particular Accounts of which no doubt you will see several, and only Observe generals, as I am ill at ease to write. Soon after or in the first Fire Colo. C. Lewis received a Mortal wound, and was brought to his tent with some Assistance. He died a few hours after, very much Regretted by the whole Army much about or soone after this hapned on the Right, I received three balls in the left Line two struck my left arm below the Elbow broke both the bones, & I find one of this is lodged in my arm. A

third entered my breast about three Inches below my left Nipple and is lodged some where in the Chest. On finding my self effectually disabled I quitted the Field. When I came to be drest, I found my Lungs forced through the wound in my breast, as long as one of my fingars. Watkins Attempted to reduce them ineffectually. He got some part returned but not the whole. Being in considerable pain, some time afterwards, I got the whole Returned by the Assistance of one of my Own Attendants. Since which I thank the Almighty I have been in a surprising state of ease. Nor did I ever know such dangerous wounds, Attended with so little inconvenience, and yet the wounds in my arm are in a bad condition. They do not digest and run but very little. What will be the consequence as yet I know not, but I write you circumstantially that you may if it is not too much trouble, write particularly to my wife. We had 7 or 800 Warriors to deal with. Never did Indians stick closer to it, nor behave bolder. The Engagement lasted from half an hour after [sunrise], to the same time before Sunset. And let me add I believe the Indians never had such a Scourging from the English before. They Scalpd many of their own dead to prevent their falling into Our hands, buried numbers, threw many into the Ohio and no doubt carried off many wounded. We found 70 Rafts. We tooke 18 or 20 Scalps, the most of them principle Warriors amongst the Shawnese &c, as we were informed by One McCulloch who came to us from his Lordship two days after the Ingagement, who viewed the Scalps & bodies & personally Knew them he says there is not a Noted Warriour left amongst the Shawnese. After the Ingagement Colo Lewis sent off some Scouts to his Lordship two of them are since Returned. His Lordship had Marchd from Hockhocking where he had been in Camp for some days. He was joined by White Eyes the Delaware who told his Lordship 700 Warriors were gon to the South, to speak with the Army there, & that they had been followed by another Nation, that they would begin with them, in the morning and their business would be over by Breakfast time. And then they would speak with his Lordship. That they came fully convinced they would beat us I think is certain. They cros'd the River & encamped the same side with us the Evening before, brought over with them their goods Deer Skins &c: took no pains to conceal themselves, And were boldly Marching to Attack Our Camp when we met them. Our Camp is situated on the Junction of the Kanhaway & Ohio in the Upper fork the Enemy in expectation of forcing us into the Ohio had lind the Opposite bank with some & the lower forks like wise was not neglected. The Enemy had brought their boys and squaas to knock us in the head I suppose, but God disappointed their Savage presumption. And tho Many brave Men lost their lives, Yet I hope in its consequences, it will be a general Good to the Country, and this engagement will be long Remembered to the Memory & Honour of those who purchas'd the Victory by their deaths. I am &c:

WM FLEMING

Be sure to write my wife the Substance of this, or enclose it to her.

[...]

In the mean time the ravage of the Indians, where ever they could carry it, was dreadful:—one Shawanese returned to his Town with the Scalps of forty men and Women and Children who he had killed. On the other hand a Party went out, with my permission, and destroyed one of the Shawanese Town, and meeting a Small Party of Indians, they killed Six or Seven of them, but this produced no Change in the designs of these People.

The real concern, principally, which the Continuation of these Miseries gave me, and, partly the Accounts Sent by the Officers of the Militia, of the Mutinous and ungovernable Spirit of their men, whom they could by no means bring to any order or discipline or even to Submit to command, determined me to go up into that part of the Country, and to exert my own immediate endeavours on this important occasion. Accordingly, as Soon as the business of the Oyer and Terminer Court in June permitted me, I sett out for Pittsburg where I arrived as has been already related. No time was lost in assembling The Delawar, Six Nations, and all the other Tribes the could be got at, or diligence neglected in conferring with them on the subject of the desolating consequences of Such enterprises as were Carrying on between the Shawense and their abettors, and our people; (I transmit to your Lordship an Account of the conferences held on this occasion in a printed copy (No. 7)) I found all those nations not only disposed to peace, but attached to our Cause, and they promised me, as your Lordship will perceive, that they would go down to the Shawanese (who with one or two less considerable Tribes only were concerned in the depredations that had been Committed) and, if I would appoint a time and place, bring them to Speak with me, and use their influence to incline them to Peace. I determined therefore to go down the Ohio; but I thought it Prudent to take a Force which might effect our purpose if our Negotiation failed: And I collected from the Militia of the Neighbouring Counties about twelve hundred men, to take with me, Sending orders to a colonel Lewis to March with as many more, of the Militia of the Southern Counties, across the Country to Join me at the Mouth of the little Kanhaway, the Place I appointed to meet the Indians at.

I passed down the river with this body of Men, and arrived at the appointed place at the Stated time. The day after Some of our friends the Delawars arrived according to their promise; but they brought us the disagreeable information, that the Shawanese would listen to no terms, and were resolved to prosecute their designs against the people of Virginia.

The Delawars, Notwithstanding, remained Steady in their attachment; and their Chief, named Captain White Eyes, offered me the assistance of himself and whole tribe; but apprehending evil effects from the Jealousy of, and natural dislike in our People to, all Indians, I accepted only of him and two or three: And I received great Service from the faithfulness, the firmness and remarkable good understanding of White Eyes.

Colonel Lewis not Joining me, and being unwilling to encrease the expence of the Country by delay, and, from the accounts we had of the numbers of the Indians, Judging the Force I had with me Sufficient to defeat them and destroy their Towns, in case they Should refuse the offers of peace; and after Sending orders to Colonel Lewis, to follow me to a place I appointed near the Indian Settlements, I crossed the Ohio and proceeded to the Shawanese Towns; in which March, one of our detached parties encountered an other of Indians laying in Ambush, of whom they killed Six or eight and took Sixteen Prisoners.

When we came up to the Towns we found them deserted, and that the main body of the Indians, to the amount of near five hundred, had Some time before gone off towards the Ohio; and we Soon learnt that they had Crossed that river, near the Mouth of the great Kanhaway, with the design of attacking the Corps under Colonel Lewis. In effect this Body, in their route to Join me, was encamped within a Mile of the Conflux of these two rivers, and near the place where the Indians Crossed, who were discovered by two men, of which they killed, of Colonel Lewis's Corps at break of Day the 10th of October. Colonel Lewis, upon receiving intelligence of their being advanced to within half a Mile of his Camp, ordered out three hundred men in two divisions, who upon their approach were immediately attacked by the Indians, and a very warm engagement ensued; Colonel Lewis found it Necessary to reinforce the divisions first Sent out, which (without the main Body of his Corps having engaged) obliged the Indians to retreat, after an Action which lasted till about one O'clock after noon, and little Skermishing till Night, under the favour of which the Indians repassed the river and escaped. Colonel Lewis lost on his side his Brother and two other Colonels of Militia, men of Character and Some Condition in their counties, and forty Six Men killed, and about eighty wounded. The loss of the Indians by their Accounts amounted to about thirty killed and some wounded.

The event of this Action, proving very different from what the Indians had promised themselves, they at once resolved to make no further efforts against a Power they saw so far Superior to theirs; but determined to throw themselves upon our Mercy: And, with the greatest expedition, they came in Search of the body with which they knew I marched, and found me near their own Towns the Day after I got there.

They presently made known their intentions, and I admitted them immediately to a conference, wherein all our differences were Settled. The terms of our reconciliation were, briefly, that the Indians should deliver up all prisoners without reserve; that they should restore all horses and other valuable effects which they had carried off; that they Should not hunt on our Side the Ohio, nor molest any Boats passing thereupon; That they Should promise to agree to such regulations, for their trade with our People, as Should be hereafter dictated by the Kings Instructions, and that they Should deliver into our hands certain Hostages, to be kept by us until we were convinced of their Sincere intention to adhere to all these Articles. The Indians, finding, contrary to their expectation, no punishment likely to follow, agreed to everything with the greatest alacrity, and gave the most solemn assurances of their quiet and peacable deportment for the future: and in return I have given them every promise of protection and good treatment on our Side.

Thus this affair, which undoubtedly was attended with circumstances of Shocking inhumanity, may be the means of producing happy effects; for it has impressed an idea of the power of the White people, upon the minds of the Indians, which they did not before entertain; and, there is reason to believe, it has extinguished the rancour which raged so violently in our People against the Indians: and I think there is a great probability that these Scenes of distress will never be renewed, than ever was before.

[…]

Source: Reuben Gold Thwaites and Louise Phelps Kellogg, eds., *Documentary History of Dunmore's War, 1774* (Madison: Wisconsin Historical Society, 1905), 253–257, 382–387.

59. Continental Congress, Two Addresses to the Six Nations, 1776–1777 [Excerpts]

Introduction

Six Native American tribes of the Iroquoian language group—the Cayugas, Mohawks, Oneidas, Onondagas, Senecas, and Tuscaroras—formed a confederation that controlled a huge expanse of territory across northern New York, Pennsylvania, and the Ohio Country. Guy Johnson, the superintendent of Indian affairs beginning in 1774, tried to recruit the Six Nations to the British side of the American Revolutionary War (1775–1783) and succeeded with four of them. Only the Oneidas and Tuscaroras were loyal to the American side. The 1776 message, directed to the Six Nations as well as the Delaware and Shawnee tribes, expressed a wish for their friendship but contained the implied threat that the Americans would meet violence with violence. The 1777 message, addressed to the Six Nations a year later, reproached those who had since begun fighting on the side of the British and asked them to reconsider. These messages failed to influence those who had decided to aid the British. Indian, British, and Tory fighters conducted brutal raids along the western frontier and into upstate New York. In 1779 George Washington ordered Major General

John Sullivan to wreak total destruction on the settlements of the enemy Iroquois.

Primary Source

Address to the Six Nations, December 7, 1776

Brothers of the Six Nations, Delawares and Shawanese,

We, the delegates of the thirteen United States of America, are extremely pleased to see you. We take you by the hand, and bid you welcome to our great council fire.

Brothers,

You say that God Almighty has been pleased to bring us together. You say well. He superintends and governs men and their actions. He now sees us. He judges of the sincerity of our hearts, and will punish those who deceive.

Brothers, Sachems [chiefs] and Warriors,

You have heard what our commissioners have said to you at Pittsburg, by our directions. You have listened to their arguments; and your own reason will suggest, that the conduct they have recommended to you, must be productive of your happiness and welfare. We think that you must be fully convinced that your safety, as nations, depends on preserving peace and friendship with the white people of this island.

We are sorry to hear of the death of your great men, and are well pleased that our commissioners have wiped the tears from your eyes, and covered the graves of our departed friends.

Our hearts are good towards all the Indians in the woods, who have friendly dispositions towards us.

We love peace, and wish that the chain of friendship between us and you may contract no rust. On our part, we will do every thing to keep it bright and strong.

But should we be attacked by any tribe of Indians in the woods, we hope to convince them that we can repel their attempts with ease. Friendship, however, with you, is what we earnestly desire. Our commissioners have told you so, and they have not deceived you.

We now inform you, that we wish to sit down with you under the same tree of peace; to water its roots and cherish its growth, so that it may shelter us and you, and our and your children.

Brothers,

We have prepared some presents for you, which our commissioners will deliver before your departure.

Address to the Six Nations, December 3, 1777

Brothers, Sachems, and Warriors of the Six Nations!

The great council of the United States call now for your attention. Open your ears, that you may hear, and your hearts, that you may understand,

Brothers, Sachems, and Warriors of the Six Nations!

When the people on the other side of the great water, without any cause, sought our destruction, and sent over their ships and their warriors to fight against us, and to take away our possessions, you might reasonably have expected us to ask for your assistance. If we are enslaved, you cannot be free. For our strength is greater than yours. If they would not spare their own brothers, of the same flesh and blood, would they spare you? If they burn our houses and ravage our lands, could yours be secure?

But, brothers, we acted on very different principles. Far from desiring you to hazard your lives in our quarrel, we advised you to sit still in ease and peace. We even entreated you to remain neuter; and, under the shade of your trees, and by the side of your streams, to smoke your pipe in safety and contentment. Though pressed by our enemies, and when their ships obstructed our supplies of arms and powder, and cloathing, we were not unmindful of your wants. Of what was necessary for our own use, we cheerfully spared you a part. More we should have done, had it been in our power.

Brothers, Cayugas, Senecas, Tascaroras, and Mohawks!

Open your ears and hear our complaints. Why have you listened to the voice of our enemies? why have you suffered Sir John Johnson and Butler to mislead you? why have you assisted General St. Leger and his warriors from the other side of the great water, by giving them a free passage through your country to annoy us; which both you and we solemnly promised should not be defiled with blood? why have you suffered so many of your nations to join them in their cruel purposes? Is this a suitable return for our love and kindness? or did you suspect, that we were too weak or too cowardly to defend our country; and join our enemies, that you might come in for a share of the plunder? what has been gained by this unprovoked treachery? what but shame and disgrace! your foolish warriors and their new allies have been defeated and driven back in every quarter; and many of them justly paid the price of their rashness with their lives. . . .

Brothers, Cayugas, Senecas, Tuscaroras, Mohawks!

Look into your hearts, and be attentive. Much are you to blame, and greatly have you wronged us. Be wise in time. Be sorry for and amend your faults. The great council, through the blood of our friends, who fell by your tomahawks at the German Flats, cries aloud against you, will yet be patient. We do not desire to destroy you. Long have we been at peace; and it is still our wish to bury the hatchet, and wipe away the blood which some of you have so unjustly shed. Till time shall be no more, we wish to smoke with you the calumet of friendship around your central council fire at Onondaga. But, brothers, mark well what we now tell you. Let it sink deep as the bottom of the sea, and never be forgotten by you or your children. If ever again you take up the hatchet to strike us; if you join our enemies in battle or council; if you give them intelligence, or encourage or permit them to pass through your country to molest or hurt any of our people, we shall look upon you as our enemies, and treat you as the worst of enemies, who, under a cloak of friendship, cover your bad designs, and, like the concealed adder, only wait for an opportunity to wound us, when we are most unprepared. . . .

Brothers, Oneidas and Onondagas!

Hearken to what we have to say to you in particular: It rejoices our hearts, that we have no reason to reproach you in common with the rest of the Six Nations. We have experienced your love, strong as the oak, and your fidelity, unchangeable as truth. You have kept fast hold of the ancient covenant-chain, and preserved it free from rust and decay, and bright as silver. Like brave men, for glory you despised danger; you stood forth, in the cause of your friends, and ventured your lives in our battles. While the sun and moon continue to give light to the world, we shall love and respect you. As our trusty friends, we shall protect you; and shall at all times consider your welfare as our own.

Brothers, of the Six Nations!

Open your ears and listen attentively. It is long ago that we explained to you our quarrel with the people on the other side of the great water. Remember that our cause is just; you and your fore fathers have long seen us allied to those people in friendship. By our labour and industry they flourished like the trees of the forest, and became exceeding rich and proud. At length, nothing would satisfy them, unless, like slaves, we would give them the power over our whole substance. Because we would not yield to such a shameful bondage, they took up the hatchet. You have seen them covering our coasts with their ships, and a part of our country with their warriors; but you have not seen us dismayed; on the contrary, you know, that we have stood firm like rocks and fought like men, who deserved to be free. . . .

Brothers: Believe us that they feel their own weakness, and that they are unable to subdue the thirteen United States. Else why have they not left our Indian brethren in peace, as they first promised, and we wished to have done? Why have they endeavoured by cunning speeches, by falsehood and misrepresentation, by strong drink and presents, to embitter the minds and darken the understandings of all our Indian friends on this great continent, from the north to the south, and to engage them to take up the hatchet against us without any provocation? The Cherokees, like some of you, were prevailed upon to strike our people. We carried the war into their country and fought them. They saw their error, they repented, and we forgave them. The United States are kind and merciful, and wish for peace with all the world. We have, therefore, renewed our ancient covenant-chain with that nation.

Brothers: The Shawanese and the Delawares give us daily proofs of their good disposition and their attachment to us; and are ready to assist us against all our enemies. The Chickasaws are among the number of our faithful friends. And the Choctaws, though remote from us, have refused to listen to the persuasions of our enemies, rejected all their offers of corruption, and continue peaceable. The Creeks are also our steady friends. . . .

Brothers, Sachems, and Warriors of the Six Nations!

Hearken to our counsel. Let us, who are born on the same great continent, love one another. Our interest is the same, and we ought to be one people, always ready to assist and to serve each other. What are the people who belong to the other side of the great water to either of us? They never came here for our sakes; but to gratify their own pride and avarice. Their business now is to kill and destroy our inhabitants, to lay waste our houses and farms. The day, we trust, will soon arrive when we shall be rid of them forever. Now is the time to hasten and secure this happy event. Let us then, from this moment, join hand and heart in the defence of our common country. Let us rise as one man and drive away our cruel oppressors. Henceforward let none be able to separate us.

If any of our people injure you, acquaint us of it, and you may depend upon full satisfaction. If any of yours hurt us, be you ready to repair the wrong or punish the aggressor. Above all, shut your ears against liars and deceivers, who, like false meteors, strive to lead you astray, and to set us at variance. Believe no evil of us, till you have taken pains to discover the truth. Our council-fire always burns clear and bright in Pennsylvania. Our commissioners and agents are near your country. We shall not be blinded by false reports or false appearances.

Source: *Journals of the Continental Congress, 1774–1789*, December 7, 1776, p. 1011, and December 3, 1777, pp. 995–996.

60. George Washington, Instructions to John Sullivan Ordering the Destruction of the Six Nations, May 31, 1779

Introduction

Of the Six Nations of the Iroquois Confederacy, the Cayugas, Mohawks, Onondagas, and Senecas joined the British side in the American Revolutionary War (1775–1783). Only the Oneidas and Tuscaroras were loyal to the American side. The British, Loyalists, and allied Indians conducted brutal raids along the western frontier and into upstate New York. The massacre of settlers in Pennsylvania's Wyoming Valley and New York's Cherry Valley stirred up public anger against the Indians. Since the military situation in the North was stalemated, General George Washington decided that he could afford to detach a force to deal with the problem. He ordered Major General John Sullivan to undertake the "total destruction and devastation" of the hostile tribes' settlements. Washington's orders demonstrate that he did not shrink from the language of total war, calling for the capture of prisoners of "every age and sex" and "the total ruinment of their settlements" and for Iroquois country to "be not only overrun, but destroyed." The campaign's only battle took place near the village of Newtown (near present-day Elmira, New York) on August 29, 1779. The Americans defeated a mixed force of Tories and Indians. Thereafter, the Americans marched into the heart of the Iroquois homeland to burn and destroy. The expedition ruined the Six Nations. The following winter, the Iroquois had to live on British charity.

However, this did not eliminate the Iroquois' ability to continue their raids. During 1780 and 1781 they struck more often and with greater brutality.

Primary Source

The Expedition you are appointed to command is to be directed against the hostile tribes of the Six Nations of Indians, with their associates and adherents. The immediate objects are the total destruction and devastation of their settlements, and the capture of as many prisoners of every age and sex as possible. It will be essential to ruin their crops now in the ground and prevent their planting more.

I would recommend, that some post in the center of the Indian Country, should be occupied with all expedition, with a sufficient quantity of provisions whence parties should be detached to lay waste all the settlements around, with instructions to do it in the most effectual manner, that the country may not be merely over-run, but destroyed.

But you will not by any means listen to any overture of peace before the total ruinment of their settlements is effected. Our future security will be in their inability to injure us and in the terror with which the severity of the chastisement they receive will inspire them.

Source: John C. Fitzpatrick, ed., *The Writings of George Washington* (Washington, DC: U.S. Government Printing Office, 1936).

61. Henry Dearborn, Account of John Sullivan's Indian Expedition, 1779

Introduction

Using bases in Canada, Indians, Britons, and Tories conducted savage raids along the western frontier and into upstate New York. The Wyoming Valley Massacre and the Cherry Valley Massacre stirred up public demand that Congress do something. The military situation to the north was stalemated, so George Washington decided that he could afford to detach a force to deal with the problem. Major General John Sullivan commanded the expedition. Washington instructed Sullivan to destroy the Iroquois settlements of the Six Nations. Colonel Henry Dearborn accompanied Sullivan's expedition. Excerpts from his Revolutionary War journals describe some of what took place. It is an account of savagery on both sides. The campaign's only battle took place near the village of Newtown (near present-day Elmira, New York) on August 29, 1779. The Americans defeated a mixed force of Tories and Indians. Thereafter the Americans marched into the heart of the Iroquois homeland to burn and destroy. The expedition ruined the Six Nations. The following winter the Iroquois had to live on British charity. However, this did not eliminate the Iroquois' ability to continue their raids. During 1780 and 1781 they struck more often and with greater brutality.

Primary Source

29th The army march'd at 9 oclock A.M. proceeded about 5 miles when our light troops discover'd a line of brestwork about 80 rods in their front, which upon reconoytering was found to extend about half a mile in length, on very advantageous ground with a learge brook in front. the river on their right, a high mountain on their left & a learge settlement in their rear call'd New Town; their works ware very artfully mask'd with green bushes, so that I think the discovering them was as accidental as it was fortunate to us. Skurmishing on both sides commence'd after we discover'd their works, cover'd by Gen¹. Hands Brigade, Gen¹. Poors Brigade & riflemen to turn the Enimies left, & fall in their rear, supported by Gen¹. Clintons Brigade: Gen¹. Maxwells Brigade to form a Corps dereserve; the left flanking division & light Infantry to pursue the enimy when they left their works.—at 3 oclock P.M. Gen¹. Poor began his rout by Collumns from the right of Reg¹s by files, we pass'd a very thick swamp, so cover'd with bushes for near a mile that the Collumns found great difficulty in keeping their order, but by Gen¹. Poors great prudence & good conduct, we proceeded in much better order than I expected we possibly could have done; after passing this swamp we inclin'd to the left, cross'd the creek that runs in front of the Enimies works:—on both sides this creek, was a learge number of new houses, but no land cleared. soon after we pass'd this creek we began to assend the mountain that cover'd the Enimies left. Immediately after we began to Assend the Mountain, we ware saluted by a brisk fire from a body of Indians who ware posted on this mountain for the purpos of preventing any troops turning the left of their works. at the same Instant that they began their fire on us, they rais'd the Indian yell, or war whoop: the rifle men kept up a scattering fire while we form'd the line of Battle, which was done exceeding quick; we then advanced rappedly with fix'd bayonets without fireing a shot, altho they kept up a steady fire on us until we gain'd the summet of the Mountain, which is about half a mile, we then gave them a full volley which oblig'd them to take to their heels: Col.⁰ Reids Reg.ᵗ which was on the left of the Brigade was more severely attackt then any other part of the Brigade, which prevented his advancing as far as the rest. after we had scowerd the top of the mountain, (in doing which Lᵗ. Cass of our Reg¹. tommohawk'd an Indian with the Indians own tomma-hawk that was slightly wounded) I being next to Col.⁰ Reid on the left, finding he still was very severely ingag'd nearly on the same ground he was first attackt on, thought proper to reverce the front of the Reg¹. & moove to his assistence. I soon discover'd a body of Indians turning his right, which I turn'd about by a full fire from the reg¹. this was a very seasonable relief to Col.⁰ Reid who at the very moment I fir'd on those that ware turning his right found himself so surrounded, that he was reduce'd to the nessessaty of

retreeting, or making a desparate push with the bayonet, the latter of which he had begun to put in execution the moment I gave him releaf; the Enimy now all left the field of action with precepetation, & in great confusion, pursued by our light Infantry about 3 miles, they lef[t] a number of their packs blankets &c on the ground.— half an hour before the action became serious with Gen¹. Poors Brigade the Artillery open'd upon their works which soon made their works too warm for them.—we found of the Enimy on the field of action 11 Indian warriers dead & one Squaw; toock on white man & one negro prisoners, from whome we learnt that Butler Commanded here, that Brant had all the Indians that could be muster'd in the five Nations, that there was about 200 whites a few of which ware British regular troops. it seems their whole force was not far from 1000.—these prisoners inform us that their loss in kill'd & wounded was very great, the most of which they according to custom, carried off.

13 March'd at 7 oclock proceed[ed] 1½ miles to a town call's Kanegsas or quicksea, consisting of 18 houses situate on an excellent Intervale near a small lake. we found a learge quantity of corn, beens, Squashes, potatoes, water Mellons, cucumbers &c &c in & about this town:—the army halted here 4 hours, to destroy the Town & corn, & to build a bridge over a creek.—at this town liv'd a very noted warrier call'd Great Tree, who has made great pretentions of friendship to us & has been to Phyladelphia & to Gen¹. Washingtons head Quarters since the war commenced, & has receiv'd a number of Presents, from Genl Washington & from Congress, yet we suppose he is with Butler against us.

A party of Rifle men & some others 26 in the whole under the command of Lᵗ. Boyd of the Rifle corps was sent last night to a town 7 miles from here to make what discoveries he could & return at day brake—4 of his men went into the town found it abandoned but found 3 or 4 scattering indians about it, one of which they kill'd & Skelp'd & then returd to Lᵗ. Boyd after sunrise who lay at some distance from the town.—he then sent 4 men to report to Gen¹. Sullivan what he had discovered, & moov'd on slowly with the remainder toward camp. after he had proceeded about half way to camp he halted some time expecting the Army along. he after halting some time sent 2 more men to Camp who discovered some scattering indians & returnd to Lᵗ. Boyd again. he then march'd on his party towards camp, discover'd some scattering Indians, one of which his men kill'd he soon found himself nearly surrounded, & attackt by two or three hundred savages & tories he after fighting them some time attemp[t] to retreet, but found it impracticable 6 or 7 of his men did make their escape, the remainder finding themselves completely surrounded ware determin'd to sell themselves as deer as possible, & bravely fought until every man was killed but 2 which ware taken one of which was Lᵗ. Boyd.

March 14th . . . after marching about 2 miles on this flat we came to the Chenesee river which we forded, passed over a body of flats on the other side & assended on to oak land, proceeded 3 miles & ariv'd at the town which we found deserted. here we found the bodies of L^t. Boyd & one other man Mangled in a most horred manner. from appeerences it seems they ware tyed to two trees near which they lay, & first severly whip'd, then their tongues ware cut out, their finger nails pluck'd off, their eyes pluck'd out, then speer'd & cut in many places, & after they had vented their hellish spite & rage, cut off their heads and left them.—this was a most horrid specticle to behold—& from which we are taught the necessaty of fighting those more than divels to the last moment rather than fall into their hands alive.—

This is much the leargest Town we have met with. it consists of more then 100 houses, is situate on an excellent piece of land in a learge bow of the river.—it appeers the savages left this place in a great hurry & confusion, as they left learge quantities of corn husk'd & some in heeps not husk'd & many other signs of confusion.

15th at 6 o'clock the whole Army ware turn'd out to destroy the corn in & about this town which we found in great abundance. we ware from 6 oclock to 2 P.M. in destroying the corn & houses. it is generally thought we have destroy'd 15000 bushels of corn at this place.—the meathod we toock to destroy it was to make learge fires with parts of houses & other wood & the pileing the corn on to the fire ading wood as we piled on the corn, which effectually destroyd the whole of it.—a woman with her child came to us to day who was taken at wyoming when that place was cut off. her husband & one child ware kill'd & skelp'd in her sight when she was taken. she informs us that butler & Brant with the tories & Indians left this place in a great hurry the 13 ins^t. & are gone to Niagara which is 80 miles from hence, where they expect we are going.—she says the Indians are very uneasey with Butler & their other leaders, & are in great distress.

Source: Frederick Cook, *Journals of the Military Expedition of Major General John Sullivan against the Six Nations of Indians in 1779* (Albany, NY: Knapp, Peck & Thomson, Printers, 1887), 87–88.

62. Promises of Land Grants to Volunteer Soldiers, 1780

Introduction

During the American Revolutionary War (1775–1783), the Americans and the British vied with one another to secure the loyalty of Indians and recruit the colonists. Lacking enough money to attract soldiers with the promise of generous pay, the colonial government authorized recruiters to promise extensive land grants to newly recruited volunteers. Inevitably the land would be carved out of Indian territories, particularly those of the Indians who joined the British side and attacked colonists settled on the western frontier. In 1778 Virginia colonel George Rogers Clark

received secret orders from Governor Patrick Henry to carry the Revolutionary War into hostile Indian territory and recruit militia in Kentucky (then a county of Virginia) for this purpose. Virginia legislators, including Thomas Jefferson, authorized Clark to offer 300 acres to each volunteer soldier and specify that the acreage would come from the conquered territory, not from friendly Indians. In the documents presented here, dated April 11, 1780, recruiters who have received a number of 560-acre land grants from Colonel Clark promise to recruit one soldier for every grant received. After the war, many American veterans sold their land grants to speculators in order to raise needed money.

Primary Source

Rec^d of Col: Ge^o R^s Clark this 11th day of Apr^l 1780 Six land Warrants Containing five Hundred & Sixty Acres of Land Each for which Warrants I promise to Delliver Col. Clark one Able Bodeyed Soldier for Each Warrant, p^r m^r

WILL SHANNON

J^{no} THRUTON SULLIVAN

Rec^d of Col: Ge^o R Clark 12th day of Aprile 1780 four land warrants cont^g five Hundred & sixty Acres Each for which I promis to Recruit four Able bodeyded Soldirers Durring the war to serve in Col Clarks Reg^t

ABRJI KELLARD

WILL SHANNON

Rec^d of Col: Ge^o R^s Clark 12th day of April 1780 twenty land warrants Containg five Hundred & sixty Acres Each for which I promis to return him twenty Able bodey^d Soldiers to serve during the war in his battalion

BU^D WORTHINGTON

WILL SHANNON.

Source: James Alton James, ed., *George Rogers Clark Papers, 1771–1781* (Springfield: Illinois State Historical Society, 1912), 37–38, 412–413.

63. Kentucky Petition for Protection from Shawnees, March 13, 1780

Introduction

The Shawnees of the Ohio Country had been barred from their Kentucky hunting grounds by treaties with the Iroquois and the Cherokees that had opened the territory to white settlement. Since the Shawnees had not been party to these treaties, they continually attacked Kentucky settlers. Virginia troops forced the Shawnees to make peace in 1774 (Kentucky was then considered part of Virginia). When the American Revolutionary War (1775–1783) broke out, British authorities in the region encouraged the Shawnees to resume their raids on Kentucky settlers and reclaim their hunting grounds. In 1778 Virginia militia colonel George Rogers Clark, who was in charge of defending the Kentucky frontier, received secret orders to carry the war into hostile Indian territory. Clark and his Kentucky recruits famously captured Kaskaskia, Kahokia, and Vincennes, British outposts north of the Ohio River. In 1780 British and Indian forces mounted attacks on Kentucky. This petition is one of several from Kentucky settlements asking Clark to assist in their defense. In August 1780 Clark led an expedition across the Ohio River and destroyed Shawnee villages and crops.

Primary Source

It is with the greatest concern That we, the Inhabitants of Bryan's Station, inform you that the Indians are again Doing mischief in our Country. Last Thursday William Bryan, a young man Belonging to this Station, was killed and scalped, as he was Coming in from hunt^g, and Two horses taken from the Company, and on Fryday the old Station of Licking was attacked fiercely. They Began Early in the morning and Continued till Late at night. Two of our men was wounded in the attack, and The Indians Carried off all the horses belonging to the station, except 2 or 3 which were in the fort, and killed almost all their cattle.

We are sure that we cannot Live in any tolerable degree of satisfaction, unless we Endeavour to carry on an Expedition against them, our Countrymen of every Station will give all the Assistance in their power, we believe; and we shall not be Backward to assist in so necessary an Enterprise. The more to facilitate the undertaking, we find ourselves Constrained to present this our address to you, Reposing special Trust in your patriotism, Courage and good Conduct. Beg you will head our men, and assist us with your great guns, with which we think we shall be able (under God) to Expel them from our Country.

We need not Exaggerate on the Cruelty and Devastation with which their foot steps are marked, as you are perfectly acquainted with their savage nature, and Every day almost produces to us fresh instances of their Rapine, and our unhappy Countrymen by them slain, are Irrefragable proofs of their malicious intentions. Therefore we Entreat you by all the ties of humanity to give us a helping hand, To take the Command of our men and your great guns, and march to the Towns of the Enemy, and Destroy them from the face of the Earth, if possible.

We from this station will send as many men as we can possibly spare, who will find themselves provision &c; and we Believe Every station will do the like, and We Believe we shall Be able to raise a Respectable Body in the Whole, which we think, by the Blessing of God, will be able to check their ravages, and we shall live in peace in satisfaction.

We beg you will take this matter into your Consideration, and give us an answer as soon as possible, as much Depends upon the Expedition of this matter, no time ought to be lost in the prosecution of it, as a few weeks, if not days, may prove fatal.

Am, Sir, Your most obed^t Servt

[not signed]

The inhabitants of Lexington having met together to consult on the contents of the above Letter this moment received from the Inhabitants of Bryan's station (situated on the North Fork of Elkhorn) it was unanimously agreed, that Col Clarke be supplicated to give his kind assistance to head our Men against those savage robbers who are again plundering our Country. You, Sir, are therefore earnestly requested by us to take the Command, to appoint a place of rendezvous, and we on our part will not be backward to give you all the assistance the strength of this garrison can possibly spare.

Signed in behalf of the inhabitants of Lexington.

Francis McConnell, John Morrison, James Nourse

P. S. Since we received the above, two men arrived at the fort chased by the Indians, which were plundering within six miles of this garrison, and a company of us are now going to march against them; but we think an expedition against the towns will be the most likely means to prevent further mischief.

[*Endorsed:*] The Inhabitants of Bryans Station Mar. 13th 1780

Source: James Alton James, ed., *George Rogers Clark Papers, 1771–1781* (Springfield: Illinois State Historical Society, 1912), 401–402.

64. Emerson Bennett, Portrayal of Simon Girty in *The Renegade* (1848), 1782 [Excerpt]

Introduction

As a child, Pennsylvania-born Simon Girty (1741–1818) was captured, along with his three brothers, and adopted by the Seneca Indians, with whom he lived for many years. As a result, he got along with Indians and was well versed in their ways. At the outbreak of the American Revolutionary War (1775–1783), Girty initially served the Americans as an interpreter, but when the Americans failed to honor his contract, he deserted to the British side in 1778, earning a reputation as a turncoat. Girty led Indian attacks on American soldiers in Kentucky and the surrounding region throughout the Revolution and again in the 1790s. In 1782 Girty was present when Indians tortured and killed the American officer William Crawford. Survivors later gave conflicting accounts of Girty's role. One account credited Girty with trying to save the prisoners, while another accused him of instigating and enjoying the torture. The latter account was widely believed and made Girty a hated figure. His exaggerated portrayal as a cardboard villain in the novel *The Renegade,* excerpted here, demonstrates the loathing that he inspired. The author, Emerson Bennett, born in Massachusetts in 1822, wrote more than 50 novels.

Primary Source

. . . As soon as mutual recognitions had passed between the prisoners, the individual habited in the British uniform stepped forward and said, jocosely:

"So, friends, we all meet again, do we, eh?—ha, ha, ha!"

At the sound of his voice, the old man and his wife, both of whom had been too intently occupied with Algerpon and Ella to notice him before, started, and turning their eyes suddenly upon him, simultaneously exclaimed:

"Mr. Williams!"

"*Sometimes* Mr. Williams," answered the other, with a strong emphasis on the first word, accompanying it with a horrible oath; "but now, when disguise is no longer necessary, Simon Girty, the renegade, by—!—ha, ha, ha!"

As he uttered these words, in a hoarse, bragadocia tone, a visible shudder of fear or disgust, or both combined, passed through the frame of each of the prisoners; and Algernon turning to him, with an expression of loathing contempt, said:

"I more than half suspected as much, when I sometime since contemplated your low-browed, hang-dog countenance. Of course we can expect no mercy at such hands."

"Mercy!" cried Girty, turning fiercely upon him, his eyes gleaming savagely, his mouth twisting into a shape intended to express the most withering contempt, while his words fairly hissed from between his tightly set teeth: "Mercy? dog! No, by h—l! for none like you! Hark ye, Mr. Reynolds! Were you in the damnable cells of the Inquisition, accused of heresy, and about to be put to the tortures, you might think yourself in Paradise compared to what you shall yet undergo!"

As he uttered these words, Ella shrieked and fell fainting to the earth. Springing to, Girty raised her in his arms, and pointing to her pale features, as he did so, continued:

"See! Mr. Reynolds, this girl loves you; I love her; we are rivals; and you, my rival, are in my power: and by—! and all the powers of darkness, you shall feel my vengeance!"

"You love her?" broke in Mrs. Younker, who, despite her previous dangerous warning, could hold her peace no longer: "You love her! you mean, contemptible, red headed puppy! I don't believe as how you knows enough to love nothing! And so you're Simon Girty, hey? that thar sneaking, red-coat renegade! Well, I reckon as how you've told the truth once; for I've hearn tell that he war an orful mean looking imp o' Satan; and I jest don't believe as how a meaner one nor yourself could be sheer'd up in the whole universal yarth o' creation."

"Rail on, old woman!" replied Girty, as he chafed the temples of Ella with his hands; "but in a little lower key, or I shall be under the necessity of ordering a stopper to your mouth; which, saving the tortures of the stake, is the worst punishment for you I can now invent. As for you, Mr. Younker," continued he, turning his face to the old man, with a peculiar expression, "you seem to have nothing to say to an old friend—ha, ha, ha!"

"Whensomever I mention the name o' Simon Girty," replied Younker, in a deliberate and startlingly solemn tone, "I al'ays call down God's curse upon the fiendish renegade—and I do so now."

"By—! old man," cried Girty, casting Ella roughly from him, and starting upright, the perfect picture of a fiend in human shape, "another word, and your brains shall be scattered to the four winds of heaven!" As he spoke, he brandished his tomahawk over the other's head, while the child before noticed, uttered a wild scream, and sprang to Mrs. Younker, at whose side she crouched in absolute terror.

"Strike!" answered Younker, mildly, with an unchanged countenance, his eye resting steadily upon the other, who could not meet his gaze in the same manner. "Strike! Simon Girty; for I'm a man that's never feared death, and don't now; besides, I reiterate all I've said, and with my dying breath pray God to curse ye!"

"Not yet!" rejoined Girty, smothering his rage, as he replaced his weapon. "Not yet, Ben Younker; for you take death too easy; and by—! I'll make it have terrors for you! But what child is this?" continued he, grasping the little girl fiercely by the arm, causing her to utter a cry of pain and fear. "By heavens! what do we with squalling children? Here, Oshasqua, I give her in your charge: and if she yelp again, brain her, by—!" and he closed with an oath.

Source: Emerson Bennett, *The Renegade* (Cincinnati: Robinson and Jones, 1848), 63–64.

65. Treaty of Paris, 1783

Introduction

Word of Cornwallis's October 19, 1781, surrender at Yorktown reached London on November 25. In March 1782 Parliament passed a resolution permitting the king to declare a truce. Britain now had to negotiate a peace with not only the United States but also with France, Spain, and Holland. The American peace commissioners—Benjamin Franklin, John Adams, John Jay, and Henry Laurens—received instructions from Congress to "be guided by the wishes of the French court" as they conducted negotiations from Paris. British officials first approached Franklin about a peace treaty in April 1782. A preliminary treaty, signed by representatives from both nations on November 30, 1782, granted to the fledgling United States nearly everything it wanted. The formal cessation of hostilities took effect on January 20, 1783. After an interval in which France and Great Britain concluded their own peace negotiations, the final Treaty of Paris was signed on September 3, 1783, and officially brought a close to the American Revolution, with Great Britain recognizing the colonies' independence. The bulk of the British Army left American soil, departing New York in November 1783. The Continental Congress ratified the Treaty of Paris on January 14, 1784. Britain also signed separate treaties with France and Spain, America's allies.

Primary Source

In the name of the most holy and undivided Trinity.

It having pleased the Divine Providence to dispose the hearts of the most serene and most potent Prince George the Third, by the grace of God, king of Great Britain, France, and Ireland, defender of the faith, duke of Brunswick and Lunebourg, arch-treasurer and prince elector of the Holy Roman Empire etc., and of the United States of America, to forget all past misunderstandings and differences that have unhappily interrupted the good correspondence and friendship which they mutually wish to restore, and to establish such a beneficial and satisfactory intercourse, between the two countries upon the ground of reciprocal advantages and mutual convenience as may promote and secure to both perpetual peace and harmony; and having for this desirable end already laid the foundation of peace and reconciliation by the Provisional Articles signed at Paris on the 30th of November 1782, by the commissioners empowered on each part, which articles were agreed to be inserted in and constitute the Treaty of Peace proposed to be concluded between the Crown of Great Britain and the said United States, but which treaty was not to be concluded until terms of peace should be agreed upon between Great Britain and France and his Britannic Majesty should be ready to conclude such treaty accordingly; and the treaty between Great Britain and France having since been concluded, his Britannic Majesty and the United States of America, in order to carry into full effect the Provisional Articles above mentioned, according to the tenor thereof, have constituted and appointed, that is to say his Britannic Majesty on his part, David Hartley, Esqr., member of the Parliament of Great Britain, and the said United States on their part, John Adams, Esqr., late a commissioner of the United States of America at the court of Versailles, late delegate in Congress from the state of Massachusetts, and chief justice of the said state, and minister plenipotentiary of the said United States to their high mightinesses the States General of the United Netherlands; Benjamin Franklin, Esqr., late delegate in Congress from the state of Pennsylvania, president of the convention of the said state, and minister plenipotentiary from the United States of America at the court of Versailles; John Jay, Esqr., late president of Congress and chief justice of the state of New York, and minister plenipotentiary from the said United States at the court of Madrid; to be plenipotentiaries for the concluding and signing the present definitive treaty; who after having reciprocally communicated their respective full powers have agreed upon and confirmed the following articles.

Article 1:

His Brittanic Majesty acknowledges the said United States, viz., New Hampshire, Massachusetts Bay, Rhode Island and Providence Plantations, Connecticut, New York, New Jersey, Pennsylvania, Maryland, Virginia, North Carolina, South Carolina and Georgia, to be free sovereign and independent states, that he treats with them as such, and for himself, his heirs, and successors, relinquishes all claims to the government, propriety, and territorial rights of the same and every part thereof.

Article 2:

And that all disputes which might arise in future on the subject of the boundaries of the said United States may be prevented, it is hereby agreed and declared, that the following are and shall be their boundaries, viz.; from the northwest angle of Nova Scotia, viz., that angle which is formed by a line drawn due north from the source of St. Croix River to the highlands; along the said highlands which divide those rivers that empty themselves into the river St. Lawrence, from those which fall into the Atlantic Ocean, to the northwesternmost head of Connecticut River; thence down along the middle of that river to the forty-fifth degree of north latitude; from thence by a line due west on said latitude until it strikes the river Iroquois or Cataraquy; thence along the middle of said river into Lake Ontario; through the middle of said lake until it strikes the communication by water between that lake and Lake Erie; thence along the middle of said communication into Lake Erie, through the middle of said lake until it arrives at the water communication between that lake and Lake Huron; thence along the middle of said water communication into Lake Huron, thence through the middle of said lake to the water communication between that lake and Lake Superior; thence through Lake Superior northward of the Isles Royal and Phelipeaux to the Long Lake; thence through the middle of said Long Lake and the water communication between it and the Lake of the Woods, to the said Lake of the Woods; thence through the said lake to the most northwesternmost point thereof, and from thence on a due west course to the river Mississippi; thence by a line to be drawn along the middle of the said river Mississippi until it shall intersect the northernmost part of the thirty-first degree of north latitude, South, by a line to be drawn due east from the determination of the line last mentioned in the latitude of thirty-one degrees of the equator, to the middle of the river Apalachicola or Catahouche; thence along the middle thereof to its junction with the Flint River, thence straight to the head of Saint Mary's River; and thence down along the middle of Saint Mary's River to the Atlantic Ocean; east, by a line to be drawn along the middle of the river Saint Croix, from its mouth in the Bay of Fundy to its source, and from its source directly north to the aforesaid highlands which divide the rivers that fall into the Atlantic Ocean from those which fall into the river Saint Lawrence; comprehending all islands within twenty leagues of any part of the shores of the

United States, and lying between lines to be drawn due east from the points where the aforesaid boundaries between Nova Scotia on the one part and East Florida on the other shall, respectively, touch the Bay of Fundy and the Atlantic Ocean, excepting such islands as now are or heretofore have been within the limits of the said province of Nova Scotia.

Article 3:

It is agreed that the people of the United States shall continue to enjoy unmolested the right to take fish of every kind on the Grand Bank and on all the other banks of Newfoundland, also in the Gulf of Saint Lawrence and at all other places in the sea, where the inhabitants of both countries used at any time heretofore to fish. And also that the inhabitants of the United States shall have liberty to take fish of every kind on such part of the coast of New-foundland as British fishermen shall use, (but not to dry or cure the same on that island) and also on the coasts, bays and creeks of all other of his Brittanic Majesty's dominions in America; and that the American fishermen shall have liberty to dry and cure fish in any of the unsettled bays, harbors, and creeks of Nova Scotia, Magdalen Islands, and Labrador, so long as the same shall remain unsettled, but so soon as the same or either of them shall be settled, it shall not be lawful for the said fishermen to dry or cure fish at such settlement without a previous agreement for that purpose with the inhabitants, proprietors, or possessors of the ground.

Article 4:

It is agreed that creditors on either side shall meet with no lawful impediment to the recovery of the full value in sterling money of all bona fide debts heretofore contracted.

Article 5:

It is agreed that Congress shall earnestly recommend it to the leg-islatures of the respective states to provide for the restitution of all estates, rights, and properties, which have been confiscated belonging to real British subjects; and also of the estates, rights, and properties of persons resident in districts in the possession on his Majesty's arms and who have not borne arms against the said United States. And that persons of any other description shall have free liberty to go to any part or parts of any of the thirteen United States and therein to remain twelve months unmolested in their endeavors to obtain the restitution of such of their estates, rights, and properties as may have been confiscated; and that Congress shall also earnestly recommend to the several states a reconsidera-tion and revision of all acts or laws regarding the premises, so as to render the said laws or acts perfectly consistent not only with justice and equity but with that spirit of conciliation which on the return of the blessings of peace should universally prevail. And

that Congress shall also earnestly recommend to the several states that the estates, rights, and properties, of such last mentioned per-sons shall be restored to them, they refunding to any persons who may be now in possession the bona fide price (where any has been given) which such persons may have paid on purchasing any of the said lands, rights, or properties since the confiscation.

And it is agreed that all persons who have any interest in con-fiscated lands, either by debts, marriage settlements, or otherwise, shall meet with no lawful impediment in the prosecution of their just rights.

Article 6:

That there shall be no future confiscations made nor any prosecu-tions commenced against any person or persons for, or by reason of, the part which he or they may have taken in the present war, and that no person shall on that account suffer any future loss or damage, either in his person, liberty, or property; and that those who may be in confinement on such charges at the time of the rati-fication of the treaty in America shall be immediately set at liberty, and the prosecutions so commenced be discontinued.

Article 7:

There shall be a firm and perpetual peace between his Brittanic Majesty and the said states, and between the subjects of the one and the citizens of the other, wherefore all hostilities both by sea and land shall from henceforth cease. All prisoners on both sides shall be set at liberty, and his Brittanic Majesty shall with all con-venient speed, and without causing any destruction, or carrying away any Negroes or other property of the American inhabitants, withdraw all his armies, garrisons, and fleets from the said United States, and from every post, place, and harbor within the same; leaving in all fortifications, the American artilery that may be therein; and shall also order and cause all archives, records, deeds, and papers belonging to any of the said states, or their citizens, which in the course of the war may have fallen into the hands of his officers, to be forthwith restored and delivered to the proper states and persons to whom they belong.

Article 8:

The navigation of the river Mississippi, from its source to the ocean, shall forever remain free and open to the subjects of Great Britain and the citizens of the United States.

Article 9:

In case it should so happen that any place or territory belonging to Great Britain or to the United States should have been con-quered by the arms of either from the other before the arrival of the said Provisional Articles in America, it is agreed that the same shall be restored without difficulty and without requiring any compensation.

Article 10:

The solemn ratifications of the present treaty expedited in good and due form shall be exchanged between the contracting parties in the space of six months or sooner, if possible, to be computed from the day of the signatures of the present treaty. In witness whereof we the undersigned, their ministers plenipotentiary, have in their name and in virtue of our full powers, signed with our hands the present definitive treaty and caused the seals of our arms to be affixed thereto.

Done at Paris, this third day of September in the year of our Lord, one thousand seven hundred and eighty-three.

D. HARTLEY (SEAL)
   JOHN ADAMS (SEAL)
   B. FRANKLIN (SEAL)
   JOHN JAY (SEAL)

Source: National Archives.

66. Joseph Brant, Message to the British Governor, 1783

Introduction

In the 1783 Treaty of Paris, which ended the American Revolutionary War (1775–1783), Great Britain granted the United States control of the territory extending from the east coast to the Mississippi River and from the northern border of Florida to the Great Lakes. The Indians who had supported the British during the war and lived in this territory were neither consulted during the negotiations nor mentioned in the treaty. Thayendanegea (1743–1807), also known as Joseph Brant, was a prominent Mohawk leader. The Mohawks were one of the Iroquois nations that had supported the British, contributing an estimated 300 warriors to the British side. Brant had led many of the most deadly attacks against the Americans. In this message to the governor of Quebec, Brant demands an explanation for the exclusion of Britain's Indian allies from the treaty. The Revolutionary War fatally weakened the Iroquois, and they never regained their power and influence. Most took refuge in Canada. The Fort Stanwix Treaty, signed in 1784, brought fighting between the United States and the Iroquois Confederacy to an end. An additional treaty was signed with the Mohawks that marked the end of Mohawk power. After the war, the United States stripped all British-allied Indians of their rights and lands, although the Indians who had supported the Americans did not fare much better in the long run.

Primary Source

Brother Asharekowa and Representatives of the King, the sachems and War Chieftains of the Six United Nations of Indians and their Allies have heard that the King, their Father, has made peace with his children the Bostonians. The Indians distinguish by Bostonians, the Americans in Rebellion, as it first began in Boston, and when they heard of it, they found that they were forgot and no mention made of them in said Peace, wherefore they have now sent me to inform themselves before you of the real truth, whether it is so or not, that they are not partakers of that Peace with the King and the Bostonians. Brother, listen with great attention to our words, we were greatly alarmed and cast down when we heard that news, and it occasions great discontent and surprise with our People; wherefore tell us the real truth from your heart, and we beg that the King will be put in mind by you and recollect what we have been when his people first saw us, and what we have since done for him and his subjects. Brother, we, the Mohawks, were the first Indian Nation that took you by the hand like friends and brothers, and invited you to live amongst us, treating you with kindness upon your debarkation in small parties. The Oneidas, our neighbors, were equally well disposed towards you and as a mark of our sincerity and love towards you we fastened your ship to a great mountain at Onondaga, the Center of our Confederacy, the rest of the Five Nations approving of it. We were then a great people, conquering all Indian Nations round about us, and you in a manner but a handful, after which you increased by degrees and we continued your friends and allies, joining you from time to time against your enemies, sacrificing numbers of our people and leaving their bones scattered in your enemies country. At last we assisted you in conquering all Canada, and then again, for joining you so firmly and faithfully, you renewed your assurances of protecting and defending ourselves, lands and possessions against any encroachment whatsoever, procuring for us the enjoyment of fair and plentiful trade of your people, and sat contented under the shade of the Tree of Peace, tasting the favour and friendship of a great Nation bound to us by Treaty, and able to protect us against all the world.

Brother, you have books and records of our mutual Treaties and Engagements, which will confirm the truth of what I have been telling, and as we are unacquainted with the art of writing, we keep it fresh in our memory by Belts of Wampum deposited in our Council House at Onondaga. We have also received an ornament for the Head, i.e. a crown, from her late Majesty, Queen Ann, as a token of her mutual and unalterable friendship and alliance with us and our Confederacy. Wherefore, we on our side have maintained an uninterrupted attachment towards you, in confidence and expectation of a Reciprocity, and to establish a Perpetual Friendship and Alliance between us, of which we can give you several instances, to wit, when a few years after the Conquest of Canada, your people in this country thought themselves confined on account of their numbers with regard to a Scarcity of Land, we were applied to for giving up some of ours, and fix a Line or mark between them and Us. We considered upon it, and relinquished a great Teritory to the King for the use of his Subjects, for a Trifling consideration, merely as a Confirmation of said Act, and as a proof of our sincere Regard towards them. This happened so late as the year 1768 at Fort Stanwix, and was gratefully Accepted and Ratified by the different Governors and Great men of the respective Colonies on the Sea Side, in presence of our Late Worthy Friend and Superintendent, Sir William Johnson, when we expected a permanent, Brotherly Love and Amity, would be the Consequence, but in vain. The insatiable thirst for Power and the next Object of dissatisfaction to the King's Subjects on the Sea Coast, and they to blind our Eyes, Sent Priests from New England amongst us, whom we took for Messengers of Peace, but we were Surprisingly undeceived when we found soon after, that they came to sow the Seeds of discord among our People, in order to alienate our ancient attachments and Alliance from the King our Father, and join them in Rebellion against him, and when they stood up against him, they first endeavored to ensnare us, the Mohawks, and the Indians of the Six Nations living on the Susquehanna River, and the Oneidas, by which division they imagined the remainder of the Confederacy would soon follow, but to not the Least effect. About this Sad Period we lost our Greatest Friend, Sir William Johnson, notwithstanding we were unalterably determined to stick to our Ancient Treaties with the Crown of England and when the Rebels attempted to insult the Families and Descendents of our late Superintendent, on whom the management of our affairs devolved, we stuck to them and Protected them as much as in our Power, conducting them to Canada with a determined Resolution inviolably to adhere to our Alliance at the Risque of our *Lives* Families and Property, the rest of the Six Nations finding the Firmness and Steadiness of us, the Mohawks, and Aughuagos, followed our Example and espoused the King's cause to this Present Instant. It is as I tell you, Brother, and would be too tedious to repeat on this Pressing Occasion the many Proofs of Fidelity we have given the King our Father. Wherefore Brother, I am now Sent in behalf of all the King's Indian Allies to receive a decisive answer from you, and to know whether they are included in the Treaty with the Americans, as faithful Allies should be or not and whether those Lands which the Great Being above has pointed out for Our Ancestors, and their descendants, and Placed them there from the beginning and where the Bones of our forefathers are laid, is secure to them, or whether the Blood of their Grand Children is to be mingled with their Bones, thro' the means of Our Allies for whom we have often so freely Bled.

Source: Colin G. Calloway, ed., *The World Turned Upside Down: Indian Voices from Early America* (Boston: St. Martin's, 1994), 167–169.

67. Benjamin Franklin, *The Savages of North America*, 1784

Introduction

The writings of Benjamin Franklin (1706–1790), one of the most accomplished and admired early Americans, reveal a sense of fairness and sympathy for Indians. From the time of first contact with the Indians of the Americas, European writers had idealized the Indians as "noble savages." Franklin, however, was more evenhanded in his assessment. Born into modest circumstances in a family of 17 children and with little formal education, Franklin became a publisher and an author and made a fortune as an inventor. His long political and diplomatic career began when he entered Pennsylvania politics. Franklin urged the colonies to unite with one another and allied Indians for mutual defense in the French and Indian War (1754–1763). One of the authors of the Declaration of Independence, Franklin traveled to France and persuaded the French to assist the Americans in the American Revolutionary War (1775–1783). After the war he again went to France to negotiate the peace treaty. *The Savages of North America* was published in England as a pamphlet in 1784 while Franklin was serving as the minister to France for the newly independent United States. In the pamphlet, Franklin satirically compares the traditional good manners among Indians with the rudeness of Americans, making the argument that the so-called savages are far from savage. Franklin returned to the United States in 1785 and two years later was instrumental in bringing about the adoption of the U.S. Constitution.

Primary Source

SAVAGES we call them, because their manners differ from ours, which we think the perfection of civility; they think the same of theirs.

Perhaps, if we could examine the manners of different nations with impartiality, we should find no people so rude, as to be without any rules of politeness; nor any so polite, as not to have some remains of rudeness.

The Indian men, when young, are hunters and warriors; when old, counsellors; for all their government is by the counsel or advice of the sages; there is no force, there are no prisons, no officers to compel obedience, or inflict punishment. Hence they generally study oratory, the best speaker having the most influence. The Indian women till the ground, dress the food, nurse and bring up the children, and preserve and hand down to posterity the memory of public transactions. These employments of men and women are accounted natural and honorable. Having few artificial wants, they have abundance of leisure for improvement by conversation. Our laborious manner of life, compared with theirs, they esteem slavish and base; and the learning, on which we value ourselves, they regard as frivolous and useless. An instance of this occurred at the treaty of Lancaster, in Pennsylvania, *anno* 1744, between the government of Virginia and the Six Nations. After the principal business was settled, the commissioners from Virginia acquainted the Indians by a speech, that there was at Williamsburg a college, with a fund for educating Indian youth; and that, if the chiefs of the Six Nations would send down half a dozen of their sons to that college, the government would take care that they should be well provided for, and instructed in all the learning of the white people. It is one of the Indian rules of politeness not to answer a public proposition the same day that it is made; they think it would be treating it as a light matter, and that they show it respect by taking time to consider it, as of a matter important. They therefore deferred their answer till the day following; when their speaker began, by expressing their deep sense of the kindness of the Virginia government, in making them that offer; "for we know," says he, "that you highly esteem the kind of learning taught in those colleges, and that the maintenance of our young men, while with you, would be very expensive to you. We are convinced, therefore, that you mean to do us good by your proposal; and we thank you heartily. But you, who are wise, must know that different nations have different conceptions of things; and you will therefore not take it amiss, if our ideas of this kind of education happen not to be the same with yours. We have had some experience of it; several of our young people were formerly brought up at the colleges of the northern provinces; they were instructed in all your sciences; but, when they came back to us, they were bad runners, ignorant of every means of living in the woods, unable to bear either cold or hunger, knew neither how to build a cabin, take a deer, nor kill an enemy, spoke our language imperfectly, were therefore neither fit for hunters, warriors, nor counsellors; they were totally good for nothing. We are however not the less obliged by your kind offer, though we decline accepting it; and, to show our grateful sense of it, if the gentlemen of Virginia will send us a dozen of their sons, we will take great care of their education, instruct them in all we know, and make *men* of them."

Having frequent occasions to hold public councils, they have acquired great order and decency in conducting them. The old men sit in the foremost ranks, the warriors in the next, and the women and children in the hindmost. The business of the women is to take exact notice of what passes, imprint it in their memories (for they have no writing), and communicate it to their children. They are the records of the council, and they preserve the tradition of the stipulations in treaties a hundred years back; which, when we compare with our writings, we always find exact. He that would speak, rises. The rest observe a profound silence. When he has finished and sits down, they leave him five or six minutes to recollect, that, if he has omitted any thing he intended to say, or has any thing to add, he may rise again and deliver it. To interrupt another, even in common conversation, is reckoned highly indecent. How different this is from the conduct of a polite British House of Commons, where scarce a day passes without some confusion, that makes the speaker hoarse in calling *to order;* and how different from the mode of conversation in many polite companies of Europe, where, if you do not deliver your sentence with great rapidity, you are cut off in the middle of it by the impatient loquacity of those you converse with, and never suffered to finish it!

The politeness of these savages in conversation is indeed carried to excess, since it does not permit them to contradict or deny the truth of what is asserted in their presence. By this means they indeed avoid disputes; but then it becomes difficult to know their minds, or what impression you make upon them. The missionaries who have attempted to convert them to Christianity, all complain of this as one of the great difficulties of their mission. The Indians hear with patience the truths of the Gospel explained to them, and give their usual tokens of assent and approbation; you would think they were convinced. No such matter. It is mere civility.

A Swedish minister, having assembled the chiefs of the Susquehanna Indians, made a sermon to them, acquainting them with the principal historical facts on which our religion is founded; such as the fall of our first parents by eating an apple, the coming of Christ to repair the mischief, his miracles and suffering, &c. When he had finished, an Indian orator stood up to thank him. "What you have told us," says he, "is all very good. It is indeed bad to eat apples. It is better to make them all into cider. We are much obliged by your kindness in coming so far, to tell us those things which you have heard from your mothers. In return, I will tell you some of those we have heard from ours." In the beginning, our fathers had only the flesh of animals to subsist on; and, if their hunting was unsuccessful, they were starving. Two of our young hunters, having killed a deer, made a fire in the woods to broil some parts of it. When they were about to satisfy their hunger, they beheld a beautiful young woman descend from the clouds, and seat herself on that hill, which you see yonder among the Blue Mountains. They said to each other, it is a spirit that perhaps has smelt our broiling venison, and wishes to eat of it; let us offer some to her. They presented her with the tongue; she was pleased with the taste of it, and said, 'Your kindness shall be rewarded; come to this place after thirteen moons, and you shall find something that will be of great benefit in nourishing you and your children to the latest generations.' They did so, and, to their surprise, found plants they had never seen before; but which, from that ancient time, have been constantly cultivated among us, to our great advantage. Where her right hand had touched the ground, they found maize; where her left hand had touched it, they found kidney-beans; and where her backside had sat on it, they found tobacco." The good missionary, disgusted with this idle tale, said, "What I delivered to you were sacred truths; but what you tell me is mere fable, fiction, and falsehood." The Indian, offended, replied, "My brother, it seems your friends have not done you justice in your education; they have not well instructed you in the rules of common civility. You saw that we, who understand and practise those rules, believed all your stories; why do you refuse to believe ours?"

When any of them come into our towns, our people are apt to crowd round them, gaze upon them, and incommode them, where they desire to be private; this they esteem great rudeness, and the effect of the want of instruction in the rules of civility and good manners. "We have," say they, "as much curiosity as you, and when you come into our towns, we wish for opportunities of looking at you; but for this purpose we hide ourselves behind bushes, where you are to pass, and never intrude ourselves into your company."

Their manner of entering one another's village has likewise its rules. It is reckoned uncivil in travelling strangers to enter a village abruptly, without giving notice of their approach. Therefore, as soon as they arrive within hearing, they stop and hollow, remaining there till invited to enter. Two old men usually come out to them, and lead them in. There is in every village a vacant dwelling, called *the strangers' house.* Here they are placed, while the old men go round from hut to hut, acquainting the inhabitants, that strangers are arrived, who are probably hungry and weary; and every one sends them what he can spare of victuals, and skins to repose on. When the strangers are refreshed, pipes and tobacco are brought; and then, but not before, conversation begins, with inquiries who they are, whither bound, what news, &c.; and it usually ends with offers of service, if the strangers have occasion for guides, or any necessaries for continuing their journey; and nothing is exacted for the entertainment.

The same hospitality, esteemed among them as a principal virtue, is practised by private persons; of which Conrad Weiser, our interpreter, gave me the following instance. He had been naturalized among the Six Nations, and spoke well the Mohock language. In going through the Indian country, to carry a message from our governor to the council at Onondaga, he called at the habitation of Canassetego, an old acquaintance, who embraced him, spread furs for him to sit on, and placed before him some boiled beans and venison, and mixed some rum and water for his drink. When he was well refreshed, and had lit his pipe, Canassetego began to converse with him; asked how he had fared the many years since they had seen each other; whence he then came; what occasioned the journey, &c. Conrad answered all his questions; and when the discourse began to flag, the Indian, to continue it, said, "Conrad, you have lived long among the white people, and know something of their customs; I have been sometimes at Albany, and have observed, that once in seven days they shut up their shops, and assemble all in the great house; tell me what it is for? What do they do there?" "They meet there," says Conrad, "to hear and learn *good things.*" "I do not doubt," says the Indian, "that they tell you so; they have told me the same; but I doubt the truth of what they say, and I will tell you my reasons. I went lately to Albany to sell my skins and buy blankets, knives, powder, rum, &c. You know I used generally to deal with Hans Hanson; but I was a little inclined this time to try some other merchants. However, I called first upon Hans, and asked him what he would give for beaver. He

said he could not give any more than four shillings a pound; 'but,' says he, 'I cannot talk on business now; this is the day when we meet together to learn *good things,* and I am going to meeting.' So I thought to myself, 'Since I cannot do any business today, I may as well go to the meeting too,' and I went with him. There stood up a man in black, and began to talk to the people very angrily. I did not understand what he said; but, perceiving that he looked much at me and at Hanson, I imagined he was angry at seeing me there; so I went out, sat down near the house, struck fire, and lit my pipe, waiting till the meeting should break up. I thought too, that the man had mentioned something of beaver, and I suspected it might be the subject of their meeting. So, when they came out, I accosted my merchant. 'Well, Hans,' says I, 'I hope you have agreed to give more than four shillings a pound.' 'No,' says he, 'I cannot give so much; I cannot give more than three shillings and sixpence.' I then spoke to several other dealers, but they all sung the same song,— three and sixpence,—three and sixpence. This made it clear to me, that my suspicion was right; and, that whatever they pretended of meeting to learn *good things,* the real purpose was to consult how to cheat Indians in the price of beaver. Consider but a little, Conrad, and you must be of my opinion. If they met so often to learn *good things,* they would certainly have learned some before this time. But they are still ignorant. You know our practice. If a white man, in travelling through our country, enters one of our cabins, we all treat him as I do you; we dry him if he is wet, we warm him if he is cold, and give him meat and drink, that he may allay his thirst and hunger; and we spread soft furs for him to rest and sleep on; we demand nothing in return. But, if I go into a white man's house at Albany, and ask for victuals and drink, they say, 'Where is your money?' and if I have none, they say, 'Get out, you Indian dog.' You see they have not yet learned those little *good things,* that we need no meetings to be instructed in, because our mothers taught them to us when we were children; and therefore it is impossible their meetings should be, as they say, for any such purpose, or have any such effect; they are only to contrive *the cheating of Indians in the price* of beaver."

Source: John Bigelow, ed., *The Works of Benjamin Franklin,* Vol. 10 (New York: Putnam, 1904), 385–394.

68. Treaty of Fort Stanwix, October 22, 1784

Introduction

Fort Stanwix, which stood at a strategic place at the head of the Mohawk River, controlled the portage between the river and Wood Creek and thus controlled the main travel route from Canada to the Mohawk Valley. This was also the heart of Iroquois country.

When the British conceded independence to the American colonies following the American Revolutionary War (1775–1783), they largely abandoned their Indian allies. During the war, the Sullivan-Clinton Expedition had marched into the Iroquois heartland and burned homes and ruined crops. The Iroquois had to flee to Canada and subsist on British charity. After the war, some Iroquois returned to their former homes. The Treaty of Fort Stanwix, signed on October 22, 1784, near Rome, New York, formally brought fighting between the United States and the Iroquois Confederacy to an end. However, the war had fatally weakened the Iroquois, and they never regained their power and influence. This treaty should not be confused with an earlier Fort Stanwix treaty signed in 1768 in which the Iroquois abandoned their claims to lands southeast of a line running from Fort Stanwix to Fort Pitt and then along the southern bank of the Ohio River to the mouth of the Tennessee River.

Primary Source

Articles concluded at Fort Stanwix, on the twenty-second day of October one thousand seven hundred and eighty-four, between Oliver Wolcott, Richard Butler, and Arthur Lee, Commissioners Plenipotentiary from the United States, in Congress assembled, on the one Part, and the Sachems and Warriors of the Six Nations, on the other.

The United States of America give peace to the Senecas, Mohawks, Onondagas and Cayugas, and receive them into their protection upon the following conditions:

ARTICLE 1. Six hostages shall be immediately delivered to the commissioners by the said nations, to remain in possession of the United States, till all prisoners, white and black, which were taken by the said Senecas, Mohawks, Onondagas and Cayugas, or by any of them, in the late war, from among the people of the United States, shall be delivered up.

ARTICLE 2. The Oneida and Tuscarora nations shall be secured in the possession of the lands on which they are settled.

ARTICLE 3. A line shall be drawn, beginning at the mouth of a creek about four miles east of Niagara, called Oyonwayea, or Johnston's Landing-Place, upon the lake named by the Indians Oswego, and by us Ontario; from thence southerly in a direction always four miles east of the carrying-path, between Lake Erie and Ontario, to the mouth of Tehoseroron or Buffaloe Creek on Lake Erie; then south to the north boundary of the state of Pennsylvania; thence west to the end of the said north boundary; then south along the west boundary of the said state, to the river Ohio; the said land from the mouth of the Oyonwayea to the Ohio, shall be the western boundary of the lands of the Six Nations, so that the Six Nations shall and do yield to the United States, all claims to the country west of the said boundary, and then they shall be secured in the peaceful possession of the lands they inhabit east and north of the same, reserving only six miles square round the fort of Oswego, to the United States, for the support of the same.

ARTICLE 4. The Commissioners of the United States, in consideration of the present circumstances of the Six Nations, and in executing of the humane and liberal views of the United States upon the signing of the above articles, will order goods to be delivered to the said Six Nations for their use and comfort.

Oliver Wolcott
    Richard Butler
    Arthur Lee

Mohawks:
    Onogwendahonji, his x mark
    Touighnatogon, his x mark

Onondagas:
    Oheadarighton, his x mark
    Kendarindgon, his x mark

Senekas:
    Tayagonendagighti, is x mark
    Tehonwaeaghrigagi, his x mark

Oneidas:
    Otyadonenghti, his x mark
    Dagaheari, his x mark

Cayuga:
    Oraghgoanendagen, his x mark

Tuscaroras:
    Ononghsawenghti, his x mark,
    Tharondawagon, his x mark

Seneka Abeal:
    Kayenthoghke, his x mark

Witness:
    Sam. Jo. Atlee
    James Dean
    Wm. Maclay
    Saml. Montgomery
    Fras. Johnston
    Derick Lane, captain
    Pennsylvaina Commissioners
    John Mercer, lieutenant
    Aaron Hill
    William Pennington, lieutenant

Alexander Campbell

Mahlon Hord, ensign

Saml. Kirkland, missionary

Haugh Peeles

Source: Fort Stanwix (Schuyler) Treaty, October 22, 1784. Part of the James Madison Papers at the Library of Congress Repository, Manuscript Division, Washington, DC 20540, http://hdl.loc.gov/loc.mss/mjm.02_0225_0226.

69. Daniel Boone, "Colonel Boone's Autobiography," 1784 [Excerpt]

Introduction

The main attraction for European immigrants to North America was the prospect of free land. The inexorable westward movement of the frontier created enormous conflict with the Indians. The English proclamation of 1763 forbade colonists from settling on land west of a line running along the crest of the Appalachian Mountains and ordered existing settlers to return east. The proclamation angered both land-hungry settlers and influential land speculators and was largely ignored. In 1775 Daniel Boone led about 30 men over the mountains into present-day Kentucky, where he established a settlement named Boonesborough. During this journey he blazed the Wilderness Road. Thousands of settlers subsequently followed this road west even while the American Revolutionary War (1775–1783) raged. In addition, Congress encouraged westward movement by offering land grants in the region to attract recruits for the army. Throughout the war, settlers in Kentucky (which became a county of Virginia in 1776) suffered repeated attacks from Indians and Loyalists, largely without assistance from the East. Boone's leadership helped them endure. In 1784 Boone published a colorful autobiography recounting some of his adventures and battles during these turbulent years in Kentucky.

Primary Source

[The following pages were dictated by Colonel Boone to John Filson, and published in 1784. Colonel Boone has been heard to say repeatedly since its publication, that "it is every word true."]

Curiosity is natural to the soul of man, and interesting objects have a powerful influence on our affections. Let these influencing powers actuate, by the permission or disposal of Providence, from selfish or social views, yet in time the mysterious will of Heaven is unfolded, and we behold our conduct, from whatsoever motives excited, operating to answer the important designs of Heaven. Thus we behold Kentucky, lately a howling wilderness, the habitation of savages and wild beasts, become a fruitful field; this region, so favorably distinguished by nature, now become the habitation of civilization, at a period unparalleled in history, in the midst of a raging war, and under all the disadvantages of emigration to a country so remote from the inhabited parts of the continent. Here, where the hand of violence shed the blood of the innocent; where the horrid yells of savages and the groans of the distressed sounded in our ears, we now hear the praises and adorations of our Creator; where wretched wigwams stood, the miserable abodes of savages, we behold the foundations of cities laid, that, in all probability, will equal the glory of the greatest upon earth. And we view Kentucky, situated on the fertile banks of the great Ohio, rising from obscurity to shine with splendor, equal to any other of the stars of the American hemisphere.

The settling of this region well deserves a place in history. Most of the memorable events I have myself been exercised in; and, for the satisfaction of the public, will briefly relate the circumstance of my adventures, and scenes of life from my first movement to this country until this day.

It was on the first of May, in the year 1769, that I resigned my domestic happiness for a time, and left my family and peaceable habitation on the Yadkin River, in North Carolina, to wander through the wilderness of America, in quest of the country of Kentucky, in company with John Finley, John Stewart, Joseph Holden, James Monay, and William Cool. We proceeded successfully, and after a long and fatiguing journey through a mountainous wilderness, in a westward direction. On the 7th of June following we found ourselves on Red River, where John Finley had formerly been trading with the Indians, and, from the top of an eminence, saw with pleasure the beautiful level of Kentucky. Here let me observe that for some time we had experienced the most uncomfortable weather, as a prelibation of our future sufferings. At this place we encamped, and made a shelter to defend us from the inclement season, and began to hunt and reconnoitre the country. We found everywhere abundance of wild beasts of all sorts, through this vast forest. The buffalo were more frequent than I have seen cattle in the settlements, browsing on the leaves of the cane, or cropping the herbage on those extensive plains, fearless, because ignorant of the violence of man. Sometimes we saw hundreds in a drove, and the numbers about the Bait springs were amazing. In this forest, the habitation of beasts of every kind natural to America, we practiced hunting with great success until the 22d day o' December following.

This day John Stewart and I had a pleasing ramble, but fortune changed the scene in the close of it. We had passed through a great forest, on which stood myriads of trees, some gay with blossoms, and others rich with fruits. Nature was here a series of wonders, and a fund of delight. Here she displayed her ingenuity and industry in a variety of flowers and fruits, beautifully colored, elegantly shaped, and charmingly flavored; and we were diverted with innumerable animals presenting themselves perpetually to our view. In the decline of the day, near Kentucky River, as we ascended the brow of a small hill, a number of Indians rushed out of a thick canebrake upon us, and made us prisoners. The time of our sorrow was now arrived, and the scene fully opened. The Indians plundered us of what we had, and kept us in confinement seven days, treating us with common savage usage. During this time we discovered no uneasiness or desire to escape, which made them less suspicious of us; but in the dead of night, as we lay in a thick canebrake by a large fire, when sleep had locked-up their senses, my situation not disposing me for rest, I touched my companion, and gently awoke him. We improved this favorable opportunity and departed, leaving them to take their rest, and speedily directed our course toward our old camp, but found it plundered, and the company dispersed and gone home. About this time my brother, Squire Boone, with another adventurer, who came to explore the country shortly after us, was wandering through the forest, determined to find me if possible, and accidentally found our camp. Notwithstanding the unfortunate circumstances of our company, and our dangerous situation, as surrounded with hostile savages, our meeting so fortunately in the wilderness made us reciprocally sensible of the utmost satisfaction. So much does friendship triumph over misfortune, that sorrows and sufferings vanish at the meeting not only of real friends, but of the most distant acquaintances, and substitute happiness in their room.

Soon after this, my companion in captivity, John Stewart, was killed by the savages, and the man that came with my brother returned home by himself. We were then in a dangerous, helpless situation, exposed daily to perils and death among savages and wild beasts—not a white man in the country but ourselves.

Thus situated, many hundred miles from our families in the howling wilderness, I believe few would have equally enjoyed the happiness we experienced. I often observed to my brother, "You see now how little nature requires to be satisfied. Felicity, the companion of content, is rather found in our own breasts than in the enjoyment of external things; and I firmly believe it requires but a little philosophy to make a man happy in whatsoever state he is. This consists in a full resignation to the will of Providence; and a resigned soul finds pleasure in a path strewed with briers and thorns."

We continued not in a state of indolence, but hunted every day, and prepared a little cottage to defend us from the winter storms. We remained there undisturbed during the winter, and on the first day of May, 1770, my brother returned home to the settlement by himself, for a new recruit of horses and ammunition, leaving me by myself, without bread, salt, or sugar, without company of my fellow-creatures, or even a horse or dog. I confess I never before was under greater necessity of exercising philosophy and fortitude. A few days I passed uncomfortably. The idea of a beloved wife and family, and their anxiety upon the account of my absence and exposed situation, made sensible impressions on my heart. A thousand dreadful apprehensions presented themselves to my view, and had undoubtedly disposed me to melancholy, if further indulged.

One day I undertook a tour through the country, and the diversity and beauties of nature I met with in this charming season, expelled every gloomy and vexatious thought. Just at the close of day the gentle gales retired, and left the place to the disposal of a profound calm. Not a breeze shook the most tremulous leaf. I had gained the summit of a commanding ridge, and, looking round with astonishing delight, beheld the ample plains, the beauteous tracts below. On the other hand, I surveyed the famous river Ohio, that rolled in silent dignity, marking the western boundary of Kentucky with inconceivable grandeur. At a vast distance I beheld the mountains lift their venerable brows, and penetrate the clouds. All things were still. I kindled a fire near a fountain of sweet water, and feasted on the loin of a buck, which a few hours before I had killed. The sullen shades of night soon overspread the whole hemisphere, and the earth seemed to gasp after the hovering moisture. My roving excursion this day had fatigued my body, and diverted my imagination. I laid me down to sleep, and I awoke not until the sun had chased away the night. I continued this tour, and in a few days explored a considerable part of the country, each day equally pleased as the first. I returned again to my old camp, which was not disturbed in my absence. I did not confine my lodging to it, but often reposed in thick canebrakes, to avoid the savages, who, I believe, often visited my camp, but, fortunately for me, in my absence. In this situation I was constantly exposed to danger and death. How unhappy such a situation for a man tormented with fear, which is vain if no danger comes, and if it does, only augments the pain! It was my happiness to be destitute of this afflicting passion, with which I had the greatest reason to be affected. The prowling wolves diverted my nocturnal hours with perpetual howlings; and the various species of animals in this vast forest, in the daytime, were continually in my view.

Thus I was surrounded by plenty in the midst of want. I was happy in the midst of dangers and inconveniences. In such a diversity, it was impossible I should be disposed to melancholy. No populous city, with all the varieties of commerce and stately structures, could afford so much pleasure to my mind as the beauties of nature I found here.

Thus, through an uninterrupted scene of sylvan pleasures, I spent the time until the 27th day of July following, when my brother, to my great felicity, met me, according to appointment, at our old camp. Shortly after, we left this place, not thinking it safe to stay there longer, and proceeded to Cumberland River, reconnoitering that part of the country until March, 1771, and giving names to the different waters.

Soon after, I returned home to my family, with a determination to bring them as soon as possible to live in Kentucky, which I esteemed a second paradise, at the risk of my life and fortune.

I returned safe to my old habitation, and found my family in happy circumstances. I sold my farm on the Yadkin, and what goods we could not carry with us; and on the 25th day of September, 1773, bade a farewell to our friends, and proceeded on our journey to Kentucky, in company with five families more, and forty men that joined us in Powel's Valley, which is one hundred and fifty miles from the now settled parts of Kentucky. This promising beginning was soon overcast with a cloud of adversity; for, upon the 10th day of October, the rear of our company was attacked by a number of Indians, who killed six, and wounded one man. Of these, my eldest son was one that fell in the action. Though we defended ourselves and repulsed the enemy, yet this unhappy affair scattered our cattle, brought us into extreme difficulty, and so discouraged the whole company, that we retreated forty miles, to the settlement on Clinch River. We had passed over two mountains, viz., Powel's and Walden's, and were approaching Cumberland mountain when this adverse fortune overtook us. These mountains are in the wilderness, as we pass from the old settlements in Virginia to Kentucky, are ranged in a southwest and northeast direction, are of a great length and breadth, and not far distant from each other. Over these, nature hath formed passes that are less difficult than might be expected, from a view of such huge piles. The aspect of these cliffs is so wild and horrid, that it is impossible to behold them without terror. The spectator is apt to imagine that nature has formerly suffered some violent convulsion, and that these are the dismembered remains of the dreadful shock; the ruins, not of Persepolis or Palmyra, but of the world!

I remained with my family on Clinch until the 6th of June, 1774, when I and one Michael Stoner were solicited by Governor Dunmore of Virginia to go to the falls of the Ohio, to conduct into the settlements a number of surveyors that had been sent thither by him some months before; this country having about this time drawn the attention of many adventurers. We immediately complied with the Governor's request, and conducted in the surveyors—completing a tour of eight hundred miles, through many difficulties, in sixty-two days.

Soon after I returned home, I was ordered to take the command of three garrisons during the campaign which Governor Dunmore carried on against the Shawanese Indians; after the conclusion of which, the militia was discharged from each garrison, and I, being relieved from my post, was solicited by a number of North Carolina gentlemen, that were about purchasing the lands lying on the south side of Kentucky River, from the Cherokee Indians, to attend their treaty at Wataga, in March, 1775, to negotiate with them, and mention the boundaries of the purchase. This I accepted; and, at the request of the same gentlemen, undertook to mark out a road in the best passage from the settlement through the wilderness to Kentucky, with such assistance as I thought necessary to employ for such an important undertaking.

I soon began this work, having collected a number of enterprising men, well armed. We proceeded with all possible expedition until we came within fifteen miles of where Boonesborough now stands, and where we were fired upon by a party of Indians, that killed two, and wounded two of our number; yet, although surprised and taken at a disadvantage, we stood our ground. This was on the 20th of March, 1775. Three days after, we were fired upon again, and had two men killed, and three wounded. Afterward we proceeded on to Kentucky River without opposition; and on the first day of April began to erect the fort of Boonesborough at a salt lick, about sixty yards from the river, on the south side.

On the fourth day, the Indians killed one of our men. We were busily employed in building this fort until the fourteenth day of June following, without any further opposition from the Indians; and having finished the works, I returned to my family on Clinch.

In a short time I proceeded to remove my family from Clinch to this garrison, where we arrived safe, without any other difficulties than such as are common to this passage; my wife and daughter being the first white women that ever stood on the banks of Kentucky River.

On the 24th day of December following, we had one man killed, and one wounded by the Indians, who seemed determined to persecute us for erecting this fortification.

On the fourteenth day of July, 1776, two of Colonel Calaway's daughters, and one of mine, were taken prisoners near the fort. I immediately pursued the Indians with only eight men, and on the 16th overtook them, killed two of the party, and recovered the girls. The same day on which this attempt was made, the Indians divided themselves into different parties, and attacked several forts, which were shortly before this time erected, doing a great deal of mischief. This was extremely distressing to the new settlers. The innocent husbandman was shot down, while busy in cultivating the soil for his family's supply. Most of the cattle around the stations were destroyed. They continued their hostilities in this manner until the 15th of April, 1777, when they attacked Boonesborough with a party of above one hundred in number, killed one man, and wounded four. Their loss in this attack was not certainly known to us. On the 4th day of July following, a party of about two hundred Indians attacked Boonesborough, killed one man and wounded two. They besieged us forty-eight hours, during which time seven of them were killed, and, at last, finding themselves not likely to prevail, they raised the siege and departed.

The Indians had disposed their warriors in different parties at this time, and attacked the different garrisons, to prevent their assisting each other, and did much injury to the distressed inhabitants.

On the 19th day of this month, Colonel Logan's fort was besieged by a party of about two hundred Indians. During this dreadful siege they did a great deal of mischief, distressed the garrison, in which were only fifteen men, killed two, and wounded one. The enemy's loss was uncertain, from the common practice which the Indians have of carrying off their dead in time of battle. Colonel Harrod's fort was then defended by only sixty-five men, and Boonesborongh by twenty-two, there being no more forts or white men in the country, except at the Falls, a considerable distance from these; and all, taken collectively, were but a handful to the numerous warriors that were everywhere dispersed through the country, intent upon doing all the mischief that savage barbarity could invent. Thus we passed through a scene of sufferings that exceeds description.

On the 25th of this month, a reinforcement of forty-five men arrived from North Carolina, and about the 20th of August following, Colonel Bowman arrived with one hundred men from Virginia. Now we began to strengthen; and hence, for the space of six weeks, we had skirmishes with Indians, in one quarter or another, almost every day.

The savages now learned the superiority of the Long Knife, as they call the Virginians, by experience; being out-generalled in almost every battle. Our affairs began to wear a new aspect, and the enemy, not daring to venture on open war, practiced secret mischief at times.

On the 1st day of January, 1778, I went with a party of thirty men to the Blue Licks, on Licking River, to make salt for the different garrisons in the country.

On the 7th day of February, as I was hunting to procure meat for the company, I met with a party of one hundred and two Indians, and two Frenchmen, on their march against Boonesborough, that place being particularly the object of the enemy. They pursued, and took me; and brought me on the 8th day to the Licks, where twenty-seven of my party were, three of them having previously returned home with the salt. I, knowing it was impossible for them to escape, capitulated with the enemy, and, at a distance, in their view, gave notice to my men of their situation, with orders not to resist, but surrender themselves captives.

The generous usage the Indians had promised before in my capitulation, was afterward fully complied with, and we proceeded with them as prisoners to Old Chilicothe, the principal Indian Town on Little Miami, where we arrived, after an uncomfortable journey, in very severe weather, on the 18th day of February, and received as good treatment as prisoners could expect from savages. On the 10th day of March following, I and ten of my men were conducted by forty Indians to Detroit, where we arrived the 30th day, and were treated by Governor Hamilton, the British commander at that post, with great humanity.

During our travels, the Indians entertained me well, and their affection for me was so great, that they utterly refused to leave me there with the others, although the Governor offered them one hundred pounds sterling for me, on purpose to give me a parole to go home. Several English gentlemen there, being sensible of my adverse fortune, and touched with human sympathy, generously offered a friendly supply for my wants, which I refused, with many thanks for their kindness—adding, that I never expected it would be in my power to recompense such unmerited generosity.

The Indians left my men in captivity with the British at Detroit, and on the 10th day of April brought me toward Old Chilicothe, where we arrived on the 25th day of the same month. This was a long and fatiguing march, through an exceedingly fertile country, remarkable for fine springs and streams of water. At Chilicothe I spent my time as comfortably as I could expect; was adopted, according to their custom, into a family, where I became a son, and had a great share in the affection of my new parents, brothers, sisters, and friends. I was exceedingly familiar and friendly with them, always appearing as cheerful and satisfied as possible, and they put great confidence in me. I often went a hunting with them, and frequently gained their applause for my activity at our shooting-matches. I was careful not to exceed many of them in shooting; for no people are more envious than they in this sport. I could observe, in their countenances and gestures, the greatest expressions of joy when they exceeded me; and, when the reverse happened, of envy. The Shawanese king took great notice of me, and treated me with profound respect and entire friendship, often intrusting me to hunt at my liberty. I frequently returned with the spoils of the woods, and as often presented some of what I had taken to him, expressive of duty to my sovereign. My food and lodging were in common with them; not so good, indeed, as I could desire, but necessity makes every thing acceptable.

I now began to meditate an escape, and carefully avoided their suspicions, continuing with them at Old Chilicothe until the 1st day of June following, and then was taken by them to the salt springs on Scioto, and kept there making salt ten days. During this time I hunted some for them, and found the land, for a great extent about this river, to exceed the soil of Kentucky, if possible, and remarkably well watered.

When I returned to Chilicothe, alarmed to see four hundred and fifty Indians, of their choicest warriors, painted and armed in a fearful manner, ready to march against Boonesborough, I determined to escape the first opportunity.

On the 16th, before sunrise, I departed in the most secret manner, and arrived at Boonesborough on the 20th, after a journey of one hundred and sixty miles, during which I had but one meal.

I found our fortress in a bad state of defense; but we proceeded immediately to repair our flanks, strengthen our gates and posterns, and form double bastions, which we completed in ten days. In this time we daily expected the arrival of the Indian army; and at length, one of my fellow-prisoners, escaping from them, arrived, informing us that the enemy had, on account of my departure, postponed their expedition three weeks. The Indians had spies out viewing our movements, and were greatly alarmed with our increase in number and fort ideations. The grand council of the nations was held frequently and with more deliberation than usual. They evidently saw the approaching hour when the Long Knife would dispossess them of their desirable habitations; and, anxiously concerned for futurity, determined utterly to extirpate the whites out of Kentucky. We were not intimidated by their movements, but frequently gave them proofs of our courage.

About the first of August, I made an incursion into the Indian country with a party of nineteen men, in order to surprise a small town up Scioto, called Paint Creek Town. We advanced within four miles thereof, when we met a party of thirty Indians on their march against Boonesborough, intending to join the others from Chilicothe. A smart fight ensued between us for some time; at length the savages gave way and fled. We had no loss on our side;

the enemy had one killed, and two wounded. We took from them three horses, and all their baggage; and being informed by two of our number that went to their town, that the Indians had entirely evacuated it, we proceeded no further, and returned with all possible expedition to assist our garrison against the other party. We passed by them on the sixth day, and on the seventh we arrived safe at Boonesborough.

On the 8th, the Indian army arrived, being four hundred and forty-four in number, commanded by Captain Duquesne, eleven other Frenchmen, and some of their own chiefs, and marched up within view of our fort, with British and French colors flying; and having sent a summons to me, in his Britannia Majesty's name, to surrender the fort, I requested two days consideration, which was granted.

It was now a critical period with us. We were a small number in the garrison—a powerful army before our walls, whose appearance proclaimed inevitable death, fearfully painted, and marking their footsteps with desolation. Death was preferable to captivity; and if taken by storm, we must inevitably be devoted to destruction. In this situation we concluded to maintain our garrison, if possible. We immediately proceeded to collect what we could of our horses and other cattle, and bring them through the posterns into the fort; and in the evening of the 9th, I returned answer that we were determined to defend our fort while a man was living. "Now," said I to their commander, who stood attentively hearing my sentiments, "we laugh at your formidable preparations; but thank you for giving us notice and time to provide for our defense. Your efforts will not prevail; for our gates shall forever deny you admittance." Whether this answer affected their courage or not I cannot tell; but contrary to our expectations, they formed a scheme to deceive us, declaring it was their orders, from Governor Hamilton, to take us captives, and not to destroy us; but if nine of us would come out and treat with them, they would immediately withdraw their forces from our walls, and return home peaceably. This sounded grateful in our ears; and we agreed to the proposal.

We held the treaty within sixty yards of the garrison, on purpose to divert them from a breach of honor, as we could not avoid suspicions of the savages. In this situation the articles were formally agreed to, and signed; and the Indians told us it was customary with them on such occasions for two Indians to shake hands with every white man in the treaty, as an evidence of entire friendship. We agreed to this also, but were soon convinced their policy was to take us prisoners. They immediately grappled us; but, although surrounded by hundreds of savages, we extricated ourselves from them, and escaped all safe into the garrison, except one that was wounded, through a heavy fire from their army. They immediately attacked us on every side, and a constant heavy fire ensued between us, day and night, for the space of nine days.

In this time the enemy began to undermine our fort, which was situated sixty yards from Kentucky River. They began at the water-mark, and proceeded in the bank some distance, which we understood by their making the water muddy with the clay; and

we immediately proceeded to disappoint their design, by cutting a trench across their subterranean passage. The enemy, discovering our countermine by the clay we threw out of the fort, desisted from that stratagem; and experience now fully convincing them that neither their power nor policy could effect their purpose, on the 20th day of August they raised the siege and departed.

During this siege, which threatened death in every form, we had two men killed, and four wounded, besides a number of cattle. We killed of the enemy thirty-seven, and wounded a great number. After they were gone, we picked up one hundred and twenty-five pounds weight of bullets, besides what stuck in the logs of our fort, which certainly is a great proof of their industry. Soon after this, I went into the settlement, and nothing worthy of a place in this account passed in my affairs for some time.

During my absence from Kentucky, Colonel Bowman carried on an expedition against the Shawanese, at Old Chilicothe, with one hundred and sixty men, in July, 1779. Here they arrived undiscovered, and a battle ensued, which lasted until ten o'clock, A. M., when Colonel Bowman, finding he could not succeed at this time, retreated about thirty miles. The Indians, in the meantime, collecting all their forces, pursued and overtook him, when a smart fight continued near two hours, not to the advantage of Colonel Bowman's party.

Colonel Harrod proposed to mount a number of horse, and furiously to rush upon the savages, who at this time fought with remarkable fury. This desperate step had a happy effect, broke their line of battle, and the savages fled on all sides. In these two battles we had nine killed, and one wounded. The enemy's loss uncertain, only two scalps being taken.

On the 22d day of June, 1780, a large party of Indians and Canadians, about six hundred in number, commanded by Colonel Bird, attacked Riddle's and Martin's stations, at the forks of Licking River, with six pieces of artillery. They carried this expedition so secretly, that the unwary inhabitants did not discover them until they fired upon the forts; and, not being prepared to oppose them, were obliged to surrender themselves miserable captives to barbarous savages, who immediately after tomahawked one man and two women, and loaded all the others with heavy baggage, forcing them along toward their towns, able or unable to march. Such as were weak and faint by the way, they tomahawked. The tender women and helpless children fell victims to their cruelty. This, and the savage treatment they received afterward, is shocking to humanity and too barbarous to relate.

The hostile disposition of the savages and their allies caused General Clarke, the commandant at the Falls of the Ohio, immediately to begin an expedition with his own regiment, and the armed force of the country, against Pecaway, the principal town of the Shawanese, on a branch of Great Miami, which he finished with great success, took seventeen scalps, and burnt the town to ashes, with the loss of seventeen men.

About this time I returned to Kentucky with my family; and here, to avoid an inquiry into my conduct, the reader being before informed of my bringing my family to Kentucky, I am under the necessity of informing him that, during my captivity with the Indians, my wife, who despaired of ever seeing me again—expecting the Indians had put a period to my life, oppressed with the distresses of the country, and bereaved of me, her only happiness—had, before I returned, transported my family and goods on horses through the wilderness, amid a multitude of dangers, to her father's house in North Carolina.

Shortly after the troubles at Boonesborough, I went to them, and lived peaceably there until this time. The history of my going home, and returning with my family, forms a series of difficulties, an account of which would swell a volume; and, being foreign to my purpose, I shall purposely omit them.

I settled my family in Boonesborough once more; and shortly after, on the 6th day of October, 1780, I went in company with my brother to the Blue Licks; and, on our return home, we were fired upon by a party of Indians. They shot him and pursued me, by the scent of their dog, three miles; but I killed the dog, and escaped. The winter soon came on, and was very severe, which confined the Indians to their wigwams.

The severities of this winter caused great difficulties in Kentucky. The enemy had destroyed most of the corn the summer before. This necessary article was scarce and dear, and the inhabitants lived chiefly on the flesh of buffalo. The circumstances of many were very lamentable; however, being a hardy race of people, and accustomed to difficulties and necessities, they were wonderfully supported through all their sufferings, until the ensuing autumn, when we received abundance from the fertile soil,

Toward spring we were frequently harassed by Indians; and in May, 1782, a party assaulted Ashton's station, killed one man, and took a negro prisoner. Captain Ashton, with twenty-five men, pursued and overtook the savages, and a smart fight ensued, which lasted two hours; but they, being superior in number, obliged Captain Ashton's party to retreat, with the loss of eight killed, and four mortally wounded; their brave commander himself being numbered among the dead.

The Indians continued their hostilities; and, about the 10th of August following, two boys were taken from Major Hoy's station. This party was pursued by Captain Holder and seventeen men, who were also defeated, with the loss of four men killed, and one wounded. Our affairs became more and more alarming. Several stations which had lately been erected in the country were continually infested with savages, stealing their horses and killing the men at every opportunity. In a field near Lexington, an Indian shot a man, and running to scalp him, was himself shot from the fort, and fell dead upon his enemy.

Every day we experienced recent mischiefs. The barbarous savage nations of Shawanese, Cherokees, Wyandots, Tawas, Delawares, and several others near Detroit, united in a war against us, and assembled their choicest warriors at Old Chilicothe, to go on the expedition, in order to destroy us, and entirely depopulate the country. Their savage minds were inflamed to mischief by two

abandoned men, Captains M'Kee and Girty. These led them to execute every diabolical scheme, and on the 15th day of August, commanded a party of Indians and Canadians, of about five hundred in number, against Bryant's station, five miles from Lexington. Without demanding a surrender, they furiously assaulted the garrison, which was happily prepared to oppose them; and, after they had expended much ammunition in vain, and killed the cattle round the fort, not being likely to make themselves masters of this place, they raised the siege, and departed in the morning of the third day after they came, with the loss of about thirty killed, and the number of wounded uncertain. Of the garrison, four were killed, and three wounded.

On the 18th day, Colonel Todd, Colonel Trigg, Major Harland and myself, speedily collected one hundred and seventy-six men, well armed, and pursued the savages. They had marched beyond the Blue Licks, to a remarkable bend of the main fork of Licking River, about forty-three miles from Lexington, where we overtook them on the 19th day. The savages observing us gave way; and we, being ignorant of their numbers, passed the river. When the enemy saw our proceedings, having greatly the advantage of us in situation, they formed the line of battle from one bend of Licking to the other, about a mile from the Blue Licks. An exceeding fierce battle immediately began, for about fifteen minutes, when we being overpowered by numbers, were obliged to retreat, with the loss of sixty-seven men, seven of whom were taken prisoners. The brave and much-lamented Colonels Todd and Trigg, Major Harland, and my second son, were among the dead. We were informed that the Indians, numbering their dead, found they had four killed more than we; and therefore four of the prisoners they had taken were, by general consent, ordered to be killed in a most barbarous manner by the young warriors, in order to train them up to cruelty; and then they proceeded to their towns.

On our retreat we were met by Colonel Logan, hastening to join us, with a number of well-armed men. This powerful assistance we unfortunately wanted in the battle; for, notwithstanding the enemy's superiority of numbers, they acknowledged that, if they had received one more fire from us, they should undoubtedly have given way. So valiantly did our small party fight, that to the memory of those who unfortunately fell in the battle, enough of honor cannot be paid. Had Colonel Logan and his party been with us, it is highly probable we should have given the savages a total defeat.

I cannot reflect upon this dreadful scene, but sorrow fills my heart. A zeal for the defense of their country led these heroes to the scene of action, though with a few men to attack a powerful army of experienced warriors. When we gave way, they pursued us with the utmost eagerness, and in every quarter spread destruction. The river was difficult to cross, and many were killed in the flight—some just entering the river, some in the water, others after crossing, in ascending the cliffs. Some escaped on horseback, a few on foot; and, being dispersed everywhere in a few hours, brought the melancholy news of this unfortunate battle to Lexington. Many widows were now made. The reader may guess what sorrow filled the hearts of the inhabitants, exceeding any thing that I am able to describe. Being reinforced, we returned to bury the dead, and found their bodies strewed everywhere, cut and mangled in a dreadful manner. This mournful scene exhibited a horror almost unparalleled: some torn and eaten by wild beasts; those in the river eaten by fishes; all in such a putrefied condition, that no one could be distinguished from another.

As soon as General Clark, then at the Falls of the Ohio—who was ever our ready friend, and merits the love and gratitude of all his countrymen—understood the circumstances of this unfortunate action, he ordered an expedition, with all possible haste, to pursue the savages, which was so expeditiously effected, that we overtook them within two miles of their towns; and probably might have obtained a great victory, had not two of their number met us about two hundred poles before we came up. These returned quick as lightning to their camp, with the alarming news of a mighty army in view. The savages fled in the utmost disorder, evacuated their towns, and reluctantly left their territory to our mercy. We immediately took possession of Old Chilicothe without opposition, being deserted by its inhabitants. We continued our pursuit through five towns on the Miami River, Old Chilicothe, Pecaway, New Chilicothe, Will's Towns, and Chilicothe—burnt them all to ashes, entirely destroyed their corn, and other fruits, and everywhere spread a scene of desolation in the country. In this expedition we took seven prisoners and five scalps, with the loss of only four men, two of whom were accidentally killed by our own army.

This campaign in some measure damped the spirits of the Indians, and made them sensible of our superiority. Their connections were dissolved, their armies scattered, and a future invasion put entirely out of their power; yet they continued to practice mischief secretly upon the inhabitants, in the exposed parts of the country.

In October following, a party made an incursion into that district called the Crab Orchard; and one of them, being advanced some distance before the others, boldly entered the house of a poor defenseless family, in which was only a negro man, a woman, and her children, terrified with the apprehensions of immediate death. The savage, perceiving their defenseless condition, without offering violence to the family, attempted to capture the negro, who happily proved an overmatch for him, threw him on the ground, and in the struggle, the mother of the children drew an axe from a corner of the cottage, and cut his head off, while her little daughter shut the door. The savages instantly appeared, and applied their tomahawks to the door. An old rusty gun-barrel, without a lock, lay in a corner, which the mother put through a small crevice, and the savages, perceiving it, fled. In the meantime, the alarm spread through the neighborhood; the armed men collected immediately, and pursued the ravagers into the wilderness. Thus Providence, by the means of this negro, saved the whole of the poor family from destruction. From that time until the happy return of peace between the United States and Great Britain, the Indians did us no mischief. Finding the great king beyond the water disappointed in his expectations, and conscious of the importance of the Long

Knife, and their own wretchedness, some of the nations immediately desired peace; to which, at present [1784], they seem universally disposed, and are sending ambassadors to General Clarke, at the Falls of the Ohio, with the minutes of their councils.

To conclude, I can now say that I have verified the saying of an old Indian who signed Colonel Henderson's deed. Taking me by the hand, at the delivery thereof—"Brother," said he, "we have given you a fine land, but I believe you will have much trouble in settling it." My footsteps have often been marked with blood, and therefore I can truly subscribe to its original name. Two darling sons and a brother have I lost by savage hands, which have also taken from me forty valuable horses, and abundance of cattle. Many dark and sleepless nights have I been a companion for owls, separated from the cheerful Society of men, scorched by the summer's sun, and pinched by the winter's cold—an instrument ordained to settle the wilderness. But now the scene is changed: peace crowns the sylvan shade.

What thanks, what ardent and ceaseless thanks are due to that all-superintending Providence which has turned a cruel war into peace, brought order out of confusion, made the fierce savages placid, and turned away their hostile weapons from our country. May the same Almighty Goodness banish the accursed monster, war, from all lands, with her hated associates, rapine and Insatiable ambition! Let peace, descending from her native heaven, bid her olives spring amid the joyful nations; and plenty, in league with commerce, scatter blessings from her copious hand!

This account of my adventures will inform the reader of the most remarkable events of this country. I now live in peace and safety, enjoying the sweets of liberty, and the bounties of Providence, with my once fellow-sufferers, in this delightful country, which I have seen purchased with a vast expense of blood and treasure: delighting in the prospect of its being, in a short time, one of the most opulent and powerful States on the continent of North America; which, with the love and gratitude of my countrymen, I esteem a sufficient reward for all my toil and dangers.

DANIEL BOONE.
Fayette County, Kentucky.

Source: "Colonel Boone's Autobiography," in Cecil B. Hartley, *Life & Times of Col. Daniel Boone* (Philadelphia: G. G. Evans, 1860), 333, 339–344, 347–350.

70. Chickasaw Treaty, 1786

Introduction

The Chickasaw Indians were a tribe of hunters and warriors who lived in towns near the headwaters of the Tombigbee River in northeastern Mississippi. They were one of the dominant tribes in the lower Mississippi River Valley. When the French began to spread out from New Orleans, the British encouraged the Chickasaws to fight against the French. Sixty years of conflict between the British-backed Chickasaws and the French and their Indian allies ensued. The Chickasaws again served as British allies during the American Revolutionary War (1775–1783) by fighting the Spanish (who were allied with the American rebels and the French) in Florida and attacking isolated American outposts. When the war ended in 1781, the British largely abandoned the Chickasaws. Without British support, the Chickasaws were vulnerable to American cries for revenge. In 1783 Congress declared that any Indians who had supported the British had forfeited their right to their land. It is noteworthy, however, that even those native peoples who had helped the American rebels during the war received little help in return once the war ended. Sporadic fighting between the Chickasaws and the Americans continued over the next five years as the Chickasaws slowly lost strength as a fighting force. This treaty was one of several signed by the Chickasaws under duress that promised to cede large tracts of their land to the United States. The treaty opened new lands to southern frontiersmen who eagerly surged into the region that was to become Alabama and Mississippi.

Primary Source

Articles of a treaty, concluded at Hopewell, on the Keowee, near Seneca Old Town, between Benjamin Hawkins, Andrew Pickens, and Joseph Martin, Commissioners Plenipotentiary of the United States of America, of the one Part; and Piomingo, Head Warrior and First Minister of the Chickasaw Nation; Mingatushka, one of the leading Chiefs; and Latopoia, first beloved Man of the said Nation, Commissioners Plenipotentiary of all the Chickasaws, of the other Part. The Commissioners Plenipotentiary of the United States of America give peace to the Chickasaw Nation, and receive them into the favor and protection of the said States, on the following conditions:

ARTICLE I. The Commissioners Plenipotentiary of the Chickasaw nation, shall restore all the prisoners, citizens of the United States, to their entire liberty, if any there be in the Chickasaw nation. They shall also restore all the negroes, and all other property taken during the late war, from the citizens, if any there be in the Chickasaw nation, to such person, and at such time and place, as the Commissioners of the United States of America shall appoint.

ARTICLE II. The Commissioners Plenipotentiary of the Chickasaws, do hereby acknowledge the tribes and the towns of the Chickasaw nation, to be under the protection of the United States of America, and of no other sovereign whosoever.

ARTICLE III. The boundary of the lands hereby allotted to the Chickasaw nation to live and hunt on, within the limits of the United States of America, is, and shall be the following, viz. Beginning on the ridge that divides the waters running into the Cumberland, from those running into the Tennessee, at a point in a line to be run north-east, which shall strike the Tennessee at the mouth of Duck river; thence running westerly along the said ridge, till it shall strike the Ohio; thence down the southern banks thereof to the Mississippi; thence down the same, to the Choctaw line or Natches district; thence along the said line, or the line of the district eastwardly as far as the Chickasaws claimed, and lived and hunted on, the twenty-ninth of November, one thousand seven hundred and eighty-two. Thence the said boundary, eastwardly, shall be the lands allotted to the Choctaws and Cherokees to live and hunt on, and the lands at present in the possession of the Creeks; saving and reserving for the establishment of a trading post, a tract or parcel of land to be laid out at the lower port of the Muscle shoals, at the mouth of Ocochappo, in a circle, the diameter of which shall be five miles on the river, which post, and the lands annexed thereto, shall be to the use and under the government of the United States of America.

ARTICLE IV. If any citizen of the United States, or other person not being an Indian, shall attempt to settle on any of the lands hereby allotted to the Chickasaws to live and hunt on, such person shall forfeit the protection of the United States of America, and the Chickasaws may punish him or not as they please.

ARTICLE V. If any Indian or Indians, or persons residing among them, or who shall take refuge in their nation, shall commit a robbery or murder, or other capital crime, on any citizen of the United States, or person under their protection, the tribe to which such offender or offenders may belong, or the nation, shall be bound to deliver him or them up to be punished according to the ordinances of the United States in Congress assembled: Provided, that the punishment shall not be greater, than if the robbery or murder, or other capital crime, had been committed by a citizen on a citizen.

ARTICLE VI. If any citizen of the United States of America, or person under their protection, shall commit a robbery or murder, or other capital crime, on any Indian, such offender or offenders shall be punished in the same manner as if the robbery or murder or other capital crime had been committed on a citizen of the United States of America; and the punishment shall be in presence of some of the Chickasaws, if any will attend at the time and place, and that they may have an opportunity so to do, due notice, if practicable, of such intended punishment, shall be sent to some one of the tribes.

ARTICLE VII. It is understood that the punishment of the innocent under the idea of retaliation is unjust, and shall not be practiced on either side, except where there is a manifest violation of this treaty; and then it shall be preceded, first by a demand of justice, and if refused, then by a declaration of hostilities.

ARTICLE VIII. For the benefit and comfort of the Indians, and for the prevention of injuries or oppressions on the part of the citizens or Indians, the United States in Congress assembled shall have the sole and exclusive right of regulating the trade with the Indians, and managing all their affairs in such manner as they think proper.

ARTICLE IX. Until the pleasure of Congress be known respecting the eighth article, all traders, citizens of the United States, shall have liberty to go to any of the tribes or towns of the Chickasaws to trade with them, and they shall be protected in their persons and property, and kindly treated.

ARTICLE X. The said Indians shall give notice to the citizens of the United States of America, of any designs which they may know or suspect to be formed in any neighboring tribe, or by any person whosoever, against the peace, trade or interests of the United States of America.

ARTICLE XI. The hatchet shall be forever buried, and the peace given by the United States of America, and friendship re-established between the said States on the one part, and the Chickasaw nation on the other part, shall be universal, and the contracting parties shall use their utmost endeavors to maintain the peace given as aforesaid, and friendship re-established. In witness of all and every thing herein contained, between the said States and Chickasaws, we, their underwritten commissioners, by virtue of our full powers, have signed this definitive treaty, and have caused our seals to be hereunto affixed. Done at Hopewell, on the Keowee, this tenth day of January, in the year of our Lord one thousand seven hundred and eighty-six.

Benjamin Hawkins (L.S.), And'w. Pickens (L.S.), Jos. Martin (L.S.), Piomingo, his x mark (L.S.), Mingatushka, his x mark (L.S.), Latopoia, his x mark (L.S.), Witness: Wm. Blount, Wm. Hazard, Sam. Taylor, James Cole, Sworn Interpreter.

Source: Library of Congress.

71. Northwest Ordinance, 1787

Introduction

In 1763 the British government barred colonists from settling the Northwest Territory (the area covered by the present-day states of Ohio, Indiana, Illinois, Michigan, and Wisconsin). After the newly formed United States took over the territory in 1783, Virginia and other states ceded their territorial claims to the federal government. Congress passed the Northwest Ordinance on July 13, 1787. The Northwest Ordinance opened the territory for settlement, provided for territorial government, established civil rights for its inhabitants, and pledged to honor Indian property rights. The ordinance also prohibited slavery in the territory and provided for the eventual admission of between three and five states from those

territories. Congress renewed the ordinance in 1789 and again in 1790 and extended it to the territory south of the Ohio River. However, the slavery prohibition did not apply south of the Ohio. The ordinance did little to settle lingering conflicts among American settlers, the territory's Indians, and British traders who wielded influence from neighboring Canada and incited Indians to resist American settlement. The Northwest Territory became a major battleground of the War of 1812.

Primary Source

An Ordinance for the government of the Territory of the United States northwest of the River Ohio.

Be it ordained by the United States in Congress assembled, That the said territory, for the purposes of temporary government, be one district, subject, however, to be divided into two districts, as future circumstances may, in the opinion of Congress, make it expedient.

Be it ordained by the authority aforesaid, That the estates, both of resident and nonresident proprietors in the said territory, dying intestate, shall descent to, and be distributed among their children, and the descendants of a deceased child, in equal parts; the descendants of a deceased child or grandchild to take the share of their deceased parent in equal parts among them: And where there shall be no children or descendants, then in equal parts to the next of kin in equal degree; and among collaterals, the children of a deceased brother or sister of the intestate shall have, in equal parts among them, their deceased parents' share; and there shall in no case be a distinction between kindred of the whole and half blood; saving, in all cases, to the widow of the intestate her third part of the real estate for life, and one third part of the personal estate; and this law relative to descents and dower, shall remain in full force until altered by the legislature of the district. And until the governor and judges shall adopt laws as hereinafter mentioned, estates in the said territory may be devised or bequeathed by wills in writing, signed and sealed by him or her in whom the estate may be (being of full age), and attested by three witnesses; and real estates may be conveyed by lease and release, or bargain and sale, signed, sealed and delivered by the person being of full age, in whom the estate may be, and attested by two witnesses, provided such wills be duly proved, and such conveyances be acknowledged, or the execution thereof duly proved, and be recorded within one year after proper magistrates, courts, and registers shall be appointed for that purpose; and personal property may be transferred by delivery; saving, however to the French and Canadian inhabitants, and other settlers of the Kaskaskies, St. Vincents and the neighboring villages who have heretofore professed themselves citizens of Virginia, their laws and customs now in force among them, relative to the descent and conveyance, of property.

Be it ordained by the authority aforesaid, That there shall be appointed from time to time by Congress, a governor, whose commission shall continue in force for the term of three years, unless sooner revoked by Congress; he shall reside in the district, and have a freehold estate therein in 1,000 acres of land, while in the exercise of his office.

There shall be appointed from time to time by Congress, a secretary, whose commission shall continue in force for four years unless sooner revoked; he shall reside in the district, and have a freehold estate therein in 500 acres of land, while in the exercise of his office. It shall be his duty to keep and preserve the acts and laws passed by the legislature, and the public records of the district, and the proceedings of the governor in his executive department, and transmit authentic copies of such acts and proceedings, every six months, to the Secretary of Congress: There shall also be appointed a court to consist of three judges, any two of whom to form a court, who shall have a common law jurisdiction, and reside in the district, and have each therein a freehold estate in 500 acres of land while in the exercise of their offices; and their commissions shall continue in force during good behavior.

The governor and judges, or a majority of them, shall adopt and publish in the district such laws of the original States, criminal and civil, as may be necessary and best suited to the circumstances of the district, and report them to Congress from time to time: which laws shall be in force in the district until the organization of the General Assembly therein, unless disapproved of by Congress; but afterwards the Legislature shall have authority to alter them as they shall think fit.

The governor, for the time being, shall be commander in chief of the militia, appoint and commission all officers in the same below the rank of general officers; all general officers shall be appointed and commissioned by Congress.

Previous to the organization of the general assembly, the governor shall appoint such magistrates and other civil officers in each county or township, as he shall find necessary for the preservation of the peace and good order in the same: After the general assembly shall be organized, the powers and duties of the magistrates and other civil officers shall be regulated and defined by the said assembly; but all magistrates and other civil officers not herein otherwise directed, shall during the continuance of this temporary government, be appointed by the governor.

For the prevention of crimes and injuries, the laws to be adopted or made shall have force in all parts of the district, and for the execution of process, criminal and civil, the governor shall make proper divisions thereof; and he shall proceed from time to time as circumstances may require, to lay out the parts of the district in which the Indian titles shall have been extinguished, into counties and townships, subject, however, to such alterations as may thereafter be made by the legislature.

So soon as there shall be five thousand free male inhabitants of full age in the district, upon giving proof thereof to the governor, they shall receive authority, with time and place, to elect a representative from their counties or townships to represent them in the general assembly: Provided, That, for every five hundred free male inhabitants, there shall be one representative, and so on progressively with the number of free male inhabitants shall the right of representation increase, until the number of representatives shall amount to twenty five; after which, the number and proportion of representatives shall be regulated by the legislature: Provided, That no person be eligible or qualified to act as a representative unless he shall have been a citizen of one of the United States three years, and be a resident in the district, or unless he shall have resided in the district three years; and, in either case, shall likewise hold in his own right, in fee simple, two hundred acres of land within the same; Provided, also, That a freehold in fifty acres of land in the district, having been a citizen of one of the states, and being resident in the district, or the like freehold and two years residence in the district, shall be necessary to qualify a man as an elector of a representative.

The representatives thus elected, shall serve for the term of two years; and, in case of the death of a representative, or removal from office, the governor shall issue a writ to the county or township for which he was a member, to elect another in his stead, to serve for the residue of the term.

The general assembly or legislature shall consist of the governor, legislative council, and a house of representatives. The Legislative Council shall consist of five members, to continue in office five years, unless sooner removed by Congress; any three of whom to be a quorum: and the members of the Council shall be nominated and appointed in the following manner, to wit: As soon as representatives shall be elected, the Governor shall appoint a time and place for them to meet together; and, when met, they shall nominate ten persons, residents in the district, and each possessed of a freehold in five hundred acres of land, and return their names to Congress; five of whom Congress shall appoint and commission to serve as aforesaid; and, whenever a vacancy shall happen in the council, by death or removal from office, the house of representatives shall nominate two persons, qualified as aforesaid, for each vacancy, and return their names to Congress; one of whom congress shall appoint and commission for the residue of the term. And every five years, four months at least before the expiration of the time of service of the members of council, the said house shall nominate ten persons, qualified as aforesaid, and return their names to Congress; five of whom Congress shall appoint and commission to serve as members of the council five years, unless sooner removed. And the governor, legislative council, and house of representatives, shall have authority to make laws in all cases, for the good government of the district, not repugnant to the principles and articles in this ordinance established and declared. And all bills, having passed by a majority in the house, and by a majority in the council, shall be referred to the governor for his assent; but no bill, or legislative act whatever, shall be of any force without his assent. The governor shall have power to convene, prorogue, and dissolve the general assembly, when, in his opinion, it shall be expedient.

The governor, judges, legislative council, secretary, and such other officers as Congress shall appoint in the district, shall take an oath or affirmation of fidelity and of office; the governor before the president of congress, and all other officers before the Governor. As soon as a legislature shall be formed in the district, the council and house assembled in one room, shall have authority, by joint ballot, to elect a delegate to Congress, who shall have a seat in Congress, with a right of debating but not voting during this temporary government.

And, for extending the fundamental principles of civil and religious liberty, which form the basis whereon these republics, their laws and constitutions are erected; to fix and establish those principles as the basis of all laws, constitutions, and governments, which forever hereafter shall be formed in the said territory: to provide also for the establishment of States, and permanent government therein, and for their admission to a share in the federal councils on an equal footing with the original States, at as early periods as may be consistent with the general interest:

It is hereby ordained and declared by the authority aforesaid, That the following articles shall be considered as articles of compact between the original States and the people and States in the said territory and forever remain unalterable, unless by common consent, to wit:

Article 1. No person, demeaning himself in a peaceable and orderly manner, shall ever be molested on account of his mode of worship or religious sentiments, in the said territory.

Article 2. The inhabitants of the said territory shall always be entitled to the benefits of the writ of habeas corpus, and of the trial by jury; of a proportionate representation of the people in the legislature; and of judicial proceedings according to the course of the common law. All persons shall be bailable, unless for capital offenses, where the proof shall be evident or the presumption great. All fines shall be moderate; and no cruel or unusual punishments shall be inflicted. No man shall be deprived of his liberty or property, but by the judgment of his peers or the law of the land; and, should the public exigencies make it necessary, for the common preservation, to take any person's property, or to demand his particular services, full compensation shall be made for the same. And, in the just preservation of rights and property, it is understood and declared, that no law ought ever to be made, or have force in the said territory, that shall, in any manner whatever, interfere with or affect private contracts or engagements, bona fide, and without fraud, previously formed.

Article 3. Religion, morality, and knowledge, being necessary to good government and the happiness of mankind, schools and the means of education shall forever be encouraged. The utmost good faith shall always be observed towards the Indians; their lands and property shall never be taken from them without their consent; and, in their property, rights, and liberty, they shall never be invaded or disturbed, unless in just and lawful wars authorized by Congress; but laws founded in justice and humanity, shall from time to time be made for preventing wrongs being done to them, and for preserving peace and friendship with them.

Article 4. The said territory, and the States which may be formed therein, shall forever remain a part of this Confederacy of the United States of America, subject to the Articles of Confederation, and to such alterations therein as shall be constitutionally made; and to all the acts and ordinances of the United States in Congress assembled, conformable thereto. The inhabitants and settlers in the said territory shall be subject to pay a part of the federal debts contracted or to be contracted, and a proportional part of the expenses of government, to be apportioned on them by Congress according to the same common rule and measure by which apportionments thereof shall be made on the other States; and the taxes for paying their proportion shall be laid and levied by the authority and direction of the legislatures of the district or districts, or new States, as in the original States, within the time agreed upon by the United States in Congress assembled. The legislatures of those districts or new States, shall never interfere with the primary disposal of the soil by the United States in Congress assembled, nor with any regulations Congress may find necessary for securing the title in such soil to the bona fide purchasers. No tax shall be imposed on lands the property of the United States; and, in no case, shall nonresident proprietors be taxed higher than residents. The navigable waters leading into the Mississippi and St. Lawrence, and the carrying places between the same, shall be common highways and forever free, as well to the inhabitants of the said territory as to the citizens of the United States, and those of any other States that may be admitted into the confederacy, without any tax, impost, or duty therefor.

Article 5. There shall be formed in the said territory, not less than three nor more than five States; and the boundaries of the States, as soon as Virginia shall alter her act of cession, and consent to the same, shall become fixed and established as follows, to wit: The western State in the said territory, shall be bounded by the Mississippi, the Ohio, and Wabash Rivers; a direct line drawn from the Wabash and Post Vincents, due North, to the territorial line between the United States and Canada; and, by the said territorial line, to the Lake of the Woods and Mississippi. The middle State shall be bounded by the said direct line, the Wabash from Post Vincents to the Ohio, by the Ohio, by a direct line, drawn due north from the mouth of the Great Miami, to the said territorial line, and by the said territorial line. The eastern State shall be bounded by the last mentioned direct line, the Ohio, Pennsylvania, and the said territorial line: Provided, however, and it is further understood and declared, that the boundaries of these three States shall be subject so far to be altered, that, if Congress shall hereafter find it expedient, they shall have authority to form one or two States in that part of the said territory which lies north of an east and west line drawn through the southerly bend or extreme of Lake Michigan. And, whenever any of the said States shall have sixty thousand free inhabitants therein, such State shall be admitted, by its delegates, into the Congress of the United States, on an equal footing with the original States in all respects whatever, and shall be at liberty to form a permanent constitution and State government: Provided, the constitution and government so to be formed, shall be republican, and in conformity to the principles contained in these articles; and, so far as it can be consistent with the general interest of the confederacy, such admission shall be allowed at an earlier period, and when there may be a less number of free inhabitants in the State than sixty thousand.

Article 6. There shall be neither slavery nor involuntary servitude in the said territory, otherwise than in the punishment of crimes whereof the party shall have been duly convicted: Provided, always, That any person escaping into the same, from whom labor or service is lawfully claimed in any one of the original States, such fugitive may be lawfully reclaimed and conveyed to the person claiming his or her labor or service as aforesaid.

Be it ordained by the authority aforesaid, That the resolutions of the 23rd of April, 1784, relative to the subject of this ordinance, be, and the same are hereby repealed and declared null and void.

> **Source:** Francis Newton Thorpe, ed., *The Federal and State Constitutions, Colonial Charters, and Other Organic Laws of the States, Territories, and Colonies Now or Heretofore Forming the United States of America,* Vol. 2 (Washington, DC: U.S. Government Printing Office, 1909).

72. Treaty of Fort Harmar, 1789

Introduction

The powerful Iroquois Confederacy included six nations: the Mohawks, the Oneidas, the Tuscaroras, the Onondagas, the Cayugas, and the Senecas. The confederacy had held a dominant political and military position by virtue of its fighting prowess, political organization, and diplomatic skills. After the destruction of their homeland during the Sullivan-Clinton Expedition (1779) in the American Revolutionary War (1775–1783), the Iroquois, who had fought on the side of the British (the Oneidas and Tuscaroras fought for the Americans), became refugees. However, fighting between Americans and the Iroquois continued. The Treaty of Fort Harmar was one of several treaties attempting to bring the fighting to an end. Representatives from the Iroquois Confederacy along with leaders of the Ottawas, Wyandots, Delawares, Chippewas, Pottawatomis, and Sauks met with Arthur St. Clair, governor of the Northwest Territory, at a site near present-day Marietta, Ohio, and signed a treaty on January 9, 1789. The treaty failed to address the major Indian concern: the incursions by New Englanders into the so-called Firelands, an area of the Western Reserves that overlapped land set aside for the Indians. St. Clair had received authorization from Secretary of War Henry Knox to relinquish certain lands set aside for white settlement in exchange for the Firelands. Instead, St. Clair used threats and bribery to reiterate the terms of previous treaties, including the 1784 Treaty of Fort Stanwix. Despite the new treaty, a great deal of hostility remained over land rights in the Ohio Valley, as the Americans expected the Iroquois

to relinquish nearly all their holdings in the region. The treaty's failure led to intensified fighting in the Northwest. The land issues remained unresolved until the War of 1812 saw the definitive end of Indian political and military power in that area covered by the Treaty of Fort Harmar.

Primary Source

Articles of a treaty made at Fort Harmar, the ninth day of January, in the year of our Lord one thousand seven hundred and eighty-nine, between Arthur St. Clair, esquire, Governor of the territory of the United States of America, northwest of the river Ohio, and Commissioner plenipotentiary of the said United States, for removing all causes of controversy, regulating trade, and settling boundaries, between the Indian nations in the northerly department and the said United States, of the one part, and the sachems and warriors of the Six Nations, of the other part:

ARTICLE I

WHEREAS the United States, in congress assembled, did, by their commissioners, Oliver Wolcott, Richard Butler, and Arthur Lee, esquires, duly appointed for that purpose, at a treaty held with the said Six Nations, viz: with the Mohawks, Oneidas, Onondagas, Tuscaroras, Cayugas, and Senekas, at fort Stanwix, on the twenty-second day of October, one thousand seven hundred and eighty-four, give peace to the said nations, and receive them into their friendship and protection: And whereas the said nations have now agreed to and with the said Arthur St. Clair, to renew and confirm all the engagements and stipulations entered into at the before mentioned treaty at fort Stanwix: and whereas it was then and there agreed, between the United States of America and the said Six Nations, that a boundary line should be fixed between the lands of the said Six Nations and the territory of the said United States, which boundary line is as follows, viz: Beginning at the mouth of a creek, about four miles east of Niagara, called Ononwayea, or Johnston's Landing Place, upon the lake named by the Indians Oswego, and by us Ontario; from thence southerly, in a direction always four miles east of the carrying place, between lake Erie and lake Ontario, to the mouth of Tehoseroton, or Buffalo creek, upon lake Erie; thence south, to the northern boundary of the state of Pennsylvania; thence west, to the end of the said north boundary; thence south, along the west boundary of the said state to the river Ohio. The said line, from the mouth of Ononwayea to the Ohio, shall be the western boundary of the lands of the Six Nations, so that the Six Nations shall and do yield to the United States, all claim to the country west of the said boundary; and then they shall be secured in the possession of the lands they inhabit east, north, and south of the same, reserving only six miles square, round the fort of Oswego, for the support of the same. The said Six Nations, except the Mohawks none of whom have attended at this time, for and in consideration of the peace then granted to them, the presents they then received, as well as in consideration of a quantity of goods, to the value of three thousand dollars, now delivered to them by the said Arthur St. Clair, the receipt whereof they do hereby acknowledge, do hereby renew and confirm the said boundary line in the words beforementioned, to the end that it may be and remain as a division line between the lands of the said Six Nations and the territory of the United States, forever. And the undersigned Indians, as well in their own names as in the name of their respective tribes and nations, their heirs and descendants, for the considerations beforementioned, do release, quit claim, relinquish, and cede, to the United States of America, all the lands west of the said boundary or division line, and between the said line and the strait, from the mouth of Ononwayea and Buffalo Creek, for them, the said United States of America, to have and to hold the same, in true and absolute propriety, forever.

ARTICLE II

The United States of America confirm to the Six Nations all the lands which they inhabit, lying east and north of the beforementioned boundary line, and relinquish and quit claim to the same and every part thereof, excepting only six miles square round the fort of Oswego, which six miles square round said fort is again reserved to the United States by these presents.

ARTICLE III

The Oneida and Tuscarora nations, are also again secured and confirmed in the possession of their respective lands.

ARTICLE IV

The United States of America renew and confirm the peace and friendship entered into with the Six Nations, (except the Mohawks) at the treaty beforementioned, held at fort Stanwix, declaring the same to be perpetual. And if the Mohawks shall, within six months, declare their assent to the same, they shall be considered as included.

Done at Harmar, on the Muskingum, the day and year first above written.

In witness whereof, the parties have hereunto, interchangeably, set their hands and seals.

Ar. St. Clair,
    Cageaga, or Dogs Round the Fire,
    Sawedowa, or The Blast,
    Kiondushowa, or Swimming Fish,
    Oneahye, or Lancing Feather,
    Sohaeas, or Falling Mountain,

Otachsaka, or Broken Tomahawk, his x mark,
Tekahias, or Long Tree, his x mark,
Oneensetee, or Loaded Man, his x mark,
Kiahtulaho, or Snake Aqueia, or Bandy Legs Kiandogewa,
    or Big Tree, his x mark,
Owenewa, or Thrown in the Water, his x mark
Gyantwaia, or Corn planter, his x mark,
Gyasota, or Big Cross, his x mark,
Kannassee, or New Arrow,
Achiout, or Half Town,
Anachout, or The Wasp, his x mark,
Chishekoa, or Wood Bug, his x mark,
Sessewa, or Big Bale of a Kettle,
Sciahowa, or Council Keeper,
Tewanias, or Broken Twig,
Sonachshowa, or Full Moon,
Cachunwase, or Twenty Canoes,
Hickonquash, or Tearing Asunder,

In presence of—
Jos. Harmar, lieutenant-colonel commanding First Regiment and brigadier-general by brevet,
    Richard Butler,
    Jno. Gibson,
    Will. M'Curdy, captain,
    Ed. Denny, ensign First U. S. Regiment,
    A. Hartshorn, ensign,
    Robt. Thompson, ensign, First U. S. Regiment,
    Fran. Belle, ensign,
    Joseph Nicholas.

SEPARATE ARTICLE.

Should a robbery or murder be committed by an Indian or Indians of the Six Nations, upon the citizens or subjects of the United States, or by the citizens or subjects of the United States, or any of them, upon any of the Indians of the said nations, the parties accused of the same shall be tried, and if found guilty, be punished according to the laws of the state, or of the territory of the United States, as the case may be, where the same was committed. And should any horses be stolen, either by the Indians of the said nations, from the citizens or subjects of the United States, or any of them, or by any of the said citizens or subjects from any of the said Indians, they may be reclaimed into whose possession soever they may have come; and, upon due proof, shall be restored, any sale in open market notwithstanding; and the persons convicted shall be punished with the utmost severity the laws will admit. And the said nations engage to deliver the persons that may be accused, of their nations, of either of the beforementioned crimes, at the nearest post of the United States, if the crime was committed within the territory of the United States; or to the civil authority of the state, if it shall have happened within any of the United States.

Ar. St. Clair.

Source: National Archives.

73. Trade and Intercourse Act, July 22, 1790

Introduction

The various treaties signed between the young United States and the Indians just beyond its western frontier proved difficult to enforce. This was due in large part to the lawless behavior of American settlers, who took by force land that had been promised to the Indians. The U.S. War Department was in charge of Indian affairs, and Secretary of War Henry Knox (former Revolutionary War hero), along with President George Washington, called on Congress to pass legislation aimed at stiffening treaty enforcement and regulating the behavior of white settlers toward Indians on the frontier. The resulting act required a license for the conduct of any trade with the Indians and imposed steep fines for noncompliance. The act also prohibited any white individual from purchasing Indian lands outside the jurisdiction of a government treaty and required that crimes by whites against Indians be subject to the same punishment as crimes against whites. The latter provision was more often flouted than honored in the ensuing decades. This act was the first in a series of such laws. Later trade and intercourse acts with similar provisions were passed in 1796, 1799, and 1802. The much more detailed 1802 act was considered to be the backbone of U.S. Indian policy and remained in effect until 1834.

Primary Source

An Act to Regulate Trade and Intercourse With the Indian Tribes.

SECTION 1. *Be it enacted by the Senate and House of Representatives of the United States of America in Congress assembled,* That no person shall be permitted to carry on any trade or intercourse with the Indian tribes, without a license for that purpose under the hand and seal of the superintendent of the department, or of such other person as the President of the United States shall appoint for that purpose; which superintendent, or other person so appointed, shall, on application, issue such license to any proper person, who shall enter into bond with one or more sureties, approved of by the superintendent, or person issuing such license, or by the President of the United States, in the penal sum of one thousand dollars, payable to the President of the United States for the time being, for the use of the United States,

conditioned for the true and faithful observance of such rules, regulations and restrictions, as now are, or hereafter shall be made for the government of trade and intercourse with the Indian tribes. The said superintendents, and persons by them licensed as aforesaid, shall be governed in all things touching the said trade and intercourse, by such rules and regulations as the President shall prescribe. And no other person shall be permitted to carry on any trade or intercourse with the Indians without such license as aforesaid. No license shall be granted for a longer term than two years. *Provided nevertheless,* That the President may make such order respecting the tribes surrounded in their settlements by the citizens of the United States, as to secure an intercourse without license, if he may deem it proper.

SEC. 2. *And be it further enacted,* That the superintendent, or person issuing such license, shall have full power and authority to recall all such licenses as he may have issued, if the person so licensed shall transgress any of the regulations or restrictions provided for the government of trade and intercourse with the Indian tribes, and shall put in suit such bonds as he may have taken, immediately on the breach of any condition in said bond: *Provided always,* That if it shall appear on trial, that the person from whom such license shall have been recalled, has not offended against any of the provisions of this act, or the regulations prescribed for the trade and intercourse with the Indian tribes, he shall be entitled to receive a new license.

SEC. 3. *And be it further enacted,* That every person who shall attempt to trade with the Indian tribes, or to be found in the Indian country with such merchandise in his possession as are usually vended to the Indians, without a license first had and obtained, as in this act prescribed, and being thereof convicted in any court proper to try the same, shall forfeit all the merchandise so offered for sale to the Indian tribes, or so found in the Indian country, which forfeiture shall be one half to the benefit of the person prosecuting, and the other half to the benefit of the United States.

SEC. 4. *And be it enacted and declared,* That no sale of lands made by any Indians, or any nation or tribe of Indians in the United States, shall be valid to any person or persons, or to any state, whether having the right of pre-emption to such lands or not, unless the same shall be made and duly executed at some public treaty, held under the authority of the United States.

SEC. 5. *And be it further enacted,* That if any citizen or inhabitant of the United States, or of either of the territorial districts of the United States, shall go into any town, settlement or territory belonging to any nation or tribe of Indians, and shall there commit any crime upon, or trespass against, the person or property of any peaceable and friendly Indian or Indians, which, if committed within the jurisdiction of any state, or within the jurisdiction of either of the said districts, against a citizen or white inhabitant thereof, would be punishable by the laws of such state or district, such offender or offenders shall be subject to the same punishment, and shall be proceeded against in the same manner as if the offence had been committed within the jurisdiction of the state or district to which he or they may belong, against a citizen or white inhabitant thereof.

SEC. 6. *And be it further enacted,* That for any of the crimes or offences aforesaid, the like proceedings shall be had for apprehending, imprisoning or bailing the offender, as the case may be, and for recognizing the witnesses for their appearance to testify in the case, and where the offender shall be committed, or the witnesses shall be in a district other than that in which the offence is to be tried, for the removal of the offender and the witnesses or either of them, as the case may be, to the district in which the trial is to be had, as by the act to establish the judicial courts of the United States, are directed for any crimes or offenses against the United States.

SEC. 7. *And be it further enacted,* That this act shall be in force for the term of two years, and from thence to the end of the next session of Congress, and no longer.

APPROVED, July 22, 1790.

Source: "An Act to Regulate Trade and Intercourse with the Indian Tribes," *U.S. Statutes at Large* 1 (1790): 137.

74. Anthony Wayne, Letter to Henry Knox on the Victory at Fallen Timbers, August 28, 1794

Introduction

The end of the American Revolutionary War (1775–1783) released pent-up demand for western land. Thousands of settlers headed west. Many of them traveled to Pittsburgh, purchased or built water craft, and then followed the Ohio River to carve out homes and farms throughout the Ohio River Valley without regard to whether the land had been promised to the Indians. Arthur St. Clair, a veteran Revolutionary War general, served as the first governor of the Northwest Territory (which included the area covered by the present-day states of Ohio, Indiana, Illinois, Michigan, and Wisconsin) from 1789 to 1802. In 1791 St. Clair was also appointed major general in command of the U.S. Army. At first the army was expected to enforce treaties by driving illegal settlers off Indian lands. The British remaining in the Northwest Territory encouraged the Indians to step up attacks on settlers. In 1790 and 1791 Washington ordered the army to go on campaign against the Miami Indians. The undermanned and poorly organized campaigns led to a costly and humiliating defeat and the replacement of St. Clair with the Revolutionary War hero Anthony Wayne. The more determined and competent Wayne trained his men well and decisively defeated the Indians at Fallen Timbers on August 20, 1794. Wayne's letter to Secretary of War Henry Knox proudly

reports on the accomplishment. The victory at Fallen Timbers led to the surrender of many western tribes, including the Miamis, Wyanadots, Chippewas, Shawnees, and Delawares, in 1795.

Primary Source

Head Quarters
 Grand Glaize, 28th August, 1794

SIR—It is with infinite pleasure that I now announce to you the brilliant success of the Federal army under my command, in a general action with the combined force of the hostile Indians, and a considerable number of the volunteers and militia of Detroit, on the 20th instant, on the banks of the Miamis, in the vicinity of the British post and garrison, at the foot of the rapids.

The army advanced from this place on the 15th instant, and arrived at Roche de Bout on the 18th; the 19th we were employed in making a temporary post for the reception of our stores and baggage, and in reconnoitering the position of the enemy, who were encamped behind a thick bushy wood and the British fort.

At 8 o'clock, on the morning of the 20th, the army again advanced in columns, agreeably to the standing order of march; the legion on the right flank, covered by the Miamis,—one brigade of mounted volunteers on the left, under Brigadier-General Todd, and the other in the rear, under Brigadier-General Barbee:—a select battalion of mounted volunteers moved in front of the legion, commanded by Major Price, who was directed to keep sufficiently advanced—so as to give timely notice for the troops to form, in case of action—it being yet undetermined whether the Indians would decide for peace or war. After advancing about five miles, Major Price's corps received so severe a fire from the enemy, who were secreted in the woods, and high grass, as to compel them to retreat.

The legion was immediately formed in two lines, principally in a close, thick wood, which extended for miles on our left; and for a very-considerable distance in front, the ground being covered with old fallen timber, probably occasioned by a tornado, which rendered it impracticable for the cavalry to act with effect; and afforded the enemy the most favorable covert for their savage mode of warfare: they were formed in three lines, within supporting distance of each other, and extending near two miles, at right angles with the river.

I soon discovered, from the weight of the fire, and extent of their lines, that the enemy were in full force in front, in possession of their favorite ground, and endeavoring to turn our left flank. I therefore gave orders for the second line to advance, to support the first, and directed Major-General Scott to gain and turn the right flank of the savages, with the whole of the mounted volunteers, by a circuitous route: at the same time I ordered the front line to advance with trailed arms, and rouse the Indians from their coverts, at the point of the bayonet; and, when up, to deliver a close and well directed fire on their backs, followed by a brisk charge, so as not to give time to load again. I also ordered Captain Miss Campbell, who commanded the legionary cavalry, to turn the left flank of the enemy next the river, and which afforded a favorable field for that corps to act in.

All those orders were obeyed with spirit and promptitude; but such was the impetuosity of the charge by the first line of infantry, that the Indians and Canadian militia and volunteers were driven from all their coverts in so short a time, that although every exertion was used by the officers of the second line of the legion, and by Generals Scott, Todd, and Barbee, of the mounted volunteers, to gain their proper positions, yet but a part of each could get up in season to participate in the action; the enemy being driven, in the course of one hour, more than two miles, through the thick woods already mentioned, by less than one half their numbers.

From every account, the enemy amounted to 2000 combatants; the troops actually engaged against them, were short of 900. This horde of savages, with their allies, abandoned themselves to flight, and dispersed with terror and dismay; leaving our victorious army in full and quiet possession of the field of battle, which terminated under the influence of the guns of the British garrison, as you will observe by the enclosed correspondence between Major Campbell, the commandant, and myself, upon the occasion.

The bravery and conduct of every officer belonging to the army, from the generals down to the ensigns, merit my highest approbation. There were, however, some whose rank and situation placed their conduct in a very conspicuous point of view, and which I observed with pleasure and the most lively gratitude: among whom I must beg leave to mention Brigadier-General Wilkinson and Colonel Hamtramck, the commandants of the right and left wings of the legion, whose brave example inspired the troops; to these, I must add the names of my faithful and gallant aids-de-camp, Captains De Butts and T. Lewis, and Lieutenant Harrison, who, with the Adjutant-General, Major Mills, rendered the most essential service by communicating my orders in every direction, and by their conduct and bravery exciting the troops to press for victory. Lieutenant Covington, upon whom the command of the cavalry now devolved, cut down two savages with his own hand, and Lieutenant Webb one, in turning the enemy's left flank.

The wounds received by Captains Slough and Prior, and Lieutenants Campbell, Smith, (an extra aid-de-camp to General Wilkinson,) of the legionary infantry, and Captain Van Rensellaer, of the dragoons, and Captain Rawlins, Lieutenant M'Kenney, and Ensign Duncan, of the mounted volunteers, bear honorable testimony of their bravery and conduct.

Captains H. Lewis and Brock, with their companies of light infantry, had to sustain an unequal fire for some time, which they supported with fortitude. In fact, every officer and soldier who had an opportunity to come into action, displayed that true bravery which will always insure success.

And here permit me to declare, that I never discovered more true spirit and anxiety for action, than appeared to pervade the whole of the mounted volunteers; and I am well persuaded that had the enemy maintained their favorite ground but for one half hour longer, they would have most severely felt the prowess of that corps.

But whilst I pay this just tribute to the living, I must not forget the gallant dead; among whom we have to lament the early death of those worthy and brave officers, Captain Miss Campbell, of the dragoons, and Lieutenant Towles, of the light infantry of the legion, who fell in the first charge.

Enclosed is a particular return of the killed and wounded. The loss of the enemy was more than double that of the Federal army. The woods were strewed, for a considerable distance, with the dead bodies of Indians and their white auxiliaries; the latter armed with British muskets and bayonets.

We remained three days and nights on the banks of the Miamis, in front of the field of battle; during which time all the houses and corn-fields were consumed and destroyed for a considerable distance, both above and below Fort Miamis, as well as within pistolshot of that garrison, who were compelled to remain tacit spectators of this general devastation and conflagration; among which were the houses, stores, and property of Colonel M'Kee, the British Indian agent, and principal stimulator of the war now existing between the United States and the savages.

The army returned to this place on the 27th, by easy marches, laying waste the villages and corn-fields for about fifty miles on each side of the Miamis. There remains yet a number of villages, and a great quantity of corn, to be consumed or destroyed upon Au Glaize and the Miamis, above this place, which will be effected in the course of a few days. In the interim, we shall improve Fort Defiance, and as soon as the escort returns with the necessary supplies from Greeneville and Fort Recovery, the army will proceed to the Miami villages, in order to accomplish the object of the campaign.

It is, however, not improbable that the enemy may make one more desperate effort against the army, as it is said that a reinforcement was hourly expected at Fort Miamis, from Niagara, as well as numerous tribes of Indians living on the margins and islands of the lakes. This is a business rather to be wished for than dreaded, whilst the army remains in force. Their numbers will only tend to confuse the savages, and the victory will be the more complete and decisive, and which may eventually insure a permanent and happy peace.

Under these impressions, I have the honor to be your most obedient and very humble servant,

ANTHONY WAYNE.

The Hon. Major General Knox,
Secretary of War.

Source: H. N. Moore, *Life and Services of Gen. Anthony Wayne* (Philadelphia: John B. Perry, 1845), 190–197.

75. Treaty of Greenville, 1795

Introduction

At the end of the American Revolutionary War (1775–1783), thousands of settlers headed west to carve out homes and farms throughout the Ohio River Valley without regard to whether the land had been promised to the Indians. Arthur St. Clair, a veteran Revolutionary War general, served as the first governor of the Northwest Territory (which included the area covered by the present-day states of Ohio, Indiana, Illinois, Michigan, and Wisconsin) and was also appointed major general in command of the U.S. Army. At first the army was expected to enforce treaties by driving illegal settlers off Indian lands. The British remaining in the Northwest Territory encouraged the Indians to step up attacks on settlers. In 1790 and 1791 President George Washington ordered the army to go on campaign against the Miami Indians. The undermanned and poorly organized campaigns led to a costly and humiliating defeat and the replacement of St. Clair with the Revolutionary War hero Anthony Wayne. Wayne trained his men well and decisively defeated the Indians at Fallen Timbers on August 20, 1794. His victory led to the 1795 Treaty of Greenville. The treaty was signed by representatives of several major tribes in the region and ceded large tracts of land covering approximately 25,000 square miles, representing more than half of present-day Ohio. Many Indian leaders objected to the treaty, however, including the rising young warrior, Tecumseh. In addition, further white expansion quickly reignited hostilities in the region.

Primary Source

A treaty of peace between the United States of America, and the tribes of Indians called the Wyandots, Delawares, Shawanees, Ottawas, Chippewas, Pattawatimas, Miamis, Eel Rivers, Weas, Kickapoos, Piankeshaws, and Kaskaskias.

To put an end to a destructive war, to settle all controversies, and to restore harmony and friendly intercourse between the said United States and Indian tribes, Anthony Wayne, major general commanding the army of the United States, and sole commissioner for the good purposes above mentioned, and the said tribes of Indians, by their sachems, chiefs, and warriors, met together at Greenville, the head quarters of the said army, have agreed on the following articles, which, when ratified by the President, with the advice and consent of the Senate of the United States, shall be binding on them and the said Indian tribes.

Article 1

Henceforth all hostilities shall cease; peace is hereby established, and shall be perpetual; and a friendly intercourse shall take place between the said United States and Indian tribes.

Article 2

All prisoners shall, on both sides, be restored. The Indians, prisoners to the United States, shall be immediately set at liberty. The people of the United States, still remaining prisoners among the Indians, shall be delivered up in ninety days from the date hereof, to the general or commanding officer at Greenville, fort Wayne, or fort Defiance; and ten chiefs of the said tribes shall remain at Greenville as hostages, until the delivery of the prisoners shall be effected.

Article 3

The general boundary line between the lands of the United States and the lands of the said Indian tribes, shall begin at the mouth of Cayahoga river, and run thence up the same to the portage, between that and the Tuscarawas branch of the Muskingum, thence down that branch to the crossing place above fort Lawrence, thence westerly to a fork of that branch of the Great Miami river, running into the Ohio, at or near which fork stood Loromie's store, and where commences the portage between the Miami of the Ohio, and St. Mary's river, which is a branch of the Miami which runs into lake Erie; thence a westerly course to fort Recovery, which stands on a branch of the Wabash; thence southwesterly in a direct line to the Ohio, so as to intersect that river opposite the mouth of Kentucke or Cuttawa river. And in consideration of the peace now established; of the goods formerly received from the United States; of those now to be delivered; and of the yearly delivery of goods now stipulated to be made hereafter; and to indemnify the United States for the injuries and expenses they have sustained during the war, the said Indian tribes do hereby cede and relinquish forever, all their claims to the lands lying eastwardly and southwardly of the general boundary line now described: and these lands, or any part of them, shall never hereafter be made a cause or pretence, on the part of the said tribes, or any of them, of war or injury to the United States, or any of the people thereof.

And for the same considerations, and as an evidence of the returning friendship of the said Indian tribes, of their confidence in the United States, and desire to provide for their accommodations, and for that convenient intercourse which will be beneficial to both parties, the said Indian tribes do also cede to the United States the following pieces of land, to wit:

1) One piece of land six miles square, at or near Loromie's store, before mentioned.

2) One piece two miles square, at the head of the navigable water or landing, on the St. Mary's river, near Girty's town.

3) One piece six miles square, at the head of the navigable water of the Auglaize river.

4) One piece six miles square, at the confluence of the Auglaize and Miami rivers, where fort Defiance now stands.

5) One piece six miles square, at or near the confluence of the rivers St. Mary's and St. Joseph's, where fort Wayne now stands, or near it.

6) One piece two miles square, on the Wabash river, at the end of the portage from the Miami of the lake, and about eight miles westward from fort Wayne.

7) One piece six miles square, at the Ouatanon, or Old Wea towns, on the Wabash river.

8) One piece twelve miles square, at the British fort on the Miami of the lake, at the foot of the rapids.

9) One piece six miles square, at the mouth of the said river, where it empties into the lake.

10) One piece six miles square, upon Sandusky lake, where a fort formerly stood.

11) One piece two miles square, at the lower rapids of Sandusky river.

12) The post of Detroit, and all the land to the north, the west and the south of it, of which the Indian title has been extinguished by gifts or grants to the French or English governments: and so much more land to be annexed to the district of Detroit, as shall be comprehended between the river Rosine, on the south, lake St. Clair on the north, and a line, the general course whereof shall be six miles distant from the west end of lake Erie and Detroit river.

13) The post of Michilimackinac, and all the land on the island on which that post stands, and the main land adjacent, of which the Indian title has been extinguished by gifts or grants to the French or English governments; and a piece of land on the main to the north of the island, to measure six miles, on lake Huron, or the strait between lakes Huron and Michigan, and to extend three miles back from the water of the lake or strait; and also, the Island De Bois Blane, being an extra and voluntary gift of the Chippewa nation.

14) One piece of land six miles square, at the mouth of Chikago river, emptying into the southwest end of lake Michigan, where a fort formerly stood.

15) One piece twelve miles square, at or near the mouth of the Illinois river, emptying into the Mississippi.

16) One piece six miles square, at the old Piorias fort and village near the south end of the Illinois lake, on said Illinois river. And whenever the United States shall think proper to survey and mark the boundaries of the lands hereby ceded to them, they shall give timely notice thereof to the said tribes of Indians, that they may appoint some of their wise chiefs to attend and see that the lines are run according to the terms of this treaty.

And the said Indian tribes will allow to the people of the United States a free passage by land and by water, as one and the other shall be found convenient, through their country, along the chain of posts hereinbefore mentioned; that is to say, from the commencement of the portage aforesaid, at or near Loromie's store, thence along said portage to the St. Mary's, and down the same to fort Wayne, and then down the Miami, to lake Erie; again, from the commencement of the portage at or near Loromie's store along the portage from thence to the river Auglaize, and down the same to its junction with the Miami at fort Defiance; again, from the commencement of the portage aforesaid, to Sandusky river, and down the same to Sandusky bay and lake Erie, and from Sandusky to the post which shall be taken at or near the foot of the Rapids of the Miami of the lake; and from thence to Detroit. Again, from the mouth of Chikago, to the commencement of the portage, between that river and the Illinois, and down the Illinois river to the Mississippi; also, from fort Wayne, along the portage aforesaid, which leads to the Wabash, and then down the Wabash to the Ohio. And the said Indian tribes will also allow to the people of the United States, the free use of the harbors and mouths of rivers along the lakes adjoining the Indian lands, for sheltering vessels and boats, and liberty to land their cargoes where necessary for their safety.

Article 4

In consideration of the peace now established, and of the cessions and relinquishments of lands made in the preceding article by the said tribes of Indians, and to manifest the liberality of the United States, as the great means of rendering this peace strong and perpetual, the United States relinquish their claims to all other Indian lands northward of the river Ohio, eastward of the Mississippi, and westward and southward of the Great Lakes and the waters, uniting them, according to the boundary line agreed on by the United States and the King of Great Britain, in the treaty of peace made between them in the year 1783. But from this relinquishment by the United States, the following tracts of land are explicitly excepted:

1st. The tract on one hundred and fifty thousand acres near the rapids of the river Ohio, which has been assigned to General Clark, for the use of himself and his warriors.

2nd. The post of St. Vincennes, on the River Wabash, and the lands adjacent, of which the Indian title has been extinguished.

3rd. The lands at all other places in possession of the French people and other white settlers among them, of which the Indian title has been extinguished as mentioned in the 3d article; and

4th. The post of fort Massac towards the mouth of the Ohio. To which several parcels of land so excepted, the said tribes relinquish all the title and claim which they or any of them may have.

And for the same considerations and with the same views as above mentioned, the United States now deliver to the said Indian tribes a quantity of goods to the value of twenty thousand dollars, the receipt whereof they do hereby acknowledge; and henceforward every year, forever, the United States will deliver, at some convenient place northward of the river Ohio, like useful goods, suited to the circumstances of the Indians, of the value of nine thousand five hundred dollars; reckoning that value at the first cost of the goods in the city or place in the United States where they shall be procured. The tribes to which those goods are to be annually delivered, and the proportions in which they are to be delivered, are the following:

1st. To the Wyandots, the amount of one thousand dollars.

2nd. To the Delawares, the amount of one thousand dollars.

3rd. To the Shawanees, the amount of one thousand dollars.

4th. To the Miamis, the amount of one thousand dollars.

5th. To the Ottawas, the amount of one thousand dollars.

6th. To the Chippewas, the amount of one thousand dollars.

7th. To the Pattawatimas, the amount of one thousand dollars, and

8th. To the Kickapoo, Wea, Eel River, Piankeshaw, and Kaskaskia tribes, the amount of five hundred dollars each.

Provided, that if either of the said tribes shall hereafter, at an annual delivery of their share of the goods aforesaid, desire that a part of their annuity should be furnished in domestic animals, implements of husbandry, and other utensils convenient for them, and in compensation to useful artificers who may reside with or near them, and be employed for their benefit, the same shall, at the subsequent annual deliveries, be furnished accordingly.

Article 5

To prevent any misunderstanding about the Indian lands relinquished by the United States in the fourth article, it is now explicitly declared, that the meaning of that relinquishment is this: the Indian tribes who have a right to those lands, are quietly to enjoy them, hunting, planting, and dwelling thereon, so long as they please, without any molestation from the United States; but when those tribes, or any of them, shall be disposed to sell their lands, or any part of them, they are to be sold only to the United States; and until such sale, the United States will protect all the said Indian tribes in the quiet enjoyment of their lands against all citizens of the United States, and against all other white persons who intrude upon the same. And the said Indian tribes again acknowledge themselves to be under the protection of the said United States, and no other power whatever.

Article 6

If any citizen of the United States, or any other white person or persons, shall presume to settle upon the lands now relinquished by the United States, such citizen or other person shall be out of the protection of the United States; and the Indian tribe, on whose land the settlement shall be made, may drive off the settler, or punish him in such manner as they shall think fit; and because such settlements, made without the consent of the United States, will be injurious to them as well as to the Indians, the United States shall be at liberty to break them up, and remove and punish the settlers as they shall think proper, and so effect that protection of the Indian lands herein before stipulated.

Article 7

The said tribes of Indians, parties to this treaty, shall be at liberty to hunt within the territory and lands which they have now ceded to the United States, without hindrance or molestation, so long as they demean themselves peaceably, and offer no injury to the people of the United States.

Article 8

Trade shall be opened with the said Indian tribes; and they do hereby respectively engage to afford protection to such persons, with their property, as shall be duly licensed to reside among them for the purpose of trade; and to their agents and servants; but no person shall be permitted to reside among them for the purpose of trade; and to their agents and servants; but no person shall be permitted to reside at any of their towns or hunting camps, as a trader, who is not furnished with a license for that purpose, under the hand and seal of the superintendent of the department northwest of the Ohio, or such other person as the President of the United States shall authorize to grant such licenses; to the end, that the said Indians may not be imposed on in their trade. And if any licensed trader shall abuse his privilege by unfair dealing, upon complaint and proof thereof, his license shall be taken from him, and he shall be further punished according to the laws of the United States. And if any person shall intrude himself as a trader, without such license, the said Indians shall take and bring him before the superintendent, or his deputy, to be dealt with according to law. And to prevent impositions by forged licenses, the said Indians shall, at least once a year, give information to the superintendent, or his deputies, on the names of the traders residing among them.

Article 9

Lest the firm peace and friendship now established, should be interrupted by the misconduct of individuals, the United States, and the said Indian tribes agree, that for injuries done by individuals on either side, no private revenge or retaliation shall take place; but instead thereof, complaint shall be made by the party injured, to the other: by the said Indian tribes or any of them, to the President of the United States, or the superintendent by him appointed; and by the superintendent or other person appointed by the President, to the principal chiefs of the said Indian tribes, or of the tribe to which the offender belongs; and such prudent measures shall then be taken as shall be necessary to preserve the said peace and friendship unbroken, until the legislature (or great council) of the United States, shall make other equitable provision in the case, to the satisfaction of both parties. Should any Indian tribes meditate a war against the United States, or either of them, and the same shall come to the knowledge of the before mentioned tribes, or either of them, they do hereby engage to give immediate notice thereof to the general, or officer commanding the troops of the United States, at the nearest post.

And should any tribe, with hostile intentions against the United States, or either of them, attempt to pass through their country, they will endeavor to prevent the same, and in like manner give information of such attempt, to the general, or officer commanding, as soon as possible, that all causes of mistrust and suspicion may be avoided between them and the United States. In like manner, the United States shall give notice to the said Indian tribes of any harm that may be meditated against them, or either of them, that shall come to their knowledge; and do all in their power to hinder and prevent the same, that the friendship between them may be uninterrupted.

Article 10

All other treaties heretofore made between the United States, and the said Indian tribes, or any of them, since the treaty of 1783, between the United States and Great Britain, that come within the purview of this treaty, shall henceforth cease and become void.

In testimony whereof, the said Anthony Wayne, and the sachems and war chiefs of the before mentioned nations and tribes of Indians, have hereunto set their hands and affixed their seals.

Done at Greenville, in the territory of the United States northwest of the river Ohio, on the third day of August, one thousand seven hundred and ninety five.

Wyandots
Tarhe, or Crane, his x mark, L.S.
J. Williams, jun., his x mark, L.S.
Teyyaghtaw, his x mark, L.S.
Haroenyou, or half king's son, his x mark, L.S.
Tehaawtorens, his x mark, L.S.
Awmeyeeray, his x mark, L.S.
Stayetah, his x mark, L.S.
Shateyyaronyah, or Leather Lips, his x mark, L.S.
Daughshuttayah, his x mark, L.S.
Shaawrunthe, his x mark, L.S.

Delawares
Tetabokshke, or Grand Glaize King, his x mark, L.S.
Lemantanquis, or Black King, his x mark, L.S.
Wabatthoe, his x mark, L.S.
Maghpiway, or Red Feather, his x mark, L.S.
Kikthawenund, or Anderson, his x mark, L.S.
Bukongehelas, his x mark, L.S.
Peekeelund, his x mark, L.S.
Wellebawkeelund, his x mark, L.S.
Peekeetelemund, or Thomas Adams, his x mark, L.S.
Kishkopekund, or Captain Buffalo, his x mark, L.S.
Amenahehan, or Captain Crow, his x mark, L.S.

Queshawksey, or George Washington, his x mark, L.S.
Weywinquis, or Billy Siscomb, his x mark, L.S.
Moses, his x mark, L.S.

Shawanees
Misquacoonacaw, or Red Pole, his x mark, L.S.
Cutthewekasaw, or Black Hoof, his x mark, L.S.
Kaysewaesekah, his x mark, L.S.
Weythapamattha, his x mark, L.S.
Nianysmeka, his x mark, L.S.
Waytheah, or Long Shanks, his x mark, L.S.
Weyapiersenwaw, or Blue Jacket, his x mark, L.S.
Nequetaughaw, his x mark, L.S.
Hahgoosekaw, or Captain Reed, his x mark, L.S.

Ottawas
Augooshaway, his x mark, L.S.
Keenoshameek, his x mark, L.S.
La Malice, his x mark, L.S.
Machiwetah, his x mark, L.S.
Thowonawa, his x mark, L.S.
Secaw, his x mark, L.S.

Chippewas
Mashipinashiwish, or Bad Bird, his x mark, L.S.
Nahshogashe, (from Lake Superior), his x mark, L.S.
Kathawasung, his x mark, L.S.
Masass, his x mark, L.S.
Nemekass, or Little Thunder, his x mark, L.S.
Peshawkay, or Young Ox, his x mark, L.S.
Nanguey, his x mark, L.S.
Meenedohgeesogh, his x mark, L.S.
Peewanshemenogh, his x mark, L.S.
Weymegwas, his x mark, L.S.
Gobmaatick, his x mark, L.S.

Ottawa
Chegonickska, an Ottawa from Sandusky, his x mark, L.S.

Pattawatimas
Thupenebu, his x mark, L.S.
Nawac, for himself and brother Etsimethe, his x mark, L.S.
Nenanseka, his x mark, L.S.
Keesass, or Run, his x mark, L.S.
Kabamasaw, for himself and brother Chisaugan,
    his x mark, L.S.
Sugganunk, his x mark, L.S.
Wapmeme, or White Pigeon, his x mark, L.S.
Wacheness, for himself and brother Pedagoshok,
    his x mark, L.S.
Wabshicawnaw, his x mark, L.S.
La Chasse, his x mark, L.S.

Meshegethenogh, for himself and brother, Wawasek, his x
mark, L.S.

Hingoswash, his x mark, L.S.

Anewasaw, his x mark, L.S.

Nawbudgh, his x mark, L.S.

Missenogomaw, his x mark, L.S.

Waweegshe, his x mark, L.S.

Thawme, or Le Blanc, his x mark, L.S.

Geeque, for himself and brother Shewinse, his x mark, L.S.

Pattawatimas of Huron

Okia, his x mark, L.S.

Chamung, his x mark, L.S.

Segagewan, his x mark, L.S.

Nanawme, for himself and brother A. Gin, his x mark, L.S.

Marchand, his x mark, L.S.

Wenameac, his x mark, L.S.

Miamis

Nagohquangogh, or Le Gris, his x mark, L.S.

Meshekunnoghquoh, or Little Turtle, his x mark, L.S.

Miamis and Eel Rivers

Peejeewa, or Richard Ville, his x mark, L.S.

Cochkepoghtogh, his x mark, L.S.

Eel River Tribe

Shamekunnesa, or Soldier, his x mark, L.S.

Miamis

Wapamangwa, or the White Loon, his x mark, L.S.

Weas, for themselves & the Piankeshaws

Amacunsa, or Little Beaver, his x mark, L.S.

Acoolatha, or Little Fox, his x mark, L.S.

Francis, his x mark, L.S.

Kickapoos and Kaskaskias

Keeawhah, his x mark, L.S.

Nemighka, or Josey Renard, his x mark, L.S.

Paikeekanogh, his x mark, L.S.

Delawares of Sandusky

Hawkinpumiska, his x mark, L.S.

Peyamawksey, his x mark, L.S.

Reyntueco, (of the Six Nations, living at Sandusky),
his x mark, L.S.

H. De Butts, first A.D.C. and Sec'ry to Major Gen. Wayne,

Wm. H. Harrison, Aid de Camp to Major Gen. Wayne,

T. Lewis, Aid de Camp to Major Gen. Wayne,

James O'Hara, Quartermaster Gen'l.

John Mills, Major of Infantry, and Adj. Gen'l. Caleb Swan,
P.M.T.U.S.

Gen. Demter, Lieut. Artillery,

Vigo,

P. Frs. La Fontaine,

Ast. Lasselle,

Sworn interpreters.

H. Lasselle,

Wm. Wells,

Js. Beau Bien,

Jacques Lasselle,

David Jones, Chaplain U.S.S.,

M. Morins,

Lewis Beaufait,

Bt. Sans Crainte,

R. Lachambre,

Christopher Miller,

Jas. Pepen,

Robert Wilson,

Baties Coutien,

Abraham Williams, his x mark,

P. Navarre,

Isaac Zane, his x mark

Source: Library of Congress, "Treaty of Greenville," in *American State Papers, Senate, 4th Congress, 1st Session*, Vol. 1, *Indian Affairs*, 562, Entry 67.

76. Treaty with the Mohawks, 1797

Introduction

The Mohawks were one of the tribes in upper New York who formed the Iroquois Confederacy. This powerful confederacy included six nations: the Mohawks, the Oneidas, the Tuscaroras, the Onondagas, the Cayugas, and the Senecas. The Iroquois Confederacy had held a dominant political and military position by virtue of its fighting prowess, political organization, and diplomatic skills. However, on the eve of the American Revolutionary War (1775–1783), the Iroquois Confederacy was in decline due to frequent warfare and desertion to Canada. During the war, the British encouraged the Iroquois to attack American settlements. Joseph Brant, or Thayendanegea, was a Mohawk chief who led many of the most deadly attacks against the Americans. The Mohawks contributed an estimated 300 warriors to the British side. In 1779 an American expedition led by General John Sullivan marched into the heart of the Iroquois homeland to burn and destroy. The expedition ruined the Six Nations. When the war ended, the British largely abandoned their Indian allies. The war had fatally weakened the Iroquois, and they never regained their power and influence. Only a handful of Iroquois returned to their former homes. Most relocated to Canada. The Fort Stanwix Treaty, signed on October 22, 1784, near Rome, New York, brought fighting between the United States and the Iroquois Confederacy to an end. An additional treaty signed with the Mohawks was a great symbolic event for the triumph of white expansionism and marked the end of Mohawk power.

Primary Source

Relinquishment to New York, by the Mohawk nation of Indians, under the sanction of the United States of America, of all claim to lands in that state.

At a treaty held under the authority of the United States, with the Mohawk nation of Indians, residing in the province of Upper Canada, within the dominions of the king of Great Britain, present, the honorable Isaac Smith, commissioner appointed by the United States to hold this treaty; Abraham Ten Broeck, Egbert Benson, and Ezra L'Hommedieu, agents for the state of New York; captain Joseph Brandt, and captain John Deserontyon, two of the said Indians and deputies, to represent the said nation at this treaty.

The said agents having, in the presence, and with the approbation of the said commissioner, proposed to and adjusted with the said deputies, the compensation as hereinafter mentioned to be made to the said nation, for their claim, to be extinguished by this treaty, to all lands within the said state: it is thereupon finally agreed and done, between the said agents, and the said deputies, as follows, that is to say: the said agents do agree to pay to the said deputies, the sum of one thousand dollars, for the use of the said nation, to be by the said deputies paid over to, and distributed among, the persons and families of the said nation, according to their usages. The sum of five hundred dollars, for the expenses of the said deputies, during the time they have attended this treaty: and the sum of one hundred dollars, for their expenses in returning, and for conveying the said sum of one thousand dollars, to where the said nation resides. And the said agents do accordingly, for and in the name of the people of the state of New York, pay the said three several sums to the said deputies, in the presence of the said commissioner. And the said deputies do agree to cede and release, and these presents witness, that they accordingly do, for and in the name of the said nation, in consideration of the said compensation, cede and release to the people of the state of New York, forever, all the right or title of the said nation to lands within the said state: and the claim of the said nation to lands within the said state, is hereby wholly and finally extinguished.

In testimony whereof, the said commissioner, the said agents, and the said deputies, have hereunto, and to two other acts of the same tenor and date, one to remain with the United States, one to remain with the said State, and one delivered to the said deputies, to remain with the said nation, set their hands and seals, at the city of Albany, in the said State, the twenty-ninth day of March, in the year one thousand seven hundred and ninety-seven.

Isaac Smith,
    Abm. Ten Broeck,
    Egbt. Benson,
    Ezra L'Hommedieu,
    Jos. Brandt,
    John Deserontyon,

Witnesses:
    Robert Yates,
    John Tayler,
    Chas. Williamson,
    Thomas Morris,
    The mark of x John Abeel, alias the Cornplanter, a chief of the Senekas.

Source: National Archives.

77. Louisiana Purchase Treaty, April 30, 1803

Introduction

Thomas Jefferson's election as president of the United States signified a changing of the guard as federalism and its support of centralized authority gave way to Jeffersonian republicanism. Ironically, early in his presidency Jefferson took an action that greatly extended presidential authority. He began negotiations to buy New Orleans and West Florida from France. Needing funds for his wars, Napoleon offered to sell all of the Louisiana Territory, a huge area extending from the Mississippi River to the Rocky Mountains. Aware that he might be overstepping his authority, Jefferson agreed to purchase the territory for about $15 million. The resulting treaty made no mention of the Indians who inhabited the territory and whose fates would now depend on the United States. Congress fiercely debated whether Jefferson had the right to make such a purchase, but in October the Senate voted its approval by a solid majority. The United States took formal possession in December 1803. The purchase doubled the size of U.S. territory, and 15 states eventually filled the area. The Louisiana Purchase also gave the United States a longer border with British-controlled Canada and a larger territory to defend in the event of war.

Primary Source

Treaty between the United States of America and the French Republic

The President of the United States of America and the First Consul of the French Republic in the name of the French People desiring to remove all Source of misunderstanding relative to objects of discussion mentioned in the Second and fifth articles of the Convention of the 8th Vendémiaire on 30 September 1800 relative to the rights claimed by the United States in virtue of the Treaty concluded at Madrid the 27 of October 1795, between His Catholic Majesty & the Said United States, & willing to Strengthen the union and friendship which at the time of the Said Convention was happily reestablished between the two nations have respectively named their Plenipotentiaries to wit The President of the United States, by and with the advice and consent of the Senate of the Said States; Robert R. Livingston Minister Plenipotentiary of the United States and James Monroe Minister Plenipotentiary and Envoy extraordinary of the Said States near the Government of the French Republic; And the First Consul in the name of the French people, Citizen Francis Barbé Marbois Minister of the public treasury who after having respectively exchanged their full powers have agreed to the following Articles.

Article I

Whereas by the Article the third of the Treaty concluded at St Ildefonso the 9th Vendémiaire on 1st October 1800 between the First Consul of the French Republic and his Catholic Majesty it was agreed as follows.

"His Catholic Majesty promises and engages on his part to cede to the French Republic six months after the full and entire execution of the conditions and Stipulations herein relative to his Royal Highness the Duke of Parma, the Colony or Province of Louisiana with the Same extent that it now has in the hand of Spain, & that it had when France possessed it; and Such as it Should be after the Treaties subsequently entered into between Spain and other States."

And whereas in pursuance of the Treaty and particularly of the third article the French Republic has an incontestible title to the domain and to the possession of the said Territory—The First Consul of the French Republic desiring to give to the United States a strong proof of his friendship doth hereby cede to the United States in the name of the French Republic for ever and in full Sovereignty the said territory with all its rights and appurtenances as fully and in the Same manner as they have been acquired by the French Republic in virtue of the above mentioned Treaty concluded with his Catholic Majesty.

Article II

In the cession made by the preceeding article are included the adjacent Islands belonging to Louisiana, all public lots and Squares, vacant lands and all public buildings, fortifications, barracks and other edifices which are not private property.—The Archives, papers & documents relative to the domain and Sovereignty of Louisiana and its dependances will be left in the possession of the Commissaries of the United States, and copies will be afterwards given in due form to the Magistrates and Municipal officers of such of the said papers and documents as may be necessary to them.

Article III

The inhabitants of the ceded territory shall be incorporated in the Union of the United States and admitted as soon as possible according to the principles of the federal Constitution to the enjoyment of all these rights, advantages and immunities of citizens of the United States, and in the mean time they shall be maintained and protected in the free enjoyment of their liberty, property and the Religion which they profess.

Article IV

There Shall be Sent by the Government of France a Commissary to Louisiana to the end that he do every act necessary as well to receive from the Officers of his Catholic Majesty the Said country and its dependances in the name of the French Republic if it has not been already done as to transmit it in the name of the French Republic to the Commissary or agent of the United States.

Article V

Immediately after the ratification of the present Treaty by the President of the United States and in case that of the first Consul's shall have been previously obtained, the commissary of the French Republic shall remit all military posts of New Orleans and other parts of the ceded territory to the Commissary or Commissaries named by the President to take possession—the troops whether of France or Spain who may be there shall cease to occupy any military post from the time of taking possession and shall be embarked as soon as possible in the course of three months after the ratification of this treaty.

Article VI

The United States promise to execute Such treaties and articles as may have been agreed between Spain and the tribes and nations of Indians until by mutual consent of the United States and the said tribes or nations other Suitable articles Shall have been agreed upon.

Article VII

As it is reciprocally advantageous to the commerce of France and the United States to encourage the communication of both nations for a limited time in the country ceded by the present treaty until general arrangements relative to commerce of both nations may be agreed on; it has been agreed between the contracting parties that the French Ships coming directly from France or any of her colonies loaded only with the produce and manufactures of France or her Said Colonies; and the Ships of Spain coming directly from Spain or any of her colonies loaded only with the produce or manufactures of Spain or her Colonies shall be admitted during the Space of twelve years in the Port of New-Orleans and in all other legal ports-of-entry within the ceded territory in the Same manner as the Ships of the United States coming directly from France or Spain or any of their Colonies without being Subject to any other or greater duty on merchandize or other or greater tonnage than that paid by the citizens of the United States.

During that Space of time above mentioned no other nation Shall have a right to the Same privileges in the Ports of the ceded territory—the twelve years Shall commence three months after the exchange of ratifications if it Shall take place in France or three months after it Shall have been notified at Paris to the French Government if it Shall take place in the United States; It is however well understood that the object of the above article is to favour the manufactures, Commerce, freight and navigation of France and of Spain So far as relates to the importations that the French and Spanish Shall make into the Said Ports of the United States without in any Sort affecting the regulations that the United States may make concerning the exportation of the produce and merchandize of the United States, or any right they may have to make Such regulations.

Article VIII

In future and for ever after the expiration of the twelve years, the Ships of France shall be treated upon the footing of the most favoured nations in the ports above mentioned.

Article IX

The particular Convention Signed this day by the respective Ministers, having for its object to provide for the payment of debts due to the Citizens of the United States by the French Republic prior to the 30th Sept. 1800 (8th Vendémiaire an 9) is approved and to have its execution in the Same manner as if it had been inserted in this present treaty, and it Shall be ratified in the same form and in the Same time So that the one Shall not be ratified distinct from the other.

Another particular Convention Signed at the Same date as the present treaty relative to a definitive rule between the contracting parties is in the like manner approved and will be ratified in the Same form, and in the Same time and jointly.

Article X

The present treaty Shall be ratified in good and due form and the ratifications Shall be exchanged in the Space of Six months after the date of the Signature by the Ministers Plenipotentiary or Sooner if possible.

In faith whereof the respective Plenipotentiaries have Signed these articles in the French and English languages; declaring nevertheless that the present Treaty was originally agreed to in the French language; and have thereunto affixed their Seals.

Done at Paris the tenth day of Floreal in the eleventh year of the French Republic; and the 30th of April 1803.

Source: "Treaty between the United States of America and the French Republic, April 30, 1803," in *Treaties and Other International Acts of the United States of America,* Vol. 2, *Documents 1–40: 1776–1818* (Washington, DC: U.S. Government Printing Office, 1931).

78. William Clark, Journal Account of the Lewis and Clark Expedition, October 19, 1805

Introduction

President Thomas Jefferson's 1803 purchase of the Louisiana Territory from France was a step in the inexorable westward movement of the U.S. border, which would eventually extend to the Pacific coast. The purchase doubled the area under U.S. control, and the president wasted no time in organizing an expedition to explore the new territory and cross the continent. Two soldiers, Captain Meriwether Lewis and Lieutenant William Clark (younger brother of the Revolutionary War frontier fighter George Rogers Clark), led the expedition, which departed Pittsburgh in the autumn of 1803, descended the Ohio River, and then in the spring of 1804 departed Illinois. Lewis and Clark brought gifts and strove to foster friendly relations with all the Indians they met during their two years in the wilderness, many of whom had never before seen white men. Both men kept journals of the expedition. This excerpt from Clark's journal describes a first meeting with Indians who initially dreaded the strangers until they saw the Indian woman Sacagewea, who served as their interpreter. The explorers returned to St. Louis in September 1806, owing much of their success to the assistance provided by the Indians they met. Clark went on to fight in the War of 1812, became governor of Missouri Territory, and served as the U.S. superintendent of Indian affairs from 1822 until his death in 1838.

Primary Source

October 19th Saturday 1805

The great chief Yel-lep-pit two other chiefs, and a Chief of Band below presented themselves to us verry early this morning. we Smoked with them, enformed them as we had all others above as well as we Could by Signs of our friendly intentions towards our red children Perticular those who opened their ears to our Councils. we gave a Medal, a Handkercheif & a String of Wompom to Yelleppit and a String of wompom to each of the others. Yelleppit is a bold handsom Indian, with a dignified countenance about 35 years of age, about 5 feet 8 inches high and well perpotiond. he requested us to delay untill the Middle of the day, that his people might Come down and See us, we excused our Selves and promised to Stay with him one or 2 days on our return which appeared to Satisfy him; great numbers of Indians Came down in Canoes to view us before we Set out which was not untill 9 oClock A M. we proceeded on passed a Island, close under the Lard Side about Six miles in length opposit to the lower point of which two Isds. are situated on one of which five Lodges vacent & Saffolds drying fish at the upper point of this Island Swift water. a Short distance below passed two Islands; one near the middle of the river on which is Seven lodges of Indians drying fish, at our approach they hid themselves in their Lodges and not one was to be seen untill we passed, they then Came out in greater numbers than is common in Lodges of their Size, it is probable that, the inhabitants of the 5 Lodges above had in a fright left their lodges and decended to this place to defend them Selves if attackted there being a bad rapid opposit the Island thro which we had to pass prevented our landing on this Island and passifying those people, about four miles below this fritened Island we arrived at the head of a verry bad rapid, we came too on the Lard Side to view the rapid before we would venter to run it, as the Chanel appeared to be close under the oppd. Shore, and it would be necessary to liten our canoe, I deturmined to walk down on the Lard Side, with the 2 Chiefs the interpreter & his woman, and derected the Small canoe to prcede down on the Lard Side to the foot of the rapid which was about 2 miles in length[.] I Sent on the Indian Chiefs &c. down and I assended a high clift about 200 feet above the water from the top of which is a leavel plain extending up the river and off for a great extent, at this place the Countrey becoms low on each Side of the river, and affords a prospect of the river and countrey below for great extent both to the right and left; from this place I descovered a high mountain of emence hight covered with Snow, this must be one of the mountains laid down by Vancouver, as Seen from the mouth of the Columbia River, from the Course which it bears which is West I take it to be Mt. St. Helens, destant 156 miles a range of mountains in the Derection crossing, a conacal mountain S. W. toped with Snow[.] This rapid I observed as I passed opposit to it to be verry bad interseped with high rock and Small rockey Islands, here I observed banks of Muscle Shells banked up in the river in Several places, I Delayed at the foot of the rapid about 2 hours for the Canoes which I Could See met with much dificuelty in passing down the rapid on the oposit Side maney places the men were obliged to get into the water and haul the canoes over Sholes—while Setting on a rock wateing for Capt Lewis I Shot a Crain which was flying over of the common kind. I observed a great number of Lodges on the opposit Side at Some distance below and Several Indians on the opposit bank passing up to where Capt. Lewis was with the Canoes, others I Saw on a knob nearly opposit to me at which place they delayed but

a Short time before they returned to their Lodges as fast as they could run, I was fearfull that those people might not be informed of us, I deturmined to take the little Canoe which was with me and proceed with the three men in it to the Lodges, on my aproach not one person was to be Seen except three men off in the plains, and they Sheared off as I aproached near the Shore, I landed in front of five Lodges which was at no great distance from each other, Saw no person the enteranc or Dores of the Lodges wer Shut with the Same materials of which they were built a mat, I approached one with a pipe in my hand entered a lodge which was the nearest to me found 32 persons men, women and a few children Setting permiscuesly in the Lodg, in the greatest agutation, Some crying and ringing there hands, others hanging their heads. I gave my hand to them all and made Signs of my friendly dispotion and offered the men my pipe to Smok and distributed a fiew Small articles which I had in my pockets,—this measure passified those distressed people verry much, I then Sent one man into each lodge and entered a Second myself the inhabitants of which I found more fritened than those of the first lodge I destributed Sundrey Small articles amongst them, and Smoked with the men, I then entered the third 4h & fifth Lodge which I found Somewhat passified, the three men, Drewer Jo. & R. Fields, haveing useed everey means in their power to convince them of our friendly disposition to them, I then Set my Self on a rock and made Signs to the men to come and Smoke with me not one Come out untill the Canoes arrived with the 2 Chiefs, one of whom spoke aloud, and as was their Custom to all we had passed the Indians came out & Set by me and Smoked They said we came from the clouds &c &c and were not men &c. &c. this time Capt. Lewis came down with the Canoes rear in which the Indian, as Soon as they Saw the Squar wife of the interperters they pointed to her and informed those who continued yet in the Same position I first found them, they imediately all came out and appeared to assume new life, the sight of This Indian woman, wife to one of our interprs. confirmed those people of our friendly intentions, as no woman ever accompanies a war party of Indians in this quarter—Capt Lewis joined us and we Smoked with those people in the greatest friendship, dureing which time one of our Old Chiefs informed them who we were from whence we Came and where we were going giveing them a friendly account of us, those people do not Speak prosisely the Same language of those above but understand them, I Saw Several Horses and persons on hors back in the plains maney of the men womin and children Came up from the Lodges below; all of them appeared pleased to See us, we traded some fiew articles for fish and berries, Dined, and proceeded on passed a Small rapid and 15 Lodges below the five, and Encamped below an Island Close under the Lard Side, nearly opposit to 24 Lodges on an Island near the middle of the river, and the Main Stard Shor Soon after we landed which was at a fiew willow trees about 100 Indians Came from the different Lodges, and a number of them brought wood which they gave us, we Smoked with all of them, and two of our Party Peter Crusat & Gibson played on the violin which delighted them greatly, we gave to the principal man a String of wompon treated them kindly for which they appeared greatfull, This Tribe can raise about 350 men their Dress are Similar to those at the fork except their robes are Smaller and do not reach lower than the waste and ¾ of them have Scercely any robes at all, the women have only a Small pece of a robe which Covers their Sholders neck and reaching down behind to their wastes, with a tite piece of leather about the waste, the brests are large and hang down verry low illy Shaped, high Cheeks flattened heads, & have but fiew orniments, they are all employed in fishing and drying fish of which they have great quantites on their Scaffolds, their habits customs &c. I could not lern. I killed a Duck that with the Crain afforded us a good Supper. the Indians continued all night at our fires[.]

This day we made 36 miles.

Source: Reuben Gold Thwaites, ed., *Original Journals of the Lewis and Clark Expedition, 1804–1806*, Vol. 3 (New York: Dodd, Mead & Company, 1904), 134–137.

79. Blue Jacket, Message on Relations with the British, 1807

Introduction

Contrary to the terms of the 1783 Treaty of Paris, British troops remained in their forts on the northwestern frontier of the United States. American settlers streamed into the Northwest Territory (which included the area covered by the present-day states of Ohio, Indiana, Illinois, Michigan, and Wisconsin) and established homes and farms without regard to whether the land had been set aside for the Indians. Although the British had abandoned their Indian allies after the American Revolutionary War (1775–1783), they still wielded some influence over them and encouraged them to step up their raids against American settlers. For their part, the Indians needed little encouragement as settlers encroached on their land. Renewed frontier warfare led to the Indians' defeat by General Anthony Wayne in 1794. As unrest in the region intensified, in 1807 Ohio governor Thomas Kirker (Ohio became a state in 1803) called a meeting with the Indians, including the Shawnees, Wyandots, Chippewas, and others. Blue Jacket, leader of the Shawnees, responded as follows to the Americans' question about Indian loyalties. He recounted that the British had repeatedly advised his people to resist the Americans and then had refused to let them take refuge in British forts when the Americans defeated them. Therefore, the Indians intended to remain neutral in any new conflict between the United States and Great Britain.

Primary Source

Brethren:—We are seated who heard you yesterday. You will get a true relation, as far as we and our connections can give it, who are as follows: Shawanoes, Wyandots, Potawatamies, Tawas, Chippewas, Winnepaus, Malominese, Malockese, Secawgoes, and one more from the north of the Chippewas. Brethren—you see all these men sitting before you, who now speak to you.

About eleven days ago we had a council, at which the tribes of Wyandots (the elder brother of the red people) spoke and said God had kindled a fire and all sat around it. In this council we talked over the treaties with the French and the Americans. The Wyandot said, the French formerly marked a line along the Alleghany mountains, southerly, to Charleston [South Carolina]. No man was to pass it from either side. When the Americans came to settle over the line, the English told the Indians to unite and drive off the French, until the war came on between the British and the Americans, when it was told them that King George, by his officers, directed them to unite and drive the Americans back.

After the treaty of peace between the English and Americans, the summer before [Gen. Anthony] Wayne's army came out, the English held a council with the Indians, and told them if they would turn out and unite as one man, they might surround the Americans like deer in a ring of fire and destroy them all. The Wyandot spoke further in the council. We see, said he, there is like to be war between the English and our white brethren, the Americans. Let us unite and consider the sufferings we have undergone, from interfering in the wars of the English. They have often promised to help us, and at last, when we could not withstand the army that came against us, and went to the English fort for refuge, the English told us, "I cannot let you in; you are painted too much, my children." It was then we saw the British dealt treacherously with us. We now see them going to war again. We do not know what they are going to fight for. Let us, my brethren, not interfere, was the speech of the Wyandot.

Further, the Wyandot said, I speak to you, my little brother, the Shawanoes at Greenville, and to you, our little brothers all around. You appear to be at Greenville to serve the Supreme Ruler of the universe. Now send forth your speeches to all our brethren far around us, and let us unite to seek for that which shall be for our eternal welfare; and unite ourselves in a band of perpetual brotherhood. These, brethren, are the sentiments of all the men who sit around you: they all adhere to what the elder brother, the Wyandot, has said, and these are their sentiments. It is not that they are afraid of their white brethren, but that they desire peace and harmony, and not that their white brethren could put them to great necessity, for their former arms were bows and arrows, by which they got their living.

Source: Edward Eggleston and Lillie Eggleston Seelye, *Tecumseh and the Shanee Prophet* (New York: Dodd, Mead, 1878), 125–127.

80. Tenskwatawa, Speech on a System of Religion, 1808

Introduction

After the American Revolutionary War (1775–1783) ended, American settlers streamed into the Northwest Territory (which included the area covered by the present-day states of Ohio, Indiana, Illinois, Michigan, and Wisconsin) and established homes and farms without regard to whether the land had been set aside for the Indians. Renewed frontier warfare led to the Indians' defeat by General Anthony Wayne in 1794, which led to the 1795 Treaty of Greenville. The treaty ceded large tracts of land representing more than half of present-day Ohio. Many Indian leaders objected to the treaty, however, including the rising young Shawnee warrior Tecumseh. In addition, further white expansion quickly reignited hostilities in the region. Tecumseh and his brother Tenskwatawa, popularly known as the Prophet, forged a massive Native American alliance in the Midwest in the early 1800s. The Prophet was the spiritual leader behind the movement and preached a gospel of Pan-Indian religion intended to unite all the tribes into a single powerful unit capable of bargaining with the Americans. The Prophet delivered this speech to the governor of Indiana Territory, William Henry Harrison, in 1808. The Prophet asserts that he has been preaching his new religion for the past three years and that he only wants his people to live in peace and give up drinking alcohol.

Primary Source

Father, It is three years since I first began with that system of religion which I now practice. The white people and some of the Indians were against me; but I had no other intention but to introduce among the Indians, those good principles of religion which the white people profess. I was spoken badly of by the white people, who reproached me with misleading the Indians; but I defy them to say that I did anything amiss.

Father, I was told that you intended to hang me. When I heard this, I intended to remember it, and tell my father, when I went to see him, and relate to him the truth.

I heard, when I settled on the Wabash, that my father, the governor, had declared that all the land between Vicennes and fort Wayne, was the property of the Seventeen Fires. I also heard that you wanted to know, my father, whether I was God or man; and that you said if I was the former, I should not steal horses. I heard this from Mr. Wells, but I believed it originated with himself.

The Great Spirit told me to tell the Indians that he had made them, and made the world—that he had placed them on it to do good, not evil.

I told all the red skins, that the way they were in was not good, and that they ought to abandon it.

That we ought to consider ourselves as one man; but we ought to live agreeably to our several customs, the red people after their mode, and the white people after theirs; particularly, that they should not drink whiskey; that it was not made for them, but the white people, who alone knew how to use it; and that it is the cause of all the mischief which the Indians suffer; and that they must always follow the directions of the Great Spirit, and we must listen to him, as it was he that made us: determine to listen to nothing that is bad: do not take up the tomahawk, should it be offered by the British, or by the long knives: do not meddle with any thing that does not belong to you, but mind your own business, and cultivate the ground, that your women and your children may have enough to live on.

I now inform you, that it is our intention to live in peace with our father and his people forever.

My father, I have informed you what we mean to do, and I call the Great Spirit to witness the truth of my declaration. The religion which I have established for the last three years, has been attended to by the different tribes of Indians in this part of the world. Those Indians were once different people; they are now but one: they are all determined to practice what I have communicated to them, that has come immediately from the Great Spirit through me.

Brother, I speak to you as a warrior. You are one. But let us lay aside this character, and attend to the care of our children, that they may live in comfort and peace. We desire that you will join us for the preservation of both red and white people. Formerly, when we lived in ignorance, we were foolish; but now, since we listen to the voice of the Great Spirit, we are happy.

I have listened to what you have said to us. You have promised to assist us: I now request you, in behalf of all the red people, to use your exertions to prevent the sale of liquor to us. We are all well pleased to hear you say that you will endeavor to promote our happiness. We give you every assurance that we will follow the dictates of the Great Spirit.

We are all well pleased with the attention that you have showed us; also with the good intentions of our father, the President. If you give us a few articles, such as needles, flints, hoes, powder, &c., we will take the animals that afford us meat, with powder and ball.

Source: Edward Eggleston and Lillie Eggleston Seelye, *Tecumseh and the Shanee Prophet* (New York: Dodd, Mead, 1878), 125–127.

81. Treaty of Fort Wayne, September 30, 1809

Introduction

After the American Revolutionary War (1775–1783) ended, American settlers streamed into the Northwest Territory (which included the area covered by the present-day states of Ohio, Indiana, Illinois, Michigan, and Wisconsin) and established homes and farms without regard to whether the land had been set aside for the Indians. Renewed frontier warfare led to the

Indians' defeat by General Anthony Wayne in 1794 and forced them to cede large tracts of land representing more than half of present-day Ohio. Continued white expansion quickly reignited hostilities in the region. Through a series of strong-arm tactics, Indiana territorial governor William Henry Harrison forced the Native Americans, including the Delawares and Miamis, in Indiana to sign the Treaty of Fort Wayne in 1809, ceding additional huge tracts of land in the region to the Americans. This area of the country remained rife with contention between whites and Indians until the War of 1812 saw the definitive end of Native American political and military power in the region. Governor Harrison led the force that won the famous Battle of Tippecanoe in 1811, went on to fight in the War of 1812, and eventually became president of the United States on the strength of his reputation as an Indian fighter.

Primary Source

A treaty between the United States of America, and the tribes of Indians called the Delawares, Putawatimies, Miamies and Eel River Miamies.

JAMES MADISON, President of the United States, by William Henry Harrison, governor and commander-in-chief of the Indiana territory, superintendent of Indian affairs, and commissioner plenipotentiary of the United States for treating with the said Indian tribes, and the Sachems, Head men and Warriors of the Delaware, Putawatimie, Miami and Eel River tribes of Indians, have agreed and concluded upon the following treaty; which, when ratified by the said President, with the advice and consent of the Senate of the United States, shall be binding on said Parties.

ARTICLE I

The Miami and Eel River tribes, and the Delawares and Putawatimies, as their allies, agree to cede to the United States all that tract of country which shall be included between the boundary line established by the treaty of Fort Wayne, the Wabash, and a line to be drawn from the mouth of a creek called Racoon Creek, emptying into the Wabash, on the south-east side, about twelve miles below the mouth of the Vermilion river, so as to strike the boundary line established by the treaty of Grouseland, at such a distance from its commencement at the north-east corner of the Vincennes tract, as will leave the tract now ceded thirty miles wide at the narrowest place. And also all that tract which shall be included between the following boundaries, viz: beginning at Fort Recovery, thence southwardly along the general boundary line, established by the treaty of Greenville, to its intersection with the boundary line established by the treaty of Grouseland; thence along said line to a point from which a line drawn parallel to the first mentioned line will be twelve miles distant from the same, and along the said parallel line to its intersection with a line to be drawn from Fort Recovery, parallel to the line established by the said treaty of Grouseland.

ARTICLE II

The Miamies explicitly acknowledge the equal right of the Delawares with themselves to the country watered by the White river. But it is also to be clearly understood that neither party shall have the right of disposing of the same without the consent of the other: and any improvements which shall be made on the said land by the Delawares, or their friends the Mochecans, shall be theirs forever.

ARTICLE III

The compensation to be given for the cession made in the first article shall be as follows, viz: to the Delawares a permanent annuity of five hundred dollars; to the Miamies a like annuity of five hundred dollars; to the Eel river tribe a like annuity of two hundred and fifty dollars; and to the Putawatimies a like annuity of five hundred dollars.

ARTICLE IV

All the stipulations made in the treaty of Greenville, relatively to the manner of paying the annuities, and the right of the Indians to hunt upon the land, shall apply to the annuities granted and the land ceded by the present treaty.

ARTICLE V

The consent of the Wea tribe shall be necessary to complete the title to the first tract of land here ceded; a separate convention shall be entered into between them and the United States, and a reasonable allowance of goods given them in hand, and a permanent annuity, which shall not be less than three hundred dollars, settled upon them.

ARTICLE VI

The annuities promised by the third article, and the goods now delivered to the amount of five thousand two hundred dollars, shall be considered as a full compensation for the cession made in the first article.

ARTICLE VII

The tribes who are party to this treaty being desirous of putting an end to the depredations which are committed by abandoned individuals of their own color, upon the cattle, horses, &c. of the more industrious and careful, agree to adopt the following regulations, viz: when any theft or other depredation shall be committed by any individual or individuals of one of the tribes above mentioned, upon the property of any individual or individuals of another tribe, the chiefs of the party injured shall make application to the agent of the United States, who is charged with the delivery of the annuities of the tribe to which the offending party belongs, whose duty it shall be to hear the proofs and allegations on either side, and determine between them: and the amount of his award shall be immediately deducted from the annuity of the tribe to which the offending party belongs, and given to the person injured, or to the chief of his village for his use.

ARTICLE VIII

The United States agree to relinquish their right to the reservation, at the old Ouroctenon towns, made by the treaty of Greenville, so far at least as to make no further use of it than for the establishment of a military post.

ARTICLE IX

The tribes who are party to this treaty, being desirous to show their attachment to their brothers the Kickapoos, agree to cede to the United States the lands on the north-west side of the Wabash, from the Vincennes tract to a northwardly extention of the line running from the mouth of the aforesaid Raccoon creek, and fifteen miles in width from the Wabash, on condition that the United States shall allow them an annuity of four hundred dollars. But this article is to have no effect unless the Kickapoos will agree to it.

In testimony whereof, the said William Henry Harrison, and the sachems and war chiefs of the before mentioned tribes, have hereunto set their hands and affixed their seals, at Fort Wayne, this thirtieth of September, eighteen hundred and nine.

William Henry Harrison

Delawares:
   Anderson, for Hockingpomskon, who is absent, his x mark,
   Anderson, his x mark,
   Petchekekapon, his x mark,
   The Beaver, his x mark,
   Captain Killbuck, his x mark,

Putawatimies:
   Winnemac, his x mark,
   Five Medals, by his son, his x mark,
   Mogawgo, his x mark,
   Shissahecon, for himself and his brother Tuthinipee, his x mark,
   Ossmeet, brother to Five Medals, his x mark,
   Nanousekah, Penamo's son, his x mark,
   Mosser, his x mark,
   Chequinimo, his x mark,
   Sackanackshut, his x mark,
   Cohengee, his x mark,

Miamies:
   Pucan, his x mark,
   The Owl, his x mark,
   Meshekenoghqua, or the Little Turtle, his x mark,
   Wapemangua, or the Loon, his x mark,
   Silver Heels, his x mark,
   Shawapenomo, his x mark,

Eel Rivers:
   Charley, his x mark,
   Sheshangomequah, or Swallow, his x mark,
   The young Wyandot, a Miami of Elk Hart, his x mark,

In presence of Peter Jones, secretary to the Commissioner,
   John Johnson, Indian agent,
   A. Heald, Capt. U. S. Army,
   A. Edwards, surgeon's mate,
   Ph. Ostrander, Lieut. U. S. Army,
   John Shaw,
   Stephen Johnston,
   J. Hamilton, sheriff of Dearborn County,
   Hendrick Aupaum, William Wells,
   John Conner,
   Joseph Barron,
   Abraham Ash, Sworn Interpreters.

Source: "A treaty between the United States of America and the Tribes of Indians called the Delawares, Putawatimies, Miamies and Eel River Miamies," *Indian Affairs: Laws and Treaties,* Vol. 11 (Washington, DC: Government Printing Office, 1904), 102.

82. Tecumseh, Speech to Governor William Henry Harrison, August 12, 1810

Introduction

In 1809 Governor William Henry Harrison of Indiana Territory met with Native American leaders at Fort Wayne and convinced them to cede nearly 3 million acres to the United States. The great Shawnee leader Tecumseh repeatedly warned Harrison against allowing white settlement of the new territory. The most powerful Native American of his day, Tecumseh forged a Pan-Indian alliance among midwestern tribes with the help of his brother, the Prophet, in the early 1800s. They hoped to prevent American expansion by arguing that by virtue of prior occupancy, Native Americans collectively held rights to the land and that no individual or tribe could sell or barter land without the consent of all.

In this 1810 speech to Governor Harrison, Tecumseh set forth the concept of collective land rights and argued that the 1809 Treaty of Fort Wayne was invalid because it involved only some of the tribes. Harrison became Tecumseh's chief adversary, leading the force that won the famous Battle of Tippecanoe in 1811. Harrison went on to fight in the War of 1812 and eventually became president of the United States on the strength of his reputation as an Indian fighter. Tecumseh joined the British in fighting the War of 1812 and fell in battle in 1813.

Primary Source

It is true I am a Shawanee. My forefathers were warriors. Their son is a warrior. From them I only take my existence; from my tribe I take nothing. I am the maker of my own fortune; and oh! that I could make that of my red people, and of my country, as great as the conceptions of my mind, when I think of the Spirit that rules the universe. I would not then come to Governor Harrison, to ask him to tear the treaty, and to obliterate the landmark; but I would say to him, Sir, you have liberty to return to your own country. The being within, communing with past ages, tells me, that once, nor until lately, there was no white man on this continent. That it then all belonged to red men, children of the same parents, placed on it by the Great Spirit that made them, to keep it, to traverse it, to enjoy its productions, and to fill it with the same race. Once a happy race. Since made miserable by the white people, who are never contented, but always encroaching. The way, and the only way to check and stop this evil, is, for all the red men to unite in claiming a common and equal right in the land, as it was at first, and should be yet; for it never was divided, but belongs to all, for the use of each. That no part has a right to sell, even to each other, much less to strangers; those who want all, and will not do with less. The white people have no right to take the land from the Indians, because they had it first; it is theirs. They may sell, but all must join. Any sale not made by all is not valid. The late sale is bad. It was made by a part only. Part do not know how to sell. It requires all to make a bargain for all. All red men have equal rights to the unoccupied land. The right of occupancy is as good in one place as in another. There cannot be two occupations in the same place. The first excludes all others. It is not so in hunting or travelling; for there the same ground will serve many, as they may follow each other all day; but the camp is stationary, and that is occupancy. It belongs to the first who sits down on his blanket or skins, which he has thrown upon the ground, and till he leaves it no other has a right.

Source: Samuel G. Drake, *The Book of the Indians* (Boston: Antiquarian Bookstore, 1841), 121.

83. Accounts of the Battle of Tippecanoe, 1811

Introduction

The Shawnee leader Tecumseh, with his brother the Prophet, set about organizing an Indian league to resist white encroachment. When Tecumseh visited southern tribes in an attempt to expand the league, alarm spread among white settlers along the western frontier. William Henry Harrison, territorial governor of Indiana, assembled a force numbering about 1,000 U.S. regulars and volunteers and marched against the Indians. On the morning of November 7, 1811, near the Indian town of Tippecanoe, the Prophet's warriors attacked Harrison's men. Although the Indians were badly outnumbered, a hard-fought battle ensued. Despite heavy losses, Harrison repulsed the Indian attack. The next day he entered the abandoned town and burned it before retreating. Harrison was thus able to claim victory. The battle further inflamed tensions between the United States and Great Britain because the British had been subsidizing the Indians. Strategically the battle was important because it upset Tecumseh's efforts to forge an Indian league against the Americans. The first of the following accounts is by Judge Isaac Naylor, who was then a 21-year-old volunteer rifleman. Also present at the battle was a Pottawatomi chief named Shabonee. Long after the battle he related his memories to a white journalist who published Shabonee's account in 1864. Confirming American suspicions of British involvement, Shabonee mentions two men dressed in red coats who came from Canada to incite the Indians to attack.

Primary Source

Account by Judge Isaac Naylor

I became a volunteer member of a company of riflemen, and on the 12th of September, 1811, we commenced our march toward Vincennes, and arrived there in about six days, marching about 120 miles. We remained there about a week and took up the march to a point on the Wabash river sixty miles above, on the east bank of the river, where we erected a stockade fort, which we named Fort Harrison. This was three miles below where the city of Terre Haute now stands. Colonel Joseph H. Davies, who commanded the dragoons, named the fort. The glorious defense of this fort nine months after by Captain Zachary Taylor was the first step in his brilliant career that afterwards made him President of the United States. A few days later we took up the march again for the seat of Indian warfare, where we arrived on the evening of November 6, 1811.

When the army arrived in view of the Prophet's town, an Indian was seen coming toward General Harrison with a white flag suspended on a pole. Here the army halted, and a parley was had between General Harrison and an Indian delegation, who assured the General that they desired peace, and solemnly promised to meet him next day in council, to settle the terms of peace and friendship between them and the United States.

General Marston G. Clark, who was then brigade major, and Waller Taylor, one of the judges of the General Court of the Territory of Indiana, and afterwards a Senator of the United States from Indiana (one of the General's aides), were ordered to select a place for the encampment, which they did. The army then marched to the ground selected about sunset. A strong guard was placed around the encampment, commanded by Captain James Bigger and three lieutenants. The troops were ordered to sleep on their arms. The night being cold, large fires were made along the lines of encampment and each soldier retired to rest, sleeping on his arms.

Having seen a number of squaws and children at the town, I thought the Indians were not disposed to fight. About ten o'clock at night Joseph Warnock and myself retired to rest, he taking one side of the fire and I the other, the other members of our company being all asleep. My friend Warnock had dreamed, the night before, a bad dream which foreboded something fatal to him or to some of his family, as he told me. Having myself no confidence in dreams, I thought but little about the matter, although I observed that he never smiled afterwards.

I awoke about four o'clock the next morning, after a sound and refreshing sleep, having heard in a dream the firing of guns and the whistling of bullets just before I awoke from my slumber. A drizzling rain was falling and all things were still and quiet throughout the camp. I was engaged in making a calculation when I should arrive at home.

In a few moments I heard the crack of a rifle in the direction of the point where now stands the Battle Ground house, which is occupied by Captain DuTiel as a tavern. I had just time to think that some sentinel was alarmed and had fired his rifle without a real cause, when I heard the crack of another rifle, followed by an awful Indian yell all around the encampment. In less than a minute I saw the Indians charging our line most furiously and shooting a great many rifle balls into our camp fires, throwing the live coals into the air three or four feet high.

At this moment my friend Warnock was shot by a rifle ball through his body. He ran a few yards and fell dead on the ground. Our lines were broken and a few Indians were found on the inside of the encampment. In a few moments they were all killed. Our lines closed up and our men in their proper places. One Indian was killed in the back part of Captain Geiger's tent, while he was attempting to tomahawk the Captain.

The sentinels, closely pursued by the Indians, came to the lines of the encampment in haste and confusion. My brother, William Naylor, was on guard. He was pursued so rapidly and furiously that he ran to the nearest point on the left flank, where he remained with a company of regular soldiers until the battle was near its termination. A young man, whose name was Daniel Pettit, was pursued so closely and furiously by an Indian as he was running from the guard fire to our lines, that to save his life he cocked his rifle as he ran and turning suddenly round, placed the muzzle of his gun against the body of the Indian and shot an ounce ball through him. The Indian fired his gun at the same instant, but it being longer than Pettit's the muzzle passed by him and set fire to a handkerchief which he had tied round his head. The Indians made four or five most fierce charges on our lines, yelling and screaming as they advanced, shooting balls and arrows into our ranks. At each charge they were driven back in confusion, carrying off their dead and wounded as they retreated.

Colonel Owen, of Shelby County, Kentucky, one of General Harrison's volunteer aides, fell early in action by the side of the General. He was a member of the legislature at the time of his death. Colonel Davies was mortally wounded early in the battle, gallantly charging the Indians on foot with his sword and pistols, according to his own request. He made this request three times of General Harrison, before he permitted him to make the charge. This charge was made by himself and eight dragoons on foot near the angle formed by the left flank and front line of the encampment. Colonel Davies lived about thirty six hours after he was wounded, manifesting his ruling passions in life—ambition, patriotism and an ardent love of military glory. During the last hours of his life he said to his friends around him that he had but one thing to regret—that he had military talents; that he was about to be cut down in the meridian of life without having an opportunity of displaying them for his own honor, and the good of his country. He was buried alone with the honors of war near the right flank of the army, inside of the lines of the encampment, between two trees. On one of these trees the letter 'D' is now visible. Nothing but the stump of the other remains. His grave was made here, to conceal it from the Indians. It was filled up to the top with earth and then covered with oak leaves. I presume the Indians never found it. This precautionary act was performed as a mark of peculiar respect for a distinguished hero and patriot of Kentucky.

Captain Spencer's company of mounted riflemen composed the right flank of the army. Captain Spencer and both his lieutenants were killed. John Tipton was elected and commissioned as captain of this company in one hour after the battle, as a reward for his cool and deliberate heroism displayed during the action. He died at Logansport in 1839, having been twice elected Senator of the United States from the State of Indiana.

The clear, calm voice of General Harrison was heard in words of heroism in every part of the encampment during the action. Colonel Boyd behaved very bravely after repeating these words: 'Huzza! My sons of gold, a few more fires and victory will be ours!'

Just after daylight the Indians retreated across the prairie toward their town, carrying off their wounded. This retreat was from the right flank of the encampment, commanded by Captains Spencer and Robb, having retreated from the other portions of the encampment a few minutes before. As their retreat became visible, an almost deafening and universal shout was raised by our men. 'Huzza! Huzza! Huzza!' This shout was almost equal to that of the savages at the commencement of the battle; ours was the shout of victory, theirs was the shout of ferocious but disappointed hope.

The morning light disclosed the fact that the killed and wounded of our army, numbering between eight and nine hundred men, amounted to one hundred and eight. Thirty-six Indians were found near our lines. Many of their dead were carried off during the battle. This fact was proved by the discovery of many Indian graves recently made near their town. Ours was a bloody victory, theirs a bloody defeat.

Soon after breakfast an Indian chief was discovered on the prairie, about eighty yards from our front line, wrapped in a piece of white cloth. He was found by a soldier by the name of Miller, a resident of Jeffersonville, Indiana. The Indian was wounded in one of his legs, the ball having penetrated his knee and passed down his leg, breaking the bone as it passed. Miller put his foot against him and he raised up his head and said: 'Don't kill me, don't kill me.' At the same time five or six regular soldiers tried to shoot him, but their muskets snapped and missed fire. Major Davis Floyd came riding toward him with dragoon sword and pistols and said he 'would show them how to kill Indians,' when a messenger came from General Harrison commanding that he should be taken prisoner. He was taken into camp, where the surgeons dressed his wounds. Here he refused to speak a word of English or tell a word of truth. Through the medium of an interpreter he said that he was a friend to the white people and that the Indians shot him, while he was coming to the camp to tell General Harrison that they were about to attack the army. He refused to have his leg amputated, though he was told that amputation was the only means of saving his life. One dogma of Indian superstition is that all good and brave Indians, when they die, go to a delightful region, abounding with deer and other game, and to be a successful hunter, he should have all his limbs, his gun and his dog. He therefore preferred death with all his limbs to life without them. In accordance with his request he was left to die, in company with an old squaw, who was found in the Indian town the next day after he was taken prisoner. They were left in one of our tents.

At the time this Indian was taken prisoner, another Indian, who was wounded in the body, rose to his feet in the middle of the prairie, and began to walk towards the woods on the opposite side. A number of regular soldiers shot at him but missed him. A man who was a member of the same company with me, Henry Huckleberry, ran a few steps into the prairie and shot an ounce ball through his body and he fell dead near the margin of the woods. Some Kentucky volunteers went across the prairie immediately and scalped him, dividing his scalp into four pieces, each one cutting a hole in each piece, putting his ramrod through the hole, and placing his part of the scalp just behind the first thimble of his gun, near its muzzle. Such was the fate of nearly all of the Indians found dead on the battle-ground, and such was the disposition of their scalps.

The death of Owen, and the fact that Davies was mortally wounded, with the remembrance also that a large portion of

Kentucky's best blood had been shed by the Indians, must be their apology for this barbarous conduct. Such conduct will be excused by all who witnessed the treachery of the Indians, and saw the bloody scenes of this battle.

Tecumseh being absent at the time of battle, a chief called White Loon was the chief commander of the Indians. He was seen in the morning after the battle, riding a large white horse in the woods across the prairie, where he was shot at by a volunteer named Montgomery, who is now living in the southwest part of this State. At the crack of his rifle the horse jumped as if the ball had hit him. The Indian rode off toward the town and we saw him no more. During the battle the prophet was safely located on a hill, beyond the reach of our balls, praying to the Great Spirit to give the victory to the Indians, having previously assured them that the Great Spirit would change our powder into ashes and sand.

We had about forty head of beef cattle when we came to the battle. They all ran off the night of the battle, or they were driven off by the Indians, so that they were all lost. We received rations for two days on the morning after the action. We received no more rations until the next Tuesday evening, being six days afterwards. The Indians having retreated to their town, we performed the solemn duty of consigning to their graves our dead soldiers, without shrouds or coffins. They were placed in graves about two feet deep, from five to ten in each grave.

General Harrison having learned that Tecumseh was expected to return from the south with a number of Indians whom he had enlisted in his cause, called a council of his officers, who advised him to remain on the battlefield and fortify his camp by a breastwork of logs around, about four feet high. This work was completed during the day and all the troops were placed immediately behind each line of the work when they were ordered to pass the watchword from right to left every five minutes, so that no man was permitted to sleep during the night. The watchword on the night before the battle was 'Wide awake,' 'Wide awake.' To me it was a long, cold, cheerless night.

On the next day the dragoons went to Prophet's town, which they found deserted by all the Indians, except an old squaw, whom they brought into the camp and left her with the wounded chief before mentioned. The dragoons set fire to the town and it was all consumed, casting up a brilliant light amid the darkness of the ensuing night. I arrived at the town when it was about half on fire. I found large quantities of corn, beans and peas. I filled my knapsack with these articles and carried them to the camp and divided them with the members of our mess, consisting of six men. Having these articles of food, we declined eating horse-flesh, which was eaten by a large portion of our men.

Shabonee's Description of the Battle of Tippecanoe

It was fully believed among the Indians that we should defeat General Harrison, and that we should hold the line of the Wabash and dictate terms to the whites. The great cause of our failure, was the Miamies, whose principal country was south of the river, and they wanted to treat with the whites so as to retain their land, and they played false to their red brethren and yet lost all. They are now surrounded and will be crushed. The whites will shortly have all their lands and they will be driven away.

In every talk to the Indians, General Harrison said:

Lay down your arms. Bury the hatchet, already bloody with murdered victims, and promise to submit to your great chief at Washington, and he will be a father to you, and forget all that is past. If we take your land, we will pay for it. But you must not think that you can stop the march of white men westward.

There was truth and justice in all that talk. The Indians with me would not listen to it. It was dictating to them. They wanted to dictate to him. They had counted his soldiers, and looked at them with contempt. Our young men said:

We are ten to their one. If they stay upon the other side, we will let them alone. If they cross the Wabash, we will take their scalps or drive them into the river. They cannot swim. Their powder will be wet. The fish will eat their bodies. The bones of the white men will lie upon every sand bar. Their flesh will fatten buzzards. These white soldiers are not warriors. Their hands are soft. Their faces are white. One half of them are calico peddlers. The other half can only shoot squirrels. They cannot stand before men. They will all run when we make a noise in the night like wild cats fighting for their young. We will fight for ours, and to keep the pale faces from our wigwams. What will they fight for? They won't fight. They will run. We will attack them in the night.

Such were the opinions and arguments of our warriors. They did not appreciate the great strength of the white men. I knew their great war chief, and some of his young men. He was a good man, very soft in his words to his red children, as he called us; and that made some of our men with hot heads mad. I listened to his soft words, but I looked into his eyes. They were full of fire. I knew that they would be among his men like coals of fire in the dry grass. The first wind would raise a great flame. I feared for the red men that might be sleeping in its way. I, too, counted his men. I was one of the scouts that watched all their march up the river from Vincennes. I knew that we were like these bushes—very many. They were like these trees; here and there one. But I knew too, when a great tree falls, it crushes many little ones. I saw some of the men shoot squirrels, as they rode along, and I said, the Indians have no such guns. These men will kill us as far as they can see. "They cannot see in the night," said our men who were determined to fight. So I held my tongue. I saw that all of our war chiefs were hot for battle with the white men. But they told General Harrison that they only wanted peace. They wanted him to come up into

their country and show their people how strong he was, and then they would all be willing to make a treaty and smoke the great pipe together. This was what he came for. He did not intend to fight the Indians. They had deceived him. Yet he was wary. He was a great war chief. Every night he picked his camping ground and set his sentinels all around, as though he expected we would attack him in the dark. We should have done so before we did, if it had not been for this precaution. Some of our people taunted him for this, and pretended to be angry that he should distrust them, for they still talked of their willingness to treat, as soon as they could get all the people. This is part of our way of making war. So the white army marched further and further into our country, unsuspicious, I think, of our treachery. In one thing we were deceived. We expected that the white warriors would come up on the south bank of the river, and then we could parley with them; but they crossed far down the river and came on this side, right up to the great Indian town that Elskatawwa had gathered at the mouth of the Tippecanoe. In the meantime he had sent three chiefs down on the south side to meet the army and stop it with a talk until he could get the warriors ready. Tecumseh had told the Indians not to fight, but when he was away, they took some scalps, and General Harrison demanded that we should give up our men as murderers, to be punished.

Tecumseh had spent months in traveling all over the country around Lake Michigan, making great talks to all the warriors, to get them to join him in his great designs upon the pale faces. His enmity was the most bitter of any Indian I ever knew. He was not one of our nation, he was a Shawnee. His father was a great warrior. His mother came from the country where there is no snow, near the great water that is salt. His father was treacherously killed by a white man before Tecumseh was born, and his mother taught him, while he sucked, to hate all white men, and when he grew big enough to be ranked as a warrior she used to go with him every year to his father's grave and make him swear that he would never cease to make war upon the Americans. To this end he used all his power of strategy, skill and cunning, both with white men and red. He had very much big talk. He was not at the battle of Tippecanoe. If he had been there it would not have been fought. It was too soon. It frustrated all his plans.

Elskatawwa was Tecumseh's older brother. He was a great medicine. He talked much to the Indians and told them what had happened. He told much truth, but some things that he had told did not come to pass. He was called "The Prophet." Your people knew him only by that name. He was very cunning, but he was not so great a warrior as his brother, and he could not so well control the young warriors who were determined to fight.

Perhaps your people do not know that the battle of Tippecanoe was the work of white men who came from Canada and urged us to make war. Two of them who wore red coats were at the Prophet's Town the day that your army came. It was they who urged Elskatawwa to fight. They dressed themselves like Indians, to show us how to fight. They did not know our mode. We wanted to attack at midnight. They wanted to wait till daylight. The battle commenced before either party was ready, because one of your sentinels discovered one of our warriors, who had undertaken to creep into your camp and kill the great chief where he slept. The Prophet said if that was done we should kill all the rest or they would run away. He promised us a horseload of scalps, and a gun for every warrior, and many horses. The men that were to crawl upon their bellies into camp were seen in the grass by a white man who had eyes like an owl, and he fired and hit his mark. The Indian was not brave. He cried out. He should have lain still and died. Then the other men fired. The other Indians were fools. They jumped up out of the grass and yelled. They believed what had been told them, that a white man would run at a noise made in the night. Then many Indians who had crept very close so as to be ready to take scalps when the white men ran, all yelled like wolves, wild cats and screech owls; but it did not make the white men run.

They jumped right up from their sleep with guns in their hands and sent a shower of bullets at every spot where they heard a noise. They could not see us. We could see them, for they had fires. Whether we were ready or not we had to fight now for the battle was begun. We were still sure that we should win. The Prophet had told us that we could not be defeated. We did not rush in among your men because of the fires. Directly the men ran away from some of the fires, and a few foolish Indians went into the light and were killed. One Delaware could not make his gun go off. He ran up to a fire to fix the lock. I saw a white man whom I knew very well—he was a great hunter who could shoot a tin cup from another man's head—put up his gun to shoot the Delaware. I tried to shoot the white man but another who carried the flag just then unrolled it so that I could not see my aim. Then I heard the gun and saw the Delaware fall. I thought he was dead. The white man thought so, too, and ran to him with his knife. He wanted a Delaware scalp. Just as he got to him the Delaware jumped up and ran away. He had only lost an ear. A dozen bullets were fired at the white man while he was at the fire, but he shook them off like an old buffalo bull.

Our people were more surprised than yours. The fight had been begun too soon. They were not all ready. The plan was to creep up through the wet land where horses could not run, upon one side of the camp, and on the other through a creek and steep bank covered with bushes, so as to be ready to use the tomahawk upon the sleeping men as soon as their chief was killed. The Indians thought white men who had marched all day would sleep. They found them awake.

The Prophet had sent word to General Harrison that day that the Indians were all peaceable, that they did not want to fight, that he might lie down and sleep, and they would treat with their white brothers in the morning and bury the hatchet. But the white men did not believe.

In one minute from the time the first gun was fired I saw a great war chief mount his horse and begin to talk loud. The fires were put out and we could not tell where to shoot, except on one side of the camp, and from there the white soldiers ran, but we did not succeed as the Prophet told us that we would, in scaring the whole army so that all the men would run and hide in the grass like young quails.

I never saw men fight with more courage than these did after it began to grow light. The battle was lost to us by an accident, or rather by two.

A hundred warriors had been picked out during the night for this desperate service, and in the great council-house the Prophet had instructed them how to crawl like snakes through the grass and strike the sentinels; and if they failed in that, then they were to rush forward boldly and kill the great war chief of the whites, and if they did not do this the Great Spirit, he said, had told him that the battle would be hopelessly lost. This the Indians all believed.

If the one that was first discovered and shot had died like a brave, without a groan, the sentinel would have thought that he was mistaken, and it would have been more favorable than before for the Indians. The alarm having been made, the others followed Elskatawwa's orders, which were, in case of discovery, so as to prevent the secret movement, they should make a great yell as a signal for the general attack. All of the warriors had been instructed to creep up to the camp through the tall grass during the night, so close that when the great signal was given, the yell would be so loud and frightful that the whole of the whites would run for the thick woods up the creek, and that side was left open for this purpose.

"You will, then," said the Prophet, "have possession of their camp and all its equipage, and you can shoot the men with their own guns from every tree. But above all else you must kill the great chief."

It was expected that this could be easily done by those who were allotted to rush into camp in the confusion of the first attack. It was a great mistake of the Prophet's redcoated advisers, to defer this attack until morning. It would have succeeded when the fires were brighter in the night. Then they could not have been put out.

I was one of the spies that had dogged the steps of the army to give the Prophet information every day. I saw all the arrangement of the camp. It was not made where the Indians wanted it. The place was very bad for the attack. But it was not that which caused the failure. It was because General Harrison changed horses. He had ridden a grey one every day on the march, and he could have been shot twenty times by scouts that were hiding along the route. That was not what was wanted, until the army got to a place where it could be all wiped out. That time had now come, and the hundred braves were to rush in and shoot the "Big chief on a white horse," and then fall back to a safer place.

This order was fully obeyed, but we soon found to our terrible dismay that the "Big chief on a white horse" that was killed was not General Harrison. He had mounted a dark horse. I know this, for I was so near that I saw him, and I knew him as well as I knew my own brother.

I think that I could then have shot him, but I could not lift my gun. The Great Spirit held it down. I knew then that the great white chief was not to be killed, and I knew that the red men were doomed.

As soon as daylight came our warriors saw that the Prophet's grand plan had failed—that the great white chief was alive riding fearlessly among his troops in spite of bullets, and their hearts melted.

After that the Indians fought to save themselves, not to crush the whites. It was a terrible defeat. Our men all scattered and tried to get away. The white horsemen chased them and cut them down with long knives. We carried off a few wounded prisoners in the first attack, but nearly all the dead lay unscalped, and some of them lay thus till the next year when another army came to bury them.

Our women and children were in the town only a mile from the battle-field waiting for victory and its spoils. They wanted white prisoners. The Prophet had promised that every squaw of any note should have one of the white warriors to use as her slave, or to treat as she pleased.

Oh how these women were disappointed! Instead of slaves and spoils of the white men coming into town with the rising sun, their town was in flames and women and children were hunted like wolves and killed by hundreds or driven into the river and swamps to hide.

With the smoke of that town and the loss of that battle I lost all hope of the red men being able to stop the whites.

I fought that day by the side of an old Ottawa chief and his son, the brother of my wife. We were in the advance party, and several of those nearest to me fell by the bullets or blows of two horsemen who appeared to be proof against our guns. At length one of these two men killed the young man and wounded the old chief, and at the same time I brought him and his horse to the ground. The horse ran, before he fell, down the bluff into the creek, quite out of the way of the whites. The man's leg was broken and he had another bad wound. I could have taken his scalp easily, but Sabaqua, the old chief, begged me not to kill him. He wanted to take him to his wife alive, in place of her son whom the white brave had killed.

I was willing enough to do this for I always respected a brave man, and this one was, beside, the handsomest white man I had ever seen. I knew him as soon as I saw him closely. I had seen him before. I went to Vincennes only one moon before the battle as a spy. I told the governor that I came for peace. This young man was there and I talked with him. He was not one of the warriors but had come because he was a great brave. He had told me, laughingly, that he would come to see me at my wigwam. I thought now that he should do it. I caught a horse—there were plenty of them that had lost their riders—and mounted the white brave with Sabaqua behind him to hold him on and started them off north. I was then

sure that we should all have to run that way as soon as it was light. The Indians were defeated. The great barrier was broken. It was my last fight. I put my body in the way. It was strong then, but it was not strong enough to stop the white men. They pushed it aside as I do this stick. I have never seen the place since where we fought that night. My heart was very big then. Tecumseh had filled it with gall. It has been empty ever since.

Source: Isaac Naylor, "The Battle of Tippecanoe," *Indiana Magazine of History* 2(4) (December 1906): 163–169. Shabonier, "Shabonee's Account of Tippecanoe," *Indiana Magazine of History* 17(4) (December 1921): 353–363.

84. Tecumseh, Speech to the Osages, 1811

Introduction

In 1809 Governor William Henry Harrison of Indiana Territory met with Indian leaders at Fort Wayne and convinced them to cede nearly 3 million acres to the United States. The great Shawnee leader Tecumseh understood that Indian efforts to defend their homelands had suffered from lack of cooperation among different tribes. Consequently, Tecumseh along with his brother, the Prophet, set about organizing an Indian league to resist white encroachment. Tecumseh traveled south to enlist the southern tribes, including the Creeks, Cherokees, and Osages. The Osages were a powerful tribe living in present-day southern Missouri and northern Arkansas. Tecumseh was a gifted orator, as the following speech that he delivered to the Osages shows. However, during Tecumseh's absence, important events were taking place back north. Governor Harrison led a 1,000-man force of U.S. regulars and volunteers against Tecumseh's capital, resulting in the Battle of Tippecanoe on November 7, 1811. The Americans narrowly defeated the Indians and then burned the capital. This battle shattered the Prophet's mystical authority, caused Tecumseh to lose prestige, and ended his dreams to forge an Indian confederation. During the War of 1812, Tecumseh was reduced to leading a handful of Indians in British service against the Americans. Tecumseh died in combat at the Battle of the Thames on October 5, 1813.

Primary Source

Brothers, we all belong to one family; we are all children of the Great Spirit; we walk in the same path; slake our thirst at the same spring; and now affairs of the greatest concern lead us to smoke the pipe around the same council fire. Brothers, we are friends; we must assist each other to bear our burdens. The blood of many of our fathers and brothers has run like water on the ground, to satisfy the avarice of the white men. We, ourselves, are threatened with a great evil; nothing will pacify them but the destruction of all the red men. Brothers, when the white men first set foot on our grounds, they were hungry; they had no place on which to spread their blankets, or to kindle their fires. They were feeble; they could do nothing for themselves. Our fathers commiserated their distress, and shared freely with them whatever the Great Spirit had given his red children. They gave them food when hungry, medicine when sick, spread skins for them to sleep on, and gave them grounds, that they might hunt and raise corn. Brothers, the white people are like poisonous serpents: when chilled, they are feeble and harmless; but invigorate them with warmth, and they sting their benefactors to death. The white people came among us feeble; and now that we have made them strong, they wish to kill us, or drive us back, as they would wolves and panthers. Brothers, the white men are not friends to the Indians: at first, they only asked for land sufficient for a wigwam; now, nothing will satisfy them but the whole of our hunting grounds, from the rising to the setting sun. Brothers, the white men want more than our hunting grounds; they wish to kill our old men, women, and little ones. Brothers, many winters ago there was no land; the sun did not rise and set; all was darkness. The Great Spirit made all things. He gave the white people a home beyond the great waters. He supplied these grounds with game, and gave them to his red children; and he gave them strength and courage to defend them. Brothers, my people wish for peace; the red men all wish for peace; but where the white people are, there is no peace for them, except it be on the bosom of our mother. Brothers, the white men despise and cheat the Indians; they abuse and insult them; they do not think the red men sufficiently good to live. The red men have borne many and great injuries; they ought to suffer them no longer. My people will not; they are determined on vengeance; they have taken up the tomahawk; they will make it fat with blood; they will drink the blood of the white people. Brothers, my people are brave and numerous; but the white people are too strong for them alone. I wish you to take up the tomahawk with them. If we all unite, we will cause the rivers to stain the great waters with their blood. Brothers, if you do not unite with us, they will first destroy us, and then you will fall an easy prey to them. They have destroyed many nations of red men, because they were not united, because they were not friends to each other. Brothers, the white people send runners amongst us; they wish to make us enemies, that they may sweep over and desolate our hunting grounds, like devastating winds, or rushing waters. Brothers, our Great Father [the King of England] over the great waters is angry with the white people, our enemies. He will send his brave warriors against them; he will send us rifles, and whatever else we want—he is our friend, and we are his children. Brothers, who are the white people that we should fear them? They cannot run fast, and are good marks to shoot at: they are only men; our fathers have killed many of them: we are not squaws, and we will stain the earth red with their blood. Brothers, the Great Spirit is angry with our enemies; he speaks in thunder, and the earth swallows

up villages, and drinks up the Mississippi. The great waters will cover their lowlands; their corn cannot grow; and the Great Spirit will sweep those who escape to the hills from the earth with his terrible breath. Brothers, we must be united; we must smoke the same pipe; we must fight each other's battles; and, more than all, we must love the Great Spirit: he is for us; he will destroy our enemies, and make all his red children happy.

Source: John D. Hunter, *Memoirs of a Captivity among the Indians* (London: Longman, Hurst, Rees, Orme, Brown and Green, 1823), 45–48.

85. Robert Dickson, Secret Canadian Correspondence about Indian Loyalties, 1812

Introduction

The War of 1812 renewed the competition between Great Britain and the United States for the territory along the western frontier, including the Ohio River Valley. The American victory in the American Revolutionary War (1775–1783) caused a loss of British control of the Ohio Valley. Great Britain had never accepted this loss and still hoped to establish a neutral Indian territory extending north from the Ohio River to the Canadian border with a western boundary encompassing the Mississippi and Missouri rivers. To preserve its alliances with various Indian tribes, British traders supplied weapons and ammunition. When a war against the United States began to appear likely, British planners assessed the extent to which various Indian tribes could contribute to their war effort against the Americans. This letter was sent from York, Canada, to the British Indian agent, Robert Dickson, who lived among the western tribes in the Missouri River Valley. Because of the risk that the Americans might intercept communications, the letter also provides guidelines about how to communicate secretly in the future. The second letter is Dickson's reply. Dickson explains that the number of warriors has declined to 250–300 because of a "scarcity of provisions" but still promises that these men are ready to march against the Americans when called. During the War of 1812, events showed that the Indians could harm the Americans along the western frontier but could not decisively influence the war's outcome.

Primary Source

Enclosure.

[Endorsement] No. i. Confidential Communication

TRANSMITTED TO Mr. ROBERT DICKSON RESIDING WITH THE INDIANS NEAR THE MISSOURI.

Memo. Sent off from York 27th Feby, and rec'd by M. D. early in June 1812.—J. B. G.

27th Feb. 1812
    Copy.

Sir,

As it is probable that war may result from the present state of affairs, it is very desirable to ascertain the degree of cooperation that you and your friends might be able to furnish, in case of such an Emergency taking place. You will be pleased to report with all practicable expedition upon the following matters.

1st. The number of your friends, that might be depended upon.

2. Their disposition towards us.

3. Would they assemble, and march under your orders.

4. State the succours you require, and the most eligible mode, for their conveyance.

5. Can Equipments be procured in your Country.

6. An immediate direct communication with you, is very much wished for.

7 Can you point out in what manner, that object may be accomplished.

8. Send without loss of time a few faithful and very confidential Agents—Selected from your friends.

9. Will you individually approach the Detroit frontier next Spring. If so, state the time and place, where we may meet.

Memo. Avoid mentioning names, in your written communications.

I owe you acknowledgements for two letters. Recollect to whom you promised, to procure, Shrubs and small trees.

Enclosure.

[Endorsement] No. 2. Confidential Communication

TRANSMITTED BY Mr. ROBERT DICKSON RESIDING WITH THE INDIANS NEAR THE MISSOURI. Received at Fort George, 14TH July.

June 18th 1812.

Queries contained in paper No. 1 answered—

No. 1. Answer. The numbers of my friends would have been more, but the unparalled scarcity of provisions of all sorts, has reduced them to 250 or 300 of all sorts of different languages.

2. Answer. All of the same disposition as the accompanying note will shew.

3. All ready to march when required under a proper person commissioned for that purpose.

4. An Express to be sent to St: Josephs on receipt of this, with Instructions either by Indians or a vessel. Provisions and all sort of proper goods required.

Flags, I doz. large medals with gorgets and a few small ones.

5. Equipments if timely notice is given, can be procured in the Country.

6. The Bearer of this will inform you of these and other matters.

7 As the Article above—No. 6.

8. Your wishes are complied with on this head—79 of their friends are left where this comes from.

9. St: Josephs will be the General Rendezvous, and all our friends shall be there about the 30th instant.

N.B.—An Expedition across to the Mississippi would be of great service and could be accomplished without much risk or difficulty—In the Event of hostilities more full communication will shortly take place—

Source: William Wood, ed., *Select British Documents of the Canadian War of 1812*, Vol. 1 (Toronto: Champlain Society, 1920), 423–424.

86. Nathan Heald, Report on Fort Dearborn Massacre, October 23, 1812 [Excerpt]

Introduction

When the War of 1812 began, the U.S. Army had small garrisons manning stockaded forts along the western frontier. These forts served as both trading posts and symbols of the country's territorial claims. One such place was Fort Dearborn (on the site of present-day Chicago). General William Hull, the American governor of the newly established Michigan Territory, dispatched a frontiersman named William Wells to Fort Dearborn to order the garrison to withdraw to Fort Wayne (in present-day Indiana). The garrison's commander, Captain Nathan Heald, began his retreat on August 15, 1812. Wells and 15 Miami Indian scouts led the way, followed by Heald with 55 regulars, 39 civilians including women and children, and a rear guard of 15 more Miami scouts. A party of presumably friendly Pottawatomi Indians initially escorted the column. However, British traders and Tecumseh's agents had convinced the Pottawatomis to turn on the Americans. An overwhelming number of Indians ambushed the column, capturing or killing all of the Americans and then burning down Fort Dearborn. The Indians tortured many of the prisoners and reportedly murdered Wells, cut out his heart, and ate it in the presence of the surviving prisoners. Because Heald was an officer and therefore valuable, he survived. Captain Heald's report of what became known as the Fort Dearborn Massacre is excerpted here.

Primary Source

Pittsburg, October 23d, 1812

Sir: I embrace this opportunity to render you an account of the garrison of Chicago.

On the 9th of August last, I received orders from General Hull to evacuate the post and proceed with my command to Detroit, by land, leaving it at my discretion to dispose of the public property as I thought proper. The neighboring Indians got the information as early as I did, and came in from all quarters in order to receive the goods in the factory store, which they understood were to be given them. On the 13th, Captain Wells, of Fort Wayne, arrived with about 30 Miamies, for the purpose of escorting us in, by the request of General Hull. On the 14th, I delivered the Indians all the goods in the factory store, and a considerable quantity of provisions which we could not take away with us. The surplus arms and ammunition I thought proper to destroy, fearing they would make bad use of it if put in their possession. I also destroyed all the liquor on hand after they began to collect. The collection was unusually large for that place; but they conducted themselves with the strictest propriety till after I left the fort. On the 15th, at 9 o'clock in the morning, we commenced our march: a part of the Miamies were detached in front, and the remainder in our rear, as guards, under the direction of Captain Wells. The situation of the country rendered it necessary for us to take the beach, with the lake on our left, and a high sand bank on our right, at about 100 yards distance.

We had proceeded about a mile and a half, when it was discovered that the Indians were prepared to attack us from behind the bank. I immediately marched up with the company to the top of the bank, when the action commenced; after firing one round, we charged, and the Indians gave way in front and joined those on our flanks. In about fifteen minutes they got possession of all our horses, provisions, and baggage of every description, and finding the Miamies did not assist us, I drew off the few men I had left, and took possession of a small elevation in the open prarie, out of shot of the bank or any other cover. The Indians did not follow me, but assembled in a body on the top of the bank, and after some consultations among themselves, made signs for me to approach them. I advanced towards them alone, and was met by one of the Potawatamie chiefs, called the Black Bird, with an interpreter. After shaking hands, he requested me to surrender, promising to spare the lives of all the prisoners. On a few moments consideration, I concluded it would be most prudent to comply with his request, although I did not put entire confidence in his promise. After delivering up our arms, we were taken back to their encampment near the fort, and distributed among the different tribes. The next morning, they set fire to the fort and left the place, taking the prisoners with them. Their number of warriors was between four and five hundred, mostly of the Potawatamie nation, and their loss, from the best information I could get, was about fifteen. Our strength was fifty-four regulars and twelve militia, out of which, twenty-six regulars and all the militia were killed in the action, and two women and twelve children. Ensign George Ronan and doctor Isaac V Van Voorhis of my company, with Captain Wells, of Fort Wayne, are, to my great sorrow, numbered among the dead. Lieutenant Lina T. Helm, with twenty-five noncommissioned officers and privates, and eleven women and children, were prisoners when we were separated. Mrs. Heald and myself were taken to the mouth of the river St. Joseph, and being both badly wounded, were permitted to reside with Mr. Burnet, an Indian trader. In a few days after our arrival there, the Indians all went off to take Fort Wayne, and in their absence, I engaged a Frenchman to take us to Michilimackinac by water, where I gave myself up as a prisoner of war, with one of my sergeants. The commanding officer, Captain Roberts, offered me every assistance in his power to render our situation comfortable while we remained there, and to enable us to proceed on our journey. To him I gave my parole of Honour, and came on to Detroit and reported myself to Colonel Proctor, who gave us a passage to Buffaloe; from that place I came by way of Presque Isle, and arrived here yesterday.

I have the honor to be yours, &c., N. Heald, Captain U.S. Infantry.

Thomas H. Cushing, Esqr., Adjutant General.

Source: E. A. Cruikshank, *Documents Relating to the Invasion of Canada and the Surrender of Detroit, 1812* (Ottawa: Government Printing Bureau, 1912), 225–227.

87. Accounts of the Iroquois Confederacy regarding the War of 1812, 1812–1813

Introduction

During the American Revolutionary War (1775–1783), the Indian tribes belonging to the Six Nations, or Iroquois Confederacy—namely the Mohawks, Oneidas, Tuscaroras, Onondagas, Cayugas, and Senecas—split into pro-American and pro-British factions. After the war, many Indians left New York to live in Canada. When the War of 1812 began, the Six Nations were again divided. The British encouraged Indians living in Canada to fight the Americans. Some Americans wanted to enlist Indians in U.S. service. The Indians of the Six Nations were caught in a bind, not wanting to fight against fellow tribesmen while worrying about the consequences of trying to stay neutral. The first document provides the Indian request for clarification of their status from the U.S. government now that war had begun. The second document provides the official response. The last document is a speech from the Seneca leader known to the white community as Red Jacket. He had earned that name during the Revolutionary War for the scarlet coat that the British gave him when he served on the British side. Red Jacket was an Indian nationalist who believed, as his speech shows, that the Six Nations were best off if their lands remained within American boundaries. At the Battle of Chippewa (July 5, 1814), New York Iroquois served in a brigade commanded by General Peter D. Porter (mentioned in Red Jacket's speech) and fought Indians belonging to the Six Nations who served with the British.

Primary Source

Address of Six Nations, Resident in New York, to the President of the United States

BROTHER,—The undersigned chiefs and warriors of the Oneida, Onondaga, Stockbridge and Tuscarora tribes of Indians, as far west as Tonawanda, regularly deputed by our respective tribes, have this day lighted up a council fire at Onondaga, the ancient council ground of the Six Confederate Nations of Indians, and have invited our white brothers of Onondaga to meet with us and hear what we have to say.

BROTHER,—We see that the tomahawk is lifted up between you and the British. We are uneasy about it, and therefore we have met and determined to tell you our minds about it:

BROTHER,—At the close of the late war Gen. Washington told us to be sober and attend to agriculture and to refrain from shedding blood: this advice was good. Our good prophet of the Seneca tribe, who is now with us in this council, has given us the same advice, and our tribe have entered into a league to follow that advice. We wish to hold fast to it and not take any part in the contest between your people and the British.

We have been repeatedly told by your agents that it was your wish that we should remain neutral, and therefore we are much surprised and disappointed in the council, lately held at Buffalo Creek, at being invited to take up the tomahawk.

BROTHER,—You must not suppose from what we have now told you that we are unfriendly to you or your people. We are your decided friends. We reside among your people. Your friends are our friends, and your enemies are our enemies.

In the former war between your people and the British, some of us took up the tomahawk on their side. When the peace took place we buried it deep, and it shall never be raised against you and your people.

BROTHER,—We are few in number and can do but little, but our hearts are good and we are willing to do what we can, and if you want our assistance say so and we will go with your people to battle.

We are anxious to know your wishes respecting us as soon as possible, because some of our young men are uneasy, and we fear they may disperse among different tribes and be hostile to you. Pray direct your communication to the chiefs and warriors of the respective tribes, to be left at Onondaga Post office.

Onondaga, Sept. 28th, 1812.

Signed by sixteen chiefs and warriors.

Speech of the President of the United States to the Six Nations

BROTHERS OF THE SIX NATIONS:—

Through our sub-agent and interpreter, Jasper Parrish, you have expressed some uneasiness with regard to the attacks of the British upon your wives and children. Be not disquieted. Should the enemy cross the Niagara river you will be removed to a place of safety. Others of your red brethren have been so removed. They were honest to us and were therefore hated and menaced by the British. They are now eating our bread in the State of Ohio and in places of safety.

MY BROTHERS,—While on this subject let me offer to you my advice that during the war you should gather yourselves together and move to your reserved tract on the head waters of the Alleghany, where you may work and sleep in safety.

MY BROTHERS,—You have also expressed some fears lest your annuities and the interest on your bank stock should not be punctually paid. Bad men have raised in you these doubts. Listen to such no longer. Have not your claims upon us been punctually paid hitherto? And can you have a better assurance of our future conduct towards you than what is furnished by your own experience of that which is past. It is true that the quantity of goods payable as part of your annuity is somewhat less than it was formerly, but this is the effect of the war forced upon us by the British. They therefore are the true causes of this evil.

MY BROTHERS,—Continue your good faith to the United States and trust to their justice and kindness.

War Department, April 8th, 1803. [sic]

By order of the President of the U. States.

Speech of Red Jacket at a Council Held at Buffalo, October 21, 1813, Addressed to Erastus Granger, Esq. Agent, Etc.

Brother, we are rejoiced to meet you in health, for which we are grateful to the Great Spirit. Brother, our feelings were hurt, that after the willingness we have shown to assist our brethren of the United States in the war in which they are engaged, our friendship should be suspected. Our dissatisfaction arose from another cause. Brother: General Porter and myself had promised our warriors that they should have pay for one month's services for guarding the land. General Wilkinson also promised them pay for their services, but went away and told them that General McClure would fulfill the promise made to them. We have not received pay according to promise. We think you were not authorized to promise us. We think we are trifled with. We were promised that all horses and cattle should be free plunder. We took horses; we had to give them up. We have been deceived. We, the Senecas and Onondagas, gave up the property we took. The Oneidas, whom you have educated and taught your habits, gave up nothing. We want you to state this to the President. We want permission to go to Washington. We are an independent nation. We have taken up arms in your favor. We want to know on what footing we stand. We know not how long the war will last. It was agreed by all at Fort George that we should send word. We want a small deputation from the friendly Indians at the westward to meet us at Washington. Let us unite, and in one season more we will drive the red coats from this island. They are foreigners. This country belongs to us and the United States. We do not fight for conquest, but we fight for our rights, for our lands and for our country. We hope our request will be granted. We trust that you will make our request known to the President and that we shall not be deceived.

Source: E. Cruikshank, ed., *The Documentary History of the Campaign upon the Niagara Frontier in the Year 1812,* Vol. 1 (Welland, Ontario: Lundy's Lane Historical Society, 1896), 21–22; *The Documentary History of the Campaign upon the Niagara Frontier in the Year 1813: Part I (1813)* (Welland, Ontario: Lundy's Lane Historical Society, 1902), 153; *The Documentary History of the Campaign upon the Niagara Frontier in the Year 1813: Part IV (1813)* (Welland, Ontario: Lundy's Lane Historical Society, 1907), 86–87.

88. Tecumseh, Speech to Henry Procter at Amherstburg during the War of 1812, September 18, 1813

Introduction

In 1810 and 1811, the great Shawnee leader Tecumseh, along with his brother, the Prophet, set about organizing an Indian league to resist white encroachment from American settlers. In 1811 Governor William Henry Harrison led a U.S. force against Tecumseh's capital. In the ensuing Battle of Tippecanoe (November 7, 1811), the Americans narrowly defeated the Indians and then burned their capital. This battle shattered the Prophet's mystical authority, caused Tecumseh to lose prestige, and ended his dream to forge an Indian confederation. During the War of 1812, Tecumseh was reduced to leading a handful of Indians in British service against the Americans. Commodore Oliver Perry's victory on Lake Erie (September 10, 1813) gave the Americans naval control of the lake. This enabled Perry's fleet to ferry Harrison's army across the lake to take the offensive against Procter's army. On September 18, 1813, an Indian council was held at Amherstburg to announce Procter's decision to retreat. Tecumseh was angered by the decision and gave an impassioned speech chastising Procter for what he saw as cowardice and offering to continue the fight against the United States without British help. The following is the text of Tecumseh's address. In spite of Tecumseh's threat, Procter continued his retreat until he reached the Thames River. Here occurred an overwhelming American victory, the Battle of the Thames, on October 5, 1813. Among the killed was Tecumseh.

Primary Source

Father, listen to your children! You have them now all before you.

The war before this, our British father gave the hatchet to his red children, when our chiefs were alive.

They are now dead. In that war, our father was thrown on his back by the Americans, and our father took them by the hand without our knowledge, and ye are afraid that our father will do so again, at this time. Summer before last, when I came forward with my red brethren, and was ready to take up the hatchet in favor of our British father, we were told not to be in a hurry, that he had not yet determined to fight the Americans.

Listen!—When war was declared, our father stood up and gave us the tomahawk, and told us that he was then ready to strike the Americans; that he wanted our assistance; and that he would certainly get us our lands back, which the Americans had taken from us.

Listen!—You told us, at that time, to bring forward our families to this place; and we did so; and you promised to take care of them, and that they should want for nothing, while the men would go and fight the enemy. That we need not trouble ourselves about the enemy's garrison; that we knew nothing about them, and that our father would attend to that part of the business. You also told your red children, that you would take good care of your garrison here, which made our hearts glad.

Listen!—When we were last at the Rapids, it is true we gave you little assistance. It is hard to fight people, who live like ground hogs. Father, listen! Our fleet has gone out; we know they have fought; we have heard the great guns: but know nothing of what has happened to our father, with one arm. *Our* ships have gone one way, and we are much astonished to see our father tying up every thing and preparing to run away the other, without letting his red children know what his intentions are. You always told us to remain here, and take care of our lands; it made our hearts glad to hear that was your wish. Our great father, the king, is our head, and you represent him. You always told us, that you would never draw your foot off British ground: But now, father, we see you are drawing back, and we are sorry to see our father doing so without seeing the enemy. We must compare our father's conduct to a fat animal, that carries its tail upon its back, but when affrighted, he drops it between his legs and runs off.

Listen, Father! The Americans have not yet defeated us by land; neither are we sure that they have done so by water; we therefore, wish to remain here, and fight our enemy, if they should make their appearance. If they defeat us, we will then retreat with our father. At the battle of the Rapids last war, the Americans certainly defeated us; and when we retreated to our father's fort at that place the gates were shut against us. We were afraid that it would now be the case; but instead of that we now see our British father preparing to march out of his garrison.

Father! You have got the arms and ammunition which our great father sent for his red children. If you have an idea of going away, give them to us, and you may go and welcome, for us. Our lives are in the hands of the Great Spirit. We are determined to defend our lands, and if it be his will, we wish to leave our bones upon them.

Source: J. Russell Jr., *The History of the War between the United States and Great Britain* (Hartford, CT: B. & J. Russell, 1815), 228.

89. Treaty of Fort Jackson, August 9, 1814

Introduction

One of several Indian treaties from the War of 1812, the Treaty of Fort Jackson was signed on August 9, 1814, in Alabama by the Creek Indians and the United States. The Creeks had suffered a devastating defeat at the hands of General Andrew Jackson of the Tennessee Militia in the Battle of Horseshoe Bend (March 27, 1814). The treaty states that the Creeks had violated the treaty of friendship they had signed in New York in 1790 and started an unprovoked war. The Creek War began as a war between two factions among the Creeks, one of which was loyal to the British. A July 1813 clash between Creeks and U.S. soldiers ensued. On August 30 a surprise Creek attack captured Fort Mims, Alabama, killing more than 500 men, women, and children. The incident, known as the Fort Mims Massacre, brought the United States into overt conflict with the Creeks. Since the United States was already embroiled in the War of 1812, southern militia prosecuted the Creek War, assisted by a friendly Creek faction and the Cherokees. Under the terms of the treaty, Jackson compelled all the Creeks, friend and enemy alike, to cede huge tracts of their land in the

Southeast and forbade them to have any contact with the British or Spanish. In return the United States promised to provide food and to honor the boundaries of the Creeks' remaining territory. After concluding the Creek War, Jackson invaded Spanish Florida and then proceeded to Louisiana for the final campaign of the War of 1812. He was elected president of the United States in 1828.

Primary Source

Articles of agreement and capitulation, made and concluded this ninth day of August, one thousand eight hundred and fourteen, between major general Andrew Jackson, on behalf of the President of the United States of America, and the chiefs, deputies, and warriors of the Creek Nation.

WHEREAS an unprovoked, inhuman, and sanguinary war, waged by the hostile Creeks against the United States, hath been repelled, prosecuted and determined, successfully, on the part of the said States, in conformity with principles of national justice and honorable warfare—And whereas consideration is due to the rectitude of proceeding dictated by instructions relating to the re-establishment of peace: Be it remembered, that prior to the conquest of that part of the Creek nation hostile to the United States, numberless aggressions had been committed against the peace, the property, and the lives of citizens of the United States, and those of the Creek nation in amity with her, at the mouth of Duck river, Fort Mimms, and elsewhere, contrary to national faith, and the regard due to an article of the treaty concluded at New-York, in the year seventeen hundred ninety, between the two nations: That the United States, previously to the perpetration of such outrages, did, in order to ensure future amity and concord between the Creek nation and the said states, in conformity with the stipulations of former treaties, fulfil, with punctuality and good faith, her engagements to the said nation: that more than two-thirds of the whole number of chiefs and warriors of the Creek nation, disregarding the genuine spirit of existing treaties, suffered themselves to be instigated to violations of their national honor, and the respect due to a part of their own nation faithful to the United States and the principles of humanity, by impostures [impostors], denominating themselves Prophets, and by the duplicity and misrepresentation of foreign emissaries, whose governments are at war, open or understood, with the United States. Wherefore,

1st—The United States demand an equivalent for all expenses incurred in prosecuting the war to its termination, by a cession of all the territory belonging to the Creek nation within the territories of the United States, lying west, south, and south-eastwardly, of a line to be run and described by persons duly authorized and appointed by the President of the United States—Beginning at a point on the eastern bank of the Coosa river, where the south boundary line of the Cherokee nation crosses the same; running from thence down the said Coosa river with its eastern bank according to its various meanders to a point one mile above the mouth of Cedar creek, at Fort Williams, thence east two miles, thence south two miles, thence west to the eastern bank of the said Coosa river, thence down the eastern bank thereof according to its various meanders to a point opposite the upper end of the great falls, (called by the natives Woetumka,) thence east from a true meridian line to a point due north of the mouth of Ofucshee, thence south by a like meridian line to the mouth of Ofucshee on the south side of the Tallapoosa river, thence up the same, according to its various meanders, to a point where a direct course will cross the same at the distance of ten miles from the mouth thereof, thence a direct line to the mouth of Summochico creek, which empties into the Chatahouchie river on the east side thereof below the Eufaulau town, thence east from a true meridian line to a point which shall intersect the line now dividing the lands claimed by the said Creek nation from those claimed and owned by the state of Georgia: Provided, nevertheless, that where any possession of any chief or warrior of the Creek nation, who shall have been friendly to the United States during the war, and taken an active part therein, shall be within the territory ceded by these articles to the United States, every such person shall be entitled to a reservation of land within the said territory of one mile square, to include his improvements as near the centre thereof as may be, which shall inure to the said chief or warrior, and his descendants, so long as he or they shall continue to occupy the same, who shall be protected by and subject to the laws of the United States; but upon the voluntary abandonment thereof, by such possessor or his descendants, the right of occupancy or possession of said lands shall devolve to the United States, and be identified with the right of property ceded hereby.

2nd—The United States will guarantee to the Creek nation, the integrity of all their territory eastwardly and northwardly of the said line to be run and described as mentioned in the first article.

3d—The United States demand, that the Creek nation abandon all communication, and cease to hold any intercourse with any British or Spanish post, garrison, or town; and that they shall not admit among them, any agent or trader, who shall not derive authority to hold commercial, or other intercourse with them, by licence from the President or authorized agent of the United States.

4th—The United States demand an acknowledgment of the right to establish military posts and trading houses, and to open roads within the territory, guaranteed to the Creek nation by the second article, and a right to the free navigation of all its waters.

5th—The United States demand, that a surrender be immediately made, of all the persons and property, taken from the citizens of the United States, the friendly part of the Creek nation, the Cherokee, Chickasaw, and Choctaw nations, to the respective owners; and the United States will cause to be immediately restored to the formerly hostile Creeks, all the property taken from them since

their submission, either by the United States, or by any Indian nation in amity with the United States, together with all the prisoners taken from them during the war.

6th—The United States demand the caption and surrender of all the prophets and instigators of the war, whether foreigners or natives, who have not submitted to the arms of the United States, and become parties to these articles of capitulation, if ever they shall be found within the territory guaranteed to the Creek nation by the second article.

7th—The Creek nation being reduced to extreme want, and not at present having the means of subsistance, the United States, from motives of humanity, will continue to furnish gratuitously the necessaries of life, until the crops of corn can be considered competent to yield the nation a supply, and will establish trading houses in the nation, at the discretion of the President of the United States, and at such places as he shall direct, to enable the nation, by industry and economy, to procure clothing.

8th—A permanent peace shall ensue from the date of these presents forever, between the Creek nation and the United States, and between the Creek nation and the Cherokee, Chickesaw, and Choctaw nations.

9th—If in running east from the mouth of Summochico creek, it shall so happen that the settlement of the Kennards, fall within the lines of the territory hereby ceded, then, and in that case, the line shall be run east on a true meridian to Kitchofoonee creek, thence down the middle of said creek to its junction with Flint River, immediately below the Oakmulgee town, thence up the middle of Flint river to a point due east of that at which the above line struck the Kitchofoonee creek, thence east to the old line herein before mentioned, to wit: the line dividing the lands claimed by the Creek nation, from those claimed and owned by the state of Georgia.

The parties to these presents, after due consideration, for themselves and their constituents, agree to ratify and confirm the preceding articles, and constitute them the basis of a permanent peace between the two nations; and they do hereby solemnly bind themselves, and all the parties concerned and interested, to a faithful performance of every stipulation contained therein.

In testimony whereof, they have hereunto, interchangeably, set their hands and affixed their seals, the day and date above written.

Andrew Jackson, major general commanding Seventh Military District, (L.S.)
    Tustunnuggee Thlucco, speaker for the Upper Creeks, his x mark, (L.S.)
    Micco Aupoegau, of Toukaubatchee, his x mark, (L.S.)

Tustunnuggee Hopoiee, speaker of the Lower Creeks, his x mark, (L.S.)

Micco Achulee, of Cowetau, his x mark, (L.S.)

William McIntosh, jr., major of Cowetau, his x mark, (L.S.)

Tuskee Eneah, of Cussetau, his x mark, (L.S.)

Faue Emautla, of Cussetau, his x mark, (L.S.)

Toukaubatchee Tustunnuggee, of Hitchetee, his x mark, (L.S.)

Noble Kinnard, of Hitchetee, his x mark, (L.S.)

Hopoiee Hutkee, of Souwagoolo, his x mark, (L.S.)

Hopoiee Hutkee, for Hopoie Yoholo, of Souwogoolo, his x mark, (L.S.)

Folappo Haujo, of Eufaulau, on Chattohochee, his x mark, (L.S.)

Pachee Haujo, of Apalachoocla, his x mark, (L.S.)

Timpoeechee Bernard, captain of Uchees, his x mark, (L.S.)

Uchee Micco, his x mark, (L.S.)

Yoholo Micco, of Kialijee, his x mark, (L.S.)

Socoskee Emautla, of Kialijee, his x mark, (L.S.)

Choocchau Haujo, of Woccocoi, his x mark, (L.S.)

Esholoctee, of Nauchee, his x mark, (L.S.)

Yoholo Micco, of Tallapoosa Eufaulau, his x mark, (L.S.)

Stinthellis Haujo, of Abecoochee, his x mark, (L.S.)

Ocfuskee Yoholo, of Toutacaugee, his x mark, (L.S.)

John O'Kelly, of Coosa, (L.S.)

Eneah Thlucco, of Immookfau, his x mark, (L.S.)

Espokokoke Haujo, of Wewoko, his x mark, (L.S.)

Eneah Thlucco Hopoiee, of Talesee, his x mark, (L.S.)

Efau Haujo, of Puccan Tallahassee, his x mark, (L.S.)

Talessee Fixico, of Ocheobofau, his x mark, (L.S.)

Nomatlee Emautla, or captain Isaacs, of Cousoudee, his x mark, (L.S.)

Tuskegee Emautla, or John Carr, of Tuskegee, his x mark, (L.S.)

Alexander Grayson, of Hillabee, his x mark, (L.S.)

Lowee, of Ocmulgee, his x mark, (L.S.)

Nocoosee Emautla, of Chuskee Tallafau, his x mark, (L.S.)

William McIntosh, for Hopoiee Haujo, of Ooseoochee, his x mark, (L.S.)

William McIntosh, for Chehahaw Tustunnuggee, of Chehahaw, his x mark, (L.S.)

William McIntosh, for Spokokee Tustunnuggee, of Otellewhoyonnee, his x mark, (L.S.)

Done at fort Jackson, in presence of—

Charles Cassedy, acting secretary,
   Benjamin Hawkins, agent for Indian affairs,
   Return J. Meigs, A.C. nation,
   Robert Butler, Adjutant General U.S. Army,
   J.C. Warren, assistant agent for Indian affairs,
   George Mayfield,
   Alexander Curnels,
   George Lovett,
   Public interpreters.

Source: "Articles of Agreement and Capitulation, Aug. 9, 1814," in *The Public Statutes at Large of the United States of America,* Vol. 7, edited by Richard Peters (Boston: Little, Brown, 1846), 120–122.

90. Treaty of Ghent, December 24, 1814

Introduction

When American and British peace negotiators met in Ghent, Belgium, in August 1814, some hard bargaining ensued. At first the British demanded the creation of an independent Indian state, disarmament of the American side of the Great Lakes, and favorable territory adjustments. When the American negotiating team firmly rejected this one-sided proposal, British negotiators dropped the proposal for an independent Indian state and proposed the principle of whoever was currently holding territory (*uti possidetis*) as the basis for boundary adjustments. Monroe told his negotiators to resist this proposal and strive for the principle of the status quo before the war began. Meanwhile, the British ministry remained committed to conducting a war of punishment and asked the Duke of Wellington to take command in British North America. Wellington declined and added that the British position of *uti possidetis* was wrong. His reply caused the British to drop that demand. In late November when the Americans learned of this change, negotiations proceeded rapidly to an acceptable conclusion, with a treaty being signed on December 24, 1814, in Ghent, Belgium, by representatives from the United States and Great Britain. Neither side gave in on any principle, and neither party relinquished any territory. The U.S. Senate ratified the Treaty of Ghent on February 16, 1815. As a result of this treaty, Indians no longer enjoyed British support in territory outside of Canada.

Primary Source

Treaty of Peace and Amity between His Britannic Majesty and the United States of America

His Britannic Majesty and the United States of America desirous of terminating the war which has unhappily subsisted between the two Countries, and of restoring upon principles of perfect reciprocity, Peace, Friendship, and good Understanding between them, have for that purpose appointed their respective Plenipotentiaries, that is to say, His Britannic Majesty on His part has appointed the Right Honourable James Lord Gambier, late Admiral of the White now Admiral of the Red Squadron of His Majesty's Fleet; Henry Goulburn Esquire, a Member of the Imperial Parliament and Under Secretary of State; and William Adams Esquire, Doctor of Civil Laws: And the President of the United States, by and with the advice and consent of the Senate thereof, has appointed John Quincy Adams, James A. Bayard, Henry Clay, Jonathan Russell, and Albert Gallatin, Citizens of the United States; who, after a reciprocal communication of their respective Full Powers, have agreed upon the following Articles.

ARTICLE THE FIRST.

There shall be a firm and universal Peace between His Britannic Majesty and the United States, and between their respective Countries, Territories, Cities, Towns, and People of every degree without exception of places or persons. All hostilities both by sea and land shall cease as soon as this Treaty shall have been ratified by both parties as hereinafter mentioned. All territory, places, and possessions whatsoever taken by either party from the other during the war, or which may be taken after the signing of this Treaty, excepting only the Islands hereinafter mentioned, shall be restored without delay and without causing any destruction or carrying away any of the Artillery or other public property originally captured in the said forts or places, and which shall remain therein upon the Exchange of the Ratifications of this Treaty, or any Slaves or other private property; And all Archives, Records, Deeds, and Papers, either of a public nature or belonging to private persons, which in the course of the war may have fallen into the hands of the Officers of either party, shall be, as far as may be practicable, forthwith restored and delivered to the proper authorities and persons to whom they respectively belong. Such of the Islands in the Bay of Passamaquoddy as are claimed by both parties shall remain in the possession of the party in whose occupation they may be at the time of the Exchange of the Ratifications of this Treaty until the decision respecting the title to the said Islands shall have been made in conformity with the fourth Article of this Treaty. No disposition made by this Treaty as to such possession of the Islands and territories claimed by both parties shall in any manner whatever be construed to affect the right of either.

ARTICLE THE SECOND.

Immediately after the ratifications of this Treaty by both parties as hereinafter mentioned, orders shall be sent to the Armies, Squadrons, Officers, Subjects, and Citizens of the two Powers to cease from all hostilities: and to prevent all causes of complaint which might arise on account of the prizes which may be taken at sea after the said Ratifications of this Treaty, it is reciprocally agreed that all vessels and effects which may be taken after the space of twelve days from the said Ratifications upon all parts of the Coast of North America from the Latitude of twenty three degrees North to the Latitude of fifty degrees North, and as far Eastward in the Atlantic Ocean as the thirty sixth degree of West Longitude from the Meridian of Greenwich, shall be restored on each side:—that the time shall be thirty days in all other parts of the Atlantic Ocean North of the Equinoctial Line or Equator:—and the same time for the British and Irish Channels, for the Gulf of Mexico, and all parts of the West Indies:—forty days for the North Seas, for the Baltic,

and for all parts of the Mediterranean—sixty days for the Atlantic Ocean South of the Equator as far as the Latitude of the Cape of Good Hope.—ninety days for every other part of the world South of the Equator, and one hundred and twenty days for all other parts of the world without exception.

ARTICLE THE THIRD.

All Prisoners of war taken on either side as well by land as by sea shall be restored as soon as practicable after the Ratifications of this Treaty as hereinafter mentioned on their paying the debts which they may have contracted during their captivity. The two Contracting Parties respectively engage to discharge in specie the advances which may have been made by the other for the sustenance and maintenance of such prisoners.

ARTICLE THE FOURTH.

Whereas it was stipulated by the second Article in the Treaty of Peace of one thousand seven hundred and eighty three between His Britannic Majesty and the United States of America that the boundary of the United States should comprehend all Islands within twenty leagues of any part of the shores of the United States and lying between lines to be drawn due East from the points where the aforesaid boundaries between Nova Scotia on the one part and East Florida on the other shall respectively touch the Bay of Fundy and the Atlantic Ocean, excepting such Islands as now are or heretofore have been within the limits of Nova Scotia, and whereas the several Islands in the Bay of Passamaquoddy, which is part of the Bay of Fundy, and the Island of Grand Menan in the said Bay of Fundy, are claimed by the United States as being comprehended within their aforesaid boundaries, which said Islands are claimed as belonging to His Britannic Majesty as having been at the time of and previous to the aforesaid Treaty of one thousand seven hundred and eighty three within the limits of the Province of Nova Scotia: In order therefore finally to decide upon these claims it is agreed that they shall be referred to two Commissioners to be appointed in the following manner: viz: One Commissioner shall be appointed by His Britannic Majesty and one by the President of the United States, by and with the advice and consent of the Senate thereof, and the said two Commissioners so appointed shall be sworn impartially to examine and decide upon the said claims according to such evidence as shall be laid before them on the part of His Britannic Majesty and of the United States respectively. The said Commissioners shall meet at St Andrews in the Province of New Brunswick, and shall have power to adjourn to such other place or places as they shall think fit. The said Commissioners shall by a declaration or report under their hands and seals decide to which of the two Contracting parties the several Islands aforesaid do respectedly belong in conformity with the true intent of the said Treaty of Peace of one thousand seven hundred and eighty three. And if the said

Commissioners shall agree in their decision both parties shall consider such decision as final and conclusive. It is further agreed that in the event of the two Commissioners differing upon all or any of the matters so referred to them, or in the event of both or either of the said Commissioners refusing or declining or wilfully omitting to act as such, they shall make jointly or separately a report or reports as well to the Government of His Britannic Majesty as to that of the United States, stating in detail the points on which they differ, and the grounds upon which their respective opinions have been formed, or the grounds upon which they or either of them have so refused, declined or omitted to act. And His Britannic Majesty and the Government of the United States hereby agree to refer the report or reports of the said Commissioners to some friendly Sovereign or State to be then named for that purpose, and who shall be requested to decide on the differences which may be stated in the said report or reports, or upon the report of one Commissioner together with the grounds upon which the other Commissioner shall have refused, declined or omitted to act as the case may be. And if the Commissioner so refusing, declining, or omitting to act, shall also wilfully omit to state the grounds upon which he has so done in such manner that the said statement may be referred to such friendly Sovereign or State together with the report of such other Commissioner, then such Sovereign or State shall decide ex parse upon the said report alone. And His Britannic Majesty and the Government of the United States engage to consider the decision of such friendly Sovereign or State to be final and conclusive on all the matters so referred.

ARTICLE THE FIFTH.

Whereas neither that point of the Highlands lying due North from the source of the River St Croix, and designated in the former Treaty of Peace between the two Powers as the North West Angle of Nova Scotia, nor the North Westernmost head of Connecticut River has yet been ascertained; and whereas that part of the boundary line between the Dominions of the two Powers which extends from the source of the River St Croix directly North to the above mentioned North West Angle of Nova Scotia, thence along the said Highlands which divide those Rivers that empty themselves into the River St Lawrence from those which fall into the Atlantic Ocean to the North Westernmost head of Connecticut River, thence down along the middle of that River to the forty fifth degree of North Latitude, thence by a line due West on said latitude until it strikes the River Iroquois or Cataraquy, has not yet been surveyed: it is agreed that for these several purposes two Commissioners shall be appointed, sworn, and authorized to act exactly in the manner directed with respect to those mentioned in the next preceding Article unless otherwise specified in the present Article. The said Commissioners shall meet at St Andrews in the Province of New Brunswick, and shall have power to adjourn to such other place or places as they shall think fit. The said Commissioners shall have

power to ascertain and determine the points above mentioned in conformity with the provisions of the said Treaty of Peace of one thousand seven hundred and eighty three, and shall cause the boundary aforesaid from the source of the River St Croix to the River Iroquois or Cataraquy to be surveyed and marked according to the said provisions. The said Commissioners shall make a map of the said boundary, and annex to it a declaration under their hands and seals certifying it to be the true Map of the said boundary, and particularizing the latitude and longitude of the North West Angle of Nova Scotia, of the North Westernmost head of Connecticut River, and of such other points of the said boundary as they may deem proper. And both parties agree to consider such map and declaration as finally and conclusively fixing the said boundary. And in the event of the said two Commissioners differing, or both, or either of them refusing, declining, or wilfully omitting to act, such reports, declarations, or statements shall be made by them or either of them, and such reference to a friendly Sovereign or State shall be made in all respects as in the latter part of the fourth Article is contained, and in as full a manner as if the same was herein repeated.

ARTICLE THE SIXTH.

Whereas by the former Treaty of Peace that portion of the boundary of the United States from the point where the fortyfifth degree of North Latitude strikes the River Iroquois or Cataraquy to the Lake Superior was declared to be "along the middle of said River into Lake Ontario, through the middle of said Lake until it strikes the communication by water between that Lake and Lake Erie, thence along the middle of said communication into Lake Erie, through the middle of said Lake until it arrives at the water communication into the Lake Huron; thence through the middle of said Lake to the water communication between that Lake and Lake Superior:" and whereas doubts have arisen what was the middle of the said River, Lakes, and water communications, and whether certain Islands lying in the same were within the Dominions of His Britannic Majesty or of the United States: In order therefore finally to decide these doubts, they shall be referred to two Commissioners to be appointed, sworn, and authorized to act exactly in the manner directed with respect to those mentioned in the next preceding Article unless otherwise specified in this present Article. The said Commissioners shall meet in the first instance at Albany in the State of New York, and shall have power to adjourn to such other place or places as they shall think fit. The said Commissioners shall by a Report or Declaration under their hands and seals, designate the boundary through the said River, Lakes, and water communications, and decide to which of the two Contracting parties the several Islands lying within the said Rivers, Lakes, and water communications, do respectively belong in conformity with the true intent of the said Treaty of one thousand seven hundred and eighty three. And both parties agree to consider such designation and decision as final and conclusive.

And in the event of the said two Commissioners differing or both or either of them refusing, declining, or wilfully omitting to act, such reports, declarations, or statements shall be made by them or either of them, and such reference to a friendly Sovereign or State shall be made in all respects as in the latter part of the fourth Article is contained, and in as full a manner as if the same was herein repeated.

ARTICLE THE SEVENTH.

It is further agreed that the said two last mentioned Commissioners after they shall have executed the duties assigned to them in the preceding Article, shall be, and they are hereby, authorized upon their oaths impartially to fix and determine according to the true intent of the said Treaty of Peace of one thousand seven hundred and eighty three, that part of the boundary between the dominions of the two Powers, which extends from the water communication between Lake Huron and Lake Superior to the most North Western point of the Lake of the Woods;—to decide to which of the two Parties the several Islands lying in the Lakes, water communications, and Rivers forming the said boundary do respectively belong in conformity with the true intent of the said Treaty of Peace of one thousand seven hundred and eighty three, and to cause such parts of the said boundary as require it to be surveyed and marked. The said Commissioners shall by a Report or declaration under their hands and seals, designate the boundary aforesaid, state their decision on the points thus referred to them, and particularize the Latitude and Longitude of the most North Western point of the Lake of the Woods, and of such other parts of the said boundary as they may deem proper. And both parties agree to consider such designation and decision as final and conclusive. And in the event of the said two Commissioners differing, or both or either of them refusing, declining, or wilfully omitting to act, such reports, declarations or statements shall be made by them or either of them, and such reference to a friendly Sovereign or State shall be made in all respects as in the latter part of the fourth Article is contained, and in as full a manner as if the same was herein revealed.

ARTICLE THE EIGHTH.

The several Boards of two Commissioners mentioned in the four preceding Articles shall respectively have power to appoint a Secretary, and to employ such Surveyors or other persons as they shall judge necessary. Duplicates of all their respective reports, declarations, statements, and decisions, and of their accounts, and of the Journal of their proceedings shall be delivered by them to the Agents of His Britannic Majesty and to the Agents of the United States, who may be respectively appointed and authorized to manage the business on behalf of their respective Governments. The said Commissioners shall be respectively paid in such manner as shall be agreed between the two contracting parties, such agreement being to be settled at the time of the Exchange of the Ratifications of this Treaty. And all other expenses attending the said Commissions shall be defrayed equally by the two parties. And in the case of death, sickness, resignation, or necessary absence, the place of every such Commissioner respectively shall be supplied in the same manner as such Commissioner was first appointed; and the new Commissioner shall take the same oath or affirmation and do the same duties. It is further agreed between the two contracting parties that in case any of the Islands mentioned in any of the preceding Articles, which were in the possession of one of the parties prior to the commencement of the present war between the two Countries, should by the decision of any of the Boards of Commissioners aforesaid, or of the Sovereign or State so referred to, as in the four next preceding Articles contained, fall within the dominions of the other party, all grants of land made previous to the commencement of the war by the party having had such possession, shall be as valid as if such Island or Islands had by such decision or decisions been adjudged to be within the dominions of the party having had such possession.

ARTICLE THE NINTH.

The United States of America engage to put an end immediately after the Ratification of the present Treaty to hostilities with all the Tribes or Nations of Indians with whom they may be at war at the time of such Ratification, and forthwith to restore to such Tribes or Nations respectively all the possessions, rights, and privileges which they may have enjoyed or been entitled to in one thousand eight hundred and eleven previous to such hostilities. Provided always that such Tribes or Nations shall agree to desist from all hostilities against the United States of America, their Citizens, and Subjects upon the Ratification of the present Treaty being notified to such Tribes or Nations, and shall so desist accordingly. And His Britannic Majesty engages on his part to put an end immediately after the Ratification of the present Treaty to hostilities with all the Tribes or Nations of Indians with whom He may be at war at the time of such Ratification, and forthwith to restore to such Tribes or Nations respectively all the possessions, rights, and privileges, which they may have enjoyed or been entitled to in one thousand eight hundred and eleven previous to such hostilities. Provided always that such Tribes or Nations shall agree to desist from all hostilities against His Britannic Majesty and His Subjects upon the Ratification of the present Treaty being notified to such Tribes or Nations, and shall so desist accordingly.

ARTICLE THE TENTH.

Whereas the Traffic in Slaves is irreconcilable with the principles of humanity and Justice, and whereas both His Majesty and the United States are desirous of continuing their efforts to promote its entire abolition, it is hereby agreed that both the contracting parties shall use their best endeavours to accomplish so desirable an object.

ARTICLE THE ELEVENTH.

This Treaty when the same shall have been ratified on both sides without alteration by either of the contracting parties, and the Ratifications mutually exchanged, shall be binding on both parties, and the Ratifications shall be exchanged at Washington in the space of four months from this day or sooner if practicable. In faith whereof, We the respective Plenipotentiaries have signed this Treaty, and have hereunto affixed our Seals.

Done in triplicate at Ghent the twenty fourth day of December one thousand eight hundred and fourteen.

GAMBIER. [Seal]
   HENRY GOULBURN [Seal]
   WILLIAM ADAMS [Seal]
   JOHN QUINCY ADAMS [Seal]
   J. A. BAYARD [Seal]
   H. CLAY [Seal]
   JON. RUSSELL [Seal]
   ALBERT GALLATIN [Seal]

Source: "Treaty of Peace and Amity between His Britannic Majesty and the United States of America, Dec. 24, 1814," in *Treaties and Other International Acts of the United States of America*, Vol. 2, *Documents 1–40: 1776–1818* (Washington, DC: U.S. Government Printing Office, 1931), 581.

91. Adams-Onís Treaty, February 22, 1819

Introduction

Negotiated by U.S. secretary of state (and future U.S. president) John Quincy Adams and Spanish diplomat Luis de Onís, the Adams-Onís Treaty transferred ownership of eastern Florida from Spain to the United States and established a definitive boundary between Spanish-held Mexico and the U.S. territory acquired in the Louisiana Purchase. The United States had already taken control of western Florida during the War of 1812. Signed on February 22, 1819, in Washington, D.C., the treaty was not ratified and put into effect until February 22, 1821. However, as early as 1818, well before the treaty was signed, Andrew Jackson had already led U.S. soldiers into eastern Florida against the Creeks and Seminoles, whom British adventurers had incited to mount raids into Georgia. Jackson's incursion into eastern Florida (known as the First Seminole War) and execution of British subjects was highly illegal and could have caused an international diplomatic crisis, but Spain was anxious to leave Florida. In 1821 Mexico won its independence from Spain, and Texas remained part of Mexico. Like so many other treaties between European powers and the United

States, this treaty gave scant regard to the Native Americans who lived on the lands covered by the treaty. In the decades to come, Florida was the site of two more wars between the United States and the Seminole Indians: the Second Seminole War (1835–1842) and the Third Seminole War (1855–1858).

Primary Source

TREATY OF AMITY, SETTLEMENT, AND LIMITS BETWEEN THE UNITED STATES OF AMERICA AND HIS CATHOLIC MAJESTY, CONCLUDED AT WASHINGTON, FEBRUARY 22, 1819; RATIFICATION ADVISED BY SENATE, FEBRUARY 24, 1819; RATIFIED BY PRESIDENT; RATIFIED BY THE KING OF SPAIN, OCTOBER 24, 1820; RATIFICATION AGAIN ADVISED BY SENATE, FEBRUARY 19, 1821; RATIFIED BY PRESIDENT, FEBRUARY 22, 1821; RATIFICATIONS EXCHANGED AT WASHINGTON, FEBRUARY 22, 1821; PROCLAIMED, FEBRUARY 22, 1821.

THE United States of America and His Catholic Majesty, desiring to consolidate, on a permanent basis, the friendship and good correspondence which happily prevails between the two parties have determined to settle and terminate all their differences and pretensions, by a treaty, which shall designate, with precision, the limits of their respective bordering territories in North America.

With this intention, the President of the United States, has furnished with their full powers, John Quincy Adams, Secretary of State of the said United States; and His Catholic Majesty has appointed the Most Excellent Lord Don Luis De Onis, Gonzales, Lopez y Vara, Lord of the town of Rayaces, Perpetual Regidor of the Corporation of the city of Salamanca, Knight Grand Cross of the Royal American Order of Isabella the Catholic, decorated with the Lys of La Vendee, Knight Pensioner of the Royal and Distinguished Spanish Order of Charles the Third, Member of the Supreme Assembly of the said Royal Order; of the Council of His Majesty; His Secretary, with Exercise of Decrees, and His Envoy Extraordinary and Minister Plenipotentiary near the United States of America;

And the said Plenipotentiaries, after having exchanged their powers, have agreed upon and concluded the following articles:

ARTICLE I

There shall be a firm and inviolable peace and sincere friendship between the United States and their citizens and His Catholic Majesty, his successors and subjects, without exception of persons or places.

ARTICLE II

His Catholic Majesty cedes to the United States, in full property and sovereignty, all the territories which belong to him, situated to the eastward of the Mississippi, known by the name of East and West Florida. The adjacent islands dependent on said provinces, all public lots and squares, vacant lands, public edifices, fortifications, barracks, and other buildings, which are not private property, archives and documents, which relate directly to the property and sovereignty of said provinces, are included in this article. The said archives and documents shall be left in possession of the commissaries or officers of the United States, duly authorized to receive them.

ARTICLE III

The boundary line between the two countries, west of the Mississippi, shall begin on the Gulph of Mexico, at the mouth of the river Sabine, in the sea, continuing north, along the western bank of that river, to the 32d degree of latitude; thence, by a line due north, to the degree of latitude where it strikes the Rio Roxo of Nachitoches, or Red River; then following the course of the Rio Roxo westward, to the degree of longitude 100 west from London and 23 from Washington; then, crossing the said Red River, and running thence by a line due north, to the river Arkansas; thence, following the course of the southern bank of the Arkansas, to its source, in latitude 42 north; and thence, by that parallel of latitude, to the South Sea. The whole being as laid down in Melish's map of the United States, published at Philadelphia, improved to the first of January, 1818. But if the source of the Arkansas River shall be found to fall north or south of latitude 42, then the line shall run from the said source due south or north, as the case may be, till it meets the said parallel of latitude 42, and thence, along the said parallel, to the South Sea: All the islands in the Sabine, and the said Red and Arkansas Rivers, throughout the course thus described, to belong to the United States; but the use of the waters, and the navigation of the Sabine to the sea, and of the said rivers Roxo and Arkansas, throughout the extent of the said boundary, on their respective banks, shall be common to the respective inhabitants of both nations.

The two high contracting parties agree to cede and renounce all their rights, claims, and pretensons, to the territories described by the said line, that is to say: The United States hereby to His Catholic Majesty, and renounce forever, all their rights, claims and pretensons, to the territories lying west and south of the above-described line; and, in like manner, His Catholic Majesty cedes to the said United States all his rights, claims, and pretensons to any territories east and north of the said line, and for himself, his heirs, and successors, renounces all claim to the said territories forever.

ARTICLE IV

To fix this line with more precision, and to place the landmarks which shall designate exactly the limits of both nations, each of the contracting parties shall appoint a Commissioner and a surveyor, who shall meet before the termination of one year from the date of the ratification of this treaty at Nachitoches, on the Red River, and proceed to run and mark the said line, from the mouth of the Sabine to the Red River, and from the Red River to the river Arkansas, and to ascertain the latitude of the source of the said river Arkansas, in conformity to what is above agreed upon and stipulated, and the line of latitude 42, to the South Sea: they shall make out plans, and keep journals of their proceedings, and the result agreed upon by them shall be considered as part of this treaty, and shall have the same force as if it were inserted therein. The two Governments will amicably agree respecting the necessary articles to be furnished to those persons, and also as to their respective escorts, should such be deemed necessary.

ARTICLE V

The inhabitants of the ceded territories shall be secured in the free exercise of their religion, without any restriction; and all those who may desire to remove to the Spanish dominions shall be permitted to sell or export their effects, at any time whatever, without being subject, in either case, to duties.

ARTICLE VI

The inhabitants of the territories which His Catholic Majesty cedes to the United States, by this treaty, shall be incorporated in the Union of the United States, as soon as may be consistent with the principles of the Federal Constitution, and admitted to the enjoyment of all the privileges, rights, and immunities of the citizens of the United States.

ARTICLE VII

The officers and troops of His Catholic Majesty, in the territories hereby ceded by him to the United States, shall be withdrawn, and possession of the places occupied by them shall be given within six months after the exchange of the ratifications of this treaty, or sooner if possible, by the officers of His Catholic Majesty to the commissioners or officers of the United States duly appointed to receive them; and the United States shall furnish the transports and escorts necessary to convey the Spanish officers and troops and their baggage to the Havana.

ARTICLE VIII

All the grants of land made before the 24th of January, 1818, by His Catholic Majesty, or by his lawful authorities, in the said territories ceded by His Majesty to the United States, shall be ratified and confirmed to the persons in possession of the lands, to the same extent that the same grants would be valid if the territories had remained under the dominion of His Catholic Majesty. But the owners in possession of such lands, who, by reason of the recent circumstances of the Spanish nation, and the revolutions in Europe, have been prevented from fulfilling all the conditions of their grants, shall complete them within the terms limited in the Same, respectively, from the date of this treaty; in default of which the said grants shall be null and void. All grants made since the said 24th of January, 1818, when the first proposal, on the part of His Catholic Majesty, for the cession of the Floridas was made, are hereby declared and agreed to be null and void.

ARTICLE IX

The two high contracting parties, animated with the most earnest desire of conciliation, and with the object of putting an end to all the differences which have existed between them, and of confirming the good understanding which they wish to be forever maintained between them, reciprocally renounce all claims for damages or injuries which they, themselves, as well as their respective citizens and subjects, may have suffered until the time of signing this treaty.

The renunciation of the United States will extend to all the injuries mentioned in the convention of the 11th of August, 1802.

(2) To all claims on account of prizes made by French privateers, and condemned by French Consuls, within the territory and jurisdiction of Spain.

(3) To all claims of indemnities on account of the suspension of the right of deposit at New Orleans in 1802.

(4) To all claims of citizens of the United States upon the Government of Spain, arising from the unlawful seizures at sea, and in the ports and territories of Spain, or the Spanish colonies.

(5) To all claims of citizens of the United States upon the Spanish Government, statements of which, soliciting the interposition of the Government of the United States, have been presented to the Department of State, or to the Minister of the United States in Spain, since the date of the convention of 1802, and until the Signature of this treaty.

The renunciation of His Catholic Majesty extends—

(1) To all the injuries mentioned in the convention of the 11th of August, 1802.

(2) To the sums which His Catholic Majesty advanced for the return of Captain Pike from the Provincias Internas.

(3) To all injuries caused by the expedition of Miranda, that was fitted out and equipped at New York.

(4) To all claims of Spanish subjects upon the Government of the United States arising from unlawful seizures at sea, or within the ports and territorial jurisdiction of the United States.

Finally, to all the claims of subjects of His Catholic Majesty upon the Government of the United States in which the interposition of his Catholic Majesty's Government has been solicited, before the date of this treaty and since the date of the convention of 1802, or which may have been made to the department of foreign affairs of His Majesty, or to His Minister in the United States.

And the high contracting parties, respectively, renounce all claim to indemnities for any of the recent events or transactions of their respective commanders and officers in the Floridas.

The United States will cause satisfaction to be made for the injuries, if any, which, by process of law, shall be established to have been suffered by the Spanish officers, and individual Spanish inhabitants, by the late operations of the American Army in Florida.

ARTICLE X

The convention entered into between the two Governments, on the 11th of August, 1802, the ratifications of which were exchanged the 21st December, 1818, is annulled.

ARTICLE XI

The United States, exonerating Spain from all demands in future, on account of the claims of their citizens to which the renunciations herein contained extend, and considering them entirely cancelled, undertake to make satisfaction for the same, to an amount not exceeding five millions of dollars. To ascertain the full amount and validity of those claims, a commission, to consist of three Commissioners, citizens of the United States, shall be appointed by the President, by and with the advice and consent of the Senate, which commission shall meet at the city of Washington, and, within the space of three years from the time of their first meeting, shall receive, examine, and decide upon the amount and validity of all the claims included within the descriptions above mentioned. The said Commissioners shall take an oath or affirmation, to be entered on the record of their proceedings, for the faithful and diligent discharge of their duties; and, in case of the death, sickness, or necessary absence of any such Commissioner, his place may be supplied by the appointment, as aforesaid, or by the President of the United States, during the recess of the Senate, of another Commissioner in his stead. The said Commissioners shall be authorized to hear and examine, on oath, every question relative to the said claims, and to receive all suitable authentic testimony concerning the same. And the Spanish Government shall furnish all such documents and elucidations as may be in their possession, for the adjustment of the said claims, according to the principles of justice, the laws of nations, and the stipulations of the treaty between the two parties of 27th October, 1795; the said documents to be specified, when demanded, at the instance of the said Commissioners.

The payment of such claims as may be admitted and adjusted by the said Commissioners, or the major part of them, to an amount not exceeding five millions of dollars, shall be made by the United States, either immediately at their Treasury, or by the creation of stock, bearing an interest of six per cent. per annum, payable from the proceeds of sales of public lands within the territories hereby ceded to the United States, or in such other manner as the Congress of the United States may prescribe by law.

The records of the proceedings of the said Commissioners, together with the vouchers and documents produced before them, relative to the claims to be adjusted and decided upon by them, shall, after the close of their transactions, be deposited in the

Department of State of the United States; and copies of them, or any part of them, shall be furnished to the Spanish Government, if required, at the demand of the Spanish Minister in the United States.

ARTICLE XII

The treaty of limits and navigation, of 1795, remains confirmed in all and each one of its articles excepting the 2, 3, 4, 21, and the second clause of the 22d article, which having been altered by this treaty, or having received their entire execution, are no longer valid.

With respect to the 15th article of the same treaty of friendship, limits, and navigation of 1795, in which it is stipulated that the flag shall cover the property, the two high contracting parties agree that this shall be so understood with respect to those Powers who recognize this principle; but if either of the two contracting parties shall be at war with a third party, and the other neutral, the flag of the neutral shall cover the property of enemies whose Government acknowledge this principle, and not of others.

ARTICLE XIII

Both contracting parties, wishing to favour their mutual commerce, by affording in their ports every necessary assistance to their respective merchant-vessels, have agreed that the sailors who shall desert from their vessels in the ports of the other, shall be arrested and delivered up, at the instance of the Consul, who shall prove, nevertheless, that the deserters belonged to the vessels that claimed them, exhibiting the document that is customary in their nation: that is to say, the American Consul in a Spanish port shall exhibit the document known by the name of articles, and the Spanish Consul in American ports the roll of the vessel; and if the name of the deserter or deserters who are claimed shall appear in the one or the other, they shall be arrested, held in custody, and delivered to the vessel to which they shall belong.

ARTICLE XIV

The United States hereby certify that they have not received any compensation from France for the injuries they suffered from her privateers, Consuls, and tribunals on the coasts and in the ports of Spain, for the satisfaction of which provision is made by this treaty; and they will present an authentic statement of the prizes made, and of their true value, that Spain may avail herself of the same in such manner as she may deem just and proper.

ARTICLE XV

The United States, to give to His Catholic Majesty, a proof of their desire to cement the relations of amity subsisting between the two nations, and to favour the commerce of the subjects of His Catholic Majesty, agree that Spanish vessels, coming laden only with productions of Spanish growth or manufactures, directly from the ports of Spain, or of her colonies, shall be admitted, for the term of twelve years, to the ports of Pensacola and St. Augustine, in the Floridas, without paying other or higher duties on their cargoes, or of tonnage, than will be paid by the vessels of the United States. During the said term no other nation shall enjoy the same privileges within the ceded territories. The twelve years shall commence three months after the exchange of the ratifications of this treaty.

ARTICLE XVI

The present treaty shall be ratified in due form, by the contracting parties, and the ratifications shall be exchanged in six months from this time, or sooner if possible.

In witness whereof we, the underwritten Plenipotentiaries of the United States of America and of His Catholic Majesty, have signed, by virtue of our powers, the present treaty of amity, settlement, and limits, and have thereunto affixed our seals, respectively.

Done at Washington this twenty-second day of February, one thousand eight hundred and nineteen.

JOHN QUINCY ADAMS [L. S.]
LUIS DE ONIS [L. S.]

> **Source:** "Treaty of Friendship, Cession of the Floridas, and Boundaries," in *Treaties, Conventions, International Acts, Protocols and Agreements between the United States of America and Other Powers, 1776–1909*, Vol. 2 (Washington, DC: U.S. Government Printing Office, 1910), 1, 651.

92. Andrew Jackson, Indian Removal Messages to Congress, 1829–1830

Introduction

Andrew Jackson's heroic military reputation in the Creek War and the War of 1812 eventually led to his election as president of the United States in 1828. President Jackson's annual messages to Congress, delivered in 1829 and 1830, announced and justified his policy of removing Indians from the Southeast—including the Choctaws and Chickasaws of Alabama and Mississippi and the Cherokees of Georgia—and resettling them on land west of the Mississippi River. Despite some public sympathy for the Native Americans, Jackson argued that if the Indians remained within existing states, they would constitute a foreign people, contradicting the prohibition of states within other states found in Article IV, Section 3, of the U.S. Constitution. Congress subsequently adopted the Indian Removal Act of 1830, which appropriated $500,000 to pay the costs of exchanging Indian lands in the East for land to the west. The U.S. Supreme Court decisions in *Cherokee Nation v. Georgia* (1831) and *Worcester v. Georgia* (1832) proved inadequate to protect Native American interests in the face of state, presidential, and congressional opposition. They were ultimately forced off their land, culminating in the devastating forced migration of 15,000 Cherokees in 1838 to present-day Oklahoma. More than 4,000 died during the journey, leading the Cherokees to call the march the Trail of Tears.

Primary Source

It gives me pleasure to announce to Congress that the benevolent policy of the government, steadily pursued for nearly thirty years, in relation to the removal of the Indians beyond the white settlements is approaching to a happy consummation. Two important tribes have accepted the provision made for their removal at the last session of Congress, and it is believed that their example will induce the remaining tribes also to seek the same obvious advantages.

The consequences of a speedy removal will be important to the United States, to individual states, and to the Indians themselves. The pecuniary advantages which it promises to the government are the least of its recommendations. It puts an end to all possible danger of collision between the authorities of the general and state governments on account of the Indians. It will place a dense and civilized population in large tracts of country now occupied by a few savage hunters. By opening the whole territory between Tennessee on the north and Louisiana on the south to the settlement of the whites it will incalculably strengthen the southwestern frontier and render the adjacent states strong enough to repel future invasions without remote aid. It will relieve the whole state of Mississippi and the western part of Alabama of Indian occupancy, and enable those states to advance rapidly in population, wealth, and power.

It will separate the Indians from immediate contact with settlements of whites; free them from the power of the states; enable them to pursue happiness in their own way and under their own rude institutions; will retard the progress of decay, which is lessening their numbers, and perhaps cause them gradually, under the protection of the government and through the influence of good counsels, to cast off their savage habits and become an interesting, civilized, and Christian community. These consequences, some of them so certain and the rest so probable, make the complete execution of the plan sanctioned by Congress at their last session an object of much solicitude.

Toward the aborigines of the country no one can indulge a more friendly feeling than myself, or would go further in attempting to reclaim them from their wandering habits and make them a happy, prosperous people. I have endeavored to impress upon them my own solemn convictions of the duties and powers of the general government in relation to the state authorities. For the justice of the laws passed by the states within the scope of their reserved powers they are not responsible to this government. As individuals we may entertain and express our opinions of their acts, but as a government we have as little right to control them as we have to prescribe laws for other nations.

With a full understanding of the subject, the Choctaw and the Chickasaw tribes have with great unanimity determined to avail themselves of the liberal offers presented by the act of Congress, and have agreed to remove beyond the Mississippi River. Treaties have been made with them, which in due season will be submitted for consideration. In negotiating these treaties, they were made to understand their true condition, and they have preferred maintaining their independence in the Western forests to submitting to the laws of the states in which they now reside. These treaties, being probably the last which will ever be made with them, are characterized by great liberality on the part of the government. They give the Indians a liberal sum in consideration of their removal, and comfortable subsistence on their arrival at their new homes. If it be their real interest to maintain a separate existence, they will there be at liberty to do so without the inconveniences and vexations to which they would unavoidably have been subject in Alabama and Mississippi.

Humanity has often wept over the fate of the aborigines of this country, and philanthropy has been long busily employed in devising means to avert it, but its progress has never for a moment been arrested, and one by one have many powerful tribes disappeared from the earth. To follow to the tomb the last of his race and to tread on the graves of extinct nations excite melancholy reflections. But true philanthropy reconciles the mind to these vicissitudes as it does to the extinction of one generation to make room for another. In the monuments and fortresses of an unknown people, spread over the extensive regions of the West, we behold the memorials of a once powerful race, which was exterminated or has disappeared to make room for the existing savage tribes. Nor is there anything in this which, upon a comprehensive view of the general interests of the human race, is to be regretted. Philanthropy could not wish to see this continent restored to the condition in which it was found by our forefathers. What good man would prefer a country covered with forests and ranged by a few thousand savages to our extensive republic, studded with cities, towns, and prosperous farms, embellished with all the improvements which art can devise or industry execute, occupied by more than 12 million happy people, and filled with all the blessings of liberty, civilization, and religion?

The present policy of the government is but a continuation of the same progressive change by a milder process. The tribes which occupied the countries now constituting the Eastern states were annihilated or have melted away to make room for the whites. The waves of population and civilization are rolling to the westward, and we now propose to acquire the countries occupied by the red men of the South and West by a fair exchange, and, at the expense of the United States, to send them to a land where their existence may be prolonged and perhaps made perpetual.

Doubtless it will be painful to leave the graves of their fathers; but what do they more than our ancestors did or than our children are now doing? To better their condition in an unknown land our forefathers left all that was dear in earthly objects. Our children by thousands yearly leave the land of their birth to seek new homes in distant regions. Does humanity weep at these painful separations from everything, animate and inanimate, with which the young heart has become entwined? Far from it. It is rather a source of joy that our country affords scope where our young population may range unconstrained in body or in mind, developing the power and faculties of man in their highest perfection. These remove hundreds and almost thousands of miles at their own expense, purchase the lands they occupy, and support themselves at their new homes from the moment of their arrival. Can it be cruel in this government when, by events which it cannot control, the Indian is made discontented in his ancient home to purchase his lands, to give him a new and extensive territory, to pay the expense of his removal, and support him a year in his new abode? How many thousands of our own people would gladly embrace the opportunity of removing to the West on such conditions? If the offers made to the Indians were extended to them, they would be hailed with gratitude and joy.

And is it supposed that the wandering savage has a stronger attachment to his home than the settled, civilized Christian? Is it more afflicting to him to leave the graves of his fathers than it is to our brothers and children? Rightly considered, the policy of the general government toward the red man is not only liberal but generous. He is unwilling to submit to the laws of the states and mingle with their population. To save him from this alternative, or perhaps utter annihilation, the general government kindly offers him a new home, and proposes to pay the whole expense of his removal and settlement.

In the consummation of a policy originating at an early period, and steadily pursued by every administration within the present century—so just to the states and so generous to the Indians—the executive feels it has a right to expect the cooperation of Congress and of all good and disinterested men. The states, moreover, have a right to demand it. It was substantially a part of the compact which made them members of our Confederacy. With Georgia there is an express contract; with the new states an implied one of equal obligation. Why, in authorizing Ohio, Indiana, Illinois, Missouri, Mississippi, and Alabama to form constitutions and become separate states, did Congress include within their limits extensive tracts of Indian lands, and, in some instances, powerful Indian tribes? Was it not understood by both parties that the power of the states was to be coextensive with their limits, and that, with all convenient dispatch, the general government should extinguish the Indian title and remove every obstruction to the complete jurisdiction of the state governments over the soil? Probably not one of those states would have accepted a separate existence—certainly it would never have been granted by Congress—had it been understood that

they were to be confined forever to those small portions of their nominal territory the Indian title to which had at the time been extinguished.

It is, therefore, a duty which this government owes to the new states to extinguish as soon as possible the Indian title to all lands which Congress themselves have included within their limits. When this is done the duties of the general government in relation to the states and the Indians within their limits are at an end. The Indians may leave the state or not, as they choose. The purchase of their lands does not alter in the least their personal relations with the state government. No act of the general government has ever been deemed necessary to give the states jurisdiction over the persons of the Indians. That they possess by virtue of their sovereign power within their own limits in as full a manner before as after the purchase of the Indian lands; nor can this government add to or diminish it.

May we not hope, therefore, that all good citizens, and none more zealously than those who think the Indians oppressed by subjection to the laws of the states, will unite in attempting to open the eyes of those children of the forest to their true condition, and by a speedy removal to relieve them from all the evils, real or imaginary, present or prospective, with which they may be supposed to be threatened.

Source: President Jackson's Message to Congress "On Indian Removal," December 6, 1830, Records of the United States Senate, 1789–1990, Record Group 46, National Archives.

93. Indian Removal Act, May 28, 1830

Introduction

President Andrew Jackson's December 1829 message to Congress set forth his justification for removing the Indians of the southeastern states to what was deemed Indian Territory in present-day Oklahoma. After bitter debates in Congress and in the press (only the issue of slavery was more divisive), Congress passed the Indian Removal Act in May 1830. The act authorized the government to make treaties with the southeastern tribes and appropriated $500,000 to compensate the Indians for any houses and other improvements they had made to their land. The Indians were promised perpetual sovereignty over their new territory. While the Choctaws and Chickasaws of Alabama and Mississippi accepted the government's offers, the Cherokees did not. President Jackson ordered the Cherokee Nation off its land in Georgia in 1833. Although the tribe fought against the order in the U.S. court system, it was eventually forced to comply. As some 15,000 Cherokees, under military escort, made their arduous journey to Oklahoma in 1838, starvation, illness, cold, and despair resulted in thousands of deaths. The Cherokees came to call the march the Trail of Tears.

Primary Source

An Act to provide for an exchange of lands with the Indians residing in any of the states or territories, and for their removal west of the river Mississippi.

Be it enacted by the Senate and House of Representatives of the United States of America, in Congress assembled, That it shall and may be lawful for the President of the United States to cause so much of any territory belonging to the United States, west of the river Mississippi, not included in any state or organized territory, and to which the Indian title has been extinguished, as he may judge necessary, to be divided into a suitable number of districts, for the reception of such tribes or nations of Indians as may choose to exchange the lands where they now reside, and remove there; and to cause each of said districts to be so described by natural or artificial marks, as to be easily distinguished from every other.

And be it further enacted, That it shall and may be lawful for the President to exchange any or all of such districts, so to be laid off and described, with any tribe or nation of Indians now residing within the limits of any of the states or territories, and with which the United States have existing treaties, for the whole or any part or portion of the territory claimed and occupied by such tribe or nation, within the bounds of any one or more of the states or territories, where the land claimed and occupied by the Indians, is owned by the United States, or the United States are bound to the state within which it lies to extinguish the Indian claim thereto.

And be it further enacted, That in the making of any such exchange or exchanges, it shall and may be lawful for the President solemnly to assure the tribe or nation with which the exchange is made, that the United States will forever secure and guaranty to them, and their heirs or successors, the country so exchanged with them; and if they prefer it, that the United States will cause a patent or grant to be made and executed to them for the same: *Provided always,* That such lands shall revert to the United States, if the Indians become extinct, or abandon the same.

And be it further enacted, That if, upon any of the lands now occupied by the Indians, and to be exchanged for, there should be such improvements as add value to the land claimed by any individual or individuals of such tribes or nations, it shall and may be lawful for the President to cause such value to be ascertained by appraisement or otherwise, and to cause such ascertained value to be paid to the person or persons rightfully claiming such improvements. And upon the payment of such valuation, the improvements so valued and paid for, shall pass to the United States, and possession shall not afterwards be permitted to any of the same tribe.

And be it further enacted, That upon the making of any such exchange as is contemplated by this act, it shall and may be lawful for the President to cause such aid and assistance to be furnished to the emigrants as may be necessary and proper to enable them to remove to, and settle in, the country for which they may have exchanged; and also, to give them such aid and assistance as may

be necessary for their support and subsistence for the first year after their removal.

And be it further enacted, That it shall and may be lawful for the President to cause such tribe or nation to be protected, at their new residence, against all interruption or disturbance from any other tribe or nation of Indians, or from any other person or persons whatever.

And be it further enacted, That it shall and may be lawful for the President to have the same superintendence and care over any tribe or nation in the country to which they may remove, as contemplated by this act, that he is now authorized to have over them at their present places of residence: *Provided,* That nothing in this act contained shall be construed as authorizing or directing the violation of any existing treaty between the United States and any of the Indian tribes.

And be it further enacted, That for the purpose of giving effect to the Provisions of this act, the sum of five hundred thousand dollars is hereby appropriated, to be paid out of any money in the treasury, not otherwise appropriated.

Source: "An Act to Provide for an Exchange of Lands with the Indians Residing in Any of the States or Territories, and for Their Removal West of the River Mississippi," in *The Public Statutes at Large of the United States of America*, Vol. 4, edited by Richard Peters (Boston: Little, Brown, 1846), 411–413.

94. *Cherokee Nation v. Georgia,* March 18, 1831 [Excerpts]

Introduction

President Andrew Jackson's December 1829 message to Congress set forth his justification for removing the Indians of the southeastern states to what was deemed Indian Territory in present-day Oklahoma. After bitter debate, Congress passed the Indian Removal Act in 1830. The act authorized the government to make land-exchange treaties with the southeastern tribes and promised the Indians perpetual sovereignty over their new territory. While the Choctaws and Chickasaws of Alabama and Mississippi accepted the government's offers, the Cherokees did not. *Cherokee Nation v. Georgia* was among the most important cases to come before the U.S. Supreme Court in its first half century. At issue was the State of Georgia's attempts to take control of Cherokee land protected by treaties between the federal government and the Cherokees. The Cherokee Nation argued that Georgia state laws did not apply to their lands because theirs was a sovereign nation. In a 4 to 2 decision, the Court recognized the Cherokees' status as a sovereign nation but not a foreign nation, a fine distinction that denied them (and by legal precedent, other Indian nations) the right to bring their case before the Court. President Jackson ordered the Cherokee Nation off its land in Georgia in

1833, and the forced migration of some 15,000 Cherokees began in 1838.

Primary Source

Mr. Chief Justice Marshall delivered the opinion of the Court.

This bill is brought by the Cherokee Nation, praying an injunction to restrain the State of Georgia from the execution of certain laws of that State which, as is alleged, go directly to annihilate the Cherokees as a political society and to seize, for the use of Georgia, the lands of the Nation which have been assured to them by the United States in solemn treaties repeatedly made and still in force.

If Courts were permitted to indulge their sympathies, a case better calculated to excite them can scarcely be imagined. A people once numerous, powerful, and truly independent, found by our ancestors in the quiet and uncontrolled possession of an ample domain, gradually sinking beneath our superior policy, our arts and our arms, have yielded their lands by successive treaties, each of which contains a solemn guarantee of the residue, until they retain no more of their formerly extensive territory than is deemed necessary to their comfortable subsistence. To preserve this remnant, the present application is made.

Before we can look into the merits of the case, a preliminary inquiry presents itself. Has this Court jurisdiction of the cause?

The third article of the Constitution describes the extent of the judicial power. The second section closes an enumeration of the cases to which it is extended, with "controversies" "between a State or the citizens thereof, and foreign states, citizens, or subjects." A subsequent clause of the same section gives the supreme Court original jurisdiction in all cases in which a State shall be a party. The party defendant may then unquestionably be sued in this Court. May the plaintiff sue in it? Is the Cherokee Nation a foreign state in the sense in which that term is used in the Constitution?

The counsel for the plaintiffs have maintained the affirmative of this proposition with great earnestness and ability. So much of the argument as was intended to prove the character of the Cherokees as a State as a distinct political society, separated from others, capable of managing its own affairs and governing itself, has, in the opinion of a majority of the judges, been completely successful. They have been uniformly treated as a State from the settlement of our country. The numerous treaties made with them by the United States recognize them as a people capable of maintaining the relations of peace and war, of being responsible in their political character for any violation of their engagements, or for any aggression committed on the citizens of the United States by any individual of their community. Laws have been enacted in the spirit of these treaties. The acts of our Government plainly recognize the Cherokee Nation as a State, and the Courts are bound by those acts.

A question of much more difficulty remains. Do the Cherokees constitute a foreign state in the sense of the Constitution?

The counsel have shown conclusively that they are not a State of the union, and have insisted that, individually, they are aliens, not owing allegiance to the United States. An aggregate of aliens composing a State must, they say, be a foreign state. Each individual being foreign, the whole must be foreign.

This argument is imposing, but we must examine it more closely before we yield to it. The condition of the Indians in relation to the United States is perhaps unlike that of any other two people in existence. In the general, nations not owing a common allegiance are foreign to each other. The term *foreign nation* is, with strict propriety, applicable by either to the other. But the relation of the Indians to the United States is marked by peculiar and cardinal distinctions which exist nowhere else.

The Indian Territory is admitted to compose a part of the United States. In all our maps, geographical treatises, histories, and laws, it is so considered. In all our intercourse with foreign nations, in our commercial regulations, in any attempt at intercourse between Indians and foreign nations, they are considered as within the jurisdictional limits of the United States, subject to many of those restraints which are imposed upon our own citizens. They acknowledge themselves in their treaties to be under the protection of the United States; they admit that the United States shall have the sole and exclusive right of regulating the trade with them, and managing all their affairs as they think proper; and the Cherokees, in particular, were allowed by the treaty of Hopewell, which preceded the Constitution, "to send a deputy of their choice, whenever they think fit, to Congress." . . .

. . . They may, more correctly, perhaps, be denominated domestic dependent nations. They occupy a territory to which we assert a title independent of their will, which must take effect in point of possession when their right of possession ceases. Meanwhile they are in a state of pupilage. Their relation to the United States resembles that of a ward to his guardian. . . .

The Court has bestowed its best attention on this question, and, after mature deliberation, the majority is of opinion that an Indian tribe or Nation within the United States is not a foreign state in the sense of the Constitution, and cannot maintain an action in the Courts of the United States. . . .

. . . But the Court is asked to do more than decide on the title. The bill requires us to control the Legislature of Georgia, and to restrain the exertion of its physical force. The propriety of such an interposition by the Court may be well questioned. It savours too much of the exercise of political power to be within the proper province of the judicial department. But the opinion on the point respecting parties makes it unnecessary to decide this question.

If it be true that the Cherokee Nation have rights, this is not the tribunal in which those rights are to be asserted. If it be true that wrongs have been inflicted, and that still greater are to be apprehended, this is not the tribunal which can redress the past or prevent the future. . . .

Source: *The Cherokee Nation v. The State of Georgia,* 30 U.S. 1 (1831).

95. Winfield Scott, Effect of the Cholera Epidemic on the Conduct of the Black Hawk War, 1832 [Excerpt]

Introduction

The influx of American settlers had pushed the Sauk and Fox Indians across the Mississippi River. Sauk warriors led by the war chief Black Hawk crossed the river into Illinois in 1831 and burned settlers' houses. Black Hawk returned a year later with some 2,000 of his people to settle in western Illinois and try to reclaim his former territory. The authorities sent regular army troops and militia to eject the Indians from Illinois. After a series of battles, the American force inflicted a decisive defeat on August 2, 1832. General Winfield Scott had earned renown for his role in the War of 1812. In premodern times, diseases killed far more people than did battle. Whenever people gathered in close contact, whether Indians or soldiers, infectious diseases spread with fatal ease. This episode in Scott's long career shows how he dealt with disastrous loss of life caused by disease. Scott arrived on the scene five days after the decisive battle of the Black Hawk War with his forces depleted by an epidemic of Asiatic cholera that had swept through his overcrowded troop transport vessels on the Great Lakes. One-third of his men were dead or unable to serve, while many others had deserted for fear of contagion. In this excerpt from his 1864 memoir, Scott—referring to himself in the third person—reports that he singlehandedly treated and cured many of his men, as the ship's doctor was drunk and had retired to his bed.

Primary Source

Ascending Lake Huron, the Asiatic cholera, the new scourge of mankind which had just before been brought to Quebec, found its way up the chain of waters, in time to infect the troops of Scott's expedition at different points on the lakes. In his particular steamer, the disease broke out suddenly, and with fatal violence. The only surgeon on board, in a panic, gulped down half a bottle of wine; went to bed, sick, and ought to have died. There was nobody left that knew anything of the healing art, or of the frightful distemper—only Scott, who, anticipating its overtaking him in the Northwest, had taken lessons from Surgeon Mower, stationed in New York—eminent in his profession, and of a highly inquiring, philosophic mind—in respect to the character, and mode of treating the disease. Thus he became the doctor on the afflicting occasion—no doubt a very indifferent one, except in labor and intrepidity. He had provided the whole expedition with the remedies suggested by Doctor Mower, which, on board his steamer, he applied, in great part, with his own hand to the sick. His principal success was in preventing a general panic, and, *mirabile dictu!* actually cured, in the incipient stage, by *command,* several individuals of that fatal preparation for the reception of the malady.

It continued several days after landing, in July, at Chicago—then but a hamlet. As soon as the troops had become sufficiently convalescent they were marched thence across the wild prairies, inhabited by nomads of Potawatamies—Indians of doubtful neutrality. Scott preceded the detachments, and on arriving at Prairie du Chien, was glad to find that Atkinson, after a most fagging march of weeks and hundreds of miles, following the devious retreat of the Hawk, finally overtook him at the mouth of the Badaxe in the act of crossing the Mississippi, with his band, and in a gallant combat, killed many of his followers, made others prisoners, and dispersed the remainder.

Source: Winfield Scott, *Memoirs of Lieut.-General Scott, LL.D.,* Vol. 1 (New York: Sheldon, 1864), 218–219.

96. Black Hawk, Surrender Speech, 1832

Introduction

The end of the War of 1812 and the 1824 completion of the Erie Canal caused settlers to pour into the Midwest. The influx of American settlers forced the Indians to cede land that had once been promised to them in perpetuity and pushed the Sauk and Fox Indians across the Mississippi River. Sauk warriors led by the war chief Black Hawk, former allies of the British in the War of 1812, crossed the river into Illinois in 1831 and burned a number of settlers' houses. Black Hawk returned a year later with some 2,000 men, women, and children to settle in western Illinois and try to reclaim his people's former territory. The authorities sent regular army troops and militia to eject the Indians from Illinois. After a series of battles, the American force inflicted a decisive defeat on August 2, 1832. The Black Hawk War lasted only 15 weeks but inflicted hundreds of Indian casualties and brought about the demise of both the Sauk and Fox tribes as political and military forces in the Midwest. Black Hawk delivered this address at the time of his surrender, stating that he was satisfied because he had fulfilled his duty to resist and avenge white encroachment. He spent a year in prison after his capture, and upon his release he and his fellow captives traveled around the country as something of a public attraction. Black Hawk dictated his autobiography to an interpreter in 1833, and it became a best seller.

Primary Source

Black-hawk is an Indian. He has done nothing for which an Indian ought to be ashamed. He has fought for his countrymen, the squaws and papooses, against white men, who came, year after year, to cheat them and take away their lands. You know the cause of our making war. It is known to all white men. They ought to be ashamed of it. The white men despise the Indians, and drive them from their homes. But the Indians are not deceitful. The white men speak bad of the Indian, and look at him spitefully. But the Indian does not tell lies; Indians do not steal.

An Indian, who is as bad as the white men, could not live in our nation; he would be put to death, and eat up by the wolves. The white men are bad schoolmasters; they carry false looks, and deal in false actions; they smile in the face of the poor Indian to cheat him; they shake them by the hand to gain their confidence, to make them drunk, to deceive them, and ruin our wives. We told them to let us alone, and keep away from us; but they followed on, and beset our paths, and they coiled themselves among us, like the snake. They poisoned us by their touch. We were not safe. We lived in danger. We were becoming like them, hypocrites and liars, adulterers, lazy drones, all talkers, and no workers.

We looked up to the Great Spirit. We went to our great father. We were encouraged. His great council gave us fair words and big promises; but we got no satisfaction. Things were growing worse. There were no deer in the forest. The opossum and beaver were fled; the springs were drying up, and our squaws and papooses without victuals to keep them from starving; we called a great council, and built a large fire. The spirit of our fathers arose and spoke to us to avenge our wrongs or die. We all spoke before the council fire. It was warm and pleasant. We set up the war-whoop, and dug up the tomahawk; our knives were ready, and the heart of Black-hawk swelled high in his bosom, when he led his warriors to battle. He is satisfied. He will go to the world of spirits contented. He has done his duty. His father will meet him there, and commend him.

Source: Samuel G. Drake, *The Aboriginal Races of North America* (Philadelphia: Charles Desilver, 1859), 657.

97. Act Creating a Commissioner of Indian Affairs, July 9, 1832

Introduction

Relations between the United States and the Indians evolved as the young American republic matured. Following the initial treaties in which Native Americans ceded land to the United States in exchange for trade goods and promises of land in the West, the government passed laws regulating trade and prohibiting unauthorized sales of Indian land. The treaties and the regulations alike were widely flouted by American settlers and traders. In 1824 the U.S. secretary of war, without consulting Congress, created a bureau of Indian Affairs as part of the War Department and appointed an official to carry out its duties. Not until 1832 did Congress pass a law both authorizing the Bureau of Indian

Affairs, which remained a part of the War Department, and creating the position of commissioner of Indian Affairs. The law also contained a prohibition against bringing any alcohol into Indian Territory. In 1849 Congress created the Department of the Interior and transferred control of Indian affairs to the new department. During the decades of Indian warfare in the West that followed the American Civil War (1861–1865), army officers and Interior Department officials traded accusations of corruption and blamed one another for undoing any gains they had made. The War Department argued repeatedly and unsuccessfully that it should resume control of Indian affairs.

Primary Source

CLXXIV.—*An Act to provide for the appointment of a commissioner of Indian Affairs, and for other purposes,* (a)

Be it enacted by the Senate and House of Representatives of the United States of America, in Congress assembled, That the President shall appoint, by and with the advice and consent of the Senate, a commissioner of Indian affairs, who shall, under the direction of the Secretary of War, and agreeably to such regulations as the President may, from time to time, prescribe, have the direction and management of all Indian affairs, and of all matters arising out of Indian relations, and shall receive a salary of three thousand dollars per annum.

Sec. 2. *And be it further enacted,* That the Secretary of War shall arrange or appoint to the said office the number of clerks necessary therefor, so as not to increase the number now employed; and such sum as is necessary to pay the salary of said commissioner for the year one thousand eight hundred and thirty-two, shall be, and the same hereby is, appropriated out of any money in the treasury.

Sec. 3. *And be it further enacted,* That all accounts and vouchers for claims and disbursements connected with Indian affairs, shall be transmitted to the said commissioner for administrative examination, and by him passed to the proper accounting officer of the Treasury Department for settlement; and all letters and packages to and from the said commissioner, touching the business of his office, shall be free of postage.

Sec. 4. *And be it further enacted,* That no ardent spirits shall be hereafter introduced, under any pretence, into the Indian country.

Sec. 5. *And be it further enacted,* That the Secretary of War shall, under the direction of the President, cause to be discontinued the services of such agents, sub-agents, interpreters, and mechanics, as may, from time to time, become unnecessary, in consequence of the emigration of the Indians, or other causes.

Approved, July 9, 1832.

Source: "An Act to Provide for the Appointment of a Commissioner of Indian Affairs, and for Other Purposes," in *The Public Statutes at Large of the United States of America,* Vol. 4, edited by Richard Peters (Boston: Little, Brown, 1846), 564.

98. Treaty with the Seminoles, 1833

Introduction

On May 9, 1832, the U.S. government made a treaty with the Seminoles under which the Seminoles agreed to leave Florida and move to land in Arkansas adjacent to that of the Creek Indians. In return for the cession of Florida, the government promised monetary compensation plus blankets and clothing. The treaty specified that the move would take place before the beginning of 1836. The follow-up treaty, signed on March 28, 1833, finalized the arrangements for removal based on a Seminole delegation's inspection and approval of the new land. Congress ratified the treaty in 1834. However, late in 1835 a band of Seminoles led by Osceola, a Creek, attacked the Indian agent who was to supervise the removal and massacred more than 100 army regulars. General Winfield Scott went on campaign to subdue the Seminoles, but by the time his column arrived, the Seminoles had gone into hiding. Scott was withdrawn and eventually sent to supervise the Cherokee removal. General Zachary Taylor also tried but failed to subdue the Seminoles. Colonel William Worth finally succeeded in ending Seminole resistance in 1842 after pursuing a scorched-earth strategy of destroying homes and crops.

Primary Source

WHEREAS, the Seminole Indians of Florida, entered into certain articles of agreement, with James Gadson, Commissioner on behalf of the United States, at Payne's landing, on the 9th day of May, 1832: the first article of which treaty or agreement provides, as follows: "The Seminoles Indians relinquish to the United States all claim to the land they at present occupy in the Territory of Florida, and agree to emigrate to the country assigned to the Creeks, west of the Mississippi river; it being understood that an additional extent of territory proportioned to their number will be added to the Creek country, and that the Seminoles will be received as a constituent part of the Creek nation, and be re-admitted to all the privileges as members of the same." And whereas, the said agreement also stipulates and provides, that a delegation of Seminoles should be sent at the expense of the United States to examine the country to be allotted them among the Creeks, and should this delegation be satisfied with the character of the country and of the favorable disposition of the Creeks to unite with them as one people, then the aforementioned treaty would be considered binding and obligatory upon the parties. And whereas a treaty was made between the United States and the Creek Indians west of the Mississippi, at Fort Gibson, on the 14th day of February 1833, by which a country was provided for the Seminoles in pursuance of the existing arrangements between the United States and that tribe. And whereas, the special delegation, appointed by the Seminoles on the 9th day of May 1832, have since examined the land designated for them by the undersigned Commissioners, on behalf of the United States, and have expressed themselves satisfied with the same, in and by their letter dated, March 1833, addressed to the undersigned Commissioners.

Now, therefore, the Commissioners aforesaid, by virtue of the power and authority vested in them by the treaty made with Creek Indians on the 14th day of February 1833, as above stated, hereby designate and assign to the Seminole tribe of Indians, for their separate future residence, forever, a tract of country lying between the Canadian river and the north fork thereof, and extending west to where a line running north and south between the main Canadian and north branch, will strike the forks of Little river, provided said west line does not extend more than twenty-five miles west from the mouth of said Little river. And the undersigned Seminole chiefs, delegated as aforesaid, on behalf of their nation hereby declare themselves well satisfied with the location provided for them by the Commissioners, and agree that their nation shall commence the removal to their new home as soon as the Government will make arrangements for their emigration, satisfactory to the Seminole nation.

And whereas, the said Seminoles have expressed high confidence in the friendship and ability of their present agent, Major Phagen, and desire that he may be permitted to remove them to their new homes west of the Mississippi; the Commissioners have considered their request, and cheerfully recommend Major Phagan as a suitable person to be employed to remove the Seminoles as aforesaid, and trust his appointment will be made, not only to gratify the wishes of the Indians but as conducive to the public welfare.

In testimony whereof, the commissioners on behalf of the United States, and the delegates of the Seminole nation, have hereunto signed their names this 28th day of March, A. D. 1833, at fort Gibson.

Montfort Stokes,
Henry L. Ellsworth,
John F. Schermerhorn.

Seminole Delegates:
    John Hick, representing Sam Jones, his x mark.
    Holata Emartta, his x mark.
    Jumper, his x mark.
    Coi Hadgo, his x mark.
    Charley Emartta, his x mark.
    Ya-ha-hadge, his x mark.
    Ne-ha-tho-clo, representing Fuch-a-lusti-hadgo, his x mark,
    On behalf of the Seminole nation.

Source: "Treaty with the Seminoles," in *The Public Statutes at Large of the United States of America,* Vol. 7, edited by Richard Peters (Boston: Little, Brown, 1846), 423–424.

99. Sam Houston, Message to the Indian Tribes of Texas, November 11, 1836

Introduction

Samuel Houston (1793–1863) was born into a military family in Virginia and enlisted as a private in the U.S. Army at age 20. He was wounded at the 1814 Battle of Horseshoe Bend while serving with Andrew Jackson. Several years after the War of 1812 ended, Houston, who had lived among the Cherokees in his youth, served as a U.S. agent to manage the removal of the Tennessee Cherokees to a reservation in Indian Territory (present-day Oklahoma). He then served as a lawyer, a legislator, and governor of Tennessee. Jackson later secured another appointment for Houston as an Indian agent to the Cherokees, in which office he worked to protect Cherokee interests. Houston went on to assignments among the Indians of Texas, emerged as a leader of the American settlers of Texas, and won fame as a military hero of the Texas Revolution. He became president of the Lone Star Republic when it became independent in 1836 and then served as the U.S. senator from Texas during 1846–1859. In this message, Houston, as president of the new republic, announces to six Indian tribes, including the Comanches, that the Mexicans are gone and that the Texans wish to live in peace. Little time would pass before the Comanches became the most-feared raiders of the Texas settlers.

Primary Source

To the Chiefs of Six Tribes
    Executive Department, Columbia, 11th Novr. 1836

To the Chiefs of the Wacos, Towacconnies, Towassies, Keebies, Ionics & Comanchies, and all other Indians wishing to be friends:

Brothers: I have heard, that you wish to talk with your white brothers and to smoke the Pipe of Peace!

Bad men have stolen horses and made war and brought trouble upon the white and red people. It is now time to be at Peace with each other and bury the Tomahawk forever. The great Chief of Mexico, Santa Anna, is our prisoner and he cannot help you to make war any more upon us. The Mexicans have told you many things, and you find they have spoken to you with two tongues. Hear my words, and walk in the white path, and you shall be happy. You shall have such things as you wish to swap for. We will pay you for what you have to sell. If you come to see me, I will give you presents that you may remember my Talk. I once gave to the Chief of the Commanchie nation, a silver medal when I was in San Antonio. I now wish to see him with his other Chiefs that we may smoke together and be friends. I send my friends to talk with all

the Chiefs of the Wacos, Towacconnies, Towassies, Kechies, Ionics and Commanchies, and to make a writing with them to bring it to a Great Council of peace.

Sam Houston.

> **Source:** A. Williams and E. Barker, eds., *The Writings of Sam Houston, 1813–1863,* Vol. 1 (Austin: University of Texas Press, 1938), 479–480.

100. John Ross, Letter to General Winfield Scott about the Cherokee Removal, August 30, 1838

Introduction

President Andrew Jackson's December 1829 message to Congress set forth his justification for removing the Indians of the southeastern states to what was deemed Indian Territory (present-day Oklahoma). After bitter debates in Congress and in the press, Congress passed the Indian Removal Act in May 1830. The act authorized the government to make treaties with the southeastern tribes and appropriated $500,000 to compensate the Indians for any houses and other improvements they had made to their land. The Indians were promised perpetual sovereignty over their new territory. When the Cherokees did not accept the government's offer, President Jackson ordered the Cherokee Nation off its land in Georgia in 1833. Although the tribe fought against the order in the U.S. court system, it was eventually forced to comply. General Winfield Scott was placed in charge of the massive 1838 removal of some 15,000 Cherokees. In this letter to Scott, Cherokee chief John Ross reports that on the very eve of their departure, the first contingent of Cherokees has discovered that their property has not yet been valued. The Cherokees feared, with good reason, that their property would not be fairly valued by government agents once the owners departed or that the government would neglect to compensate them at all.

Primary Source

TO WINFIELD SCOTT

Cherokee Agency Aug. 30th 1838

Sir

On the 24th Inst. I had the honor to receive through your aid de camp Colo. H. B. Shaw, a communication in reference to the claims of the Cherokees presented to you.

In that communication you were pleased to direct, Or "advise, that the claimants should go in person to the Commissioners." That course has been taken, by many of Our people in pursuance of your advice, and some difficulties having arisen, I deem it my duty respectfully to present them to you.

In the extract of a letter from the Commissioners, with which I am favored, in your communication, it is said, that "All these improvements have been, long since, valued by the Agents of the Government, and placed on the register of payments." But on application made by the Cherokees of the first detachment, just on the eve of starting to the West, it was discovered that many of their improvements have not been so valued. The Cherokees presented a Statement of their claims accompanyed by ample proof of their correctness, but the Commissioners rejected them and said they will send Agents to value the places. It will readily be perceived, that embarrassment and confusion and loss, must result from such a course. The Cherokee owners of the improvements being already organized for emigration and just on the eve of starting, with their Detachments, would not feel satisfied that after their departure, agents should go out alone, without any person to point out the property to be valued. Nor would they feel satisfied, even were there a prospect that the property could be correctly ascertained; that the amount of valuation, should in accordance with the system heretofore pursued by those Gentlemen, be placed on the registers of payment and left open to the depredations of exparte claims often fictitious against the real owner of the same name: and as was the case affording no security whatever, that the owner would ever receive payment for his property such having been the fact in the cases of several applicants for payment. And if, for the information of the valuing agents, the Cherokees were now allowed to go to every part of the country to point our their property, the progress of emigration would be retarded and derangements in the Detachments would in all probability ensue. I beg leave, with submission, to call your attention to the manner in which payments have been made to those who have made application to the commissioners. One half only of the amount has been paid and that, in funds, which will be uncurrent as soon as they pass the limits of Tennessee.

I wish also, very respectfully to say, that the Cherokee people have claims against the U. States for spoliations of various kinds, the presentation of which for adjudication, has been prevented, by the pressure of their preparatory arrangements for removal.

And with regard to the observation in the Commissioners letter, in reference to the valuations made by their Agents, "that those, thus made, are far more liberal than Mr. Ross and his associates have made them," I have only to observe, that we have made no assessments at all but merely described the property, so that the principles of appraisement, recognized by the Govt. might be applied to them.

Source: Gary E. Moulton, ed., *The Papers of Chief John Ross,* Vol. 1 (Norman: University of Oklahoma Press, 1985), 665–666.

101. Winfield Scott, Address to the Cherokee People regarding Removal, 1838

Introduction

President Andrew Jackson's December 1829 message to Congress set forth his justification for removing the Indians of the southeastern states to what was deemed "Indian country" in present-day Oklahoma. After bitter debates in Congress and in the press, Congress passed the Indian Removal Act in May 1830. The act authorized the government to make treaties with the southeastern tribes and appropriated half a million dollars to compensate the Indians for any houses and other improvements they had made to their land. The Indians were promised perpetual sovereignty over their new territory. When the Cherokees refused the government's offer, President Jackson ordered the Cherokee Nation off its land in Georgia in 1833. Although the tribe fought against the order in the U.S. court system, it was eventually forced to comply. General Winfield Scott was placed in charge of the military escort for the massive migration of some 15,000 Cherokees. In this excerpt from his 1864 memoir, Scott reproduces his address to the Cherokee people in which he exhorts them to comply with his orders. He follows this with his description of a peaceful migration, which gives little indication of the hardships and deaths endured on the Trail of Tears.

Primary Source

MAJOR-GENERAL SCOTT, of the United States' Army, sends to the Cherokee people remaining in North Carolina, Georgia, Tennessee, and Alabama this ADDRESS.

Cherokees:—The President of the United States has sent me, with a powerful army, to cause you, in obedience to the treaty of 1835, to join that part of your people who are already established in prosperity on the other side of the Mississippi. Unhappily, the two years which were allowed for the purpose, you have suffered to pass away without following, and without making any preparation to follow, and now, or by the time that this solemn *address* shall reach your distant settlements, the emigration must be commenced in haste, but, I hope, without disorder. I have no power, by granting a farther delay, to correct the error that you have committed. The full moon of May is already on the wane, and before another shall have passed away, every Cherokee man, woman, and child, in those States, must be in motion to join their brethren in the far West.

My friends—This is no sudden determination on the part of the President, whom you and I must now obey. By the treaty, the emigration was to have been completed on or before the 23d of this month, and the President has constantly kept you warned, during the two years allowed, through all his officers and agents in this country, that the treaty would be enforced.

I am come to carry out that determination. My troops already occupy many positions in the country that you are to abandon, and thousands and thousands are approaching from every quarter, to render resistance and escape alike hopeless. All those troops, regular and militia, are your friends. Receive them and confide in them as such. Obey them when they tell you that you can remain no longer in this country. Soldiers are as kind-hearted as brave, and the desire of every one of us is to execute our painful duty in mercy. We are commanded by the President to act toward you in that spirit, and such is also the wish of the whole people of America.

Chiefs, head men, and warriors—Will you then, by resistance, compel us to resort to arms? God forbid! Or will you, by flight, seek to hide yourselves in mountains and forests, and thus oblige us to hunt you down? Remember that, in pursuit, it may be impossible to avoid conflicts. The blood of the white man, or the blood of the red man, may be spilt, and if spilt, however accidentally, it may be impossible for the discreet and humane among you, or among us, to prevent a general war and carnage. Think of this, my Cherokee brethren! I am an old warrior, and have been present at many a scene of slaughter; but spare me, I beseech you, the horror of witnessing the destruction of the Cherokees.

Do not, I invite you, even wait for the close approach of the troops; but make such preparations for emigration as you can, and hasten to this place, to Ross's Landing, or to Gunter's Landing, where you will all be received in kindness by officers selected for the purpose. You will find food for all, and clothing for the destitute, at either of those places, and thence at your ease, and in comfort, be transported to your new homes according to the terms of the treaty.

This is the address of a warrior to warriors. May his entreaties be kindly received, and may the God of both prosper the Americans and Cherokees, and preserve them long in peace and friendship with each other.

WINFIELD SCOTT.

Source: Winfield Scott, *Memoirs of Lieut.-General Scott, LL.D.,* Vol. 1 (New York: Sheldon, 1864), 323–329.

102. Accounts of Missionaries to Oregon, 1837

Introduction

Missionaries Narcissa Whitman (1808–1847) and Eliza Spalding (1807–1851) and their husbands made the overland trip across the Rocky Mountains in 1836 to establish Presbyterian missions among the Indians of Oregon Territory. They were the first white women to make that journey, which originated in western New York and took seven months. Their diaries reveal their great faith in the importance of their mission. To lead the heathen Indians to salvation was their sacred duty and justified the sacrifice of the comforts of home. Mrs. Whitman proved unsuited to frontier mission life. She had to fight her aversion to the Indians and wrote home to complain about their fleas. The Indians in turn found her haughty. However, pride and faith made it impossible for her to abandon her post (near present-day Walla Walla, Washington). Beginning in 1843, hundreds of American immigrants surged into Oregon. The Whitmans' aid to the settlers aroused the Indians' suspicions. The 1847 immigrants brought measles, which took the lives of the vulnerable Cayuses surrounding the mission but did not kill white people. Dr. Whitman's failure to save the chief's children culminated in the massacre of November 29, 1847, in which both of the Whitmans and 12 others were murdered and dozens were taken hostage. The massacre set off the Cayuse War. At her mission 120 miles distant, Eliza Spalding was at first beloved by the Nez Perces. She worked indefatigably teaching their children, but the influx of white immigrants gave rise to unrest there as well. The Spaldings abandoned their mission after the Whitman Massacre and settled on land in the Willamette Valley. Mrs. Spalding likely died of tuberculosis at the age of 43.

Primary Source

From the Diary of Mrs. Whitman

Wieletpoo Jan 2 1837—Universal fast day. Through the kind Providence of God we are permitted to celebrate this day in heathen lands. It has been one of peculiar interest to us, so widely separated from kindred souls, alone, in the thick darkness of heathenism. We have just finished a separate room for ourselves with a stove in it, lent by Mr. P for our use this winter. Thus I am spending my winter as comfortably as heart could wish, & have suffered less from excessive cold than in many winters previous in New York. Winters are not very severe here. Usually they have but little snow say there is more this winter now on the ground than they have had for many years previous & that the winter is nearly over. After a season of worship during which I felt great depressure of spirits, we visited the lodges. All seemed well pleased as I had not been to any of them before. We are on the lands of the Old Chief Umtippe who with a lodge or two are now absent for a few days hunting deer. But a few of the Cayuses winter here. They appear to seperate in small companies, makes their cashes of provision in the fall & remain for the winter, & besides they are not well united. The young Chief Towerlooe is of another family & is more properly the ruling chief. He is Uncle to the young Cayuse Halket now at Red River Mission whom we expect to return this fall & to whom the chieftainship belongs by inheritance. The Old Chief Umtippe has been a savage creature in his day. His heart is still the same, full of all manner of hypocracy deceit and guile. He is a mortal beggar as all Indians are. If you ask a favour of him, sometimes it is granted or not just as he feels, if granted it must be well paid for.

A few days ago he took it into his head to require pay for teaching us the language & forbid his people from coming & talking with us for fear we should learn a few words of them. The Cayuses as well as the Nez Perces are very strict in attending to their worship which they have regularly every morning at day break & eve at twilight and once on the Sab. They sing & repeat a form of prayers very devoutly after which the Chief gives them a talk. The tunes & prayers were taught them by a Roman Catholic trader. Indeed their worship was commenced by him. As soon as we became settled we established a meeting among them on the Sab in our own house. Did not think it best to interfere with their worship but during the time had a family bible class & prayer meeting. Many are usually in to our family worship especially evenings, when we spend considerable time in teaching them to sing. About 12 or 14 boys come regularly every night & are delighted with it.

SAB JAN 29—Our meeting to day with the Indians was more interesting than usual. I find that as we succeed in their language in communicating the truth to them so as to obtain a knowledge of their views & feelings, my heart becomes more & more interested in them. They appear to have a partial knowledge of the leading truths of the Bible; of sin, so far as it extends to outward actions, but know [no] knowledge of the heart.

FEB 1st—Husband has gone to Walla W to stay & is not expected to return untill tomorrow eve, & I am alone for the first time to sustain the family altar, in the midst of a room full of native youth & boys, who have come in to sing as usual. After worship several gathered close around me as if anxious I should tell them some thing about the Bible. I had been reading the 12th chap of Acts, & with Richards help endeavoured to give them an account of Peters imprisonment &c, as well as I could. O that I had full possession of their language so that I could converse with them freely.

FEB 18th—Anniversary of our marriage. I find it perfectly natural to suffer my thoughts to dwell upon scenes that transpired one year ago from the present time. One year since I have heard a lisp even of my beloved friends in Angelica, & who can tell how many are sleeping in their graves by this time. Ah! it would be like cold water to a thirsty soul indeed, to know how you all do. It is delightful weather now. . . .

From the Diary of Mrs. Spalding

MARCH 20, 1837—Our prospects of usefulness among the people appear very promising. They seem to manifest an increasing interest in instruction, particularly the story of the cross. I have prepared some paintings representing several important events recorded in scripture, these we find a great help in communicating instruction to ignorant minds, whose language, as yet, we speak very imperfectly. The children in particular are interested in learning to read, several are beginning to read in the testament. O may

this people soon have the word of God in their Own language to peruse, & embrace the truth to become a people, civilized, Christianized & saved.

JUNE 15th, 1837—We feel happy & satisfied with our situation & employment, though it removes us from almost all we hold dear on earth. The privilege of laboring to introduce the blessings of the Gospel of Our adorable Redeemer among the destitute heathen will more than compensate for all we have laid aside for this blessed object.

We find this people anxious to receive instruction & to have their children educated. We have taken 8 native children into our family—as yet they appear promising. We hope to come into circumstances soon to do more to benefit the children for they are our hope of the nation. May the Lord help us to labor successfully for the promotion of his cause among this people & send us fellow laborers, & may this great harvest now ripe soon be gathered & saved in the kingdom of our Redeemer.

DEC. 3d, 1837—Through the astonishing mercy of God, I am now enjoying comfortable health. On the 15th of last month, I was made the joyful mother of a daughter. My illness has not been severe, or protracted, & the little one is still spared to us & appears in good health—for these, & the nameless other mercies myself & husband have been made the recipient of, we would call upon our souls & all the powers within us to bless the Lord—& while we bless the Lord for mercies past, we would remember that we are to seek from Him all that we shall ever need. We would humbly pray God to remember us in relation to the little one he has in great mercy committed to our care & seek heavenly wisdom and grace to aid us in discharging the accountable duties of parents. Last sabbath, she with brother & sister Whitman's little daughter were given to God, in the covenant of baptism. O, may they indeed receive the blessings promised to Abraham's seed.

Source: Clifford Merrill Drury, ed., *First White Women over the Rockies*, Vol. 1 (Glendale, CA: Arthur H. Clark, 1963), 123–124, 138, 203.

103. Felix Huston, Report on the Battle of Plum Creek, August 12, 1840

Introduction

When Mexico won independence from Spain in 1821, Mexico encouraged Americans to settle in its northern province of Texas. Thousands of Americans migrated to Texas, and in 1836 they declared their independence from Mexico. After several hard-fought battles, Texas became an independent republic the same year. Having defeated the Mexican Army, the settlers still had to contend with constant and brutal raids by the Comanches, the dominant tribe in Texas. Prior to the Battle of Plum Creek on August 12, 1840, the Comanches had recently destroyed two towns and plundered hundreds of head of livestock. Texan settlers gained revenge at the Battle of Plum Creek. Indian casualties were high, including more than 80 killed and many women and children taken prisoner. Texan forces retook 1 white captive and a great deal of stolen livestock. Texas Militia general Felix Huston reports in this letter to the U.S. secretary of war that at the cost of 1 man killed and 7 wounded, he has "given the Comanches a lesson they will long remember." It took one more battle to convince the Comanches to cease their raids in Texas and turn their attention to Mexico. The Comanches and their allies so thoroughly terrorized northern Mexico that the 1848 treaty ending the Mexican-American War (1846–1848) contained the promise that the Americans would prevent Indian raids into Mexico. As U.S. troops tried to keep this promise, Comanches again began raiding within Texas.

Primary Source

To Hon. T. B. Archer, Secretary of War

I arrived here yesterday evening and found Captain Caldwell encamped on Plum Creek with about one hundred men. This morning I was requested to take command, which I did with the consent of the men. I organized them into companies, under command of Captains Caldwell, Bird and Ward. About six o'clock the spies reported that the Indians were approaching Plum Creek. I crossed above the trail about three miles and passed down on the west side; on arriving near the trail I was joined by Colonel Burleson with about one hundred men, under the command of Colonel Jones, Lieutenant-Colonel Wallace and Major Hardeman. I immediately formed into two lines, the right commanded by Colonel Anderson and the left commanded by Captain Caldwell, with a reserve commanded by Major Hardeman, with Captain Ward's company. On advancing near the Indians they formed for action, with a front of woods on their right (which they occupied), their lines nearly a quarter of a mile into the prairie. I dismounted my men and a handsome fire was opened—the Indian chiefs cavorting around in splendid style, in front and flank, finely mounted, and dressed in all the splendor of Comanche warfare. At this time several Indians fell from their horses, and we had three or four of our men wounded. I ordered Colonel Burleson, with the right wing, to move around the point of woods, and Captain Caldwell, with the left wing, to charge into the woods; which movements were executed in gallant style. The Indians did not stand the charge, and fled at all points. From that time there was a warm and spirited pursuit for fifteen miles, the Indians scattered, mostly abandoning their horses and taking to the thickets. Nothing could exceed the animation of the men, and the cool and steady manner in which they would dismount and deliver their fire. Upwards of forty Indians were killed, two prisoners (a squaw and child) taken—we have taken upwards of two hundred horses and mules,

and many of them heavily packed with the plunder of Linnville and the lower country. There is still a large number of good horses and mules which are not gathered up. Of the captives taken by the Indians below we have only been able to retake one—Mrs. Watts of Linnville, who was wounded by the Indians with an arrow when they fled. Mrs. Crosby was speared and we understand that all the others were killed. We have lost one killed and seven wounded, one mortally. I cannot speak too highly of the Colorado, Guadalupe and Lavaca militia, assembled so hastily together and without organization. I was assisted by Major Izod, Colonel Bell, Captain Howard and Captain Nell, as volunteer aids, all of whom rendered essential service. Colonel Burleson acted with that cool, deliberate and prompt courage and conduct which he has so often and gallantly displayed in almost every Indian and Mexican battle since the war commenced. Captain Caldwell, also a tried Indian fighter, led on his wing to the charge with a bold front and a cheerful heart. Colonel Jones, Lieutenant-Colonel Wallace, Major Hardeman, and each of the captains commanding companies, acted with the utmost courage and firmness.

To conclude, I believe we have given the Comanches a lesson which they will long remember; near four hundred of their brave warriors have been defeated by half their number, and I hope and trust that this will be the last of their depredations on our frontier. On tomorrow I contemplate embodying as many men as I can, and if we have a sufficient number of good horses, pursue the Indians in the hopes that we may overtake them before they reach the mountains. Colonel Moore joined us this evening with about one hundred and seventy men; horses very hard ridden. I have the honor to be your most obedient servant.

FELIX HUSTON, Major-General T.M.

> **Source:** *Journals of the House of Representatives of the Republic of Texas: Fifth Congress, First Session, 1840–1841* (Austin: Cruger and Wing, 1841), Appendix, 141ff.

104. Texas Annexation Act, March 1, 1845

Introduction

When Mexico won independence from Spain in 1821, Mexico encouraged Americans to settle in its northern province of Texas. Thousands of Americans (many with their slaves) moved to Texas, and in 1836 they won their independence from Mexico. The republic applied for annexation to the United States, but northerners resisted this because they objected to the expansion of slavery. The election of James K. Polk, who favored annexation, as president of the United States brought about the March 1, 1845, Texas Annexation Act. Texas officially joined the United States on

December 29, 1845. The annexation of Texas infuriated the Mexican government. The failure of diplomatic efforts to resolve the disputes between the two countries, particularly the issue of Texas's southern border, led to the Mexican-American War (1846–1848). The American victory in 1848 added a vast new territory to the nation, encompassing parts of present-day New Mexico, Arizona, Nevada, California, Utah, Wyoming, and Colorado. The U.S. Army had to expand in order to protect the ensuing influx of American settlers throughout the West. The soldiers garrisoning the far-flung network of forts and outposts had to develop new modes of warfare to meet the challenge of pursuing hostile Indians over great expanses of untracked land.

Primary Source

Joint Resolution for annexing Texas to the United States.

Resolved by the Senate and House of Representatives of the United States of America in Congress assembled, That Congress doth consent that the territory properly included within, and rightfully belonging to the Republic of Texas, may be erected into a new state, to be called the state of Texas, with a republican form of government, to be adopted by the people of said republic, by deputies in Convention assembled, with the consent of the existing government, in order that the same may be admitted as one of the states of this Union.

2. And be it further resolved, That the foregoing consent of Congress is given upon the following conditions, and with the following guarantees, to wit: First—said state to be formed, subject to the adjustment by this government of all questions of boundary that may arise with other governments; and the constitution thereof, with the proper evidence of its adoption by the people of said republic of Texas, shall be transmitted to the President of the United States, to be laid before Congress for its final action, on or before the first day of January, one thousand eight hundred and forty-six. Second—said state, when admitted into the Union, after ceding to the United States all public edifices, fortifications, barracks, ports and harbors, navy and navy-yards, docks, magazines, arms, armaments, and all other property and means pertaining to the public defence belonging to said republic of Texas, shall retain all the public funds, debts, taxes, and dues of every kind which may belong to or be due and owing said republic; and shall also retain all the vacant and unappropriated lands lying within its limits, to be applied to the payment of the debts and liabilities of said republic of Texas; and the residue of said lands, after discharging said debts and liabilities, to be disposed of as said state may direct; but in no event are said debts and liabilities to become a charge upon the government of the United States. Third—New states, of convenient size, not exceeding four in number, in addition to said state of Texas, and having sufficient population, may hereafter, by the consent of said state, be formed out of the territory thereof, which shall be entitled to admission under the provisions of the federal constitution. And such states as may be formed out of that portion of said territory lying south of thirty-six degrees

thirty minutes north latitude, commonly known as the Missouri compromise line, shall be admitted into the Union with or without slavery, as the people of each state asking admission may desire. And in such state or states as shall be formed out of said territory north of said Missouri compromise line, slavery, or involuntary servitude, (except for crimes) shall be prohibited.

3. And be it further resolved, That if the President of the United States shall in his judgment and discretion deem it most advisable, instead of proceeding to submit the foregoing resolution to the Republic of Texas, as an overture on the part of the United States for admission, to negotiate with that Republic; then, Be it resolved, that a state, to be formed out of the present Republic of Texas, with suitable extent and boundaries, and with two representatives in Congress, until the next apportionment of representation, shall be admitted into the Union, by virtue of this act, on an equal footing with the existing states, as soon as the terms and conditions of such admission, and the cession of the remaining Texan territory to the United States shall be agreed upon by the governments of Texas and the United States: And that the sum of one hundred thousand dollars be, and the same is hereby, appropriated to defray the expenses of missions and negotiations, to agree upon the terms of said admission and cession, either by treaty to be submitted to the Senate, or by articles to be submitted to the two Houses of Congress, as the President may direct.

J W JONES
Speaker of the House of Representatives.

WILLIE P. MANGUM
President, pro tempore, of the Senate.

Approv'd March 1. 1845
JOHN TYLER

Source: *Treaties and Other International Acts of the United States of America,* Vol. 4, *Documents 80–121: 1836–1846* (Washington, DC: U.S. Government Printing Office, 1934).

105. John O'Sullivan, Manifest Destiny, July 1845 [Excerpts]

Introduction

In July 1845 the *Democratic Review* published this article by New York journalist John L. O'Sullivan in which he argues that the United States should annex Texas. This was O'Sullivan's first use of the words "manifest destiny" to describe the inevitability of American expansion across the continent. O'Sullivan did not support going to war against Mexico to take territory by force. Rather, he believed that American expansion would happen naturally and without violence as pioneers established their civilization wherever they settled. He predicted that California would soon be populated and controlled by Americans whether or not the United States went to war with Mexico. O'Sullivan makes no mention of the necessity of using force against native peoples. Five months later, in December 1845, O'Sullivan used the words again in a similar context in the *New York Morning News*. This time, discussing the ongoing border dispute between the United States and Great Britain, he argued that the United States was entitled to claim all of Oregon in order to fulfill its "manifest destiny." It was this second use of the term that seized the imagination of the American public and established the term as a slogan for 19th-century expansionism. Political opponents of American expansionism mocked the term "manifest destiny" but in so doing inadvertently brought it to public attention and widespread use.

Primary Source

The Great Nation of Futurity

The American people having derived their origin from many other nations, and the Declaration of National Independence being entirely based on the great principle of human equality, these facts demonstrate at once our disconnected position as regards any other nation; that we have, in reality, but little connection with the past history of any of them, and still less with all antiquity, its glories, or its crimes. On the contrary, our national birth was the beginning of a new history, the formation and progress of an untried political system, which separates us from the past and connects us with the future only; and so far as regards the entire development of the natural rights of man, in moral, political, and national life, we may confidently assume that our country is destined to be the great nation of futurity.

It is so destined, because the principle upon which a nation is organized fixes its destiny, and that of equality is perfect, is universal. It presides in all the operations of the physical world, and it is also the conscious law of the soul—the self-evident dictates of morality, which accurately defines the duty of man to man, and consequently man's rights as man. Besides, the truthful annals of any nation furnish abundant evidence, that its happiness, its greatness, its duration, were always proportionate to the democratic equality in its system of government.

[...]

What friend of human liberty, civilization, and refinement, can cast his view over the past history of the monarchies and aristocracies of antiquity, and not deplore that they ever existed? What philanthropist can contemplate the oppressions, the cruelties, and injustice inflicted by them on the masses of mankind, and not turn with moral horror from the retrospect?

America is destined for better deeds. It is our unparalleled glory that we have no reminiscences of battlefields, but in defence

of humanity, of the oppressed of all nations, of the rights of conscience, the rights of personal enfranchisement. Our annals describe no scenes of horrid carnage, where men were led on by hundreds of thousands to slay one another, dupes and victims to emperors, kings, nobles, demons in the human form called heroes. We have had patriots to defend our homes, our liberties, but no aspirants to crowns or thrones; nor have the American people ever suffered themselves to be led on by wicked ambition to depopulate the land, to spread desolation far and wide, that a human being might be placed on a seat of supremacy.

We have no interest in the scenes of antiquity, only as lessons of avoidance of nearly all their examples. The expansive future is our arena, and for our history. We are entering on its untrodden space, with the truths of God in our minds, beneficent objects in our hearts, and with a clear conscience unsullied by the past. We are the nation of human progress, and who will, what can, set limits to our onward march? Providence is with us, and no earthly power can. We point to the everlasting truth on the first page of our national declaration, and we proclaim to the millions of other lands that "the gates of hell"—the powers of aristocracy and monarchy—"shall not prevail against it."

The far-reaching, the boundless future will be the era of American greatness. In its magnificent domain of space and time, the nation of many nations is destined to manifest to mankind the excellence of divine principles; to establish on earth the noblest temple ever dedicated to the worship of the Most High—the Sacred and the True. Its floor shall be a hemisphere—its roof the firmament of the star-studded heavens, and its congregation [a] Union of many Republics, comprising hundreds of happy millions, calling, owning no man master, but governed by God's natural and moral law of equality, the law of brotherhood—of "peace and good will amongst men."

[...]

Yes, we are the nation of progress, of individual freedom, of universal enfranchisement. Equality of rights is the cynosure of our union of States, the grand exemplar of the correlative equality of individuals; and while truth sheds its effulgence, we cannot retrograde, without dissolving the one and subverting the other. We must onward to the fulfilment of our mission—to the entire development of the principle of our organization—freedom of conscience, freedom of person, freedom of trade and business pursuits, universality of freedom and equality. This is our high destiny, and in nature's eternal, inevitable decree of cause and effect we must accomplish it. All this will be our future history, to establish on earth the moral dignity and salvation of man—the immutable truth and beneficence of God. For this blessed mission to the nations of the world, which are shut out from the life-giving light of truth, has America been chosen; and her high example shall smite unto death the tyranny of kings, hierarchs, and oligarchs, and carry the glad tidings of peace and good will where myriads now endure an existence scarcely more enviable than that of beasts of the field. Who, then, can doubt that our country is destined to be *the great nation* of futurity?

Source: "The Great Nation of Futurity," in *The United States Magazine and Democratic Review,* Vol. 6 (Washington, DC: Langtree and O'Sullivan, 1839), 426–430.

106. Lansford W. Hastings, *The Emigrants' Guide to Oregon and California,* 1845 [Excerpt]

Introduction

Lansford W. Hastings, a young Ohio lawyer who longed for adventure, traveled overland to Oregon in 1842. Disappointed with what he found, he went on to California the following spring. His book is a piece of promotional literature designed to attract settlers to California, and his critics charged him with extremely biased reporting. However, the book's 1845 publication caught the expansionist public mood, and the book sold well. In this excerpt Hastings describes the Indians of Oregon Territory and the peaceful coexistence of American settlers with British traders. Beginning in 1843, hundreds of American settlers surged into Oregon. Writing two years before the Indian massacre at the Whitman mission, Hastings describes the Indians as posing no threat to settlers beyond minor theft and calls a fire at the Whitman mission entirely accidental. While the United States and Great Britain threatened war over Oregon Territory, they came to terms and signed a treaty a few months after Hastings's book was published. It then became the Americans' responsibility to prosecute the Cayuse War (1847–1848). Through his writing and by personal persuasion, Hastings played a part in the population of California by Americans. After the American Civil War (1861–1865), Hastings promoted the idea of a Confederate colony in Brazil. He died sometime in the 1870s while sailing to Brazil.

Primary Source

The most numerous and important tribes, of the Western section, are the Shatshet, Squamish, Toando, Chalams, Classet, Chenook, Clatsop, Klackamus, Klackatats, Kallapuyas, Umpquas, Killamucks, Rogues, Klamets, Shasty and Celkilis tribes, which like all other tribes of the country, have, by many, been thought to be migratory, and wandering tribes, but this appears not to be the case. They are always to be found within their own proper territories, sometimes passing and re-passing, however, from fishing to fishing, or from hunting ground to hunting ground; yet, their usual haunts are very seldom, if ever, entirely abandoned. They all subsist almost entirely upon fish, which they are enabled to take in any abundance, and at any, and every season of the year. Some of them

also hunt, but hunting appears to require too much active exertion, to comport with their inherent and hereditary indolence, therefore, as a means of livelihood, it is not very generally adopted. They generally live in small huts, constructed in the most simple, and artless manner imaginable. Uprights of about eight feet in length are obtained, which are inserted about one foot into the ground, side by side, forming either a square or circular enclosure, of about ten feet in diameter. At the side of these uprights, about two feet from the ground, and also about five feet from the ground, poles are placed horizontally, and attached by means of barks or withes [*sic*] to the uprights, when the walls are completed. The roof or cover, is of bark or branches and twigs of trees, which, thrown on in the roughest manner, completes these primitive, rude dwellings, of the Oregon aborigines. These Indians are of much service to the settlers, as they can be employed for a mere nominal compensation, to perform various kinds of labor, at many kinds of which, they are very expert, especially paddling canoes, rowing boats, hunting and driving horses, and bearing dispatches. With the exception of those in the extreme northern and southern portions of the country, they are entirely friendly and inoffensive. Such is the character, particularly of those, in the immediate neighborhood of the different settlements, yet, it is true, that the settlers here, are not entirely free from the little pilferings, and low treachery, to which all Indians are, more or less addicted. They very seldom steal any thing but food and clothing, though they frequently drive the horses of the settlers off, in order that they may be employed to find them, and this they do, in order to obtain food and clothing, as a reward for their services. The word friendly, is here used, in the sense in which it is used upon a former page, signifying merely, that they will make no unprovoked attack upon your person, or that they will not kill you; but not that they will not steal, for stealing appears to be an inborn vice, to which all barbarous Indians, are habitually addicted. The statement, which I have seen in several of our western papers, in reference to the burning of Dr. Whitman's mill, by the Indians, as an act of war or hostility, is entirely unfounded. The burning of this mill, occurred while I was in that country, and it was wholly accidental; no fault or design whatever, was attributed to the Indians. It is also reported, that all the various tribes in the neighborhood of the settlements, are combining, for the purpose of making a simultaneous attack, upon the settlers. This report is also, without foundation, for that unanimity of feeling does not exist among them, which would be indispensable to such a combination. But it they were hostile, and should combine, for warlike purposes, still, no danger whatever, would be apprehended from them, for they have neither the means, nor courage, to enable them to prosecute an efficient warfare.

A civil organization has recently taken place in Oregon, and an infant republic is now, in full operation. Several attempts had been made to effect an organization, prior to the spring of 1843, but they had all proved ineffectual. The present organization took place, in the spring of 1843, in accordance with the expressed wishes, of a great majority of all the settlers. An election was held, during the same spring, when the various officers, such as members of the legislature, a supreme judge, justices of the peace, sheriffs, constables, a treasurer, a secretary, and the different prothonotaries [*sic*], were elected. No executive was elected, consequently, the government must, of course, prove very inefficacious; though it was designed merely, as a substitute for a government, until the United States shall afford them a government, more enlarged, and more effective; to which event, the people of Oregon look forward, with a deep, and abiding interest. The legislature convened in the month of May 1843, at which time, it adopted the statute laws of Iowa, with such alterations and amendments, as local circumstances, seemed to require. Neither the officers of the Hudson's Bay Company, nor any persons in the service of that company, took any part in this governmental organization, nor did many of the Canadians or half-breeds, who had formerly been engaged in the service of that company. The reason assigned by the gentlemen of that company, for the neutral course which they pursued, was that they were British subjects, and hence, amenable to the laws of that government, which were already extended to that country, and in full force; therefore, whatever necessity might exist, on the part of American citizens, to enact a temporary code of laws, no such necessity existed on the part of British subjects. Those gentlemen, no doubt, pursued the proper course, in reference to their duty, as British subjects, for it is strictly true, that by an act of parliament, the jurisdiction and laws of Upper Canada, are extended over all that country, occupied by the British fur traders, whether such country is owned, or claimed by the British government. In accordance with this law, several gentlemen of the Hudson's Bay Company, were appointed, and now officiate, as justices of peace; having jurisdiction of all civil matters of controversy, where the amount claimed, does not exceed two hundred pounds sterling. The jurisdiction of these justices, in criminal cases, only extend to the examination of those who stand charged with the commission of criminal offences; against whom, if sufficient evidence is found, they are sent to Upper Canada, for final trial. This jurisdiction does not extend, as some have supposed, to the citizens of the United States; but, as is thus seen, there are two distinct forms of government, now established in Oregon, which will most likely, conflict, and thereby, produce serious consequences, if they are long continued.

Great Britain, then, has already done, by actual legislation, what our government seems willing to concede, that we have no right to do, under the existing circumstances. Although Great Britain, has already extended the jurisdiction and laws of Canada, over that country, when it is proposed to extend the jurisdiction and laws of Iowa, over the same country; or in any other manner to establish a government there; it is insisted that the government of the United States, has not the right.

Source: Lansford W. Hastings, *The Emigrants' Guide to Oregon and California* (Cincinnati: George Conclin, 1845), 60–61.

107. Oregon Treaty, June 15, 1846

Introduction

The United States and Great Britain threatened to go to war over Oregon Territory, even as the Mexican-American War (1846–1848) began over a Texas border dispute. However, the two nations came to terms and signed this treaty in which they agreed on a border that divided the territory between the United States and Canada. The treaty extended the dominion of the United States to the Pacific coast and opened the floodgates to thousands of immigrants. Inevitably, the settlers clashed with the Indians residing in Oregon. Oregon Territory was officially established in 1848, but it took Congress two years to extend the laws governing national Indian policy to the new territory. (Washington was separated from Oregon and became Washington Territory in 1853.) Some 42,000 Indians of 35 tribes lived in the territory. Many attacked the growing population of American settlers, leading to more than a decade of war extending from 1847 to 1858. Delay in ratifying treaties caused further troubles when whites began occupying Indian lands regardless of their legal status. By 1858, the Indians of Oregon had been overpowered and confined to reservations.

Primary Source

The United States of America and her Majesty the Queen of the United Kingdom of Great Britain and Ireland, deeming it to be desirable for the future welfare of both countries that the state of doubt and uncertainty which has hitherto prevailed respecting the sovereignty and government of the territory on the northwest coast of America, lying westward of the Rocky or Stony Mountains, should be finally terminated by an amicable compromise of the rights mutually asserted by the two parties over the said territory, have respectively named plenipotentiaries to treat and agree concerning the terms of such settlement—that is to say: the President of the United States of America has, on his part, furnished with full powers James Buchanan, Secretary of State of the United States, and her Majesty the Queen of the United Kingdom of Great Britain and Ireland has, on her part, appointed the Right Honorable Richard Pakenham, a member of her Majesty's Most Honorable Privy Council, and her Majesty's Envoy Extraordinary and Minister Plenipotentiary to the United States; who, after having communicated to each other their respective full powers, found in good and due form, have agreed upon and concluded the following articles:—

Article I.

From the point on the forty-ninth parallel of north latitude, where the boundary laid down in existing treaties and conventions between the United States and Great Britain terminates, the line of boundary between the territories of the United States and those of her Britannic Majesty shall be continued westward along the said forty-ninth parallel of north latitude to the middle of the channel which separates the continent from Vancouver's Island, and thence southerly through the middle of the said channel, and of Fuca's Straits, to the Pacific Ocean: *Provided, however,* That the navigation of the whole of the said channel and straits, south of the forty-ninth parallel of north latitude, remain free and open to both parties.

Article II.

From the point at which the forty-ninth parallel of north latitude shall be found to intersect the great northern branch of the Columbia River, the navigation of the said branch shall be free and open to the Hudson's Bay Company, and to all British subjects trading with the same, to the point where the said branch meets the main stream of the Columbia, and thence down the said main stream to the ocean, with free access into and through the said river or rivers, it being understood that all the usual portages along the line thus described shall, in like manner, be free and open. In navigating the said river or rivers, British subjects, with their goods and produce, shall be treated on the same footing as citizens of the United States; it being, however, always understood that nothing in this article shall he construed as preventing, or intended to prevent, the government of the United States from making any regulations respecting the navigation of the said river or rivers not inconsistent with the present treaty.

Article III.

In the future appropriation of the territory south of the forty-ninth parallel of north latitude, as provided in the first article of this treaty, the possessory rights of the Hudson's Bay Company, and of all British subjects who may be already in the occupation of land or other property lawfully acquired within the said territory, shall be respected.

Article IV.

The farms, lands, and other property of every description, belonging to the Puget's Sound Agricultural Company, on the north side of the Columbia River, shall be confirmed to the said company. In case, however, the situation of those farms and lands should be considered by the United States to be of public and political importance, and the United States government should signify a desire to obtain possession of the whole, or of any part thereof, the property so required shall be transferred to the said government, at a proper valuation, to be agreed upon between the parties.

Article V.

The present treaty shall be ratified by the President of the United States, by and with the advice and consent of the Senate thereof, and by her Britannic Majesty; and the ratifications shall he exchanged at London, at the expiration of six months from the date hereof, or sooner, if possible.

In witness whereof, the respective Plenipotentiaries have signed the same, and have affixed thereto the seals of their arms.

Done at Washington, the fifteenth day of June, in the year of our Lord one thousand eight hundred and forty-six.

JAMES BUCHANAN. [L. S.]
RICHARD PAKENHAM. [L. S.]

Source: "Treaty with Great Britain, in Regard to Limits Westward of the Rocky Mountains," in *The Statutes at Large and Treaties of the United States of America: From March 1, 1845, to March 3, 1851,* Vol. 9, edited by George Minot (Boston: Little, Brown, 1851), 869.

108. Treaty of Guadalupe Hidalgo, February 2, 1848

Introduction

Signed on February 2, 1848, by representatives from the United States and Mexico and ratified the following month, the Treaty of Guadalupe Hidalgo ended the Mexican-American War (1846–1848). Mexico had suffered badly in the war and was compelled to relinquish vast amounts of land in what is today the southwestern United States (parts of present-day New Mexico, Arizona, Nevada, California, Utah, Wyoming, and Colorado) and abandon all claims to Texas. In exchange, the United States paid Mexico $15 million and promised to prevent Indians from raiding across the border into Mexico, a task at which the U.S. Army had only mixed success. The territory of the continental United States now extended to its present-day borders. The army had to expand along with the nation in order to protect American settlers throughout the West. The soldiers garrisoning the far-flung network of forts and outposts had to develop new modes of warfare to meet the challenge of pursuing hostile Indians over great expanses of untracked land. The additional territory secured by the treaty also ignited the fires of sectional controversy by raising questions regarding the expansion of slavery.

Primary Source

Treaty of Peace, Friendship, Limits, and Settlement between the United States of America and the United Mexican States Concluded at Guadalupe Hidalgo, February 2, 1848; Ratification Advised by Senate, with Amendments, March 10, 1848; Ratified by President, March 16, 1848; Ratifications Exchanged at Queretaro, May 30, 1848; Proclaimed, July 4, 1848.

IN THE NAME OF ALMIGHTY GOD

The United States of America and the United Mexican States animated by a sincere desire to put an end to the calamities of the war which unhappily exists between the two Republics and to establish Upon a solid basis relations of peace and friendship, which shall confer reciprocal benefits upon the citizens of both, and assure the concord, harmony, and mutual confidence wherein the two people should live, as good neighbors have for that purpose appointed their respective plenipotentiaries, that is to say: The President of the United States has appointed Nicholas P. Trist, a citizen of the United States, and the President of the Mexican Republic has appointed Don Luis Gonzaga Cuevas, Don Bernardo Couto, and Don Miguel Atristain, citizens of the said Republic; Who, after a reciprocal communication of their respective full powers, have, under the protection of Almighty God, the author of peace, arranged, agreed upon, and signed the following: Treaty of Peace, Friendship, Limits, and Settlement between the United States of America and the Mexican Republic.

ARTICLE I

There shall be firm and universal peace between the United States of America and the Mexican Republic, and between their respective countries, territories, cities, towns, and people, without exception of places or persons.

ARTICLE II

Immediately upon the signature of this treaty, a convention shall be entered into between a commissioner or commissioners appointed by the General-in-chief of the forces of the United States, and such as may be appointed by the Mexican Government, to the end that a provisional suspension of hostilities shall take place, and that, in the places occupied by the said forces, constitutional order may be reestablished, as regards the political, administrative, and judicial branches, so far as this shall be permitted by the circumstances of military occupation.

ARTICLE III

Immediately upon the ratification of the present treaty by the Government of the United States, orders shall be transmitted to the commanders of their land and naval forces, requiring the latter (provided this treaty shall then have been ratified by the Government of the Mexican Republic, and the ratifications exchanged) immediately to desist from blockading any Mexican ports and requiring the former (under the same condition) to commence, at the earliest moment practicable, withdrawing all troops of the United States then in the interior of the Mexican Republic, to points that shall be selected by common agreement, at a distance from the seaports not exceeding thirty leagues; and such evacuation of the interior of the Republic shall be completed with the least possible delay; the Mexican Government hereby binding itself to afford every facility in its power for rendering the same convenient to the troops, on their march and in their new positions, and for

promoting a good understanding between them and the inhabitants. In like manner orders shall be despatched to the persons in charge of the custom houses at all ports occupied by the forces of the United States, requiring them (under the same condition) immediately to deliver possession of the same to the persons authorized by the Mexican Government to receive it, together with all bonds and evidences of debt for duties on importations and on exportations, not yet fallen due. Moreover, a faithful and exact account shall be made out, showing the entire amount of all duties on imports and on exports, collected at such custom-houses, or elsewhere in Mexico, by authority of the United States, from and after the day of ratification of this treaty by the Government of the Mexican Republic; and also an account of the cost of collection; and such entire amount, deducting only the cost of collection, shall be delivered to the Mexican Government, at the city of Mexico, within three months after the exchange of ratifications.

The evacuation of the capital of the Mexican Republic by the troops of the United States, in virtue of the above stipulation, shall be completed in one month after the orders there stipulated for shall have been received by the commander of said troops, or sooner if possible.

ARTICLE IV

Immediately after the exchange of ratifications of the present treaty all castles, forts, territories, places, and possessions, which have been taken or occupied by the forces of the United States during the present war, within the limits of the Mexican Republic, as about to be established by the following article, shall be definitely restored to the said Republic, together with all the artillery, arms, apparatus of war, munitions, and other public property, which were in the said castles and forts when captured, and which shall remain there at the time when this treaty shall be duly ratified by the Government of the Mexican Republic. To this end, immediately upon the signature of this treaty, orders shall be despatched to the American officers commanding such castles and forts, securing against the removal or destruction of any such artillery, arms, apparatus of war, munitions, or other public property. The city of Mexico, within the inner line of intrenchments surrounding the said city, is comprehended in the above stipulation, as regards the restoration of artillery, apparatus of war, & c.

The final evacuation of the territory of the Mexican Republic, by the forces of the United States, shall be completed in three months from the said exchange of ratifications, or sooner if possible; the Mexican Government hereby engaging, as in the foregoing article to use all means in its power for facilitating such evacuation, and rendering it convenient to the troops, and for promoting a good understanding between them and the inhabitants.

If, however, the ratification of this treaty by both parties should not take place in time to allow the embarcation of the troops of the United States to be completed before the commencement of the sickly season, at the Mexican ports on the Gulf of Mexico, in such case a friendly arrangement shall be entered into between the General-in-Chief of the said troops and the Mexican Government, whereby healthy and otherwise suitable places, at a distance from the ports not exceeding thirty leagues, shall be designated for the residence of such troops as may not yet have embarked, until the return of the healthy season. And the space of time here referred to as, comprehending the sickly season shall be understood to extend from the first day of May to the first day of November.

All prisoners of war taken on either side, on land or on sea, shall be restored as soon as practicable after the exchange of ratifications of this treaty. It is also agreed that if any Mexicans should now be held as captives by any savage tribe within the limits of the United States, as about to be established by the following article, the Government of the said United States will exact the release of such captives and cause them to be restored to their country.

ARTICLE V

The boundary line between the two Republics shall commence in the Gulf of Mexico, three leagues from land, opposite the mouth of the Rio Grande, otherwise called Rio Bravo del Norte, or Opposite the mouth of its deepest branch, if it should have more than one branch emptying directly into the sea; from thence up the middle of that river, following the deepest channel, where it has more than one, to the point where it strikes the southern boundary of New Mexico; thence, westwardly, along the whole southern boundary of New Mexico (which runs north of the town called Paso) to its western termination; thence, northward, along the western line of New Mexico, until it intersects the first branch of the river Gila; (or if it should not intersect any branch of that river, then to the point on the said line nearest to such branch, and thence in a direct line to the same); thence down the middle of the said branch and of the said river, until it empties into the Rio Colorado; thence across the Rio Colorado, following the division line between Upper and Lower California, to the Pacific Ocean.

The southern and western limits of New Mexico, mentioned in the article, are those laid down in the map entitled "Map of the United Mexican States, as organized and defined by various acts of the Congress of said republic, and constructed according to the best authorities. Revised edition. Published at New York, in 1847, by J. Disturnell," of which map a copy is added to this treaty, bearing the signatures and seals of the undersigned Plenipotentiaries. And, in order to preclude all difficulty in tracing upon the ground the limit separating Upper from Lower California, it is agreed that the said limit shall consist of a straight line drawn from the middle of the Rio Gila, where it unites with the Colorado, to a point on the coast of the Pacific Ocean, distant one marine league due south of the southernmost point of the port of San Diego, according to the plan of said port made in the year 1782 by Don Juan Pantoja, second sailing-master of the Spanish fleet, and published at Madrid in the year 1802, in the atlas to the voyage of the schooners Sutil and Mexicana; of which plan a copy is hereunto added, signed and sealed by the respective Plenipotentiaries.

In order to designate the boundary line with due precision, upon authoritative maps, and to establish upon the ground landmarks which shall show the limits of both republics, as described in the present article, the two Governments shall each appoint a commissioner and a surveyor, who, before the expiration of one year from the date of the exchange of ratifications of this treaty, shall meet at the port of San Diego, and proceed to run and mark the said boundary in its whole course to the mouth of the Rio Bravo del Norte. They shall keep journals and make out plans of their operations; and the result agreed upon by them shall be deemed a part of this treaty, and shall have the same force as if it were inserted therein. The two Governments will amicably agree regarding what may be necessary to these persons, and also as to their respective escorts, should such be necessary.

The boundary line established by this article shall be religiously respected by each of the two republics, and no change shall ever be made therein, except by the express and free consent of both nations, lawfully given by the General Government of each, in conformity with its own constitution.

ARTICLE VI

The vessels and citizens of the United States shall, in all time, have a free and uninterrupted passage by the Gulf of California, and by the river Colorado below its confluence with the Gila, to and from their possessions situated north of the boundary line defined in the preceding article; it being understood that this passage is to be by navigating the Gulf of California and the river Colorado, and not by land, without the express consent of the Mexican Government.

If, by the examinations which may be made, it should be ascertained to be practicable and advantageous to construct a road, canal, or railway, which should in whole or in part run upon the river Gila, or upon its right or its left bank, within the space of one marine league from either margin of the river, the Governments of both republics will form an agreement regarding its construction, in order that it may serve equally for the use and advantage of both countries.

ARTICLE VII

The river Gila, and the part of the Rio Bravo del Norte lying below the southern boundary of New Mexico, being, agreeably to the fifth article, divided in the middle between the two republics, the navigation of the Gila and of the Bravo below said boundary shall be free and common to the vessels and citizens of both countries; and neither shall, without the consent of the other, construct any work that may impede or interrupt, in whole or in part, the exercise of this right; not even for the purpose of favoring new methods of navigation. Nor shall any tax or contribution, under any denomination or title, be levied upon vessels or persons navigating the same or upon merchandise or effects transported thereon, except in the case of landing upon one of their shores. If, for the purpose of making the said rivers navigable, or for maintaining them in such state, it should be necessary or advantageous to establish any tax or contribution, this shall not be done without the consent of both Governments.

The stipulations contained in the present article shall not impair the territorial rights of either republic within its established limits.

ARTICLE VIII

Mexicans now established in territories previously belonging to Mexico, and which remain for the future within the limits of the United States, as defined by the present treaty, shall be free to continue where they now reside, or to remove at any time to the Mexican Republic, retaining the property which they possess in the said territories, or disposing thereof, and removing the proceeds wherever they please, without their being subjected, on this account, to any contribution, tax, or charge whatever.

Those who shall prefer to remain in the said territories may either retain the title and rights of Mexican citizens, or acquire those of citizens of the United States. But they shall be under the obligation to make their election within one year from the date of the exchange of ratifications of this treaty; and those who shall remain in the said territories after the expiration of that year, without having declared their intention to retain the character of Mexicans, shall be considered to have elected to become citizens of the United States.

In the said territories, property of every kind, now belonging to Mexicans not established there, shall be inviolably respected. The present owners, the heirs of these, and all Mexicans who may hereafter acquire said property by contract, shall enjoy with respect to it guarantees equally ample as if the same belonged to citizens of the United States.

ARTICLE IX

The Mexicans who, in the territories aforesaid, shall not preserve the character of citizens of the Mexican Republic, conformably with what is stipulated in the preceding article, shall be incorporated into the Union of the United States and be admitted at the proper time (to be judged of by the Congress of the United States) to the enjoyment of all the rights of citizens of the United States, according to the principles of the Constitution; and in the mean time, shall be maintained and protected in the free enjoyment of their liberty and property, and secured in the free exercise of their religion without restriction.

ARTICLE X

[Stricken out]

ARTICLE XI

Considering that a great part of the territories, which, by the present treaty, are to be comprehended for the future within the limits of the United States, is now occupied by savage tribes, who will hereafter be under the exclusive control of the Government of the United States, and whose incursions within the territory of Mexico would be prejudicial in the extreme, it is solemnly agreed that all such incursions shall be forcibly restrained by the Government of the United States whensoever this may be necessary; and that when they cannot be prevented, they shall be punished by the said Government, and satisfaction for the same shall be exacted all in the same way, and with equal diligence and energy, as if the same incursions were meditated or committed within its own territory, against its own citizens.

It shall not be lawful, under any pretext whatever, for any inhabitant of the United States to purchase or acquire any Mexican, or any foreigner residing in Mexico, who may have been captured by Indians inhabiting the territory of either of the two republics; nor to purchase or acquire horses, mules, cattle, or property of any kind, stolen within Mexican territory by such Indians.

And in the event of any person or persons, captured within Mexican territory by Indians, being carried into the territory of the United States, the Government of the latter engages and binds itself, in the most solemn manner, so soon as it shall know of such captives being within its territory, and shall be able so to do, through the faithful exercise of its influence and power, to rescue them and return them to their country or deliver them to the agent or representative of the Mexican Government. The Mexican authorities will, as far as practicable, give to the Government of the United States notice of such captures; and its agents shall pay the expenses incurred in the maintenance and transmission of the rescued captives; who, in the mean time, shall be treated with the utmost hospitality by the American authorities at the place where they may be. But if the Government of the United States, before receiving such notice from Mexico, should obtain intelligence, through any other channel, of the existence of Mexican captives within its territory, it will proceed forthwith to effect their release and delivery to the Mexican agent, as above stipulated.

For the purpose of giving to these stipulations the fullest possible efficacy, thereby affording the security and redress demanded by their true spirit and intent, the Government of the United States will now and hereafter pass, without unnecessary delay, and always vigilantly enforce, such laws as the nature of the subject may require. And, finally, the sacredness of this obligation shall never be lost sight of by the said Government, when providing for the removal of the Indians from any portion of the said territories, or for its being settled by citizens of the United States; but, on the contrary, special care shall then be taken not to place its Indian occupants under the necessity of seeking new homes, by committing those invasions which the United States have solemnly obliged themselves to restrain.

ARTICLE XII

In consideration of the extension acquired by the boundaries of the United States, as defined in the fifth article of the present treaty, the Government of the United States engages to pay to that of the Mexican Republic the sum of fifteen millions of dollars.

Immediately after the treaty shall have been duly ratified by the Government of the Mexican Republic, the sum of three millions of dollars shall be paid to the said Government by that of the United States, at the city of Mexico, in the gold or silver coin of Mexico. The remaining twelve millions of dollars shall be paid at the same place, and in the same coin, in annual installments of three millions of dollars each, together with interest on the same at the rate of six per centum per annum. This interest shall begin to run upon the whole sum of twelve millions from the day of the ratification of the present treaty by the Mexican Government, and the first of the installments shall be paid at the expiration of one year from the same day. Together with each annual installment, as it falls due, the whole interest accruing on such installment from the beginning shall also be paid.

ARTICLE XIII

The United States engage, moreover, to assume and pay to the claimants all the amounts now due them, and those hereafter to become due, by reason of the claims already liquidated and decided against the Mexican Republic, under the conventions between the two republics severally concluded on the eleventh day of April, eighteen hundred and thirty-nine, and on the thirtieth day of January, eighteen hundred and forty-three; so that the Mexican Republic shall be absolutely exempt, for the future, from all expense whatever on account of the said claims.

ARTICLE XIV

The United States do furthermore discharge the Mexican Republic from all claims of citizens of the United States, not heretofore decided against the Mexican Government, which may have arisen previously to the date of the signature of this treaty; which discharge shall be final and perpetual, whether the said claims be rejected or be allowed by the board of commissioners provided for in the following article, and whatever shall be the total amount of those allowed.

ARTICLE XV

The United States, exonerating Mexico from all demands on account of the claims of their citizens mentioned in the preceding article, and considering them entirely and forever canceled, whatever their amount may be, undertake to make satisfaction for the same, to an amount not exceeding three and one-quarter millions of dollars. To ascertain the validity and amount of those claims, a board of commissioners shall be established by the Government of

the United States, whose awards shall be final and conclusive; provided, that in deciding upon the validity of each claim, the board shall be guided and governed by the principles and rules of decision prescribed by the first and fifth articles of the unratified convention, concluded at the city of Mexico on the twentieth day of November, one thousand eight hundred and forty-three; and in no case shall an award be made in favour of any claim not embraced by these principles and rules.

If, in the opinion of the said board of commissioners or of the claimants, any books, records, or documents, in the possession or power of the Government of the Mexican Republic, shall be deemed necessary to the just decision of any claim, the commissioners, or the claimants through them, shall, within such period as Congress may designate, make an application in writing for the same, addressed to the Mexican Minister of Foreign Affairs, to be transmitted by the Secretary of State of the United States; and the Mexican Government engages, at the earliest possible moment after the receipt of such demand, to cause any of the books, records, or documents so specified, which shall be in their possession or power (or authenticated copies or extracts of the same), to be transmitted to the said Secretary of State, who shall immediately deliver them over to the said board of commissioners; provided that no such application shall be made by or at the instance of any claimant, until the facts which it is expected to prove by such books, records, or documents, shall have been stated under oath or affirmation.

ARTICLE XVI

Each of the contracting parties reserves to itself the entire right to fortify whatever point within its territory it may judge proper so to fortify for its security.

ARTICLE XVII

The treaty of amity, commerce, and navigation, concluded at the city of Mexico, on the fifth day of April, A. D. 1831, between the United States of America and the United Mexican States, except the additional article, and except so far as the stipulations of the said treaty may be incompatible with any stipulation contained in the present treaty, is hereby revived for the period of eight years from the day of the exchange of ratifications of this treaty, with the same force and virtue as if incorporated therein; it being understood that each of the contracting parties reserves to itself the right, at any time after the said period of eight years shall have expired, to terminate the same by giving one year's notice of such intention to the other party.

ARTICLE XVIII

All supplies whatever for troops of the United States in Mexico, arriving at ports in the occupation of such troops previous to the final evacuation thereof, although subsequently to the restoration of the custom-houses at such ports, shall be entirely exempt from duties and charges of any kind; the Government of the United States hereby engaging and pledging its faith to establish and vigilantly to enforce, all possible guards for securing the revenue of Mexico, by preventing the importation, under cover of this stipulation, of any articles other than such, both in kind and in quantity, as shall really be wanted for the use and consumption of the forces of the United States during the time they may remain in Mexico. To this end it shall be the duty of all officers and agents of the United States to denounce to the Mexican authorities at the respective ports any attempts at a fraudulent abuse of this stipulation, which they may know of, or may have reason to suspect, and to give to such authorities all the aid in their power with regard thereto; and every such attempt, when duly proved and established by sentence of a competent tribunal. They shall be punished by the confiscation of the property so attempted to be fraudulently introduced.

ARTICLE XIX

With respect to all merchandise, effects, and property whatsoever, imported into ports of Mexico, whilst in the occupation of the forces of the United States, whether by citizens of either republic, or by citizens or subjects of any neutral nation, the following rules shall be observed:

1) All such merchandise, effects, and property, if imported previously to the restoration of the custom-houses to the Mexican authorities, as stipulated for in the third article of this treaty, shall be exempt from confiscation, although the importation of the same be prohibited by the Mexican tariff.

(2) The same perfect exemption shall be enjoyed by all such merchandise, effects, and property, imported subsequently to the restoration of the custom-houses, and previously to the sixty days fixed in the following article for the coming into force of the Mexican tariff at such ports respectively; the said merchandise, effects, and property being, however, at the time of their importation, subject to the payment of duties, as provided for in the said following article.

(3) All merchandise, effects, and property described in the two rules foregoing shall, during their continuance at the place of importation, and upon their leaving such place for the interior, be exempt from all duty, tax, or imposts of every kind, under whatsoever title or denomination. Nor shall they be there subject to any charge whatsoever upon the sale thereof.

(4) All merchandise, effects, and property, described in the first and second rules, which shall have been removed to any place in the interior, whilst such place was in the occupation of the forces of the United States, shall, during their continuance therein, be exempt from all tax upon the sale or consumption thereof, and from every kind of impost or contribution, under whatsoever title or denomination.

(5) But if any merchandise, effects, or property, described in the first and second rules, shall be removed to any place not occupied at the time by the forces of the United States, they shall, upon their introduction into such place, or upon their sale or consumption there, be subject to the same duties which, under the Mexican laws, they would be required to pay in such cases if they had been imported in time of peace, through the maritime custom-houses, and had there paid the duties conformably with the Mexican tariff.

(6) The owners of all merchandise, effects, or property, described in the first and second rules, and existing in any port of Mexico, shall have the right to reship the same, exempt from all tax, impost, or contribution whatever.

With respect to the metals, or other property, exported from any Mexican port whilst in the occupation of the forces of the United States, and previously to the restoration of the custom-house at such port, no person shall be required by the Mexican authorities, whether general or state, to pay any tax, duty, or contribution upon any such exportation, or in any manner to account for the same to the said authorities.

ARTICLE XX

Through consideration for the interests of commerce generally, it is agreed, that if less than sixty days should elapse between the date of the signature of this treaty and the restoration of the custom-houses, conformably with the stipulation in the third article, in such case all merchandise, effects and property whatsoever, arriving at the Mexican ports after the restoration of the said custom-houses, and previously to the expiration of sixty days after the day of signature of this treaty, shall be admitted to entry; and no other duties shall be levied thereon than the duties established by the tariff found in force at such custom-houses at the time of the restoration of the same. And to all such merchandise, effects, and property, the rules established by the preceding article shall apply.

ARTICLE XXI

If unhappily any disagreement should hereafter arise between the Governments of the two republics, whether with respect to the interpretation of any stipulation in this treaty, or with respect to any other particular concerning the political or commercial relations of the two nations, the said Governments, in the name of those nations, do promise to each other that they will endeavour, in the most sincere and earnest manner, to settle the differences so arising, and to preserve the state of peace and friendship in which the two countries are now placing themselves, using, for this end, mutual representations and pacific negotiations. And if, by these means, they should not be enabled to come to an agreement, a resort shall not, on this account, be had to reprisals, aggression, or hostility of any kind, by the one republic against the other, until the Government of that which deems itself aggrieved shall have maturely considered, in the spirit of peace and good neighbourship, whether it would not be better that such difference should be settled by the arbitration of commissioners appointed on each side, or by that of a friendly nation. And should such course be proposed by either party, it shall be acceded to by the other, unless deemed by it altogether incompatible with the nature of the difference, or the circumstances of the case.

ARTICLE XXII

If (which is not to be expected, and which God forbid) war should unhappily break out between the two republics, they do now, with a view to such calamity, solemnly pledge themselves to each other and to the world to observe the following rules; absolutely where the nature of the subject permits, and as closely as possible in all cases where such absolute observance shall be impossible:

(1) The merchants of either republic then residing in the other shall be allowed to remain twelve months (for those dwelling in the interior), and six months (for those dwelling at the seaports) to collect their debts and settle their affairs; during which periods they shall enjoy the same protection, and be on the same footing, in all respects, as the citizens or subjects of the most friendly nations; and, at the expiration thereof, or at any time before, they shall have full liberty to depart, carrying off all their effects without molestation or hindrance, conforming therein to the same laws which the citizens or subjects of the most friendly nations are required to conform to. Upon the entrance of the armies of either nation into the territories of the other, women and children, ecclesiastics, scholars of every faculty, cultivators of the earth, merchants, artisans, manufacturers, and fishermen, unarmed and inhabiting unfortified towns, villages, or places, and in general all persons whose occupations are for the common subsistence and benefit of mankind, shall be allowed to continue their respective employments, unmolested in their persons. Nor shall their houses or goods be burnt or otherwise destroyed, nor their cattle taken, nor their fields wasted, by the armed force into whose power, by the events of war, they may happen to fall; but if the necessity arise to take anything from them for the use of such armed force, the same shall be paid for at an equitable price. All churches, hospitals, schools, colleges, libraries, and other establishments for charitable and beneficent purposes, shall be respected, and all persons connected with the same protected in the discharge of their duties, and the pursuit of their vocations.

(2) In order that the fate of prisoners of war may be alleviated all such practices as those of sending them into distant, inclement or unwholesome districts, or crowding them into close and noxious places, shall be studiously avoided. They shall not be confined in dungeons, prison ships, or prisons; nor be put in irons, or bound or otherwise restrained in the use of their limbs. The officers shall enjoy liberty on their paroles, within convenient districts, and have comfortable quarters; and the common soldiers shall be disposed in cantonments, open and extensive enough for air and exercise and lodged in barracks as roomy and good as are provided by the party in whose power they are for its own troops. But if any officer shall break his parole by leaving the district so assigned him, or any other prisoner shall escape from the limits of his cantonment after they shall have been designated to him, such individual, officer, or other prisoner, shall forfeit so much of the benefit of this article as provides for his liberty on parole or in cantonment. And if any officer so breaking his parole or any common soldier so escaping from the limits assigned him, shall afterwards be found in arms previously to his being regularly exchanged, the person so offending shall be dealt with according to the established laws of war. The officers shall be daily furnished, by the party in whose power they are, with as many rations, and of the same articles, as are allowed either in kind or by commutation, to officers of equal rank in its own army; and all others shall be daily furnished with such ration as is allowed to a common soldier in its own service; the value of all which supplies shall, at the close of the war, or at periods to be agreed upon between the respective commanders, be paid by the other party, on a mutual adjustment of accounts for the subsistence of prisoners; and such accounts shall not be mingled with or set off against any others, nor the balance due on them withheld, as a compensation or reprisal for any cause whatever, real or pretended. Each party shall be allowed to keep a commissary of prisoners, appointed by itself, with every cantonment of prisoners, in possession of the other; which commissary shall see the prisoners as often as he pleases; shall be allowed to receive, exempt from all duties and taxes, and to distribute, whatever comforts may be sent to them by their friends; and shall be free to transmit his reports in open letters to the party by whom he is employed. And it is declared that neither the pretense that war dissolves all treaties, nor any other whatever, shall be considered as annulling or suspending the solemn covenant contained in this article. On the contrary, the state of war is precisely that for which it is provided; and, during which, its stipulations are to be as sacredly observed as the most acknowledged obligations under the law of nature or nations.

ARTICLE XXIII

This treaty shall be ratified by the President of the United States of America, by and with the advice and consent of the Senate thereof; and by the President of the Mexican Republic, with the previous approbation of its general Congress; and the ratifications shall be exchanged in the City of Washington, or at the seat of Government of Mexico, in four months from the date of the signature hereof, or sooner if practicable. In faith whereof we, the respective Plenipotentiaries, have signed this treaty of peace, friendship, limits, and settlement, and have hereunto affixed our seals respectively. Done in quintuplicate, at the city of Guadalupe Hidalgo, on the second day of February, in the year of our Lord one thousand eight hundred and forty-eight.

N. P. TRIST
LUIS P. CUEVAS
BERNARDO COUTO
MIGL. ATRISTAIN

Source: Treaty of Peace, Friendship, Limits and Settlement with the Republic of Mexico. February 2, 1848. *United States Treaties and Other International Agreements,* vol. 9 (Washington, DC: Government Printing Office, 1950), 922.

109. James Polk, Message to Congress on the Discovery of Gold in California, December 5, 1848

Introduction

In his message to Congress at the end of 1848, President James K. Polk had many favorable developments on which to report. Victory in the war with Mexico had expanded the United States to encompass parts of present-day New Mexico, Arizona, Nevada, California, Utah, Wyoming, and Colorado. After lauding the temperate climate, fertility, and strategic importance of Texas and the nation's new acquisitions, Polk confirmed the electrifying discovery of gold in California. Lieutenant William T. Sherman, the future American Civil War (1861–1865) general, was serving as an aide to the American military governor of California, Colonel Richard Mason, in 1848. The war with Mexico was not yet officially ended when reports of gold discoveries began circulating in California, and American soldiers stationed there deserted in droves to search for gold. Sherman and Mason visited a mine and engaged a special courier to carry a sample of gold to the president. Polk's December announcement began the gold rush in earnest. Thousands of gold seekers pouring into California, closely followed by settlers, sealed the fate of those Indians who had survived Spanish and Mexican rule. Mining polluted the water and interfered with fishing, and miners and settlers depleted wild game and took Indian land by force. Thousands of California Indians died of starvation, disease, and violence.

Primary Source

[. . .]

The area of these several Territories, according to a report carefully prepared by the Commissioner of the General Land Office from the most authentic information in his possession, and which is herewith transmitted, contains 1,193,061 square miles, or 763,559,040 acres; while the area of the remaining twenty-nine States and the territory not yet organized into States east of the Rocky Mountains contains 2,059,513 square miles, or 1,318,126,058 acres. These estimates show that the territories recently acquired, and over which our exclusive jurisdiction and

dominion have been extended, constitute a country more than half as large as all that which was held by the United States before their acquisition. If Oregon be excluded from the estimate, there will still remain within the limits of Texas, New Mexico, and California 851,598 square miles, or 545,012,720 acres, being an addition equal to more than one-third of all the territory owned by the United States before their acquisition, and, including Oregon, nearly as great an extent of territory as the whole of Europe, Russia only excepted. The Mississippi, so lately the frontier of our country, is now only its center. With the addition of the late acquisitions, the United States are now estimated to be nearly as large as the whole of Europe. It is estimated by the Superintendent of the Coast Survey in the accompanying report that the extent of the seacoast of Texas on the Gulf of Mexico is upward of 400 miles; of the coast of Upper California on the Pacific, of 970 miles, and of Oregon, including the Straits of Fuca, of 650 miles, making the whole extent of seacoast on the Pacific 1,620 miles and the whole extent on both the Pacific and the Gulf of Mexico 2,020 miles. The length of the coast on the Atlantic from the northern limits of the United States around the capes of Florida to the Sabine, on the eastern boundary of Texas, is estimated to be 3,100 miles; so that the addition of seacoast, including Oregon, is very nearly two-thirds as great as all we possessed before, and, excluding Oregon, is an addition of 1,370 miles, being nearly equal to one-half of the extent of coast which we possessed before these acquisitions. We have now three great maritime fronts—on the Atlantic, the Gulf of Mexico, and the Pacific—making in the whole an extent of seacoast exceeding 5,000 miles. This is the extent of the seacoast of the United States, not including bays, sounds, and small irregularities of the main shore and of the sea islands. If these be included, the length of the shore line of coast, as estimated by the Superintendent of the Coast Survey in his report, would be 33,063 miles. It would be difficult to calculate the value of these immense additions to our territorial possessions. Texas, lying contiguous to the western boundary of Louisiana, embracing within its limits a part of the navigable tributary waters of the Mississippi and an extensive seacoast, could not long have remained in the hands of a foreign power without endangering the peace of our southwestern frontier. Her products in the vicinity of the tributaries of the Mississippi must have sought a market through these streams, running into and through our territory, and the danger of irritation and collision of interests between Texas as a foreign state and ourselves would have been imminent, while the embarrassments in the commercial intercourse between them must have been constant and unavoidable. Had Texas fallen into the hands or under the influence and control of a strong maritime or military foreign power, as she might have done, these dangers would have been still greater. They have been avoided by her voluntary and peaceful annexation to the United States. Texas, from her position, was a natural and almost indispensable part of our territories. Fortunately, she has been restored to our country, and now constitutes one of the States of our Confederacy, "upon an equal footing with the original States." The salubrity of climate, the fertility of soil, peculiarly adapted to the production of some of our most valuable staple commodities, and her commercial advantages must soon make her one of our most populous States. New Mexico, though situated in the interior and without a seacoast, is known to contain much fertile land, to abound in rich mines of the precious metals, and to be capable of sustaining a large population. From its position it is the intermediate and connecting territory between our settlements and our possessions in Texas and those on the Pacific Coast. Upper California, irrespective of the vast mineral wealth recently developed there, holds at this day, in point of value and importance, to the rest of the Union the same relation that Louisiana did when that fine territory was acquired from France forty-five years ago. Extending nearly ten degrees of latitude along the Pacific, and embracing the only safe and commodious harbors on that coast for many hundred miles, with a temperate climate and an extensive interior of fertile lands, it is scarcely possible to estimate its wealth until it shall be brought under the government of our laws and its resources fully developed. From its position it must command the rich commerce of China, of Asia, of the islands of the Pacific, of western Mexico, of Central America, the South American States, and of the Russian possessions bordering on that ocean. A great emporium will doubtless speedily arise on the Californian coast which may be destined to rival in importance New Orleans itself. The depot of the vast commerce which must exist on the Pacific will probably be at some point on the Bay of San Francisco, and will occupy the same relation to the whole western coast of that ocean as New Orleans does to the valley of the Mississippi and the Gulf of Mexico. To this depot our numerous whale ships will resort with their cargoes to trade, refit, and obtain supplies. This of itself will largely contribute to build up a city, which would soon become the center of a great and rapidly increasing commerce. Situated on a safe harbor, sufficiently capacious for all the navies as well as the marine of the world, and convenient to excellent timber for shipbuilding, owned by the United States, it must become our great Western naval depot. It was known that mines of the precious metals existed to a considerable extent in California at the time of its acquisition. Recent discoveries render it probable that these mines are more extensive and valuable than was anticipated. The accounts of the abundance of gold in that territory are of such an extraordinary character as would scarcely command belief were they not corroborated by the authentic reports of officers in the public service who have visited the mineral district and derived the facts which they detail from personal observation. Reluctant to credit the reports in general circulation as to the quantity of gold, the officer commanding our forces in California visited the mineral district in July last for the purpose of obtaining accurate information on the subject. His report to the War Department of the result of his examination and the facts obtained on the spot is herewith laid before Congress. When he visited the country there were about 4,000 persons engaged in collecting gold. There is every reason to believe that the number of persons so employed

has since been augmented. The explorations already made warrant the belief that the supply is very large and that gold is found at various places in an extensive district of country. Information received from officers of the Navy and other sources, though not so full and minute, confirms the accounts of the commander of our military force in California. It appears also from these reports that mines of quicksilver are found in the vicinity of the gold region. One of them is now being worked, and is believed to be among the most productive in the world. The effects produced by the discovery of these rich mineral deposits and the success which has attended the labors of those who have resorted to them have produced a surprising change in the state of affairs in California. Labor commands a most exorbitant price, and all other pursuits but that of searching for the precious metals are abandoned. Nearly the whole of the male population of the country have gone to the gold districts. Ships arriving on the coast are deserted by their crews and their voyages suspended for want of sailors. Our commanding officer there entertains apprehensions that soldiers can not be kept in the public service without a large increase of pay. Desertions in his command have become frequent, and he recommends that those who shall withstand the strong temptation and remain faithful should be rewarded. This abundance of gold and the all-engrossing pursuit of it have already caused in California an unprecedented rise in the price of all the necessaries of life. That we may the more speedily and fully avail ourselves of the undeveloped wealth of these mines, it is deemed of vast importance that a branch of the Mint of the United States be authorized to be established at your present session in California. Among other signal advantages which would result from such an establishment would be that of raising the gold to its par value in that territory. A branch mint of the United States at the great commercial depot on the west coast would convert into our own coin not only the gold derived from our own rich mines, but also the bullion and specie which our commerce may bring from the whole west coast of Central and South America. The west coast of America and the adjacent interior embrace the richest and best mines of Mexico, New Granada, Central America, Chile, and Peru. The bullion and specie drawn from these countries, and especially from those of western Mexico and Peru, to an amount in value of many millions of dollars, are now annually diverted and carried by the ships of Great Britain to her own ports, to be recoined or used to sustain her national bank, and thus contribute to increase her ability to command so much of the commerce of the world. If a branch mint be established at the great commercial point upon that coast, a vast amount of bullion and specie would flow thither to be recoined, and pass thence to New Orleans, New York, and other Atlantic cities. The amount of our constitutional currency at home would be greatly increased, while its circulation abroad would be promoted. It is well known to our merchants trading to China and the west coast of America that great inconvenience and loss are experienced from the fact that our coins are not current at their par value in those countries. The powers of Europe, far removed from the west coast of America by the Atlantic Ocean, which intervenes, and by a tedious and dangerous navigation around the southern cape of the continent of America, can never successfully compete with the United States in the rich and extensive commerce which is opened to us at so much less cost by the acquisition of California. The vast importance and commercial advantages of California have heretofore remained undeveloped by the Government of the country of which it constituted a part. Now that this fine province is a part of our country, all the States of the Union, some more immediately and directly than others, are deeply interested in the speedy development of its wealth and resources. No section of our country is more interested or will be more benefited than the commercial, navigating, and manufacturing interests of the Eastern States. Our planting and farming interests in every part of the Union will be greatly benefited by it. As our commerce and navigation are enlarged and extended, our exports of agricultural products and of manufactures will be increased, and in the new markets thus opened they can not fail to command remunerating and profitable prices.

[...]

Source: James D. Richardson, ed., *Messages and Papers of the Presidents,* Vol. 4 (Washington, DC: U.S. Government Printing Office, 1897), 634–637.

110. Testimonials to Congress on the Efficacy of the Colt Revolver against Indians, 1851

Introduction

The brutal raids of the Comanches, the dominant tribe in Texas, terrorized American settlers. Comanche raiders burned settlements, stole livestock, and murdered with abandon. What lives they spared were spent in cruel captivity. The Comanches dominated close combat with their superior mobility and firepower. The Texas Rangers were finally able to tip the balance in their own favor when they acquired repeating five-shot pistols, or revolvers, invented by Samuel Colt in 1836. By the mid-1840s, revolver-armed Texans could kill many times their own number. As a result, the Comanches became unwilling to meet American troops in direct combat. Thereafter, the army had to develop new modes of warfare to meet the challenge of pursuing hostile Indians over great expanses of untracked land and bringing them to battle. The revolver figured in the War Department's planning as it equipped cavalry troopers to serve on the Texas frontier. This 1851 report by the congressional Committee on Military Affairs contains testimonials by army officers and others, all of whom greatly preferred the repeating pistol to the single-shot pistol.

The Colt revolver, the legendary six-shooter or Peacemaker, soon became the weapon of choice for soldiers and civilians alike on the frontier.

Primary Source

The Committee on Military Affairs, to whom was referred the reply of the Secretary of War to the resolution of the Senate of September 30, 1850, directing him to ascertain the opinion of the Officers of the Ordnance Bureau, and of the United States mounted regiments, as to the relative efficiency of the REPEATING PISTOLS, invented by Samuel Colt, and other inventors, their adaptation to the service, and the propriety of substituting the most improved repeating pistol for the common dragoon pistol now in use, respectfully report:—

THAT they have examined the documents submitted by the Secretary of War, and find that, in conformity with the request of the said resolution, a board of United States ordnance officers were convened at Washington City, by General Talcott, chief of the Ordnance Bureau, on the 13th of November last, to "make trial of such repeating and other arms as might be presented for that purpose." Due notice of the assembling of the board and its object was given to ALL inventors of repeating pistols and other arms, who were known to the Ordnance Bureau, and they were respectfully invited to attend with samples of their arms. Inquiries were also addressed to those officers who were supposed to be the most experienced in the use of repeating pistols, and their opinions collected as to the merits of such arms. Colt's, Leavitt's, Warner's, and Perry's were submitted for examination and fully tested, and the result of these enquiries and experiments has been to establish the superiority of Colt's repeating pistol over all others, and, with some slight alterations and improvements, its admirable adaptation to the dragoon service. Those repeating arms first constructed by Mr. Colt, were too complicated and easily deranged to be fit for rough service. Previous, however, to the year 1840, they had been so much improved, that many highly experienced officers recommended their trial in the army and navy, believing them to be admirably adapted for such service. In the progress of improvement, complexity has yielded to simplicity, and delicacy to strength, as appears by the inspection returns of Major Thornton, a member of the board of ordnance officers. He reports that only one pistol failed in the inspection trial out of the last two thousand and eighty-two tested in 1850; and even this failure was attributed to the imperfect metal of the particular arm. These improvements by Mr. Colt, in the construction of the repeating-arms, have encouraged the department to adopt them gradually into the service—first in the ranger troops employed in Mexico, and afterward in the mounted riflemen; until at this time they have grown into general favor with the army and country; and there are numerous requisitions for them upon the department, which the government has not the arms to supply.

On the Texan frontier and on the several routes to California, the Indian tribes are renewing their murderous warfare, and a general Indian war is likely to ensue, unless bodies of mounted men, efficiently equipped for such service, are employed against them. Experience has proved that it is difficult to contend successfully against savages with the usual arms of mounted men— the ordinary dragoon pistol and Hall's carbine. General Harney, who employed Colt's pistol successfully in Florida, says: "It is the only weapon with which we can hope ever to subdue those wild and daring tribes, unless we can have at least three regiments of dragoons on the Texas frontier alone;" and those officers who have recently returned from the frontier corroborate this statement by declaring, that a dragoon armed with Colt's repeating pistol and a musquetoon, or perhaps Sharp's rifle, would be the most efficient and the most formidable for frontier service; and particularly when encounters with the savages occur, as they generally do, in prairies, defiles, and mountain gorges. The advantages of repeating-arms in such encounters are incalculable. A few bold men, well skilled in the use of these weapons, can, under such circumstances, encounter and scatter almost any number of savages.

The committee take occasion, in this connection, to refer to the report of Brevet Brigadier General Talcott, colonel of ordnance; the report of the board of ordnance officers; and to the abstract from the opinions of various experienced officers of the army in relation to this subject—all of which accompany this report, and testify to the efficiency and adaptation of Colt's repeating pistol to the service of mounted troops. The committee accordingly recommend that COLT'S repeating pistols be substituted, under the direction and in the discretion of the department, in lieu of the common dragoon pistol now in use in the service, and that a sufficient quantity be purchased, so far as the same can be done within the present regular appropriations, to supply such demands as may be made upon and allowed by the department.

No. 1.

A summary of the reports of the board of officers convened to examine the various kinds of repeating fire-arms, and their adaptation to the cavalry service of the United States army.

"The board of ordnance officers, convened by order of Brigadier General George Talcott, colonel of ordnance, dated November 6, 1850, for the purpose of making trial of such repeating, and other arms, as might be presented for that purpose, in pursuance of the resolution of the Senate, and directions of the Secretary of War, have the honor to report, that the following pistols were presented, examined, and tried by them during their session at the Washington arsenal since the 13th instant, viz: 1st. Colt's, 2d. Leavitt's; 3d. Warner's; 4th. Perry's. That the first three are similar in principle, viz: with a revolving cylinder, containing six charges and one barrel; the fourth is constructed on a different plan, the breech being hung upon trunnions upon which it revolves.

"From the opportunities of experimenting with Colt's pistol, and from its use in service, the inventor has been able to remedy defects and strengthen weak parts; and the inspection reports accompanying this, of such pistols as were made during the past year, show that the material is of a better quality than that used in the previous manufacture of his pistol; and the trials made by this board are conclusive evidence to their minds, that, when made of really good materials, they are capable of meeting all reasonable demands of service.

"The common cavalry pistol is seldom successfully used in action; but for frontier or other service, where a small number of men are often exposed to the attack of a much stronger force, a pistol susceptible of repeating its discharge, would be of great efficiency; and its advantages over the common dragoon pistol on such occasions, have been proved in several instances.

"From the examination and trials which they have made of these arms, the board are of opinion that Colt's revolving pistol is better adapted to the service of mounted troops than any other pistol offered to their notice, and may be advantageously substituted for the present cavalry pistol."

BREVET COL. R. L. BAKER,
    MAJ. A. MORDECAI, *Ordnance.*
    COL. BENJ. HUGER, *Board*
    MAJ. W. A. THORNTON, *of Practice.*
    LIEUT. COL. TALCOTT,
    [...]

No. 3.

General Harney, under date of November 8, 1850, says:—.
    "I consider the arm perfect for the dragoon service, particularly when opposed to the western prairie Indians. It is the only weapon with which we can hope ever to subdue these wild and daring tribes, unless we can have at least *three* regiments of dragoons on the *Texas frontier alone.* I consider Colt's repeating pistol *equal,* in *every* respect, to any other pistol now in use, and *very greatly* superior in almost every respect.

"In 1837 or 1838, Mr. Colt took some of his rifles to Florida. A board of officers was ordered to examine them, and report on their efficiency, &c. The report was favorable, and General Jessup ordered the purchase of fifty, and they were placed in my hands. They were very delicately made, easily put out of order, and very difficult to repair. They were the first ever used or manufactured. Thirty-odd of them were lost at Caloosa Hatchee, all at the time in good order; and most of the others, with but little repairs, would be still good, and were turned over to the ordnance officer at Baton Rouge in 1842 or '43. During the whole of this time they were in constant use, *and not one single accident to the injury of any person occurred; and I honestly believe that but for these arms, the Indians would now be luxuriating in the everglades of Florida.*"

No. 4

Captain M. E. Van Buren, of mounted rifles, under date of November 4, 1850, says:—

"Within the past ten years, I have had opportunities of becoming familiar with Colt's pistol, having carried one on the march to Oregon, and also when accompanying Colonel Loring in his pursuit of deserters in March and April last, when we were exposed to almost incessant rains, and having used or practiced with it almost daily. This experience, with that which I had previously acquired, has led me to adopt the most favorable opinion of Colt's repeating pistol as to efficiency and adaptation to the service of our mounted troops.

"Colt's revolver possesses the following advantages over the common dragoon pistol: It contains five more shots at one loading; it has greater length of range and accuracy of aim, and these give greater confidence and morale to the soldier. . . . It is less liable to premature discharge than any other percussion arm with which I am acquainted. If the common dragoon pistol, capped ready for use, be carried in the holster at half cock, the cap is very liable to come off. If the hammer be let down on the cap, to secure it, there is great danger of premature discharge at any gait faster than a walk. Colt's pistol is free from these objections. The position of the cones secures the caps in their place, without the necessity of letting down the hammer; and the hammer being down upon the pan, it would require more motion than the pistol is likely to get in the holster, to pull the hammer back far enough to revolve the chamber and present a cap to the hammer.

"I do not think this pistol more liable to get out of order than any other. I certainly found mine, which was put to very severe tests in the way of use and exposure, and to which I gave no more care than I would have given to any other kind of pistol, always in efficient condition."

[. . .]

No. 10.

Washington City, *Feb.* 1850.

Dear Sir: In reply to your letter of the 25th inst., I will state that Colt's repeating pistols are preferred in California, over any other kind of arms. In fact, there is no part of the Union, where they are so highly esteemed. Every man in that country would have one if he could get it. I am sure that thousands could have been sold there during the last summer. The Indians in the gorges of the Sierra Nevada are terrified into honest habits, by the miners in that region being armed with these pistols.

WM. M. GWIN,
    U. S. Senator from California.

[. . .]

No. 46.

Brevet Lieutenant Colonel Hooker, Assistant Adjutant General, U. S. Army, reports "that Colt's repeating pistol appears to give greater satisfaction in time of war than any weapon that has fallen under my observation.

"During the war with Mexico our officers were extremely anxious to provide themselves with Colt's pistols, and so great was the demand, I have known them to sell for $140 each. I regard it as an invaluable arm, particularly for mounted officers and cavalry. For the last description of force it seems to possess all the advantage of the carbine, without any of the objections to that arm. My opinion of the pistol is formed from my own experience, as well as that of officers who served with me."

[. . .]

No. 63.

Major O. Cross, Quarter Master, United States Army, states that, "While on a march to Columbia river, I considered Colt's six-shooter as an invaluable weapon, particularly on the western prairies, where you frequently meet hostile bands of Indians. While on this long march, when hunting or running buffalo, I seldom ever saw any other pistols used.

"The Indians throughout the route seem to look on it as a great curiosity, and expressed much astonishment when shown to them, and explained as to the mode of using it. This pistol was much sought after by the emigrants, and sold in Oregon at from sixty to eighty dollars. In all the towns through which I have traveled in Mexico, Colt's 'six-shooters' have been prized very highly.

"I have been much on the prairies of the west, and have visited many Indian tribes, and consider it by far the best pistol I have ever examined. I would wish no other for mounted troops."

[. . .]

No. 75.

Captain H. W. Benharn, Corps of Engineers, U. S. Army, reports: "I consider Colt's many chambered pistol indispensable in the holsters of every mounted officer or soldier. While serving on reconnoitering parties, during our recent war with Mexico, in which I was generally escorted by parties of the Texan rangers, (of which troops we had several companies, unsurpassed in the world, I can not but believe for such duties, and who had used Colt's arms for several years, whenever they could obtain them,) we always felt that we were not properly armed without these weapons, and with them, thought ourselves fully competent to cope with four or five times our numbers armed in any other manner. And with all due deference to any opinion that may be entertained by those who have had more experience in regular cavalry service, than officers in our army have been able to acquire, I have long been of the opinion, that these arms must eventually supersede the use of carbines and carbineers; for I can not conceive that there would be one occasion in a hundred, where the cavalry soldier would require, or could use any other weapon than one of Colt s largest size pistols."

No. 76.

Captain S. G. French, Assistant Quarter-master, U. S. Army, reports that, "During more than a year's service on the frontiers of Texas and Mexico, I had ample opportunity to test the use of Colt's repeating pistols. Their 'range,' certainty and *precision* of firing, commend their general use. Another advantage they have over the ordinary pistol, is the great confidence they always give persons thus armed, and the corresponding dread they create in parties to attack men so prepared with the means of defense. Such confidence was reposed in those pistols, that whenever I had occasion to send small parties in advance, or to employ express-riders to carry the mails through the Indian country, it was always made a condition, that they should be furnished with Colt's revolvers; otherwise they would not risk their lives in such service. I might add, as a further proof of their efficiency for protection, that while other arms were cheap and abundant, Colt's revolvers would command three times their original cost; and often, persons thus armed, would not part with them for any consideration."

[…]

No. 82.

Major G. T. Howard, late of Texas Regiment, and Captain Sutton, late of Texas Rangers, state: "We deem Colt's repeating pistols to be the greatest improvement in small arms of the age. We have been familiar with the use of this effective invention, on the frontiers of Texas, since 1839, and we do unhesitatingly affirm, that they give the combatant more confidence and a greater spirit of defiance in those hand to hand struggles with the prairie Indians, than any other arm now in use.

"Those prairie tribes ride with boldness and wonderful skill, and are, perhaps, unsurpassed, as irregular cavalry. They are so dexterous in the use of the bow, that a single Indian, at full speed, is capable of keeping an arrow constantly in the air, between himself and the enemy; therefore, to encounter such an expert antagonist, with any certainty of doing execution, requires an impetuous charge, skillful horsemanship, and a rapid discharge of shots, such as can only be delivered with Colt's six shooters. They are the only weapon which has enabled the experienced frontiers-man to defeat the mounted Indian in his own peculiar mode of warfare; in those encounters which, though soon over, require a steady nerve, the greatest possible precision and celerity of movement, there is no time to reload fire-arms, even were it possible to do so, and manage your horse, in the midst of a quick and wily enemy, ever on the watch and ready to lance the first man who may loose the least control of his animal. In this description of service, Colt's revolver asserts its great and unquestionable superiority over all other weapons. We state, and with entire assurance of the fact, that Colt's six-shooter is the arm which has rendered the name of Texas ranger, a check and terror to the hostile bands of our frontier Indians. With our citizens they are considered unparalleled in the force and accuracy of their shooting, and are esteemed an invaluable weapon in offensive operations against the marauding tribes which depredate upon our frontier settlements.

"As for the difficulty of keeping these pistols in order, which is sometimes raised as an objection, we have never discovered any. They can only become unfit for service in the hands of men who never possessed the proper pride of a soldier, or where discipline must be most egregiously neglected."

[…]

No. 87.

Commodore Thomas Ap. C. Jones, United States Navy, reports: "It is now about nine years, if I rightly remember, since a number of Colt's repeating-arms were, by order of the Secretary of the Navy, put on board my flag ship, then bound on a cruise to the Pacific. It was on that cruise that I made the first demonstration on California, Monterey, and I think on my return home, I stated how much I felt myself strengthened while in occupation of the town of Monterey against the Mexican General's threatened attack, by having an hundred each of Colt's carbines and dragoon pistols, in the hands of my small party in possession of the town and fort. Even at that day I considered Colt's pistols nearly or quite perfect, but the subsequent improvements, I am inclined to think, render them as nearly perfect as can be expected. During my late cruise, while in California, I witnessed some of the most remarkable shooting with one of Colt's new Dragoon pistols I ever saw; it beating, at a very long musket range, a U. S. musket, and a first rate *western Virginia bear rifle*. These facts I state, believing them to be worth more than all else I could say."

[…]

No. 95.

Charles H. Haswell, Engineer in Chief, United States Navy, reports that: "From an extended acquaintance with the operation of Colt's repeating pistol, I am of the opinion that it combines the essential points of facility of loading, and rapidity of discharge, in a degree that renders it indispensable as an arm of attack or defense, and it has not any disadvantages of construction that invalidate these points."

[...]

Source: *Report as to the Relative Efficiency of the Repeating Pistols.* United States. Congress. Senate. Committee on Military Affairs—January 30, 1851.

111. Treaty of Fort Laramie, September 17, 1851

Introduction

The expansion of the United States from sea to sea unleashed a great migration of Americans across the Indian territory of the Great Plains. Subsequently, the U.S. government focused on how to dissuade the Indians from attacking the migrants. Signed at Fort Laramie in Wyoming Territory in 1851, this Treaty of Fort Laramie treaty attempted to establish relations with seven northern Plains Indian tribes, including the Sioux, and secure their promise not to interfere with American overland migrants, roads, forts, and trading posts. At the same time, the treaty specified the territories assigned to the seven tribes and exacted a promise that they would not fight among themselves. In return, the United States was to protect the Indians from harm by Americans and to provide financial and material assistance to the Indians for the purpose of taking up agriculture. The government was pursuing a policy of trying to integrate the Indians into American society by giving them incentives to adopt American ways. The U.S. government signed another Treaty of Fort Laramie in 1868, also with the Sioux and allied tribes. This second treaty established for the Sioux an extensive reservation in present-day South Dakota, but the peace was similarly short-lived. Just eight years later war with the Sioux broke out, due in no small part to the discovery of gold deposits in the Black Hills of South Dakota.

Primary Source

Articles of a treaty made and concluded at Fort Laramie, in the Indian Territory, between D. D. Mitchell, superintendent of Indian affairs, and Thomas Fitzpatrick, Indian agent, commissioners specially appointed and authorized by the President of the United States, of the first part, and the chiefs, headmen, and braves of the following Indian nations, residing south of the Missouri River, east of the Rocky Mountains, and north of the lines of Texas and New Mexico, viz, the Sioux or Dahcotahs, Cheyennes, Arrapahoes, Crows, Assinaboines, Gros-Ventre Mandans, and Arrickaras, parties of the second part, on the seventeenth day of September, A. D. one thousand eight hundred and fifty-one.*

ARTICLE 1.

The aforesaid nations, parties to this treaty, having assembled for the purpose of establishing and confirming peaceful relations amongst themselves, do hereby covenant and agree to abstain in future from all hostilities whatever against each other, to maintain good faith and friendship in all their mutual intercourse, and to make an effective and lasting peace.

ARTICLE 2.

The aforesaid nations do hereby recognize the right of the United States Government to establish roads, military and other posts, within their respective territories.

ARTICLE 3.

In consideration of the rights and privileges acknowledged in the preceding article, the United States bind themselves to protect the aforesaid Indian nations against the commission of all depredations by the people of the said United States, after the ratification of this treaty.

ARTICLE 4.

The aforesaid Indian nations do hereby agree and bind themselves to make restitution or satisfaction for any wrongs committed, after the ratification of this treaty, by any band or individual of their people, on the people of the United States, whilst lawfully residing in or passing through their respective territories.

ARTICLE 5.

The aforesaid Indian nations do hereby recognize and acknowledge the following tracts of country, included within the metes and boundaries hereinafter designated, as their respective territories, viz:

The territory of the Sioux or Dahcotah Nation, commencing the mouth of the White Earth River, on the Missouri River: thence in a southwesterly direction to the forks of the Platte River: thence up the north fork of the Platte River to a point known as the Red Bute, or where the road leaves the river; thence along the range of mountains known as the Black Hills, to the head-waters of Heart River; thence down Heart River to its mouth; and thence down the Missouri River to the place of beginning.

The territory of the Gros Ventre, Mandans, and Arrickaras Nations, commencing at the mouth of Heart River; thence up the Missouri River to the mouth of the Yellowstone River; thence up the Yellowstone River to the mouth of Powder River in a south-easterly direction, to the head-waters of the Little Missouri River;

thence along the Black Hills to the head of Heart River, and thence down Heart River to the place of beginning.

The territory of the Assinaboin Nation, commencing at the mouth of Yellowstone River; thence up the Missouri River to the mouth of the Muscle-shell River; thence from the mouth of the Muscle-shell River in a southeasterly direction until it strikes the head-waters of Big Dry Creek; thence down that creek to where it empties into the Yellowstone River, nearly opposite the mouth of Powder River, and thence down the Yellowstone River to the place of beginning.

The territory of the Blackfoot Nation, commencing at the mouth of Muscle-shell River; thence up the Missouri River to its source; thence along the main range of the Rocky Mountains, in a southerly direction, to the head-waters of the northern source of the Yellowstone River; thence down the Yellowstone River to the mouth of Twenty-five Yard Creek; thence across to the head-waters of the Muscle-shell River, and thence down the Muscle-shell River to the place of beginning.

The territory of the Crow Nation, commencing at the mouth of Powder River on the Yellowstone; thence up Powder River to its source; thence along the main range of the Black Hills and Wind River Mountains to the head-waters of the Yellowstone River; thence down the Yellowstone River to the mouth of Twenty-five Yard Creek; thence to the head waters of the Muscle-shell River; thence down the Muscle-shell River to its mouth; thence to the head-waters of Big Dry Creek, and thence to its mouth.

The territory of the Cheyennes and Arrapahoes, commencing at the Red Bute, or the place where the road leaves the north fork of the Platte River; thence up the north fork of the Platte River to its source; thence along the main range of the Rocky Mountains to the head-waters of the Arkansas River; thence down the Arkansas River to the crossing of the Santa Fé road; thence in a northwesterly direction to the forks of the Platte River, and thence up the Platte River to the place of beginning.

It is, however, understood that, in making this recognition and acknowledgement, the aforesaid Indian nations do not hereby abandon or prejudice any rights or claims they may have to other lands; and further, that they do not surrender the privilege of hunting, fishing, or passing over any of the tracts of country heretofore described.

ARTICLE 6.

The parties to the second part of this treaty having selected principals or head-chiefs for their respective nations, through whom all national business will hereafter be conducted, do hereby bind themselves to sustain said chiefs and their successors during good behavior.

ARTICLE 7.

In consideration of the treaty stipulations, and for the damages which have or may occur by reason thereof to the Indian nations, parties hereto, and for their maintenance and the improvement of their moral and social customs, the United States bind themselves to deliver to the said Indian nations the sum of fifty thousand dollars per annum for the term of ten years, with the right to continue the same at the discretion of the President of the United States for a period not exceeding five years thereafter, in provisions, merchandise, domestic animals, and agricultural implements, in such proportions as may be deemed best adapted to their condition by the President of the United States, to be distributed in proportion to the population of the aforesaid Indian nations.

ARTICLE 8.

It is understood and agreed that should any of the Indian nations, parties to this treaty, violate any of the provisions thereof, the United States may withhold the whole or a portion of the annuities mentioned in the preceding article from the nation so offending, until, in the opinion of the President of the United States, proper satisfaction shall have been made.

In testimony whereof the said D. D. Mitchell and Thomas Fitzpatrick commissioners as aforesaid, and the chiefs, headmen, and braves, parties hereto, have set their hands and affixed their marks, on the day and at the place first above written.

D. D. Mitchell
   Thomas Fitzpatrick
   Commissioners.

Sioux:
   Mah-toe-wha-you-whey, his x mark.
   Mah-kah-toe-zah-zah, his x mark.
   Bel-o-ton-kah-tan-ga, his x mark.
   Nah-ka-pah-gi-gi, his x mark.
   Mak-toe-sah-bi-chis, his x mark.
   Meh-wha-tah-ni-hans-kah, his x mark.

Cheyennes:
   Wah-ha-nis-satta, his x mark.
   Voist-ti-toe-vetz, his x mark.
   Nahk-ko-me-ien, his x mark.
   Koh-kah-y-wh-cum-est, his x mark.

Arrapahoes:
   Bè-ah-té-a-qui-sah, his x mark.
   Neb-ni-bah-seh-it, his x mark.
   Beh-kah-jay-beth-sah-es, his x mark.

Crows:

Arra-tu-ri-sash, his x mark.

Doh-chepit-seh-chi-es, his x mark.

Assinaboines:

Mah-toe-wit-ko, his x mark.

Toe-tah-ki-eh-nan, his x mark.

Mandans and Gros Ventres:

Nochk-pit-shi-toe-pish, his x mark.

She-oh-mant-ho, his x mark.

Arickarees:

Koun-hei-ti-shan, his x mark.

Bi-atch-tah-wetch, his x mark.

In the presence of—

A. B. Chambers, secretary.

S. Cooper, colonel, U. S. Army.

R. H. Chilton, captain, First Drags.

Thomas Duncan, captain, Mounted Riflemen.

Thos. G. Rhett, brevet captain R. M. R.

W. L. Elliott, first lieutenant R. M. R.

C. Campbell, interpreter for Sioux.

John S. Smith, interpreter for Cheyennes.

Robert Meldrum, interpreter for the Crows.

H. Culbertson, interpreter for Assiniboines and Gros Ventres.

Francois L'Etalie, interpreter for Arickarees.

John Pizelle, interpreter for the Arrapahoes.

B. Gratz Brown.

Robert Campbell.

Edmond F. Chouteau

* This treaty as signed was ratified by the Senate with an amendment changing the annuity in Article 7 from fifty to ten years, subject to acceptance by the tribes. Assent of all tribes except the Crows was procured (see Upper Platte C., 570, 1853, Indian Office) and in subsequent agreements this treaty has been recognized as in force.

Source: "Treaty of Fort Laramie with Sioux, Etc., 1851," in *Indian Affairs: Laws and Treaties,* Vol. 2, *Treaties,* edited by Charles J. Kappler (Washington, DC: U.S. Government Printing Office, 1904), 549–596.

112. Apache Treaty, July 1, 1852

Introduction

American troops occupied New Mexico during the Mexican-American War (1846–1848), and New Mexico officially became U.S. territory at the end of the war. The Apaches, who had been implacable enemies of the Spanish and then the Mexicans, were willing to accept the American presence as preferable to that of Mexico. This treaty establishes friendly relations in perpetuity with several Apache leaders, including the famous Mangas Coloradas (who was summarily executed by American troops in 1863). The treaty also attempts to honor a provision in the 1848 treaty with Mexico by prohibiting Apache raids into Mexico. Like other such treaties, it provides for safe passage through Indian territory and asserts the American right to build forts, agencies, and trading posts. In exchange, the United States makes a vague promise to provide gifts. However, reports of gold brought miners who trespassed on Apache land and provoked violent confrontations. Soon the Apaches were at war, attacking and destroying American property. The Apaches were elusive enemies whom the Americans could only rarely bring to battle. Apache resistance to the American presence persisted for decades. The last Apache bands did not surrender until 1886, and some Apaches spent 27 years as prisoners of war.

Primary Source

ARTICLE 1.

Said nation or tribe of Indians through their authorized Chiefs aforesaid do hereby acknowledge and declare that they are lawfully and exclusively under the laws, jurisdiction, and government of the United States of America, and to its power and authority they do hereby submit.

ARTICLE 2.

From and after the signing of this Treaty hostilities between the contracting parties shall forever cease, and perpetual peace and amity shall forever exist between said Indians and the Government and people of the United States; the said nation, or tribe of Indians, hereby binding themselves most solemnly never to associate with or give countenance or aid to any tribe or band of Indians, or other persons or powers, who may be at any time at war or enmity with the government or people of said United States.

ARTICLE 3.

Said nation, or tribe of Indians, do hereby bind themselves for all future time to treat honestly and humanely all citizens of the United States, with whom they have intercourse, as well as all persons and powers, at peace with the said United States, who may be lawfully among them, or with whom they may have any lawful intercourse.

ARTICLE 4.

All said nation, or tribe of Indians, hereby bind themselves to refer all cases of aggression against themselves or their property and territory, to the government of the United States for adjustment, and to conform in all things to the laws, rules, and regulations of said government in regard to the Indian tribes.

ARTICLE 5.

Said nation, or tribe of Indians, do hereby bind themselves for all future time to desist and refrain from making any "incursions within the Territory of Mexico" of a hostile or predatory character; and that they will for the future refrain from taking and conveying into captivity any of the people or citizens of Mexico, or the animals or property of the people or government of Mexico; and that they will, as soon as possible after the signing of this treaty, surrender to their agent all captives now in their possession.

ARTICLE 6.

Should any citizen of the United States, or other person or persons subject to the laws of the United States, murder, rob, or otherwise maltreat any Apache Indian or Indians, he or they shall be arrested and tried, and upon conviction, shall be subject to all the penalties provided by law for the protection of the persons and property of the people of the said States.

ARTICLE 7.

The people of the United States of America shall have free and safe passage through the territory of the aforesaid Indians, under such rules and regulations as may be adopted by authority of the said States.

ARTICLE 8.

In order to preserve tranquility and to afford protection to all the people and interests of the contracting parties, the government of the United States of America will establish such military posts and agencies, and authorize such trading houses at such times and places as the said government may designate.

ARTICLE 9.

Relying confidently upon the justice and the liberality of the aforesaid government, and anxious to remove every possible cause that might disturb their peace and quiet, it is agreed by the aforesaid Apaches that the government of the United States shall at its earliest convenience designate, settle, and adjust their territorial boundaries, and pass and execute in their territory such laws as may be deemed conducive to the prosperity and happiness of said Indians.

ARTICLE 10.

For and in consideration of the faithful performance of all the stipulations herein contained, by the said Apache Indians, the government of the United States will grant to said Indians such donations, presents, and implements, and adopt such other liberal and humane measures as said government may deem meet and proper.

ARTICLE 11.

This Treaty shall be binding upon the contracting parties from and after the signing of the same, subject only to such modifications and amendments as may be adopted by the government of the United States; and, finally, this treaty is to receive a liberal construction, at all times and in all places, to the end that the said Apache Indians shall not be held responsible for the conduct of others, and that the government of the United States shall so legislate and act as to secure the permanent prosperity and happiness of said Indians.

In faith whereof we the undersigned have signed this Treaty, and affixed thereunto our seals, at the City of Santa Fe, this the first day of July in the year of our Lord one thousand eight hundred and fifty-two.

E. V. Summer,
Bvt. Col. U.S.A. commanding Ninth Department In charge of Executive Office of New Mexico.

John Greiner,
Act. Supt. Indian Affairs, New Mexico.

Capitan Vuelta, his x mark
Cuentas Azules, his x mark
Blancito, his x mark
Negrito, his x mark
Capitan Simon, his x mark
Mangus Colorado, his x mark

Witnesses:
    F. A. Cunningham,
    Paymaster, U.S.A.
    J. C. McFerran, 1st Lt. 3d Inf. Act. Ast. Adj. Gen.
    Caleb Sherman.
    Fred. Saynton.
    Chas. McDougall.
    Surgeon, U.S.A.
    S. M. Baird.

Witness to the signing of Mangus Colorado:
    John Pope,
    Bvt. Capt. T. E.

Source: "Treaty with the Apaches," in U.S. Statutes at Large 10 (1852): 979.

113. Gadsden Purchase Treaty, December 30, 1853

Introduction

Signed in 1853 by representatives from the United States and Mexico, the Gadsden Purchase Treaty transferred ownership of a small strip of land covering about 30,000 square miles in the Southwest (part of present-day New Mexico and Arizona) from Mexico to the United States for the sum of $10 million. Mexico desperately needed money, and the United States wanted the land for the southern route of the transcontinental railroad as proposed by James Gadsden, a South Carolinian and U.S. minister to Mexico. The purchase agreement also dealt with lingering tensions from the Mexican-American War (1846–1848). As part of the war-ending Treaty of Guadelupe Hidalgo in 1848, the United States had promised to prevent Indian raids into Mexico but had failed to do so. Mexico wanted the United States to honor this clause but agreed to nullify it as part of the Gadsden Purchase. The purchase marked the final acquisition in the continental expansion of the United States and also served as one more inflammatory issue in the ongoing sectional controversy, as northerners objected to the possibility of the transcontinental railroad being constructed on a southern route.

Primary Source

A PROCLAMATION.

WHEREAS a treaty between the United States of America and the Mexican Republic was concluded and signed at the City of Mexico on the thirtieth day of December, one thousand eight hundred and fifty-three; which treaty, as amended by the Senate of the United States, and being in the English and Spanish languages, is word for word as follows:

IN THE NAME OF ALMIGHTY GOD:

The Republic of Mexico and the United States of America desiring to remove every cause of disagreement which might interfere in any manner with the better friendship and intercourse between the two countries, and especially in respect to the true limits which should be established, when, notwithstanding what was covenanted in the treaty of Guadalupe Hidalgo in the year 1848, opposite interpretations have been urged, which might give occasion to questions of serious moment: to avoid these, and to strengthen and more firmly maintain the peace which happily prevails between the two republics, the President of the United States has, for this purpose, appointed James Gadsden, Envoy Extraordinary and Minister Plenipotentiary of the same, near the Mexican government, and the President of Mexico has appointed as Plenipotentiary "ad hoc" his excellency Don Manuel Diez de Bonilla, cavalier grand cross of the national and distinguished order of Guadalupe, and Secretary of State, and of the office of Foreign Relations, and Don Jose Salazar Ylarregui and General Mariano Monterde as scientific commissioners, invested with full powers for this negotiation, who, having communicated their respective full powers, and finding them in due and proper form, have agreed upon the articles following:

ARTICLE I.

The Mexican Republic agrees to designate the following as her true limits with the United States for the future: retaining the same dividing line between the two Californias as already defined and established, according to the 5th article of the treaty of Guadalupe Hidalgo, the limits between the two republics shall be as follows: Beginning in the Gulf of Mexico, three leagues from land, opposite the mouth of the Rio Grande, as provided in the 5th article of the treaty of Guadalupe Hidalgo; thence, as defined in the said article, up the middle of that river to the point where the parallel of 31° 47' north latitude crosses the same; thence due west one hundred miles; thence south to the parallel of 31° 20' north latitude; thence along the said parallel of 31° 20' to the 111th meridian of longitude west of Greenwich; thence in a straight line to a point on the Colorado River twenty English miles below the junction of the Gila and Colorado rivers; thence up the middle of the said river Colorado until it intersects the present line between the United States and Mexico.

For the performance of this portion of the treaty, each of the two governments shall nominate one commissioner, to the end that, by common consent the two thus nominated, having met in the city of Paso del Norte, three months after the exchange of the ratifications of this treaty, may proceed to survey and mark out upon the land the dividing line stipulated by this article, where it shall not have already been surveyed and established by the mixed commission, according to the treaty of Guadalupe, keeping a journal and making proper plans of their operations. For this purpose, if they should judge it necessary, the contracting parties shall be at liberty each to unite to its respective commissioner, scientific or other assistants, such as astronomers and surveyors, whose concurrence shall not be considered necessary for the settlement of a true line of division between the two Republics; that line shall be alone established upon which the commissioners may fix, their consent in this particular being considered decisive and an integral part of this treaty, without necessity of ulterior ratification or approval, and without room for interpretation of any kind by either of the parties contracting.

The dividing line thus established shall, in all time, be faithfully respected by the two governments, without any variation therein, unless of the express and free consent of the two, given in conformity to the principles of the law of nations, and in accordance with the constitution of each country respectively.

In consequence, the stipulation in the 5th article of the treaty of Guadalupe upon the boundary line therein described is no longer of any force, wherein it may conflict with that here established, the said line being considered annulled and abolished wherever it may not coincide with the present, and in the same manner remaining in full force where in accordance with the same.

ARTICLE II.

The government of Mexico hereby releases the United States from all liability on account of the obligations contained in the eleventh article of the treaty of Guadalupe Hidalgo; and the said article and the thirty-third article of the treaty of amity, commerce, and navigation between the United States of America and the United Mexican States concluded at Mexico, on the fifth day of April, 1831, are hereby abrogated.

ARTICLE III.

In consideration of the foregoing stipulations, the Government of the United States agrees to pay to the government of Mexico, in the city of New York, the sum of ten millions of dollars, of which seven millions shall be paid immediately upon the exchange of the ratifications of this treaty, and the remaining three millions as soon as the boundary line shall be surveyed, marked, and established.

ARTICLE IV.

The provisions of the 6th and 7th articles of the treaty of Guadalupe Hidalgo having been rendered nugatory, for the most part, by the cession of territory granted in the first article of this treaty, the said articles are hereby abrogated and annulled, and the provisions as herein expressed substituted therefor. The vessels, and citizens of the United States shall, in all time, have free and uninterrupted passage through the Gulf of California, to and from their possessions situated north of the boundary line of the two countries. It being understood that this passage is to be by navigating the Gulf of California and the river Colorado, and not by land, without the express consent of the Mexican government; and precisely the same provisions, stipulations, and restrictions, in all respects, are hereby agreed upon and adopted, and shall be scrupulously observed and enforced by the two contracting governments in reference to the Rio Colorado, so far and for such distance as the middle of that river is made their common boundary line by the first article of this treaty.

The several provisions, stipulations, and restrictions contained in the 7th article of the treaty of Guadalupe Hidalgo shall remain in force only so far as regards the Rio Bravo del Forte, below the initial of the said boundary provided in the first article of this treaty; that is to say, below the intersection of the 31° 47' 30" parallel of latitude, with the boundary line established by the late treaty dividing said river from its mouth upwards, according to the fifth article of the treaty of Guadalupe.

ARTICLE V.

All the provisions of the eighth and ninth, sixteenth and seventeenth articles of the treaty of Guadalupe Hidalgo, shall apply to the territory ceded by the Mexican Republic in the first article of the present treaty, and to all the rights of persons and property, both civil and ecclesiastical, within the same, as fully and as effectually as if the said articles were herein again recited and set forth.

ARTICLE VI.

No grants of land within the territory ceded by the first article of this treaty bearing date subsequent to the day—twenty-fifth of September—when the minister and subscriber to this treaty on the part of the United States, proposed to the Government of Mexico to terminate the question of boundary, will be considered valid or be recognized by the United States, or will any grants made previously be respected or be considered as obligatory which have not been located and duly recorded in the archives of Mexico.

ARTICLE VII.

Should there at any future period (which God forbid) occur any disagreement between the two nations which might lead to a rupture of their relations and reciprocal peace, they bind themselves in like manner to procure by every possible method the adjustment of every difference; and should they still in this manner not succeed, never will they proceed to a declaration of war, without having previously paid attention to what has been set forth in article twenty-one of the treaty of Guadalupe for similar cases; which article, as well as the twenty-second is here reaffirmed.

ARTICLE VIII.

The Mexican Government having on the 5th of February, 1853, authorized the early construction of a plank and railroad across the Isthmus of Tehuantepec, and, to secure the stable benefits of said transit way to the persons and merchandise of the citizens of Mexico and the United States, it is stipulated that neither government will interpose any obstacle to the transit of persons and merchandise of both nations; and at no time shall higher charges be made on the transit of persons and property of citizens of the United States, than may be made on the persons and property of other foreign nations, nor shall any interest in said transit way, nor in the proceeds thereof, be transferred to any foreign government.

The United States, by its agents, shall have the right to transport across the isthmus, in closed bags, the mails of the United States not intended for distribution along the line of communication; also the effects of the United States government and its citizens, which may be intended for transit, and not for distribution on the isthmus, free of custom-house or other charges by the Mexican government. Neither passports nor letters of security will be required of persons crossing the isthmus and not remaining in the country.

When the construction of the railroad shall be completed, the Mexican government agrees to open a port of entry in addition to the port of Vera Cruz, at or near the terminus of said road on the Gulf of Mexico.

The two governments will enter into arrangements for the prompt transit of troops and munitions of the United States, which that government may have occasion to send from one part of its territory to another, lying on opposite sides of the continent.

The Mexican government having agreed to protect with its whole power the prosecution, preservation, and security of the work, the United States may extend its protection as it shall judge wise to it when it may feel sanctioned and warranted by the public or international law.

ARTICLE IX.

This treaty shall be ratified, and the respective ratifications shall be exchanged at the city of Washington within the exact period of six months from the date of its signature, or sooner, if possible.

In testimony whereof, we, the plenipotentiaries of the contracting parties, have hereunto affixed our hands and seals at Mexico, the thirtieth (30th) day of December, in the year of our Lord one thousand eight hundred and fifty-three, in the thirty-third year of the independence of the Mexican republic, and the seventy-eighth of that of the United States.

JAMES GADSDEN,
MANUEL DIEZ DE BONILLA
JOSE SALAZAR YLARBEGUI
J. MARIANO MONTERDE,

And whereas the said treaty, as amended, has been duly ratified on both parts, and the respective ratifications of the same have this day been exchanged at Washington, by WILLIAM L. MARCY, Secretary of State of the United States, and SENOR GENERAL DON JUAN N. ALMONTE, Envoy Extraordinary and Minister Plenipotentiary of the Mexican Republic, on the part of their respective Governments:

Now, therefore, be it known that I, FRANKLIN PIERCE, President of the United States of America, have caused the said treaty to be made public, to the end that the same, and every clause and article thereof, may be observed and fulfilled with good faith by the United States and the citizens thereof

In witness whereof I have hereunto set my hand and caused the seal of the United States to be affixed.

Done at the city of Washington, this thirtieth day of June, in the year of our Lord one thousand eight hundred and fifty-four, and of the Independence of the United States the seventy-eighth.

BY THE PRESIDENT:
FRANKLIN PIERCE,

W. L. MARCY, Secretary of State.

Source: "Treaty with Mexico," in U.S. Statutes at Large 10 (1853): 1031.

114. Chief Seattle, Speech to the Governor, 1854

Introduction

Beginning in 1843, hundreds of American immigrants surged into what was called Oregon Territory, in the Pacific Northwest. By 1846, Great Britain and the United States had agreed on a border between American and Canadian territory, unleashing an annual influx of thousands of Americans. Oregon Territory was officially established in 1848, and Washington became a separate territory in 1853. The Indians who lived in the northwest territories numbered about 42,000 and belonged to several dozen tribes. Many attacked the growing population of American settlers, and a state of nearly continuous warfare existed for more than a decade. Seattle, the leader of Native Americans in the Puget Sound region of Washington, remained loyal to the Americans during the years of conflict, and the Americans named their new town after him in 1853. Chief Seattle delivered this speech in 1854 at a reception for Washington's territorial governor. The elderly chief spoke no English, but a well-known pioneer and Indian guide named Dr. Henry A. Smith translated Seattle's words for the gathering. In 1887 Smith published a version of the speech in a local newspaper. Seattle speaks of the ultimate fate of his people, saying that they are destined to give way to the white man and disappear. He signed a treaty ceding land and accepting a reservation in 1855. By 1858, the rest of the Indians of the Northwest had been confined to reservations.

Primary Source

Yonder sky has wept tears of compassion on our fathers for centuries untold, and which, to us, looks eternal, may change. To-day it is fair, to-morrow it may be overcast with clouds. My words are like the stars that never set. What Seattle says the great chief, Washington, [the Indians in early times thought that Washington was still alive. They knew the name to be that of a president, and when they heard of the president at Washington they mistook the name of the city for the name of the reigning chief. They thought, also, that King George was still England's monarch, because the Hudson bay traders called themselves "King George men." This innocent deception the company was shrewd enough not to explain away for the Indians had more respect for them than they would have had, had they known England was ruled by a woman. Some of us have learned better.] can rely upon, with as much certainty as our pale-face brothers can rely upon the return of the seasons. The son of the white chief says his father sends us greetings of friendship and good-will. This is kind, for we know he has little need of our friendship in return, because his people are many. They are like the grass that covers the prairies, while my people are few, and resemble the scattering trees of a storm-swept plain.

The great, and I presume also good, white chief sends us word that he wants to buy our lands but is willing to allow us to reserve enough to live on comfortably. This indeed appears generous, for the red man no longer has rights that he need respect, and the offer may be wise, also, for we are no longer in need of a great country. There was a time when our people covered the whole land as the waves of a windruffled sea cover its shell-paved floor. But that time has long since passed away with the greatness of tribes almost forgotten. I will not mourn over our untimely decay, nor reproach my pale-face brothers with hastening it, for we, too, may have been somewhat to blame.

When our young men grow angry at some real or imaginary wrong and disfigure their faces with black paint, their hearts, also are disfigured and turn black, and then their cruelty is relentless and knows no bounds, and our old men are not able to restrain them.

But let us hope that hostilities between the red man and his pale face brothers may never return. We would have everything to lose and nothing to gain.

True it is that revenge, with our young braves, is considered gain, even at the cost of their own lives, but old men who stay at home in times of war, and old women who have sons to lose, know better.

Our great father Washington, for I presume he is now our father as well as yours, since George has moved his boundaries to the north; our great and good father, I say, sends us word by his son, who, no doubt, is a great chief among his people, that if we do as he desires, he will protect us. His brave armies will be to us a bristling wall of strength, and his great ships of war will fill our harbors so that our ancient enemies far to the northward, the Simsiams and Hydas, will no longer frighten our women and old men. Then he will be our father and we will be his children. But can this ever be? Your God loves your people and hates mine; he folds his strong arms lovingly around the white man and leads him as a father leads his infant son, but he has forsaken his red children; he makes your people wax strong every day, and soon they will fill the land; while our people are ebbing away like a fast-receding tide, that will never flow again. The white man's God cannot love his red children or he would protect them. They seem to be orphans and can look nowhere for help. How then can we become brothers? How can your father become our father and bring us prosperity and awaken in us dreams of returning greatness?

Your God seems to us to be partial. He came to the white man. We never saw Him; never even heard His voice; He gave the white man laws but He had no word for His red children whose teeming millions filled this vast continent as the stars fill the firmament. No, we are two distinct races and must ever remain so. There is little in common between us. The ashes of our ancestors are sacred and their final resting place is hallowed ground, while you wander away from the tombs of your fathers seemingly without regret.

Your religion was written on tables of stone by the iron finger of an angry God, lest you might forget it. The red man could never remember nor comprehend it.

Our religion is the traditions of our ancestors, the dreams of our old men, given them by the great Spirit, and the visions of our sachems, and is written in the hearts of our people.

Your dead cease to love you and the homes of their nativity as soon as they pass the portals of the tomb. They wander far off beyond the stars, are soon forgotten and never return. Our dead never forget the beautiful world that gave them being. They still love its winding rivers, its great mountains and its sequestered vales, and they ever yearn in tenderest affection over the lonely hearted living and often return to visit and comfort them.

Day and night cannot dwell together. The red man has ever fled the approach of the white man, as the changing mists on the mountain side flee before the blazing morning sun.

However, your proposition seems a just one, and I think my folks will accept it and will retire to the reservation you offer them, and we will dwell apart and in peace, for the words of the great white chief seem to be the voice of nature speaking to my people out of the thick darkness that is fast gathering around them like a dense fog floating inward from a midnight sea.

It matters but little where we pass the remainder of our days. They are not many. The Indian's night promises to be dark. No bright star hovers about the horizon. Sad-voiced winds moan in the distance. Some grim Nemesis of our race is on the red man's trail, and wherever he goes he will still hear the sure approaching footsteps of the fell destroyer and prepare to meet his doom, as does the wounded doe that hears the approaching footsteps of the hunter. A few more moons, a few more winters and not one of all the mighty hosts that once filled this broad land or that now roam in fragmentary bands through these vast solitudes will remain to weep over the tombs of a people once as powerful and as hopeful as your own.

But why should we repine? Why should I murmur at the fate of my people? Tribes are made up of individuals and are no better than they. Men come and go like the waves of the sea. A tear, a tamanamus, a dirge, and they are gone from our longing eyes forever. Even the white man, whose God walked and talked with him, as friend to friend, is not exempt from the common destiny. We may be brothers after all. We shall see.

We will ponder your proposition, and when we have decided we will tell you. But should we accept it, I here and now make this the first condition: That we will not be denied the privilege, without molestation, of visiting at will the graves of our ancestors and friends. Every part of this country is sacred to my people. Every hillside, every valley, every plain and grove has been hallowed by some fond memory or some sad experience of my tribe. Even the rocks that seem to lie dumb as they swelter in the sun along the silent seashore in solemn grandeur thrill with memories of past events connected with the fate of my people, and the very dust under your feet responds more lovingly to our footsteps than to yours, because it is the ashes of our ancestors, and our bare feet are conscious of the sympathetic touch, for the soil is rich with the life of our kindred.

The sable braves, and fond mothers, and glad-hearted maidens, and the little children who lived and rejoiced here, and whose very names are now forgotten, still love these solitudes, and their deep fastnesses at eventide grow shadowy with the presence of dusky spirits. And when the last red man shall have perished from the earth and his memory among white men shall have become a myth, these shores shall swarm with the invisible dead of my tribe, and when your children's children shall think themselves alone in the field, the store, the shop, upon the highway or in the silence of the woods they will not be alone. In all the earth there is no place dedicated to solitude. At night, when the streets of your cities and villages shall be silent, and you think them deserted, they will throng with the returning hosts that once filled and still love this beautiful land. The white man will never be alone. Let him be just and deal kindly with my people, for the dead are not altogether powerless.

Source: Frederic James Grant, ed., *History of Seattle, Washington* (New York: American Publishing and Engraving Co., 1891), 434–436.

115. George Crook, Service in the Northwest, 1854–1857

Introduction

Beginning in 1843, hundreds of American immigrants surged into what was called Oregon Territory, in the Pacific Northwest. By 1846, Great Britain and the United States had agreed on a border between American and Canadian territory, unleashing an annual influx of thousands of Americans. Oregon Territory was officially established in 1848. The Indians who lived in the northwest territories numbered some 42,000 and belonged to several dozen tribes. Many resisted the growing population of American settlers, who took what land they wanted regardless of its legal status. A state of nearly continuous warfare existed for most of a decade. The Indians of southern Oregon and northern California were also subject to unprovoked attacks by miners seeking gold. Once U.S. Army troops arrived, they were sometimes even called upon to defend Indians from American violence. In his autobiography (published long after his death), George Crook (1828–1890), writing of his service in the Pacific Northwest between 1854 and 1857, described how his sympathies were often with the Indians. However, by the time of the 1857 engagement recounted here, Crook

was boasting of his "first Indian," referring to his first kill. By 1858, the Indians of the Northwest had been confined to reservations. Crook had a long military career, becoming a Union general in the American Civil War (1861–1865) and earning a reputation as a legendary Indian fighter in the postwar decades.

Primary Source

[. . .]

Scattered over the country were a few Shasta Indians, generally well disposed, but more frequently forced to take the war path or sink all self respect, by the outrages of the whites perpetrated upon them. The country was over-run by people from all nations in search of the mighty dollar. Greed was almost unrestrained, and from the nature of our government there was little or no law that these people were bound to respect. It was of no unfrequent occurrence for an Indian to be shot down in cold blood, or a squaw to be raped by some brute. Such a thing as a white man being punished for outraging an Indian was unheard of. It was the fable of the wolf and lamb every time. The consequence was that there was scarcely ever a time that there was not one or more wars with the Indians somewhere on the Pacific Coast. There were a good many Indians about Fort Jones and vicinity from whom I soon learned their grievances. It is hard to believe now the wrongs these Indians had to suffer in those days. I doubt now if there is a single one left to tell their tale. The trouble with the army was that the Indians would confide in us as friends, and we had to witness this unjust treatment of them without the power to help them. Then when they were pushed beyond endurance and would go on the war path we had to fight when our sympathies were with the Indians.

[. . .]

He reported upon his return to Fort Jones that there were no Indians in the country, etc. etc. I fully realized the situation, and knew that there were plenty of Indians, and that my only show was to find where the Indians were, without their knowledge, and to attack them by surprise. I furthermore was satisfied that they watched our movements all the time, and kept out of our way. I also reasoned that seeing Capt. Judah going out of the country with the most of the troops, they would be off their guard. I had by this time learned enough about Indian craft to have confidence in my being able to hold my own with them, so, shortly after Judah left, I took two soldiers and went off on a scout to see if I couldn't locate some of their camps. I went in a southeasterly direction from the ferry, and on the second day I came on to a small rancheria. Some of the Indians wanted to talk with me, but I would not let them approach me. Telling them I was going to Yreka, of which they seemed to know the name, I was in hopes of throwing them off their guard, and I went back to camp and got all my men. I left my camp after dark so we would not be seen. I reached the vicinity of the rancheria next day sometime, and lay concealed all that day.

Sometime during the night we left camp, intending to surround the Indians just at daylight next morning. The guide, Dick Pugh, and I went ahead to locate the rancheria, while the sergeant was to follow with the company. By some mistake we became separated, so all that night was spent in hunting each other. The next morning we found each other in the same camp we had left the night previous. So the next night we again moved close to the rancheria, and surrounded it by daylight next morning, but all were gone. Just when they had left I could not tell, as a heavy rainstorm had obliterated all sign. I then sent the company with the guide under a low range of bluffs, while I rode out a little to the left to examine a dim trail I had seen on my recent scout. I had not proceeded far before I saw a squaw track which had just been made. It had doubled on its track, and was on a run, evidently having either seen me or the command. I followed it in hopes of capturing her to get information as to the whereabouts of her people. I soon saw several other tracks all running in the same direction, and also saw a lot of plunder abandoned by them. Directly saw some buck tracks. By this time I could follow them at a gallop. The chase had now become so exciting that I thought but little of the danger. Soon I saw the Indians running ahead of me. I rode up to a buck, dismounted, and wounded him, and remounted, and killed him with my pistol. Just then the Indians rose up all about me, and came towards me with frightful yells, letting fly a shower of arrows at me. I had an old muzzle-loading rifle which was now empty, and one barrel of my pistol had snapped. I thought discretion the better part of valor, so I put spurs to my horse, and ran out of the only opening left, about 100 yards, and a big Indian, seemed to me about ten feet high, was running his best to close this up. He had his hair tucked back of his ears, which gave him a particularly ferocious look. His arrows flew all around me with such a velocity that they did not appear over a couple of inches long. I must have run a couple of miles before I found the command. They being under the bluff had heard nothing. We at once returned to where I had left the Indians, but they had all fled except one old squaw who was lying beside the dead buck I had killed. This was my first Indian.

Source: Martin F. Schmitt, ed., *General George Crook: His Autobiography* (Norman: University of Oklahoma Press, 1946), 15–16, 39.

116. Jefferson Davis, Annual Report of the Secretary of War on the Proposed Transcontinental Railroad, December 3, 1855 [Excerpt]

Introduction

Jefferson Davis (1808–1889), the future president of the Confederate States of America, served as the U.S. secretary of war from 1853 to 1857. He had fought in the Mexican-American War (1846–1848), which had added a vast territory to the United States. While secretary of war, Davis worked to realize his vision of a transcontinental railroad that could quickly move troops to defend the West Coast from foreign attack. His War Department sent out teams to survey several possible routes. In this excerpt from his annual report of 1855, Davis refers to the railroad survey reports and adds his observations about the availability of water for agriculture along the proposed routes as they cross the arid plains. Although the water studies were first undertaken to support railroad construction, Davis's vision reached beyond matters of war. He cites the possibility of employing irrigation and sinking artesian wells in order to "reclaim" land that he calls "barren" and "waste" and using the arid lands for agriculture. The transcontinental railroad, completed in 1869, carried settlers and agriculture from coast to coast. Though furiously resisted by the Indians, the American conquest of the Plains and its water resources was inevitable. It is known today that agriculture on the Plains, supported by irrigation and artesian wells, is drawing down and depleting the underground aquifers, forcing farmers to drill deeper and deeper to obtain water.

Primary Source

The reports of the officers employed under the appropriations made for explorations and surveys to ascertain the most practicable and economical route for a railroad from the Mississippi river to the Pacific ocean were submitted to Congress on the 27th of February last, with a report from this department, giving a general sketch of the country over which they extended, a recapitulation of their results, and a comparison of their distinguishing characteristics; from which it was concluded that of the routes examined, the most practicable and economical was that of the thirty-second parallel. A report is herewith submitted from the officer in this department charged with the revision of the work of the several parties, and I refer to it for additional information derived from materials collected, on a further examination of them by himself, and the several officers who made the particular surveys, as well as for the results of explorations carried on during the past year. When the report was made, in February last, many of the maps, drawings, and scientific papers, intended to form part of the report, and which could only be prepared after an elaborate examination of the materials collected, had not been completed for want of time, and it became necessary to substitute hastily prepared drawings and preliminary reports. This was particularly the case with regard to the work on the route of the thirty-fifth parallel. A minute examination of the material collected in that survey has resulted in showing the route more practicable than it was at first represented to be, and in reducing to nearly one-half the original estimates of the officer in charge of the survey, which indeed seemed, when they were submitted, to be extravagant, and were noted in the report from this department as probably excessive. Another feature of interest developed in the course of the further examination of the work on the route of the thirty-second parallel is, that the Colorado desert, which is traversed by the route for a distance of 133 miles, and which, in the report referred to, was noted as consisting of a soil that needed only water to render it highly productive, is, in fact, the delta of the Colorado river, and, according to barometric levels, is so much lower than that stream as to be easily irrigated from it. Thus there is every reason to believe 4,500 square miles of soil of great fertility, of which nearly one-half is in our territory, may be brought into cultivation in one unbroken tract along the route. Under the appropriation made at the last session for the continuation of these surveys and other purposes, three parties have been in the field during the past season. One of these was directed to make examinations connected with the routes of the 32d and 35th parallels. This survey has greatly improved the aspect of the former route by changing the line for nearly half the distance between the Rio Grande and the Pimas villages on the Gila river from barren ground to cultivable valleys, and entirely avoiding a *Jornada* of eighty miles, which occurs in that section; also by the discovery of an eminently practicable route through cultivable country from the plains of Los Angeles, along the coast and through the Salinas valley, to San Francisco. The connection originally proposed between these points was by way of the valley of San Joaquin and the Great Basin. The attention of this party was also directed to an examination into the practicability of procuring water along certain parts of the route where it is now deficient. The report shows that it may be obtained by common wells at distances of about twenty miles. From the result of this exploration, moreover, it appears practicable to obtain, at a small expense, a good wagon road, supplied with water by common wells, from the Rio Grande down the San Pedro and Gila and across the Colorado desert. Such a road would be of great advantage in military operations, would facilitate the transportation of the mail across that country, and relieve emigrants pursuing that route from much of the difficulty and suffering which they now encounter. A second party was charged with the duty of testing the practicability of procuring water by artesian wells on the Llano Estacado, an arid plain which has been heretofore described as a desert. The experiment has so far demonstrated its practicability as to leave little doubt of its final success; it will be continued, however, until the problem shall have been fully solved. The examinations into the feasibility of causing subterranean streams to flow upon the surface from artesian wells, though undertaken in connection with the practicability of a railroad, if they should prove entirely successful, will have a value beyond their connection with that object in the reclamation of a region which is now a waste, and its adaptation to the pastoral, and, perhaps, the agricultural uses of man.

Source: Dunbar Rowland, ed., *Jefferson Davis, Constitutionalist: His Letters, Papers, and Speeches,* Vol. 2 (Jackson: Mississippi Department of Archives and History, 1923), 565–566.

117. Abner Doubleday, Service in Florida during the Third Seminole War, 1855–1858 [Excerpt]

Introduction

Abner Doubleday (1819–1893) is best remembered for his purported invention of baseball. (Historians fiercely disagree on whether or not the game originated with Doubleday, but all original documentation relating to his role in the game was consumed in a fire.) An 1842 West Point graduate, Doubleday entered the U.S. Army as an artillery officer. He served with Zachary Taylor in Mexico and in 1854 went to Texas to garrison a fort on the Rio Grande. The border garrisons were intended to intercept the attacks of hostile Indians, but the Indians easily evaded them. Similarly, two years later in Florida during the Third Seminole War (1855–1858), the remaining Seminoles eluded the army's attempts to capture and remove them. Doubleday's account of his Florida service candidly describes the difficulties that the soldiers encountered while trying to locate the Seminoles. The account is excerpted from the first of his three volumes of reminiscences about his army service. The outbreak of the American Civil War (1861–1865) found Doubleday on duty at Fort Sumter, where he fired the first Union shot of the war. Among his postwar assignments was command of a black infantry regiment in Texas. Doubleday retired from active duty in 1873 after more than 30 years of service.

Primary Source

One morning soon after our arrival just before breakfast I was standing near the stables when Col Dimick made his appearance in a soldiers overcoat and said to me, "Do you ride?" I replied in the affirmative and he said, "Get a horse from the Qtr Ms dept and let us ride out a little ways." I complied with his request and we rode out. It gave me a taste of his quality as an Indian campaigner. We scoured the country for a long distance were gone all day and did not return until night. I was very much fatigued and glad to break my long fast. The Indians might easily have cut us off for we took no precautions. We soon found that Dimick was addicted to these long excursions and whenever we saw him put on that overcoat we knew what we had to expect.

I am afraid if the statistics of the money spent in Florida were made out it could easily be shown that it cost more than $100,000 to capture or kill one Indian. I believe it would have been much cheaper to let the matter out by contract. In saying this I do not mean to disparage the skill or gallantry of the officers of the army for they were actuated by a strong sense of duty and did all in their power but the material furnished us was not suitable for the business. The German and Irish emigrants who enlisted at this time composed the bulk of our forces and were almost necessarily ignorant of anything like woodcraft. How could a soldier loaded down with his musket and cartridge box his canteen and haversack succeed in catching wholly unencumbered Indians who knew every path and stream and culvert and who were not encumbered with any commissariat. They managed to find food enough where ever they were. The arrow root of which covered the country the inner bark of certain trees wild plums and the cabbage palmetto were always available. The waters swarmed with fish and the woods with game.

In order to send out scouting parties intelligently Brannan and myself were directed to make a road north to New River some 30 miles distant and I set myself to making a map of the surrounding country for I was fond of that kind of business and always liked to have all the localities around me on paper. We did not see or hear anything of the Seminoles for some time and as their trail was frequently found fresh at a crossing about 3 miles up the river I was sent there to try and open communication with them. I put up a pole bent it towards the sun at 3 PM. made 7 notches in it and leaving some tobacco and other presents then called wampum. I then put up a white flag and returned. All this meant that in a week from that day I would like to meet them then under a white flag. They looked at the arrangement and took the presents but did not meet us.

They knew they could outrun us and easily escape pursuit and they therefore were not at all afraid of us. One day one of them actually came to the edge of a thicket and was seen by some camp woman looking in at evening parade. The woman screamed the occurrence was reported the long roll was beaten and I put out with my co after that Indian. I deployed my men in open order and went into a hammock where the Indian had taken refuge. I soon found myself in difficulty. Some of the men went forward in open spaces and made rapid progress while others were detained by obstacles while several including myself were tied up in the wild vines and had great difficulty in moving at all. The Indians under such circumstances lay down and worm themselves down like snakes through the thickets for they have no impediments: haversacks or canteens or cartridge boxes to bother them. I saw that my co was rapidly becoming dispersed and at last gave up the attempt in despair to catch this particular Indian. The bugles were blown a long time before I could reassemble the men.

Col Dimick now organized and kept up a set of scouting expeditions. He usually left one co to guard the post and went out with the other. He would keep along the road Brannan and myself had cut and we would examine the country east of the Everglades. We would ramp all day through the woods wading in the edge of the Everglades and return at night worn out with fatigue. Then we would cut a few palmetto leaves as a bed and lie down in our blankets heedless of snakes which were abundant or alligators which came around at night. We found plenty of these animals but no Indians.

An expedition was formed to go up to Lake Okeechobee and look there for them. On the way there I saw a long morass which runs parallel to the coast and is about 200 yards wide. On the other side there was a beautiful rolling country and as it had not been inspected I thought I would try and make my way over there. It proved an awful undertaking. The mud was very soft and deep and had it not been for the trees which were frequent we would not have got across it. Panting breathlessly and worn out we held on to the branches of these trees to prevent ourselves from going under. I was amused at the wit of 2 Irish soldiers who were floundering through the deepest part. One of them, covered with mud, said, "Denis, I think I'll stop here and open shop." "And what will you sell" said Denis. "*Artificial flowers!*" When I got over I found a beautiful country with plenty of game but no sign of Indians and it was not at all agreeable to return but we succeeded in getting over at a narrower and less difficult place. On this expedition I was struck with the different degrees of memory of localities in the soldiers. I tested them with my pocket compass. Some would lose the way before they had gone 200 yards, others seemed to have an almost magical power of direction: they never varied in their course and if awakened in the darkest night would start off unerringly on the proper route. And this reminds me of an incident which occurred on this expedition. We were on our way back from the lake and had made several days journey. Although we saw no traces of Indians Dimick kept up the scouting parties so zealously that he put one of my Lieuts on a mule gave him ten men on other mules that were disabled and unable to march and directed him to make a scout but to return to the command at night. The Lieut said to me, one of his friends, this is all nonsense. It is merely to look well on the map of an exploration which is to be sent to Genl Harney. We scouted this country before and we know there are no Indians here. I am not going to kill myself and the men for nothing. Our march is north east. Very well I shall take my men out of sight of you all then take the north east course and follow you into camp and get in early. Night came but the mule party did not make its appearance. Ten o'clock came and still there were no signs of them. We made huge fires to attract their attention and Dimick began to grumble. If I send my young men out on scouts I want them to be reasonable about it. They are altogether too zealous to keep their men out so late as this. About 2 o'clock that night the mule party made its appearance. The Lieut had kept going all day and as evening came on he thought he would join us. He had no sense of locality whatever and relied entirely on his compass but there was a bugler with him who had the faculty very largely developed and who watched his proceedings with a sorrowful eye. At last the Lieut said I think I will go over to that rising ground; the bugler forgot the restraints of discipline and said "Oh don't Lieut!" "Don't" said the Lieut, "why not I think our men are over there." "Oh no lieut we have been going away from them all day. We have got back to Lake Okechobee again. If you go over there you will see the lake." "Why bless me how is this" said the Lieut. Great Heavens I have been going N.W. all day instead of N.E.

Genl Harney who commanded the Dept now organized a large expedition to cross Florida from Tampa Bay making a considerable circuit to join us at Fort Dallas. This force was under command of Capt Pemberton who had distinguished himself on Worth's staff in the Mexican War. He subsequently became the celebrated General who defended Vicksburg against Grant. A certain number of wagons were to be sent him to carry his provisions and tools but he would not wait for them and started without them. The consequence was that each soldier was loaded down with 10 days provisions. The weather was hot the marches fatiguing and the soldiers wasted or lost their provisions so that when five days had elapsed they still had a long distance to go and were out of food. They were obliged to eat one of the officer's horses and the tail of an alligator and they had a few palmetto cabbages. There was hardly any game in the vicinity at the time so that they were half starved and became very weak as they approached New River some 30 miles from Fort Dallas if I remember rightly. Brannan and myself had made a good road that far and had bridged all the streams but New River was wide and Pemberton's command had no way of crossing it. One officer, Lieut Lee a relative of Robert E. Lee swam over and finding a good road on the other side kept on until he reached Fort Dallas and told us the plight Pemberton was in. Provisions were at once sent out and the men were so eager that they ate the meat raw. Lee who was excessively hungry and who arrived at dawn of day went to the sutlers store and ate crackers and cheese there until breakfast was cooked. He ate a very hearty breakfast and he went back to the sutler's store and ate whatever he could find then until dinner. He then ate a hearty dinner and it was said went back again to the sutlers store and kept on eating until supper time. A dangerous experiment but it did not seem to injure him in the present instance. Before the expedition started our company was filled up with recruits from Governor's Island. To teach them to fire I put up a picture of an Indian on canvas leaned it against a tree and made them practice at it. They were mostly Irish and not used to firing and it was amusing to see their gratification when they hit it. I heard one of them say, "If that was old Billy Bowlegs himself its little he'd trouble the country after this." The tree against which proved to be an India rubber tree the first I had ever seen. We reached Okeechobee at last but saw no signs to indicate that our foemen were residing in that vicinity. The scenery was flat and uninteresting but the broad sheet of water was a pleasant sight after so much journey through pine forests. After this expedition Pemberton's forces returned to the east side of Florida and we settled down to our usual drills, parades, and scouting. Dimick who was afraid of nothing else had a great antipathy to snakes. The sight of one would make him sick and they are very abundant in Florida. It was not at all an uncommon circumstance to see them projecting their heads from holes under the roofs of the houses. We made preparations one day to go on a scout and as the youngsters thought they would have a better time and more freedom without the comd. officer than with him they got up a conspiracy to scare him with snake stories. They asked me what I was going to do with that reata (long rope made of horse hair which I had brought from Texas). I answered that I put it around my sleeping place at night to keep the snakes off for they were never known to crawl over this kind of rope probably mistaking for a snake of another kind. My answer opened the way and they told some terrible snake stories apropos of the place we were going to. Dimick shuddered but did not give up the expedition. After all they were not so far wrong for while he was out he got caught in a narrow path with a huge rattlesnake on each side of him and escaped by giving some prodigious leaps. We had no success in the Indian question whatever. How could we have. They kept out of our way and let us wander around. There were only about 150 warriors in the whole vast peninsula and it was impossible to surprise them with the material we had principally as I stated German or Irish emigrants who finding themselves penniless in our large cities and had enlisted to get bread. These men were wholly ignorant of wood craft and consequently were no match for the savages. The sensible thing to do would have been to organize some bands of Western Indians discipline and feed them well and they would have soon routed the Seminoles out of their nests. However at last Dimick had a gleam of hope. He received information that Billy Bowlegs and his warriors about 120 men were congregated on a large island in the Everglades so he directed me to take about 60 men and attack him. We were furnished with a supply of boats for that purpose. The island we were to seek was said to be marked with a large tree which rose from the top of a hill in such a way as to be a land mark and overlook the whole country. The Everglades is a curious fresh water swamp. Streams, rivers, and lakes are every where interspersed with islands. For several days I searched these islands as we penetrated the center of this inland sea but we found no signs of an enemy. At last as we reached the central part I saw a large island which seemed to answer the description which had been given of the stronghold of the savages and prepared to attack it. There was a high place on it and a large tree there which overlooked the surrounding country. I waited at a small island for all my boats to come up so that I could organize a strong attack. Unfortunately I did not examine the small island where we were organizing for the attack, for I had examined all the others in vain and my attention was fixed on the large island. There was a dense thicket in this small island. Behind this thicket a parry of Seminoles were in ambush. We did not know it at the time but ascertained it when we came back there. As soon as all was ready we started for the main island. As we approached it we saw plenty of Indian sign. The officers drew out their revolvers and we jumped into the water waist deep struggled through the high grass and charged up the slope but the Indians had left a day or two previously. They had made quite a residence of the place but probably their scouts had notified them of our coming. In order to ascend the large tree in the center I made a carpenter belonging to my company cut some short sticks and nail each one into the trunk of the tree so that we could go up this impromptu ladder. Every nail driven in brought out a milk white fluid which proved to be India rubber. We ascended to the top and had a fine view of the Everglades but saw no enemy. We then went back to the little island I have mentioned and there found very recent signs of them. Part of a deer had been cooked there arrow root was lying about on the ground and a number of small stakes showed that the Indians had become civilized enough to use mosquito bars. We found bear and alligators very abundant in this vast swamp. As we lay down at night the latter would come grunting around our boats and one of the crews said that one of these large creatures made an attempt to enter. At night as we lay down the uproar around us was fearful. Birds of all kinds were making the night hideous with discordant sounds. The alligators were grunting and occasionally the prolonged wail of a panther would be heard. We returned without having captured any Indians.

Source: Joseph E. Chance, ed., *My Life in the Old Army: The Reminiscences of Abner Doubleday* (Fort Worth: Texas Christian University Press, 1998), 183–189.

118. Philip Sheridan, The Indian Attack and Reprisal in the Pacific Northwest, 1856 [Excerpts]

Introduction

Philip Sheridan (1831–1888), a future hero and Union general during the American Civil War (1861–1865), was a lieutenant at the time he served in the Pacific Northwest. American immigrants had been pouring into the region since 1843. Oregon Territory was officially established in 1848, and Washington became a separate territory in 1853. The Indians who lived in the northwest territories numbered some 42,000 and belonged to several dozen tribes, including the Yakima, Walla Walla, Cayuse, and Nez Perce tribes. Many tried to resist the growing population of American settlers, and a state of nearly continuous warfare went on until 1858, when most of the Indians of the Northwest were confined to reservations. In his memoirs, published just after his death, Sheridan recounted the March 26, 1856, incident known as the Cascades Massacre and its aftermath. Yakima warriors attacked and killed 14 settlers—men, women, and children—at the Cascades of the Columbia River between Vancouver and the Dalles and lay siege to their cabins and a blockhouse. Sheridan and some 40 cavalry rode to the relief of the surviving settlers who had taken shelter in the blockhouse. When reinforcements arrived bringing a mountain howitzer, the Yakimas fled, leaving behind their allies, a band of Cascade Indians. Sheridan arrested 13 of the men. They were quickly tried by a military commission, and 9 of them were hanged.

Primary Source

The regiment moved from Fort Vancouver by boat, March 25, 1856, and landed at the small town called the Dalles, below the mouth of the Des Chutes River at the eastern base of the Cascade Range, and just above where the Columbia River enters those mountains. This rendezvous was to be the immediate point of departure, and all the troops composing the expedition were concentrated there.

On the morning of March 26 the movement began, but the column had only reached Five Mile Creek when the Yakimas, joined by many young warriors, free lances from other tribes, made a sudden and unexpected attack at the Cascades of the Columbia, midway between Vancouver and the Dalles, killed several citizens, women and children, and took possession of the Portage by besieging the settlers in their cabins at the Upper Cascades, and those who sought shelter at the Middle Cascades in the old military block-house, which had been built some years before as a place of refuge under just such circumstances. These points held out, and were not captured, but the landing at the Lower Cascades fell completely into the hands of the savages. Straggling settlers from the Lower Cascades made their way down to Fort Vancouver, distant about thirty-six miles, which they reached that night; and communicated the condition of affairs. As the necessity for early relief to the settlers and the re-establishment of communication with the Dalles were apparent, all the force that could be spared was ordered out, and in consequence I immediately received directions to go with my detachment of dragoons, numbering about forty effective men, to the relief of the middle blockhouse, which really meant to retake the Cascades.

[…]

When the Indians attacked the people at the Cascades on the 26th, word was sent to Colonel Wright, who had already got out from the Dalles a few miles on his expedition to the Spokane country. He immediately turned his column back, and soon after I had landed and communicated with the beleaguered block-house the advance of his command arrived under Lieutenant-Colonel Edward J. Steptoe. I reported to Steptoe, and related what had occurred during the past thirty-six hours, gave him a description of the festivities that were going on at the lower Cascades, and also communicated the intelligence that the Yakimas had been joined by the Cascade Indians when the place was first attacked. I also told him it was my belief that when he pushed down the main shore the latter tribe without doubt would cross over to the island we had just left, while the former would take to the mountains. Steptoe coincided with me in this opinion, and informing me that Lieutenant Alexander Piper would join my detachment with a mountain howitzer, directed me to convey the command to the island and gobble up all who came over to it.

Lieutenant Piper and I landed on the island with the first boatload, and after disembarking the howitzer we fired two or three shots to let the Indians know we had artillery with us, then advanced down the island with the whole of my command, which had arrived in the mean time; all of the men were deployed as skirmishers except a small detachment to operate the howitzer. Near the lower end of the island we met, as I had anticipated, the entire body of Cascade Indianmen, women, and children—whose homes were in the vicinity of the Cascades. They were very much frightened and demoralized at the turn events had taken, for the Yakimas at the approach of Steptoe had abandoned them, as predicted, and fled to the mountains. The chief and head-men said they had had nothing to do with the capture of the Cascades, with the murder of men at the upper landing, nor with the massacre of men, women, and children near the block-house, and put all the blame on the Yakimas and their allies. I did not believe this, however, and to test the truth of their statement formed them all in line with their muskets in hand. Going up to the first man on the right I accused him of having engaged in the massacre, but was met by a vigorous denial. Putting my forefinger into the muzzle of his gun, I found unmistakable signs of its having been recently discharged. My finger was black with the stains of burnt powder, and holding it up to the Indian, he had nothing more to say in the face of such positive evidence of his guilt. A further examination proved that all the guns were in the same condition. Their arms were at once taken possession of, and leaving a small force to look after the women and children and the very old men, so that there could be no possibility of escape, I arrested thirteen of the principal miscreants, crossed the river to the lower landing, and placed them in charge of a strong guard.

Late in the evening the steamboat, which I had sent back to Vancouver, returned, bringing to my assistance from Vancouver, Captain Henry D. Wallen's company of the Fourth Infantry and a company of volunteers hastily organized at Portland, but as the Cascades had already been retaken, this reinforcement was too late to participate in the affair. The volunteers from Portland, however, were spoiling for a fight, and in the absence of other opportunity desired to shoot the prisoners I held (who, they alleged, had killed a man named Seymour), and proceeded to make their arrangements to do so, only desisting on being informed that the Indians were my prisoners, subject to the orders of Colonel Wright, and would be protected to the last by my detachment. Not long afterward Seymour turned up safe and sound, having fled at the beginning of the attack on the Cascades, and hid somewhere in the thick underbrush until the trouble was over, and then made his way back to the settlement. The next day I turned my prisoners over to Colonel Wright, who had them marched to the upper landing of the Cascades, where, after a trial by a military commission, nine of them were sentenced to death and duly hanged. I did not see them executed, but was afterward informed that, in the absence of the usual mechanical apparatus used on such occasions, a tree with a convenient limb under which two empty barrels were placed, one on top of the other, furnished a rude but certain substitute. In executing the sentence each Indian in turn was made to stand on the top barrel, and after the noose was adjusted the lower barrel was knocked away, and the necessary drop thus obtained. In this way the whole nine were punished. Just before death they all acknowledged their guilt by confessing their participation in the massacre at the block-house, and met their doom with the usual stoicism of their race.

Source: P. H. Sheridan, *Personal Memoirs of P. H. Sheridan,* Vol. 1 (New York: Charles L. Webster, 1888), 72–73, 80–84.

119. Nez Perce Treaties, 1855, 1863, and 1868

Introduction

American immigrants began surging into the Pacific Northwest in 1843. Oregon Territory was officially established in 1848, and Washington became a separate territory in 1853. The Indians who lived in the northwest territories numbered about 42,000 and belonged to several dozen tribes. Many tried to resist the growing population of American settlers, and a state of nearly continuous warfare went on until 1858, when most of the Indians of the Northwest were confined to reservations. The Nez Perces, however, maintained friendly relations with the Americans. The first of these three treaties with the Nez Perces, made by the Washington and Oregon territories' superintendents of Indian affairs, provides for the tribe to cede land and receive a reservation, money, and goods. The 1863 treaty amends the previous treaty by reducing the size of the Nez Perce Reservation, promises to make restitution for any improvements built on the ceded land, and offers additional money and goods. The treaty also permits individual male Nez Perces to receive 20-acre allotments of land. The treaty of 1868 allows individual Nez Perces to remain on allotments outside of reservation boundaries. But in a decision typical of the time, government authorities decided to remove the Nez Perces from their home reservation to one in Idaho in order to make way for white settlement. When Chief Joseph and his people refused to move, the army was ordered to remove them by force, which led to war in 1877.

Primary Source

1855 Treaty

Articles of agreement and convention made and concluded at the treaty ground, Camp Stevens, in the Walla-Walla Valley, this eleventh day of June, in the year one thousand eight hundred and fifty-five, by and between Isaac I. Stevens, governor and superintendent of Indian affairs for the Territory of Washington, and Joel Palmer, superintendent of Indian affairs for Oregon Territory, on the part of the United States, and the undersigned chiefs, headmen, and delegates of the Nez Perce tribe of Indians occupying lands lying partly in Oregon and partly in Washington Territories, between the Cascade and Bitter Root Mountains, on behalf of, and acting for said tribe, and being duly authorized thereto by them, it being understood that Superintendent Isaac I. Stevens assumes to treat only with those of the above-named tribe of Indians residing within the Territory of Washington, and Superintendent Palmer with those residing exclusively in Oregon Territory.

ARTICLE I

The said Nez Perce tribe of Indians hereby cede, relinquish and convey to the United States all their right, title, and interest in and to the country occupied or claimed by them, bounded and described as follows, to wit:

Commencing at the source of the Wo-na-ne-she or southern tributary of the Paleuse River; thence down that river to the main Paleuse; thence in a southerly direction to the Snake River, at the mouth of the Tucanon River; thence up the Tucanon to its source in the Blue Mountains; thence southerly along the ridge of the Blue Mountains; thence to a point on Grand Ronde River, midway between Grand Ronde and the mouth of the Well-low-how River; thence along the divide between the waters of the Well-low-how and Powder River; thence to the crossing of Snake River, at the mouth of Powder River; thence to the Salmon River, fifty miles above the place known (as) the "crossing of the Salmon River;" thence due north to the summit of the Bitter Root Mountains; thence along the crest of the Bitter Root Mountains to the place of beginning.

ARTICLE II

There is, however, reserved from the lands above ceded for the use and occupation of the said tribe, and as a general reservation for other friendly tribes and bands of Indians in Washington Territory, not to exceed the present numbers of the Spokane, Walla-Walla, Cayuse, and Umatilla tribes and bands of Indians, the tract of land included within the following boundaries, to wit:

Commencing where the Moh ha-na-she or southern tributary of the Palouse River flows from the spurs of the Bitter Root Mountains; thence down said tributary to the mouth of the Ti-nat-pan-up Creek; thence southerly to the crossing of the Snake River ten miles below the mouth of the Al-po-wa-wi River; thence to the source of the Al-po-wa-wi River in the Blue Mountains; thence along the crest of the Blue Mountains; thence to the crossing of the Grand Rondo River, midway between the Grand Ronde and the mouth of the Woll-low-how River; thence along the divide between the waters of the Woll-low-how and Powder Rivers; thence to the crossing of the Snake River fifteen miles below the

mouth of the Powder River; thence to the Salmon River above the crossing; thence by the spurs of the Bitter Root Mountains to the place of beginning.

All which tract shall be set apart, and, so far as necessary, surveyed and marked out for the exclusive use and benefit of said tribe as an Indian reservation; nor shall any white man, excepting those in the employment of the Indian Department, be permitted to reside upon the said reservation without permission of the tribe and the superintendent and agent; and the said tribe agrees to remove to and settle upon the same within one year after the ratification of this treaty.

In the mean time it shall be lawful for them to reside upon any ground not in the actual claim and occupation of citizens of the United States, and upon any ground claimed or occupied, if with the permission of the owner or claimant, guarantying, however, the right to all citizens of the United States to enter upon and occupy as settlers any lands not actually occupied and cultivated by said Indians at this time, and not included in the reservation above named.

And provided that any substantial improvement heretofore made by any Indian, such as fields enclosed and cultivated, and houses erected upon the lands hereby ceded, and which he may be compelled to abandon in consequence of this treaty, shall be valued under the direction of the President of the United States, and payment made therefor in money, or improvements of an equal value be made for said Indian upon the reservation, and no Indian will be required to abandon the improvements aforesaid, now occupied by him, until their value in money or improvements of equal value shall be furnished him as aforesaid.

ARTICLE III

And provided that, if necessary for the public convenience, roads may be run through the said reservation, and, on the other hand, the right of way, with free access from the same to the nearest public highway, is secured to them, as also the right, in common with citizens of the United States, to travel upon all public highways.

The use of the Clear Water and other streams flowing through the reservation is also secured to citizens of the United States for rafting purposes, and as public highways. The exclusive right of taking fish in all the streams where running through or bordering said reservation is further secured to said Indians; as also the right of taking fish at all usual and accustomed places in common with citizens of the Territory; and of erecting temporary buildings— for curing, together with the privilege of hunting, gathering roots and berries, and pasturing their horses and cattle upon open and unclaimed land.

ARTICLE IV

In consideration of the above cession, the United States agree to pay to the said tribe in addition to the goods and provisions distributed to them at the time of signing this treaty, the sum of two hundred thousand dollars, in the following manner, that is to say, sixty thousand dollars, to be expended under the direction of the President of the United States, the first year after the ratification of this treaty, in providing for their removal to the reserve, breaking up and fencing farms, building houses, supplying them with provisions and a suitable outfit, and for such other objects as he may deem necessary, and the remainder in annuities, as follows: for the first five years after the ratification of this treaty, ten thousand dollars each year, commencing September 1, 1856; for the next five years, eight thousand dollars each year; for the next five years, six thousand each year, and for the next five years, four thousand dollars each year.

All which said sums of money shall be applied to the use and benefit of the said Indians, under the direction of the President of the United States, who may from time to time determine, at his discretion, upon what beneficial objects to expend the same for them. And the superintendent of Indian affairs, or other proper officer, shall each year inform the President of the wishes of the Indians in relation thereto.

ARTICLE V

The United States further agree to establish, at suitable points within said reservation, within one year after the ratification hereof, two schools, erecting the necessary buildings, keeping the same in repair, and providing them with furniture, books, and stationery, one of which shall be an agricultural and industrial school, to be located at the agency, and to be free to the children of said tribe, and to employ one superintendent of teaching and two teachers; to build two blacksmiths' shops, to one of which shall be attached a tin-shop and to the other a gunsmith's shop; one carpenter's shop, one wagon and plough maker's shop, and to keep the same in repair, and furnished with the necessary tools; to employ one superintendent of farming and two farmers, two blacksmiths, one tinner, one gunsmith, one carpenter, one wagon and plough maker, for the instruction of the Indians in trades, and to assist them in the same; to erect one saw-mill and one flouring-mill, keeping the same in repair, and furnished with the necessary tools and fixtures, and to employ two millers; to erect a hospital, keeping the same in repair, and provided with the necessary medicines and furniture, and to employ a physician; and to erect, keep in repair, and provide with the necessary furniture the buildings required for the accommodation of the said employees. The said buildings and establishments to be maintained and kept in repair as aforesaid, and the employees to be kept in service for the period of twenty years.

And in view of the fact that the head chief of the tribe is expected, and will be called upon, to perform many services of a public character, occupying much of his time, the United States further agrees to pay to the Nez Perce tribe five hundred dollars per year for the term of twenty years, after the ratification hereof, as a salary for such person as the tribe may select to be its head chief. To build for him, at a suitable point on the reservation, a comfortable house, and properly furnish the same, and to plough and fence for his use ten acres of land. The said salary to be paid to, and the said house to be occupied by, such head chief so long as he may be elected to that position by his tribe, and no longer. And all the expenditures and expenses contemplated in this fifth article of this treaty shall be defrayed by the United States, and shall not be deducted from the annuities agreed to be paid to said tribes nor shall the cost of transporting the goods for the annuity-payments be a charge upon the annuities, but shall be defrayed by the United States.

ARTICLE VI

The President may from time to time, at his discretion, cause the whole, or such portions of such reservation as he may think proper, to be surveyed into lots, and assign the same to such individuals or families of the said tribe as are willing to avail themselves of the privilege, and will locate on the same as a permanent home, on the same terms and subject to the same regulations as are provided in the sixth article of the treaty with the Omahas in the year 1854, so far as the same may be applicable.

ARTICLE VII

The annuities of the aforesaid tribe shall not be taken to pay the debts of individuals.

ARTICLE VIII

The aforesaid tribe acknowledge their dependence upon the Government of the United States, and promise to be friendly with all citizens thereof, and pledge themselves to commit no depredations on the property of such citizens; and should any one or more of them violate this pledge, and the fact be satisfactorily proved before the agent, the property taken shall be returned, or in default thereof, or if injured or destroyed, compensation may be made by the Government out of the annuities.

Nor will they make war on any other tribe except in self-defense, but will submit all matters of difference between them and the other Indians to the Government of the United States, or its agent, for decision, and abide thereby; and if any of the said Indians commit any depredations on any other Indians within the Territory of Washington, the same rule shall prevail as that prescribed in this article in cases of depredations against citizens.

And the said tribe agrees not to shelter or conceal offenders against the laws of the United States, but to deliver them up to the authorities for trial.

ARTICLE IX

The Nez Perces desire to exclude from their reservation the use of ardent spirits, and to prevent their people from drinking the same;

and therefore it is provided that any Indian belonging to said tribe who is guilty of bringing liquor into said reservation, or who drinks liquor, may have his or her proportion of the annuities withheld from him or her for such time as the President may determine.

ARTICLE X

The Nez Perce Indians having expressed in council a desire that William Craig should continue to live with them, he having uniformly shown himself their friend, it is further agreed that the tract of land now occupied by him, and described in his notice to the register and receiver of the land-office of the Territory of Washington, on the fourth day of June last, shall not be considered a part of the reservation provided for in this treaty, except that it shall be subject in common with the lands of the reservation to the operations of the intercourse act.

ARTICLE XI

This treaty shall be obligatory upon the contracting parties as soon as the same shall be ratified by the President and Senate of the United States.

In testimony whereof, the said Isaac I. Stevens, governor and superintendent of Indian affairs for the Territory of Washington, and Joel Palmer, superintendent of Indian affairs for Oregon Territory, and the chiefs, headmen, and delegates of the aforesaid Nez Perce tribe of Indians, have hereunto set their hands and seals, at the place, and on the day and year hereinbefore written.

Isaac I. Stevens, Governor and Superintendent Washington Territory.
Joel Palmer, Superintendent Indian Affairs.
Aleiya, or Lawyer, Head-chief of the Nez Perces,
Appushwa-hite, or Looking-glass, his x mark.
Joseph, his x mark.
James, his x mark.
Red Wolf, his x mark.
Timothy, his x mark.
U-ute-sin-male-cun, his x mark.
Spotted Eagle, his x mark.
Stoop-toop-nm or Cut-hair, his x mark.
Tah-moh-moh-kin, his x mark.
Tippelanecbupooh, his x mark.
Hah-hah-stilpilp, his x mark.
Cool-cool-shua-nin, his x mark.
Silish, his x mark.
Toh-toh-molewit, his x mark.
Tuky-in-lik-it, his x mark.
Te-holc-hole-soot, his x mark.
Ish-coh-tim, his x mark.
Wee-as-cus, his x mark.
Hah-hah-stoore-tee, his x mark.

Eee-maht-sin-pooh, his x mark.
Tow-wish-au-il-pilp, his x mark.
Kay-kay-mass, his x mark.
Speaking Eagle, his x mark.
Wat-ti-wat-ti-wah-hi, his x mark.
Howh-no-tah-kun, his x mark.
Tow-wish-wane, his x mark.
Wahpt-tah-shooshe, his x mark.
Bead Necklace, his x mark.
Koos-koos-tas-kut, his x mark.
Levi, his x mark.
Pee-oo-pe-whi-hi, his x mark.
Pee-oo-pee-iecteim, his x mark.
Pee-poome-kah, his x mark.
Hah-hah-stlil-at-me, his x mark.
Wee-yoke-sin-ate, his x mark.
Wee-ah-ki, his x mark.
Necalahtsin, his x mark.
Suck-on-tie, his x mark.
Ip-nat-tam-moose, his x mark.
Jason, his x mark.
Kole-kole-til-ky, his x mark.
In-mat-tute-kah-ky, his x mark.
Moh-see-chee, his x mark.
George, his x mark.
Nicke-el-it-may-ho, his x mark.
Say-i-ee-ouse, his x mark.
Wis-tasse-cut, his x mark.
Ky-ky-soo-te-lum, his x mark.
Ko-ko-whay-nee, his x mark.
Kwin-to-kow, his x mark.
Pee-wee-au-ap-tah, his x mark.
Wee-at-tenat-il-pilp, his x mark.
Pee-oo-pee-u-il-pilp, his x mark.
Wah-tass-tum-mannee, his x mark.
Tu-wee-si-ce, his x mark.
Lu-ee-sin-kah-koose-sin, his x mark.
Hah-tal-ee-kin, his x mark.

Signed and sealed in presence of

James Doty, secretary of treaties,
W. T. Wm. C. McKay, secretary of treaties, O. T.
W. H. Tappan, sub-Indian agent,
William Craig, interpreter,
A. D. Pamburn, interpreter,
Wm. McBean,
Geo. C. Bornford,
C. Chirouse, O. M. T.
Mie. Cles. Pandosy,
Lawrence Kip,
W. H. Pearson.

1863 Treaty

Articles of agreement made and concluded at the council-ground, in the valley of the Lapwai, W. T. on the ninth day of June, one thousand eight hundred and sixty-three; between the United States of America, by C. H. Hale, superintendent of Indian affairs, and Charles Hutchins and S. D. Howe, U. S. Indian agents for the Territory of Washington, acting on the part and in behalf of the United States, and the Nez Perce Indians, by the chiefs, head-men, and delegates of said tribe, such articles being supplementary and amendatory to the treaty made between the United States and said tribe on the 11th day of June, 1855.

ARTICLE I

The said Nez Perce tribe agree to relinquish, and do hereby relinquish, to the United States the lands heretofore reserved for the use and occupation of the said tribe, saving and excepting so much thereof as is described in Article 2 for a new reservation.

ARTICLE II

The United States agree to reserve for a home, and for the sole use and occupation of said tribe, the tract of land included within the following boundaries, to wit:

Commencing at the northeast corner of Lake Wa-ha, and running thence, northerly, to a point on the north bank of the Clearwater River, three miles below the mouth of the Lapwai, thence down the north bank of the Clearwater to the mouth of the Hatwai Creek; thence, due north, to a point seven miles distant; thence, eastwardly, to a point on the north fork of the Clearwater, seven miles distant from its mouth; thence to a point on Oro Fino Creek, five miles above its mouth; thence to a point on the north fork of the south fork of the Clearwater, five miles above its mouth; thence to a point on the south fork of the Clearwater, one mile above the bridge, on the road leading to Elk City, (so as to include all the Indian farms now within the forks); thence in a straight line, westwardly, to the place of beginning.

All of which tract shall be set apart, and the above-described boundaries shall be surveyed and marked out for the exclusive use and benefit of said tribe as an Indian reservation, nor shall any white man, excepting those in the employment of the Indian Department, be permitted to reside upon the said reservation without permission of the tribe and the superintendent and agent; and the said tribe agrees that so soon after the United States shall make the necessary provision for fulfilling the stipulations of this instrument as they can conveniently arrange their affairs, and not to exceed one year from its ratification, they will vacate the country hereby relinquished, and remove to and settle upon the lands herein reserved for them, (except as may be hereinafter provided.) In the meantime it shall be lawful for them to reside upon any ground now occupied or under cultivation by said Indians at this time, and not included in the reservation above named.

And it is provided, that any substantial improvement heretofore made by any Indian, such as fields enclosed and cultivated, or houses erected upon the lands hereby relinquished, and which he may be compelled to abandon in consequence of this treaty, shall be valued under the direction of the President of the United States, and payment therefor shall be made in stock or in improvements of an equal value for said Indian upon the lot which may be assigned to him within the bounds of the reservation, as he may choose, and no Indian will be required to abandon the improvements aforesaid, now occupied by him, until said payment or improvement shall have been made.

And it is further provided, that if any Indian living on any of the land hereby relinquished should prefer to sell his improvements to any white man, being a loyal citizen of the United States, prior to the same being valued as aforesaid, he shall be allowed so to do, but the sale or transfer of said improvements shall be made in the presence of, and with the consent and approval of, the agent or superintendent, by whom a certificate of sale shall be issued to the party purchasing, which shall set forth the amount of the consideration in kind. Before the issue of said certificate, the agent or superintendent shall be satisfied that a valuable consideration is paid, and that the party purchasing is of undoubted loyalty to the United States Government. No settlement or claim made upon the improved lands by any Indian will be permitted, except as herein provided, prior to the time specified for their removal. Any sale or transfer thus made shall be in the stead of payment for improvements from the United States.

ARTICLE III

The President shall, immediately after the ratification of this treaty, cause the boundary-lines to be surveyed, and properly marked and established; after which, so much of the lands hereby reserved as may be suitable for cultivation shall be surveyed into lots of twenty acres each, and every male person of the tribe who shall have attained the age of twenty-one years, or is the head of a family, shall have the privilege of locating upon one lot as a permanent home for such person, and the lands so surveyed, shall be allotted under such rules and regulations as the President shall prescribe, having such reference to their settlement as may secure adjoining each other the location of the different families pertaining to each band, so far as the same may be practicable. Such rules and regulations shall be prescribed by the President, or under his direction, as will insure to the family, in case of the death of the head thereof, the possession and enjoyment of such permanent home, and the improvements thereon.

When the assignments as above shall have been completed, certificates shall be issued by the Commissioner of Indian Affairs, or under his direction, for the tracts assigned in severalty, specifying the names of the individuals to whom they have been assigned respectively, and that said tracts are set apart for the perpetual and exclusive use and benefit of such assignees and their heirs. Until otherwise provided by law, such tracts shall be exempt from levy, taxation, or sale, and shall be alienable in fee, or leased, or otherwise disposed of, only to the United States, or to persons then being members of the Nez Perce tribe, and of Indian blood, with the permission of the President, and under such regulations as the Secretary of the Interior or the Commissioner of Indian Affairs shall prescribe; and if any such person or family shall at any time neglect or refuse to occupy and till a portion of the land so assigned, and on which they have located, or shall rove from place to place, the President may cancel the assignment, and may also withhold from such person or family their proportion of the annuities or other payments due them until they shall have returned to such permanent home, and resumed the pursuits of industry; and in default of their return, the tract may be declared abandoned, and thereafter assigned to some other person or family of such tribe.

The residue of the land hereby reserved shall be held in common for pasturage for the sole use and benefit of the Indians: Provided, however, That from time to time, as members of the tribe may come upon the reservation, or may become of proper age, after the expiration of the time of one year after the ratification of this treaty, as aforesaid, and claim the privileges granted under this article, lots may be assigned from the lands thus held in common, wherever the same may be suitable for cultivation. No State or territorial legislature shall remove the restriction herein provided for, without the consent of Congress, and no State or territorial law to that end shall be deemed valid until the same has been specially submitted to Congress for its approval.

ARTICLE IV

In consideration of the relinquishment herein made the United States agree to pay to the said tribe, in addition to the annuities provided by the treaty of June 11, 1855, and the goods and provisions distributed to them at the time of signing this treaty, the sum of two hundred and sixty-two thousand and five hundred dollars, in manner following, to wit:

First. One hundred and fifty thousand dollars, to enable the Indians to remove and locate upon the reservation, to be expended in the ploughing of land, and the fencing of the several lots, which may be assigned to those individual members of the tribe who will accept the same in accordance with the provisions of the preceding article, which said sum shall be divided into four annual installments, as follows: For the first year after the ratification of this treaty, seventy thousand dollars; for the second year, forty thousand dollars; for the third year, twenty-five thousand dollars; for the fourth year, fifteen thousand dollars.

Second. Fifty thousand dollars to be paid the first year after the ratification of this treaty in agricultural implements, to include wagons or carts, harness, and cattle, sheep, or other stock, as may be deemed most beneficial by the superintendent of Indian affairs, or agent, after ascertaining the wishes of the Indians in relation thereto.

Third. Ten thousand dollars for the erection of a saw and flouring mill, to be located at Kamia, the same to be erected within one year after the ratification hereof.

Fourth. Fifty thousand dollars for the boarding and clothing of the children who shall attend the schools, in accordance with such rules or regulations as the Commissioner of Indian Affairs may prescribe, providing the schools and boarding-houses with necessary furniture, the purchase of necessary wagons, teams, agricultural implements, tools, &c., for their use, and for the fencing of such lands as may be needed for gardening and farming purposes, for the use and benefit of the schools, to be expended as follows: The first year after the ratification of this treaty, six thousand dollars; for the next fourteen years, three thousand dollars each year; and for the succeeding year, being the sixteenth and last installment, two thousand dollars.

Fifth. A further sum of two thousand five hundred dollars shall be paid within one year after the ratification hereof, to enable the Indians to build two churches, one of which is to be located at some suitable point on the Kamia, and the other on the Lapwai.

ARTICLE V

The United States further agree, that in addition to a head chief the tribe shall elect two subordinate chiefs, who shall assist him in the performance of his public services, and each subordinate chief shall have the same amount of land ploughed and fenced, with comfortable house and necessary furniture, and to whom the same salary shall be paid as is already provided for the head chief in article 5 of the treaty of June 11, 1855, the salary to be paid and the houses and land to be occupied during the same period and under like restrictions as therein mentioned.

And for the purpose of enabling the agent to erect said buildings, and to plough and fence the land, as well as to procure the necessary furniture, and to complete and furnish the house, &c., of the head chief, as heretofore provided, there shall be appropriated, to be expended within the first year after the ratification hereof, the sum of two thousand five hundred dollars.

And inasmuch as several of the provisions of said art. 5th of the treaty of June 11, 1855, pertaining to the erection of schoolhouses, hospital, shops, necessary buildings for employee(s) and for the agency, as well as providing the same with necessary furniture, tools, &c., have not yet been complied with, it is hereby stipulated that there shall be appropriated, to be expended for the purposes herein specified during the first year after the ratification hereof, the following sums, to wit:

First. Ten thousand dollars for the erection of the two schools, including boarding-houses and the necessary out-buildings; said schools to be conducted on the manual-labor system as far as practicable.

Second. Twelve hundred dollars for the erection of the hospital, and providing the necessary furniture for the same.

Third. Two thousand dollars for the erection of a blacksmith's shop, to be located at Kamia, to aid in the completion of the smith's shop at the agency, and to purchase the necessary tools, iron, steel, &c.; and to keep the same in repair and properly stocked with necessary tools and materials, there shall be appropriated thereafter, for the fifteen years next succeeding, the sum of five hundred dollars each year.

Fourth. Three thousand dollars for erection of houses for employee(s), repairs of mills, shops, &c., and providing necessary furniture, tools, and materials. For the same purpose, and to procure from year to year the necessary articles that is to say, saw-logs, nails, glass, hardware, &c.—there shall be appropriated thereafter, for the twelve years next succeeding, the sum of two thousand dollars each year; and for the next three years, one thousand dollars each year.

And it is further agreed that the United States shall employ, in addition to those already mentioned in art. 5th of the treaty of June 11, 1855, two matrons to take charge of the boarding-schools, two assistant teachers, one farmer, one carpenter, and two millers.

All the expenditures and expenses contemplated in this treaty, and not otherwise provided for, shall be defrayed by the United States.

ARTICLE VI

In consideration of the past services and faithfulness of the Indian chief, Timothy, it is agreed that the United States shall appropriate the sum of six hundred dollars, to aid him in the erection of a house upon the lot of land which may be assigned to him, in accordance with the provisions of the third article of this treaty.

ARTICLE VII

The United States further agree that the claims of certain members of the Nez Perce tribe against the Government for services rendered and for horses furnished by them to the Oregon mounted volunteers, as appears by certificate issued by W. H. Fauntleroy, A. R. Qr. M. and Com. Oregon volunteers, on the 6th of March, 1856, at Camp Cornelius, and amounting to the sum of four thousand six hundred and sixty-five dollars, shall be paid to them in full, in gold coin.

ARTICLE VIII

It is also understood that the aforesaid tribe do hereby renew their acknowledgments of dependence upon the Government of the United States, their promises of friendship, and other pledges, as set forth in the eighth article of the treaty of June 11, 1855; and further, that all the provisions of said treaty which are not abrogated or specifically changed by any article herein contained, shall

remain the same to all intents and purposes as formerly, the same obligations resting upon the United States, the same privileges continued to the Indians outside of the reservation, and the same rights secured to citizens of the U. S. as to right of way upon the streams and over the roads which may run through said reservation, as are therein set forth.

But it is further provided, that the United States is the only competent authority to declare and establish such necessary roads and highways, and that no other right is intended to be hereby granted to citizens of the United States than the right of way upon or over such roads as may thus be legally established: Provided, however, That the roads now usually traveled shall, in the mean time, be taken and deemed as within the meaning of this article, until otherwise enacted by act of Congress or by the authority of the Indian Department.

And the said tribe hereby consent, that upon the public roads which may run across the reservation there may be established, at such points as shall be necessary for public convenience, hotels, or stage-stands, of the number and necessity of which the agent or superintendent shall be the sole judge, who shall be competent to license the same, with the privilege of using such amount of land for pasturage and other purposes connected with such establishment as the agent or superintendent shall deem necessary, it being understood that such lands for pasturage are to be enclosed, and the boundaries thereof described in the license.

And it is further understood and agreed that all ferries and bridges within the reservation shall be held and managed for the benefit of said tribe.

Such rules and regulations shall be made by the Commissioner of Indian Affairs, with the approval of the Secretary of the interior, as shall regulate the travel on the highways, the management of the ferries and bridges, the licensing of public houses, and the leasing of lands, as herein provided, so that the rents, profits, and issues thereof shall inure to the benefit of said tribe, and so that the persons thus licensed, or necessarily employed in any of the above relations, shall be subject to the control of the Indian Department, and to the provisions of the act of Congress "to regulate trade and intercourse with the Indian tribes, and to preserve peace on the frontiers."

All timber within the bounds of the reservation is exclusively the property of the tribe, excepting that the U. S. Government shall be permitted to use thereof for any purpose connected with its affairs, either in carrying out any of the provisions of this treaty, or in the maintaining of its necessary forts or garrisons. The United States also agree to reserve all springs or fountains not adjacent to, or directly connected with, the streams or rivers within the lands hereby relinquished, and to keep back from settlement or entry so much of the surrounding land as may be necessary to prevent the said springs or fountains being enclosed; and, further, to preserve a perpetual right of way to and from the same, as watering places, for the use in common of both whites and Indians.

ARTICLE IX

Inasmuch as the Indians in council have expressed their desire that Robert Newell should have confirmed to him a piece of land lying between Snake and Clearwater Rivers, the same having been given to him on the 9th day of June, 1861, and described in an instrument of writing bearing that date, and signed by several chiefs of the tribe, it is hereby agreed that the said Robert Newell shall receive from the United States a patent for the said tract of land.

ARTICLE X

This treaty shall be obligatory upon the contracting parties as soon as the same shall be ratified by the President and Senate of the United States.

In testimony whereof the said C. H. Hale, superintendent of Indian affairs, and Charles Hutchins and S. D. Howe, United States Indian agents in the Territory of Washington, and the chiefs, headmen, and delegates of the aforesaid Nez Perce tribe of Indians, have hereunto set their hands and seals at the place and on the day and year hereinbefore written.

Calvin H. Hale, Superintendent Indian Affairs, Wash.
T. Chas. Hutchins, United States Indian agent, Wash. T.
S. D. Howe, United States Indian agent, Wash. T.
Lawyer, Head Chief Nez Perces Nation.
Ute-sin-male-e-cum, x
Ha-harch-tuesta, x
Tip-ulania-timecca, x
Es-coatum, x
Timothy, x
Levi, x
Jason, x
Ip-she-ne-wish-kin, (Capt. John) x
Weptas-jurnp-ki, x
We-as-cus, x
Pep-hoom-kan, (Noah) x
Shin-ma-sha-ho-soot, x
Nie-ki-lil-meh-hoom, (Jacob) x
Stoop-toop-nin, x
Su-we-cus, x
Wal-la-ta-mana, x
He-kaikt-il-pilp, x
Whis-tas-ket, x
Neus-ne-keun, x
Kul-lou-o-haikt, x
Wow-en-am-ash-il-pilp, x
Kan-pow-e-een, x
Watai-watai-wa-haikt, x
Kup-kup-pellia, x
Wap-tas-ta-mana, x

Peo-peo-ip-se-wat, x
Louis-in-ha-cush-nim, x
Lam-lim-si-lilp-nim, x
Tu-ki-lai-kish, x
Sah-kan-tai, (Eagle) x
We-ah-se-nat, x
Hin-mia-tun-pin, x
Ma-hi-a-kim, x
Shock-lo-turn-wa-haikt, (Jonah) x
Kunness-tak-mal, x
Tu-lat-sy-wat-kin, x
Tuck-e-tu-et-as, x
Nic-a-las-in, x
Was-atis-ill-pilp, x
Wow-es-en-at-im, x
Hiram, x
Howlish-wampum, x
Wat-ska-leeks, x
Wa-lai-tus, x
Ky-e-wee-pus, x
Ko-ko-il-pilp, x
Reuben, x
Tip-la-la-na-uy-kalatsekin, x
Wish-la-na-ka-nin, x
Me-tat-ueptas, (Three Feathers) x
Ray-kay-mass, x

Signed and sealed in presence of

George F. Whitworth, Secretary.
Justus Steinberger, Colonel U. S. Volunteers.
R. F. Malloy, Colonel Cavalry, O.V.
J. S. Rinearson, Major First Cavalry Oregon Volunteers.
William Kapus, First Lieutenant and Adjutant First W. T. Infantry U. S. Volunteers.
Harrison Olmstead.
Jno. Owen, (Bitter Root).
James O'Neill.
J. B. Buker, M.D.
George W. Elber.
A. A. Spalding, assistant interpreter.
Perrin B. Whitman, interpreter for the council.

1868 Treaty

Whereas certain amendments are desired by the Nez Perce tribe of Indians to their treaty concluded at the council ground in the valley of the Lapwai, in the Territory of Washington, on the ninth day of June, in the year of our Lord one thousand eight hundred and sixty-three; and whereas the United States are willing to assent to said amendments; it is therefore agreed by and between

Nathaniel G. Taylor, commissioner, on the part of the United States, thereunto duly authorized, and Lawyer, Timothy, and Jason, chiefs of said tribe, also being thereunto duly authorized, in manner and form following, that is to say:

ARTICLE I

That all lands embraced within the limits of the tract set apart for the exclusive use and benefit of said Indians by the 2d article of said treaty of June 9th, 1863, which are susceptible of cultivation and suitable for Indian farms, which are not now occupied by the United States for military purposes, or which are not required for agency or other buildings and purposes provided for by existing treaty stipulations, shall be surveyed as provided in the 3d article of said treaty of June 9th, 1863, and as soon as the allotments shall be plowed and fenced, and as soon as schools shall be established as provided by existing treaty stipulations, such Indians now residing outside the reservation as may be decided upon by the agent of the tribe and the Indians themselves, shall be removed to and located upon allotments within the reservation:

Provided, however, That in case there should not be a sufficient quantity of suitable land within the boundaries of the reservation to provide allotments for those now there and those residing outside the boundaries of the same, then those residing outside, or as many thereof as allotments cannot be provided for, may remain upon the lands now occupied and improved by them, provided, that the land so occupied does not exceed twenty acres for each and every male person who shall have attained the age of twenty-one years or is the head of a family, and the tenure of those remaining upon lands outside the reservation shall be the same as is provided in said 3d article of said treaty of June 9th, 1863, for those receiving allotments within the reservation; and it is further agreed that those now residing outside of the boundaries of the reservation and who may continue to so reside shall be protected by the military authorities in their rights upon the allotments occupied by them, and also in the privilege of grazing their animals upon surrounding unoccupied lands.

ARTICLE II

It is further agreed between the parties hereto that the stipulations contained in the 8th article of the treaty of June 9th, 1863, relative to timber, are hereby annulled as far as the same provides that the United States shall be permitted to use thereof in the maintaining of forts or garrisons, and that the said Indians shall have the aid of the military authorities to protect the timber upon their reservation, and that none of the same shall be cut or removed without the consent of the head-chief of the tribe, together with the consent of the agent and superintendent of Indian affairs, first being given in writing, which written consent shall state the part of the reservation upon which the timber is to be cut, and also the quantity, and the price to be paid therefor.

ARTICLE III

It is further hereby stipulated and agreed that the amount due said tribe for school purposes and for the support of teachers that has not been expended for that purpose since the year 1864, but has been used for other purposes, shall be ascertained and the same shall be reimbursed to said tribe by appropriation by Congress, and shall be set apart and invested in United States bonds and shall be held in trust by the United States, the interest on the same to be paid to said tribe annually for the support of teachers.

In testimony whereof the said Commissioner on the part of the United States and the said chiefs representing said Nez Perce tribe of Indians have hereunto set their hands and seals this 13th day of August, in the year of our Lord one thousand eight hundred and sixty-eight, at the city of Washington, D.C.

N. G. Taylor, Commissioner Indian Affairs
Lawyer, Head Chief Nez Perces.
Timothy, his x mark, Chief.
Jason, his x mark, Chief.

In presence of:
Charles E. Mix.
Robert Newell, United States Agent.
W. R. Irwin.

> **Source:** Treaty with the Nez Perce, 1855, June 11, 1855, 12 Stats., 957; Treaty with the Nez Perce, 1863, June 9, 1863, 14 Stats., 647; Treaty with the Nez Perce, 1868, August 13, 1868, 15 Stats., 693.

120. John Bell Hood, Engaging the Comanches in Texas, 1857

Introduction

John Bell Hood (1831–1879), a future Confederate general during the American Civil War (1861–1865), was a U.S. Army lieutenant in California when he received an appointment to join the newly formed 2nd Cavalry on the Texas frontier in 1855. He had just gone into partnership with Lieutenant George Crook to purchase land on which to grow wheat. However, Hood jumped at the chance to see active service and left for Texas after first borrowing money from San Francisco banker William T. Sherman. Since the 1820s, Americans had been settling on Comanche hunting grounds with little regard for ownership. The Comanches raided the settlements, stealing livestock, burning houses, and killing men, women, and children. After a quick strike, they would melt into the arid wilderness, defying the cavalry's attempts at pursuit and avoiding battle. Most Texans wanted only to exterminate the

Comanches. Not until 1854 did Texas make an effort to settle the Comanches on a reservation, but only about one-fourth of them complied while the rest continued raiding. In this excerpt from his memoirs, Hood recounts his experience of leading a cavalry detachment on a scouting expedition to find and engage Comanches. The intense heat and scarcity of water during the drought-afflicted summer of 1857 drained horses and soldiers alike. After 15 grueling days, they were about to turn back when a band of Comanches and Lipans attacked. Hood's outnumbered men forced them to retreat, at great cost to both. The fight at Devil's River earned Hood a promotion but did little to change the overall situation.

Primary Source

After the lapse of several months, and having grown weary of the routine duties of camp life, I determined to change the scene and start on a scouting expedition in search of the red men of the forests. Preparations were accordingly made, and I left Fort Mason on the morning of the 5th of July, 1857, in command of twenty-five men of Company "G" Second Cavalry, with an Indian guide, compass in hand and supplies for thirty days. I passed out upon the plains by the head of the Llano river, and marched thence to the country bordering on the Concha rivers. After an absence of ten days and an exploration of these different streams, I discovered an Indian trail, apparently about two or three days old, and indications warranting the belief that fifteen or twenty ponies belonged to the party which was moving in the direction of Mexico, via the head waters of Devil's river. I was young and buoyant in spirit; my men were well mounted and all eager for a chase as well as a fray. It was soon apparent that we would be forced to pass over a portion of the staked plains or desert lying between the Concha rivers and Mexico; that in order to overtake the Indians we would most likely have great fatigue and privation to endure, as we could expect to find but little water during the pursuit. However, in the conviction that we could live for a short time wherever Indians could subsist, we began the chase on the morning of the 17th of July, marched about forty miles, and camped that night upon the dry plains without water or the sight of game, so frequently in view the previous day, and without even the chirp of a bird to cheer us on our journey, we knew not exactly whither. At early dawn the following morning the march was resumed; we passed during the day a water-hole utterly unfit for use, and went into bivouac that night with the same surroundings, fully fifty miles further out in the desert. Our canteens were now empty, and the outlook was somewhat dismal. At daybreak on the 19th, "to horse" was sounded and the journey continued. About noon a deer was seen bounding over the prairie, and with the sight went forth a shout of joy from the men, who then felt confident that fresh water was not very far distant. The trail had moreover become much more distinct; this encouragement, together with the hope of quenching their thirst, reinspirited the soldiers. A few hours later another pool was reached, but not of that purity which was desirable. The odor of the water was such as

to oblige one to hold his breath whilst he partook of the distasteful but refreshing draught. The canteens were, notwithstanding, again filled, as well as the sleeves of all the waterproof coats we possessed. The pursuit was continued, and at dark we bivouacked after a forced march of probably sixty miles. Several of the horses began to show, by this time, great fatigue and leg-weariness. The following morning the lofty peaks of the mountains near Devil's river could be seen afar off, and all possible speed was made as we recognized that the line between the United States and Mexico was not far distant. About noon we reached another stagnant water-hole near the foot of a range of hills in proximity to the rugged and mountainous country about the head waters of Devil's river, along the banks of which stream passes the stage road from San Antonio to El Paso. Here we discovered that another party of Indians had joined that of which we were in pursuit. The deserted camp indicated that there were not less than fifty warriors in number. They had eaten one of their mules or horses, and this sign, together with others about their bivouac, bore clear evidence that the party had become formidable. The trail from this point was not only much larger, but presented a fresher appearance. The arms of the men were therefore carefully inspected, every preparation made for action, and the chase quickly resumed. The horses were much fatigued, and some of them were scarcely able to keep their places in the line of march; consequently the pursuit was not as rapid as it had been the three days previous. The march over the hills and up the mountains increased moreover their leg-weariness to such extent that about 3 pm. I abandoned all hope of overtaking the Indians before they crossed the Rio Grande, which river was then not far distant. This condition of the horses and the thirst of the soldiers led me to the determination to quit the trail and go immediately in search of fresh water. We were at this time well up on the high and rough range of mountains bordering on Devil's river, and after leaving the trail a distance of nigh one mile, I perceived on a parallel range about two miles off a few Indians waving a large white flag apparently hoisted from a mound. Orders from Washington had been issued before I left Fort Mason, notifying all United States troops that a party of Tonkaways were expected at the reservation, near Camp Cooper, and that they would, in the event of meeting a body of our soldiers upon the frontier, raise a white flag, upon which signal they were to be allowed to pass unmolested. I therefore became convinced that these Indians were either the Tonkaways or a hostile body endeavoring by an infamous ruse to throw me off my guard, to entrap and massacre my entire party.

Notwithstanding the condition of the men and the horses, I determined to pass over upon the ridge occupied by the red men, move toward them, and ascertain the meaning of this demonstration. I had at this time but seventeen men for action, the remainder having halted in rear, owing to the inability of their horses to advance further without rest. I moved across to the opposite ridge and, as a precautionary measure, formed line and marched forward in readiness to talk or fight. Every man was armed with an Army rifle and a six-shooter; a few of us had sabers and two revolvers, whilst I was armed with a double barrel shot-gun loaded with buck shot, and two Navy six-shooters. As we passed over a mound about one hundred and fifty or two hundred yards distant from the one occupied by friend or foe—we knew not which—the flag, seemingly a sheet, was still waving aloft and a few Indians were lounging about with every appearance of a party desirous of peace.

The ground in that vicinity was rough and partially covered with a growth of Spanish bayonets which afforded a secure place of concealment. Feeling that in the event of an attack I had better chances of success mounted than dismounted, for the reason that my fighting force in the latter instance would have been lessened by the number of men required to hold and guard the horses in rear, and sharing the belief which generally prevailed in my regiment that twenty well-armed soldiers should be able to successfully engage four times their number of Indians, I continued to move forward slowly upon the immediate right of my line. When we were within about twenty or thirty paces of the mound occupied by the Indians, four or five of them advanced towards us with the flag; suddenly they threw it to the ground and fired upon us. Simultaneously from a large heap of dry grass, weeds and leaves, burst forth, in our immediate front, a blaze of fire some thirty feet in height, and, with a furious yell, the warriors instantly rose up round about us, whilst others charged down the slope in our midst, even seizing some of our horses by the bridle reins. At the same moment a mounted party attacked the left of our line with lances. Thus began a most desperate struggle. The warriors were all painted, stripped to the waist, with either horns or wreaths of feathers upon their heads; they bore shields for defense, and were armed with rifles, bows and arrows. The quick and sharp report of our rifles, the smoke and cracking noise of the fire, together with the great odds against us, the shouts of the soldiers and the yells of the Indians, betokened the deadly peril from which seemingly naught but a miracle could effect our deliverance. Each man, after discharging his rifle, drew his revolver and used it with terrible effect as the warriors, in many instances, were within a few feet of the muzzle of our arms. Stubbornly did my brave men hold their ground; again and again they drove the enemy back to the edge and in rear of the burning mass of weeds in our front, when finally the Indians charged desperately and forced our line back a few paces in the centre. Having discharged my shotgun, I rode at once with revolver in hand to that point, rallied the soldiers, who again drove them back, whilst our horses, in some instances, were beaten over the head with shields. The contest was at such close quarters that a warrior bore off a rifle which had been used and hung by one of the men upon his saddle. Meantime the Indians as quickly as they discharged their arms, handed them to their squaws, who ran to the rear, reloaded and returned them. At this juncture I was pierced in the left hand with an arrow which passed through the reins and the fourth finger, pinning my hand to the bridle. I instantly broke the spear head and threw it aside. Unmindful of the fact that the feathers could not pass through the wound, I pulled the arrow in the direction in which it had been shot,

and was compelled finally in order to free myself of it to seize the feathered in lieu of the barbed end.

Thus raged this hand to hand conflict until all our shots were expended, and it was found that owing to the restiveness of the horses we could not reload while mounted. We then fell back about fifty yards and dismounted for that purpose. Soon afterward arose from beyond the burning heap one continuous mourning howl, such as can alone come forth from the heart of the red man in deep distress. These sounds of sorrow revealed to me that we were in little danger of a renewal of the assault, and I was, I may in truth say, most thankful for the truce thus proclaimed. Two of our men had been killed and four, besides myself, severely wounded; we had also one horse killed and several disabled. Had the combat been renewed I would have had, after leaving a guard with the horses, but five or six men to fight on foot.

Nightfall was approaching; the Indians gathered up their dead and wounded, and moved off toward the Rio Grande. Our thirst, which was great at the beginning of the combat, had now become intense from excitement and loss of blood. I therefore moved at once to Devil's river, where we bivouacked about 10 p. m., and sent a messenger to Camp Hudson for supplies and medical aid.

Thus closed this terrible scene, and often since have I felt most grateful that our horses were so broken down, as but for their condition they would, doubtless, when beaten over the head with shields, have become totally unmanageable, and have caused the massacre of my entire command. I attribute also our escape to the fact that the Indians did not have the self-possession to cut our bridle reins, which act would have proved fatal to us. We were nigh meeting a similar fate to that of the gallant Custer and his noble band.

I learned after the fight, through other Indians as well as through my guide, that the party which attacked us were Comanches and Lipans.

Source: J. B. Hood, *Advance and Retreat: Personal Experiences in the United States and Confederate State Armies* (New Orleans: G. T. Beauregard, 1880), 8–13.

121. Helen Hunt Jackson, Dramatization of the Plight of the Mission Indians, 1850s

Introduction

Helen Hunt Jackson's 1881 book *A Century of Dishonor* mobilized public opinion in favor of reforming Indian policy. In it she argued for protection of Indian rights to equal treatment under the law and secure title to their land. Jackson also coauthored an 1883 report to the commissioner of Indian Affairs on the deplorable living conditions endured by the Mission Indians of California. Beginning in the late 1700s, some 20 Franciscan missions established in Spanish-controlled California forced the indigenous peoples to labor for the mission and to convert to Catholicism. "Mission Indians" was a name applied to several dozen village-dwelling native peoples who had fallen under the sway of the Franciscans. Although the Mission Indians had few rights to land ownership or self-determination under Spanish and Mexican rule, after the U.S. victory in the Mexican-American War (1846–1848), Americans settled in their territory and seized their farms with impunity. Jackson's romantic novel *Ramona,* published in 1884, dramatized their plight. The novel is set in California in the decades immediately following the Mexican-American War. In this excerpt, the Indian loved by the heroine tells her of the Americans laying claim to his village and driving his family off. In 1891 Congress finally passed a law to establish reservations, with the right of individual ownership, for the long-neglected Mission Indians in California.

Primary Source

At the first words of Ramona's sentence, Alessandro threw his arms around her again. As she said "love," his whole frame shook with emotion.

"My Señorita!" he whispered, "my Señorita! how shall I tell you! How shall I tell you!"

"What is there to tell, Alessandro?" she said. "I am afraid of nothing, now that you are here, and not dead, as I thought."

But Alessandro did not speak. It seemed impossible. At last, straining her closer to his breast, he cried: "Dearest Señorita! I feel as if I should die when I tell you,—I have no home; my father is dead; my people are driven out of their village. I am only a beggar now, Señorita; like those you used to feed and pity in Los Angeles convent!" As he spoke the last words, he reeled, and, supporting himself against the tree, added: "I am not strong, Señorita; we have been starving."

Ramona's face did not reassure him. Even in the dusk he could see its look of incredulous horror. He misread it.

"I only came to look at you once more," he continued. "I will go now. May the saints bless you, my Señorita, always. I think the Virgin sent you to me to-night. I should never have seen your face if you had not come."

While he was speaking, Ramona had buried her face in his bosom. Lifting it now, she said, "Did you mean to leave me to think you were dead, Alessandro?"

"I thought that the news about our village must have reached you," he said, "and that you would know I had no home, and could not come, to seem to remind you of what you had said. Oh, Señorita, it was little enough I had before to give you! I don't know how I dared to believe that you could come to be with me; but I loved you so much, I had thought of many things I could do; and—" lowering his voice and speaking almost sullenly— "it is the saints, I believe, who have punished me thus for having resolved to leave my people, and take all I had for myself and you. Now they have left me nothing;" and he groaned.

"Who?" cried Ramona. "Was there a battle? Was your father killed?" She was trembling with horror.

"No," answered Alessandro. "There was no battle. There would have been, if I had had my way; but my father implored me not to resist. He said it would only make it hard for us in the end. The sheriff too, he begged me to let it all go on peaceably, and help him keep the people quiet. He felt terribly to have to do it. It was Mr. Rothsaker, from San Diego. We had often worked for him on his ranch. He knew all about us. Don't you recollect, Señorita, I told you about him,—how fair he always was, and kind too? He has the biggest wheat-ranch in Cajon; we've harvested miles and miles of wheat for him. He said he would have rather died, almost, than have had it to do; but if we resisted, he would have to order his men to shoot. He had twenty men with him. They thought there would be trouble; and well they might,—turning a whole village full of men and women and children out of their houses, and driving them off like foxes. If it had been any man but Mr. Rothsaker, I would have shot him dead, if I had hung for it; but I knew if he thought we must go, there was no help for us."

"But, Alessandro," interrupted Ramona, "I can't understand. Who was it made Mr. Rothsaker do it? Who has the land now?"

"I don't know who they are," Alessandro replied, his voice full of anger and scorn. "They're Americans,—eight or ten of them. They all got together and brought a suit, they call it, up in San Francisco; and it was decided in the court that they owned all our land. That was all Mr. Rothsaker could tell about it. It was the law, he said, and nobody could go against the law."

"Oh," said Ramona, "that's the way the Americans took so much of the Señora's land away from her. It was in the court up in San Francisco; and they decided that miles and miles of her land, which the General had always had, was not hers at all. They said it belonged to the United States Government."

"They are a pack of thieves and liars, every one of them!" cried Alessandro. "They are going to steal all the land in this country; we might all just as well throw ourselves into the sea, and let them have it. My father has been telling me this for years. He saw it coming; but I did not believe him. I did not think men could be so wicked; but he was right. I am glad he is dead. That is the only thing I have to be thankful for now. One day I thought he was going to get well, and I prayed to the Virgin not to let him. I did not want him to live. He never knew anything clear after they took him out of his house. That was before I got there. I found him sitting on the ground outside. They said it was the sun that had turned him crazy; but it was not. It was his heart breaking in his bosom. He would not come out of his house, and the men lifted him up and carried him out by force, and threw him on the ground; and then they threw out all the furniture we had; and when he saw them doing that, he put his hands up to his head, and called out, 'Alessandro! Alessandro!' and I was not there! Señorita, they said it was a voice to make the dead hear, that he called with; and nobody could stop him. All that day and all the night he kept on calling. God! Señorita, I wonder I did not die when they told me! When I got there, some one had built up a little booth of tule over his head, to keep the sun off. He did not call any more, only for water, water. That was what made them think the sun had done it. They did all they could; but it was such a dreadful time, nobody could do much; the sheriff's men were in great hurry; they gave no time. They said the people must all be off in two days. Everybody was running hither and thither. Everything out of the houses in piles on the ground. The people took all the roofs off their houses too. They were made of the tule reeds; so they would do again. Oh, Señorita, don't ask me to tell you any more! It is like death. I can't!"

Ramona was crying bitterly. She did not know what to say. What was love, in face of such calamity? What had she to give to a man stricken like this?

"Don't weep, Señorita," said Alessandro, drearily. "Tears kill one, and do no good."

"How long did your father live?" asked Ramona, clasping her arms closer around his neck. They were sitting on the ground now, and Ramona, yearning over Alessandro, as if she were the strong one and he the one to be sheltered, had drawn his head to her bosom, caressing him as if he had been hers for years. Nothing could have so clearly shown his enfeebled and benumbed condition, as the manner in which he received these caresses, which once would have made him beside himself with joy. He leaned against her breast as a child might.

"He! He died only four days ago. I stayed to bury him, and then I came away. I have been three days on the way; the horse, poor beast, is almost weaker than I. The Americans took my horse," Alessandro said.

Source: Helen Jackson, *Ramona: A Story* (Boston: Little, Brown, 1898), 236–239.

122. Texas Ordinance of Secession, February 1, 1861

Introduction

Americans began settling in Texas during the 1820s while it was still a province of Mexico, laying claim to Comanche hunting grounds without regard to ownership. Throughout the years of the Texas Republic and American statehood, the Comanches raided the settlements, stealing livestock, burning houses, and killing men, women, and children. After a quick strike, they would melt into the arid wilderness, defying the army's attempts at pursuit and avoiding battle. The deployment of U.S. cavalry troops to the Texas frontier during the 1850s did little to make settlement in Texas less perilous. Key to the eventual secession of Texas from the United States in 1861 was the more populous eastern part of the state and its embrace of slavery. However, the first words of the Texas Ordinance of Secession cite the failure of the

federal government to protect the lives and property of Texans from Indians. Although much of the population opposed secession, including Governor Sam Houston, the state seceded on the 25th anniversary of its declaration of independence from Mexico. While Texas Militia and then Confederate soldiers plotted to capture the U.S. Army troops who had tried to protect Texas, Union-loyal soldiers left their posts to return to duty in the North, and others resigned their commissions and turned south.

Primary Source

An Ordinance:

To dissolve the union between the State of Texas and the other States, united under the compact styled "The Constitution of the United States of America."

Whereas,

the Federal Government has failed to accomplish the purposes of the compact of union between these States, in giving protection either to the persons of our people upon an exposed frontier, or to the property of our citizens; and, whereas, the action of the Northern States of the Union is violative of the compact between the States and the guarantees of the Constitution; and whereas the recent developments in Federal affairs, make it evident that the power of the Federal Government is sought to be made a weapon with which to strike down the interests and prosperity of the people of Texas and her Sister slaveholding States, instead of permitting it to be, as was intended, our shield against outrage and aggression:

Therefore,

Section 1

We, the People of the State of Texas, by Delegates in Convention assembled, do declare and ordain, that the Ordinance adopted by our Convention of Delegates, on the Fourth day of July, A.D. 1845, and afterwards ratified by us, under which the Republic of Texas was admitted into Union with other States and became a party to the compact styled "The Constitution of the United States of America" be, and is hereby repealed and annulled; That all the powers, which by said compact were delegated by Texas to the Federal Government, are revoked and resumed; That Texas is of right absolved from all restraints and obligations incurred by said compact, and is a separate Sovereign State, and that her citizens and people are absolved from all allegiance to the United States, or the Government thereof.

Section 2

This ordinance shall be submitted to the people of Texas for ratification or rejection by the qualified voters thereof, on the 23rd day of February 1861, and unless rejected by a majority of the votes cast, shall take effect and be in force on and after the 2nd day of March, A.D. 1861. Provided, that in the Representative District of El Paso, said election may be held on the 19th day of February, A.D. 1861.

Adopted in Convention, at Austin City, the first day of February, A.D. 1861.

Source: *The Constitution of the State of Texas, as Amended in 1861, the Constitution of the Confederate States of America, the Ordinances of the Texas Convention, and an Address to the People of Texas* (Austin: Printed by John Marshall, State Printer, 1861), 18–19.

123. Homestead Act, May 20, 1862 [Excerpt]

Introduction

The Homestead Act granted 160 acres of land, at no cost, to anyone who lived on and worked the land for at least five years. Any person over the age of 21 who was the head of a family and was a born or soon to be naturalized American citizen could avail themselves of a grant by essentially becoming a squatter on the unclaimed public lands in the West. The decades-long drive for free distribution of public land had been stoutly resisted. Easterners did not want to lose laborers and feared that the value of their own property would fall. People in the slaveholding states saw homesteading as a threat to the spread of slavery. The outbreak of the American Civil War (1861–1865) removed the major political obstacle to passage of the act posed by the slaveholding states. The 1862 act specifically denied homesteading privileges to people who had borne arms against the United States or aided the nation's enemies, effectively excluding Confederates. However, the act was amended after the war to include former Confederates. The Homestead Act was subject to abuse, with speculators erecting mere shacks and fraudulently claiming ownership, only to sell the free land for a profit. The act was the greatest single factor in the rapid settlement of the Great Plains after the Civil War, with more than 1 million people claiming more than 80 million acres from 1863 to 1900. This in turn resulted in decades of warfare with the Plains Indians.

Primary Source

Be it enacted, That any person who is the head of a family, or who has arrived at the age of twenty-one years, and is a citizen of the United States, or who shall have filed his declaration of intention to become such, as required by the naturalization laws of the United States, and who has never borne arms against the United States Government or given aid and comfort to its enemies, shall, from and after the first of January, eighteen hundred and sixty-three, be entitled to enter one quarter-section or a less quantity of unappropriated public lands, upon which said person may have filed a pre-emption claim, or which may, at the time the application is made, be subject to pre-emption at one dollar and twenty-five cents, or less, per acre; or eighty acres or less of such unappropriated lands, at two dollars and fifty cents per acre, to be located in a body, in conformity to the legal subdivisions of the public lands, and after the same shall have been surveyed: *Provided,* That any person owning or residing on land may, under the provisions of this act, enter other land lying contiguous to his or her said land, which shall not, with the land so already owned and occupied, exceed in the aggregate one hundred and sixty acres.

Sec. 2. That the person applying for the benefit of this act shall, upon application to the register of the land office in which he or she is about to make such entry, make affidavit before the said register or receiver that he or she is the head of a family, or is twenty-one or more years of age, or shall have performed service in the Army or Navy of the United States, and that he has never borne arms against the Government of the United States or given aid and comfort to its enemies, and that such application is made for his or her exclusive use and benefit, and that said entry is made for the purpose of actual settlement and cultivation, and not, either directly or indirectly, for the use or benefit of any other person or persons whomsoever, and upon filing the said affidavit with the register or receiver, and on payment of ten dollars, he or she shall thereupon be permitted to enter the quantity of land specified: *Provided, however,* That no certificate shall be given or patent issued therefor until the expiration of five years from the date of such entry; and if, at the expiration of such time, or at any time within two years thereafter, the person making such entry—or if he be dead, his widow; or in case of her death, his heirs or devisee; or in case of a widow making such entry, her heirs or devisee, in case of her death—shall prove by two credible witnesses that he, she or they have resided upon or cultivated the same for the term of five years immediately succeeding the time of filing the affidavit aforesaid, and shall make affidavit that no part of said land has been alienated, and that he has borne true allegiance to the Government of the United States; then, in such case, he, she, or they, if at that time a citizen of the United States, shall be entitled to a patent, as in other cases provided for by law: *And provided, further,* That in case of the death of both father and mother, leaving an infant child or children under twenty-one years of age, the right and fee shall inure to the benefit of said infant child or children; and the executor, administrator, or guardian may, at any time within two years after the death of the surviving parent, and in accordance with the laws of the States in which such children for the time being have their domicile, sell said land for the benefit of said infants, but for no other purpose; and the purchaser shall acquire the absolute title by the purchase, and be entitled to a patent from the United States, on payment of the office fees and sum of money herein specified. . . .

Source: Act of May 20, 1862 (Homestead Act), Public Law 37-64, 05/20/1862; Record Group 11; General Records of the United States Government; National Archives.

124. Little Crow, Speech on the Eve of the Minnesota Sioux Uprising, August 18, 1862

Introduction

In 1851 the Sioux had signed treaties ceding land in exchange for money and goods. Widespread treaty violations, official corruption, and nonpayment of promised annuities led to the Minnesota (Santee) Sioux Uprising of 1862, one of the bloodiest Indian wars in American history. The uprising began at a time when U.S. Army regulars had been withdrawn from the western territories to prosecute the American Civil War (1861–1865) in the East. Multiple bands of Sioux joined forces to attack and kill several hundred white settlers in August 1862. In this speech before the attack, Chief Little Crow announces his intention of going to war despite the near certainty of defeat. Noting that the white men are fighting among themselves, he predicts that they will nevertheless defeat the Sioux. The task of retaliation for the Sioux attack fell to a volunteer brigade that went on campaign and captured more than 1,000 Sioux in a matter of weeks. In a single day in a series of brief show trials, military tribunals condemned 303 Sioux to death. President Abraham Lincoln commuted most of the sentences: 38 Sioux were hanged in a mass execution on December 26, 1862, while the rest were imprisoned for four years, during which 1 in 3 of them died. Minnesota's white population resented Lincoln's intervention. The Sioux reservations were confiscated, and the Sioux were exiled to Nebraska. Little Crow and a small band of his followers escaped to Canada. When Little Crow returned to Minnesota the following summer, a settler shot and killed him.

Primary Source

Taoyateduta is not a coward, and he is not a fool! When did he run away from his enemies? When did he leave his braves behind him on the warpath and turn back to his tepee? When you ran away from your enemies, he walked behind on your trail with his face to the Ojibways and covered your backs as a she-bear covers her cubs! Is Taoyateduta without scalps? Look at his war feathers! Behold the scalp locks of your enemies hanging there on his lodgepoles! Do they call him a coward? Taoyateduta is not a coward, and he is not a fool. Braves, you are like little children: you know not what you are doing.

You are full of the white man's devil water. You are like dogs in the Hot Moon when they run mad and snap at their own shadows. We are only little herds of buffalo left scattered; the great herds that once covered the prairies are no more. See!—the white men are like the locusts when they fly so thick that the whole sky is a snowstorm. You may kill one—two—ten; yes, as many as the leaves in the forest yonder, and their brothers will not miss them. Kill one—two—ten, and ten times ten will come to kill you. Count your fingers all day long and white men with guns in their hands will come faster than you can count.

Yes, they fight among themselves—away off. Do you hear the thunder of their big guns? No; it would take you two moons to run down to where they are fighting, and all the way your path would be among white soldiers as thick as tamaracks in the swamps of the Ojibways. Yes, they fight among themselves, but if you strike at them they will all turn on you and devour you and your women and little children just as the locusts in their time fall on the trees and devour all the leaves in one day.

You are fools. You cannot see the face of your chief; your eyes are full of smoke. You cannot hear his voice; your ears are full of roaring waters. Braves, you are little children—you are fools. You will die like the rabbits when the hungry wolves hunt them in the Hard Moon.

Taoyateduta is not a coward: he will die with you.

Source: Hanford Lennox Gordon, *Indian Legends and Other Poems* (Salem, MA: Salem Press Company, 1910), 382–383.

125. Accounts of Chickasaws in Confederate Service, October–November 1864

Introduction

As in previous wars among white people (the French and Indian War, the American Revolutionary War, the War of 1812), Indian individuals and tribes chose sides during the American Civil War (1861–1865) and fought for either the Union or the Confederacy. Despite the fact that most Indian nations had long since been forced to move beyond the western frontiers of the warring states, some deemed it in their interest to join one side or the other, while some preferred to remain neutral. Union and Confederate forces both tried to recruit the Cherokees, Creeks, Choctaws, Chickasaws, and Seminoles, now residing in Indian Territory (present-day Oklahoma), and some tribes themselves split into two factions. The Indian regiments raised by each side fought mostly for control of Indian Territory and the borderlands of the adjacent states. The Cherokee Nation split in two, with Stand Watie—promoted to brigadier general—leading the Confederate faction. The Chickasaw and Choctaw nations fought for the Confederates. The first document below is an act by the Chickasaw legislature calling for volunteers—and failing that, conscription—to Confederate service. The second document is the Chickasaw governor's proclamation calling for volunteers. The third document is a letter from Confederate general Samuel Maxey, who was highly effective as commander of Indian Territory.

Primary Source

Chickasaw Nation Act Calling for Confederate Volunteers and Conscription

HEADQUARTERS DISTRICT OF INDIAN TERRITORY
Fort Towson, C. N., October 27, 1864.

The following acts of the Legislature of the Chickasaw Nation, with the proclamation of Governor Pratt, are published for the information of all concerned:

By order of Maj. Gen. S. B. Maxey:
    M. L. BELL,
    Assistant Adjutant-General.

ACT OF CONSCRIPTION.

First. *Be it enacted by the Legislature of the Chickasaw Nation,* That from and after the passage of this act the Governor be, and he is hereby, required to issue his proclamation calling upon all able-bodied free male citizens of this nation to volunteer in the service of the Confederate States.

Second. *Be it further enacted,* That should not the people respond to the call of the Governor for volunteers for the C. S. service in one month from the passage of the act, all able-bodied free male citizens of this nations between the ages of eighteen and forty five years of age shall be conscripted according to the conscript act of the Confederate states.

Third. *Be it further enacted,* That the lieutenant colonel commanding the Chickasaw Battalion shall have power, and he is hereby authorized, to appoint enrolling officers, whose duty it shall be to enroll all able-bodied free male citizens, as specified in the second section of this act, according to the conscript act of the Confederate States.

Fourth. *Be it further enacted,* That no free male citizen of this nation between the ages specified in the second section of this act shall be allowed to enlist in any Caddo, Comanche or Osage company now in the service of Confederate States.

Passed the House October 11, 1864.

WM. McLish,
    Speaker of the House.

Attest:
    S. S. Gamble.
    Clerk of the House.

Passed the Senate with the amendment October 11, 1864.

    Edmund Perry.
    President pro tempore of the Senate.

Attest:
    B. F. Perry.
    Clerk of the Senate.
    Approved October 11, 1864.

Horace Pratt.
    Governor of the Chickasaw Nation.

Alex Rennie.
    National Secretary.

Approved October 8, 1864.

HORACE PRATT,
    Governor of the Chickasaw Nation.

ALEX. RENNIE,
    National Secretary.

Be it enacted by the Legislature of the Chickasaw Nation, That from and after the passage of this act all civil officers of this nation shall be exempt from military duty.

Second. *Be it further enacted,* That all judges, clerks, sheriffs and constables of this nation shall be exempt from militia duty, provided, however, that in case of a threatened invasion of our country all shall respond to the call of the Governor.

Passed the Senate October 8, 1864.

WM. Kemp.
    President of the Senate.

Attest:
    B. F. Perry.
    Secretary Senate.

Passed the House October 8, 1864.

WM. McLish
    Speaker of the House.

Attest:
    S. S. Gamble,
        Clerk of the House.
    Approved October 8, 1864.

Horace Pratt.
    Governor of the Chickasaw Nation.

Alex Rennie.
    National Secretary.

Chickasaw Governor's Proclamation Calling for Volunteers

PROCLAMATION.

Whereas, the necessities of the times, our treaty stipulations with the Confederate States of America, and a call from the President of the Confederate States require the Chickasaw Nation to furnish troops for the C. S. service, according to the fifty-first article of the treaty made at North Fork, C. N., July 12, 1861, between the Confederate States of America and the Choctaw and Chickasaw Nation, to co-operate with our allied Indian forces now in the field for the defense of our country;

and

Whereas, the Legislature of the Chickasaw Nation did, on the 11th day of October, 1864, pass an act of conscription, to take effect within thirty days from the passage of that act:

Now, therefore, I, Horace Pratt, Governor of the Chickasaw Nation, do issue this my proclamation, in accordance with the first section of that act, calling upon all able bodied free male citizens to volunteer in the service of the Confederate States and fill up the ranks of the First Chickasaw Regiment before the 12th day of November next, and thereby avoid conscription and raise the honor of the Chickasaw Nation, as on the 12th day of November the conscription act goes into effect. And I am justified in stating, for the information of all Concerned, that efforts are being made by the proper officers to furnish the soldiers with good and comfortable clothing, as well as tents and other articles necessary, as soon as possible.

HORACE PRATT,
    Governor Chickasaw Nation.

ALEXANDER RENNIE
    National Secretary.
    Tishomingo, October 12, 1864

Letter from Confederate General Samuel Maxey

HEADQUARTERS DISTRICT OF INDIAN TERRITORY,
    Fort Towson, C. N., November 12, 1864.
    General E. KIRBY SMITH.
    Shreveport, La.:

GENERAL: I returned to this place from my tour yesterday evening. I went to the session of the grand council of the Indians in alliance with the Confederacy, held at Armstrong Academy, upon the invitation of Governor P. P. Pitchlynn, the present principal chief of the Choctaw Nation. Before starting I notified Mr. Israel Folsom, president of the council, of the day I would arrive. Upon my arrival a resolution was presented requesting me to deliver an address upon the condition of the Territory on Saturday last at 10 a. m. This was delivered to me at my camp on Friday evening by the committee, Col. D. N. McIntosh, First Creek Regiment, and Col. W. P. Adair, Second Cherokee Regiment, delegates from their respective nations. In compliance with the request of the council, as contained in the resolution, I addressed that body on Saturday in a speech of three hours. The delegations from the different tribes and nations were full, and as a general rule, from the leading nations, and would compare favorably in point of intelligence and talent with similar bodies in the States. I was only in the council chamber on the above occasion, but have learned from various sources that the session was harmonious, closing on Thursday evening last. I am convinced from what I saw and have heard from intelligent members, that a general confidence in the ultimate success of our cause pervaded the members, and a general determination to comply religiously with the terms of the treaty. The council, by resolution after I left, fully indorsed my administration, civil and military. I have been furnished with official copies of their resolutions relating to myself, and respectfully forward to you copies. In view of the efforts of a few to bring about a change of district commanders, this action of the general grand council of the allied nations was very gratifying. My course has been indorsed by the department commander, the Commissioner of Indian Affairs, the council of the tribes and nations in alliance, the people in the contiguous portions of Texas and Arkansas, and above all, by my own conscience, and whatever action the War Department or the President may see fit to take, I shall now rest satisfied. The command of this district is not desirable. There are more embarrassing elements to contend with here than elsewhere, and the labor, physical and mental, is very great. I was, however, unwilling to be relieved by any order that has the appearance of censure. So far as my own reputation is concerned, it will not be increased or diminished by the action of the War Department, whatever it may be. I went into this war for the good of the country, and have as much interest in success as the President or any other citizen. No position in the Army that could be conferred, however high, would be accepted in time of peace, and when that glorious time comes round again I shall gladly retire to my citizen home and wonted civil pursuits. As to the opinions that may be entertained of me, I have all my life through endeavored to be governed by the advice of Cardinal Wolsey to Cromwell:

Be just, and fear not.
> Let all the ends thou aim'st at be thy country's.
> Thy God's and truth's: then, if thou fall'st, O, Cromwell!
> Thou fall'st a blessed martyr.

And when I have the blessing of an approving conscience I care very little for the opinions of men. In this case this council has done what its members conceive but simple justice. I feel assured that you will be pleased at this action. It sustains you to the full in your own course.

Very sincerely, your friend,

S.B. Maxey,
Major General

Source: *The War of the Rebellion: A Compilation of the Official Records of the Union and Confederate Armies,* Series I, Vol. 53 (Washington, DC: U.S. Government Printing Office, 1898), 1024–1026.

126. Report of the Southern Treaty Commission, October 30, 1865

Introduction

As in previous wars among white people, Indian individuals and tribes chose sides during the American Civil War (1861–1865) and fought for either the Union or the Confederacy, although some tried to remain neutral. Union and Confederate forces both tried to recruit the Cherokees, Creeks, Choctaws, Chickasaws, and Seminoles residing in Indian Territory (present-day Oklahoma). The Indian regiments raised by each side fought mostly for control of Indian Territory and the borderlands of the adjacent states. The Cherokee Nation split in two, while the Chickasaw and Choctaw nations fought for the Confederates. When the Civil War ended, the U.S. government sent a special delegation to Fort Smith in Indian Territory, where the commissioner of Indian affairs was to negotiate the terms for future relations with the tribes of the territory as well as those of Kansas and the western Plains. The commissioner stated that supporters of the Confederacy had forfeited any benefits provided by previous treaties with the United States but that the government was willing to reestablish relations. Among the conditions required for renewal of relations was the emancipation of all slaves held by Indians. The Indians' main objection to the proposed terms was the one requiring that all tribes in Indian Territory be consolidated under a single government as a territory of the United States. It took until the following year for most of the tribes to agree on treaty terms.

Primary Source

Report of D. N. Cooley, as president of the southern treaty commission.
Department of the Interior,
Office of Indian Affairs, October 30, 1865.

Sir: As president of the commission designated by the President to negotiate, under your instructions, "a treaty or treaties with all or any of the nations, tribes, or bands of Indians now located in the Indian country or in the State of Kansas, and also with the Indians of the plains west of Kansas and the said Indian country," I have the honor to submit the following:

The commission, as designated, consisted of myself; Elijah Sells, superintendent for the southern Indians; honorable Mr. Edmunds, Commissioner of the General Land Office; Thomas Wistar, of Pennsylvania; Major General W. S. Harney, United States army; Major General Herron; Colonel Ely S. Parker, of Lieutenant General Grant's staff; associated in the capacity of secretary and assistant secretaries were Mr. Mix, chief clerk of the Indian bureau, and Messrs. Irwin and Cook, who were detailed as employees of the government. Messrs. Edmunds and Herron declined to accompany the commission for reasons which I understand were regarded as satisfactory to the department. The residue of the commission, excepting General Harney, who arrived at Fort Smith by water communication from St. Louis, left Leavenworth, Kansas, on the day of August, en route by land for Fort Smith, under arrangements made by Major General Dodge, commanding at Fort Leavenworth. The party reached Fort Smith on the evening of the September, and every facility in his power was afforded it by Brigadier General Bussy, in command at the post, and the officers connected with him.

So soon as the necessary arrangements could be effected for preparing a room in one of the buildings within the walls of the fort for the occupancy of the commission as a council chamber, intelligence was imparted to the different delegations who had informally communicated their arrival that tbe council would open on Friday, the 8th day of September. The council was accordingly convened on that day, when there appeared representatives from loyal members of the following named tribes, viz: Creeks, Osages, Quapaws. Senecas, and Senecas and Shawnees of the Neosho agency, Cherokees, Seminoles, Shawnees, and Wyandotts, from Kansas, Chickasaws and Ohoctaws.

The United States agents present were: Major Snow, for Osages, Quapaws, Senecas, Senecas and Shawnees; George A. Reynolds, Seminoles; Isaac Colman, Choctaws and Chickasaws; Justin Harlan, Cherokees; J. W. Dunn, Creeks; Milo Gookins, Wichitas and other affiliated tribes located within the country leased by Chickasaws and Choctaws; and J. B. Abbott for Shawnees in Kansas.

(It is proper here to remark that the delegation from the disloyal Indians had not arrived; and that the Delawares, and Sacs and Foxes, located in Kansas, who were expected, were not present at any of the councils.)

The council was called to order by me, as president of the commission; after which the blessing of the Great Spirit over our deliberations was invoked by Rev. Lewis Downing, acting chief of the Cherokee nation. When Mr. Downing had concluded, I addressed the council as follows:

Brothers: It is proper that thanks should be returned to the Great Spirit, the creator of us all, that our lives have been preserved to meet upon this occasion. This, as you saw, has been done in our style of addressing the Great Spirit. We have thanked Him for His goodness in keeping us in good health, and for putting it into your minds to meet us at this time. We trust that His wisdom may guide us all in the deliberations on every question that may come before us.

We are glad to meet so many of our brothers in council, and pray the Great Spirit to keep you all in health, and to preserve your wives and children during your absence, and return us all safely to our homes when our council shall terminate.

Brothers: You will listen further: your Great Father the President, hearing that the Indians in the southwest desired to meet commissioners sent by him, in council, to renew their allegiance to the United States, and to settle difficulties among themselves which have arisen in consequence of a portion of the several tribes uniting with wicked white men who have engaged in war, has sent the commissioners now before you to hear and consider any matter which you may desire to lay before us, and to make a treaty of peace and amity with all his red children who may desire his favor and protection.

Portions of several tribes and nations have attempted to throw off their allegiance to the United States, and have made treaty stipulations with the enemies of the government, and have been in open war with those who remained loyal and true, and at war with the United States. All such have rightfully forfeited all annuities and interests in the lands in the Indian territory; but with the return of peace, after subduing and punishing severely in battle those who caused the rebellion, the President is willing to hear his erring children in extenuation of their great crime. He has authorized us to make new treaties with such nations and tribes as are willing to be at peace among themselves and with the United States.

The President has been deeply pained by the course of those who have violated their plighted faith and treaty obligations by engaging in war with those in rebellion against the United States.

He directs us to say to those who remain true, and who have aided him in punishing the rebels, he is well pleased with you, and your rights and interests will be protected by the United States.

The President directs us to express to you the hope that your dissensions may soon all be healed, and your people soon again united, prosperous, and happy.

We are now ready to hear anything you may wish to say in reply.

The response and explanations of the different nations and tribes will be found in the proceedings of the council, hereto appended.

On the second day [Saturday, September 9], after council met, I addressed the Indians, in which I stated that the commissioners had considered the talks of the Indians on the preceding day, and had authorized me to submit the following statement and propositions, as the basis on which the United States were prepared to negotiate with them:

"Brothers: We are instructed by the President to negotiate a treaty or treaties with any or all of the nations, tribes, or bands of Indians in the Indian territory, Kansas, or of the plains west of the Indian territory and Kansas.

"The following named nations and tribes have by their own acts, by making treaties with the enemies of the United States at the dates hereafter named, forfeited all right to annuities, lands, and protection by the United States.

"The different nations and tribes having made treaties with the rebel government are as follows, viz: The Creek nation, July 10, 1861; Choctaws and Chickasaws, July 12, 1861; Seminoles, August 1, 1861; Shawnees, Delawares, Wichitas and affiliated tribes residing in leased territory, August 12, 1861; the Comanches of the Prairie, August 12, 1861; the Great Osages, October 21, 1861; the Senecas, Senecas and Shawnees, (Neosho agency,) October 4, 1861; the Quapaws, October 4, 1861; the Cherokees, October 7, 1861.

"By these nations having entered into treaties with the so-called Confederate States, and the rebellion being now ended, they are left without any treaty whatever or treaty obligations for protection by the United States.

"Under the terms of the treaties with the United States, and the law of Congress of July 5, 1862, all these nations and tribes forfeited and lost all their rights to annuities and lands. The President, however, does not desire to take advantage of or enforce the penalties for the unwise actions of these nations.

"The President is anxious to renew the relations which existed at the breaking out of the rebellion.

"We, as representatives of the President, are empowered to enter into new treaties with the proper delegates of the tribes located within the socalled Indian territory, and others above named, living west and north of the Indian territory.

"Such treaties must contain substantially the following stipulations:

"1. Each tribe must enter into a treaty for permanent peace and amity with themselves, each nation and tribe, and with the United States.

"2. Those settled in the Indian territory must bind themselves, when called upon by the government, to aid in compelling the Indians of the plains to maintain peaceful relations with each other, with the Indians in the territory, and with the United States.

"3. The institution of slavery, which has existed among several of the tribes, must be forthwith abolished, and measures taken for the unconditional emancipation of all persons held in bondage, and for their incorporation into the tribes on an equal footing with the original members, or suitably provided for.

"4. A stipulation in the treaties that slavery, or involuntary servitude, shall never exist in the tribe or nation, except in punishment of crime.

"5. A portion of the lands hitherto owned and occupied by you must be set apart for the friendly tribes in Kansas and elsewhere, on such terms as may be agreed upon by the parties and approved by government, or such as may be fixed by the government.

"6. It is the policy of the government, unless other arrangement be made, that all the nations and tribes in the Indian territory be formed into one consolidated government after the plan proposed by the Senate of the United States, in a bill for organizing the Indian territory.

"7. No white person, except officers, agents, and employees of the government, or of any internal improvement authorized by the government, will be permitted to reside in the territory, unless formally incorporated with some tribes, according to the usages of the band.

"BROTHERS: You have now heard and understand what are the views and wishes of the President; and the commissioners, as they told you yesterday, will expect definite answers from each of you upon the questions submitted.

"As we said yesterday, we say again, that, in any event, those who have always been loyal, although their nation may have gone over to the enemy, will be liberally provided for and dealt with."

I then caused copies of the statement and propositions to be prepared and furnished to each agent, with instructions that they be fully interpreted and explained to them.

Source: *Report of the Commissioner of Indian Affairs for the Year 1865* (Washington, DC: U.S. Government Printing Office, 1865), 296–299.

127. U.S. Congress, Joint Commission on the Conduct of the War, Report on the Sand Creek Massacre, 1865

Introduction

The brutal Sand Creek Massacre of November 29, 1865, saw the murder of close to 200 Cheyenne and allied Indians, most of them women and children. At the time Cheyenne bands still actively resisted American settlement in Colorado, so feelings ran high against them. However, the Indians at Sand Creek had previously surrendered their weapons and cooperated with the U.S. government. Local authorities had led them to believe that they were under U.S. protection. Colonel John M. Chivington planned and led the attack. He ordered his Colorado volunteers to slaughter every Indian in the Sand Creek village and to take no prisoners.

At first Chivington reported victory against a well-armed enemy, but eyewitness accounts of atrocities—including soldiers displaying Indian body parts as trophies—soon surfaced and led to a congressional investigation in 1865. The Joint Committee on the Conduct of the War, whose conclusions are excerpted here, heard testimony about Chivington's calculated cruelty, ruled the attack a massacre, and called for charges against those responsible. No charges were ever brought. The entire history of warfare against the Indians on the American frontier included indiscriminate slaughter of friendly Indians by whites. Such episodes invariably turned friend into foe and prolonged wars. The massacre on Sand Creek prolonged war with the Cheyennes and their allies for years to come.

Primary Source

In the summer of 1864, Governor [John] Evans, of Colorado Territory, as acting superintendent of Indian Affairs, sent notice to the various bands and tribes of Indians within his jurisdiction that such as desired to be considered friendly to the whites should at once repair to the nearest military post in order to be protected from the soldiers who were to take the field against the hostile Indians.

About the close of the summer, some Cheyenne Indians, in the neighborhood of the Smoke Hills, sent word to Major [Edward W.] Wynkoop, the commandant of the post of Fort Lyon, that they had in their possession, and were willing to deliver up, some white captives they had purchased of other Indians. Major Wynkoop, with a force of over 100 men, visited these Indians and received the white captives. On his return he was accompanied by a number of the chiefs and leading men of the Indians, whom he had invited to visit Denver for the purpose of conferring with the authorities there in regard to keeping peace. Among them were Black Kettle and White Antelope of the Cheyennes, and some chiefs of the Arapahoes. The council was held and these chiefs stated that they were very friendly to the whites, and always had been, and that they desired peace. Governor Evans and Colonel Chivington, the commander of that military district, advised them to repair to Fort Lyon and submit to whatever terms the military commander there should impose. This was done by the Indians, who were treated somewhat as prisoners of war, receiving rations, and being obliged to remain within certain bounds.

All the testimony goes to show that the Indians, under the immediate control of Black Kettle and White Antelope of the Cheyennes, and Left Hand of the Arapahoes, were and had been friendly to the whites, and had not been guilty of any acts of hostility or depredation. The Indian agents, the Indian interpreter and others examined by your committee, all testify to the good character of those Indians. Even Governor Evans and Major [Scott A.] Anthony, though evidently willing to convey to your committee a false impression of the character of those Indians, were forced, in spite of their prevarication, to admit that they knew of nothing they [the Indians] had done which rendered them deserving of punishment.

A northern band of the Cheyennes, known as the Dog Soldiers, had been guilty of acts of hostility; but all the testimony goes to prove that they had no connexion with Black Kettle's band, but acted in spite of his authority and influence. Black Kettle and his band denied all connexion with or responsibility for the Dog Soldiers, and Left Hand and his band of Arapahoes were equally friendly.

These Indians, at the suggestion of Governor Evans and Colonel Chivington, repaired to Fort Lyon and placed themselves under the protection of Major Wynkoop. They were led to believe that they were regarded in the light of friendly Indians, and would be treated as such so long as they conducted themselves quietly.

The treatment extended to those Indians by Major Wynkoop does not seem to have satisfied those in authority there, and for some cause, which does not appear, he was removed, and Major Scott J. Anthony was assigned to the command of Fort Lyon; but even Major Anthony seems to have found it difficult at first to pursue any different course toward the Indians he found there. They were entirely within the power of the military. Major Anthony having demanded their arms, which they surrendered to him, they conducted themselves quietly, and in every way manifested a disposition to remain at peace with the whites. For a time even he continued issuing rations to them as Major Wynkoop had done; but it was determined by Major Anthony (whether upon his own motion or as the suggestion of others does not appear) to pursue a different course towards these friendly Indians. They were called together and told that rations could no longer be issued to them, and they had better go where they could obtain subsistence by hunting. At the suggestion of Major Anthony (and from one in his position a suggestion was the equivalent to a command) these Indians went to a place on Sand Creek, about thirty-five miles from Fort Lyon, and there established their camp, their arms being restored to them. He told them that he then had no authority to make peace with them; but in case he received such authority he would inform them of it. In his testimony he says:

"I told them they might go back on Sand creek, or between there and the headwaters of the Smoky Hill, and remain there until I received instructions from the department headquarters, from General [Samuel R.] Curtis; and that in case I did receive any authority to make peace with them I would go right over and let them know it. *I did not state to them that I would give them notice in case we intended to attack them.* They went away with that understanding, and in case I received instructions from department headquarters I was to let them know it."

To render the Indians less apprehensive of any danger, One Eye, a Cheyenne chief, was allowed to remain with them to obtain information for the use of the military authorities. He was employed at $125 a month, and several times brought to Major Anthony, at Fort Lyon, information of proposed movements of other, hostile bands. Jack Smith, a half-breed son of John S. Smith, an Indian interpreter, employed by the government, was also there for the same purpose. A U.S. soldier was allowed to remain there,

and two days before the massacre Mr. Smith, the interpreter, was permitted to go there with goods to trade with the Indians. Everything practicable seems to have been done to remove from the minds of the Indians any fear of approaching danger; and when Colonel Chivington commenced his movement he took all of the precautions in his power to prevent these Indians learning of his approach. For some days all travel on that route was forcibly stopped by him, not even the mail being allowed to pass. On the morning of 28 November he appeared at Fort Lyon with over 700 mounted men and two pieces of artillery. One of his first acts was to throw a guard around the post to prevent any one from leaving it. At this place Major Anthony joined him with 125 men and two pieces of artillery.

That night, the entire party started from Fort Lyon, and, by a forced march, arrived at the Indian camp, on Sand creek, shortly after daybreak. The Indian camp consisted of about 100 lodges of Cheyennes, under Black Kettle, and from 8 to 10 lodges of Arapahoes under Left Hand. It is estimated that each lodge contained five or more persons, and that more than one-half were women and children.

Upon observing the approach of the soldiers, Black Kettle, the head chief, ran up to the top of his lodge an American flag, which had been presented to him some years before by Commissioner [of Indian Affairs Alfred B.] Greenwood, with a small white flag under it, as he had been advised to do in case he met with any troops on the prairies. Mr. Smith, the interpreter, supposing that they might be strange troops, unaware of the character of the Indians encamped there, advanced from his lodge to meet them, but was fired upon, and returned to his lodge.

And then the scene of murder and barbarity began—men, women, and children were indiscriminately slaughtered. In a few minutes all the Indians were flying over the plain in terror and confusion. A few who endeavored to hide themselves under the bank of the creek were surrounded and shot down in cold blood, offering but feeble resistance. From the sucking babe to the old warrior, all who were overtaken were deliberately murdered. Not content with killing women and children, who were incapable of offering any resistance, the soldiers indulged in acts of barbarity of the most revolting character; such, it is to be hoped, as never before disgraced the acts of men claiming to be civilized. No attempt was made by the officers to restrain the savage cruelty of the men under their command, but they stood by and witnessed these acts without one word of reproof, if they did not incite their commission. For more than two hours the work of murder and barbarity was continued, until more than one hundred dead bodies, three fourths of them women and children, lay on the plain as evidences of the fiendish malignity and cruelty of the officers who had sedulously and carefully plotted the massacre, and of the soldiers who had so faithfully acted out the spirit of their officers.

It is difficult to believe that beings in the form of men, and disgracing the uniform of United States soldiers and officers, could commit or countenance the commission of such acts of cruelty and barbarity as are detailed in the testimony, but which your committee will not specify in the report. It is true that there seems to have existed among the people inhabiting the region of country a hostile feeling towards the Indians. Some of the Indians had committed acts of hostility towards the whites; but no effort seems to have been made by the authorities there to prevent these hostilities, other than by the commission of even worse acts. The hatred of the whites to the Indians would seem to have been inflamed and excited to the utmost; the bodies of persons killed at a great distance—whether by Indians or not, is not certain—were brought to the capital of the Territory and exposed to the public gaze for the purpose of inflaming still more the already excited feeling of the people. Their cupidity was appealed to, for the governor in a proclamation calls upon all, "either individually or in such parties as they may organize," "to kill and destroy as enemies of the country, wherever they may be found, all such hostile Indians," authorizing them to "hold to their own private use and benefit all the property of said hostile Indians that they may capture." What Indians he would ever term friendly it is impossible to tell. His testimony before your committee was characterized by such prevarication and shuffling as has been shown by no witness they have examined during the four years they have been engaged in their investigations; and for the evident purpose of avoiding admission that he was fully aware that the Indians massacred so brutally at Sand creek, were then, and had been, actuated by the most friendly feelings towards the whites, and had done all in their power to restrain those less friendly disposed.

The testimony of Major Anthony, who succeeded an officer disposed to treat these Indians with justice and humanity, is sufficient of itself to show how unprovoked and unwarranted was this massacre. He testifies that he found these Indians in the neighborhood of Fort Lyon when he assumed command of that post; that they professed their friendliness to the whites, and their willingness to do whatever he demanded of them; that they delivered their arms up to him; and they went to and encamped upon the place designated by him; that they gave him information from time to time of acts of hostility which were meditated by other and hostile bands, and in every way conducted themselves properly and peaceably, and yet he says it was fear and not principle which prevented his killing them while they were completely in his power. And when Colonel Chivington appeared at Fort Lyon, on his mission of murder and barbarity, Major Anthony made haste to accompany him with men and artillery, although Colonel Chivington had no authority whatever over him.

As to Colonel Chivington, your committee can hardly find fitting terms to describe his conduct. Wearing the uniform of the United States, which should be the emblem of justice and humanity; holding the important position of commander of a military district, and therefore having the honor of the government to that extent in his keeping, he deliberately and executed a foul and dastardly massacre which would have disgraced the veriest savage among those who were the victims of his cruelty. Having full knowledge of their friendly character, having himself been instrumental to some extent in placing them in their position of fancied security, he took advantage of their inapprehension and defenceless condition to gratify the worst passions that ever cursed the heart of man. It is thought by some that desire for political preferment prompted him to this cowardly act; that he supposed that by pandering to the inflamed passions of an excited population he could recommend himself to their regard and consideration. Others think it was to avoid being sent where there was more of danger and hard service to be performed; that he was willing to get up a show of hostility on the part of the Indians by committing himself acts which savages themselves would never premeditate. Whatever may have been his motive, it is to be hoped that the authority of this government will never again be disgraced by acts such as he and those acting with him have been guilty of committing.

There were *hostile* Indians not far distant, against which Colonel Chivington could have led the force under his command. Major Anthony testifies that but three or four days' march from his post were several hundreds of Indians, generally believed to be engaged in acts of hostility towards the whites. And he deliberately testifies that only the fear of them prevented him from killing those who were friendly and entirely within his reach and control. It is true that to reach them required some days of hard marching. It was not to be expected that they could be surprised as easily as those on Sand creek; and the warriors among them were almost, if not quite, as numerous as the soldiers under the control of Colonel Chivington. Whatever influence this may have had upon Colonel Chivington, the truth is that he surprised and murdered in cold blood, the unsuspecting men, women, and children on Sand Creek, who had every reason to believe they were under the protection of the United States authorities, and then returned to Denver and boasted of the brave deeds he and the men under his command had performed.

The Congress of the United States, at its last session, authorized the appointment of a commission to investigate all matters relating to the administration of Indian Affairs within the limits of the United States. Your committee most sincerely trust that the result of their inquiry will be the adoption of measures which will render impossible the employment of officers, civil and military, such as have heretofore made the administration of Indian Affairs in this country a byword and reproach.

In conclusion, your committee are of the opinion that for the purpose of vindicating the cause of justice and upholding the honor of the nation, prompt and energetic measures should be at once taken to remove from office those who have thus disgraced the government by whom they are employed, and to punish, as their crimes deserve, those who have been guilty of these brutal and cowardly acts.

Source: United States Congress, Senate, "Report of the Secretary of War, Sand Creek Massacre," Senate Executive Document No. 26, 39th Cong., 2nd Sess., 1867.

128. Ely S. Parker, Letter to Ulysses S. Grant on the "Indian Problem," ca. 1866 [Excerpts]

Introduction

Ely S. Parker (1828–1895) was a Seneca Indian from New York, the son of a chief and a tribal leader in his own right. Parker, trained as a lawyer and an engineer, moved to Illinois, where he struck up a friendship with Ulysses S. Grant, then a shopkeeper. When Parker tried to volunteer for the Union Army, he was rejected on the basis of his race. Grant interceded to get him a commission. After serving as an army engineer and then as an aide to Grant, Parker became Grant's military secretary in 1864 and was present at Robert E. Lee's surrender in April 1865. After the war, Parker remained on Grant's staff and rose to the rank of brigadier general. During this period Parker wrote the letter to Grant that is excerpted here. In it Parker presents his ideas for dealing with Indian affairs in the West. He suggests transferring the Bureau of Indian Affairs back to the War Department, establishing a permanent government and boundaries for Indian Territory, and setting up a commission to ensure prompt payment of the annuities promised to Indians and encourage them to take up agriculture and assimilate into white society. Parker served as President Grant's commissioner of Indian affairs from 1869 to 1871, the first Indian to hold that office. While in office, Parker was responsible for designing and implementing Grant's Peace Policy.

Primary Source

General: In compliance with your request, I have the honor to submit the following proposed plan for the establishment of a permanent and perpetual peace, and for settling all matters of differences between the United States and the various Indian tribes.

First. The transfer of the Indian Bureau from the Interior Department back to the War Department, or military branch of the government, where it originally belonged, until within the last few years.

The condition and disposition of all the Indians west of the Mississippi river, as developed in consequence of the great and rapid influx of immigration by reason of the discovery of the precious metals throughout the entire west, renders it of the utmost importance that military supervision should be extended over the Indians. Treaties have been made with a very large number of the tribes, and generally reservations have been provided as homes for them. Agents appointed from civil life have generally been provided to protect their lives and property, and to attend to the prompt and faithful observance of treaty stipulations. But as the hardy pioneer and adventurous miner advanced into the inhospitable regions occupied by the Indians in search of the precious metals, they found no rights possessed by the Indians that they were bound to respect. The faith of treaties solemnly entered into

were totally disregarded, and Indian territory wantonly violated. If any tribe remonstrated against the violation of their natural treaty rights, members of the tribe were inhumanely shot down and the whole treated as mere dogs. Retaliation generally followed, and bloody Indian wars have been the consequence, costing many lives and much treasure. In all troubles arising in this manner the civil agents have been totally powerless to avert the consequences, and when too late the military have been called in to protect the whites and punish the Indians, when if, in the beginning, the military had had the supervision of the Indians, their rights would not have been improperly molested, or if disturbed in their quietude by any lawless whites, a prompt and summary check to any further aggressions could have been given. In cases where the government promises the Indians the quiet and peaceable possession of a reservation, and precious metals are discovered or found to exist upon it, the military alone can give the Indians the needed protection and keep the adventurous miner from encroaching upon the Indians until the government has come to some understanding with them. In such cases the civil agent is absolutely powerless.

Most . . . Indian treaties contain stipulations for the payment annually to Indians of annuities, either in money or goods, or both, and agents are appointed to make these payments whenever government furnishes them the means. I know of no reason why officers of the army could not make these payments as well as civilians. The expense of agencies would be saved, and, I think, the Indians would be more honestly dealt by. An officer's honor and interest is at stake, which impels him to discharge his duty honestly and faithfully, while civil agents have none of these incentives, the ruling passion with them being generally to avoid all trouble and responsibility, and to make as much money as possible out of their offices.

In the retransfer of this bureau I would provide for the complete abolishment of the system of Indian traders, which, in my opinion, is a great evil to Indian communities. I would make government the purchaser of all articles usually brought in by Indians, giving them a fair equivalent for the same in money or goods at cost prices. In this way it would be an easy matter to regulate the sale of issue of arms and ammunition to Indians, a question which of late has agitated the minds of the civil and military authorities. If the entry of large numbers of Indians to any military post is objectionable, it can easily be arranged that only limited numbers shall be admitted daily. . . .

Second. The next measure I would suggest is the passage by Congress of a plan of territorial government for the Indians, as was submitted last winter, or a similar one. When once passed it should remain upon the statute-books as the permanent and settled policy of the government. The boundaries of the Indian territory or territories should be well defined by metes and bounds, and should remain inviolate from settlement by any except Indians and government employees.

The subject of the improvement and civilization of the Indians, and the maintenance of peaceful relations with them, has engaged the serious consideration of every administration since the birth of the American republic; and, if I recollect aright, President Jefferson was the first to inaugurate the policy of removal of the Indians from the States to the country west of the Mississippi; and President Monroe, in furtherance of this policy, recommended that the Indians be concentrated, as far as was practicable, and civil governments established for them, with schools for every branch of instruction in literature and the arts of civilized life. The plan of removal was adopted as the policy of the government, and, by treaty stipulation, affirmed by Congress; lands were set apart for tribes removing into the western wilds, and the faith of a great nation pledged that the homes selected by Indians should be and remain their homes forever, unmolested by the hand of the grasping and avaricious white man; and, in some cases, the government promised that the Indian homes and lands should never be incorporated within the limits of any new State that might be organized. How the pledges so solemnly given and the promises made were kept, the history of the western country can tell. It is presumed that humanity dictated the original policy of the removal and concentration of the Indians in the west to save them from threatened extinction. But to-day, by reason of the immense augmentation of the American population, and the extension of their settlements throughout the entire west, covering both slopes of the Rocky mountains, the Indian races are more seriously threatened with a speedy extermination than ever before in the history of the country. And, however much such a deplorable result might be wished for by some, it seems to me that the honor of a Christian nation and every sentiment of humanity dictate that no pains should be spared to avert such an appalling calamity befalling a portion of the human race. The establishment of the Indians upon any one territory is perhaps impracticable, but numbers of them can, without doubt, be consolidated in separate districts of the country, and the same system of government made to apply to each. By the concentration of tribes, although in several and separate districts, government can more readily control them and more economically press and carry out the plans for their improvement and civilization, and a better field be offered for philanthropic aid and Christian instruction. Some system of this kind has, at different periods in the history of our government, been put forward, but never successfully put into execution. A renewal of the attempt, with proper aids, it seems to me cannot fail of success.

Third. The passage by Congress of an act authorizing the appointment of an inspection board, or commission, to hold office during good behavior, or until the necessity for their services is terminated by the completion of the retransfer of the Indian Bureau to the War Department. It shall be the duty of this board to examine the account of the several agencies, see that every cent due the Indians is paid to them promptly as may be promised in treaties, and that proper and suitable goods and implements of agriculture are delivered to them when such articles are due; to make semi-annual reports, with such suggestions as, in their judgment, might seem necessary to the perfect establishment of a

permanent and friendly feeling between the people of the United States and the Indians.

This commission could undoubtedly be dispensed with in a few years, but the results of their labors might be very important and beneficial, not only in supervising and promptly checking the delinquencies of incompetent and dishonest agents, but it would be a most convincing proof to the Indians' mind that the government was disposed to deal honestly and fairly by them. Such a commission might, indeed, be rendered wholly unnecessary if Congress would consent to the next and fourth proposition which I submit in this plan.

Fourth. The passage of an act authorizing the appointment of a permanent Indian commission, to be a mixed commission, composed of such white men as possessed in a large degree the confidence of their country, and a number of the most reputable educated Indians, selected from different tribes. The entire commission might be composed of ten members, and, if deemed advisable, might be divided so that five could operate north and five south of a given line, but both to be governed by the same general instructions, and impressing upon the Indians the same line of governmental policy. It shall be made their duty to visit all the Indian tribes within the limits of the United States, whether, to do this, it requires three, five, or ten years. They shall hold talks with them, setting forth the great benefits that would result to them from a permanent peace with the whites, from their abandonment of their nomadic mode of life, and adopting agricultural and pastoral pursuits, and the habits and modes of civilized communities. Under the directions of the president the commission shall explain to the various tribes the advantages of their consolidation upon some common territory, over which Congress shall have extended the ægis of good, wise, and wholesome laws for their protection and perpetuation. It would be wise to convince the Indians of the great power and number of the whites; that they cover the whole land, to the north, south, east and west of them. I believe they could easily understand that although this country was once wholly inhabited by Indians, the tribes, and many of them once powerful, who occupied the countries now constituting the States east of the Mississippi, have, one by one, been exterminated by their abortive attempts to stem the western march of civilization.

They could probably be made to comprehend that the waves of population and civilization are upon every side of them; that it is too strong for them to resist; and that, unless they fall in line with the current of destiny as it rolls and surges around them, they must succumb and be annihilated by its overwhelming force. In consequence of the gradual extinction of the Indian races, and the failure of almost every plan heretofore attempted for the amelioration of their condition, and the prolongation of their national existence, and also because they will not abandon their savage tastes and propensities, it has of late years become somewhat common, not only for the press, but in the speeches of men of intelligence, and some occupying high and responsible positions, to advocate the policy of their immediate and absolute extermination. Such a proposition, so revolting to every sense of humanity and Christianity, it seems to me could not for one moment be entertained by any enlightened nation. On the contrary, the honor of the national character and the dictates of a sound policy, guided by the principles of religion and philanthropy, would urge the adoption of a system to avert the extinction of a people, however unenlightened they may be. The American government can never adopt the policy of a total extermination of the Indian race within her limits, numbering, perhaps, less than four hundred thousand, without a cost of untold treasure and lives of her people, beside exposing herself to the abhorrence and censure of the entire civilized world.

Source: Ely S. Parker, "Letter to Ulysses S. Grant (1864)," Senate Executive Document No. 13, 40th Cong., 1st Sess., 42–47.

129. Frances Carrington, Account of the Fort Phil Kearny Massacre, 1866

Introduction

When gold was discovered in Montana, the army attempted to establish a more direct route to the mines. Known as the Bozemen Trail, the route passed through land that had been reserved by treaty for the Sioux, Cheyennes, and Arapahos. When Colonel Henry B. Carrington and his troops began work on the trail before a new treaty was signed, Red Cloud of the Sioux cut off the negotiations. Carrington established Fort Phil Kearny in Wyoming in 1866, and its garrison—which included several soldiers' families—existed in a state of siege. On December 21, 1866, when the Sioux attacked a party of woodcutters, Captain William Fetterman led 80 men to their rescue. The Sioux then lured the soldiers into an ambush and killed every man. This account of the event that became known as the Fetterman Massacre is taken from a book about life on the frontier by an army wife. At the time of the massacre that made her a widow, the author, Frances Carrington, was actually Mrs. Grummond, whose husband, Lieutenant George Grummond, commanded the cavalry detachment in Fetterman's doomed relief column. The first Mrs. Carrington, Margaret (who wrote a memoir of her own, *An Army Wife on the Frontier*) befriended the newly widowed Mrs. Grummond. After Margaret's death in 1870, Colonel Carrington married Frances.

Primary Source

The usual "reveille" broke the stillness of the sunrise hour, to be followed in turn by "sick call" and "guard-mounting," the latter accompanied by the music of the full band, always a grateful and cheering accompaniment. Had the vision been limited to our immediate environment it would only suggest the ordinary routine exercises and functions of almost any frontier garrison in time of peace.

The wood-train moved out a little later than usual to the Pinery to begin the formal duty of the day, but with a stronger guard than before, numbering ninety men. It had gone but a short distance beyond view from the fort when the picket on Pilot Hill signaled many Indians, and that the train already had been forced to go into corral. This was not an unusual alarm, but a never-failing signal that would bring every man out of quarters with eyes and ears alert until a detail could be suitably organized and sent to its relief. Indians actually appeared for the first time, on several hills at once, although in small numbers; but the glass of Colonel Carrington revealed others in the thickets along the Big Piney Creek just in front of the fort. Their object seemed to be to test the watchfulness of the garrison and gain information as to the strength of the force that would leave the stockade in aid of the endangered wood-party. Several case-shots fired from a mountain howitzer exploded over their hiding-places, dismounted some and scattered others who broke for the hills and ravines to the north in hot haste. The "gun that shoots twice" and distributes more than eighty one-ounce balls as though dropped from the sky was entirely too mysterious and realistic for the Indian to linger within its range.

In the meantime, Brevet Lieutenant Colonel Fetterman, the senior Captain at the Post, claimed that his seniority as captain entitled him to command the relieving party, and his request was complied with. He also was given the choice of his own company and such additional details as he might select for himself. Captain Frederick Brown, just promoted and about to leave for the East, had been the district and regimental quartermaster in charge of all stock and properties and was always foremost in their protection, so that he asked for "one more chance," as he called it, "to bring in the scalp of Red Cloud himself." Permission was given, and Lieutenant Grummond, who had commanded the mounted infantry and cavalry after the death of Lieutenant Bingham, asked leave to take the cavalry detachment. His request also was granted. The entire force thus assembled at headquarters, therefore, consisted of eighty-one men, including three officers and two citizen frontiersmen, who were already acting as scouts in the quartermaster's department.

I was standing in front of my door next the commanding officer's headquarters and both saw and heard all that transpired. I was filled with dread and horror at the thought that after my husband's hairbreadth escape scarcely three weeks before he could be so eager to fight the Indians again.

The instructions of Colonel Carrington to Fetterman were distinctly and peremptorily given within my hearing and were repeated on the parade-ground when the line was formed, "Support the wood-train, relieve it, and report to me." To my husband was given the order, "Report to Captain Fetterman, implicitly obey orders, and never leave him." Solicitude on my behalf prompted Lieutenant Wands to urge my husband "for his family's sake to be prudent and avoid rash movements, or any pursuit;" and with these orders ringing in their ears they left the gate. Before they were out of hearing Colonel Carrington sprang upon the *banquet* inside the stockade (the sentry walk), halted the column, and in clear tones, heard by everybody, repeated his orders more minutely, "Under no circumstances must you cross Lodge Trail Ridge;" and the column moved quickly from sight.

I stood for a time, moments indeed, almost dazed, my heart filled with strange forebodings, then turned, entered my little house, and closed my door. The ladies, in turn, soon called to cheer me and, as I thought, with labored effort, to satisfy me that all would be well. They insisted that there was no more cause than usual for anxiety when troops were sent out, and the orders had been so explicit that any serious fight seemed absolutely impossible. And yet the recollection of the fateful action on the 6th and the danger experienced at that time came over me with such a tide of apprehension that no reassuring words could dissipate its gloom.

Shortly after the detachment left the gates, the Colonel, finding that Fetterman in his haste had gone without a surgeon ordered one to overtake the command forthwith. He started indeed, but soon returned with the information that the wood-train had broken corral and moved on safely to the Pinery, but that Fetterman had gone beyond the crest of Lodge Trail Ridge and that so many Indians were in sight he could not possibly reach him.

It became evident that the train had been threatened by a decoy party, and that when Fetterman followed its retirement thousands who had lain in ambush were assembling for his destruction.

Before leaving the watch-tower on his house, the Colonel sounded the general alarm and every man in the garrison either reported to his company's quarters or such other position assigned to him in an extreme emergency. It was a fixed rule that girths should be loosened and bits taken from the mouths of the horses so that there would never be delay when they were required for active service. Captain Ten Eyck was ordered to move at once with utmost speed with infantry and a supply wagon, and such mounted men as could be spared to guard the wagon and act as scouts. The Colonel himself inspected the men, and they were ready in very few minutes and moved at double-quick step all in a solid body to the crossing. At this crossing, as at the previous fight on the 6th of December, the ice broke through over the swift current, but without serious injury to men or horses and they pushed on.

Meanwhile, suddenly, out of silence so intense as to be torture to all who watched for any sound however slight, from the field of exposure a few shots were heard, followed up by increasing rapidity, and showing that a desperate fight was going on in the valley beyond the ridge just in the locality of the fight of the 6th, and in the very place where the command was forbidden to go. Then followed a few quick volleys, then scattering shots, and then, dead silence.

Less than half an hour had passed, and the silence was dreadful.

Of course we could see nothing of Captain Ten Eyck's men after they crossed the creek, and from his position in the wooded low ground and ravine opening just beyond the crossing he could neither hear nor see anything to guide his march until gaining some higher position which could be reached both by his loaded wagon and his mounted men. Much depended upon the actual distance from the fort where the last shots were fired and whether the sudden ceasing of the firing did not indicate a complete repulse of the Indian attack.

Hope sprang up in our aching hearts with the thought that Captain Ten Eyck had probably reached them in good time, and that the Indians had been repulsed. I shall never forget the face of Colonel Carrington as he descended from the lookout when the firing ceased. The howitzers were put in position and loaded with grape, or case-shot, and all things were in readiness for whatever might betide. He seemed to try to impress us with the assurance that no apprehension could be entertained as to the safety of the fort itself, but encouraged all to wait patiently and be ready for the return of the troops.

How different was the reality, soon to be realized!

Ten Eyck's relieving command, which had disappeared in the brush at the crossing of the creek, reached the summit of the hill opposite the fort, when all at once we saw the Colonel's Orderly, Sample, who had been sent with Ten Eyck, mounted upon one of the commander's own horses, break away from the command and dash down the hill towards the fort as fast as he could urge his horse.

Sample brought the written message from Captain Ten Eyck that "Keno Valley was full of Indians, that several hundred were on the road below, and westward, yelling and challenging him to come down to battle, but that nothing could be seen of Fetterman." He asked for a howitzer, but no one of his company could handle its ammunition and men could not be spared to move it.

The Indians who thus dared him to another fight were, as was afterwards learned, on the very field of the dreadful carnage finishing their deadly work. The message was not allowed to be published in full, but its tenor was tacitly understood to be that a terrible disaster had taken place. The evening gun was fired at sunset as usual, but what of us women! Agonizing fear possessed me! The ladies clustered in Mrs. Wands' cabin as night drew on, all speechless from absolute stagnation and terror. Then the crunching of wagon wheels startled us to our feet. The gates opened. Wagons were slowly driven within, bearing their dead but precious harvest from the field of blood and carrying forty-nine lifeless bodies to the hospital, with the heart-rending news, almost tenderly whispered by the soldiers themselves, that "*no more were to come in,*" and that "probably not a man of Fetterman's command survived."

In answer to the dispatch brought by Sample the Colonel replied in part as follows:

"Forty well-armed men, with 3000 rounds, ambulances, etc., left before your courier came in. You must unite with Fetterman, fire slowly, and keep men in hand. I ordered the wood-train in, which will give fifty men to spare."

Ten Eyck at once advanced toward the threatening Indians, who quickly vacated the field of struggle, and he was thus enabled to rescue as many as he did, and bring them in safely without the loss of a man. If the Indians had renewed the battle, his party also would have been among the victims.

Mrs. Carrington herself tenderly took me to her arms and home where in silence we awaited the unfolding of this deadly sorrow.

Source: Frances C. Carrington, *My Army Life and the Fort Phil. Kearney Massacre* (Philadelphia: J. B. Lippincott, 1911), 142–148.

130. Creation of the Indian Peace Commission, July 20, 1867

Introduction

The end of the American Civil War (1861–1865) had unleashed another flood of westward-bound pioneers, miners, and settlers, few of whom were inclined to honor the treaties setting aside land for Indians. The Indians in turn met the trespasses with violent resistance. The coming of peace between the states permitted the U.S. Army to turn its full attention to Indian outbreaks on the Plains. Vast distances, harsh climate, and topography combined to challenge the officers and men charged with making the frontier safe for white settlement. However, it was impossible to deploy enough men to defend every square mile of the West and the entire length of every wagon trail or railroad. Congress decided that the best solution for securing the frontier was to make peace with as many tribes as possible. To this end Congress established the Indian Peace Commission, consisting of three army officers and three civilian officials. The commission's task was to meet with the headmen of all hostile tribes east of the Rocky Mountains, learn the causes of their hostility, make treaties, establish Indian reservations, and encourage the Indians to take up agriculture in imitation of white society. Six months after its creation, the commission issued a report that harshly condemned the nation's past treatment of the Indians.

Primary Source

CHAP. XXXII.—*An Act to establish Peace with certain Hostile Indian Tribes.*
July 20, 1867.

Be it enacted by the Senate and House of Representatives of the United States of America in Congress assembled, That the President of the United States be, and he is hereby, authorized to appoint a commission to consist of three officers of the army not below the rank of brigadier general and who, together with N. G. Taylor, Commissioner of Indian Affairs, John B. Henderson, Chairman of the Committee of Indian Affairs of the Senate, S. F. Tappan, and John B. Sanborn, shall have power and authority to call together the chiefs and headmen of such bands or tribes of Indians as are now waging war against the United States or committing

depredations upon the people thereof, to ascertain the alleged reasons for their acts of hostility, and in their discretion, under the direction of the President, to make and conclude with said bands or tribes such treaty stipulations, subject to the action of the Senate, as may remove all just causes of complaint on their part, and at the same time establish security for person and property along the lines of railroad now being constructed to the Pacific and other thoroughfares of travel to the western Territories, and such as will most likely insure civilization for the Indians and peace and safety for the whites.

SEC. 2. *And be it further enacted,* That said commissioners are required to examine and select a district or districts of country having sufficient area to receive all the Indian tribes now occupying territory subject to the east of the Rocky mountains, not now peacefully residing on permanent reservations under treaty stipulations, to which the government has the right of occupation or to which said commissioners can obtain the right of occupation, and in which district or districts there shall be sufficient tillable or grazing land to enable the said tribes, respectively, to support themselves by agricultural and pastoral pursuits. Said district or districts, when so selected, and the selection approved by Congress, shall be and remain permanent homes for said Indians to be located thereon, and no person[s] not members of said tribes shall ever be permitted to enter thereon without the permission of the tribes interested, except officers and employees of the United States:

Provided, That the district or districts shall be so located as not to interfere with travel on highways located by authority of the United States, nor with the route of the Northern Pacific Railroad, the Union Pacific Railroad, the Union Pacific Railroad Eastern Division, or the proposed route of the Atlantic and Pacific Railroad by the way of Albuquerque.

SEC. 3. *And be it further enacted,* That the following sums of money are hereby appropriated out of any moneys in the treasury, to wit: To carry out the provisions of the preceding sections of this act, one hundred and fifty thousand dollars; to enable the Secretary of the Interior to subsist such friendly Indians as may have separated or may hereafter separate themselves from the hostile bands or tribes and seek the protection of the United States, three hundred thousand dollars.

SEC. 4. *And be it further enacted,* That the Secretary of War be required to furnish transportation, subsistence, and protection to the commissioners herein named during the discharge of their duties.

SEC. 5. *And be it further enacted,* That if said commissioners fail to secure the consent of the Indians to remove to the reservations and fail to secure peace, then the Secretary of War, under the direction of the President, is hereby authorized to accept the services of mounted volunteers from the Governors of the several States and Territories, in organized companies and battalions, not exceeding four thousand men in number, and for such term of service as, in his judgment, may be necessary for the suppression of Indian hostilities.

SEC. 6. *And be it further enacted,* That all volunteers so accepted be placed upon the same footing, in respect to pay, clothing, subsistence, and equipment, as the troops of the regular army.

SEC. 7. *And be it further enacted,* That said commissioners report their doings under this act to the President of the United States, including any such treaties and all correspondence as well as evidence by them taken.

APPROVED, July 20, 1867.

Source: "An Act to Establish Peace with Certain Hostile Indian Tribes," in *United States Statutes at Large,* Vol. 15, edited by George P. Sanger (Boston: Little, Brown, 1869), 17–18.

131. Medicine Lodge Treaty with the Kiowas, Comanches, and Apaches, October 1867

Introduction

Treaties made between U.S. authorities and Indian tribes were often proven futile soon after they were signed. On the one side, the Indian chieftains who signed the treaties were not empowered to speak for their entire tribes and frequently had only limited influence over their young warriors. On the other side were pioneers and settlers who trespassed on land that had been reserved for Indians by treaty and then when inevitably attacked clamored for protection from the overstretched U.S. Army. In addition, treaties provided for food and subsidies to help support Indians on the reservations, but the government often failed to deliver them, forcing the Indians to resume hunting or starve. The newly appointed Indian Peace Commission made three treaties at Medicine Lodge in Kansas with representatives of the Cheyennes, Kiowas, Arapahos, Apaches, and Comanches. Presented below is the treaty involving the Kiowas, Comanches, and Apaches. Among the signers of the treaty involving the Cheyennes was Black Kettle, surviving head of the band slaughtered at Sand Creek in 1864, who still hoped to pursue the path of peace. The treaties were an expression of the prevailing U.S. policy of concentrating Indians on reservations. A generalized outbreak of Indian raids occurred in the months following the treaty negotiations. The army then had the task of forcing onto reservations those Indians who refused to accept them. General Philip Sheridan's brutal winter campaign against the four tribes was intended to force compliance with the treaties.

Primary Source

Articles of a treaty concluded at the Council Camp on Medicine Lodge Creek, seventy miles south of Fort Larned, in the State of Kansas, on the twenty-first day of October, eighteen hundred and sixty-seven, by and between the United States of America,

represented by its commissioners duly appointed thereto to-wit: Nathaniel G. Taylor, William S. Harney, C. C. Augur, Alfred S. (H). Terry, John B. Sanborn, Samuel F. Tappan, and J. B. Henderson, of the one part, and the Kiowa, Comanche, and Apache Indians, represented by their chiefs and headmen duly authorized and empowered to act for the body of the people of said tribes (the names of said chiefs and headmen being hereto subscribed) of the other part, witness:

Whereas, on the twenty-first day of October, eighteen hundred and sixty-seven, a treaty of peace was made and entered into at the Council Camp, on Medicine Lodge Creek, seventy miles south of Fort Larned, in the State of Kansas, by and between the United States of America, by its commissioners Nathaniel G. Taylor, William S. Harney, C. C. Augur, Alfred H. Terry, John B. Sanborn, Samuel F. Tappan, and J. B. Henderson, of the one part, and the Kiowa and Comanche tribes of Indians, of the Upper Arkansas, by and through their chiefs and headmen whose names are subscribed thereto, of the other part, reference being had to said treaty; and whereas, since the making and signing of said treaty, at a council held at said camp on this day, the chiefs and headmen of the Apache nation or tribe of Indians express to the commissioners on the part of the United States, as aforesaid, a wish to be confederated with the said Kiowa and Comanche tribes, and to be placed, in every respect, upon an equal footing with said tribes; and whereas, at a council held at the same place and on the same day, with the chiefs and headmen of the said Kiowa and Comanche Tribes, they consent to the confederation of the said Apache tribe, as desired by it, upon the terms and conditions hereinafter set forth in this supplementary treaty: Now, therefore, it is hereby stipulated and agreed by and between the aforesaid commissioners, on the part of the United States, and the chiefs and headmen of the Kiowa and Comanche tribes, and, also, the chiefs and headmen of the said Apache tribe, as follows, to-wit:

ARTICLE I

The said Apache tribe of Indians agree to confederate and become incorporated with the said Kiowa and Comanche Indians, and to accept as their permanent home the reservation described in the aforesaid treaty with said Kiowa and Comanche tribes, concluded as aforesaid at this place, and they pledge themselves to make no permanent settlement at any place, nor on any lands, outside of said reservation.

ARTICLE II

The Kiowa and Comanche tribes, on their part, agree that all the benefits and advantages arising from the employment of physicians, teachers, carpenters, millers, engineers, farmers, and blacksmiths, agreed to be furnished under the provisions of their said treaty, together with all the advantages to be derived from the construction of agency buildings, warehouses, mills, and other structures, and also from the establishment of schools upon their said reservation, shall be jointly and equally shared and enjoyed by the said Apache Indians, as though they had been originally a part of said tribes; and they further agree that all other benefits arising from said treaty shall be jointly and equally shared as aforesaid.

ARTICLE III

The United States, on its part, agrees that clothing and other articles named in Article X. of said original treaty, together with all money or other annuities agreed to be furnished under any of the provisions of said treaty, to the Kiowa and Comanches, shall be shared equally by the Apaches. In all cases where specific articles of clothing are agreed to be furnished to the Kiowas and Comanches, similar articles shall be furnished to the Apaches, and a separate census of the Apaches shall be annually taken and returned by the agent, as provided for the other tribes. And the United States further agrees, in consideration of the incorporation of said Apaches, to increase the annual appropriation of money, as provided for in Article X. of said treaty, from twenty-five thousand to thirty thousand dollars; and the latter amount shall be annually appropriated, for the period therein named, for the use and benefit of said three tribes, confederated as herein declared; and the clothing and other annuities, which may from time to time be furnished to the Apaches, shall be based upon the census of the three tribes, annually to be taken by the agent, and shall be separately marked, forwarded, and delivered to them at the agency house, to be built under the provisions of said original treaty.

ARTICLE IV

In consideration of the advantages conferred by this supplementary treaty upon the the Apache tribe of Indians, they agree to observe and faithfully comply with all the stipulations and agreements entered into by the Kiowas and Comanches in said original treaty. They agree, in the same manner, to keep the peace toward the whites and all other persons under the jurisdiction of the United States, and to do and perform all other things enjoined upon said tribes by the provisions of said treaty; and they hereby give up and forever relinquish to the United States all rights, privileges, and grants now vested in them, or intended to be transferred to them, by the treaty between the United States and the Cheyenne and Arapahoe tribes of Indians, concluded at the camp on the Little Arkansas River, in the State of Kansas, on the fourteenth day of October, one thousand eight hundred and sixty-five, and also by the supplementary treaty, concluded at the same place on the seventeenth day of the same month, between the United States, of the one part, and the Cheyenne, Arapahoe, and Apache tribes, of the other part.

In testimony of all which, the said parties have hereunto set their hands and seals at the place and on the day herein before stated.

N. G. Taylor, President of Indian Commission.
Wm. S. Harney, Brevet Major-General, Commissioner, &c.
C. C. Augur, Brevet Major-General.
Alfred H. Terry, Brevet Major-General and Brigadier-General.
John B. Sanborn.
Samuel F. Tappan.
J. B. Henderson.

On the part of the Kiowas:
    Satanka, or Sitting Bear, his x mark,
    Sa-tan-ta, or White Bear, his x mark,
    Wah-toh-konk, or Black Eagle, his x mark,
    Ton-a-en-ko, or Kicking Eagle, his x mark,
    Fish-e-more, or Stinking Saddle, his x mark,
    Ma-ye-tin, or Woman's Heart, his x mark,
    Sa-tim-gear, or Stumbling Bear, his x mark,
    Sa-pa-ga, or One Bear, his x mark,
    Cor-beau, or The Crow, his x mark,
    Sa-ta-more, or Bear Lying Down, his x mark,

On the part of the Comanches:
    Parry-wah-say-men, or Ten Bears, his x mark,
    Tep-pe-navon, or Painted Lips, his x mark,
    To-she-wi, or Silver Brooch, his x mark,
    Cear-chi-neka, or Standing Feather, his x mark,
    Ho-we-ar, or Gap in the Woods, his x mark,
    Tir-ha-yah-gua-hip, or Horse's Back, his x mark,
    Es-a-man-a-ca, or Wolf's Name, his x mark,
    Ah-te-es-ta, or Little Horn, his x mark,
    Pooh-yah-to-yeh-be, or Iron Mountain, his x mark,
    Sad-dy-yo, or Dog Fat, his x mark,

On the part of the Apaches:
    Mah-vip-pah, Wolf's Sleeve, his x mark,
    Kon-zhon-ta-co, Poor Bear, his x mark,
    Cho-se-ta, or Bad Back, his x mark,
    Nah-tan, or Brave Man, his x mark,
    Ba-zhe-ech, Iron Shirt, his x mark,
    Til-la-ka, or White Horn, his x mark,

Attest:
    Ashton S. H. White, secretary.
    Geo. B. Willis, reporter.
    Philip McCusker, interpreter.
    John D. Howland, clerk Indian Commission.
    Sam'l S. Smoot, United States surveyor.
    A. A. Taylor.
    J. H. Leavenworth, United States Indian agent.

Thos. Murphy, superintendent Indian affairs.
Joel H. Elliott, major, Seventh U.S. Cavalry.

Source: "Treaty with the Kiowa Indians, October 21, 1867," in George P. Sanger, ed., *United States Statutes at Large,* Vol. 15 (Boston: Little, Brown, 1869), 589–592.

132. Fort Laramie Treaty, April 29, 1868

Introduction

The Indian Peace Commission, which included the victorious Civil War general William T. Sherman, signed this treaty with the Sioux and their allies at Fort Laramie in Wyoming Territory. The treaty established for the Sioux an extensive reservation in present-day South Dakota and provided for the assignment of an agent, construction of public amenities such as a school and a gristmill, the payment of annuities, and the allotment of farmland and subsidies to individual Indians. In turn the Sioux promised not to attack neighboring American settlers or to interfere with the construction of railroads. The treaty also provided that no further land cessions would be valid without the consent of three-fourths of all adult Sioux males. Just eight years later war with the Sioux broke out, due in no small part to the 1874 discovery of gold deposits on Sioux reservation land in the Black Hills of South Dakota. In 1877 the federal government essentially confiscated the Black Hills by forcing on the Sioux a treaty signed by only a small percentage of the tribe. An earlier treaty signed at Fort Laramie in 1851 had attempted to establish relations with the northern Plains Indians and secure their promise of safety for American overland migrants.

Primary Source

ARTICLES OF A TREATY MADE AND CONCLUDED BY AND BETWEEN

Lieutenant General William T. Sherman, General William S. Harney, General Alfred H. Terry, General O. O. Augur, J. B. Henderson, Nathaniel G. Taylor, John G. Sanborn, and Samuel F. Tappan, duly appointed commissioners on the part of the United States, and the different bands of the Sioux Nation of Indians, by their chiefs and headmen, whose names are hereto subscribed, they being duly authorized to act in the premises.

ARTICLE I.

From this day forward all war between the parties to this agreement shall for ever cease. The government of the United States desires peace, and its honor is hereby pledged to keep it. The Indians desire peace, and they now pledge their honor to maintain it.

If bad men among the whites, or among other people subject to the authority of the United States, shall commit any wrong upon the person or property of the Indians, the United States will, upon proof made to the agent, and forwarded to the Commissioner of Indian Affairs at Washington city, proceed at once to cause the offender to be arrested and punished according to the laws of the United States, and also reimburse the injured person for the loss sustained.

If bad men among the Indians shall commit a wrong or depredation upon the person or property of any one, white, black, or Indian, subject to the authority of the United States, and at peace therewith, the Indians herein named solemnly agree that they will, upon proof made to their agent, and notice by him, deliver up the wrongdoer to the United States, to be tried and punished according to its laws, and, in case they willfully refuse so to do, the person injured shall be reimbursed for his loss from the annuities, or other moneys due or to become due to them under this or other treaties made with the United States; and the President, on advising with the Commissioner of Indian Affairs, shall prescribe such rules and regulations for ascertaining damages under the provisions of this article as in his judgment may be proper, but no one sustaining loss while violating the provisions of this treaty, or the laws of the United States, shall be reimbursed therefor.

ARTICLE II.

The United States agrees that the following district of country, to wit, viz: commencing on the east bank of the Missouri river where the 46th parallel of north latitude crosses the same, thence along low-water mark down said east bank to a point opposite where the northern line of the State of Nebraska strikes the river, thence west across said river, and along the northern line of Nebraska to the 104th degree of longitude west from Greenwich, thence north on said meridian to a point where the 46th parallel of north latitude intercepts the same, thence due east along said parallel to the place of beginning; and in addition thereto, all existing reservations of the east bank of said river, shall be and the same is, set apart for the absolute and undisturbed use and occupation of the Indians herein named, and for such other friendly tribes or individual Indians as from time to time they may be willing, with the consent of the United States, to admit amongst them; and the United States now solemnly agrees that no persons, except those herein designated and authorized so to do, and except such officers, agents, and employees of the government as may be authorized to enter upon Indian reservations in discharge of duties enjoined by law, shall ever be permitted to pass over, settle upon, or reside in the territory described in this article, or in such territory as may be added to this reservation for the use of said Indians, and henceforth they will and do hereby relinquish all claims or right in and to any portion of the United States or Territories, except such as is embraced within the limits aforesaid, and except as hereinafter provided.

ARTICLE III.

If it should appear from actual survey or other satisfactory examination of said tract of land that it contains less than 160 acres of tillable land for each person who, at the time, may be authorized to reside on it under the provisions of this treaty, and a very considerable number of such persons shall be disposed to commence cultivating the soil as farmers, the United States agrees to set apart, for the use of said Indians, as herein provided, such additional quantity of arable land, adjoining to said reservation, or as near to the same as it can be obtained, as may be required to provide the necessary amount.

ARTICLE IV.

The United States agrees, at its own proper expense, to construct, at some place on the Missouri river, near the centre of said reservation where timber and water may be convenient, the following buildings, to wit, a warehouse, a store-room for the use of the agent in storing goods belonging to the Indians, to cost not less than $2,500; an agency building, for the residence of the agent, to cost not exceeding $3,000; a residence for the physician, to cost not more than $3,000; and five other buildings, for a carpenter, farmer, blacksmith, miller, and engineer—each to cost not exceeding $2,000; also, a school-house, or mission building, so soon as a sufficient number of children can be induced by the agent to attend school, which shall not cost exceeding $5,000.

The United States agrees further to cause to be erected on said reservation, near the other buildings herein authorized, a good steam circular saw-mill, with a grist-mill and shingle machine attached to the same, to cost not exceeding $8,000.

ARTICLE V.

The United States agrees that the agent for said Indians shall in the future make his home at the agency building; that he shall reside among them, and keep an office open at all times for the purpose of prompt and diligent inquiry into such matters of complaint by and against the Indians as may be presented for investigation under the provisions of their treaty stipulations, as also for the faithful discharge of other duties enjoined on him by law. In all cases of depredation on person or property he shall cause the evidence to be taken in writing and forwarded, together with his findings, to the Commissioner of Indian Affairs, whose decision, subject to the revision of the Secretary of the Interior, shall be binding on the parties to this treaty.

ARTICLE VI.

If any individual belonging to said tribes of Indians, or legally incorporated with them, being the head of a family, shall desire to commence farming, he shall have the privilege to select, in the presence and with the assistance of the agent then in charge, a tract of land within said reservation, not exceeding three hundred and twenty acres in extent, which tract, when so selected, certified, and recorded in the "Land Book" as herein directed, shall cease to be held in common, but the same may be occupied and held in the exclusive possession of the person selecting it, and of his family, so long as he or they may continue to cultivate it.

Any person over eighteen years of age, not being the head of a family, may in like manner select and cause to be certified to him or her, for purposes of cultivation, a quantity of land, not exceeding eighty acres in extent, and thereupon be entitled to the exclusive possession of the same as above directed.

For each tract of land so selected a certificate, containing a description thereof and the name of the person selecting it, with a certificate endorsed thereon that the same has been recorded, shall be delivered to the party entitled to it, by the agent, after the same shall have been recorded by him in a book to be kept in his office, subject to inspection, which said book shall be known as the "Sioux Land Book."

The President may, at any time, order a survey of the reservation, and, when so surveyed, Congress shall provide for protecting the rights of said settlers in their improvements, and may fix the character of the title held by each. The United States may pass such laws on the subject of alienation and descent of property between the Indians and their descendants as may be thought proper. And it is further stipulated that any male Indians over eighteen years of age, of any band or tribe that is or shall hereafter become a party to this treaty, who now is or who shall hereafter become a resident or occupant of any reservation or territory not included in the tract of country designated and described in this treaty for the permanent home of the Indians, which is not mineral land, nor reserved by the United States for special purposes other than Indian occupation, and who shall have made improvements thereon of the value of two hundred dollars or more, and continuously occupied the same as a homestead for the term of three years, shall be entitled to receive from the United States a patent for one hundred and sixty acres of land including his said improvements, the same to be in the form of the legal subdivisions of the surveys of the public lands. Upon application in writing, sustained by the proof of two disinterested witnesses, made to the register of the local land office when the land sought to be entered is within a land district, and when the tract sought to be entered is not in any land district, then upon said application and proof being made to the Commissioner of the General Land Office, and the right of such Indian or Indians to enter such tract or tracts of land shall accrue and be perfect from the date of his first improvements thereon, and shall continue as long as he continues his residence and improvements and no longer. And any Indian or Indians receiving a patent for land under the foregoing provisions shall thereby and from thenceforth become and be a citizen of the United States and be entitled to all the privileges and immunities of such citizens, and shall, at the same time, retain all his rights to benefits accruing to Indians under this treaty.

ARTICLE VII.

In order to insure the civilization of the Indians entering into this treaty, the necessity of education is admitted, especially of such of them as are or may be settled on said agricultural reservations, and they, therefore, pledge themselves to compel their children, male and female, between the ages of six and sixteen years, to attend school, and it is hereby made the duty of the agent for said Indians to see that this stipulation is strictly complied with; and the United States agrees that for every thirty children between said ages, who can be induced or compelled to attend school, a house shall be provided, and a teacher competent to teach the elementary branches of an English education shall be furnished, who will reside among said Indians and faithfully discharge his or her duties as a teacher. The provisions of this article to continue for not less than twenty years.

ARTICLE VIII.

When the head of a family or lodge shall have selected lands and received his certificate as above directed, and the agent shall be satisfied that he intends in good faith to commence cultivating the soil for a living, he shall be entitled to receive seeds and agricultural implements for the first year, not exceeding in value one hundred dollars, and for each succeeding year he shall continue to farm, for a period of three years more, he shall be entitled to receive seeds and implements as aforesaid, not exceeding in value twenty-five dollars. And it is further stipulated that such persons as commence farming shall receive instruction from the farmer herein provided for, and whenever more than one hundred persons shall enter upon the cultivation of the soil, a second blacksmith shall be provided, with such iron, steel, and other material as may be needed.

ARTICLE IX.

At any time after ten years from the making of this treaty, the United States shall have the privilege of withdrawing the physician, farmer, blacksmith, carpenter, engineer, and miller herein provided for, but in case of such withdrawal, an additional sum thereafter of ten thousand dollars per annum shall be devoted to the education of said Indians, and the Commissioner of Indian Affairs shall, upon careful inquiry into their condition, make such rules and regulations for the expenditure of said sums as will best promote the education and moral improvement of said tribes.

ARTICLE X.

In lieu of all sums of money or other annuities provided to be paid to the Indians herein named under any treaty or treaties heretofore made, the United States agrees to deliver at the agency house on the reservation herein named, on or before the first day of August of each year, for thirty years, the following articles, to wit:

For each male person over 14 years of age, a suit of good substantial woollen clothing, consisting of coat, pantaloons, flannel shirt, hat, and a pair of home-made socks.

For each female over 12 years of age, a flannel shirt, or the goods necessary to make it, a pair of woollen hose, 12 yards of calico, and 12 yards of cotton domestics.

For the boys and girls under the ages named, such flannel and cotton goods as may be needed to make each a suit as aforesaid, together with a pair of woollen hose for each.

And in order that the Commissioner of Indian Affairs may be able to estimate properly for the articles herein named, it shall be the duty of the agent each year to forward to him a full and exact census of the Indians, on which the estimate from year to year can be based.

And in addition to the clothing herein named, the sum of $10 for each person entitled to the beneficial effects of this treaty shall be annually appropriated for a period of 30 years, while such persons roam and hunt, and $20 for each person who engages in farming, to be used by the Secretary of the Interior in the purchase of such articles as from time to time the condition and necessities of the Indians may indicate to be proper. And if within the 30 years, at any time, it shall appear that the amount of money needed for clothing, under this article, can be appropriated to better uses for the Indians named herein, Congress may, by law, change the appropriation to other purposes, but in no event shall the amount of the appropriation be withdrawn or discontinued for the period named. And the President shall annually detail an officer of the army to be present and attest the delivery of all the goods herein named, to the Indians, and he shall inspect and report on the quantity and quality of the goods and the manner of their delivery. And it is hereby expressly stipulated that each Indian over the age of four years, who shall have removed to and settled permanently upon said reservation, one pound of meat and one pound of flour per day, provided the Indians cannot furnish their own subsistence at an earlier date. And it is further stipulated that the United States will furnish and deliver to each lodge of Indians or family of persons legally incorporated with them, who shall remove to the reservation herein described and commence farming, one good American cow, and one good well-broken pair of American oxen within 60 days after such lodge or family shall have so settled upon said reservation.

ARTICLE XI.

In consideration of the advantages and benefits conferred by this treaty and the many pledges of friendship by the United States, the tribes who are parties to this agreement hereby stipulate that they will relinquish all right to occupy permanently the territory outside their reservations as herein defined, but yet reserve the right to hunt on any lands north of North Platte, and on the Republican Fork of the Smoky Hill river, so long as the buffalo may range thereon in such numbers as to justify the chase. And they, the said Indians, further expressly agree:

1st. That they will withdraw all opposition to the construction of the railroads now being built on the plains.

2d. That they will permit the peaceful construction of any railroad not passing over their reservation as herein defined.

3d. That they will not attack any persons at home, or travelling, nor molest or disturb any wagon trains, coaches, mules, or cattle belonging to the people of the United States, or to persons friendly therewith.

4th. They will never capture, or carry off from the settlements, white women or children.

5th. They will never kill or scalp white men, nor attempt to do them harm.

6th. They withdraw all pretence of opposition to the construction of the railroad now being built along the Platte river and westward to the Pacific ocean, and they will not in future object to the construction of railroads, wagon roads, mail stations, or other works of utility or necessity, which may be ordered or permitted by the laws of the United States. But should such roads or other works be constructed on the lands of their reservation, the government will pay the tribe whatever amount of damage may be assessed by three disinterested commissioners to be appointed by the President for that purpose, one of the said commissioners to be a chief or headman of the tribe.

7th. They agree to withdraw all opposition to the military posts or roads now established south of the North Platte river, or that may be established, not in violation of treaties heretofore made or hereafter to be made with any of the Indian tribes.

ARTICLE XII.

No treaty for the cession of any portion or part of the reservation herein described which may be held in common, shall be of any validity or force as against the said Indians unless executed and signed by at least three-fourths of all the adult male Indians occupying or interested in the same, and no cession by the tribe shall be understood or construed in such manner as to deprive, without his consent, any individual member of the tribe of his rights to any tract of land selected by him as provided in Article VI of this treaty.

ARTICLE XIII.

The United States hereby agrees to furnish annually to the Indians the physician, teachers, carpenter, miller, engineer, farmer, and blacksmiths, as herein contemplated, and that such appropriations shall be made from time to time, on the estimate of the Secretary of the Interior, as will be sufficient to employ such persons.

ARTICLE XIV.

It is agreed that the sum of five hundred dollars annually for three years from date shall be expended in presents to the ten persons of said tribe who in the judgment of the agent may grow the most valuable crops for the respective year.

ARTICLE XV.

The Indians herein named agree that when the agency house and other buildings shall be constructed on the reservation named, they will regard said reservation their permanent home, and they will make no permanent settlement elsewhere; but they shall have the right, subject to the conditions and modifications of this treaty, to hunt, as stipulated in Article XI hereof.

ARTICLE XVI.

The United States hereby agrees and stipulates that the country north of the North Platte river and east of the summits of the Big Horn mountains shall be held and considered to be unceded Indian territory, and also stipulates and agrees that no white person or persons shall be permitted to settle upon or occupy any portion of the same; or without the consent of the Indians, first had and obtained, to pass through the same; and it is further agreed by the United States, that within ninety days after the conclusion of peace with all the bands of the Sioux nation, the military posts now established in the territory in this article named shall be abandoned, and that the road leading to them and by them to the settlements in the Territory of Montana shall be closed.

ARTICLE XVII.

It is hereby expressly understood and agreed by and between the respective parties to this treaty that the execution of this treaty and its ratification by the United States Senate shall have the effect, and shall be construed as abrogating and annulling all treaties and agreements heretofore entered into between the respective parties hereto, so far as such treaties and agreements obligate the United States to furnish and provide money, clothing, or other articles of property to such Indians and bands of Indians as become parties to this treaty, but no further.

In testimony of all which, we, the said commissioners, and we, the chiefs and headmen of the Brule band of the Sioux nation, have hereunto set our hands and seals at Fort Laramie, Dakota Territory, this twenty-ninth day of April, in the year one thousand eight hundred and sixty-eight.

N. G. TAYLOR,
W. T. SHERMAN, *Lt. Genl.*
WM. S. HARNEY, *Bvt. Maj. Gen. U. S. A.*
JOHN B. SANBORN,
S. F. TAPPAN,
C. C. AUGUR, *Bvt. Maj. Gen.*
ALFRED H. TERRY, *Bvt. M. Gen. U. S. A.*

Attest:

A. S. H. White, *Secretary.*

Executed on the part of the Brule band of Sioux by the chiefs and headman whose names are hereto annexed, they being thereunto duly authorized, at Fort Laramie, D. T., the twenty-ninth day of April, in the year A. D. 1868.

MA-ZA-PON-KASKA, his X mark, Iron Shell.

WAH-PAT-SHAH, his X mark, Red Leaf.

HAH-SAH-PAH, his X mark, Black Horn.

ZIN-TAH-GAH-LAT-SKAH, his X mark, Spotted Tail.

ZIN-TAH-SKAH, his X mark, White Tail.

ME-WAH-TAH-NE-HO-SKAH, his X mark, Tall Mandas.

SHE-CHA-CHAT-KAH, his X mark, Bad Left Hand.

NO-MAH-NO-PAH, his X mark, Two and Two.

TAH-TONKA-SKAH, his X mark, White Bull.

CON-RA-WASHTA, his X mark, Pretty Coon.

HA-CAH-CAH-SHE-CHAH, his X mark, Bad Elk.

WA-HA-KA-ZAH-ISH-TAH, his X mark, Eye Lance.

MA-TO-HA-KE-TAH, his X mark, Bear that looks behind.

BELLA-TONKA-TONKA, his X mark, Big Partisan.

MAH-TO-HO-HONKA, his X mark, Swift Bear.

TO-WIS-NE, his X mark, Cold Place.

ISH-TAH-SKAH, his X mark, White Eye.

MA-TA-LOO-ZAH, his X mark, Fast Bear.

AS-HAH-KAH-NAH-ZHE, his X mark, Standing Elk.

CAN-TE-TE-KI-YA, his X mark, The Brave Heart.

SHUNKA-SHATON, his X mark, Day Hawk.

TATANKA-WAKON, his X mark, Sacred Bull.

MAPIA SHATON, his X mark, Hawk Cloud.

MA-SHA-A-OW, his X mark, Stands and Comes.

SHON-KA-TON-KA, his X mark, Big Dog.

Attest:

Ashton S. H. White, *Secretary of Commission.*

George B. Withs, *Phonographer to Commission.*

Geo. H. Holtzman.

John D. Howland.

James C. O'Connor.

Char. E. Guern, *Interpreter.*

Leon T. Pallardy, *Interpreter.*

Nicholas Janis, *Interpreter.*

Executed on the part of the Ogallalla band of Sioux by the chiefs and headmen whose names are hereto subscribed, they being thereunto duly authorized, at Fort Laramie, the 25th day of May, in the year A. D. 1868.

TAH-SHUN-KA-CO-QUI-PAH, his X mark, Man-afraid-of-his-horses.

SHA-TON-SKAH, his X mark, White Hawk.

SHA-TON-SAPAH, his X mark, Black Hawk.

E-GA-MON-TON-KA-SAPAH, his X mark, Black Tiger.

OH-WAH-SHE-CHA, his X mark, Bad Wound.

PAH-GEE, his X mark, Grass.

WAH-NON-REH-CHE-GEH, his X mark, Ghost Heart.

CON-REEH, his X mark, Crow.

OH-HE-TE-KAH, his X mark, The Brave.

TAH-TON-KAH-HE-YO-TA-KAH, his X mark, Sitting Bull.

SHON-KA-OH-WAH-MEN-YE, his X mark, Whirlwind Dog.

HA-KAH-KAH-TAH-MIECH, his X mark, Poor Elk.

WAM-BU-LEE-WAH-KON, his X mark, Medicine Eagle.

CHON-GAH-MA-HE-TO-HANS-KA, his X mark, High Wolf.

WAH-SE-CHUN-TA-SHUN-KAH, his X mark, American Horse.

MAH-HAH-MAH-HA-MAK-NEAR, his X mark, Man that walks under the ground.

MAH-TO-TOW-PAH, his X mark, Four Bears.

MA-TO-WEE-SHA-KTA, his X mark, One that kills the bear.

OH-TAH-KEE-TOKA-WEE-CHAKTA, his X mark, One that kills in a hard place.

TAH-TON-KAH-TA-MIECH, his X mark, The Poor Bull.

OH-HUNS-EE-GA-NON-SKEN, his X mark, Mad Shade.

SHAH-TON-OH-NAH-OM-MINNE-NE-OH-MINNE, his X mark, Whirling Hawk.

MAH-TO-CHUN-KA-OH, his X mark, Bear's Back.

CHE-TON-WEE-KOH, his X mark, Fool Hawk.

WAH-HOH-KE-ZA-AH-HAH, his X mark, One that has the lance.

SHON-GAH-MANNI-TOH-TAN-KA-SEH, his x mark, Big Wolf Foot.

EH-TON-KAH, his X mark, Big Mouth.

MA-PAH-CHE-TAH, his X mark, Bad Hand.

WAH-KE-YUN-SHAH, his X mark, Red Thunder.

WAK-SAH, his X mark, One that Cuts Off.

CHAH-NOM-QUI-YAH, his X mark, One that Presents the Pipe.

WAH-KE-KE-YAN-PUH-TAH, his X mark, Fire Thunder.

MAH-TO-NONK-PAH-ZE, his X mark, Bear with Yellow Ears.

CON-REE-TEH-KA, his X mark, The Little Crow.

HE-HUP-PAH-TOH, his X mark, The Blue War Club.

SHON-KEE-TOH, his X mark, The Blue Horse.

WAM-BALLA-OH-CONQUO, his X mark, Quick Eagle.

TA-TONKA-SUPPA, his X mark, Black Bull.

MOH-TOH-HA-SHE-NA, his X mark, The Bear Hide.

Attest:

S. E. Ward.

Jas. C. O'Connor.

J. M. Sherwood.

W. C. Slicer.

Sam Deon.

H. M. Mathews.

Joseph Bissonette, *Interpreter.*

Nicholas Janis, *Interpreter.*

Lefroy Jott, *Interpreter.*

Antoine Janis, *Interpreter.*

Executed on the part of the Minneconjon band of Sioux by the chiefs and headmen whose names are hereunto subscribed, they being thereunto duly authorized.

HEH-WON-GE-CHAT, his X mark, One Horn.

OH-PON-AH-TAH-E-MANNE, his X mark, The Elk that bellows Walking.

HEH-HO-LAH-REH-CHA-SKAH, his X mark, Young White Bull.

WAH-CHAH-CHUM-KAH-COH-KEE-PAH, his X mark, One that is Afraid of Shield.

HE-HON-NE-SHAKTA, his X mark, The Old Owl.

MOC-PE-A-TOH, his X mark, Blue Cloud.

OH-PONG-GE-LE-SKAH, his X mark, Spotted Elk.

TAH-TONK-KA-HON-KE-SCHNE, his X mark, Slow Bull.

SHONK-A-NEE-SHAH-SHAH-A-TAH-PE, his X mark, The Dog Chief.

MA-TO-TAH-TA-TONK-KA, his X mark, Bull Bear.

WOM-BEH-LE-TON-KAH, his X mark, The Big Eagle.

MA-TOH-EH-SCHNE-LAH, his X mark, The Lone Bear.

MAH-TOH-KE-SU-YAH, his X mark, The One who Remembers the Bear.

MA-TOH-OH-HE-TO-KEH, his X mark, The Brave Bear.

EH-CHE-MA-HEH, his X mark, The Runner.

TI-KI-YA, his X mark, The Hard.

HE-MA-ZA, his X mark, Iron Horn.

Attest:

Jas. C. O'Connor,

Wm. D. Brown,

Nicholas Janis, *Interpreter.*

Antoine Janis, *Interpreter.*

Executed on the part of the Yanctonais band of Sioux by the chiefs and headmen whose names are hereto subscribed, they being thereunto duly authorized:

MAH-TO-NON-PAH, his X mark, Two Bears.

MA-TO-HNA-SKIN-YA, his X mark, Mad Bear.

HE-O-PU-ZA, his X mark, Louzy.

AH-KE-CHE-TAH-CHE-CA-DAN, his X mark, Little Soldier.

MAH-TO-E-TAN-CHAN, his X mark, Chief Bear.

CU-WI-H-WIA, his X mark, Rotten Stomach.

SKUN-KA-WE-TKO, his X mark, Fool Dog.

ISH-TA-SAP-PAH, his X mark, Black Eye.

IH-TAN-CHAN, his X mark, The Chief.

I-A-WI-CA-KA, his X mark, The one who Tells the Truth.

AH-KE-CHE-TAH, his X mark, The Soldier.

TA-SHI-NA-GI, his X mark, Yellow Robe.

NAH-PE-TON-KA, his X mark, Big Hand.

CHAN-TEE-WE-KTO, his X mark, Fool Heart.

HOH-GAN-SAH-PA, his X mark, Black Catfish.

MAH-TO-WAH-KAN, his X mark, Medicine Bear.

SHUN-KA-KAN-SHA, his X mark, Red Horse.

WAN-RODE, his X mark, The Eagle.

CAN-HPI-SA-PA, his X mark, Black Tomahawk.

WAR-HE-LE-RE, his X mark, Yellow Eagle.

CHA-TON-CHE-CA, his X mark, Small Hawk, or Long Fare.

SHU-GER-MON-E-TOO-HA-SKA, his X mark, Tall Wolf.

MA-TO-U-TAH-KAH, his X mark, Sitting Bear.

HI-HA-CAH-GE-NA-SKENE, his X mark, Mad Elk.

Arapahoes.

LITTLE CHIEF, his X mark.

TALL BEAR, his X mark.

TOP MAN, his X mark.

NEVA, his X mark.

THE WOUNDED BEAR, his X mark.

THIRLWIND, his X mark.

THE FOX, his X mark.

THE DOG BIG MOUTH, his X mark.

SPOTTED WOLF, his X mark.

SORREL HORSE, his X mark.

BLACK COAL, his X mark.

BIG WOLF, his X mark.

KNOCK-KNEE, his X mark.

BLACK CROW, his X mark.

THE LONE OLD MAN, his X mark.

PAUL, his X mark.

BLACK BULL, his X mark.

BIG TRACK, his X mark.

THE FOOT, his X mark.

BLACK WHITE, his X mark.

YELLOW HAIR, his X mark.

LITTLE SHIELD, his X mark.

BLACK BEAR, his X mark.

WOLF MOCASSIN, his X mark.

BIG ROBE, his X mark.

WOLF CHIEF, his X mark.

Witnesses:

Robert P. McKibbin, *Capt. 4 Inf. Bvt. Lieut. Col. U. S. A. Comdg. Ft. Laramie.*

Wm. H. Powell, *Bvt. Maj. Capt. 4th Inf.*

Henry W. Patterson, *Capt. 4th Infy.*

Theo. E. True, *2d Lieut. 4th Inf.*

W. G. Bullock.

Chas. E. Guern, *Special Indian Interpreter for the Peace Commission.*

FORT LARAMIE, WG. T., *Nov. 6, 1868.*

MAKH-PI-AH-LU-TAH, his X mark, Red Cloud.

WA-KI-AH-WE-CHA-SHAH, his X mark, Thunder Man.

MA-ZAH-ZAH-GEH, his X mark, Iron Cane.

WA-UMBLE-WHY-WA-KA-TUYAH, his X mark, High Eagle.

KO-KE-PAH, his X mark, Man Afraid.

WA-KI-AH-WA-KOU-AH, his X mark, Thunder Flying
    Running.

Witnesses:

W. McE. DYE, *Bvt. Col. U. S. A. Comg.*

A. B. CAIN, *Capt. 4 Inf. Bt. Maj. U. S. A.*

ROBT. P. McKIBBIN, *Capt. 4 Inf. Bvt. Lt. Col. U. S. A.*

JNO. MILLER, *Capt. 4th Inf.*

G. L. LUHN, *1st Lieut. 4th Inf. Bvt. Capt. U. S. A.*

H. C. SLOAN, *2d Lt. 4th Inf.*

WHITTINGHAM COX, *1st Lieut. 4th Infy.*

A. W. VOGDES, *1st Lt. 4th Infy.*

BUTLER D. PRICE, *2d Lt. 4th Inf.*

HEADQRS., FORT LARAMIE, *Novr. 6, '68.*

Executed by the above on this date.

All of the Indians are Ogallalaha excepting Thunder Man and Thunder Flying Running, who are Brulés.

WM. McE. DYE, *Maj. 4th Infy. and Bvt. Col. U. S. A. Cong.*

Attest:

JAS. C. O'CONNOR.

NICHOLAS JANIS, *Interpreter.*

FRANC. LA FRAMBOISE, *Interpreter.*

P. J. DE SMET, S. J., *Missionary among the Indians.*

SAML. D. HINMAN, B. D., *Missionary.*

Executed on the part of the Uncpapa band of Sioux, by the chiefs and headmen whose names are hereto ascribed, they being thereunto duly authorized.

CO-KAM-I-YA-YA, his x mark, The Man that Goes in the Middle.

MA-TO-CA-WA-WEKSA, his x mark, Bear Rib.

TA-TO-KA-IN-YAN-KE, his x mark, Running Antelope.

KAN-GI-WA-KI-TA, his x mark, Looking Crow.

A-KI-CI-TA-HAN-SKA, his x mark, Long Soldier.

WA-KU-TE-MA-NI, his x mark, The One who Shoots Walking.

UN-KCA-KI-KA, his x mark, The Magpie.

KAN-GI-O-TA, his x mark, Plenty Crow.

HE-MA-ZA, his x mark, Iron Horn.

SHUN-KA-I-NA-PIN, his x mark, Wolf Necklace.

I-WE-HI-YU, his x mark, The Man who Bleeds from the Mouth.

HE-HA-KA-PA, his x mark, Elk Head.

I-ZU-ZA, his x mark, Grind Stone.

SHUN-KA-WI-TKO, his x mark, Fool Dog.

MA-KPI-YA-PO, his x mark, Blue Cloud.

WA-MLN-PI-LU-TA, his x mark, Red Eagle.

MA-TO-CAN-TE, his x mark, Bear's Heart.

A-KI-CI-TA-I-TAU-CAN, his x mark, Chief Soldier.

Attest:

JAS. C. O'CONNOR.

NICHOLAS JANIS, *Interpreter.*

FRANC. LA FRAMBOIS[E], *Interpreter.*

P. J. DE SMET, S. J., *Missy. among the Indians.*

SAML. D. HINMAN, B. D., *Missionary.*

Executed on the part of the Blackfeet band of Sioux by the chiefs and headmen whose names are hereto subscribed, they being thereunto duly authorized.

CAN-TE-PE-TA, his x mark, Fire Heart.

WAH-MDI-KTE, his x mark, The One who Kills Eagle.

SHO-TA, his x mark, Smoke.

WAN-MDI-MA-NI, his x mark, Walking Eagle.

WA-SHI-CUN-YA-TA-PI, his x mark, Chief White Man.

KAN-GI-I-YO-TAN-KE, his x mark, Sitting Crow.

PE-JI, his x mark, The Grass.

KDA-MA-NI, his x mark, The One that Battles as he Walks.

WAH-HAN-KA-SA-PA, his x mark, Black Shield.

CAN-TE-NON-PA, his x mark, Two Hearts.

Attest:

JAS. C. O'CONNOR.

NICHOLAS JANIS, *Interpreter.*

FRANC. LA FRAMBOISE, *Interpreter.*

P. J. DE SMET, S. J., *Missy. among the Indians.*

SAML. D. HINMAN, B. D., *Missionary.*

Executed on the part of the Cutheads band of Sioux by the chiefs and headmen whose names are hereto subscribed, they being thereunto duly authorized.

TO-KA-IN-YAN-KA, his x mark, The One who Goes Ahead
    Running.

TA-TAN-KA-WA-KIN-YAN, his x mark, Thunder Bull.

SIN-TO-MIN-SA-PA, his x mark, All over Black.

CAN-I-CA, his x mark, The One who Took the Stick.

PA-TAN-KA, his x mark, Big Head.

Attest:

JAS. C. O'CONNOR.

NICHOLAS JANIS, *Interpreter.*

FRANC. LA FRAMBOIS[E], *Interpreter.*

P. J. DE SMET, S. J., *Missy. among the Indians.*

SAML. D. HINMAN, B. D., *Missionary.*

Executed on the part of the Two Kettle band of Sioux by the chiefs and headmen whose names are hereto subscribed, they being thereunto duly authorized.

MA-WA-TAN-NI-HAN-SKA, his x mark, Long Mandan.
CAN-KPE-DU-TA, his x mark, Red War Club.
CAN-KA-GA, his x mark, The Log.

Attest:
    JAS. C. O'CONNOR.
    NICHOLAS JANIS, *Interpreter.*
    FRANC. LA FRAMBOISE, *Interpreter.*
    P. J. DE SMET, S. J., *Missy. among the Indians.*
    SAML. D. HINMAN, B. D., *Missionary.*

Executed on the part of the Sans Arch band of Sioux by the chiefs and headmen whose names are hereto annexed, they being thereunto duly authorized.

HE-NA-PIN-WA-NI-CA, his x mark, The One that has
    Neither Horn.
WA-INLU-PI-LU-TA, his x mark, Red Plume.
CI-TAN-GI, his x mark, Yellow Hawk.
HE-NA-PIN-WA-NI-CA, his x mark, No Horn.

Attest:
    JAS. C. O'CONNOR.
    NICHOLAS JANIS, *Interpreter.*
    FRANC. LA FRAMBOIS[E], *Interpreter.*
    P. J. DE SMET, S. J., *Missy. among the Indians.*
    SAML. D. HINMAN, B. D., *Missionary.*

Executed on the part of the Santee band of Sioux by the chiefs and headmen whose names are hereto subscribed, they being thereunto duly authorized.

WA-PA-SHAW, his x mark, Red Ensign.
WAH-KOO-TAY, his x mark, Shooter.
HOO-SHA-SHA, his x mark, Red Legs.
O-WAN-CHA-DU-TA, his x mark, Scarlet all over.
WAU-MACE-TAN-KA, his x mark, Big Eagle.
CHO-TAN-KA-E-NA-PE, his x mark, Flute-player.
TA-SHUN-KE-MO-ZA, his x mark, His Iron Dog.

Attest:
    SAML. D. HINMAN, B. D., *Missionary.*
    J. N. CHICKERING, *2d Lt. 22d Infy., Bvt. Capt. U. S. A.*
    P. J. DE SMET, S. J.
    NICHOLAS JANIS, *Interpreter.*
    FRANC. LA FRAMBOISE, *Interpreter.*

And whereas, the said treaty having been submitted the Senate of the United States for the constitutional action thereon, the Senate did, on the sixteenth day of February, one thousand eight hundred and sixty-nine, advise and consent to the ratification of the same, by a resolution in the words and figures following, to wit:

IN EXECUTIVE SESSION, SENATE OF THE UNITED STATES, *February 16, 1869.*

Resolved (two thirds of the senators present concurring), That the Senate advise and consent to the ratification of the treaty between the United States and the different bands of the Sioux nation of Indians, made and concluded the 29th April, 1868.
    Attest: GEO. C. GORHAM, *Secretary.*

Now, therefore, be it known that I, ANDREW JOHNSON, President of the United States of America, do in pursuance of the advice and consent of the Senate, as expressed in its resolution of the sixteenth of February, one thousand eight hundred and sixty-nine, accept, ratify, and confirm the said treaty.

In testimony whereof I have hereto signed my name, and caused the seal of the United States to be affixed.

Done at the city of Washington, this twenty-fourth day of February, in the year of our Lord one thousand eight hundred and sixty-nine, and of the Independence of the United States of America, the ninety-third.

ANDREW JOHNSON.

By the President:
WILLIAM H. SEWARD, *Secretary of State.*

> **Source:** "Treaty with the Sioux Indians," in *United States Statutes at Large,* Vol. 15, edited by George P. Sanger (Boston: Little, Brown, 1869), 635–647.

133. De Benneville Randolph Keim, The Winter Campaign against Black Kettle, 1868–1869

Introduction

The former Union Civil War hero General Philip Sheridan (1831–1888) became a renowned postwar Indian fighter. Faced with hit-and-run raids by highly mobile Plains Indians, Sheridan planned a winter campaign against the hostile Indians of the Great Plains. His planned campaign employed the concept of total war by attacking Indians while they were concentrated in their villages for the winter. By destroying their villages, livestock, and reserves of food, Sheridan's attack affected the entire enemy population. After a grueling march through blizzard conditions, the U.S. 7th Cavalry, led by George Armstrong Custer, descended on a Cheyenne village on November 29, 1868. The cavalry troopers killed as many warriors as they could (including the would-be peacemaker Black Kettle, who was shot in the back while fleeing with his wife), made prisoners of the women and children, destroyed massive amounts of armaments and property, and shot 700 ponies. This account is excerpted from a book by war reporter De Benneville Randolph Keim. Keim rode with Union troops and covered more than two dozen Civil War battles, including Sherman's march through Georgia in 1864, and later traveled with Sheridan on his campaign against the Plains Indians. The resulting book was Keim's most successful.

Primary Source

Each savage resolved to sell his life as dearly as possible. Each officer and trooper knew, with him, it was victory or torture and certain death.

During the excitement of the fight the continued absence of Elliot and his party was not observed. Firing was heard in the direction he had taken, but supposed to be Indians signaling. When the conflict with Black Kettle's warriors lulled, the question ran along the line, "where is Elliot? where is Elliot?" No one answered. He had last been seen disappearing over the "divide."

The alarm carried by the fugitives, whom Elliott and his men were pursuing, aroused the warriors of the villages which were situated on the same stream lower down. The fight with Black Kettle's warriors had not ended when a large party of Kiowas and Arrapahoes, under Satanta and Little Raven, came to the assistance of the Cheyennes. This display of force from so unexpected a quarter was a surprise to the troopers and solved at once the fate of Elliott. There was now no doubt that he and his party had struck the approaching Kiowas and Arrapahoes, coming to the rescue of the Cheyennes, and had been cut off by them. There is no question that each man of this ill fated band parted with his life as dearly as possible, and died at his post. For these unfortunate men, there was no possibility of escape. Their alternative was death by some friendly bullet, or death by the horrible torture which the hellish ingenuity of the savage alone can invent.

The reinforcements from the other villages opened their attack with considerable vigor. In order to keep them at bay, while the troopers were still engaged with Black Kettle, Weir was detached to oppose them. The savages fought with unexampled bravery, in hopes of succoring those of their allies still surviving the fight, but without success. They could not withstand the discipline and bravery of the troopers. Under the supreme impulse of self-preservation, the hostile reinforcements fled, to save themselves, their families, and their possessions from the inevitable doom of the Cheyennes. The detachment of cavalry pursued the retreating Kiowas and Arrapahoes as far as prudence, and the necessity of co-operating with the rest of the troops, would admit.

The victory was complete. One band of the most powerful and relentless of the hostile tribes had been destroyed. The captures were immense. Two white children were released from a fearful bondage. A white woman and a boy, ten years of age, held captive, were killed by the savages when the fight commenced. In the midst of the conflict, the bullets falling around in a perfect shower, a squaw, with demoniac fury, knife in hand, as if looking for an object upon which to revenge the loss of the day, fell upon an innocent captive child, and, with one terrible gash, completely disemboweled it—the warm, smoking entrails falling upon the snow.

Three days had now elapsed since leaving the train. The display of strength made by the Indians, caused a natural anxiety in regard to the safety of the supplies and the inadequate force left to protect them. These considerations fixed the resolution of Custer to hasten back to his wagons.

While all that was left of Black Kettle's village was being destroyed, seven hundred ponies, belonging to the late chief and his warriors, were shot. Two hundred were taken for the captive squaws and children, or brought in as trophies of the victory.

On the return march, no Indians were seen. They were, evidently, in great alarm at the just and terrible punishment meted out to the Cheyennes. Night and morning the captives set up their mourning songs, but received no response from lurking warriors.

At the first camp on the return, according to custom, the Osages hung their scalps outside their tents and fired several volleys over them. All the savages have a superstition that such demonstrations of hostility drive away the spirits of those from whom the scalps were taken, and that, in the event of the neglect of so important a precaution, these spirits would come and rob them of the hard-earned and ghastly evidences of their prowess.

So decisive an achievement as the battle of the Washita, was not without its sacrifices. Like all other deeds in the records of war, victory and defeat alike close up with a melancholy list of dead and suffering. Of the killed, were Elliott and Hamilton, and nineteen enlisted men. Of the wounded, were Barnitz, seriously but not mortally, and thirteen enlisted men.

The loss sustained by the savages, was one hundred and three warriors left on the ground. In property, eight hundred and seventy-five horses, ponies, and mules; two hundred and forty-one saddles, some of very fine and costly workmanship; five hundred and seventy-three buffalo robes; three hundred and ninety buffalo skins for lodges; one hundred and sixty untanned robes; thirty-five revolvers; forty-seven rifles; thirty-five pounds of powder; one thousand and fifty pounds of lead; four thousand arrows and arrow-heads; seventy-five spears; three hundred pounds of bullets; four hundred and seventy blankets; seven hundred pounds of tobacco; besides axes, bullet-moulds, lariats, saddle-bags, &c.

Having no means of transportation, the bulk of these captures were destroyed in the village before leaving. Among the warriors killed, were sixteen chiefs, including Black Kettle and Little Rock, two of the most influential warriors among the Cheyennes. Three squaws and three children, one boy and two girls, were wounded.

The banks of the Washita were silent. The charred remains of the village, and the stark corpses of the warriors, were the only vestiges of Black Kettle's band. The wolf, prowling in the midst of the blackened ruins of the Indian lodge, now alone disturbed the solitary haunts of the once proud and fierce warrior.

Source: De B. Randolph Keim, *Sheridan's Troopers on the Borders: A Winter Campaign on the Plains* (Philadelphia: David McKay, 1885), 118–120.

134. Emanuel Stance, Report on Engagement, May 26, 1870

Introduction

In 1866 Congress authorized the formation of four African American regiments as part of the regular army: the 9th Cavalry, the 10th Cavalry, the 24th Infantry, and the 25th Infantry. They were sent west to serve on the frontier, and the Indians came to call them buffalo soldiers, a name that the soldiers soon proudly adopted. In addition to fighting the Indians of the Plains and in the Southwest, the buffalo soldiers built roads, escorted the mail, and dealt with frontier outlaws. Emanuel Stance was the first black soldier to receive the Medal of Honor. Born into slavery in Louisiana sometime during the 1840s, Stance enlisted in the U.S. Army in October 1866. Since he was highly literate, as demonstrated by his letters below, promotion came quickly. Stance was a sergeant in the 9th U.S. Cavalry on May 20, 1870, when he led a 10-man patrol out of Fort McKavett, Texas. His patrol twice engaged with superior numbers of Indians and captured a total of 15 horses from them. The three documents presented here are Stance's report on his patrol, his commander's report to headquarters that resulted in the medal, and Stance's gracious letter accepting the medal. Stance was the first of 18 black soldiers who received the Medal of Honor for service on the frontier. A strict disciplinarian but also hot-tempered and a hard drinker, Stance was murdered in 1887, probably by his own men.

Primary Source

Fort McKavett, Texas
May 26, 1870
Lieutenant B. M. Custer
Post Adjutant

Lieutenant:

I have the honor to make the following report of a scout after Indians made in compliance with Special Orders No. 73, extract 2, Headquarters Post of Fort McKavett, Texas, May 19, 70. I left camp on the 20th of May taking the Kickapoo road. When some fourteen (14) miles out I discovered a party of Indians making across the hills having a herd of horses with them. I charged them

and after slight skirmishing they abandoned the herd and took to the mountains. Having secured the horses—9 in number—I resumed my march to Kickapoo Springs and camped for the night. The following morning, I decided to return to the Post with my captured stock, as they would embarrass further operations, as my command was small numbering ten all told. I accordingly started about 6 o'clock A.M., when about two miles from Kickapoo, I discovered a party of Indians about 20 in number, making for a couple of Government teams, which were about three miles in advance of me. They evidently meant to capture the stock as there was only a small guard with the teams. I immediately attacked them by charging them. They tried hard to make a stand to get their herd of horses off, but I set the Spencers to talking and whistling about their ears so lively that they broke in confusion and fled to the hills, leaving us their herd of five horses. Resuming the march towards Camp, they skirmished along my left flank to the eight mile water hole, evidently being determined to take the stock. I turned my little command loose on them at this place, and after a few volleys they left me to continue my march in peace.

I reached camp at 2 P.M. of the 21st with 15 head of horses captured from the Indians. The casualties of this scout was one horse slightly wounded.

I have the honor to be, Very respectfully
Your Obt. Servant
Emanuel Stance
Sergeant, Co. "F," 9 Cavalry

Endorsement
Headquarters Fort McKavett. Texas,
June 1, 1870

Respectfully forwarded to HdQrs Sub Dist. of the Pecos. The gallantry displayed by the Sergeant and his party as well as good judgment used on both occasions, deserves much praise. As this is the fourth and fifth encounter that Sergt. Stance has had with Indians within the past two years, in all of which occasions he has been mentioned for good behavior by his immediate Commanding Officer it is a pleasure to commend him to higher authority.

Henry Carroll.
Captain 9 Cavalry
Commanding Post
Fort McKavett, Texas
July 24, 1870

To the
Adjutant General
United States Army
Washington, D.C.

General:

I have the honor to acknowledge the receipt of a communication of July 9, 1870, from The Adjutant General's Office, inclosing my Medal of Honor. I will cherish the gift as a thing of priceless value and endeavor by my future conduct to merit the high honor conferred upon me.

I have the honor to be,
very respectfully,
Your obedient Servant

Emanuel Stance
Sergeant F Co, 9th Cavy

Source: Frank N. Schubert, ed., *Voices of the Buffalo Soldier* (Albuquerque: University of New Mexico Press, 2003), 36–38.

135. Ulysses S. Grant, Peace Policy, December 5, 1870

Introduction

After the American Civil War (1861–1865), the U.S. government considered new approaches to pacifying the Indians and making the West safe for white settlement. Ely Parker, a Seneca Indian and an aide to Ulysses S. Grant, emphasized secure boundaries for Indian reservations and prompt payment of promised annuities so as to encourage Indians to take up agriculture. When Grant became president of the United States in 1869, he appointed Parker commissioner of Indian affairs, the first Indian to hold that office. Parker was responsible for designing and implementing the Grant administration's peace policy, which Grant described in this excerpt from his 1870 message to Congress. Many Indian agencies had been staffed by political appointees whose corruption disgraced the government. Their diversion of goods and money intended for Indians had made reservation life one of deprivation and misery, forcing a return to hunting and raiding. Under the new policy, the government appointed Christian missionaries whom, it was hoped, would be honest, would look after the Indians' spiritual and physical well-being, and would gently guide them to assimilate into white society. The displaced agents and disgruntled army officers objected to the loss of authority and drove Parker from office with false accusations of corruption. On the part of the missionaries, interdenominational turf battles and overemphasis on religion at the expense of material well-being also helped to defeat the peace policy.

Primary Source

Reform in the management of Indian affairs has received the special attention of the Administration from its inauguration to the present day. The experiment of making it a missionary work was tried with a few agencies given to the denomination of Friends, and has been found to work most advantageously. All agencies and superintendencies not so disposed of were given to officers of the Army. The act of Congress reducing the Army renders Army officers ineligible for civil positions. Indian agencies being civil offices, I determined to give all the agencies to such religious denominations as had heretofore established missionaries among the Indians, and perhaps to some other denominations who would undertake the work on the same terms; that is, as a missionary work. The societies selected are allowed to name their own agents, subject to the approval of the Executive, and are expected to watch over them and aid them as missionaries, to Christianize and civilize the Indian, and to train him in the arts of peace. The Government watches over the official acts of these agents, and requires of them as strict an accountability as if they were appointed in any other manner. I entertain the confident hope that the policy now pursued will, in a few years, bring all the Indians upon reservations, where they will live in houses, have school-houses and churches, and will be pursuing peaceful and self-sustaining avocations, and where they may be visited by the law abiding white man with the same impunity that he now visits the civilized white settlements. I call your special attention to the report of the Commissioner of Indian Affairs for full information on this subject.

Source: Edward McPherson, *A Handbook of Politics for 1872* (Washington, DC: Philp & Solomons, 1872), 21.

136. John G. Bourke, The Use of Apache Scouts, 1873–1886

Introduction

George Crook (1828–1890), a Union general in the American Civil War (1861–1865), earned a reputation as an effective Indian fighter in the postwar decades. He assumed command of the Department of Arizona in 1871. John G. Bourke (1843–1896), author of the memoir excerpted here, was a cavalry captain who served as Crook's aide-de-camp from 1870 to 1886. Here Bourke describes Crook's employment of Apache scouts, an innovative strategy that brought him victory in the Apache campaign of 1872–1873. Until he recruited Indian scouts in the autumn of 1872, Crook's troopers had been unsuccessfully pursuing the fast-moving Apaches after their hit-and-run raids. The scouts located the Apaches in two of their strongholds, the troopers surprised them there, and Crook received the surrender of more than 2,000 Apaches in 1873. On Crook's recommendation, 10 of his scouts received the Medal of Honor. In 1875 Crook was transferred to command of the Department of the Platte and fought against the Sioux. He returned to his Arizona command in 1882. Although Crook brought many of the Apaches onto reservations, Geronimo remained at large. Arizona settlers complained that Crook was too sympathetic to Indians. Frustrated by the lack of government support, Crook asked to be reassigned in 1886 and was replaced by General Nelson Miles. Crook spent his remaining years advocating for Indian rights.

Primary Source

The presence of the Indian scouts saved the white soldiers a great deal of extra fatigue, for the performance of which the Apaches were better qualified. It was one of the fundamental principles upon which General Crook conducted all his operations, to enlist as many of the Indians as could be induced to serve as scouts, because by this means he not only subtracted a considerable element from those in hostility and received hostages, as it were, for the better behavior of his scouts' kinsmen, but he removed from the shoulders of his men an immense amount of arduous and disagreeable work, and kept them fresh for any emergency that might arise. The Apaches were kept constantly out on the flanks, under the white guides, and swept the country of all hostile bands. The white troops followed upon the heels of the Indians, but at a short distance in the rear, as the native scouts were better acquainted with all the tricks of their calling, and familiar with every square acre of the territory. The longer we knew the Apache scouts, the better we liked them. They were wilder and more suspicious than the Pimas and Maricopas, but far more reliable, and endowed with a greater amount of courage and daring. I have never known an officer whose experience entitled his opinion to the slightest consideration, who did not believe as I do on this subject. On this scout Captain Hamilton was compelled to send back his Maricopas as worthless; this was before he joined Brown at MacDowell.

Source: John G. Bourke, *On the Border with Crook* (New York: Scribner, 1902), 202–203.

137. John G. Bourke, The Military Telegraph in the Far West, 1870s

Introduction

The long military career of George Crook (1828–1890) encompassed service in the Pacific Northwest in the 1850s, command of Union troops in the American Civil War (1861–1865), and service in the Indian campaigns of the West. John G. Bourke (1843–1896), author of the memoir excerpted here, was a cavalry captain who served as Crook's aide-de-camp from 1870 to 1886. Here Bourke describes the spread of military telegraph lines across Arizona. The first transcontinental telegraph line had been completed in 1861. Branch lines connecting various points throughout Arizona were completed in the mid-1870s. The instantaneous communication enabled by the telegraph at first awed the Apaches, but they soon learned how to disable it. Telegraphy became a useful tool in the Indian Wars because it allowed the army to report the movements of the enemy and send troops to intercept them. Because they knew the land better and traveled lighter, Indian warriors enjoyed superior mobility compared to army troops. The telegraph helped the army compensate for this disadvantage. In 1875 Crook was transferred out of Arizona and was sent to command the campaigns against the Sioux. In 1882 he returned to command of the Department of Arizona. Arizona settlers complained that Crook was too sympathetic to Indians. Frustrated by the lack of government support, Crook asked to be reassigned in 1886 and was replaced by General Nelson Miles. Crook spent his remaining years advocating for Indian rights.

Primary Source

. . . The military telegraph line was built from San Diego, California, to Fort Yuma, California, thence to Maricopa Wells, Arizona, where it bifurcated, one line going on to Prescott and Fort Whipple, the other continuing eastward to Tucson, and thence to San Carlos and Camp Apache, or rather to the crossing of the Gila River, fifteen miles from San Carlos.

For this work, the most important ever undertaken in Arizona up to that time, Congress appropriated something like the sum of fifty-seven thousand dollars, upon motion of Hon. Richard C. McCormick, then Delegate; the work of construction was superintended by General James J. Dana, Chief Quartermaster of the Department of Arizona, who managed the matter with such care and economy that the cost was some ten or eleven thousand dollars less than the appropriation. The citizens of Arizona living nearest the line supplied all the poles required at the lowest possible charge. When it is understood that the total length of wire stretched was over seven hundred miles, the price paid (less than forty-seven thousand dollars) will show that there was very little room for excessive profit for anybody in a country where all transportation was by wagon or on the backs of mules across burning deserts and over lofty mountains. The great task of building this line was carried out successfully by Major George F. Price, Fifth Cavalry, since dead, and by Lieutenant John F. Trout, Twenty-third Infantry.

One of the first messages transmitted over the wire from Prescott to Camp Apache was sent by an Apache Indian, to apprise his family that he and the rest of the detachment with him would reach home on a certain day. To use a Hibernicism, the wire to Apache did not go to Apache, but stopped at Grant, at the time of which I am writing. General Crook sent a message to the commanding officer at Camp Grant, directing him to use every endeavor to have the message sent by the Apache reach its destination, carrying it with the official dispatches forwarded by courier to Camp Apache. The family and friends of the scout were surprised and bewildered at receiving a communication sent over the white man's talking wire (Pesh-bi-yalti), of which they had lately been hearing so much; but on the day appointed they all put on their thickest coats of face paint, and donned their best bibs and tuckers, and sallied out on foot and horseback to meet the incoming party, who were soon descried descending the flank of an adjacent steep mountain. That was a great day for Arizona; it impressed upon the minds of the savages the fact that the white man's arts were superior to those which their own "Medicine Men" pretended to possess, and made them see that it would be a good thing for their own interests to remain our friends.

The Apaches made frequent use of the wire. A most amusing thing occurred at Crook's headquarters, when the Apache chief "Pitone," who had just come up from a mission of peace to the Yumas, on the Colorado, and who had a grievance against "Pascual," the chief of the latter tribe, had the operator, Mr. Strauchon, inform "Pascual" that if he did not do a certain thing which he had promised to do, the Apaches would go on the war-path, and fairly wipe the ground with the Yumas. There couldn't have been a quainter antithesis of the elements of savagery and enlightenment than the presence of that chief in the telegraph office on such a mission. The Apaches learned after a while how to stop the communication by telegraph, which they did very adroitly by pulling down the wire, cutting it in two, and tying the ends together with a rubber band, completely breaking the circuit. The linemen would have to keep their eyes open to detect just where such breaks existed.

Source: John G. Bourke, *On the Border with Crook* (New York: Scribner, 1902), 232–233.

138. George Crook, Discovery of Gold in the Black Hills, 1875

Introduction

George Crook (1828–1890), a Union general in the American Civil War (1861–1865), earned a reputation as an effective Indian fighter in the postwar decades. He assumed command of the Department of Arizona in 1871. In 1875 he was transferred to command of the Department of the Platte. As he describes in this passage from his memoirs, one of his first duties was to go to the Black Hills of South Dakota, Sioux reservation land on which gold had been discovered the previous year, and eject the trespassing prospectors. Crook found that the gold seekers felt entitled to do whatever they pleased on reservation land, and some sneaked back onto the reservation at the first opportunity. The government tried to negotiate a new treaty that would give them the Black Hills, but the Sioux were unwilling to negotiate and give up land that was sacred to them. Angered by the miners' trespassing, Indians left the reservation. When they defied the government's order to return, the army moved against them, and years of war ensued. In 1877 the federal government essentially confiscated the Black Hills by forcing on the Sioux a treaty signed by only a small percentage of the tribe.

Primary Source

The discovery of gold in the Black Hills was attracting much attention amongst the people of the country. Many expeditions were being fitted out with the view of going into that country. As it was on the Sioux reservation, the authorities in Washington were anxious to prevent this violation of the treaty stipulations. Several parties were prevented from going in. General Sheridan, in command of the Division of the Missouri, issued an order directing the troops to arrest any such persons attempting to go into the Black Hills, and to destroy all their transportation, guns and property generally. But notwithstanding all these precautions, many had sifted in.

I was ordered to proceed to that country and eject these people. About the middle of July I started for the Black Hills from Cheyenne, via Fort Laramie in ambulances. Our party consisted of Major Stanton and his clerk, Gen. J. E. Smith and son, George Wilson, and myself. Col. R. I. Dodge was already in that country with an expedition exploring the country, or rather he was escorting some persons, supposed to be scientific, who represented the Interior Department, who were examining the country for the purpose of determining whether the precious metals really existed in paying quantities or not.

I found a good many sovereign citizens scattered about the Hills, prospecting, while others had commenced mining. There was more or less feeling amongst them with what they regarded as an interference with the rights of a sovereign citizen of "these here United States" to go where he pleased and do as he pleased. I circulated around amongst them, got them to come and have a talk, when I explained the whole affair to them, that I was merely executing an unpleasant duty and that I had no feeling in the matter, and advised them to go peaceably. I issued a proclamation warning them to leave the country. I had suggested that as the claims which they had taken up were invalid and would not hold in case the land was thrown up to settlement without a relocation, I advised them to agree amongst themselves to respect each other's claims when it became lawful for them to go into this country. Most of them left, but a few dodged the troops that I left under the command of Capt. Pollock, 9th Infantry. The Black Hills was then a most interesting and beautiful country. It was like an oasis in the desert, for here was a broken piece of country covered with a beautiful growth of timber, filled with game of all kinds, surrounded as far as the eye could see with bare, uninteresting plains. Nothing of importance occurred until the beginning of 1876, when I received instructions to compel the Sioux and Cheyenne Indians, who were off their reservation, to go on it. They were consequently notified that they must either go on the reservation by such a time, or else the troops would attack them wherever found. I might say that these Indians were continually committing depredations on the surrounding country, were insolent, and claimed the whole of Wyoming and part of the adjacent territories, and declined to be restrained in their freedom in the slightest particular. Sometime during the fall a commission comprised of Senator Allison and other members of Congress assembled at Red Cloud agency to treat with these Indians for the Black Hills country.

Source: Martin F. Schmitt, ed., *General George Crook: His Autobiography* (Norman: University of Oklahoma Press, 1946), 188–189.

139. Fanny Dunbar Corbusier, The Removal of Apaches to San Carlos Reservation, 1876

Introduction

The U.S. Army in the Southwest, under the command of George Crook, had brought a period of peace to Arizona by 1875. Soon after Crook's transfer to Dakota, white settlers in Arizona engineered the seizure of the desirable land occupied by several Apache reservations in the highlands of Arizona and New Mexico. Various bands of Apaches were ordered to move to a reservation at San Carlos in the desolate, inhospitable southeastern Arizona lowlands. Forced to leave the ancestral land that had been promised to them in perpetuity, where they had lived in relative contentment, and to coexist on a single reservation among their traditional enemies, the Apaches rightly viewed the transfer as a betrayal. At San Carlos they suffered from the extreme heat, brackish water, and insect-borne diseases. As a result, the Chiricahua Apaches, led by Victorio, left the reservation and went on the warpath. In the memoir excerpted here, an army officer's wife describes the forced transfer in 1876, the Apaches' reaction, and her husband's role in it. The author, Fanny Dunbar Corbusier, was married to an army surgeon, William Henry Corbusier, and accompanied him to all his duty stations during his 39-year career. Her memoir covers the years 1860 to 1908 and encompasses the Indian wars in the American West through the Spanish-American War (1896–1898) and service in the Philippines.

Primary Source

The Indians had been successful at truck farming under the direction of army officers and were contemplating the extension of their patches in the spring. If left where they were, they would soon have been self-supporting, but the Indian Department sent a special Commissioner, Colonel L. E. Dudley, who had been an officer in the Civil War, to remove them to the San Carlos Reservation. They were very happy in their own country and did not wish to go where their enemies were numerous. Colonel Dudley tried to convince them that the change would be for their good and that he came from General Grant in Washington, who said they must go. They did not believe him and came to Father to know why they should

leave the country that had always belonged to them and which the Government had promised should be theirs and their children's forever.

Father assured them that General Grant said that they must go. We heard the wails of the women all night, and in the morning the chiefs returned and told Father they would go if he went with them. After he had promised, they had another talk with the Commissioner and consented to move.

In the latter part of February, when the day came for them to start, they gathered what belongings that they could carry. The very young children, old people, and sick were put into their cone-shaped baskets to be carried on the backs of the strong ones. One old man carried his old sick wife on his back in one of these baskets. The recommendations of Father and others to take the Indians around the mountains by wagon road was [were] ignored, and the march across rivers and over high mountains was begun.

They moved along slowly in a long, silent, sad procession. When they reached Camp Verde, sixteen miles down the Verde River, Father had not yet come up and they refused to go on unless he was with them. After he had joined them, they went on, but silently. Second Lieutenant George O. Eaton, Fifth United States Cavalry, was in command of a detachment of men that went along as a guard and one was needed as very poor arrangements had been made for feeding the Indians.

Before they reached San Carlos they were fighting hungry. One morning, after the food had all given out, a bullet whizzed over the commissioner's head as a warning. He left quickly, promising to send back food very soon. When Father left them at San Carlos, the women and children cried and the men begged him to stay with them or come back, as they were among their old enemies and they did not know the white man at the Agency.

Source: Patricia Y. Stallard, ed., *Fanny Dunbar Corbusier: Recollections of Her Army Life, 1869–1908* (Norman: University of Oklahoma Press, 2003), 62–63.

140. Elizabeth Custer, Account of Corruption among Indian Agents, 1870s

Introduction

Elizabeth Bacon Custer (1842–1933) wed the gallant but headstrong Civil War cavalryman, George Armstrong Custer, in 1864. She accompanied him to his duty stations throughout their marriage, which ended with his defeat and death at the infamous Battle of the Little Bighorn in 1876. After authorities, up to President Ulysses S. Grant, questioned Custer's judgment in the wake of the disaster, Custer's widow devoted the rest of her long life to defending his reputation and burnishing his image. Elizabeth

Custer outlived her late husband's critics and by sheer determination prevented any serious investigation into his conduct for more than 50 years. Her three memoirs—"*Boots and Saddles*" (1885), excerpted here; *Following the Guidon* (1890); and *Tenting on the Plains* (1893)—brought her financial security and kept an idealized image of Custer before the public. Here she describes an instance, one of many throughout the post–Civil War West, of corruption among Indian agents and their diversion of Indian rations for their own profit. Like many army men, Custer sympathized with the plight of the Indians in being deprived of their rations by civilian officials. In this episode, the reservation Sioux appealed to Custer for help, and the general wired Washington for permission to feed them from abundant army rations. The secretary of war refused permission because feeding the Indians from army rations would have discredited the Interior Department, whose job it was to feed the Indians. This decision and others like it drove Indians to flee their reservations and go to war.

Primary Source

The Indians came several times from the reservation for council, but the occasion that made the greatest impression upon me was toward the spring. They came to implore the general for food. In the fall the steamer bringing them supplies was detained in starting. It had hardly accomplished half the distance before the ice impeded its progress and it lay out in the channel, frozen in, all winter. The suffering among the Indians was very great. They were compelled to eat their dogs and ponies to keep from starving. Believing a personal appeal would be effectual, they asked to come to our post for a council.

The Indian band brought their great orator Running Antelope. He was intensely dignified and fine looking. His face when he spoke was expressive and animated, contrary to all the precedents of Indian oratory we had become familiar with. As he stood among them all in the general's room, he made an indelible impression on my memory. The Indians' feet are unusually small; sometimes their vanity induces them to put on women's shoes. The hands are slender and marvelously soft, considering their life of exposure. Their speech is full of gesture, and the flexible wrist makes their movements expressive. A distinguished scholar, speaking of the aid the hand is to an orator, calls it the "second face." It certainly was so with Running Antelope. He described the distressing condition of the tribe with real eloquence. While he spoke, lifting his graceful hands toward Heaven in appeal, one of my husband's birds that was uncaged floated down and alighted on the venerable warrior's head. It had been so petted, no ordinary movement startled the little thing. It maintained its poise, spreading its wings to keep its balance, as the Indian moved his head in gesture. The orator saw that the faces of the Indians showed signs of humor, but he was ignorant of what amused them. His inquiring eyes saw no solution in the general's, for, fearing to disconcert him, General Custer controlled every muscle in his face. Finally the bird whirled up to his favorite resting place on the horn of the buffalo head,

and the warrior understood the unusual sight of a smile from his people.

His whole appeal was most impressive, and touched the quick sympathies of my husband. He was a sincere friend of the reservation Indian. The storehouses at our post were filled with supplies, and he promised to telegraph to the Great Father for permission to give them rations until spring. Meantime, he promised them all they could eat while they awaited at the post the answer to the dispatch. Not content with a complaint of their present wrongs, Running Antelope went off into an earnest denunciation of the agents, calling them dishonest.

One of the Indians, during the previous summer, with fox-like cunning had lain out on the dock all day apparently sleeping, while he watched the steamer unloading supplies for them. A mental estimate was carefully made of what came off the boat and compared as carefully afterward with what was distributed. There was an undeniable deficit. A portion that should have been theirs was detained, and they accused the agent of keeping it. The general interrupted and asked the interpreter to say that the Great Father selected the agents from among good men before sending them out from Washington. Running Antelope quickly responded, "They may be good men when they leave the Great Father, but they get to be desperate cheats by the time they reach us." I shall have to ask whoever reads to substitute another more forcible adjective, such as an angry man would use, in place of "desperate." The Indian language is not deficient in abusive terms and epithets.

When the council was ended and the Indians were preparing to leave, my husband asked me to have Mary put everything we had ready to eat on the dining-room table. The manner in which Running Antelope folded his robe around him and strode in a stately way down the long parlor was worthy of a Roman emperor.

I had been so impressed by his oratory and lordly mien that I could hardly believe my eyes, or descend from the lofty state of mind into which he had taken me, when I saw him at table and realized what he was doing. After gorging himself, he emptied the plates and swept all the remains from before the plates of the other chiefs into the capacious folds of his robe. This he rebelted at the waist, so that it formed a very good temporary haversack. With an air signifying "to the victor belong the spoils," he swept majestically out of the house.

The answer came next day from the secretary of war that the Department of the Interior, which had the Indians in charge, refused to allow any army supplies to be distributed. They gave as a reason that it would involve complexities in their relations with other departments. It was a very difficult thing for the general to explain to the Indians. They knew that both army and Indians were fed from the same source, and they could not comprehend what difference it could make when a question of starvation was pending. They could not be told, what we all knew, that had the War Department made good the deficiencies it would have reflected discredit on the management of the Department of the Interior.

The chiefs were compelled to return to their reservations, where long ago all the game had been shot and many of their famishing tribe were driven to join the hostiles. We were not surprised that the warriors were discouraged and desperate and that the depredations of Sitting Bull on the settlements increased with the new accessions to his numbers.

Source: Elizabeth B. Custer, *"Boots and Saddles": Or, Life in Dakota with General Custer* (New York: Harper and Brothers, 1885), 225–228.

141. John G. Bourke, Account of an Attack on a Sioux Village, 1876

Introduction

George Crook (1828–1890), a Union general in the American Civil War (1861–1865), earned a reputation as an effective Indian fighter in the postwar decades. He assumed command of the Department of Arizona in 1871. In 1875 he was transferred to command of the Department of the Platte. John G. Bourke (1843–1896), author of the memoir excerpted here, was a cavalry captain who served as Crook's aide-de-camp from 1870 to 1886. Here Bourke recounts episodes that took place in March 1876 in the campaign against the Sioux. Gold had been discovered on an 1874 army expedition into the Black Hills of South Dakota, land that had been reserved to the Sioux. The army tried but failed to prevent prospectors from trespassing on the reservation. Angered by white encroachment, Indians left the reservation. When they defied the government's order to return, the army moved against them. These passages describe an attack by Crook's men on the village of the Sioux war leader Crazy Horse, the attack's unsatisfactory outcome, and the soldiers' slaughter of 100 ponies captured from the Indians. Crazy Horse took part in the Battle of the Little Bighorn a few months later and surrendered to Crook in May 1877. Also in 1877, the federal government essentially confiscated the Black Hills by forcing on the Sioux a treaty signed by only a small percentage of the tribe.

Primary Source

Just as we approached the edge of the village we came upon a ravine some ten feet in depth and of a varying width, the average being not less than fifty. We got down this deliberately, and at the bottom and behind a stump saw a young boy about fifteen years old driving his ponies. He was not ten feet off. The youngster wrapped his blanket about him and stood like a statue of bronze, waiting for the fatal bullet; his features were as immobile as if cut in stone. The American Indian knows how to die with as much stoicism as the East Indian. I leveled my pistol. "Don't shoot," said Egan, "we must make no noise." We were up on the bench upon which the village

stood, and the war-whoop of the youngster was ringing wildly in the winter air, awakening the echoes of the bald-faced bluffs. The lodges were not arranged in any order, but placed where each could secure the greatest amount of protection from the configuration of the coves and nooks amid the rocks. The ponies close to the village trotted off slowly to the right and left as we drew near; the dogs barked and howled and scurried out of sight; a squaw raised the door of her lodge, and seeing the enemy yelled with all her strength, but as yet there had been not one shot fired.

[. . .]

Crook reached camp about noon of the 18th of March, and it goes without saying that his presence was equal to that of a thousand men. He expressed his gratification upon hearing of our successful finding of "Crazy Horse's" village, as that chief was justly regarded as the boldest, bravest, and most skilful warrior in the whole Sioux nation; but he could not conceal his disappointment and chagrin when he learned that our dead and wounded had been needlessly abandoned to the enemy, and that with such ample supplies of meat and furs at hand our men had been made to suffer from hunger and cold, with the additional fatigue of a long march which could have been avoided by sending word to him. Crook, with a detachment from the four companies left with him, had come on a short distance in advance of Hawley's and Dewees's battalions, and run in upon the rear-guard of the Cheyennes and Sioux who had stampeded so many of the ponies from Reynolds's bivouac; the General took sight at one of the Indians wearing a war-bonnet and dropped him out of the saddle; the Indian's comrades seized him and took off through the broken country, but the pony, saddle, buffalo robe, blanket, and bonnet of the dead man fell into our hands, together with nearly a hundred of the ponies; which were driven along to our forlorn camp at the confluence of the Lodge Pole and the Powder.

There was nothing for Crook to do but abandon the expedition, and return to the forts, and reorganize for a summer campaign. We had no beef, as our herd had been run off on account of the failure to guard it; we were out of supplies, although we had destroyed enough to last a regiment for a couple of months; we were encumbered with sick, wounded, and cripples with frozen limbs, because we had not had sense enough to save the furs and robes in the village; and the enemy was thoroughly aroused, and would be on the *qui vive* for all that we did. To old Fort Reno, by way of the valley of the Powder, was not quite ninety miles. The march was uneventful, and there was nothing to note beyond the storms of snow and wind, which lasted, with some spasmodic intermissions, throughout the journey. The wind blew from the south, and there was a softening of the ground, which aggravated the disagreeable features by adding mud to our other troubles. The Indians hung round our camps every night, occasionally firing a shot at our fires, but more anxious to steal back their ponies than to fight. To remove all excuse for their presence Crook ordered that the throats of the captured ponies be cut, and this was done on two different nights: first, some fifty being knocked in the head with axes, or having their throats cut with the sharp knives of the scouts, and again, another "bunch" of fifty being shot before sundown. The throat-cutting was determined upon when the enemy began firing in upon camp, and was the only means of killing the ponies without danger to our own people. It was pathetic to hear the dismal trumpeting (I can find no other word to express my meaning) of the dying creatures, as the breath of life rushed through severed windpipes. The Indians in the bluffs recognized the cry, and were aware of what we were doing, because with one yell of defiance and a parting volley, they left us alone for the rest of the night.

Steaks were cut from the slaughtered ponies and broiled in the ashes by the scouts; many of the officers and soldiers imitated their example. Prejudice to one side, the meat is sweet and nourishing, not inferior to much of the stringy beef that used to find its way to our markets.

Source: John G. Bourke, *On the Border with Crook* (New York: Scribner, 1902), 273, 280–281.

142. Red Horse, Account of the Battle of the Little Bighorn, 1876

Introduction

Angered by white encroachment and starving due to nondelivery of promised food rations, Indians of the northern Plains defied government orders and left their reservations. In 1876 General Philip Sheridan ordered three converging columns to move against the Sioux and their allies. On June 25, 1876, Brigadier General George Armstrong Custer (1839–1876) and his 7th Cavalry discovered the major Sioux encampment on Little Bighorn Creek. Custer did not realize how large a force he confronted and, without waiting for more troops to arrive, ordered Major Marcus Reno and his detachment to charge. As the outnumbered Reno was fought to a standstill, Custer's force charged from another direction. Custer and all of his more than 200 men died in the ensuing combat. The nation was shocked by the defeat. Custer's judgment and Reno's actions came under scrutiny, but most importantly, the army turned its full might against the Indians of the northern Plains. In 1881 Red Horse, a Sioux war chief, gave this eyewitness account to army physician Charles McChesney. At McChesney's request, Red Horse created 42 illustrations. There is some agreement between Red Horse's account of the battle and the account by army interpreter Frederick Frances Girard. Red Horse's account (translated from sign language) and pictures were eventually published in a congressional document as part of a report on Plains Indian language.

Primary Source

Five springs ago I, with many Sioux Indians, took down and packed up our tipis and moved from Cheyenne river to the Rosebud river, where we camped a few days; then took down and packed up our lodges and moved to the Little Bighorn river and pitched our lodges with the large camp of Sioux.

The Sioux were camped on the Little Bighorn river as follows: The lodges of the Uncpapas were pitched highest up the river under a bluff. The Santee lodges were pitched next. The Oglala's lodges were pitched next. The Brule lodges were pitched next. The Minneconjou lodges were pitched next. The Sans Arcs' lodges were pitched next. The Blackfeet lodges were pitched next. The Cheyenne lodges were pitched next. A few Arikara Indians were among the Sioux (being without lodges of their own). Two-Kettles, among the other Sioux (without lodges).

I was a Sioux chief in the council lodge. My lodge was pitched in the center of the camp. The day of the attack I and four women were a short distance from the camp digging wild turnips. Suddenly one of the women attracted my attention to a cloud of dust rising a short distance from camp. I soon saw that the soldiers were charging the camp. To the camp I and the women ran. When I arrived a person told me to hurry to the council lodge. The soldiers charged so quickly we could not talk [council]. We came out of the council lodge and talked in all directions. The Sioux mount horses, take guns, and go fight the soldiers. Women and children mount horses and go, meaning to get out of the way.

Among the soldiers was an officer who rode a horse with four white feet. [This officer was evidently Capt. French, Seventh Cavalry.] The Sioux have for a long time fought many brave men of different people, but the Sioux say this officer was the bravest man they had ever fought. I don't know whether this was Gen. Custer or not. Many of the Sioux men that I hear talking tell me it was. I saw this officer in the fight many times, but did not see his body. It has been told me that he was killed by a Santee Indian, who took his horse. This officer wore a large-brimmed hat and a deerskin coat. This officer saved the lives of many soldiers by turning his horse and covering the retreat. Sioux say this officer was the bravest man they ever fought. I saw two officers looking alike, both having long yellowish hair.

Before the attack the Sioux were camped on the Rosebud river. Sioux moved down a river running into the Little Bighorn river, crossed the Little Bighorn river, and camped on its west bank.

This day [day of attack] a Sioux man started to go to Red Cloud agency, but when he had gone a short distance from camp he saw a cloud of dust rising and turned back and said he thought a herd of buffalo was coming near the village.

The day was hot. In a short time the soldiers charged the camp. [This was Maj. Reno's battalion of the Seventh Cavalry.] The soldiers came on the trail made by the Sioux camp in moving, and crossed the Little Bighorn river above where the Sioux crossed, and attacked the lodges of the Uncpapas, farthest up the river. The women and children ran down the Little Bighorn river a short distance into a ravine. The soldiers set fire to the lodges. All the Sioux now charged the soldiers and drove them in confusion across the Little Bighorn river, which was very rapid, and several soldiers were drowned in it. On a hill the soldiers stopped and the Sioux surrounded them. A Sioux man came and said that a different party of Soldiers had all the women and children prisoners. Like a whirlwind the word went around, and the Sioux all heard it and left the soldiers on the hill and went quickly to save the women and children.

From the hill that the soldiers were on to the place where the different soldiers [by this term Red-Horse always means the battalion immediately commanded by General Custer, his mode of distinction being that they were a different body from that first encountered] were seen was level ground with the exception of a creek. Sioux thought the soldiers on the hill [i.e., Reno's battalion] would charge them in rear, but when they did not the Sioux thought the soldiers on the hill were out of cartridges. As soon as we had killed all the different soldiers the Sioux all went back to kill the soldiers on the hill. All the Sioux watched around the hill on which were the soldiers until a Sioux man came and said many walking soldiers were coming near. The coming of the walking soldiers was the saving of the soldiers on the hill. Sioux can not fight the walking soldiers [infantry], being afraid of them, so the Sioux hurriedly left.

The soldiers charged the Sioux camp about noon. The soldiers were divided, one party charging right into the camp. After driving these soldiers across the river, the Sioux charged the different soldiers [i.e., Custer's] below, and drive them in confusion; these soldiers became foolish, many throwing away their guns and raising their hands, saying, "Sioux, pity us; take us prisoners." The Sioux did not take a single soldier prisoner, but killed all of them; none were left alive for even a few minutes. These different soldiers discharged their guns but little. I took a gun and two belts off two dead soldiers; out of one belt two cartridges were gone, out of the other five.

The Sioux took the guns and cartridges off the dead soldiers and went to the hill on which the soldiers were, surrounded and fought them with the guns and cartridges of the dead soldiers. Had the soldiers not divided I think they would have killed many Sioux. The different soldiers [i.e., Custer's battalion] that the Sioux killed made five brave stands. Once the Sioux charged right in the midst of the different soldiers and scattered them all, fighting among the soldiers hand to hand.

One band of soldiers was in rear of the Sioux. When this band of soldiers charged, the Sioux fell back, and the Sioux and the soldiers stood facing each other. Then all the Sioux became brave and charged the soldiers. The Sioux went but a short distance before they separated and surrounded the soldiers. I could see the officers riding in front of the soldiers and hear them shooting. Now the Sioux had many killed. The soldiers killed 136 and wounded 160 Sioux. The Sioux killed all these different soldiers in the ravine.

The soldiers charged the Sioux camp farthest up the river. A short time after the different soldiers charged the village below. While the different soldiers and Sioux were fighting together the Sioux chief said, "Sioux men, go watch soldiers on the hill and prevent their joining the different soldiers." The Sioux men took the clothing off the dead and dressed themselves in it. Among the soldiers were white men who were not soldiers. The Sioux dressed in the soldiers' and white men's clothing fought the soldiers on the hill.

The banks of the Little Bighorn river were high, and the Sioux killed many of the soldiers while crossing. The soldiers on the hill dug up the ground [i.e., made earth-works], and the soldiers and Sioux fought at long range, sometimes the Sioux charging close up. The fight continued at long range until a Sioux man saw the walking soldiers coming. When the walking soldiers came near the Sioux became afraid and ran away.

Source: J. W. Powell, *Tenth Annual Report of the Bureau of Ethnology, 52d Congress, 2d Session, House Doc. 116* (Washington, DC: U.S. Government Printing Office, 1893), 564–566.

143. Frederick Frances Girard, Account of the Battle of the Little Bighorn, 1876

Introduction

On June 25, 1876, Brigadier General George Armstrong Custer (1839–1876) and his 7th Cavalry discovered the major Sioux encampment on Little Bighorn Creek. Custer apparently did not realize how large a force he confronted and, without waiting for additional troops to arrive, ordered Major Marcus Reno and his detachment to charge. As the outnumbered Reno was fought to a standstill, Custer's force charged from another direction. Custer and all of his more than 200 men died in the ensuing combat. The nation was shocked by the defeat. Custer's judgment and Reno's actions came under scrutiny, but most importantly, the army turned its full might against the Indians of the northern Plains. This account by army interpreter Frederick Frances Girard agrees in some respects with the Sioux account given by Red Horse. Girard notes that Reno appeared to give up when he might have kept fighting and that the arrival of General Alfred Terry with the rest of the intended attack column caused the Indians to retreat. Girard later testified against Reno in a court of inquiry, blaming him for his seeming inaction during the slaughter. However, the court cleared Reno of wrongdoing, and historians argue that Reno was too outnumbered to come to Custer's aid. Custer's Last Stand remains a focal point for mythologists and historians, both professional and amateur.

Primary Source

On June 22d, Custer's command left the mouth of the Rosebud looking for Indians. On June 24th, we broke camp and marched all day and in evening went into camp. The men had supper and grazed their horses and then marched all night till 4 A.M., when a halt was called. The horses remained saddled but the soldiers slept on the ground as best they could. Two Arikara scouts arrived from Lieutenant Varnum, who had been sent out to reconnoitre and locate Indian camps. They brought word of a very large camp down in Little Big Horn Valley, but the Indians had discovered us and were on the run. Custer ordered me to go with him and the two Arikara scouts who had come in from Varnum and two of our scouts, to where Lieutenant Varnum was. About daybreak we reached Varnum and could see the large black mass moving in front and down the Little Big Horn and a dense cloud of dust over all and behind. The camp we had found was the smaller camp (the larger camp was downstream farther), and was on the way to the larger camp and this led us all to believe that the Indians were stampeded. Custer and his party with Varnum and his scouts started back to rejoin the command at a sharp gait. Before reaching his troops, about half way back, Tom Custer met us at the head of the troops and Custer addressed him saying: "Tom, who in the devil moved these troops forward? My orders and intentions were to remain in camp all day and make a night attack on the Indians but they have discovered us and are on the run." After joining the troops, Custer with his officers held a consultation and decided it would be better to follow the Indians so he divided his command into three battalions, one under his own command, Benteen in command of the second, and Reno of the third. Benteen he sent to the left of the command to overlook the ridges as we marched down the valley. He then ordered Reno to take his command and try to overtake the Indians and bring them to battle while he himself would support him. Custer said: "Take the scouts with you." Reno started on the double quick down the valley until he came to the Little Big Horn. Up to that time we were all still under the impression that the Indians were running away. Upon reaching the ford of the Little Big Horn, I discovered that the Indians were coming back to give us battle and called Reno's attention to this change in their movements. Reno halted for a few seconds and ordered the men forward. Thinking that Custer should know of this change of front on the part of the Indians, I rode back at once to tell Custer the news. At an abrupt turn I met Cook, Custer's adjutant, ahead of his command, who said: "Gerard, what's up?"

On hearing the news he ordered me back to Reno's command and rode to inform Custer of the change in the front on the part of the Indians. I rejoined Reno's command just as he was drawing up his men on the skirmish line. The men were almost six feet apart along the brow of a hill below which was a belt of timber. As the Indians came charging back the men used the timber for cover and the Indians rode by on the left and around to the higher ground at the rear and left. Not more than four rounds had been fired before they saw Custer's command dashing along the hills one mile to their rear. Reno then gave the order: "The Indians are taking us in the rear, mount and charge." This was then about 1:30 P.M. I was surprised at this change of position as we had excellent cover and could hold off the Indians indefinitely, but the orders were to mount and charge. Charley Reynolds was killed as he rode up the slope at the left and Isaiah a little farther out. Reno led his men in Indian file back to the ford above which he had seen Custer's command pass. The Indians picked off the troops at will; it was a rout not a charge. All the men were shot in the back, some men fell before high ground was reached. As soon as the hill was gained, Benteen and his command came up and the demoralization of Reno's men affected his own men and no attempt was made to go to Custer's aid. They remained where they were though it was about 2 P.M. and no Indians attacked them for more than an hour.

After Reno's command left, I found in the timber Lieutenant de Rudio, Sergeant O'Neill and Wm. Jackson, a half-breed Blackfoot scout, who were also cut off from the command. All the afternoon we could hear the troop volleys, but the scattering fire of the Indians gradually predominated till we were sure that the Indians had won. The fight where Reno's men were began shortly after 4 and kept up till dark. We remained where we were till dark and then struck out west thinking Reno's command had returned. We missed the morning ford and tried the ford Reno used to retreat by but the dead bodies made the horses snort and the water looked too deep so they returned and found a new ford. As we mounted the bank we saw a match lit and called out: "There are the troops, Hello!" and then the match was put out. As we neared the old crossing we saw the Indian lances against the sky and the Indians hearing us turn off suddenly, called out, "Are you afraid, we are not white troops." De Rudio and O'Neill lay down and hid in the brush at this point while Jackson and I rode down and across the stream straight against a cut bank. Both horses threw their riders, our guns were lost, but finally a ford was found and just at dawn we rode out on the prairie. At the left we could hear more Indians coming across the Little Big Horn, coming down to attack Reno. Then we galloped hard to the bunch of willows at the right and reached it before the Indians came out of the water. Here we remained till dark. About 11 A.M. we saw them attack Reno's camp. About one hour before sunset a great talking and confusion arose, the Indians evidently saw Terry coming and began to fall back. Some left for their village to gather their families while others rode away up the Little Big Horn. The retreating warriors passed by hundreds close to where we lay hid in the willows.

Source: O. G. Libby, ed. *The Arikara Narrative of the Campaign against the Hostile Dakotas* (Cedar Rapids, IA: Torch, 1920), 171–175.

144. John G. Bourke, The Surrender of Crazy Horse, 1877

Introduction

George Crook (1828–1890), a Union general in the American Civil War (1861–1865), earned a reputation as an effective Indian fighter in the postwar decades. Crook assumed command of the Department of the Platte in 1875. John G. Bourke (1843–1896), author of the memoir excerpted here, was a cavalry captain who served as Crook's aide-de-camp from 1870 to 1886. Bourke describes in candid detail the surrender of the Sioux war chief Crazy Horse. Gold had been discovered on an 1874 army expedition into the Black Hills of South Dakota, land that had been reserved for the Sioux. The army tried but failed to prevent prospectors from trespassing on the reservation. Angered by white encroachment, Indians left the reservation. When they defied the government's order to return, the army moved against them. Crazy Horse led the 1866 Fetterman Massacre, the 1876 Battle of the Rosebud, and the 1876 Battle of Little Bighorn, the latter of which brought the wrath of the U.S. Army and sealed the fate of the Sioux. Crazy Horse surrendered to Crook in May 1877. In September of that year Crazy Horse died in a scuffle with guards, although it is unknown who inflicted the fatal wound. Also in 1877, the federal government essentially confiscated the Black Hills by forcing on the Sioux a treaty signed by only a small percentage of the tribe.

Primary Source

On the 6th of May, 1877, shortly after meridian, "Crazy Horse's" band approached the agency, descending the hills in the following order: First, Lieutenant William P. Clarke, with the agency Indians—that is, "Red Cloud" and his Indian soldiers; next, "Crazy Horse," at the head of his warriors, having abreast of him "Little Big Man," "Little Hawk," "He Dog," "Old Hawk," and "Bad Road." Stringing along behind, for a distance of nearly two miles, came the old men with the women and children, lodges, ponies, dogs, and other plunder. Lieutenant Clarke had gone out early in the morning to a point seven or eight miles from the post to meet the incoming party. "Crazy Horse," upon learning who he was, remained silent, but was not at all ungracious or surly. He dismounted from his pony, sat down upon the ground, and said that then was the best time for smoking the pipe of peace. He then held out his left hand to Clarke, telling him: "Cola [friend], I shake with this hand because my heart is on this side; I want this peace to last forever." The principal warriors were then presented, each shaking hands. "Crazy Horse" had given his feather bonnet and all other regalia of the war-path to "Red Cloud," his brother-in-law, as he had no

further use for them. "He Dog" took off his own war bonnet and scalp shirt and put them upon Clarke in sign of friendly good-will. The most perfect discipline was maintained, and silence reigned from the head of the cavalcade to the farthest "travois."

When the post was reached, the warriors began to intone a peace chant, in whose refrain the squaws and older children joined, and which lasted until a halt was ordered and the work of turning over ponies and surrendering arms began. An enumeration disclosed the fact that "Crazy Horse" had with him not quite twenty-five hundred ponies, over three hundred warriors, one hundred and forty-six lodges, with an average of almost two families in each, and between eleven hundred and eleven hundred and fifty people all told, not counting the very considerable number who were able to precede the main body, on account of having fatter and stronger ponies. Lieutenant Clarke, in firm but quiet tones, informed the new arrivals that everything in the shape of a fire-arm must be given up, and to insure this being done he would wait until after the squaws had pitched their "tepis," and then make the collection in person. One hundred and seventeen fire-arms, principally cavalry carbines and Winchesters, were found and hauled away in a cart. "Crazy Horse" himself gave up three Winchesters, and "Little Hawk" two. By what seemed to be a curious coincidence, "Little Hawk" wore [a] pendent at his neck[,] the silver medal given to his father at the Peace Conference on the North Platte, in 1817; it bore the effigy of President Monroe. Some of the other chiefs, in surrendering, laid sticks down upon the ground, saying: "Cola, this is my gun, this little one is a pistol; send to my lodge and get them." Every one of these pledges was redeemed by the owner. There was no disorder and no bad feeling, which was remarkable enough, considering that so many of "Crazy Horse's" band had never been on a reservation before. Everything ran along as smooth as clockwork, such interpretation as was necessary being made by Frank Gruard and Billy Hunter; Clarke, however, needed little help, as he could converse perfectly in the sign language. Just behind the knoll overlooking the flat upon which "Crazy Horse's" village had been erected, every one of the Cheyenne warriors was in the saddle, armed to the teeth, and ready to charge down upon "Crazy Horse" and settle their score with him, at the first sign of treachery.

"Crazy Horse's" warriors were more completely disarmed than any other bands coming under my observation, not so much in the number of weapons as in the pattern and condition; to disarm Indians is always an unsatisfactory piece of business, so long as the cowboys and other lawless characters in the vicinity of the agencies are allowed to roam over the country, each one a travelling arsenal. The very same men who will kill unarmed squaws and children, as *was* done in January, 1891, near Pine Ridge Agency, will turn around and sell to the bucks the arms and ammunition which they require for the next war-path. At the very moment when Crook was endeavoring to deprive the surrendering hostiles of deadly weapons, Colonel Mason captured a man with a vehicle loaded with metallic cartridges, brought up from Cheyenne or Sidney, to be disposed of to the young men at Spotted Tail. As with cartridges, so with whiskey: the western country has too many reprobates who make a nefarious living by the sale of vile intoxicants to savages; this has been persistently done among the Sioux, Mojaves, Hualpais, Navajos, and Apaches, to my certain knowledge. Rarely are any of these scoundrels punished. The same class of men robbed the Indians with impunity; "Spotted Tail" lost sixty head of ponies which the Indian scouts trailed down to North Platte, where they were sold among the stock-raisers. The arrest of the thieves was confided to the then sheriff of Sidney, who, somehow, always failed to come up with them; possibly the fact that he was the head of the gang himself may have had something to do with his nonsuccess, but that is hard to say.

"Crazy Horse" took his first supper at Red Cloud Agency with Frank Gruard, who had been his captive for a long time and had made his escape less than two years previously. Frank asked me to go over with him. When we approached the chief's "tepi," a couple of squaws were grinding coffee between two stones, and preparing something to eat. "Crazy Horse" remained seated on the ground, but when Frank called his name in Dakota, "Tashnnca-uitco," at the same time adding a few words I did not understand, he looked up, arose, and gave me a hearty grasp of his hand. I saw before me a man who looked quite young, not over thirty years old, five feet eight inches high, lithe and sinewy, with a scar in the face. The expression of his countenance was one of quiet dignity, but morose, dogged, tenacious, and melancholy. He behaved with stolidity, like a man who realized he had to give in to Fate, but would do so as sullenly as possible. While talking to Frank, his countenance lit up with genuine pleasure, but to all others he was, at least in the first days of his coming upon the reservation, gloomy and reserved. All Indians gave him a high reputation for courage and generosity. In advancing upon an enemy, none of his warriors were allowed to pass him. He had made hundreds of friends by his charity towards the poor, as it was a point of honor with him never to keep anything for himself, excepting weapons of war. I never heard an Indian mention his name save in terms of respect. In the Custer massacre, the attack by Reno had at first caused a panic among women and children, and some of the warriors, who started to flee, but "Crazy Horse," throwing away his rifle, brained one of the incoming soldiers with his stone war-club and jumped upon his horse.

"Little Hawk," who appeared to rank next to "Crazy Horse" in importance, was much like his superior in size and build, but his face was more kindly in expression and he more fluent in speech; he did most of the talking. "Little Big Man" I did not like in those days; principally on account of his insolent behavior to the members of the Allison Commission at this same agency, during the summer. In appearance he was crafty, but withal a man of considerable ability and force. He and I became better friends afterwards, and exchanged presents. I hold now his beautiful calumet and a finely-beaded tobacco bag, as well as a shirt trimmed with human scalps, which was once the property of "Crazy Horse."

As it is never too soon to begin a good work, Mr. Thomas Moore, the Chief of Transportation, was busy the next morning in teaching the Sioux squaws how to make bread out of the flour issued to them, which used to be wasted, fed to their ponies, or bartered off at the trader's store.

Source: John G. Bourke, *On the Border with Crook* (New York: Scribner, 1902), 412–414.

145. Chief Joseph, Surrender Speech, October 15, 1877

Introduction

American immigrants began surging into the Pacific Northwest in 1843. Oregon Territory was officially established in 1848, and Washington became a separate territory in 1853. The Indians who lived in the northwestern territories numbered about 42,000 and belonged to several dozen tribes. Many tried to resist the growing population of American settlers, and a state of nearly continuous warfare went on until 1858, when most of the Indians of the Northwest were confined to reservations. The Nez Perces, however, maintained friendly relations with the Americans. But in a decision typical of the time, U.S. government authorities decided to remove the Nez Perces from their home reservation in Washington and Oregon to a reservation in Idaho in order to make way for white settlement. While some Nez Perces complied, Chief Joseph and his people refused to move. The army was ordered to remove them by force, which led to war in 1877. The army pursued the band for more than 1,000 miles across the mountains. Over the course of four months, Chief Joseph's band of Nez Perces conducted guerrilla warfare, striking and then melting into the wilderness. Their mobility was limited by the presence of women and children. Meanwhile, the army used the telegraph to quickly summon reinforcements. Chief Joseph surrendered in Montana on October 15, 1877, with this brief speech.

Primary Source

At his surrender in the Bear Paw Mountains, 1877

Tell General Howard that I know his heart. What he told me before I have in my heart. I am tired of fighting. Our chiefs are killed. Looking Glass is dead, Tu-hul-hil-sote is dead. The old men are all dead. It is the young men who now say yes or no. He who led the young men is dead. It is cold and we have no blankets. The little children are freezing to death. My people—some of them have run away to the hills and have no blankets and no food. No one knows where they are—perhaps freezing to death. I want to have time to look for my children and see how many of them I can find. Maybe I shall find them among the dead. Hear me, my chiefs, my heart is sick and sad. From where the sun now stands I will fight no more against the white man.

Source: Norman B. Wood, *Lives of Famous Indian Chiefs* (Aurora, IL: American Indian Historical Publishing Company, 1906), 520.

146. Fanny Dunbar Corbusier, The Pursuit of the Cheyennes, 1878

Introduction

In the memoir excerpted here, an army officer's wife describes several events that she witnessed near the Pine Ridge Agency in southern Dakota Territory in 1878. The author, Fanny Dunbar Corbusier, was married to an army surgeon, William Henry Corbusier, and accompanied him to all his duty stations during his 39-year career. The Sioux, Cheyennes, and Arapahos had signed a treaty at Fort Laramie in Wyoming Territory in 1868. The treaty established reservations and provided for the assignment of an agent, construction of public amenities such as a school and a gristmill, the payment of annuities, and the allotment of farmland and subsidies to individual Indians. In turn the Indians promised not to attack neighboring American settlers. Although some Indians settled down to farming, as described here, white encroachment on Indian lands and nondelivery of rations by corrupt agents frequently led to unrest and breakouts. This was invariably followed by the army going in pursuit to force their return to the reservation. The author describes her husband's work to prevent fraud as well as a Cheyenne breakout and recapture in 1878. Mrs. Corbusier's memoir covers the years 1860 to 1908 and encompasses the Indian Wars in the American West through the Spanish-American War (1896–1898) and service in the Philippines.

Primary Source

The Ogala Indians, who had been removed from the Red Cloud Agency the year before to the Missouri River, where the Indian Bureau wished to establish them, would not remain there. [They] returned in the fall of 1878 to their old country and located themselves about twenty miles by wagon road northeast from Camp Sheridan, and here the Pine Ridge Agency buildings were erected.

He proved himself well fitted for the position, managing them and their affairs in such a manner that he soon gained their confidence, and as long as they were under his charge, they remained peaceful and contented. He procured wagons for them and had them haul their own supplies, furnished by the Government, from the Missouri River. They built houses, dug wells, began to cook on stoves and adopt other ways of the white man. He enforced the laws by means of police of their own people. All white men living with Indian women—squaw men, as they were called—that wished to remain on the reservation were required to marry them according to our customs. [A]nd be it said to the credit of these men that with few exceptions they complied with his order without any demur, and the very few that went away soon returned to marry their faithful companions and give their children a legal status. These women were gentle, industrious, and made these men good wives.

The tepee belongs to the woman, and if her husband misbehaves, she can and does turn him out. Even American Horse, a chief, was once disciplined in this manner by his squaw. They did not whip their children, and the boys were treated with great consideration. A boy would consider it an indignity to be struck by a woman. I knew a Piute boy to take poison parsnip because his mother whipped him, and Father had great difficulty in saving his life. The boys were taught very early to ride horseback, to use the bow and arrow and the girls to perform the simple duties that would later be required of them. They carried their babies strapped in a hoo-pa on their backs, suspended from a strap that is passed around the forehead. Jugs of water were carried by them in the same manner.

Four missionaries established themselves at the Agency, three of them Episcopalians and one Roman Catholic. Two of the former, [the] Reverend John Robinson and the Reverend Wolcort, frequently came over to hold services for us, and a French Jesuit to minister to the men. The latter was cultured and very agreeable and we always entertained him, as we did the clergymen of our own denomination, but one day a rough, red-faced man came to our door instead of our gentle friend, who told us that the latter had been sent to France for discipline, as he was too liberal in his ideas and associated too intimately with Protestants. We did not entertain the new man, and the work that the other had been carrying on very successfully at the Agency was annulled by him, much to the advantage of the men of the other denomination.

Many of the supplies sent by the Government to Indians had never reached them, so Army officers were detailed as inspectors to witness the issue of all of their annuities and report upon their quality. Father was selected for that duty at Pine Ridge Agency. Every ten days he would get up before four A.M., eat his breakfast, and drive the twenty miles so as to arrive at the Agency by seven A.M., at which hour he would begin to receive the cattle.

Formerly the cattle would frequently be let out at night, and in the morning the Indians would find the corral empty. Then to pacify them, the contractor would present them with a few head, or a herd of scrawny steers would be delivered in which were three or four fat ones, and one of the latter would be slaughtered, weighed on steelyards, and its weight taken as the average for the whole bunch. The Indians would fare very well if they received even two-thirds of the beef to which they were entitled.

To prevent any further fraud, Father saw that the corrals were so well constructed that the palisades could not be pulled up by the cowboys with their lariats. The cattle were kept over night without water and in the morning weighed on platform scales, run into a chute, and there cross arrows branded on each one, so that if any did escape they could be identified. They were then run into another corral from which the head of each family received all that belonged to him. When a steer was released from the corral, they would chase him about as if he were a buffalo before killing him, and we heard that formerly Indians were sometimes accidentally shot while engaged at their customary sport. It was a long time before this steer-baiting could be stopped.

[...]

In September 1878, three hundred Cheyenne Indians under Lone Wolf, Wild Hog, and Dull Knife set out from the Cheyenne and Arapaho Reservation near Camp Reno, in the Indian Territory to return north to their old home in Dakota. Troops were sent after them, but they moved so rapidly that before they could be intercepted they were well up in Nebraska, had committed many depredations on the way, and killed forty or more men, women, and children. When they reached the Union Pacific Railroad, nearly one half of them, mostly young men, headed by Lone Wolf, left the older people and later surrendered. The others, under Wild Hog and Dull Knife, continued on their way to the old Red Cloud Agency.

The Twenty-Third Infantry under Major Alexander J. Dallas pursued them from the south up through the Sand Hills across the Niobrara River until they were headed off on the north by troops from the Third and Seventh Cavalry when they entrenched themselves on Chadron Creek, about eighteen miles west from Camp Sheridan. A mountain howitzer sent from our Post soon dislodged them, and they were induced, October 24, to give up their arms and were taken over to Fort Robinson, where the 49 men and 100 women and children were confined in an old building. They, however, managed to get ten rifles and five pistols into the prison by taking them apart and having their women and children hide the pieces and ammunition in their clothing.

An attempt was made to separate Wild Hog from his people, when they barricaded the windows and doors, and at night. On January 9, he made a dash for freedom. Some of them were shot down while crossing the parade ground. Dull Knife was wounded in the leg and escaped to Pine Ridge, and the others fortified themselves among the rocks and did not surrender to troops A, C, B, F, H, and L, Third Cavalry, until not a man was left alive and very few women and children were not wounded of the 150 confined, 64 were killed, 58 were taken to the Pine Ridge Agency, 2 were sent back to the Indian Territory, and 7 supposed killed, as they could not be otherwise accounted for.

Probably 100 soldiers were engaged, and 11 of them were killed or died of their wounds. Captain Henry W. Wessels [Wessels] Jr., Third Cavalry, and nine enlisted men were wounded. The prisoners passed through our Post on their way to Pine Ridge and remained over the night of March 15, 1879. The oldest male among them could not have been fourteen years of age, and he was wounded. They were a pitiable sight. Father dressed their wounds and we took them cakes, sweets, and such food as their captors did not have to give to them.

Source: Patricia Y. Stallard, ed., *Fanny Dunbar Corbusier: Recollections of Her Army Life, 1869–1908* (Norman: University of Oklahoma Press, 2003), 86–90.

147. *Standing Bear v. Crook,* May 12, 1879

Introduction

Treaties made between U.S. authorities and Indian tribes were often proven futile soon after they were signed. Early treaties sought to remove Indians from eastern lands desired by settlers and send them to unwanted land to the west. During the 1850s, treaties established reservations for Indians, promised food and subsidies to help support them on the reservations, and encouraged Indians to settle down to farming. However, whites demanded access to desirable reservation land, forcing the removal of Indians to yet another reservation, and the government often failed to deliver the promised food and goods, forcing the Indians to resume hunting or starve. The army then had the task of enforcing government policy. In this case, the Ponca tribe had been forced in 1877 to leave its Dakota Territory reservation and move to Indian Territory (present-day Oklahoma). Standing Bear led a group of Poncas back to their former home. General George Crook, commander of the Department of the Platte, arrested Standing Bear and his followers, who then sued for a writ of habeus corpus—a basic civil right enjoyed by white Americans—to secure their release. Judge Elmer S. Dundy of the U.S. Circuit Court in Nebraska ruled in Standing Bear's favor, saying that since the Poncas were not at war with the United States, they could not be jailed for moving from one place to another. Historically when Indians resorted to the white judicial system, the system most often failed them.

Primary Source

DUNDY, J.—During the fifteen years in which I have been engaged in administering the laws of my country, I have never been called upon to hear or decide a case that appealed so strongly to my sympathy as the one now under consideration. On the one side, we have a few of the remnants of a once numerous and powerful, but now weak, insignificant, unlettered, and generally despised race; on the other, we have the representative of one of the most powerful, most enlightened, and most christianized nations of modern times. On the one side, we have the representatives of this wasted race coming into this national tribunal of ours, asking for justice and liberty to enable them to adopt our boasted civilization, and to pursue the arts of peace, which have made us great and happy as a nation; on the other side, we have this magnificent, if not magnanimous, government, resisting this application with the determination of sending these people back to the country which is to them less desirable than perpetual imprisonment in their own native land. But I think it is creditable to the heart and mind of the brave and distinguished officer who is made respondent herein to say that he has no sort of sympathy in the business in which he is forced by his position to bear a part so conspicuous; and, so far as I am individually concerned, I think it not improper to say that, if the strongest possible sympathy could give the relators title to freedom, they would have been restored to liberty the moment the arguments in their behalf were closed. No examination or further thought would then have been necessary or expedient. But in a country where liberty is regulated by law, something more satisfactory and enduring than mere sympathy must furnish and constitute the rule and basis of judicial action. It follows that this case must be examined and decided on principles of law, and that unless the relators are entitled to their discharge under the constitution or laws of the United States, or some treaty made pursuant thereto, they must be remanded to the custody of the officer who caused their arrest, to be returned to the Indian Territory, which they left without the consent of the government.

On the 8th of April, 1879, the relators, Standing Bear and twenty-five others, during the session of the court held at that time at Lincoln, presented their petition, duly verified, praying for the allowance of a writ of *habeas corpus* and their final discharge from custody there under.

The petition alleges, in substance, that the relators are Indians who have formerly belonged to the Ponca tribe of Indians, now located in the Indian Territory; that they had some time previously withdrawn from the tribe, and completely severed their tribal relations therewith, and had adopted the general habits of the whites, and were then endeavoring to maintain themselves by their own exertions, and without aid or assistance from the general government; that whilst they were thus engaged, and without being guilty of violating any of the laws of the United States, they were arrested and restrained of their liberty by order of the respondent, George Crook.

The writ was issued and served on the respondent on the 8th day of April, and, the distance between the place where the writ was made returnable and the place where the relators were confined being more than twenty miles, ten days were allotted in which to make return.

On the 18th of April the writ was returned, and the authority for the arrest and detention is therein shown. The substance of the return to the writ, and the additional statement since filed, is that the relators are individual members of, and connected with, the Ponca tribe of Indians; that they had fled or escaped from a reservation situated some place within the limits of the Indian Territory—had departed therefrom without permission from the government; and, at the request of the secretary of the interior, the general of the army had issued an order which required the respondent to arrest and return the relators to their tribe in the Indian Territory, and that, pursuant to the said order, he had caused the relators to be arrested on the Omaha Indian reservation, and that they were in his custody for the purpose of being returned to the Indian Territory.

It is claimed upon the one side, and denied upon the other, that the relators had withdrawn and severed, for all time, their connection with the tribe to which they belonged; and upon this point alone was there any testimony produced by either party hereto. The other matters stated in the petition and the return to the writ are conceded to be true; so that the questions to be determined are purely questions of law.

On the 8th of March, 1859, a treaty was made by the United States with the Ponca tribe of Indians, by which a certain tract of country, north of the Niobrara river and west of the Missouri, was set apart for the permanent home of the said Indians, in which the government agreed to protect them during their good behavior. But just when, or how, or why, or under what circumstances, the Indians left their reservation in Dakota and went to the Indian Territory, does not appear.

The district attorney very earnestly questions the jurisdiction of the court to issue the writ, and to hear and determine the case made herein, and has supported his theory with an argument of great ingenuity and much ability. But, nevertheless, I am of the opinion that his premises are erroneous, and his conclusions, therefore, wrong and unjust. The great respect I entertain for that officer, and the very able manner in which his views were presented, make it necessary for me to give somewhat at length the reasons which lead me to this conclusion.

The district attorney discussed at length the reasons which led to the origin of the writ of *habeas corpus,* and the character of the proceedings and practice in connection therewith in the parent country. It was claimed that the laws of the realm limited the right to sue out this writ to the *free subjects* of the kingdom, and that none others came within the benefits of such beneficent laws; and, reasoning from analogy, it is claimed that none but American citizens are entitled to sue out this high prerogative writ in any of the federal courts. I have not examined the English laws regulating the suing out of the writ, nor have I thought it necessary so to do. Of this I will only observe that if the laws of England are as they are claimed to be, they will appear at a disadvantage when compared with our own. This only proves that the laws of a limited monarchy are sometimes less wise and humane than the laws of our own republic—that whilst the parliament of Great Britain was legislating in behalf of the favored few, the congress of the United States was legislating in behalf of all mankind who come within our jurisdiction.

Section 751 of the revised statutes declares that "the supreme court and the circuit and district courts shall have power to issue writs of *habeas corpus.*" Section 752 confers the power to issue writs on the judges of said courts, within their jurisdiction, and declares this to be "for the purpose of inquiry into the cause of restraint of liberty." Section 753 restricts the power, limits the jurisdiction, and defines the cases where the writ may properly issue. That may be done under this section where the prisoner "is in custody under or by color of authority of the United States, . . . or is in custody for an act done or omitted in pursuance of a law of the United States, . . . or in custody in violation of the constitution or of a law or treaty of the United States." Thus, it will be seen that when a *person* is in custody or deprived of his liberty under color of authority of the United States, or in violation of the constitution or laws or treaties of the United States, the federal judges have jurisdiction, and the writ can properly issue. I take it that the true construction to be placed upon this act is this, that in *all* cases where federal officers, civil or military, have the custody and control of a person claimed to be unlawfully restrained of liberty, they are *then* restrained of liberty under color of authority of the United States, and the federal courts can properly proceed to determine the question of unlawful restraint, because no other courts can properly do so. In the other instance, the federal courts and judges can properly issue the writ in *all* cases where the *person* is alleged to be in custody in violation of the constitution or a law or treaty of the United States. In such a case, it is wholly immaterial what *officer,* state or federal, has custody of the person seeking the relief. These relators may be entitled to the writ in either case. Under the first paragraph they certainly are—that is, if an Indian can be entitled to it at all—because they are in custody of a federal officer, under color of authority of the United States. And they may be entitled to the writ under the other paragraph, before recited, for the reason, as they allege, that they are restrained of liberty in violation of a provision of their treaty, before referred to. Now, it must be borne in mind that the *habeas corpus* act describes applicants for the writ as "*persons*" or "*parties,*" who may be entitled thereto. It nowhere describes them as *citizens,* nor is citizenship in any way or place made a qualification for suing out the writ, and, in the absence of express provision or necessary implication which would require the interpretation contended for by the district attorney, I should not feel justified in giving the words *person* and *party* such a narrow construction. The most natural, and therefore most reasonable, way is to attach the same meaning to *words* and *phrases* when found in a statute that is attached to them when and where found in general use. If we do so in this instance, then the question cannot be open to serious doubt. Webster describes a person as "a living soul; a self-conscious being; a moral agent; especially a living human being; a man, woman, or child; an individual of the human race." This is comprehensive enough, it would seem, to include even an Indian. In defining certain generic terms, the 1st section of the revised statutes declares that the word *person* includes copartnerships and corporations. On the whole, it seems to me quite evident that the comprehensive language used in this section is intended to apply to all mankind—as well the relators as the more favored white race. This will be doing no violence to language, or to the spirit or letter of the law, nor to the intention, as it is believed, of the law-making power of the government. I must hold, then, that *Indians,* and consequently the relators, are

persons, such as are described by and included within the laws before quoted. It is said, however, that this is the first instance on record in which an Indian has been permitted to sue out and maintain a writ of *habeas corpus* in a federal court, and *therefore* the court must be without jurisdiction in the premises. This is a *non sequitur.* I confess I do not know of another instance where this has been done, but I can also say that the occasion for it perhaps has never before been so great. It may be that the Indians think it wiser and better, in the end, to resort to this peaceful process than it would be to undertake the hopeless task of redressing their own alleged wrongs by force of arms. Returning reason, and the sad experience of others similarly situated, have taught them the folly and madness of the arbitrament of the sword. They can readily see that any serious resistance on their part would be the signal for their utter extermination. Have they not, then, chosen the wiser part by resorting to the very tribunal erected by those they claim have wronged and oppressed them? This, however, is not the tribunal of their own choice, but it is the *only* one into which they can lawfully go for deliverance. It cannot, therefore, be fairly said that because no Indian ever before invoked the aid of this writ in a federal court, the rightful authority to issue it does not exist. Power and authority rightfully conferred do not necessarily cease to exist in consequence of long non-user. Though much time has elapsed, and many generations have passed away, since the passage of the original *habeas corpus* act, from which I have quoted, it will not do to say that these Indians cannot avail themselves of its beneficent provisions simply because none of their ancestors ever sought relief there under.

Every *person* who comes within our jurisdiction, whether he be European, Asiatic, African, or "native to the manor born," must obey the laws of the United States. Every one who violates them incurs the penalty provided thereby. When a *person* is charged, in a proper way, with the commission of crime, we do not inquire upon the trial in what country the accused was born, nor to what sovereign or government allegiance is due, nor to what race he belongs. The questions of guilt and innocence only form the subjects of inquiry. An Indian, then, especially off from his reservation, is amenable to the criminal laws of the United States, the same as all other persons. They being subject to arrest for the violation of our criminal laws, and being *persons* such as the law contemplates and includes in the description of parties who may sue out the writ, it would indeed be a sad commentary on the justice and impartiality of our laws to hold that Indians, though natives of our own country, cannot test the validity of an alleged illegal imprisonment in this manner, as well as a subject of a foreign government who may happen to be sojourning in this country, but owing it no sort of allegiance. I cannot doubt that congress intended to give to *every person* who might be unlawfully restrained of liberty under color of authority of the United States, the right to the writ and a discharge thereon. I conclude, then, that, so far as the issuing of the writ is concerned, it was properly issued, and that the relators are within the jurisdiction conferred by the *habeas corpus* act.

A question of much greater importance remains for consideration, which, when determined, will be decisive of this whole controversy. This relates to the right of the government to arrest and hold the relators for a time, for the purpose of being returned to a point in the Indian Territory from which it is alleged the Indians escaped. I am not vain enough to think that I can do full justice to a question like the one under consideration. But, as the matter furnishes so much valuable material for discussion, and so much food for reflection, I shall try to present it as viewed from my own standpoint, without reference to consequences or criticisms, which, though not specially invited, will be sure to follow.

A review of the policy of the government adopted in its dealings with the friendly tribe of Poncas, to which the relators at one time belonged, seems not only appropriate, but almost indispensable to a correct understanding of this controversy. The Ponca Indians have been at peace with the government, and have remained the steadfast friends of the whites, for many years. They lived peaceably upon the land and in the country they claimed and called their own.

On the 12th of March, 1858, they made a treaty with the United States, by which they ceded all claims to lands, except the following tract: "Beginning at a point on the Niobrara river, and running due north so as to intersect the Ponca river twenty-five miles from its mouth; thence from said point of intersection up and along the Ponca river twenty miles; thence due south to the Niobrara river; and thence down and along said river to the place of beginning; which tract is hereby reserved for the future homes of said Indians." In consideration of this cession, the government agreed "to protect the Poncas in the possession of the tract of land reserved for their future homes, and their persons and property thereon, during good behavior on their part." Annuities were to be paid them for thirty years, houses were to be built, schools were to be established, and other things were to be done by the government, in consideration of said cession. (See 12 Stats. at Large, p. 997.)

On the 10th of March, 1865, another treaty was made, and a part of the other reservation was ceded to the government. Other lands, however, were, to some extent, substituted therefore, "by way of rewarding them for their constant fidelity to the government, and citizens thereof, and with a view of returning to the said tribe of Ponca Indians their old burying-grounds and cornfields." This treaty also provides for paying $15,080 for spoliations committed on the Indians. (See 14 Stats. at Large, p. 675.)

On the 29th day of April, 1868, the government made a treaty with the several bands of Sioux Indians, which treaty was ratified by the senate on the 16th of the following February, in and by which the reservations set apart for the Poncas under former treaties were completely absolved. (15 Stats. at Large, p. 635.) This was done without consultation with, or knowledge or consent on the part of, the Ponca tribe of Indians.

On the 15th of August, 1876, congress passed the general Indian appropriation bill, and in it we find a provision authorizing the secretary of the interior to use $25,000 for the removal of the Poncas to the Indian Territory, and providing them a home therein, with consent of the tribe. (19 Stats. at Large, p. 192.)

In the Indian appropriation bill passed by congress on the 27th day of May, 1878, we find a provision authorizing the secretary of the interior to expend the sum of $30,000 for the purpose of removing and locating the Ponca Indians on a new reservation, near the Kaw river.

No reference has been made to any other treaties or laws, under which the right to arrest and remove the Indians is claimed to exist.

The Poncas lived upon their reservation in southern Dakota, and cultivated a portion of the same, until two or three years ago, when they removed therefrom, but whether by force or otherwise does not appear. At all events, we find a portion of them, including the relators, located at some point in the Indian Territory. *There*, the testimony seems to show, is where the trouble commenced. Standing Bear, the principal witness, states that out of five hundred and eighty-one Indians who went from the reservation in Dakota to the Indian Territory, one hundred and fifty-eight died within a year or so, and a great proportion of the others were sick and disabled, caused, in a great measure, no doubt, from change of climate; and to save himself and the survivors of his wasted family, and the feeble remnant of his little band of followers, he determined to leave the Indian Territory and return to his old home, where, to use his own language, "he might live and die in peace, and be buried with his fathers." He also states that he informed the agent of their final purpose to leave, never to return, and that he and his followers had finally, fully, and forever severed his and their connection with the Ponca tribe of Indians, and had resolved to disband as a tribe, or band, of Indians, and to cut loose from the government, go to work, become self-sustaining, and adopt the habits and customs of a higher civilization. To accomplish what would seem to be a desirable and laudable purpose, all who were able so to do went to work to earn a living. The Omaha Indians, who speak the same language, and with whom many of the Poncas have long continued to intermarry, gave them employment and ground to cultivate, so as to make them self-sustaining. And it was when at the Omaha reservation, and when *thus* employed, that they were arrested by order of the government, for the purpose of being taken back to the Indian Territory. They claim to be unable to see the justice, or reason, or wisdom, or *necessity,* of removing them by force from their own native plains and blood relations to a far-off country, in which they can see little but new-made graves opening for their reception. The land from which they fled in fear has no attractions for them. The love of home and native land was strong enough in the minds of these people to induce them to brave every peril to return and live and die where they had been reared. The bones of the dead son of Standing Bear were not to repose in the land they hoped to be leaving forever, but were carefully preserved and protected, and formed a part of what was to them a melancholy procession homeward. Such instances of parental affection, and such love of home and native land, may be *heathen* in origin, but it seems to me that they are not unlike *christian* in principle.

What is here stated in this connection is mainly for the purpose of showing that the relators did all they could to separate themselves from their tribe and to sever their tribal relations, for the purpose of becoming self-sustaining and living without support from the government. This being so, it presents the question as to whether or not an Indian can withdraw from his tribe, sever his tribal relation therewith, and terminate his allegiance thereto, for the purpose of making an independent living and adopting our own civilization.

If Indian tribes are to be regarded and treated as separate but dependent nations, there can be no serious difficulty about the question. If they are not to be regarded and treated as separate, dependent nations, then no allegiance is owing from an individual Indian to his tribe, and he could, therefore, withdraw therefrom at any time. The question of expatriation has engaged the attention of our government from the time of its very foundation. Many heated discussions have been carried on between our own and foreign governments on this great question, until diplomacy has triumphantly secured the right to every person found within our jurisdiction. This right has always been claimed and admitted by our government, and it is now no longer an open question. It can make but little difference, then, whether we accord to the Indian tribes a national character or not, as in either case I think the individual Indian possesses the clear and God-given right to withdraw from his tribe and forever live away from it, as though it had no further existence. If the right of expatriation was open to doubt in this country down to the year 1868, certainly since that time no sort of question as to the right can now exist. On the 27th of July of that year congress passed an act, now appearing as section 1999 of the revised statutes, which declares that: "Whereas, the right of expatriation is a natural and inherent right of all people, indispensable to the enjoyment of the rights of life, liberty, and the pursuit of happiness; and, whereas, in the recognition of this principle the government has freely received emigrants from all nations, and invested them with the rights of citizenship. . . . Therefore, any declaration, instruction, opinion, order, or decision of any officer of the United States which denies, restricts, impairs, or questions the right of expatriation, is declared inconsistent with the fundamental principles of the republic."

This declaration must forever settle the question until it is reopened by other legislation upon the same subject. This is, however, only reaffirming in the most solemn and authoritative manner a principle well settled and understood in this country for many years past.

In most, if not all, instances in which treaties have been made with the several Indian tribes, where reservations have been set apart for their occupancy, the government has either reserved the right or bound itself to protect the Indians thereon. Many of the treaties expressly prohibit white persons being on the reservations unless specially authorized by the treaties or acts of congress for the purpose of carrying out treaty stipulations.

Laws passed for the government of the Indian country, and for the purpose of regulating trade and intercourse with the Indian tribes, confer upon certain officers of the government almost unlimited power over the persons who go upon the reservations without lawful authority. Section 2149 of the revised statutes authorizes and requires the commissioner of Indian affairs, with the approval of the secretary of the interior, to remove from any "tribal reservation" any person being thereon without authority of law, or whose presence within the limits of the reservation may, in the judgment of the commissioner, be detrimental to the peace and welfare of the Indians. The authority here conferred upon the commissioner fully justifies him in causing to be removed from Indian reservations *all* persons thereon in violation of law, or whose presence thereon may be detrimental to the peace and welfare of the Indians upon the reservations. This applies as well to an Indian as to a white person, and manifestly for the same reason, the object of the law being to prevent unwarranted interference between the Indians and the agent representing the government. Whether such an extensive discretionary power is wisely vested in the commissioner of Indian affaire or not, need not be questioned. It is enough to know that the power rightfully exists, and, where existing, the exercise of the power must be upheld. If, then, the commissioner has the right to cause the expulsion from the Omaha Indian reservation of all persons thereon who are there in violation of law, or whose presence may be detrimental to the peace and welfare of the Indians, then he must of necessity be authorized to use the necessary force to accomplish his purpose. Where, then, is he to look for this necessary force? The military arm of the government is the most natural and most potent force to be used on such occasions, and section 2150 of the revised statutes specially authorizes the use of the army for this service. The army, then, it seems, is the proper force to employ when intruders and trespassers who go upon the reservations are to be ejected therefrom.

The first subdivision of the revised statutes last referred to provides that "the military forces of the United States may be employed, in such manner and under such regulations as the president may direct, in the apprehension of every person who may be in the Indian country in violation of law, and in conveying him immediately from the Indian country, by the nearest convenient and safe route, to the civil authority of the territory or judicial district in which such person shall be found, to be proceeded against in due course of law." . . . This is the authority under which the military can be lawfully employed to remove intruders from an Indian reservation. What may be done by the troops in such cases is here fully and clearly stated; and it is *this* authority, it is believed, under which the respondent acted.

All Indian reservations held under treaty stipulations with the government must be deemed and taken to be a part of the *Indian country,* within the meaning of our laws on that subject. The relators were found upon the Omaha Indian reservation. That being a part of the Indian country, and they not being a part of the Omaha tribe of Indians, they were there without lawful authority, and if the commissioner of Indian affairs deemed their presence detrimental to the peace and welfare of the Omaha Indians, he had lawful warrant to remove them from the reservation, and to employ the necessary military force to effect this object in safety.

General Crook had the rightful authority to remove the relators from the reservation, and must stand justified in removing them therefrom. But when the troops are thus employed they must exercise the authority in the *manner* provided by the section of the law just read. This law makes it the duty of the troops to convey the parties arrested, by the nearest convenient and safe route, *to the civil authority of the territory or judicial district in which such persons shall be found, to be proceeded against in due course of law.* The *duty* of the military authorities is here very clearly and sharply defined, and no one can be justified in departing therefrom, especially in time of peace. As General Crook had the right to arrest and remove the relators from the Omaha Indian reservation, it follows, from what has been stated, that the law required him to convey them to this city and turn them over to the marshal and United States attorney, to be proceeded against in due course of law. Then proceedings could be instituted against them in either the circuit or district court, and if the relators had incurred a penalty under the law, punishment would follow; otherwise, they would be discharged from custody. But this course was not pursued in this case; neither was it intended to observe the laws in that regard, for General Crook's orders, emanating from higher authority, expressly required him to apprehend the relators and remove them by force to the Indian Territory, from which it is alleged they escaped. But in what General Crook has done in the premises no fault can be imputed to him. He was simply obeying the orders of his superior officers, but the orders, as we think, lack the necessary authority of law, and are, therefore, not binding on the relators.

I have searched in vain for the semblance of any authority justifying the commissioner in attempting to remove by force any Indians, whether belonging to a tribe or not, to any place, or for any other purpose than what has been stated. Certainly, without some specific authority found in an act of congress, or in a treaty with the Ponca tribe of Indians, he could not lawfully force the relators back to the Indian Territory, to remain and die in that country, against their will. In the absence of all treaty stipulations or laws of the United States authorizing such removal, I must conclude that no such arbitrary authority exists. It is true, if the relators are to be regarded as a part of the great nation of Ponca Indians, the government might, in time of war, remove them to any place of safety so long as the war should last, but perhaps no longer, unless they were charged with the commission of some crime. This is a war power merely, and exists in time of war only. Every nation exercises the right to arrest and detain an alien enemy during the existence of a war, and all subjects or citizens of the hostile nations are subject to be dealt with under this rule.

But it is not claimed that the Ponca tribe of Indians are at war with the United States, so that this war power might be used against them; in fact, they are amongst the most peaceable and

friendly of all the Indian tribes, and have at times received from the government unmistakable and substantial recognition of their long-continued friendship for the whites. In time of peace the war power remains in abeyance, and must be subservient to the civil authority of the government until something occurs to justify its exercise. No fact exists, and nothing has occurred, so far as the relators are concerned, to make it necessary or lawful to exercise such an authority over them. If they could be removed to the Indian Territory by force, and kept there in the same way, I can see no good reason why they might not be taken and kept by force in the penitentiary at Lincoln, or Leavenworth, or Jefferson City, or any other place which the commander of the forces might, in his judgment, see proper to designate. I cannot think that any such arbitrary authority exists in this country.

The reasoning advanced in support of my views, leads me to conclude:

1st. That an *Indian* is a Person within the meaning of the laws of the United States, and has, therefore, the right to sue out a writ of *habeas corpus* in a federal court, or before a federal judge, in all cases where he may be confined or in custody under color of authority of the United States, or where he is restrained of liberty in violation of the constitution or laws of the United States.

2d. That General George Crook, the respondent, being commander of the military department of the Platte, has the custody of the relators, under color of authority of the United States, and in violation of the laws thereof.

3d. That no rightful authority exists for removing by force any of the relators to the Indian Territory, as the respondent has been directed to do.

4th. That the Indians possess the inherent right of expatriation, as well as the more fortunate white race, and have the inalienable right to "*life, liberty,* and the pursuit of happiness," so long as they obey the laws and do not trespass on forbidden ground. And,

5th. Being restrained of liberty under color of authority of the United States, and in violation of the laws thereof, the relators must be discharged from custody, and it is so ordered.

Ordered Accordingly.

Source: United States ex rel Standing Bear v. Crook 25 F. Cas. 695 (C.C. Nebr. 1879) (No. 14891).

148. Fanny Dunbar Corbusier, Description of a Sioux Religious Ceremony, 1879

Introduction

In the memoir excerpted here, an army officer's wife describes the Sun Dance, the main Sioux religious ceremony, that she attended with her family in the summer of 1879. The author, Fanny Dunbar

Corbusier, was married to an army surgeon, William Henry Corbusier, and accompanied him to all his duty stations during his 39-year career. Despite the centuries-long untiring and sometimes successful efforts of missionaries to convert Native Americans to Christianity, native religious practices continued, often coexisting with Christianity. The Oglala Sioux, who held their Sun Dance at Pine Ridge in Dakota Territory (near the border with Nebraska) were one of the numerous subgroups of the northern Plains people known as the Sioux. The Sioux signed treaties with the United States in 1851 and 1868, both of which were violated by white settlers and miners. In response the Sioux mounted a determined resistance to white occupation of their lands. The army responded with additional troops and eventually forced most of the Sioux onto reservations. There they suffered from hunger and deprivation as corrupt government agents diverted their food rations for their own profit. In their suffering, the defeated Sioux provided fertile ground for the growth of the messianic Ghost Dance religion in 1890.

Primary Source

In June 1879, about the time of the year that the sun was farthest north, the Oglalas held their customary yearly ceremony known as the Sun Dance, and we all went over to Pine Ridge to witness it. Efforts had been made to have the Indians discontinue it, but the whites had given them no better method of communing with the spirit world and the sun, the source of all life, so they continued to worship in their own fashion.

We arrived early on the plain east of the Agency and saw the great tribal circle of tepees, each band in its proper place. Several mounted men in their war bonnets of eagle feathers reaching nearly to the ground seemed to be delivering messages as they passed from the south around the circle west, thence north, and afterward east. After watching the people preparing to leave their camp to attend the commemorations, we drove to a large circular enclosure of poles, branches of trees, and canvas, having only one opening, and that on the east. Then seeing many Indians moving south, we followed them to the hills and seated ourselves near the summit of one that overlooked a grove of trees not far away.

Very soon we heard the chanting of many voices, and a long line of mounted Indian warriors in their war bonnets, war shirts, blue leggings trimmed in various colors came into view, and behind them or to their right came other lines of mounted men until there were at least one thousand all told. They dismounted and after them followed their women and children, some on horseback, some in wagons, and others leading ponies hauling travois which held their babies. Large drums were brought forward, placed on the ground, and each one was surrounded by five or six men and women. We were on the east and extreme left of the line and only a few feet from one of the bands.

After the men had seated themselves the chanting was resumed, accompanied by the beating of the drums, the high-pitched voices of the women mingling with the deep tones of the men. Occasionally the drumming and singing would stop and a man would arise and count a "coup," which when ended would be followed by the triumphant yells of the people and quick beating of the drum. A "coup" is a deed of prowess of which a warrior boasts; it may be of a horse stealing trip or the killing of an enemy, and to strike an armed foe with a bow is considered a grand "coup." There was a tall, spare Indian named "No-Flesh," whom we had frequently seen before. . . . [W]hen he counted a "coup" and yelled, [he] showed his teeth between his thin lips, and the expression on his thin face was as if he was relating some horrible act of barbarity but I did not learn what it was.

A tree was selected at the foot of a hill on the far side of the valley and women approached to lay their hands upon it, a declaration that they had led irreproachful lives during the last year. It was afterward cut by men and women, and when it had fallen it was cleared of its branches except near the top, where a few were allowed to remain. It was then taken to the enclosure accompanied by the horsemen, who when nearby dashed ahead yelling as if elated at the success of some great undertaking. The tree was erected in the centre, and a bundle of some sort in a bunch of sage was fastened high up, and just beneath it the figure of a man about a foot long. After we had seated ourselves in the shade of brush and canvas, not far from the south of the entrance, a large drum was placed in position nearer the entrance and surrounded by some six or eight men and women who began to chant, beating time on the drum.

The eight or ten penitents who were to undergo the ordeal entered in single file soon afterward, the head one carrying in front of him the skull of a buffalo bull. They passed us, went to the west side where they seated themselves in a row placing some sticks and the buffalo skull in front of them to form a sort of altar. Then Red Cloud arose and, facing the pole, looked upward while supplicating the sun that their women might bear many boys, that the grass might be abundant, buffalo plentiful, and that they should have a great increase in the number of their horses.

The dancing then began and was to continue four days and four nights, during which time the men were to fast, neither eating nor drinking, but they could smoke tobacco. It actually didn't last more than three days. Always facing the east and looking up at the pole and into the sun until it had passed the meridian, the dancers, each with a whistle made from a leg bone of a turkey between his lips to blow short blasts while keeping time with his feet, moved forward and back hour after hour, until too exhausted to stand up. When one would fall, a great yelling took place and the drums were beaten the harder and faster.

One man after a while was approached by a medicine man, who raised a fold of the skin from the upper part of his chest, ran the blade of his knife through, pushed in a wooden skewer and fastened it to a rope, and the other end of which was attached to the pole high up. As the man danced again he threw himself backward in his efforts to tear out the piece of wood. He fainted several times and lay still for a while, to rise again and dance. The medicine man at length examined the wound, and when the man made the next attempt to free himself, he broke loose. We suspected that the medicine man cut enough of the skin to make the task easier. A fire was kept up the whole time on the east of the pole, and when it needed replenishing, a man would come in with wood, count a "coup," and lay it on the fire.

About noon food was brought in for the onlookers. We partook of some of it, and when the god [dog] meat came around, Lieutenant Charles G. Starr, First Infantry, said he would eat some of it if I would, so I ate a small piece. The boys ate it without any demur.

In the interval between the dancing, horses were given away by the dancers and others. Sometimes the horses were brought in, but oftener sticks as pledges for horses were given to be reclaimed afterward. When a poor old woman received a horse, she would cry out praises for the donor and say that he was a brave man. A man is not considered brave by them unless he is good to the poor, no matter what feats of daring he may have performed. The dancers underwent this sort of penance to fulfill a vow made to the sun in return for some favor or mercy they had asked and received.

Source: Patricia Y. Stallard, ed., *Fanny Dunbar Corbusier: Recollections of Her Army Life, 1869–1908* (Norman: University of Oklahoma Press, 2003), 94–97.

149. Luther Standing Bear, Account of Attendance at Carlisle Indian School, 1879

Introduction

The Carlisle Indian School was founded in 1879 as a humanitarian experiment in forced assimilation of Indian youths and became a model for other Indian boarding schools. Emphasis at the Carlisle Indian School was on English and occupational skills along with other typical subjects, music, and sports. On arrival, Indian children had their long hair cut off and were given new names, were made to wear clothing typical of white people, were required to attend church, were forbidden to speak their native languages, and were fed a white person's diet. Many children died from the multiple shocks to their systems, exacerbated by homesickness. The first students were recruited from among the Sioux, who sent their children to Carlisle reluctantly but voluntarily, while others, such as the children of captured Apaches, were forced to attend. Of the thousands of children who attended the school, some remembered it with horror, and others remembered it with gratitude. The school's most famous alumnus was the athlete Jim Thorpe. This excerpt is from a memoir by one of the earliest students, Luther Standing Bear (1868–1939), an Oglala Sioux born on Pine Ridge Reservation in South Dakota. At first miserable, he grew determined to learn the ways of white men. After leaving school, he

operated a store on the reservation, traveled with Buffalo Bill's Wild West Show, wrote several books, and acted in westerns. The Carlisle Indian School operated until 1918.

Primary Source

At the age of eleven years, ancestral life for me and my people was most abruptly ended without regard for our wishes, comforts, or rights in the matter. At once I was thrust into an alien world, into an environment as different from the one into which I had been born as it is possible to imagine, to remake myself, if I could, into the likeness of the invader.

By 1879, my people were no longer free, but were subjects confined on reservations under the rule of agents. One day there came to the agency a party of white people from the East. Their presence aroused considerable excitement when it became known that these people were school teachers who wanted some Indian boys and girls to take away with them to train as were white boys and girls.

Now. father was a 'blanket Indian,' but he was wise. He listened to the white strangers, their offers and promises that if they took his Son they would care well for him, teach him how to read and write, and how to wear white man's clothes. But to father all this was just 'sweet talk,' and I know that it was with great misgivings that he left the decision to me and asked if I cared to go with these people. I of course shared with the rest of my tribe a distrust of the white people, so I know that for all my dear father's anxiety he was proud to hear me say 'Yes.' That meant that I was brave.

I could think of no reason why white people wanted Indian boys and girls except to kill them, and not having the remotest idea of what a school was, I thought we were going East to die. But so well had courage and bravery been trained into us that it became a part of our unconscious thinking and acting, and personal life was nothing when it came time to do something for the tribe. Even in our play and games we voluntarily put ourselves to various tests in the effort to grow brave and fearless, for it was most discrediting to be called *can'l wanka,* or a coward. Accordingly there were few cowards, most Lakota men preferring to die in the performance of some act of bravery than to die of old age. Thus, in giving myself up to go East I was proving to my father that he was honored with a brave son. In my decision to go, I gave up many things dear to the heart of a little Indian boy, and one of the things over which my child mind grieved was the thought of saying good-bye to my pony. I rode him as far as I could on the journey, which was to the Missouri River, where we took the boat. There we parted from our parents, and it was a heart-breaking scene, women and children weeping. Some of the children changed their minds and were unable to go on the boat, but for many who did go it was a final parting.

On our way to school we saw many white people, more than we ever dreamed existed, and the manner in which they acted when they saw us quite indicated their opinion of us. It was only about three years after the Custer battle, and the general opinion was that the Plains people merely infested the earth as nuisances, and our being there simply evidenced misjudgment on the part of Wakan Tanka. Whenever our train stopped at the railway stations, it was met by great numbers of white people who came to gaze upon the little Indian 'savages.' The shy little ones sat quietly at the car windows looking at the people who swarmed on the platform. Some of the children wrapped themselves in their blankets, covering all but their eyes. At one place we were taken off the train and marched a distance down the street to a restaurant. We walked down the street between two rows of uniformed men whom we called soldiers, though I suppose they were policemen. This must have been done to protect us, for it was surely known that we boys and girls could do no harm. Back of the rows of uniformed men stood the white people craning their necks, talking, laughing, and making a great noise. They yelled and tried to mimic us by giving what they thought were war-whoops. We did not like this, and some of the children were naturally very much frightened. I remember how I tried to crowd into the protecting midst of the jostling boys and girls. But we were all trying to be brave, yet going to what we thought would end in death at the hands of the white people whom we knew had no love for us. Back on the train the older boys sang brave songs in an effort to keep up their spirits and ours too. In my mind I often recall that scene—eighty-odd blanketed boys and girls marching down the street surrounded by a jeering, unsympathetic people whose only emotions were those of hate and fear; the conquerors looking upon the conquered. And no more understanding us than if we had suddenly been dropped from the moon.

At last at Carlisle the transforming, the 'civilizing' process began. It began with clothes. Never, no matter what our philosophy or spiritual quality, could we be civilized while wearing the moccasin and blanket. The task before us was not only that of accepting new ideas and adopting new manners, but actual physical changes and discomfort has to be borne uncomplainingly until the body adjusted itself to new tastes and habits. Our accustomed dress was taken and replaced with clothing that felt cumbersome and awkward. Against trousers and handkerchiefs we had a distinct feeling—they were unsanitary and the trousers kept us from breathing well. High collars, stiff-bosomed shirts, and suspenders fully three inches in width were uncomfortable, while leather boots caused actual suffering. We longed to go barefoot, but were told that the dew on the grass would give us colds. That was a new warning for us, for our mothers had never told us to beware of colds, and I remember as a child coming into the tipi with moccasins full of snow. Unconcernedly I would take them off my feet, pour out the snow, and put them on my feet again without any thought of sickness, for in that time colds, catarrh, bronchitis, and la grippe were unknown. But we were soon to know them. Then, red flannel undergarments were given us for winter wear, and for me, at least, discomfort grew into actual torture. I used to endure it

as long as possible, then run upstairs and quickly take off the flannel garments and hide them. When inspection time came, I ran and put them on again, for I knew that if I were found disobeying the orders of the school I should be punished. My niece once asked me what it was that I disliked the most during those first bewildering days, and I said, 'red flannel.' Not knowing what I meant, she laughed, but I still remember those horrid, sticky garments which we had to wear next to the skin, and I still squirm and itch when I think of them. Of course, our hair was cut, and then there was much disapproval. But that was part of the transformation process and in some mysterious way long hair stood in the path of our development. For all the grumbling among the bigger boys, we soon had our heads shaven. How strange I felt! Involuntarily, time and time again, my hands went to my head, and that night it was a long time before I went to sleep. If we did not learn much at first, it will not be wondered at, I think. Everything was queer, and it took a few months to get adjusted to the new surroundings.

Almost immediately our names were changed to those in common use in the English language. Instead of translating our names into English and calling Zinkcaziwin, Yellow Bird, and Wanbli K'Jeska, Spotted Eagle, which in itself would have been educational, we were just John, Henry, or Maggie, as the case might be. I was told to take a pointer and select a name for myself from the list written on the blackboard. I did, and since one was just as good as another, and as I could not distinguish any difference in them, I placed the pointer on the name Luther. I then learned to call myself by that name and got used to hearing others call me by it, too. By that time we had been forbidden to speak our mother tongue, which is the rule in all boarding schools. This rule is uncalled for, and today is not only robbing the Indian, but America of a rich heritage. The language of a people is part of their history. Today we should be perpetuating history instead of destroying it, and this can only be effectively done by allowing and encouraging the young to keep it alive. A language unused, embalmed, and reposing only in a book, is a dead language. Only the people themselves, and never the scholars, can nourish it into life.

Of all the changes we were forced to make, that of diet was doubtless the most injurious, for it was immediate and drastic. White bread we had for the first meal and thereafter, as well as coffee and sugar. Had we been allowed our own simple diet of meat, either boiled with soup or dried, and fruit, with perhaps a few vegetables, we should have thrived. But the change in clothing, housing, food, and confinement combined with lonesomeness was too much, and in three years nearly one half of the children from the Plains were dead and through with all earthly schools. In the graveyard at Carlisle most of the graves are those of little ones.

Source: Reprinted from *Land of the Spotted Eagle* by Luther Standing Bear by permission of the University of Nebraska Press. Copyright, 1933 by Luther Standing Bear. Renewal copyright, 1960, by May Jones.

150. Helen Hunt Jackson, *A Century of Dishonor*, 1881 [Excerpts]

Introduction

Helen Hunt Jackson's book *A Century of Dishonor* mobilized public opinion in favor of reforming Indian policy. She argued for protection of Indian rights to equal treatment under the law, secure title to their land, and the eventual conferral of full citizenship. Jackson also coauthored a report in 1883 to the commissioner of Indian affairs on the deplorable living conditions endured by the Mission Indians of California. Beginning in the late 1700s, some 20 Franciscan missions established in Spanish-controlled California forced the indigenous peoples to labor for the mission and to convert to Catholicism. "Mission Indians" was a name applied to several dozen village-dwelling native peoples who had fallen under the sway of the Franciscans. Many of these peoples were nearly extirpated by disease and deprivation. The majority of the survivors were Shoshones and Yumas. Although they had few rights to land ownership or self-determination under Spanish and Mexican rule, after the U.S. victory in the Mexican-American War (1846–1848), Americans settled in the Mission Indians' territory and seized their farms with impunity. Jackson's romantic novel *Ramona* published in 1884, dramatized their plight. In 1891 Congress passed a law to establish reservations for the Mission Indians in California.

Primary Source

There are within the limits of the United States between two hundred and fifty and three hundred thousand Indians, exclusive of those in Alaska. The names of the different tribes and bands, as entered in the statistical table of the Indian Office Reports, number nearly three hundred. One of the most careful estimates which have been made of their numbers and localities gives them as follows: "In Minnesota and States east of the Mississippi, about 32,500; in Nebraska, Kansas, and the Indian Territory, 70,650; in the Territories of Dakota, Montana, Wyoming, and Idaho, 65,000; in Nevada and the Territories of Colorado, New Mexico, Utah, and Arizona, 84,000; and on the Pacific slope, 48,000."

Of these, 130,000 are self-supporting on their own reservations, "receiving nothing from the Government except interest on their own moneys, or annuities granted them in consideration of the cession of their lands to the United States."

. . . Of the remainder, 84,000 are partially supported by the Government—the interest money due them and their annuities, as provided by treaty, being inadequate to their subsistence on the reservations where they are confined. . . .

There are about 55,000 who never visit an agency, over whom the Government does not pretend to have either control or care. These 55,000 "subsist by hunting, fishing, on roots, nuts, berries, etc., and by begging and stealing"; and this also seems to dispose of the accusation that the Indian will not "work for a living." There

remains a small portion, about 31,000, that are entirely subsisted by the Government.

There is not among these three hundred bands of Indians one which has not suffered cruelly at the hands either of the Government or of white settlers. The poorer, the more insignificant, the more helpless the band, the more certain the cruelty and outrage to which they have been subjected. This is especially true of the bands on the Pacific slope. These Indians found themselves of a sudden surrounded by and caught up in the great influx of gold-seeking settlers, as helpless creatures on a shore are caught up in a tidal wave. There was not time for the Government to make treaties; not even time for communities to make laws. The tale of the wrongs, the oppressions, the murders of the Pacific-slope Indians in the last thirty years would be a volume by itself, and is too monstrous to be believed.

It makes little difference, however, where one opens the record of the history of the Indians; every page and every year has its dark stain. The story of one tribe is the story of all, varied only in differences of time and place; but neither time nor place makes any difference in the main facts. Colorado is as greedy and unjust in 1880 as was Georgia in 1830, and Ohio in 1795; and the United States Government breaks promises now as deftly as then, and with an added ingenuity from long practice.

One of its strongest supports in so doing is the wide-spread sentiment among the people of dislike to the Indian, of impatience with his presence as a "barrier to civilization" and distrust of it as a possible danger. The old tales of the frontier life, with its horrors of Indian warfare, have gradually, by two or three generations' telling, produced in the average mind something like an hereditary instinct of questioning and unreasoning aversion which it is almost impossible to dislodge or soften. . . .

President after president has appointed commission after commission to inquire into and report upon Indian affairs, and to make suggestions as to the best methods of managing them. The reports are filled with eloquent statements of wrongs done to the Indians, of perfidies on the part of the Government; they counsel, as earnestly as words can, a trial of the simple and unperplexing expedients of telling truth, keeping promises, making fair bargains, dealing justly in all ways and all things. These reports are bound up with the Government's Annual Reports, and that is the end of them. . . .

The history of the Government connections with the Indians is a shameful record of broken treaties and unfulfilled promises. The history of the border white man's connection with the Indians is a sickening record of murder, outrage, robbery, and wrongs committed by the former, as the rule, and occasional savage outbreaks and unspeakably barbarous deeds of retaliation by the latter, as the exception.

Taught by the Government that they had rights entitled to respect, when those rights have been assailed by the rapacity of the white man, the arm which should have been raised to protect them has ever been ready to sustain the aggressor.

The testimony of some of the highest military officers of the United States is on record to the effect that, in our Indian wars, almost without exception, the first aggressions have been made by the white man. . . . Every crime committed by a white man against an Indian is concealed and palliated. Every offense committed by an Indian against a white man is borne on the wings of the post or the telegraph to the remotest corner of the land, clothed with all the horrors which the reality or imagination can throw around it. Against such influences as these the people of the United States need to be warned.

To assume that it would be easy, or by any one sudden stroke of legislative policy possible, to undo the mischief and hurt of the long past, set the Indian policy of the country right for the future, and make the Indians at once safe and happy, is the blunder of a hasty and uninformed judgment. The notion which seems to be growing more prevalent, that simply to make all Indians at once citizens of the United States would be a sovereign and instantaneous panacea for all their ills and all the Government's perplexities, is a very inconsiderate one. To administer complete citizenship of a sudden, all round, to all Indians, barbarous and civilized alike, would be as grotesque a blunder as to dose them all round with any one medicine, irrespective of the symptoms and needs of their diseases. It would kill more than it would cure. Nevertheless, it is true, as was well stated by one of the superintendents of Indian Affairs in 1857, that, "so long as they are not citizens of the United States, their rights of property must remain insecure against invasion. The doors of the federal tribunals being barred against them while wards and dependents, they can only partially exercise the rights of free government, or give to those who make, execute, and construe the few laws they are allowed to enact, dignity sufficient to make them respectable. While they continue individually to gather the crumbs that fall from the table of the United States, idleness, improvidence, and indebtedness will be the rule, and industry, thrift, and freedom from debt the exception. The utter absence of individual title to particular lands deprives every one among them of the chief incentive to labor and exertion—the very mainspring on which the prosperity of a people depends."

All judicious plans and measures for their safety and salvation must embody provisions for their becoming citizens as fast as they are fit, and must protect them till then in every right and particular in which our laws protect other "persons" who are not citizens. . . .

However great perplexity and difficulty there may be in the details of any and every plan possible for doing at this late day anything like justice to the Indian, however hard it may be for good statesmen and good men to agree upon the things that ought to be done, there certainly is, or ought to be, no perplexity whatever, or difficulty whatever, in agreeing upon certain things that ought not to be done, and which must cease to be done before the first steps can be taken toward righting the wrongs, curing the ills, and wiping out the disgrace to us of the present conditions of our Indians.

Cheating, robbing, breaking promises—these three are clearly things which must cease to be done. One more thing, also, and that is the refusal of the protection of the law to the Indian's rights of property, "of life, liberty, and the pursuit of happiness."

When these four things have ceased to be done, time, statesmanship, philanthropy, and Christianity can slowly and surely do the rest. Till these four things have ceased to be done, statesmanship and philanthropy alike must work in vain, and even Christianity can reap but small harvest.

Source: Helen Hunt Jackson, *A Century of Dishonor* (New York. Harper and Bros., 1881), 336–342.

151. Sarah Winnemucca Hopkins, Petition to Congress, 1883

Introduction

Sarah Winnemucca Hopkins (ca. 1844–1891), a Northern Paiute, was born in western Nevada. Fluent in both spoken and written English, she founded and operated a school for her people, worked as an interpreter for the U.S. Army, and became a prominent lecturer on the plight of Indians. Her speeches and writings highlighted reservation conditions and the hardship caused by corrupt government officials. She was a figure of controversy among her own people, some of whom viewed her as a traitor and a tool of the army during the Bannock War of 1878. Peaceable Northern Paiutes had lived on the Malheur Reservation in southern Oregon along with the Bannock Indians. When a corrupt government agent took over Malheur, selling supplies meant for Indians and allowing whites to settle on reservation land, the Bannocks left the reservation and began raiding the neighboring whites. In 1879 the government forcibly moved the Paiutes and Bannocks to the Yakama Reservation in Washington. The secretary of the interior promised the Paiutes that they could return to Malheur, but the agent at Yakama would not permit them to leave. This petition is appended to Hopkins's autobiography, the first such book by an Indian woman. Hopkins petitioned Congress in 1883 to restore the Malheur Reservation to the Northern Paiutes, but by then her people had already scattered to several other reservations in the region, and Malheur was closed.

Primary Source

NOTE.—Mrs. Hopkins has met with so much intelligent sympathy and furtherance that she has been encouraged to make the following petition to the next Congress, which a Massachusetts representative will present in the hope that it will help to shape aright the new Indian policy, by means of the discussion it will receive:—

"Whereas, the tribe of Piute Indians that formerly occupied the greater part of Nevada, and now diminished by its sufferings and wrongs to one-third of its original number, has always kept its promise of peace and friendliness to the whites since they first entered their country, and has of late been deprived of the Malheur Reservation decreed to them by President Grant:—

"I, SARAH WINNEMUCCA HOPKINS, grand-daughter of Captain Truckee, who promised friendship for his tribe to General Fremont, whom he guided into California, and served through the Mexican war,—together with the undersigned friends who sympathize in the cause of my people,—do petition the Honorable Congress of the United States to restore to them said Malheur Reservation, which is well watered and timbered, and large enough to afford homes and support for them all, where they can enjoy lands in severalty without losing their tribal relations, so essential to their happiness and good character, and where their citizenship, implied in this distribution of land, will defend them from the encroachments of the white settlers, so detrimental to their interests and their virtues. And especially do we petition for the return of that portion of the tribe arbitrarily removed from the Malheur Reservation, after the Bannock war, to the Yakima Reservation on Columbia River, in which removal families were ruthlessly separated, and have never ceased to pine for husbands, wives, and children, which restoration was pledged to them by the Secretary of the Interior in 1880, but has not been fulfilled."

[Signatures.]

Whoever shall be interested by this little book or by Mrs. Hopkins's living word, will help to the end by copying the petition and getting signatures to it, and sending the lists before the first of December to my care, 54 Bowdoin street, Boston. For the weight of a petition is generally measured by its length. Several hundred names have already been sent in.

Source: Sarah Winnemucca Hopkins, *Life among the Paiutes: Their Wrongs and Claims* (New York: Putnam, 1883), 247.

152. Daklugie, Aspects of Apache Culture, 1880s [Excerpts]

Introduction

Asa (Ace) Daklugie (ca. 1870–1955) was the son of Juh (1825–1883), who was leader of the Nednhis, the most militant of the Chiricahua Apaches, and was also the nephew of Geronimo (his mother's brother). When Daklugie was still a young boy, white settlers in Arizona engineered the seizure of the desirable land occupied by several Apache reservations in the highlands of Arizona and New Mexico. Various bands of Apaches were ordered to move to a reservation at San Carlos in the desolate and inhospitable southeastern Arizona lowlands. Juh's band elected instead to go to Mexico, where they lived life on the move for nearly a decade.

Near the end of Daklugie's life, his wife persuaded him to talk to the white historian Eve Ball (1890–1984) about his early days. In these excerpts from the resulting book, Daklugie describes episodes from his band's raiding days in Mexico, the Apache aversion to scalping, and his father's prophetic vision of the Apaches' ultimate defeat. Daklugie and his people became prisoners of war in 1886 and were sent to Florida. Shortly after his arrival there, Daklugie was sent to the Carlisle Indian School, where he was given the hated name Asa and where he spent about eight years. There he decided to learn how to care for cattle, which seemed to him less degrading than farming. In childhood he had been betrothed to Ramona—daughter of another Apache chief, Chihuahua—who was also at Carlisle. He married her after they left Carlisle for Fort Sill, Oklahoma.

Primary Source

The last mule load consisted of two huge cowhide bags full of the yellow and white metals that the White Eyes love. When they were emptied before my father, he was indignant. He asked who had been so foolish as to bring that useless stuff. Didn't we know that bullets made of either were worthless? The stuff was of no value to us except for the making of children's toys.

Nana took pieces of the ore in his wrinkled hands and held them so that they reflected the firelight. "This," he said, referring to the silver, "is the white iron, not forbidden to us. But this yellow stuff is sacred to Ussen. We are permitted to pick it up from the surface of Mother Earth, but not to grovel in her body for it. To do so is to incur the wrath of Ussen. The Mountain Gods dance and shake their mighty shoulders, destroying everything near. The Mexicans and the greedy White Eyes are superstitious about this stuff. The love of life is strong in all people, but to them it is not so strong as their greed for gold. For it, they risk their lives."

"But, my father," said Martine, "I have lived among the Mexicans at Casas Grandes. I know they value this stuff. White Eyes will exchange ammunition, food, anything for it."

Nana nodded, "I know," he said. "Nevertheless, it is this stuff that will bring our people to ruin and cause us to lose first our land and then our lives. But right now, it has value."

"If my father approves, then," said Juh, "let it be divided. Guns last a long time, but ammunition must be constantly replaced. If it will provide for us for awhile, why should we not use it?"

When the women and children had finished their meal, Juh asked that Nana relate the account of the attack upon the Mexican mining village. Nana declined, asking that Geronimo do so. This is the account my uncle gave:

We reached the canyon in which the village is located after dark. Martine guided us to Fun. Kaytennae was assigned the honor of determining when all of the people had entered the church and of killing the guard. He was to kill the guard with a knife, which is noiseless. Fun climbed again to the roof of the Medicine Man's lodge with something wrapped in a bundle. In the upper story he quietly dug a hole in the adobe floor.

At dawn the Medicine Man made lights in the big room. Through a partially opened door we watched him at the feet of his God. He arose, went to a rope, and the pulling sent out loud noises. Many people began coming. We lay hidden until we made sure that everybody in the village had entered. When the door had been closed, we silently carried logs and stones with which to barricade both that door and a smaller one so that neither could be opened from the inside. Juh signaled to Fun on the roof. He had made a chili bomb by grinding red peppers on a metate and mixing into the ground peppers a very soft and inflammable wood. He had wrapped the mixture in a piece of his shirt. He quietly enlarged the opening in the ceiling of the big room until it would admit his bundle. With fire sticks he ignited it and, when it was burning well, dropped the flaming bundle into the room below and covered the hole with a blanket.

Soon there were noises of coughing and sneezing, blows on the door, and sounds of frantic attempts to open it. Fun slipped quickly to the ground.

We waited until the noises inside decreased before we released our captive women and children from the prison. But we did not release those Mexicans who were in the church. We left guards at the church while we went through the houses for what we needed. The women and children that we had released from the prison helped us go through the houses and pack the items on the mules. Horses were taken for those who had none. Among the non-Apache prisoners were boys young enough to be trained as warriors. They are to be treated as our own.

My brother Juh, the Nednhi chief, has brought home supplies sufficient not only for his own, but he insists that his guests share them. You know that of all the plunder divided tonight Juh took none. A great chief is one who supplies the needs of his people, not one who robs them of what they have. Let this be remembered and told to your children's children.

But Geronimo had not finished. He went on: "The Nednhi have done well. They have destroyed the enemy with the loss of only two brave warriors. They have avenged the deaths of their people, and much honor is due Juh for his conduct of the raid. Much honor is due Fun and Martine. They have proved their courage and skill as scouts. And let not Kaytennae's good work be forgotten. I have spoken."

The women refilled the small wicker cups and, when the men had drunk, departed from the circle. Fresh logs were placed on the fire and the space about it was cleared for the victory dance. After the singers and drummers again took their places, my father led, followed by his Nednhi. Then came Nana and the Chihenne; then Chihuahua and the Chokonen; and last Geronimo and his few Bedonkohes. Though my uncle Geronimo exercised the prerogatives of a chief, he was never elected to that position. In later days, when Naiche was chief of the Chiricahua, Geronimo continued to direct the fighting but scrupulously required the warriors to render to Naiche the respect due a chief. He acted as leader of war parties, but acted rather in the relationship of general to commander-in-chief. And Geronimo did his share of the fighting.

The long line danced about the fire clockwise, in single file. All joined in the singing, but above the rest I could hear the powerful voice of Juh. The difficulty he sometimes had in speaking did not affect his singing.

The men improvised steps and poses. Some gave pantomimes of their own ideas of fighting, using a rifle to gesticulate. Others knelt momentarily, fired an arrow or a bullet, or mimicked the thrust of a lance. Each performed as he chose, without effort to duplicate the actions of another.

"I am glad," murmured my mother, "that they have brought no scalps. Scalps have always sickened me."

"You have seen them, then?" I asked. "A few times, a very few. Not until after my brother Geronimo returned to his camp in Mexico to find his beautiful wife Alope, his children, and his mother butchered and scalped did he take one. After that, he did it rarely, and never except in retaliation. I hope that when you become a warrior you will remember that Victorio has permitted no scalping and that you will not."

I sat thinking.

"Victorio permits no scalping regardless of the provocation, and he has suffered no dishonor because of that. Other tribes of Apaches do very little of it. You will not lose face by not permitting it. Will you give me your promise?"

I loved my mother, but a promise cannot be broken. I had never seen any scalping, but how could I know what I might have to do when I became a man? Apaches must protect their women and children. Ussen commanded that. White Eyes may care nothing about how they go through eternity, but Apaches do. The dead do not suffer by scalping, but they must appear in the Happy Place without their hair. There was no greater punishment for one's enemies. My mother did not press me for a promise, but added, "Do not forget to pray before you sleep."

I was told that the men caused landslides that covered all of that village and made a lake of the river. No White Eye will ever find that gold.

[. . .]

My father took his band to visit the great canyon [Del Cobre] and there we experienced a prophetic vision. There my father's warriors assembled and built their ceremonial fire near the edge of the cliff, overlooking the gorge. Many were seated, but a few stood along the wall. To my people, this was a place sacred to Ussen. They had been fighting, running, hiding, and fighting again until they were war-weary and discouraged. They had come to this place to pray for the guidance of Ussen and to seek His aid in renewing their courage and energy. From the past experiences of our people, we knew that Ussen considers this place sacred and that He answers prayers rising from it.

As was our custom, we looked through the thin blue smoke across that wide, wide chasm. When everybody was silent, my father, Juh, lifted his eyes and arms in prayer, and the warriors did also. When the supplication was ended, our eyes were fixed on the opposite wall, far, far away. At first we could see nothing, but gradually a black spot appeared and seemed to grow larger and closer. It looked like an opening in the immense wall opposite us. It was. It was the opening to a big cave, one inaccessible from the rim and equally so from below. Nothing but a bird could have reached the entrance to that cavern.

As we watched, a thin white cloud descended and stopped just below the opening in the cliff. Every person there knew that this was a message from Ussen.

"We have seen His sign," said Juh. We watched as thousands of soldiers in blue uniforms began marching eight abreast into the great opening. This lasted for a long time, for there seemed to be an endless number of soldiers. The cave must have extended far into the cliff, for none returned.

The vision, for that is what it was, lasted until dusk.

We returned to the mesa where Juh had camped. The Medicine Men, of whom my father was head, consulted, and one said, "There were many, many soldiers, all Blue Coats. They signify the government of the United States. Ussen sent the vision to warn us that we will be defeated, and perhaps all killed by the government. Their strength in numbers, with their more powerful weapons, will make us indeed join the Dead. Eventually they will exterminate us.

"That is the meaning of the vision." Juh said, "We must gather together all Apaches—the Chokonen, the Nednhi, the Chihenne, the Bedonkohe, the Tonto, and the Mescaleros. And we must bind them into a strong force, just as these soldiers are strong. With our courage in fighting and our skill, we must oppose the enemy who has driven us from our country. We must not give up. We must fight to the last man. We must remain free men or die fighting. There is no choice."

I did not at first intend telling of this vision, for you do not understand the ways of Ussen. And the White Eyes ridicule anything they do not understand. They have everything in books, but much of what has been written about the Apaches is wrong, for it has been written by our enemies. And you have not asked the Apaches what happened. Consequently, you White Eyes have everything in books and nothing in heads.

On our way north my father was drowned, but his warriors obeyed his wishes and runners were sent to the chiefs of the various tribes to enlist their help in saving our people. But too many, like Loco, had given up, even though they were brave fighting men. They had given up so that those of their tribes who still lived might survive. There was only one leader remaining who did not give up and that was Geronimo. And now the descendants of the fainthearted blame him for the twenty-seven years of captivity just because their fathers did not have the fighting spirit and the courage to risk death as he did. They submitted to living—or rather to starving—on reservations like dumb, craven things. And today they dare criticize the fighting men.

We were few, and poorly equipped, but we did not quit.

Our women and children were butchered and still we did not quit.

You say that finally Geronimo did? You've been reading books! Sometime I am going to tell you just how and why he did give up and how bitterly he regretted having done so. For the time finally came that he, too, knew that the vision must be fulfilled.

Source: Eve Ball, *Indeh: An Apache Odyssey* (Provo, UT: Brigham Young University Press, 1980), 11–12, 76–77.

153. William T. Sherman, Report on the End of the Indian Problem, 1883 [Excerpt]

Introduction

The military career of William Tecumseh Sherman (1820–1891) spanned four decades of warfare. After graduating from West Point in 1840, he served in California through the Mexican-American War (1846–1848) and the beginning of the California Gold Rush. Sherman resigned in 1853 and remained in California as a civilian banker. He returned east in 1859 to serve as superintendent of a military school in Louisiana but at the start of the American Civil War (1861–1865) went north and rejoined the U.S. Army as a colonel. The press notoriously targeted the abrasive Sherman, leaking his military plans and branding him insane. He emerged from this dark period to excel while serving under Ulysses S. Grant, earning steady promotions. Most famously, Sherman destroyed Atlanta and led the March to the Sea, which broke the back of Southern resistance. Sherman served as commanding general of the U.S. Army from 1869 to 1883. While arguing for fair treatment of Indians living on reservations, he promoted total war against those who remained hostile. In this excerpt from his final report to Congress, he states that the Indian Wars are over and that the Indian problem has been resolved for all time. He credits the army, the westward march of American settlement, and the completion of the transcontinental railroad.

Primary Source

. . . I now regard the Indians as substantially eliminated from the problem of the Army. There may be spasmodic and temporary alarms, but such Indian wars as have hitherto disturbed the public peace and tranquility are not probable. The Army has been a large factor in producing this result, but it is not the only one. Immigration and the occupation by industrious farmers and miners of land vacated by the aborigines have been largely instrumental to that end, but the railroad which used to follow in the rear now goes forward with the picket-line in the great battle of civilization with barbarism, and has become the greater cause. I have in former reports, for the past fifteen years, treated of this matter, and now, on the eve of withdrawing from active participation in public affairs, I beg to emphasize much which I have spoken and written heretofore. The recent completion of the last of the four great transcontinental lines of railway has settled forever the Indian question, the Army question, and many others which have hitherto troubled the country. . . .

Source: *Report of the United States Pacific Railway Commission,* Vol. 5 (Washington, DC: U.S. Government Printing Office, 1887), 2594–2595.

154. Manuelito, Speech on Navajo History, February 25, 1886

Introduction

Manuelito (ca. 1818–1893), as white people called him, was a leading war chief of the Navajos. His career spanned decades of raids and counterraids against neighboring tribes as well as the Mexicans, followed by the Americans. In this 1886 speech he looks back on his people's history. The ancestral territory of the Navajos ranged through northern Arizona and New Mexico. The Navajos belong to the same linguistic group as the Apaches but were more sedentary and raised livestock and crops. A series of treaties with the United States whittled down Navajo landholdings and increased unrest. The U.S. Army unleashed a scorched-earth campaign against the Navajos in 1863, sending Colonel Kit Carson to do the job. In 1864 after destroying their crops and herds, the army marched more than 8,000 Navajos to Fort Sumner, south of Santa Fe, New Mexico. There they endured hunger and cramped, squalid conditions for four years, and hundreds died. After the American public learned of conditions at Fort Sumner, the government sent General William T. Sherman to negotiate the 1868 Treaty of Bosque Redondo, which returned the Navajos to a larger reservation on a portion of their ancestral territory. The Navajos refer to that entire period as the Long Walk. Then and now, the larger reservation is too arid to produce enough food for the entire Navajo population.

Primary Source

When our fathers lived they heard that the Americans were coming across the great river westward. Now we are settling among the powerful people. We heard of the guns and powder and lead—first flint locks, then percussion caps, and now repeating rifles. We first saw the Americans at Cottonwood Wash. We had wars with the Mexicans and Pueblos. We captured mules from the Mexicans, and had many mules. The Americans came to trade with us. When the Americans first came we had a big dance, and they danced with our women. We also traded. The Americans went back to Santa Fe, which the Mexicans then held. Afterwards we heard that the Mexicans had reached Santa Fe, and that the Mexicans had disarmed them and made them prisoners. This is how the Mexican war began. Had the Mexicans let the Americans alone they would not have been defeated by the Americans. Then there were many soldiers at Santa Fe, and the Mexican governor was driven away. They did not kill the governor. Therefore we like the Americans. The Americans fight fair, and we like them. Then the soldiers built the fort here, and gave us an agent who advised us to behave well. He told us to live peaceably with the whites; to keep our promises. They wrote down promises, and so always remember them. From then on we had sheep and horses. We had lots of horses, and felt good; we had a fight with the Americans, and were whipped. At that time we thought we had a big country, extending over a great deal of land. We fought for that country because we did not want to lose it, but we made a mistake. We lost nearly everything, but we had some beads left, and with them we thought we were rich. I have always advised the young men to avoid war. I am ashamed for having gone to war. The American nation is too powerful for us to fight. When we had a fight for a few days we felt fresh, but in a short time we were worn out, and the soldiers starved us out. Then the Americans gave us something to eat, and we came in from the mountains and went to Texas. We were there for a few years; many of our people died from the climate. Then we became good friends with the white people. The Comanches wanted us to fight, but we would not join them. One day the soldiers went after the Comanches. I and the soldiers charged on the Comanches, but the Comanches drove us back, and I was left alone to fight them; so the white men came in twelve days to talk with us, as our people were dying off. People from Washington held a council with us. He explained how the whites punished those who disobeyed the law. We promised to obey the laws if we were permitted to get back to our own country. We promised to keep the treaty you read to us to-day. We promised four times to do so. We all said "yes" to the treaty, and he gave us good advice. He was General [William T.] Sherman. We told him we would try to remember what he said. He said: "I want all you people to look at me." He stood up for us to see him. He said if we would do right we could look people in the face. Then he said: "My children, I will send you back to your homes." The nights and days were long before it came time for us to go to our homes. The day before we were to start we went a little way towards home, because we were so anxious to start. We came back and the Americans gave us a little stock to start with and we thanked them for that. We told the drivers to whip the mules, we were in such a hurry. When we saw the top of the mountain from Albuquerque we wondered if it was our mountain, and we felt like talking to the ground, we loved it so, and some of the old men and women cried with joy when they reached their homes. The agent told us here how large our reservation was to be. A small piece of land was surveyed off to us, but we think we ought to have had more. Then we began to talk about more land, and we went to Washington to see about our land. Some backed out of going for fear of strange animals and from bad water, but I thought I might as well die there as here. I thought I could do something at Washington about the land. I had a short talk with the Commissioner. We were to talk with him the next day, but the agent brought us back without giving us a chance to say what we wanted. I saw a man whom I called my younger brother; he was short and fat; and we came back on foot. So Ganada-Mucho thought he would go on to Washington and fix things up, and he got sick and couldn't stand it, and came back without seeing the Commissioner. I tell these things in order that you might know what troubles we have had, and how little satisfaction we got. Therefore we have told you that the reservation was not large enough for our sheep and horses; what the others have told you is true. It is true about the snow on the mountains in the center of the reservation. It is nice there in the summer, but we have to move away in the winter. But we like to be at the mountains in the summer because there is good water and grass there, but in the winter we always move our camps. We like the southern part of the country because the land is richer. We can have farms there. We want the reservation to be extended below the railroad on the south, and also in an easterly direction.

We all appreciate the goods issued to us by the Government. At first we did not understand, now we know how to use plows and scrapers. We have good use for these things and wagons. We can then make new farms and raise crops. We are thankful for what the Government sends. We give nothing back to the whites. When we make blankets our women sell them. They look well in white men's rooms on the bed or walls. If I had a good horse I would keep the blankets myself. When any man comes from the East, we tell him our troubles. There are some bad men, both whites and Indians, whom we cannot keep from doing mischief. The whites control them by laws, and we talk ours into being good. I am glad the young men have freed their minds; now we old men have our say.

Source: Wayne Moquin and Charles Van Doren, *Great Documents in American Indian History* (New York: Praeger, 1973), 256.

155. Nelson Miles, Account of the Surrender of Geronimo, September 4, 1886

Introduction

Nelson Miles (1839–1925) enlisted in the U.S. Army at the outbreak of the American Civil War (1861–1865). Involved in many of the major campaigns, he rose to the rank of brigadier general and received the Medal of Honor for his conduct at Chancellorsville. Miles replaced General George Crook as commander of the Department of Arizona in 1886 while Geronimo (1829–1909) remained at large. Crook had negotiated surrender terms with Geronimo, but the U.S. government had refused to ratify them. Geronimo then refused to surrender, and Crook asked to be relieved. Miles wrote a sweeping memoir that also attempted to provide a complete history of this era. In this excerpt he describes the surrender of Geronimo. Miles sent all the resistant Apaches east as prisoners of war along with many who had cooperated with the government, most notoriously the Apache scouts who had assisted the army against their own people. Crook never forgave Miles for imprisoning the scouts. Miles went on to become commander of the U.S. Army in 1895, had one last engagement in the Spanish-American War (1896–1898), and retired in 1903. Geronimo, military leader of the Chiricahua Apaches, was thought by his people to have supernatural powers. His entire family had been massacred by Mexican troops in 1858. The Mexicans gave him the name Geronimo during the ensuing years as he sought revenge.

Primary Source

Every movement indicated power, energy and determination. In everything he did, he had a purpose. Of course after being hunted over these desolate valleys, mountain crests and dark ravines until he was worn down, he was anxious to make the best terms possible. His greatest anxiety seemed to be to know whether we would treat him fairly and without treachery, or, as soon as he and his followers were in our hands, order them shot to death, as had been the fate of some of his people. He first wanted to surrender as they had been accustomed to surrender before, by going back to Apache and taking their property, arms, stolen stock, and everything with them. I replied to this proposal that I was there to confirm what Captain Lawton had told them, and that was that they must surrender absolutely as prisoners of war. They could not go back to Fort Apache as they had done on previous occasions, but whatever we told them to do that they must conform to. "And more than that," I said, "it is of no use for you to ask to go back to Fort Apache, for there are no Apaches there now."

"What, no Apaches in the White Mountains?" he asked in surprise.

"No," I said.

"Where have they gone?" he asked.

"I have moved them all out of the country," I replied. "You have been at war with the white people for many years, and have been engaged in constant hostilities. I have thought it best that you should be removed from this country to some place where these hostilities cannot be resumed."

This seemed to dishearten him more than any other fact of the situation. The idea that there were no Apaches in the White Mountains was something that he had not anticipated, and he seemed to be wholly unmanned. He then said:

"We are going to do whatever you say and will request but one condition."

"What is that?" I asked.

"That you will spare our lives."

I saw at once that he still entertained the idea that we might kill them if they surrendered, and said to him:

"It is not the custom of officers of the United States army to misuse or destroy their prisoners. So long as you are our prisoners we shall not kill you but shall treat you justly. After that you must look to the President of the United States, who is the great father of all the Indians as well as of all the white people. He has control especially over Indians. He is a just man, and will treat you justly and fairly."

I did not try to explain to this savage the fact that I had no pardoning power; that I had no authority to mitigate the punishment for their crimes, or if they were tried and convicted to pardon them, but that that authority was one of the prerogatives of the chief magistrate alone. Therefore, I merely told him that he must rely upon the President for the character of his treatment, and that I was going move him, as I had already had the other Indians, out of the country. I explained to him that his people were then in three places. Part of them in Florida, part had recently been at Fort Apache, and part were then with him; but that we were going to move all to some one place.

To illustrate this to him, I picked up from the sand three pebbles in front of me, and placing them on the ground separated them so as to form the three points of a triangle, each representing a part of the tribe, and showed him that we were moving two portions of the tribe toward the third pebble which formed the apex of the triangle; I showed him that I could not tell what their future would be, but that one thing was positive: he must do whatever he was directed to do. He assented to this and said he would bring his camp in early the following morning.

He impressed me with a belief in his sincerity, and I allowed him to return to his camp, not far distant. It was one of those times when one has to place confidence even in a savage. When he mounted his horse and turned his back to us I realized we had very little control over him; still, he had placed his brother in our hands as a pledge of his good faith.

True to his word he brought in his band next morning. But Natchez, who was a younger man and the hereditary chief of the Apaches, still remained out. Why he had done so I did not know, and it gave me some concern. I had a conversation with Geronimo in which I induced him to talk quite freely, and then tried to explain to him the uselessness of contending against the military authority of the white race, owing to our many superior advantages. I told him that we had the use of steam, and could move troops with great rapidity from one part of the country to another; that we also had the telegraph and the heliostat, both superior to any of their methods of communication. He wanted to know what that was, and I said I would explain it to him.

We were then near a pool of water with no cover overhead. The operator had placed his heliostat on an extemporized tripod made by placing three sticks together. I said to Geronimo:

"We can watch your movements and send messages over the tops of these mountains in a small part of one day, and over a distance which it would take a man mounted on a swift pony twenty days to travel."

Geronimo's face assumed an air of curiosity and incredulity, and he said:

"How is that?"

I told him I would show him, and, taking him down to the heliostat, asked the operator to open communication with the nearest station which was about fifteen miles away in an air line. He immediately turned his instrument upon that point and flashed a signal of attention. As quick as thought the sunlight was flashed back again.

As I have previously had occasion to remark, when an Indian sees something that he cannot comprehend, he attributes it to some superior power beyond his knowledge and control, and immediately feels that he is in the presence of a spirit. As those stalwart warriors in Montana in using the telephone for the first time had given it the name of the "whispering spirit," so this type of the wild southern savage attributed the power he saw to something more than a mere human being. He told me that he had observed these flashes upon the mountain heights, and believing them to be spirits, had avoided them by going around those points of the mountains, never realizing that it was a subtle power used by his enemies, and that those enemies were themselves located upon these lofty points of observation and communication. I explained to him that it, the instrument, was not only harmless, but of great use, and said to him:

"From here to that point is a distance of nearly a day's march. From that point we can communicate all over this country. I can send a message back to Fort Bowie, sixty-five miles away, or to Fort Apache, nearly three hundred miles from here, and get an answer before the sun goes down in the west."

He comprehended its power and immediately put my statement to the test by saying:

"If you can talk with Fort Bowie, do this: I sent my brother to you there as a guarantee of my good faith; now tell me if my brother is all right." I said to the operator:

"Open communication with Fort Bowie and ask the officer in command, Major Beaumont, or Captain Thompson, my Adjutant-General, if Geronimo's brother is at Fort Bowie.

"Now," I said to Geronimo, "you must wait, for that inquiry with the reply will have to be repeated six times."

In a short time the answer came back that Geronimo's brother was there, was well, and waiting for him to come. This struck the savage with awe, and evidently made a strong impression upon him. I noticed that he said something to one of the warriors close by him, at which the warrior quietly turned upon his heel, walked back a short distance to where his pony was lariated, jumped on his back, and rode rapidly back in the direction of the mountains from whence Geronimo had come. This excited my curiosity, and I asked the interpreter, who was standing near by, what Geronimo said to that young warrior. The interpreter replied: "He told him to go and tell Natchez that there was a power here which he could not understand; and to come in, and come quick." The heliostat had performed its last and best work, and in a few hours Natchez came riding down from the mountains with his band of warriors and their families and came into camp, though with much hesitation and reserve. They dismounted within a short distance of the camp and Natchez with an elastic, active step came forward, with an expression on his face of awe and uncertainty, and yet expressing a desire to do what was expected of him. All his acts were graceful and courtly. He exhibited a dignified reserve, and though he appeared to be anxious, yet seemed always conscious that he was the hereditary chief, and son of the great Cochise. His father had been one of the most noted men in that country, and had been at the head of the Apaches for many years. Natchez was a tall, slender, lithe fellow, six feet two, straight as an arrow, and, I judge, was of about the age of thirty or thirty-five years, suspicious, watchful and dignified in every movement.

The Indians that surrendered with Geronimo have probably never been matched since the days of Robin Hood. Many of the warriors were outlaws from their own tribes, and their boys of from twelve to eighteen were the very worst and most vicious of all. They were clad in such a way as to disguise themselves as much as possible. Masses of grass, bunches of weeds, twigs or small boughs were fastened under their hatbands very profusely, and also upon their shoulders and backs. Their clothing was trimmed in such a way that when lying upon the ground in a bunch of grass or at the head of a ravine, if they remained perfectly silent it was as impossible to discover them as if they had been a bird or a serpent. It was in this way that they were wont to commit their worst crimes. An unsuspecting ranchman or miner going along a road or trail would pass within a few feet of these concealed Apaches, and the first intimation he would have of their presence would be a bullet through his heart or brain. The Indians, when captured, were abundantly supplied with stolen property and were well mounted on Mexican horses. One difficulty that would have been found in case they had been turned over to the civil courts for trial and punishment would have been this: Indictments would probably have been found against the principal Indians, but the young men and boys who had undoubtedly committed the larger number of crimes would have escaped, and remaining in that country would have returned to the warpath. Many of these were afterward sent to the Carlisle school, and their improvement was very marked and of a permanent character.

Source: Nelson Miles, *Personal Recollections and Observations of General Nelson A. Miles* (Chicago: Werner Co., 1897), 521–525.

156. Eugene Chihuahua, Apache Account of Imprisonment in Florida, 1880s

Introduction

In September 1886 after the final surrender of the Chiricahua Apaches, the U.S. government confiscated the last of their land and sent them by train to Fort Marion and Fort Pickens in Florida as prisoners of war. Eugene Chihuahua, around 11 years old at the time, was a son of the famous chief Chihuahua, who had at one time served as an army scout. Unlike most of the other Apache children, Eugene was not forced to go to the Carlisle Indian School because his father pleaded to keep one child with him. In later life Eugene recounted his memories to the white historian Eve Ball (1890–1984). In this excerpt from Ball's resulting book, Eugene describes the misery of prison life in Florida. The prisoners suffered from insufficient food, the unaccustomed diet, the damp climate, and mosquitos. The humidity was especially intolerable to a people accustomed to the arid Southwest. The following year they were moved to Mount Vernon Barracks, Alabama, where they endured even greater discomfort from the damp climate and contracted malaria. Nearly half perished. They remained there until 1894, when the government transferred them to Fort Sill, Oklahoma. The government still considered them prisoners but thought it more humane to remove them from the humid Southeast. The Apaches were prisoners of war for 27 years before they finally received reservations in Oklahoma and New Mexico in 1913.

Primary Source

My father would not leave Fort Bowie until the officer's promise to bring my brother from Fort Apache to us was kept. For once White Eye kept his word. He sent men and a horse for Tom, and they brought him to us. Then we were hauled to Bowie, the little station on the railroad twenty miles north of the old Apache Pass where they had built the fort. They took everything we possessed except the rags on our backs.

We had seen trains, of course, but I think no member of my father's band had ever ridden on one. I had hidden and watched them go snorting by and wondered what they were like inside. I was afraid of the engine. When it screeched and came snorting to the platform it seemed to me as if it squatted and crouched as though about to pounce on us. I don't know what day it was when they drove about seventy-five of us on that thing. The guards went, too. But they did not ship us in boxcars as has been reported. We were in places with seats that turned down at night and formed a place to sleep. And they gave us food.

Everybody was miserable. Old Nana went about telling us that, though our land and homes had been stolen from us, now families could be together, and that in two years we could go back home. When the wife of Naiche and the wife of Geronimo heard that they began to wail and say that they would never see their husbands again. Nana told them that they should not lose hope, for it was very likely that the others would be put with us, and perhaps before very long. And it comforted them because Nana never lied. It was like going into the Death Hole, for nobody knows what that is like, nor will anyone until he gets there.

The one bit of hope was our faith in the promise made by General Crook. For though he was our enemy, he was an honest enemy. Chihuahua told us that Nantan Lupan did not speak with a forked tongue, and that we could rely upon the word of the Tan Wolf. But Nantan Lupan was not on that train, and nobody knew what those guards might do.

The Mexicans could enslave many tribes, but not the Apache. Nobody could force us to work or to endure slavery. True, sometimes captured Apaches became vaqueros for a time, but only long enough that they might escape from their captors. Those forced for a time to grub in the earth starved themselves to death—women as well as men. And now, here we were, going like the wind into what we did not know, nor could we help ourselves if we knew. All we had was that tiny glimmer of hope based upon the word of a White Eye.

I knew that trains had to stop and get water, but not why. I expected that the one taking us away might do that at Lordsburg, but it did not. Deming then? As we approached the station, guards stood at both ends of the cars with leveled guns. And though the train seemed about to stop as we got near the station, it whipped up and went fast. Years later I learned that a bunch of ruffians had been in ambush there to take us off the train and kill us. To my surprise I learned that the guards were there to help us as well as to take us into captivity.

One of the soldiers who spoke Spanish talked with Chihuahua and told him about Florida. He said that there was Big Water there, so wide that nobody could even see across it. Nana told us that there is no water so wide but that his horse could swim it, so we knew that the guard was a liar. In fact we thought that, with the exception of Crook, Britton Davis, and George Wratten, all white men were.

My father, before he resigned from the scouts, had been over that country west of El Paso. He had gone that far, walking ahead of the soldiers to do their fighting for them. From El Paso the soldiers had gone back by train and left the scouts to bring their horse cannon. As he finished speaking a cannon was fired and we thought somebody was shooting at the train to kill us. The guards told Chihuahua that it was a salute to an officer on that train but I do not know who he was.

The train was going slowly as we passed Fort Bliss. At that time there were just two or three little adobe buildings, not much bigger than chicken houses. It was not where it is now; it was between the railroad and the Rio Bravo [Rio Grande].

I don't know how long we were on that train before they put us off in the night, but we were in Florida, St. Augustine. They put us on a flat place close to a big water and let us camp there, I don't know how long. It was muggy and hot. Mosquitoes almost ate us alive. We were so miserable that we did not care how soon thy might kill us. Nana tried to keep us encouraged by telling us that every day brought us one step closer to the time we could go home. He never failed to remind us that no matter how we suffered we were still Apaches and must never complain. Also he said that we were to do whatever we were told and not let anybody know how we hated the White Eyes, because to antagonize them would only make things worse for us.

That place by the Big Water was bad, bad; but it was not nearly so bad as that old fort where they took us. It looked like something in Mexico and had rooms underground. People have said that the Apaches were cruel, but they never shut people up in traps as White Eyes did. They were merciful and killed them. Those were awful places and smelled bad, but when they put tents on top for us that was much better.

Then they took all the men and big boys away from the women and children and put us on that island. That's when my father gave up ever going back. They put us in a big boat and took us to that island where there was a lighthouse. I think that lighthouse was to scare boats away. It scared me, but I didn't say a word.

A guard told us that there was a boy [buoy] out there but we didn't see one; we just saw a big ball painted red and blue bobbing up and down in the water. The man said that on one side of the line it belonged to one tribe and on the other side to another. But there wasn't any line, either.

They left us on that island with some food; but before they went they showed us how to put oil in the lamps, trim the wicks, and light them. Every morning we climbed up to that light and put it out. Then we had to fill the lamp and light it again each evening. I liked that. There was nothing else to do but fish.

Boys always have to cook for warriors. When we opened those boxes, there was flour, coffee, and some sugar; there were some White Eye beans that we didn't like, but we at least got to eat something. And no meat. What were we going to eat? "Fish," the man said. He brought fishing tackle. The water was full of fish, but we don't eat fish; we don't eat anything that grows under water. And we don't eat pork. (I liked bacon but if my mother had known she would have died. Back home there was a scout we called Coche Sergeant because he ate pork.) How long have you ever gone without food? Eighteen hours? Just wait till you have starved eighteen days; then maybe you'll eat anything you can get, like we did.

We were out there a long time. There was nothing to do but fish. A boat came sometimes to bring more food. We couldn't swim back to land; it was too far. We wanted to die.

One day a boat came with food and oil, and it took Chihuahua and me back to that fort. And we saw my mother and my brothers and sister. An officer was picking out Apache children to take away with him. Everybody was frantic. First they didn't let wives and husbands be together; now they were going to take the children away from the mothers.

There were many more people there, mostly Chiricahua, but some Warm Springs too; they had been rounded up at Fort Apache and shipped out there on a train. There must have been nearly four hundred. That place where they put us was covered with tents till you could hardly move. But at least they were not living down in those damp, dark places under the ground.

Some men were drilling like soldiers. But nobody got enough to eat. And everybody was scared. So were we when we learned why; they were going to take the children away to a place they called a school to teach them how to live.

They didn't take quite all, but every one of Chihuahua's children was to go. My father knew the interpreter Concepción. My father asked Concepcíon to tell the officer to leave him one child or he would die. Finally they said he could keep one, just one. Then he and my mother had to decide which one, and that was hard to do. My mother said that it must be a man child because he might be a chief if they ever got back home. So they picked me to stay. The rest had to go.

They knew what White Eyes were going to do to the girls and they wanted to save them, but there was no place to hide them. What were they going to do? Nana told them: One man would take a friend's daughter and say that she was another wife, because wives didn't have to go unless their husbands went too. And they did that and saved some from being taken away.

I had one sister, Ramona. She was about fifteen, almost full grown. When she was just a little girl Juh and Chihuahua promised each other that when she was old enough she was to marry Daklugie, Juh's son. But what was going to happen to her at that place where they were taking her?

They took nearly all away—most on a train, some on a boat.

Then the officer told Chihuahua that his children were going on a train. They let us go to the station when they took my brothers and sister. When the train pulled in we could see a guard standing between two cars. And behind him, who do you think was there? Daklugie. They were sending him, too. Then we knew that Mangus had given up, too.

His group had been sent to Pensacola, where they had been put with Geronimo's band. That meant that, except for a few who had run away to the Blue Mountains in Mexico, all our people had given up.

I don't remember when they took us back to that island, but one day a man came out and told Chihuahua that an officer wanted to see him.

Chihuahua was sent to the officer and I went with him. Whether or not it was a court-martial I don't know, but I don't think so; because if this officer knew my father had resigned from the army he did not say it. Maybe Britton had not reported my father. Chihuahua always thought that when the Fat Boy learned that he had been fooled by Chato and Mickey Free he himself resigned. That's when he took that job managing that big ranch down in Mexico.

The officer asked my father about ambushing and killing a lot of soldiers at a pass. Chihuahua did not lie; standing tall and looking proud, he said, "I did it! My warriors and me, we did it. Aieee! I am proud of it. I just wish that we had killed every one of them!"

"Why did you do this?" asked the officer.

"Why did they kill my mother? Why did they kill the women of my warriors' families? If they wanted to fight, why didn't they fight men? Why just women and children? Your soldiers were not fighting men; they were fighting women!" And Chihuahua turned his back to the officer and sat down on his blanket. And he sat tall and proud to hear the death sentence.

"Chihuahua," said the officer, "You are a brave man. You speak the truth. I like that. I have looked at our record and I know that you are telling the truth. I cannot blame you for what you did. Had I been in your place I hope that I might have had the courage act as you did. Much as I should like to let you go back to your own country I cannot do that. But this I can do for you; as long as you live nobody can say to you 'Bring wood!' 'Carry water!' Nobody can force you to work."

My father answered, "You will not be with me. How will others know that I am not to do these things?"

"I will give you the uniform of a captain in the cavalry. You have been a scout and have worn the uniform."

"Not the pants," said Chihuahua, "Nor the hat; nor the boots."

"But I do this on condition that you wear the uniform, all of it!" He smiled and added, "That includes the trousers."

It was degrading for a Chiricahua to wear the pants, and my father hated them; but he cut out the seat and wore his breechclout over them, so that down the side the stripe showed. The jacket he liked because the double bars of the captain's rank shone on his shoulders.

And nobody bothered Chihuahua. Neither did they Geronimo. He had no double bar, but he was Geronimo, and as long as either lived they did not work. It was not intended by Ussen that Apache warriors work.

Source: Eve Ball, *Indeh: An Apache Odyssey* (Provo, UT: Brigham Young University Press, 1980), 125–129.

157. Dawes Act, February 8, 1887

Introduction

Considered the most important piece of U.S. federal legislation dealing with Native American land rights, the Dawes Act became law on February 8, 1887. Also known as the General Allotment Act, it was named after its principal congressional sponsor, Senator Henry Dawes of Massachusetts. The act provided for the subdivision and allocation of Indian reservation land into individual holdings. In addition, Indians not residing on reservations could apply to local land offices for title to nonreservation land. In passing the act, Congress was responding in part to public demands for reform by conferring on Indians the right to secure individual land ownership. However, the Dawes Act also extended the jurisdiction of U.S. laws over reservations. This provision undermined tribal authority in an attempt to make Indian reservations more similar to white society. Another underlying purpose was to encourage Indians to settle in one place and take up agriculture. The law gave rise to widespread abuses that resulted in the Indians losing some 90 million acres—two-thirds of their total land—by selling it to white speculators. Not until 1934, however, did the federal government pass legislation to supersede the Dawes Act and reestablish the authority of traditional tribal structures.

Primary Source

An act to provide for the allotment of lands in severalty to Indians on the various reservations, and to extend the protection of the laws of the United States and the Territories over the Indians, and for other purposes.

Be it enacted by the Senate and House of Representatives of the United States of America in Congress assembled, That in all cases where any tribe or band of Indians has been, or shall hereafter be, located upon any reservation created for their use, either by treaty stipulation or by virtue of an act of Congress or executive order setting apart the same for their use, the President of the United States be, and he hereby is, authorized, whenever in his opinion any reservation or any part thereof of such Indians is advantageous for agricultural and grazing purposes, to cause said reservation, or any part thereof, to be surveyed, or resurveyed if necessary, and to allot the lands in said reservation in severalty to any Indian located thereon in quantities as follows:

To each head of a family, one-quarter of a section;

To each single person over eighteen years of age, one-eighth of a section;

To each orphan child under eighteen years of age, one-eighth of a section; and

To each other single person under eighteen years now living, or who may be born prior to the date of the order of the President directing an allotment of the lands embraced in any reservation, one-sixteenth of a section: *Provided,* That in case there is not sufficient land in any of said reservations to allot lands to each individual of the classes above named in quantities as above provided, the lands embraced in such reservation or reservations shall be allotted to each individual of each of said classes pro rata in accordance with the provisions of this act: *And provided further,* That where the treaty or act of Congress setting apart such reservation provides the allotment of lands in severalty in quantities in excess of those herein provided, the President, in making allotments upon such reservation, shall allot the lands to each individual Indian belonging thereon in quantity as specified in such treaty or act: *And provided further,* That when the lands allotted are only valuable for grazing purposes, an additional allotment of such grazing lands, in quantities as above provided, shall be made to each individual.

SEC. 2. That all allotments set apart under the provisions of this act shall be selected by the Indians, heads of families selecting for their minor children, and the agents shall select for each orphan child, and in such manner as to embrace the improvements of the Indians making the selection. Where the improvements of two or more Indians have been made on the same legal subdivision of land, unless they shall otherwise agree, a provisional line may be run dividing said lands between them, and the amount to which each is entitled shall be equalized in the assignment of the remainder of the land to which they are entitled under this act: *Provided,* That if any one entitled to an allotment shall fail to make a selection within four years after the President shall direct that allotments may be made on a particular reservation, the Secretary of the Interior may direct the agent of such tribe or band, if such there be, and if there be no agent, then a special agent appointed for that purpose, to make a selection for such Indian, which selection shall be allotted as in cases where selections are made by the Indians, and patents shall issue in like manner.

SEC. 3. That the allotments provided for in this act shall be made by special agents appointed by the President for such purpose, and the agents in charge of the respective reservations on which the allotments are directed to be made, under such rules and regulations as the Secretary of the Interior may from time to time prescribe, and shall be certified by such agents to the Commissioner of Indian Affairs, in duplicate, one copy to be retained in the Indian Office and the other to be transmitted to the Secretary of the Interior for his action, and to be deposited in the General Land Office.

SEC. 4. That where any Indian not residing upon a reservation, or for whose tribe no reservation has been provided by treaty, act of Congress, or executive order, shall make settlement upon any surveyed or unsurveyed lands of the United States not otherwise appropriated, he or she shall be entitled, upon application to the local land-office for the district in which the lands are located, to have the same allotted to him or her, and to his or her children, in quantities and manner as provided in this act for Indians residing upon reservations; and when such settlement is made upon unsurveyed lands, the grant to such Indians shall be adjusted upon the survey of the lands so as to conform thereto; and patents shall be issued to them for such lands in the manner and with the restrictions as herein provided. And the fees to which the officers of such local land-office would have been entitled had such lands been entered under the general laws for the disposition of the public lands shall be paid to them, from any moneys in the Treasury of the United States not otherwise appropriated, upon a statement of an account in their behalf for such fees by the Commissioner of the General Land Office, and a certification of such account to the Secretary of the Treasury by the Secretary of the Interior.

SEC. 5. That upon the approval of the allotments provided for in this act by the Secretary of the Interior, he shall cause patents to issue therefor in the name of the allottees, which patents shall be of the legal effect, and declare that the United States does and will hold the land thus allotted, for the period of twenty-five years, in trust for the sole use and benefit of the Indian to whom such allotment shall have been made, or, in case of his decease, of his heirs according to the laws of the State or Territory where such land is located, and that at the expiration of said period the United States will convey the same by patent to said Indian, or his heirs as aforesaid, in fee, discharged of said trust and free of all charge or incumbrance whatsoever: *Provided,* That the President of the United States may in any case in his discretion extend the period. And if any conveyance shall be made of the lands set apart and allotted as herein provided, or any contract made touching the same, before the expiration of the time above mentioned, such conveyance or contract shall be absolutely null and void: *Provided,* That the law of descent and partition in force in the State or Territory where such lands are situate shall apply thereto after patents therefor have been executed and delivered, except as herein otherwise provided; and the laws of the State of Kansas regulating the descent and partition of real estate shall, so far as practicable, apply to all lands in the Indian Territory which may be allotted in severalty under the provisions of this act: *And provided further,* That at any time after lands have been allotted to all the Indians of any tribe as herein provided, or sooner if in the opinion of the President it shall be for the best interests of said tribe, it shall be lawful for the Secretary of the Interior to negotiate with such Indian tribe for the purchase and release by said tribe, in conformity with the treaty or statute under which such reservation is held, of such portions of its reservation not allotted as such tribe shall, from time to time, consent to sell, on such terms and conditions as shall be considered just and equitable between the United States and said tribe of Indians, which purchase shall not be complete until ratified by Congress, and the form and manner of executing such release prescribed by Congress: *Provided however,* That all lands adapted to agriculture, with or without irrigation so sold or released to the United States by any Indian tribe shall be held by the United States for the sole purpose of securing homes to actual settlers and shall be disposed of by the United States to actual and bona fide settlers only tracts not exceeding one hundred and sixty acres to any one person, on such terms as Congress shall prescribe, subject to grants which Congress may make in aid of education: *And provided further,* That no patents shall issue therefor except to the person so taking the same as and for a homestead, or his heirs, and after the expiration of five years occupancy thereof as such homestead; and any conveyance of said lands taken as a homestead, or any contract touching the same, or

lien thereon, created prior to the date of such patent, shall be null and void. And the sums agreed to be paid by the United States as purchase money for any portion of any such reservation shall be held in the Treasury of the United States for the sole use of the tribe or tribes of Indians; to whom such reservations belonged; and the same, with interest thereon at three per cent per annum, shall be at all times subject to appropriation by Congress for the education and civilization of such tribe or tribes of Indians or the members thereof. The patents aforesaid shall be recorded in the General Land Office, and afterward delivered, free of charge, to the allottee entitled thereto. And if any religious society or other organization is now occupying any of the public lands to which this act is applicable, for religious or educational work among the Indians, the Secretary of the Interior is hereby authorized to confirm such occupation to such society or organization, in quantity not exceeding one hundred and sixty acres in any one tract, so long as the same shall be so occupied, on such terms as he shall deem just; but nothing herein contained shall change or alter any claim of such society for religious or educational purposes heretofore granted by law. And hereafter in the employment of Indian police, or any other employees in the public service among any of the Indian tribes or bands affected by this act, and where Indians can perform the duties required, those Indians who have availed themselves of the provisions of this act and become citizens of the United States shall be preferred.

SEC. 6. That upon the completion of said allotments and the patenting of the lands to said allottees, each and every number of the respective bands or tribes of Indians to whom allotments have been made shall have the benefit of and be subject to the laws, both civil and criminal, of the State or Territory in which they may reside; and no Territory shall pass or enforce any law denying any such Indian within its jurisdiction the equal protection of the law. And every Indian born within the territorial limits of the United States to whom allotments shall have been made under the provisions of this act, or under any law or treaty, and every Indian born within the territorial limits of the United States who has voluntarily taken up, within said limits, his residence separate and apart from any tribe of Indians therein, and has adopted the habits of civilized life, is hereby declared to be a citizen of the United States, and is entitled to all the rights, privileges, and immunities of such citizens, whether said Indian has been or not, by birth or otherwise, a member of any tribe of Indians within the territorial limits of the United States without in any manner affecting the right of any such Indian to tribal or other property.

SEC. 7. That in cases where the use of water for irrigation is necessary to render the lands within any Indian reservation available for agricultural purposes, the Secretary of the Interior be, and he is hereby, authorized to prescribe such rules and regulations as he may deem necessary to secure a just and equal distribution thereof among the Indians residing upon any such reservation; and no other appropriation or grant of water by any riparian proprietor shall be permitted to the damage of any other riparian proprietor.

SEC. 8. That the provisions of this act shall not extend to the territory occupied by the Cherokees, Creeks, Choctaws, Chickasaws, Seminoles, and Osage, Miamies and Peorias, and Sacs and Foxes, in the Indian Territory, nor to any of the reservations of the Seneca Nation of New York Indians in the State of New York, nor to that strip of territory in the State of Nebraska adjoining the Sioux Nation on the south added by executive order.

SEC. 9. That for the purpose of making the surveys and resurveys mentioned in section two of this act, there be, and hereby is, appropriated, out of any moneys in the Treasury not otherwise appropriated, the sum of one hundred thousand dollars, to be repaid proportionately out of the proceeds of the sales of such land as may be acquired from the Indians under the provisions of this act.

SEC. 10. That nothing in this act contained shall be so construed to affect the right and power of Congress to grant the right of way through any lands granted to an Indian, or a tribe of Indians, for railroads or other highways, or telegraph lines, for the public use, or condemn such lands to public uses, upon making just compensation.

SEC. 11. That nothing in this act shall be so construed as to prevent the removal of the Southern Ute Indians from their present reservation in Southwestern Colorado to a new reservation by and with consent of a majority of the adult male members of said tribe.

Source: "Dawes Act of 1887," U.S. Statutes at Large 24 (1887): 388–391.

158. Documents concerning the Ghost Dance, 1890

Introduction

The Ghost Dance religion originated with a Paiute medicine man, Wovoka, who promised that the white man would disappear, the buffalo would return, the Indian dead would be resurrected, and the Indians would be restored to their land and their traditional way of life. To bring this about, the Indians would have to remain peaceful and take part in the Ghost Dance ritual. The religion spread rapidly, and the Sioux embraced it with particular fervor. Black Elk (1863–1950), a Sioux medicine man and a cousin of Crazy Horse, became a leading participant in the Ghost Dance movement. In 1932 he recounted the events of his life to author John Neihardt. In this excerpt from the resulting book, *Black Elk Speaks,* Black Elk recalls the spread of the Ghost Dance during the summer of 1890 and describes his vision in which he learned how to make "ghost

shirts," which were believed to give protection against bullets. The second document is a translation by ethnologist James Mooney of songs that accompanied the Ghost Dance. Mooney's report, originally published by the U.S. government in 1896, is a leading source of information about the Ghost Dance religion.

Primary Source

Black Elk's Vision

Then the father was a spotted eagle dancing on ahead of me with his wings fluttering, and he was making the shrill whistle that is his. My body did not move at all, but I looked ahead and floated fast toward where I looked. There was a ridge right in front of me, and I thought I was going to run into it, but I went right over it. On the other side of the ridge I could see a beautiful land where many, many people were camping in a great circle. I could see that they were happy and had plenty. Everywhere there were drying racks full of meat. The air was clear and beautiful with a living light that was everywhere. All around the circle, feeding on the green, green grass, were fat and happy horses; and animals of all kinds were scattered all over the green hills, and singing hunters were returning with their meat. I floated over the tepees and began to come down feet first at the center of the hoop where I could see a beautiful tree all green and full of flowers. When I touched the ground, two men were coming toward me, and they wore holy shirts made and painted in a certain way. They came to me and said: "It is not yet time to see your father, who is happy. You have work to do. We will give you something that you shall carry back to your people, and with it they shall come to see their loved ones." I knew it was the way their holy shirts were made that they wanted me to take back. They told me to return at once, and then I was out in the air again, floating fast as before. When I came right over the dancing place, the people were still dancing, but it seemed they were not making any sound. I had hoped to see the withered tree in bloom, but it was dead. Then I fell back into my body, and as I did this I heard voices all around and above me, and I was sitting on the ground. Many were crowding around, asking me what vision I had seen. I told them just what I had seen, and what I brought back was the memory of the holy shirts the two men wore. That evening some of us got together at Big Road's tepee and decided to use the ghost shirts I had seen. So the next day I made ghost shirts all day long and painted them in the sacred manner of my vision. As I made these shirts, I thought how in my vision everything was like old times and the tree was flowering, but when I came back the tree was dead. And I thought that if this world would do as the vision teaches, the tree could bloom here too.

The Ghost Dance Religion

Maka' Sito'Maniyas
　The whole world is coming,
　A nation is coming, a nation is coming,
　The Eagle has brought the message to the tribe.

The father says so, the father says so.
Over the whole earth they are coming.
The buffalo are coming, the buffalo are coming,
The Crow has brought the message to the tribe,
The father says so, the father says so.

Le' Na Wa'Kas

It is I who make these sacred things,
Says the father, says the father.
It is I who make the sacred shirt,
Says the father, says the father.
It is I who made the pipe,
Says the father, says the father.

Source: Reprinted by permission from *Black Elk Speaks: Being the Life Story of a Holy Man of the Oglala Sioux, the Premier Edition,* edited by John G. Neihardt, the State University of New York Press © 2008, State University of New York. All rights reserved; James Mooney, The Ghost-Dance Religion and the Sioux Outbreak of 1890 (Washington DC: Government Printing Office), 1072.

159. Sitting Bull, Speech on Keeping Treaties, 1890

Introduction

Sitting Bull (ca. 1831–1890), a renowned warrior and chief of the Sioux Nation from the mid-1860s until his death, had led his people and the allied Cheyennes and Arapahos in their steadfast resistance to white encroachment on the northern Plains. Despite military victories, starvation forced his surrender in 1881. This excerpt is taken from a speech he made in 1890 in which he explains that he will not cede any more land to the United States. The Sioux had embraced the rapidly spreading Ghost Dance religion with particular fervor. The religion promised that the white man would disappear, the buffalo would return, the Indian dead would be resurrected, and the Indians would be restored to their land and their traditional way of life. The U.S. agent at the Pine Ridge Reservation asked for military protection, fearing that the religious fervor would lead to a violent uprising. Concerned about Sitting Bull's influence, the army ordered his arrest. On December 15, 1890, Sitting Bull was shot and killed while his followers tried to prevent his arrest. His people fled the reservation but returned to surrender two weeks later. The confrontation the next day at Wounded Knee marked the end of the Indian Wars.

Primary Source

What treaty that the whites have kept has the red man broken? Not one. What treaty that the whites ever made with us red men have they kept? Not one. When I was a boy the Sioux owned the world. The sun rose and set in their lands. They sent 10,000 horsemen to

battle. Where are the warriors to-day? Who slew them? Where are our lands? Who owns them? What white man can say I ever stole his lands or a penny of his money? Yet they say I am a thief. What white woman, however lonely, was ever when a captive insulted by me? Yet they say I am a bad Indian. What white man has ever seen me drunk? Who has ever come to me hungry and gone unfed? Who has ever seen me beat my wives or abuse my children? What law have I broken? Is it wrong for me to love my own? Is it wicked in me because my skin is red; because I am a Sioux; because I was born where my fathers lived; because I would die for my people and my country?

Source: W. Fletcher Johnson, *The Red Record of the Sioux: Life of Sitting Bull* (Edgewood Publishing Company, 1891), 201.

160. Nelson Miles, Correspondence regarding Sioux Unrest, December 19, 1890

Introduction

Sitting Bull (ca. 1831–1890) was a renowned warrior and chief of the Sioux Nation from the mid-1860s until his death. Despite military victories, starvation forced his surrender in 1881. Confined to their South Dakota reservation and suffering from inadequate rations, in 1890 the Sioux embraced the rapidly spreading Ghost Dance religion with particular fervor. The religion promised that the white man would disappear, the buffalo would return, and the Indians would be restored to their land and their traditional way of life. Fearing that the religious fervor would lead to a violent uprising, the U.S. agent at Pine Ridge Reservation cabled Washington to demand military protection. Only days after the army's botched attempt to arrest Sitting Bull on December 15, 1890, General Nelson A. Miles wrote these letters. In them he pinpoints the real cause of Sioux unrest: not religious fervor but instead bad faith on the part of the U.S. government. The Sioux had been forced to cede yet another portion of their land and had not received the promised food rations. Miles argues that he and his troops can deal with the hostile elements only if Congress will honor the treaty and see to it that the peaceful Indians are well fed.

Primary Source

Rapid City, South Dakota, December 19, 1890
Senator Dawes,
Washington, District of Columbia:

You may be assured of the following facts that cannot not be gainsaid:

First. The forcing process of attempting to make large bodies of Indians self-sustaining when the government was cutting down their rations and their crops almost a failure, is one cause of the difficulty.

Second. While the Indians were urged and almost forced to sign a treaty presented to them by the commission authorized by Congress, in which they gave up a valuable portion of their reservation which is now occupied by white people, the government has failed to fulfill its part of the compact, and instead of an increase or even a reasonable supply for their support, they have been compelled to live on half and two-thirds rations, and received nothing for the surrender of their lands, neither has the government given any positive assurance that they intend to do any differently with them in the future.

Congress has been in sessions several weeks and could, if it were disposed, in a few hours confirm the treaties that its commissioners have made with these Indians and appropriate the necessary funds for its fulfillment and thereby give an earnest of their good faith or intention to fulfill their part of the compact. Such action, in my judgment, is essential to restore confidence with the Indians and give peace and protection to the settlements. If this be done, and the President authorized to place the turbulent and dangerous tribes of Indians under the control of the military, Congress need not enter into details, but can safely trust the military authorities to subjugate and govern, and in the near future make self-sustaining, any or all of the Indian tribes of this country.

Rapid City, South Dakota, December 19, 1890
General John M. Schofield,
Commanding the Army, Washington, District of Columbia:

Replying to your long telegram, one point is of vital importance— the difficult Indian problem can not be solved permanently at this end of the line. It requires the fulfillment by Congress of the treaty obligations which the Indians were entreated and coerced into signing. They signed away a valuable portion of their reservation, and it is now occupied by white people, for which they have received nothing. They understood that ample provision would be made for their support: instead, their supplies have been reduced, and much of the time they have been living on half and two-thirds rations. Their crops, as well as the crops of the white people, for two years have been almost a total failure. The disaffection is widespread, especially among the Sioux, while the Cheyennes have been on the verge of starvation and were forced to commit depredations to sustain life. These facts are beyond question, and the evidence is positive and sustained by thousands of witnesses. Serious difficulty has been gathering for years. Congress has been in session several weeks and could in a single hour confirm the treaties and appropriate the necessary funds for their fulfillment, which their commissioners and the highest officials of the government have guaranteed to these people, and unless the officers of

the army can give some positive assurance that the government intends to act in good faith with these people, the loyal element will be diminished and the hostile element increased. If the government will give some positive assurance that it will fulfill its part of the understanding with these 20,000 Sioux Indians, they can safely trust the military authorities to subjugate, control and govern these turbulent people, and I hope that you will ask the Secretary of War and the Chief Executive to bring the matter directly to the attention of Congress.

Source: James Mooney, *The Ghost-Dance Religion and the Sioux Outbreak of 1890* (Washington, DC: Government Printing Office, 1896), 835–836.

161. Indian and White Accounts of the Battle of Wounded Knee, 1890

Introduction

Confined to their South Dakota reservation and suffering from inadequate rations, in 1890 the Sioux embraced the rapidly spreading Ghost Dance religion with particular fervor. The U.S. agent at the Pine Ridge Reservation demanded military protection, fearing that a violent uprising was imminent. The army ordered the arrest of Sitting Bull, and he was killed on December 15, 1890, when his followers tried to prevent his arrest. His people then fled the reservation but returned to surrender two weeks later. Black Elk (1863–1950), a Sioux medicine man and a cousin of Crazy Horse, was a leading participant in the Ghost Dance movement. In this excerpt from the 1932 book *Black Elk Speaks,* he describes the December 29, 1890, massacre of his people at Wounded Knee. Most of the surrendering Indians had stacked their arms, but the soldiers were confiscating the weapons that a few men had concealed. A concealed rifle went off, a scuffle ensued, and a soldier was shot. U.S. troops turned their guns on the Indians at close range, mowed them down, and then pursued and killed those who tried to flee. The U.S. troops killed more than 150 Sioux, many of them women and children. In the second excerpt, published in 1899, author Annie Tallent expresses the white prejudices of the time. In her telling, the Indians, by prearrangement, drew their concealed weapons and opened fire on the soldiers.

Primary Source

Black Elk's Account

Then I rode over the ridge and the others after me, and we were crying: "Take courage! It is time to fight!" The soldiers who were guarding our relatives shot at us and then ran away fast, and some more cavalrymen on the other side of the gulch did too. We got our relatives and sent them across the ridge to the northwest where they would be safe. I had no gun, and when we were charging, I just held the sacred bow out in front of me with my right hand. The bullets did not hit us at all. We found a little baby lying all alone near the head of the gulch. I could not pick her up just then, but I got her later and some of my people adopted her. I just wrapped her up tighter in a shawl that was around her and left her there. It was a safe place, and I had other work to do. The soldiers had run eastward over the hills where there were some more soldiers, and they were off their horses and lying down. I told the others to stay back, and I charged upon them holding the sacred bow out toward them with my right hand. They all shot at me and I could hear bullets all around me, but I ran my horse right close to them, and then swung around. Some soldiers across the gulch began shooting at me too, but I got back to the others and was not hurt at all. By now many other Lakotas, who had heard the shooting, were coming up from Pine Ridge, and we all charged on the soldiers. They ran eastward toward where the trouble began. We followed down along the dry gulch, and what we saw was terrible. Dead and wounded women and children and little babies were scattered all along there where they had been trying to run away. The soldiers had followed along the gulch, as they ran, and murdered them in there. Sometimes they were in heaps because they had huddled together, and some were scattered all along. Sometimes bunches of them had been killed and torn to pieces where the wagon guns hit them. I saw a little baby trying to suck its mother, but she was bloody and dead. There were two little boys at one place in this gulch. They had guns and they had been killing soldiers all by themselves. We could see the soldiers they had killed. The boys were all alone there, and they were not hurt. These were very brave little boys. When we drove the soldiers back, they dug themselves in, and we were not enough people to drive them out from there. In the evening they marched off up Wounded Knee Creek, and then we saw all that they had done there. Men and women and children were heaped and scattered all over the flat at the bottom of the little hill where the soldiers had their wagon-guns, and westward up the dry gulch all the way to the high ridge, the dead women and children and babies were scattered. When I saw this I wished that I had died too, but I was not sorry for the women and children. It was better for them to be happy in the other world, and I wanted to be there too. But before I went there I wanted to have revenge. I thought there might be a day, and we should have revenge. After the soldiers marched away, I heard from my friend, Dog Chief, how the trouble started, and he was right there by Yellow Bird when it happened. This is the way it was: In the morning the soldiers began to take all the guns away from the Big Foots, who were camped in the flat below the little hill where the mound and burying ground are now. The people had stacked most of their guns, and even their knives, by the tepee where Big Foot was lying sick. Soldiers were on the little hill and all around, and there were soldiers across the dry gulch to the south and over east along Wounded Knee Creek

too. The people were nearly surrounded, and the wagon guns were pointing at them. Some had not yet given up their guns, and so the soldiers were searching all the tepees, throwing things around and poking into everything. There was a man called Yellow Bird, and he and another man were standing in front of the tepee where Big Foot was lying sick. They had white sheets around and over them, with eyeholes to look through, and they had guns under these. An officer came to search them. He took the other man's gun, and then started to take Yellow Bird's. But Yellow Bird would not let go. He wrestled with the officer, and while they were wrestling, the gun went off and killed the officer. Wasichus and some others have said he meant to do this, but Dog Chief was standing right there, and he told me it was not so. As soon as the gun went off, Dog Chief told me, an officer shot and killed Big Foot who was lying sick inside the tepee. Then suddenly nobody knew what was happening, except that the soldiers were all shooting and the wagon-guns began going off right in among the people. Many were shot down right there. The women and children ran into the gulch and up west, dropping all the time, for the soldiers shot them as they ran. There were only about a hundred warriors and there were nearly five hundred soldiers. The warriors rushed to where they had piled their guns and knives. They fought soldiers with only their hands until they got their guns. Dog Chief saw Yellow Bird run into a tepee with his gun, and from there he killed soldiers until the tepee caught fire. Then he died full of bullets. It was a good winter day when all this happened. The sun was shining. But after the soldiers marched away from their dirty work, a heavy snow began to fall. The wind came up in the night. There was a big blizzard, and it grew very cold. The snow drifted deep in the crooked gulch, and it was one long grave of butchered women and children and babies, who had never done any harm and were only trying to run away.

Annie Tallent's Account

Regarding this as a lack of good faith, and suspecting treachery on the part of the desperate band, Capt. Whiteside ordered his dismounted troopers to close in about the Indians, which they did, taking a stand within twenty feet of them, in an almost complete square, when, like a flash, they drew their concealed guns from beneath their blankets, and fired a deadly volley into the closed ranks of the soldiers. Exasperated at this base treachery, the soldiers, scarcely waiting for the word of command, opened a terrific fire on the Indians, who fell before it as falls the grain before the sickle of the reaper.

Source: Reprinted by permission from *Black Elk Speaks: Being the Life Story of a Holy Man of the Oglala Sioux, the Premier Edition,* edited by John G. Neihardt, the State University of New York Press © 2008, State University of New York. All rights reserved; Annie D. Tallent, The Black Hills; or, The Last Hunting Ground of the Dakotahs (St. Louis: Nixon-Jones Printing Co., 1899), 710.

162. Frederick Jackson Turner, "The Significance of the Frontier in American History," 1893 [Excerpts]

Introduction

In July 1893 U.S. historian Frederick Jackson Turner delivered a paper to the American Historical Association, which was meeting at the World's Columbian Exposition in Chicago. That paper served as the foundation for this essay, which was published shortly thereafter. The 1890 U.S. census report had announced the end of the western frontier, and the killings at Wounded Knee had ended all Indian resistance to American control of all land within U.S. borders. Turner emphasized the vital role played by the existence of the frontier on the formation of American society and a uniquely American character. He argued that the availability of open land in the West, by always offering the opportunity for a fresh start, had fostered equal opportunity and democratic government. Turner also described how taking up residence beyond the frontier turned Europeans into Americans and how the frontier toughened and transformed settlers before they in turn transformed the frontier into an outpost of a uniquely American civilization. The closing of the frontier would thus change the course of American history in unknown ways. Turner was the first historian to express these now-familiar ideas. Later historians have attributed the American public's enthusiasm for the Spanish-American War (1896–1898) and subsequent expansionism to the collective need for a new frontier.

Primary Source

(On the occasion of the World's Columbian Exhibition)

Up to our own day American history has been in a large degree the history of the colonization of the Great West. The existence of an area of free land, continuous recession, and the advance of American settlements westward, explain American development.

Behind institutions, behind constitutional forms and modifications lie the vital forces that call these organs into life and shape them to meet changing conditions. The peculiarity of American institutions is the fact that they have been compelled to adapt themselves to the changes of an expanding people—to the changes involved in crossing a continent, this winning a wilderness, and in developing at each area of this progress out of the primitive economic and political conditions of the frontier into the complexity of city life. . . . Thus American development has exhibited not merely advance along a single line, but a return to primitive conditions on a continually advancing frontier line, and a new development for that area. American social development has been continually beginning over again on the frontier. This perennial rebirth, this fluidity of American life, this expansion westward with its new opportunities, its continuous touch with the simplicity of primitive society, furnish the forces dominating American character. The true point of view in the history of this nation is not the Atlantic coast, it is the Great West. . . .

. . . The frontier is the line of most rapid and effective Americanization. The wilderness masters the colonist. It finds him a European in dress, industries, tools, modes of travel, and thought. It takes him from the railroad car and puts him in the birch canoe. It strips off the garments of civilization and arrays him in the hunting shirt and the moccasin. It puts him in the log cabin of the Cherokee and Iroquois and runs an Indian palisade around him. Before long he has gone to planting Indian corn and plowing with a sharp stick; he shouts the war cry and takes the scalp in orthodox Indian fashion. In short, at the frontier the environment is at first too strong for the man. He must accept the conditions which it furnishes, or perish, and so he fits himself into the Indian clearings and follows the Indian trails. Little by little he transforms the wilderness but the outcome is not the old Europe, not simply the development of Germanic germs, any more than the first phenomenon was a case of reversion to the Germanic mark. The fact is, that here is a new product that is American. At first, the frontier was the Atlantic coast. It was the frontier of Europe in a very real sense. Moving westward, the frontier became more and more American. As successive terminal moraines result from successive glaciations, so each frontier leaves its traces behind it, and when it becomes a settled area the region still partakes of the frontier characteristics. Thus the advance of the frontier has meant a steady movement away from the influence of Europe, a steady growth of independence on American lines. And to study this advance, the men who grew up under these conditions, and the political, economic, and social results, is to study the really American part of our history. . . .

. . . Since the days when the fleet of Columbus sailed into the waters of the New World, America has been another name for opportunity, and the people of the United States have taken their tone from the incessant expansion which has not only been open but has been forced upon them. He would be a rash prophet who should assert that the expansive character has now entirely ceased. Movement has been its dominant fact, and unless this training has no effect upon a people, the American energy will continually demand a wider field for its exercise. But never again will such gifts of free land offer themselves. For a moment, at the frontier, the bonds of custom are broken and unrestraint is triumphant. There is not tabula rasa. The stubborn American environment is there with its imperious summons to accept its conditions; the inherited ways of doing things are also there; and yet, in spite of environment, and in spite of custom, each frontier did indeed furnish a new field of opportunity, a gate of escape from the bondage of the past; and freshness and confidence, and scorn of older society, impatience of its restraints and its ideas, and indifference to its lessons, have accompanied the frontier. What the Mediterranean Sea was to the Greeks, breaking the bond of custom, offering new experiences, calling out new institutions and activities, that, and more, the ever retreating frontier has been to the United States directly, and to the nations of Europe more remotely. And now, four centuries from the discovery of America, at the end of a hundred years of life under the Constitution, the frontier has gone, and with its going has closed the first period in American history.

Source: Frederick Jackson Turner, *The Frontier in American History* (New York: Henry Holt, 1920), 1–38.

163. Documents concerning the Indian Citizenship Act, 1924 and 1933

Introduction

The Indian Citizenship Act conferred U.S. citizenship on all Indians born in the United States while ensuring that they would retain their rights to tribal land. Until the passage of this law, U.S. citizenship was granted on a case-by-case basis to Indians who had severed their tribal affiliations, joined the U.S. armed forces, or assimilated into white society. Several states used various legal loopholes to deny the Indians full citizenship rights, such as the right to vote, until well into the 1940s. Indians did not greet this act with universal rejoicing. For example, the Oglala Sioux author Luther Standing Bear (1868–1939) viewed the act with derision, calling it little more than an attempt to make the government look good. In this excerpt from his memoirs he calls the act a hoax, saying that the need for such an act simply reveals the Indians' enslaved status and that the existence of reservations and government agents proves that Indians have not attained all the rights of citizenship. Luther Standing Bear was born on the Pine Ridge Reservation in South Dakota. He reluctantly attended the Carlisle Indian School. After leaving school, he operated a store on the reservation, traveled with Buffalo Bill's Wild West Show, wrote several books, and acted in westerns.

Primary Source

Indian Citizenship Act of 1924

BE IT ENACTED by the Senate and house of Representatives of the United States of America in Congress assembled, That all non citizen Indians born within the territorial limits of the United States be, and they are hereby, declared to be citizens of the United States: Provided That the granting of such citizenship shall not in any manner impair or otherwise affect the right of any Indian to tribal or other property. Approved, June 2, 1924. [H. R. 6355.] [Public, No. 175.] SIXTY-EIGHTH CONGRESS. Sess. I. CHS. 233. 1924. See House Report No. 222, Certificates of Citizenship to Indians, 68th Congress, 1st Session, Feb. 22, 1924. Note: This statute has been codified in the United States Code at Title 8, Sec. 1401(b).

Comments by Luther Standing Bear regarding the Indian Citizenship Act

Worse and worse have become reservation conditions under a system that was bad from the beginning. Such a deplorable state of affairs could only continue to exist because of several reasons, mainly because of slight public concern for the Indian; because of the declaration of President Coolidge on June 5, 1924, that presumably made the Indian a citizen of the United States, and because the mass of people think and say, "The Government takes care of the Indian."

The very act of signing the bill disclosed the fact that a bonded and enslaved people lived in the "land of the free and the home of the brave," even though it was then more than half a century since slavery was supposed to have been wiped from the land. The bill signed by President Coolidge supposedly gave the Indian the same rights enjoyed by other men, but it was just another hoax. The reservation still remains, the agent is still on the job. Indian children are still wrested from their mother's arms to be sent away, young "citizens" still go to segregated schools where they are refused the right to speak their native tongue, the Indian Bureau politicians still fatten on Indian money and the Indian is still being robbed. My people of South Dakota have been in dire straits, and during the past two years the old have rapidly passed away, unable to endure the cold of winter insufficiently clothed, and have slowly become undermined in health by starvation while the public sleeps on the thought that "the Government takes care of the Indian." The twenty million dollars public appropriation disbursed last year among the various tribes was but a crumb thrown into a starving mouth. Each Sioux received the sum of seven dollars and a half, and when I talked to the agent about it this summer (1931) he admitted that it came at a most needed time. But public appropriations never have and never will supply the Sioux people with the need to have their reservation freed from the white cattle-raiser and given cattle of their own to raise; nor can the doling of such pittances to any tribe effect the needed relief and reform.

Source: Indian Citizenship Act (43 U.S. Stats. At Large, Ch. 233, p. 253 (1924); *Land of the Spotted Eagle* by Luther Standing Bear by permission of the University of Nebraska Press. Copyright 1933 by Luther Standing Bear. Renewal copyright 1960 by May Jones.

164. Indian Reorganization Act, June 18, 1934

Introduction

John Collier, the commissioner of Indian affairs, campaigned for the reform of Indian policy and the reversal of the abuses under the allotment system established by the Dawes Act. The Dawes Act of 1887 had tried to assimilate Indians into American society by promoting individual land ownership and agricultural pursuits while diminishing the authority of tribal leadership. Individual land ownership had the unintended result of Indians losing land by selling it to speculators. Collier reported that since 1887 Indians had lost some 90 million acres (two-thirds of their total land area), which had resulted in widespread economic ruin and despair. The Indian Reorganization Act, also called the Wheeler-Howard Act, restored reservation lands to collective tribal ownership and allocated funds to purchase back allotments for the benefit of the tribes. However, the act provided for two notable exceptions: any lands included in federal reclamation projects and Papago land in Arizona, which the government wished to open to mining operations. The act also provided for self-government on Indian reservations and financial assistance for education, vocational training, and economic development.

Primary Source

(Wheeler-Howard Act—48 Stat. 984—25 U.S.C. § 461 *et seq*)

—An Act to conserve and develop Indian lands and resources; to extend to Indians the right to form business and other organizations; to establish a credit system for Indians; to grant certain rights of home rule to Indians; to provide for vocational education for Indians; and for other purposes.

BE IT ENACTED by the Senate and House of Representatives of the United States of America in Congress assembled, That hereafter no land of any Indian reservation, created or set apart by treaty or agreement with the Indians, Act of Congress, Executive order, purchase, or otherwise, shall be allotted in severalty to any Indian.

Sec. 2. The existing periods of trust placed upon any Indian lands and any restriction on alienation thereof are hereby extended and continued until otherwise directed by Congress.

Sec. 3. The Secretary of the Interior, if he shall find it to be in the public interest, is hereby authorized to restore to tribal ownership the remaining surplus lands of any Indian reservation heretofore opened, or authorized to be opened, to sale, or any other form of disposal by Presidential proclamation, or by any of the public land laws of the United States; Provided, however, That valid rights or claims of any persons to any lands so withdrawn existing on the date of the withdrawal shall not be affected by this Act: Provided further, That this section shall not apply to lands within any reclamation project heretofore authorized in any Indian reservation: Provided further, That the order of the Department of the interior signed, dated, and approved by Honorable Ray Lyman Wilbur, as Secretary of the Interior, on October 28, 1932, temporarily withdrawing lands of the Papago Indian Reservation in Arizona from all forms of mineral entry or claim under the public land mining laws is hereby revoked and rescinded, and the lands of the said Papago Indian Reservation are hereby restored to exploration and location, under the existing mining laws of the United States, in accordance with the express terms and provisions declared and set forth in the Executive orders establishing said Papago Indian Reservation: Provided further, That the damages shall be paid to the Papago Tribe for loss of any improvements of any land located for mining in such a sum as may be determined by the Secretary of the Interior but not exceed the cost of said improvements: Provided further, That a yearly rental not to exceed five cents per acre shall be paid to the Papago Indian Tribe: Provided further, That in the event that any person or persons, partnership, corporation, or association, desires a mineral patent, according to the mining laws of the United States, he or they shall first deposit in the treasury of the United States to the credit of the Papago Tribe the sum of $1.00 per acre in lieu of annual rental, as hereinbefore provided, to compensate for the loss or occupancy of the lands withdrawn by the requirements of mining operations: Provided further, That patentee shall also pay into the Treasury of the United States to the credit of the Papago Tribe damages for the loss of improvements not heretofore said in such a sum as may be determined by the Secretary of the Interior, but not to exceed the cost thereof; the payment of $1.00 per acre for surface use to be refunded to patentee in the event that the patent is not required.

Nothing herein contained shall restrict the granting or use of permits for easements or rights-of-way; or ingress or egress over the lands for all proper and lawful purposes; and nothing contained therein, except as expressly provided, shall be construed as authority by the Secretary of the Interior, or any other person, to issue or promulgate a rule or regulation in conflict with the Executive order of February 1, 1917, creating the Papago Indian Reservation in Arizona or the Act of February 21, 1931 (46 Stat. 1202).

Sec. 4. Except as herein provided, no sale, devise, gift, exchange or other transfer of restricted Indian lands or of shares in the assets of any Indian tribe or corporation organized hereunder, shall be made or approved: Provided, however, That such lands or interests may, with the approval of the Secretary of the Interior, be sold, devised, or otherwise transferred to the Indian tribe in which the lands or shares are located or from which the shares were derived or to a successor corporation; and in all instances such lands or interests shall descend or be devised, in accordance with the then existing laws of the State, or Federal laws where applicable, in which said lands are located or in which the subject matter of the corporation is located, to any member of such tribe or of such corporation or any heirs of such member: Provided further, That the Secretary of the Interior may authorize voluntary exchanges of lands of equal value and the voluntary exchange of shares of equal value whenever such exchange, in his judgement, is expedient and beneficial for or compatible with the proper consolidation of Indian lands and for the benefit of cooperative organizations.

Sec. 5. The Secretary of the Interior is hereby authorized, in his discretion, to acquire through purchase, relinquishment, gift, exchange, or assignment, any interest in lands, water rights or surface rights to lands, within or without existing reservations, including trust or otherwise restricted allotments whether the allottee be living or deceased, for the purpose of providing lands for Indians.

For the acquisition of such lands, interests in lands, water rights, and surface rights, and for expenses incident to such acquisition, there is hereby authorized to be appropriated, out of any funds in the Treasury not otherwise appropriated, a sum not to exceed $2,000,000 in any one fiscal year: Provided, That no part of such funds shall be used to acquire additional land outside of the exterior boundaries of Navajo Indian Reservation for the Navajo Indians in Arizona and New Mexico, in the event that the proposed Navajo boundary extension measures now pending in congress and embodied in the bills (S. 2531 and H.R. 8927) to define the exterior boundaries of the Navajo Indian Reservation in Arizona, and for other purposes, and the bills (S. 2531 and H.R. 8982) to define the exterior boundaries of the Navajo Indian Reservation in New Mexico and for other purposes, or similar legislation, become law.

The unexpended balances of any appropriations made pursuant to this section shall remain available until expended.

Title to any lands or rights acquired pursuant to this Act shall be taken in the name of the United States in trust for the Indian tribe or individual Indian for which the land is acquired, and such lands or rights shall be exempt from State and local taxation.

Sec. 6. The Secretary of the Interior is directed to make rules and regulations for the operation and management of Indian forestry units on the principle of sustained-yield management, to restrict the number of livestock grazed on Indian range units to the estimated carrying capacity of such ranges, and to promulgate such other rules and regulations as may be necessary to protect the range from deterioration, to prevent soil erosion, to assure full utilization of the range, and like purposes.

Sec. 7. The Secretary of the Interior is hereby authorized to proclaim new Indian reservations on lands acquired pursuant to any authority conferred by this Act, or to add such lands to existing reservations: Provided, That lands added to existing reservations shall be designated for the exclusive use of Indians entitled by enrollment or by tribal membership to residence at such reservations.

Sec. 8. Nothing contained in this Act shall be construed to relate to Indian holdings of allotments or homesteads upon the public domain outside of the geographic boundaries of any Indian reservation now existing or established hereafter.

Sec. 9. There is hereby authorized to be appropriated, out of any funds in the Treasury not otherwise appropriated, such sums as may be necessary, but not to exceed $250,000 in any fiscal year, to be expended at the order of the Secretary of the Interior, in defraying the expenses of organizing Indian chartered corporations or other organizations created under this Act.

Sec. 10. There is hereby authorized to be appropriated, out of any funds in the Treasury not otherwise appropriated, the sum of $10,000,000 to be established as a revolving fund from which the Secretary of the Interior, under such rules and regulations as he may prescribe, may make loans to Indian chartered corporations for the purpose of promoting the economic development of such tribes and of their members, and may defray the expenses of administering such loans. Repayment of amounts loaned under this authorization shall be credited to the revolving fund and shall be available for the purposes for which the fund is established. A report shall be made annually to Congress of transactions under this authorization.

Sec. 11. There is hereby authorized to be appropriated, out of any funds in the United States Treasury not otherwise appropriated, a sum not to exceed $250,000 annually, together with any unexpended balances of previous appropriations made pursuant to this section, for loans to Indians for the payment of tuition and other expenses in recognized vocational and trade schools: Provided, That not more than $50,000 of such sum shall be available for loans to Indian students in high schools and colleges. Such loans shall be reimbursable under rules established by the Commissioner of Indian Affairs.

Sec. 12. The Secretary of the Interior is directed to establish standards of health, age, character, experience, knowledge, and ability for Indians who may be appointed, without regard to civil-service laws, to the various positions maintained, now or hereafter, by the Indian office, in the administrative functions or services affecting any Indian tribe. Such qualified Indians shall hereafter have the preference to appointment to vacancies in any such positions.

Sec. 13. The provisions of this Act shall not apply to any of the Territories, colonies, or insular possessions of the United States, except that sections 9, 10, 11, 12, and 16 shall apply to the Territory of Alaska: Provided, That Sections 2, 4, 7, 16, 17, and 18 of this Act shall not apply to the following named Indian tribes, together with members of other tribes affiliated with such named located in the State of Oklahoma, as follows: Cheyenne, Arapaho, Apache, Comanche, Kiowa, Caddo, Delaware, Wichita, Osage, Kaw, Otoe, Tonkawa, Pawnee, Ponca, Shawnee, Ottawa, Quapaw, Seneca, Wyandotte, Iowa, Sac and Fox, Kickapoo, Pottawatomi, Cherokee, Chickasaw, Choctaw, Creek, and Seminole. Section 4 of this Act shall not apply to the Indians of the Klamath Reservation in Oregon.

Sec. 14. The Secretary of the Interior is hereby directed to continue the allowance of the articles enumerated in section 17 of the Act of March 2, 1889 (25 Stat. L. 891), or their commuted cash value under the Act of June 10, 1886 (29 Stat. L. 334), to all Sioux Indians who would be eligible, but for the provisions of this Act, to receive allotments of lands in severalty under section 19 of the Act of May 29, 1908 (25 (35) Stat. L. 451), or under any prior Act, and who have the prescribed status of the head of a family or single person over the age of eighteen years, and his approval shall be final and conclusive, claims therefor to be paid as formerly from the permanent appropriation made by said section 17 and carried on the books of the Treasury for this purpose. No person shall receive in his own right more than one allowance of the benefits, and application must be made and approved during the lifetime of the allottee or the right shall lapse. Such benefits shall continue to be paid upon such reservation until such time as the lands available therein for allotment at the time of the passage of this Act would have been exhausted by the award to each person receiving such benefits of an allotment of eighty acres of such land.

Sec. 15. Nothing in this Act shall be construed to impair or prejudice any claim or suit of any Indian tribe against the United States. It is hereby declared to be the intent of Congress that no expenditures for the benefit of Indians made out of appropriations authorized by this Act shall be considered as offsets in any suit brought to recover upon any claim of such Indians against the United States.

Sec. 16. Any Indian tribe, or tribes, residing on the same reservation, shall have the right to organize for its common welfare, and may adopt an appropriate constitution and bylaws, which shall become effective when ratified by a majority vote of the adult members of the tribe, or of the adult Indians residing on such reservation, as the case may be, at a special election authorized by the Secretary of the Interior under such rules and regulations as he may prescribe. Such constitution and bylaws when ratified as aforesaid and approved by the Secretary of the Interior shall be revocable by an election open to the same voters and conducted in the same manner as hereinabove provided. Amendments to the constitution and bylaws may be ratified and approved by the Secretary in the same manner as the original constitution and bylaws.

In addition to all powers vested in any Indian tribe or tribal council by existing law, the constitution adopted by said tribe shall also vest in such tribe or its tribal council the following rights and powers: To employ legal counsel, the choice of counsel and fixing of fees to be subject to the approval of the Secretary of the Interior; to prevent the sale, disposition, lease, or encumbrance of tribal lands, interests in lands, or other tribal assets without the consent of the tribe; and to negotiate with the Federal, State, and local Governments. The Secretary of the Interior shall advise such tribe or its tribal council of all appropriation estimates or Federal projects for the benefit of the tribe prior to the submission of such estimates to the Bureau of the Budget and the Congress.

Sec. 17. The Secretary of the Interior may, upon petition by at least one-third of the adult Indians, issue a charter of incorporation to such tribe: Provided, That such charter shall not become operative until ratified at a special election by a majority vote of the adult Indians living on the reservation. Such charter may convey to the incorporated tribe the power to purchase, take by gift, or bequest, or otherwise, own, hold, manage, operate, and dispose of property of every description, real and personal, including the power to purchase restricted Indian lands and to issue in exchange therefor interests in corporate property, and such further powers as may be incidental to the conduct of corporate business, not inconsistent with law, but no authority shall be granted to sell, mortgage, or lease for a period exceeding ten years any of the land included in the limits of the reservation. Any charter so issued shall not be revoked or surrendered except by Act of Congress.

Sec. 18. This Act shall not apply to any reservation wherein a majority of the adult Indians, voting at a special election duly called by the Secretary of the Interior, shall vote against its application. It shall be the duty of the Secretary of the Interior, within one year after the passage and approval of this Act, to call such an election, which election shall be held by secret ballot upon thirty days' notice.

Sec. 19. The term "Indian" as used in this Act shall include all persons of Indian descent who are members of any recognized Indian tribe now under Federal jurisdiction, and all persons who are descendants of such members who were, on June 1, 1934, residing within the present boundaries of any reservation, and shall further include all other persons of one-half or more Indian blood. For the purposes of this Act, Eskimos and other aboriginal peoples of Alaska shall be considered Indians. The term "tribe" wherever used in this Act shall be construed to refer to any Indian tribe, organized band, pueblo, or the Indians residing on one reservation. The words "adult Indians" wherever used in this Act shall be construed to refer to Indians who have attained the age of twenty-one years.

Approved, June 18, 1934.

Amendments to the Wheeler-Howard Act (Indian Reorganization Act), June 18, 1934

Section 15 of the Indian Reorganization Act was modified in part by the following provisions contained in the Act of August 12, 1935 (Public Law 260—74th Congress, 1st Session):

Sec. 2. In all suits now pending in the Court of claims by an Indian tribe or band which have not been tried or submitted, and in any suit hereafter filed in the Court of Claims by any such tribe or band, the Court of Claims is hereby directed to consider and to offset against any amount found due the said tribe or band all sums expended gratuitously by the United States for the benefit of the said tribe or band; and in all cases now pending or hereafter filed in the Court of Claims in which an Indian tribe or band is party plaintiff, wherein the duty of the court is merely to report its finding of fact and conclusions to Congress, the said Court of Claims is hereby directed to include in its report a statement of the amount of money which has been expended by the United States gratuitously for the benefit of the said tribe or band: Provided, that the expenditures made prior to the date of the law, treaty, agreement, or Executive order under which the claims asserted; and expenditures under the Act of June 18, 1934 (48 Stat. L. 984), except expenditures under appropriations made pursuant to section 5 of such Act, shall not be charged as offsets against any claim on behalf of an Indian tribe or tribes now pending in the Court of Claims or hereafter filed.

Sec. 19. The term "Indian" as used in this Act shall include all persons of Indian descent who are members of any recognized Indian tribe now under Federal jurisdiction, and all persons who are descendants of such members who were, on June 1, 1934, residing within the present boundaries of any Indian reservation, and shall further include all other persons of one-half or more Indian blood. For the purposes of this Act, Eskimos and other aboriginal peoples of Alaska shall be considered Indians. The term "tribe" wherever used in this Act shall be construed to refer to any Indian tribe, organized band, pueblo, or the Indians residing on one reservation. The words "adult Indians" wherever used in this Act shall be construed to refer to Indians who have attained the age of twenty-one years.

Source: Indian Reorganization Act, U.S. Code 25, §§ 461 et seq.

165. Lyndon Johnson, Message to Congress on Indian Self-Determination, March 6, 1968

Introduction

President Lyndon B. Johnson, in keeping with his overall domestic policy regarding minority groups, sought to make American Indians full and equal participants in American society. The following is an excerpt from his "Special Message to Congress on the Problems of the American Indian: 'The Forgotten American.'" Johnson sought to discard the model of a paternalistic government providing services to be passively accepted by Indians and replace it with Indian self-determination and self-help in partnership with the government. He asked Congress to appropriate $500 million for Indian programs and established a centralized council to coordinate Indian programs scattered among various departments, including the Department of the Interior, the Department of Agriculture, the Commerce Department, the Labor Department, the Department of Housing, and the Department of Health, Education, and Welfare. Johnson hoped to develop Indian leadership and tribal self-government, raise the standard of living, and promote freedom of choice, whether the choice was to remain on a reservation or live and work elsewhere. He was the first U.S. president to articulate the concept of Indian self-determination, a major change of direction that has remained the keystone of federal Indian policy. In the ensuing decades, tribal governments have taken over programs formerly operated by the Bureau of Indian Affairs.

Primary Source

To the Congress of the United States:

Mississippi and Utah—the Potomac and the Chattahoochee—Appalachia and Shenandoah . . . The words of the Indian have become our words—the names of our states and streams and landmarks.

His myths and his heroes enrich our literature. His lore colors our art and our language. For two centuries, the American Indian has been a symbol of the drama and excitement of the earliest America.

But for two centuries, he has been an alien in his own land.

Relations between the United States Government and the tribes were originally in the hands of the War Department. Until 1871, the United States treated the Indian tribes as foreign nations.

It has been only 44 years since the United States affirmed the Indian's citizenship: the full political equality essential for human dignity in a democratic society.

It has been only 22 years since Congress enacted the Indian Claims Act, to acknowledge the Nation's debt to the first Americans for their land.

But political equality and compensation for ancestral lands are not enough. The American Indian deserves a chance to develop his talents and share fully in the future of our Nation.

There are about 600,000 Indians in America today. Some 400,000 live on or near reservations in 25 States. The remaining 200,000 have moved to our cities and towns. The most striking fact about the American Indians today is their tragic plight:

—Fifty thousand Indian families live in unsanitary, dilapidated dwellings: many in huts, shanties, even abandoned automobiles.

—The unemployment rate among Indians is nearly 40 percent—more than ten times the national average.

—Fifty percent of Indian schoolchildren—double the national average—drop out before completing high school.

—Indian literacy rates are among the lowest in the Nation; the rates of sickness and poverty are among the highest.

—Thousands of Indians who have migrated into the cities find themselves untrained for jobs and unprepared for urban life.

—The average age of death of an American Indian today is 44 years; for all other Americans, it is 65.

The American Indian, once proud and free, is torn now between white and tribal values; between the politics and language of the white man and his own historic culture. His problems, sharpened by years of defeat and exploitation, neglect and inadequate effort, will take many years to overcome.

But recent landmark laws—the Economic Opportunity Act, the Elementary and Secondary Education Act, the Manpower Development and Training Act—have given us an opportunity to deal with the persistent problems of the American Indian. The time has come to focus our efforts on the plight of the American Indian through these and the other laws passed in the last few years.

No enlightened Nation, no responsible government, no progressive people can sit idly by and permit this shocking situation to continue.

I propose a new goal for our Indian programs: A goal that ends the old debate about "termination" of Indian programs and stresses self-determination; a goal that erases old attitudes of paternalism and promotes partnership self-help.

Our goal must be:

—A standard of living for the Indians equal to that of the country as a whole.
—Freedom of Choice: An opportunity to remain in their homelands, if they choose, without surrendering their dignity; an opportunity to move to the towns and cities of America, if they choose, equipped with the skills to live in equality and dignity.
—Full participation in the life of modern America, with a full share of economic opportunity and social justice.

I propose, in short, a policy of maximum choice for the American Indian: a policy expressed in programs of self-help, self-development, self-determination.

To start toward our goal in Fiscal 1969, I recommend that the Congress appropriate one-half a billion dollars for programs targeted at the American Indian—about 10 percent more than Fiscal 1968.

Strengthened Federal Leadership

In the past four years, with the advent of major new programs, several agencies have undertaken independent efforts to help the American Indian. Too often, there has been too little coordination between agencies; and no clear, unified policy which applied to all.

To launch an undivided, Government-wide effort in this area, I am today issuing an Executive Order to establish a National Council on Indian Opportunity.[1]

The Chairman of the Council will be the Vice President who will bring the problems of the Indians to the highest levels of Government. The Council will include a cross section of Indian leaders, and high government officials who have programs in this field:

—The Secretary of the Interior, who has primary responsibility for Indian Affairs.
—The Secretary of Agriculture, whose programs affect thousands of Indians.
—The Secretary of Commerce, who can help promote economic development of Indian lands.

—The Secretary of Labor, whose manpower programs can train more Indians for more useful employment.
—The Secretary of Health, Education, and Welfare, who can help Indian communities with two of their most pressing needs—health and education.
—The Secretary of Housing and Urban Development, who can bring better housing to Indian lands.
—The Director of the Office of Economic Opportunity, whose programs are already operating in several Indian communities.

The Council will review Federal programs for Indians, make broad policy recommendations, and ensure that programs reflect the needs and desires of the Indian people. Most important, I have asked the Vice President, as Chairman of the Council, to make certain that the American Indian shares fully in all our federal programs.

Self-Help and Self-Determination

The greatest hope for Indian progress lies in the emergence of Indian leadership and initiative in solving Indian problems. Indians must have a voice in making the plans and decisions in programs which are important to their daily life.

Within the last few months we have seen a new concept of community development—a concept based on self-help—work successfully among Indians. Many tribes have begun to administer activities which Federal agencies had long performed in their behalf:

—On the Crow Creek, Lower Brule, and Fort Berthold reservations in the Dakotas and on reservations in several other states, imaginative new work-experience programs, operated by Indians themselves, provide jobs for Indians once totally dependent on welfare.
—The Warm Springs Tribes of Oregon ran an extensive program to repair flood damage on their reservation.
—The Oglala Sioux of South Dakota and the Zunis of New Mexico are now contracting to provide law enforcement services for their communities.
—The Navajos—who this year celebrate the 100th anniversary of their peace treaty with the United States—furnish many community services normally provided by the Federal government, either through contract or with funds from their own Treasury.

Passive acceptance of Federal service is giving way to Indian involvement. More than ever before, Indian needs are being identified from the Indian viewpoint—as they should be.

This principle is the key to progress for Indians—just as it has been for other Americans. If we base our programs upon it, the day will come when the relationship between Indians and the Government will be one of full partnership—not dependency.

Education

The problems of Indian education are legion:

—Ten percent of American Indians over age 14 have had no schooling at all.

—Nearly 60 percent have less than an eighth grade education.

—Half of our Indian children do not finish high school today.

—Even those Indians attending school are plagued by language barriers, by isolation in remote areas, by lack of a tradition of academic achievement.

Standard schooling and vocational training will not be enough to overcome the educational difficulties of the Indians. More intensive and imaginative approaches are needed.

The legislation enacted in the past four years gives us the means to make the special effort now needed in Indian education: The Elementary and Secondary Education Act, the Education Professions Development Act, the Vocational Education Act, and the Higher Education Act.

The challenge is to use this legislation creatively.

I have directed the Secretary of the Interior and the Secretary of Health, Education, and Welfare:

—To work together to make these programs responsive to the needs of Indians.

—To develop a concentrated effort in Indian education with State and local agencies. This is critical if the two-thirds of Indian schoolchildren in non-Indian public schools are to get the special help they sorely need.

Pre-School Programs

In the past few years we as a Nation have come to recognize the irreplaceable importance of the earliest years in a child's life. Preschool education and care—valuable for all children—are urgently needed for Indian children.

We must set a goal to enroll every four and five-year-old Indian child in a pre-school program by 1971.

For 1969, I am requesting funds to:

—Make the Head Start Program available to 10,000 Indian children.

—Establish, for the first time, kindergartens for 4,500 Indian youngsters next September.

To encourage Indian involvement in this educational process, I am asking the Secretary of the Interior to assure that each of these kindergartens employ local Indian teacher aides as well as trained teachers.

Federal Indian Schools

Since 1961, we have undertaken a substantial program to improve the 245 Federal Indian schools, which are attended by over 50,000 children. That effort is now half completed. It will continue.

But good facilities are not enough.

I am asking the Secretary of the Interior, in cooperation with the Secretary of Health, Education, and Welfare, to establish a model community school system for Indians. These schools will:

—Have the finest teachers, familiar with Indian history, culture and language.

—Feature an enriched curriculum, special guidance and counseling programs, modern instruction materials, and a sound program to teach English as a second language.

—Serve the local Indian population as a community center for activities ranging from adult education classes to social gatherings.

To reach this goal, I propose that the Congress appropriate $5.5 million to attract and hold talented and dedicated teachers at Indian schools and to provide 200 additional teachers and other professionals to enrich instruction, counseling and other programs.

To help make the Indian school a vital part of the Indian community, I am directing the Secretary of the Interior to establish Indian school boards for Federal Indian Schools. School board members—selected by their communities—will receive whatever training is necessary to enable them to carry out their responsibilities.

Higher Education

Indian youth must be given more opportunities to develop their talents fully and to pursue their ambitions free of arbitrary barriers to learning and employment. They must have a chance to become professionals: doctors, nurses, engineers, managers and teachers.

For the young Indian of today will eventually become the bridge between two cultures, two languages, and two ways of life.

Therefore, we must open wide the doors of career training and higher education to all Indian students who qualify.

To reach this goal:

—I am requesting $3 million in Fiscal 1969 for college scholarship grants, to include for the first time living allowances for Indian students and their families to help capable young Indians meet the costs of higher education.

—I am asking the Secretary of Health, Education, and Welfare to make a special and sustained effort to assure that our regular scholarship and loan programs are available to Indian high school graduates.

—I am asking the Director of the Office of Economic Opportunity to establish a special Upward Bound program for Indian high school students.

Health and Medical Care

The health level of the American Indian is the lowest of any major population group in the United States:

—The infant mortality rate among Indians is 34.5 per 1,000 births—12 points above the National average,

—The incidence of tuberculosis among Indians and Alaska natives is about five times the National average.

—More than half of the Indians obtain water from contaminated or potentially dangerous sources, and use waste disposal facilities that are grossly inadequate.

—Viral infections, pneumonia, and malnutrition—all of which contribute to chronic ill health and mental retardation—are common among Indian children.

We have made progress. Since 1963:

—The infant death rate has declined 21 percent.

—Deaths from tuberculosis are down 29 percent.

—The number of outpatient visits to clinics and health centers rose 16 percent. But much more remains to be done.

I propose that the Congress increase health programs for Indians by about ten percent, to $112 million in Fiscal 1969, with special emphasis on child health programs.

But if we are to solve Indian health problems, the Indian people themselves must improve their public health and family health practices. This will require a new effort to involve Indian families in a crusade for better health.

Recent experience demonstrates that Indians have been successful in working side by side with health professionals:

—They have organized tribal health committees to review Indian health problems and design programs for solving them.

—They have launched new programs in sanitation, mental health, alcoholism, and accident control.

—A cooperative Indian-government project to provide safe water and disposal systems for 44,000 Indians and Alaska native families has proved successful. For every Federal dollar spent, Indian Americans have contributed another 40 cents in labor, materials and actual funds.

I am directing the Secretary of Health, Education, and Welfare to build a "community participation" component into every Federal health program for Indians which lends itself to this approach.

Essential to this effort will be a large, well-trained corps of community health aides drawn from the Indian population: nursing assistants, health record clerks, medical-social aides and nutrition workers. These community health aides can greatly assist professional health workers in bringing health services to Indian communities.

I recommend that the Congress appropriate funds to train and employ more than 600 new community Indian health aides in the Public Health Service.

These aides will serve nearly 200,000 Indians and Alaska natives in their home communities, teaching sound health practices to the Indian people in several critical fields: pre-natal health, child care, home sanitation and personal hygiene.

Our goal is first to narrow, then to close the wide breach between the health standards of Indians and other Americans. But before large investments in Federally-sponsored health services can pay lasting dividends, we must build a solid base of Indian community action for better health.

Jobs and Economic Development

The plight of the Indians gives grim testimony to the devastating effects of unemployment on the individual, the family, and the community:

—Nearly 40 percent of the labor force on Indian lands is chronically unemployed, compared with a national unemployment rate of 3.5 percent.

—Of the Indians who do work, a third are underemployed in temporary or seasonal jobs.

—Fifty percent of Indian families have cash incomes below $2,000 a year; 75 percent have incomes below $3,000.

With rare exception, Indian communities are so underdeveloped that there is little, if any, opportunity for significant social or economic progress.

Two percent of all the land in the United States is Indian land. Indian lands are about the size of all the New England States and a small slice of New York. But many of their resources—oil, gas, coal, uranium, timber, water—await development.

The economic ills of Indian areas can have a major impact upon neighboring regions as well. It is not only in the best interests of the Indians, but of the entire Nation, to expand Indian economic opportunity.

Jobs

Special employment programs have been established to help meet the needs of Indians. In 1967 alone, more than 10,000 men and women received training and other help to get jobs under the Indian Bureau's programs—double the number served four years ago. These programs:

—Provide all-expenses-paid training and placement for Indian adults.

—Develop projects in cooperation with private industry, in which families prepare together for the transition from welfare dependency to useful, productive work.

To meet the increasing demand, I propose that the Indian Vocational Training Program be expanded to the full authorization of $25 million in Fiscal 1969—nearly double the funds appropriated last year.

In the State of the Union message, I proposed a 25 percent increase—to $2.1 billion—in our manpower training programs for Fiscal 1969.

As a part of this effort, I have asked the Secretary of Labor to expand the Concentrated Employment Program to include Indian reservations.

Area Development

The economic development of potentially productive Indian areas suffers from a lack of base capital to permit Indians to take advantage of sound investment opportunities and to attract private capital.

The Indian Resources Development Act, now pending before Congress, contains provisions to spark this kind of investment.

The central feature of this Act is an authorization of $500 million for an Indian loan guaranty and insurance fund and for a direct loan revolving fund. These funds would:

—Provide the foundation for the economic development of Indian lands.
—Encourage light industry to locate on or near Indian reservations.
—Permit better development of natural resources.
—Encourage development of the tourist potential on many reservations.

The Indian Resources Development Act would also permit the issuance of Federal corporate charters to Indian tribes or groups of Indians. This charter gives them the means to compete with other communities in attracting outside investment.

I urge the Congress to enact this program for the economic development of Indian resources.

Roads for Economic Development

Without an adequate system of roads to link Indian areas with the rest of our Nation, community and economic development, Indian self-help programs, and even education cannot go forward as rapidly as they should.

Large areas inhabited by Indians are virtually inaccessible. For example, on the vast Navajo-Hopi area there are only 30 percent as many miles of surfaced roads per 1,000 square miles as in rural areas of Arizona and New Mexico.

The woefully inadequate road systems in Indian areas must be improved. Good roads are desperately needed for economic development. And good roads may someday enable the Indian people to keep their young children at home, instead of having to send them to far-away boarding schools.

I propose an amendment to the Federal Highway Act increasing the authorization for Indian road construction to $30 million annually beginning in Fiscal 1970.

Essential Community Services

Housing

Most Indian housing is far worse than the housing in many slums of our large cities.

To begin our attack on the backlog of substandard housing:

—I have asked the Secretary of Housing and Urban Development to increase Indian home construction by an additional 1,000 units this coming year, for a total of 2,500 annually.
—I propose that the Congress double the Fiscal 1968 appropriations—to $6 million in 1969—for a broad home improvement program.

These steps are a strong start toward improving living conditions among Indians, while we deal with the underlying causes of inadequate housing. But the present housing law is too rigid to meet the special needs and conditions of our Indian population.

I am therefore submitting legislation to open the door for more Indians to receive low-cost housing aid, and to extend the loan programs of the Farmers Home Administration to tribal lands. In addition:

—The Secretary of Housing and Urban Development will review construction standards for Indian homes to ensure flexibility in design and construction of Indian housing.
—The Secretaries of the Interior and Housing and Urban Development will explore new low-cost techniques of construction suitable to a stepped-up Indian housing program.

Community Action

Programs under the Economic Opportunity Act have improved morale in Indian communities. They have given tribes new opportunities to plan and carry out social and economic projects. Community action programs, particularly Head Start, deserve strong support.

I am asking the Congress to provide $22.7 million in Fiscal 1969 for these important efforts.

Water and Sewer Projects

Shorter life expectancy and higher infant mortality among Indians are caused in large part by unsanitary water supplies and contamination from unsafe waste disposal.

The Federal Government has authority to join with individual Indians to construct these facilities on Indian lands. The government contributes the capital. The Indian contributes the labor.

To step up this program, I recommend that the Congress increase appropriations for safe water and sanitary waste disposal facilities by 30 percent—from $10 million in Fiscal 1968 to $13 million in Fiscal 1969.

Civil Rights

A Bill of Rights for Indians

In 1934, Congress passed the Indian Reorganization Act, which laid the groundwork for democratic self-government on Indian reservations. This Act was the forerunner of the tribal constitutions—the charters of democratic practice among the Indians.

Yet few tribal constitutions include a bill of rights for individual Indians. The basic individual rights which most Americans enjoy in relation to their government—enshrined in the Bill of Rights of the Constitution of the United States—are not safeguarded for Indians in relation to their tribes.

A new Indian Rights Bill is pending in the Congress. It would protect the individual rights of Indians in such matters as freedom of speech and religion, unreasonable search and seizure, a speedy and fair trial, and the right to habeas corpus. The Senate passed an Indian Bill of Rights last year. I urge the Congress to complete action on that Bill of Rights in the current session.

In addition to providing new protection for members of tribes, this bill would remedy another matter of grave concern to the American Indian.

Fifteen years ago, the Congress gave to the States authority to extend their criminal and civil jurisdictions to include Indian reservations—where jurisdiction previously was in the hands of the Indians themselves.

Fairness and basic democratic principles require that Indians on the affected lands have a voice in deciding whether a State will assume legal jurisdiction on their land.

I urge the Congress to enact legislation that would provide for tribal consent before such extensions of jurisdiction take place.

Off-Reservation Indians

Most of us think of Indians as living in their own communities—geographically, socially and psychologically remote from the main current of American life.

Until World War II, this was an accurate picture of most Indian people. Since that time, however, the number of Indians living in towns and urban centers has increased to 200,000.

Indians in the towns and cities of our country have urgent needs for education, health, welfare, and rehabilitation services, which are far greater than that of the general population.

These needs can be met through Federal, State and local programs. I am asking the new Council on Indian Opportunity to study this problem and report to me promptly on actions to meet the needs of Indians in our cities and towns.

Alaskan Native Claims

The land rights of the native people of Alaska—the Aleuts, Eskimos and Indians—have never been fully or fairly defined.

Eighty-four years ago, Congress protected the Alaska natives in the use and occupancy of their lands. But then, and again when Alaska was given statehood, Congress reserved to itself the power of final decision on ultimate title.

It remains our unfinished task to state in law the terms and conditions of settlement, so that uncertainty can be ended for the native people of Alaska.

Legislation is now pending to resolve this issue. I recommend prompt action on legislation to:

—Give the native people of Alaska title to the lands they occupy and need to sustain their villages.
—Give them rights to use additional lands and water for hunting, trapping and fishing to maintain their traditional way of life, if they so choose.
—Award them compensation commensurate with the value of any lands taken from them.

The First Americans

The program I propose seeks to promote Indian development by improving health and education, encouraging long-term economic growth, and strengthening community institutions.

Underlying this program is the assumption that the Federal government can best be a responsible partner in Indian progress by treating the Indian himself as a full citizen, responsible for the pace and direction of his development.

But there can be no question that the government and the people of the United States have a responsibility to the Indians.

In our efforts to meet that responsibility, we must pledge to respect fully the dignity and the uniqueness of the Indian citizen.

That means partnership—not paternalism.

We must affirm the right of the first Americans to remain Indians while exercising their rights as Americans.

We must affirm their right to freedom of choice and self-determination.

We must seek new ways to provide Federal assistance to Indians—with new emphasis on Indian self-help and with respect for Indian culture.

And we must assure the Indian people that it is our desire and intention that the special relationship between the Indian and his government grow and flourish. For, the first among us must not be last.

I urge the Congress to affirm this policy and to enact this program.

LYNDON B. JOHNSON
The White House
March 6, 1968

[1] Executive Order 11399 "Establishing the National Council on Indian Opportunity" is printed in the Weekly Compilation of Presidential Documents, the Federal Register, and the Code of Federal Regulations (4 Weekly Comp. Pres. Docs., p. 448; 33 F.R. 4245; 3 CFR, 1968 Comp. p. 105).

Source: Lyndon B. Johnson, *Public Papers of the Presidents of the United State: Lyndon B. Johnson, 1968–69,* Vol. 1 (Washington, DC: U.S. Government Printing Office, 1970), 336–337, 143–144.

166. Bureau of Indian Affairs, Procedures for Establishing the Existence of an Indian Tribe, October 2, 1978

Introduction

The oldest bureau in the federal government, the Bureau of Indian Affairs (BIA) was originally established in 1824 as part of the War Department. In 1849 Congress created the Department of the Interior and transferred control of the BIA to the new department. The Interior Department has retained control of the BIA ever since, despite War Department attempts to resume control. Through a number of skillful administrators, the BIA had grown to one of the largest divisions of the federal government by the turn of the 20th century. The BIA's main mission is to protect the rights and land of Native Americans and to facilitate federal programs to assist the Native Americans while not infringing on the tribes' right to govern themselves. The BIA has had to balance the goal of Indian self-determination with that of promoting full participation in American society. Although the BIA has traditionally been managed and staffed by white employees, it has hired substantially more Native Americans since the 1970s. As the movement for Indian self-determination gained momentum through the second half of the 20th century, nonrecognized Indian groups have campaigned for official recognition as tribes. In response the BIA issued these guidelines for establishing tribal status that include eligibility for federal benefits, the right to self-government, and legal obligations.

Primary Source

Section 1. Definitions.

As used in this part:

Area Office means a Bureau of Indian Affairs Area Office.

Assistant Secretary means the Assistant Secretary—Indian Affairs, or that officer's authorized representative.

Autonomous means the exercise of political influence or authority independent of the control of any other Indian governing entity. Autonomous must be understood in the context of the history, geography, culture and social organization of the petitioning group.

Board means the Interior Board of Indian Appeals.

Bureau means the Bureau of Indian Affairs.

Community means any group of people which can demonstrate that consistent interactions and significant social relationships exist within its membership and that its members are differentiated from and identified as distinct from nonmembers. Community must be understood in the context of the history, geography, culture and social organization of the group.

Continental United States means the contiguous 48 states and Alaska.

Continuously or continuous means extending from first sustained contact with non-Indians throughout the group's history to the present substantially without interruption.

Department means the Department of the Interior.

Documented petition means the detailed arguments made by a petitioner to substantiate its claim to continuous existence as an Indian tribe, together with the factual exposition and all documentary evidence necessary to demonstrate that these arguments address the mandatory criteria in Section 7(a) through (g).

Historically, historical or history means dating from first sustained contact with non-Indians.

Indian group or group means any Indian or Alaska Native aggregation within the continental United States that the Secretary of the Interior does not acknowledge to be an Indian tribe.

Indian tribe, also referred to herein as tribe, means any Indian or Alaska Native tribe, band, pueblo, village, or community within the continental United States that the Secretary of the Interior presently acknowledges to exist as an Indian tribe.

Indigenous means native to the continental United States in that at least part of the petitioner's territory at the time of sustained contact extended into what is now the continental United States.

Informed party means any person or organization, other than an interested party, who requests an opportunity to submit comments or evidence or to be kept informed of general actions regarding a specific petitioner.

Interested party means any person, organization or other entity who can establish a legal, factual or property interest in an acknowledgment determination and who requests an opportunity to submit comments or evidence or to be kept informed of general actions regarding a specific petitioner. "Interested party" includes the governor and attorney general of the state in which a petitioner is located, and may include, but is not limited to, local governmental units, and any recognized Indian tribes and unrecognized Indian groups that might be affected by an acknowledgment determination.

Letter of intent means an undocumented letter or resolution by which an Indian group requests Federal acknowledgment as an Indian tribe and expresses its intent to submit a documented petition.

Member of an Indian group means an individual who is recognized by an Indian group as meeting its membership criteria and who consents to being listed as a member of that group.

Member of an Indian tribe means an individual who meets the membership requirements of the tribe as set forth in its governing document or, absent such a document, has been recognized as a member collectively by those persons comprising the tribal governing body, and has consistently maintained tribal relations with the tribe or is listed on the tribal rolls of that tribe as a member, if such rolls are kept.

Petitioner means any entity that has submitted a letter of intent to the Secretary requesting acknowledgment that it is an Indian tribe.

Political influence or authority means a tribal council, leadership, internal process or other mechanism which the group has used as a means of influencing or controlling the behavior of its members in significant respects, and/or making decisions for the group which substantially affect its members, and/or representing the group in dealing with outsiders in matters of consequence. This process is to be understood in the context of the history, culture and social organization of the group.

Previous Federal acknowledgment means action by the Federal government clearly premised on identification of a tribal political entity and indicating clearly the recognition of a relationship between that entity and the United States.

Secretary means the Secretary of the Interior or that officer's authorized representative.

Sustained contact means the period of earliest sustained non-Indian settlement and/or governmental presence in the local area in which the historical tribe or tribes from which the petitioner descends was located historically.

Tribal relations means participation by an individual in a political and social relationship with an Indian tribe.

Tribal roll, for purposes of these regulations, means a list exclusively of those individuals who have been determined by the tribe to meet the tribe's membership requirements as set forth in its governing document. In the absence of such a document, a tribal roll means a list of those recognized as members by the tribe's governing body. In either case, those individuals on a tribal roll must have affirmatively demonstrated consent to being listed as members.

Section 2. Purpose.

The purpose of this part is to establish a departmental procedure and policy for acknowledging that certain American Indian groups exist as tribes. Acknowledgment of tribal existence by the Department is a prerequisite to the protection, services, and benefits of the Federal government available to Indian tribes by virtue of their status as tribes. Acknowledgment shall also mean that the tribe is entitled to the immunities and privileges available to other federally acknowledged Indian tribes by virtue of their government-to-government relationship with the United States as well as the responsibilities, powers, limitations and obligations of such tribes. Acknowledgment shall subject the Indian tribe to the same authority of Congress and the United States to which other federally acknowledged tribes are subjected.

Section 3. Scope.

(a) This part applies only to those American Indian groups indigenous to the continental United States which are not currently acknowledged as Indian tribes by the Department. It is intended to apply to groups that can establish a substantially continuous tribal existence and which have functioned as autonomous entities throughout history until the present.

(b) Indian tribes, organized bands, pueblos, Alaska Native villages, or communities which are already acknowledged as such and are receiving services from the Bureau of Indian Affairs may not be reviewed under the procedures established by these regulations.

(c) Associations, organizations, corporations or groups of any character that have been formed in recent times may not be acknowledged under these regulations. The fact that a group that meets the criteria in Section 7 (a) through (g) has recently incorporated or otherwise formalized its existing autonomous political process will be viewed as a change in form and have no bearing on the Assistant Secretary's final decision.

(d) Splinter groups, political factions, communities or groups of any character that separate from the main body of a currently acknowledged tribe may not be acknowledged under these regulations. However, groups that can establish clearly that they have functioned throughout history until the present as an autonomous tribal entity may be acknowledged under this part, even though they have been regarded by some as part of or have been associated in some manner with an acknowledged North American Indian tribe.

(e) Further, groups which are, or the members of which are, subject to congressional legislation terminating or forbidding the Federal relationship may not be acknowledged under this part.

(f) Finally, groups that previously petitioned and were denied Federal acknowledgment under these regulations or under previous regulations in Part of this title, may not be acknowledged under these regulations. This includes reorganized or reconstituted petitioners previously denied, or splinter groups, spin-offs, or component groups of any type that were once part of petitioners previously denied.

(g) Indian groups whose documented petitions are under active consideration at the effective date of these revised regulations may choose to complete their petitioning process either under these regulations or under the previous acknowledgment regulations in part of this title. This choice must be made by April 26, 1994. This option shall apply to any petition for which a determination is not final and effective. Such petitioners may request a suspension of consideration under Section 10(g) of not more than 180 days in order to provide additional information or argument.

Section 4. Filing a letter of intent.

(a) Any Indian group in the continental United States that believes it should be acknowledged as an Indian tribe and that it can satisfy the criteria in Section 7 may submit a letter of intent.

(b) Letters of intent requesting acknowledgment that an Indian group exists as an Indian tribe shall be filed with the Assistant Secretary—Indian Affairs, Department of the Interior, 1849 C Street, NW., Washington, DC 20240. Attention: Branch of Acknowledgment and Research, Mail Stop 2611-MIB. A letter of intent may be filed in advance of, or at the same time as, a group's documented petition.

(c) A letter of intent must be produced, dated and signed by the governing body of an Indian group and submitted to the Assistant Secretary.

Section 5. Duties of the Department.

(a) The Department shall publish in the Federal Register, no less frequently than every three years, a list of all Indian tribes entitled to receive services from the Bureau by virtue of their status as Indian tribes. The list may be published more frequently, if the Assistant Secretary deems it necessary.

(b) The Assistant Secretary shall make available revised and expanded guidelines for the preparation of documented petitions by September 23, 1994. These guidelines will include an explanation of the criteria and other provisions of the regulations, a discussion of the types of evidence which may be used to demonstrate particular criteria or other provisions of the regulations, and general suggestions and guidelines on how and where to conduct research. The guidelines may be supplemented or updated as necessary. The Department's example of a documented petition format, while preferable, shall not preclude the use of any other format.

(c) The Department shall, upon request, provide petitioners with suggestions and advice regarding preparation of the documented petition. The Department shall not be responsible for the actual research on behalf of the petitioner.

(d) Any notice which by the terms of these regulations must be published in the Federal Register, shall also be mailed to the petitioner, the governor of the state where the group is located, and to other interested parties.

(e) After an Indian group has filed a letter of intent requesting Federal acknowledgment as an Indian tribe and until that group has actually submitted a documented petition, the Assistant Secretary may contact the group periodically and request clarification, in writing, of its intent to continue with the petitioning process.

(f) All petitioners under active consideration shall be notified, by April 16, 1994 of the opportunity under Section 3(g) to choose whether to complete their petitioning process under the provisions of these revised regulations or the previous regulations as published, on September 5, 1978, at 43 FR 39361.

(g) All other groups that have submitted documented petitions or letters of intent shall be notified of and provided with a copy of these regulations by July 25, 1994.

Section 6. General provisions for the documented petition.

(a) The documented petition may be in any readable form that contains detailed, specific evidence in support of a request to the Secretary to acknowledge tribal existence.

(b) The documented petition must include a certification, signed and dated by members of the group's governing body, stating that it is the group's official documented petition.

(c) A petitioner must satisfy all of the criteria in paragraphs (a) through (g) of Section 7 in order for tribal existence to be acknowledged. Therefore, the documented petition must include thorough explanations and supporting documentation in response to all of the criteria. The definitions in Section 1 are an integral part of the regulations, and the criteria should be read carefully together with these definitions.

(d) A petitioner may be denied acknowledgment if the evidence available demonstrates that it does not meet one or more criteria. A petitioner may also be denied if there is insufficient evidence that it meets one or more of the criteria. A criterion shall be considered met if the available evidence establishes a reasonable likelihood of the validity of the facts relating to that criterion. Conclusive proof of the facts relating to a criterion shall not be required in order for the criterion to be considered met.

(e) Evaluation of petitions shall take into account historical situations and time periods for which evidence is demonstrably limited or not available. The limitations inherent in demonstrating the historical existence of community and political influence or authority shall also be taken into account. Existence of community and political influence or authority shall be demonstrated on a substantially continuous basis, but this demonstration does not require meeting these criteria at every point in time. Fluctuations in tribal activity during various years shall not in themselves be a cause for denial of acknowledgment under these criteria.

(f) The criteria in Section 7 (a) through (g) shall be interpreted as applying to tribes or groups that have historically combined and functioned as a single autonomous political entity.

(g) The specific forms of evidence stated in the criteria in Section 7 (a) through (c) and Section 7(e) are not mandatory requirements. The criteria may be met alternatively by any suitable evidence that demonstrates that the petitioner meets the requirements of the criterion statement and related definitions.

Section 7. Mandatory criteria for Federal acknowledgment.

The mandatory criteria are:

(a) The petitioner has been identified as an American Indian entity on a substantially continuous basis since 1900. Evidence that the group's character as an Indian entity has from time to time been denied shall not be considered to be conclusive evidence that this criterion has not been met. Evidence to be relied upon in determining a group's Indian identity may include one or a combination of the following, as well as other evidence of identification by other than the petitioner itself or its members.

(1) Identification as an Indian entity by Federal authorities.

(2) Relationships with State governments based on identification of the group as Indian.

(3) Dealings with a county, parish, or other local government in a relationship based on the group's Indian identity.

(4) Identification as an Indian entity by anthropologists, historians, and/or other scholars.

(5) Identification as an Indian entity in newspapers and books.

(6) Identification as an Indian entity in relationships with Indian tribes or with national, regional, or state Indian organizations.

(b) A predominant portion of the petitioning group comprises a distinct community and has existed as a community from historical times until the present.

(1) This criterion may be demonstrated by some combination of the following evidence and/or other evidence that the petitioner meets the definition of community set forth in Section 1:

(i) Significant rates of marriage within the group, and/or, as may be culturally required, patterned out-marriages with other Indian populations.

(ii) Significant social relationships connecting individual members.

(iii) Significant rates of informal social interaction which exist broadly among the members of a group.

(iv) A significant degree of shared or cooperative labor or other economic activity among the membership.

(v) Evidence of strong patterns of discrimination or other social distinctions by non-members.

(vi) Shared sacred or secular ritual activity encompassing most of the group.

(vii) Cultural patterns shared among a significant portion of the group that are different from those of the non-Indian populations with whom it interacts. These patterns must function as more than a symbolic identification of the group as Indian. They may include, but are not limited to, language, kinship organization, or religious beliefs and practices.

(viii) The persistence of a named, collective Indian identity continuously over a period of more than 50 years, notwithstanding changes in name.

(ix) A demonstration of historical political influence under the criterion in Section 7(c) shall be evidence for demonstrating historical community.

(2) A petitioner shall be considered to have provided sufficient evidence of community at a given point in time if evidence is provided to demonstrate any one of the following:

(i) More than 50 percent of the members reside in a geographical area exclusively or almost exclusively composed of members of the group, and the balance of the group maintains consistent interaction with some members of the community;

(ii) At least 50 percent of the marriages in the group are between members of the group;

(iii) At least 50 percent of the group members maintain distinct cultural patterns such as, but not limited to, language, kinship organization, or religious beliefs and practices;

(iv) There are distinct community social institutions encompassing most of the members, such as kinship organizations, formal or informal economic cooperation, or religious organizations; or

(v) The group has met the criterion in Section 7(c) using evidence described in Section 7(c)(2).

(c) The petitioner has maintained political influence or authority over its members as an autonomous entity from historical times until the present.

(1) This criterion may be demonstrated by some combination of the evidence listed below and/or by other evidence that the petitioner meets the definition of political influence or authority in Section 1.

(i) The group is able to mobilize significant numbers of members and significant resources from its members for group purposes.

(ii) Most of the membership considers issues acted upon or actions taken by group leaders or governing bodies to be of importance.

(iii) There is widespread knowledge, communication and involvement in political processes by most of the group's members.

(iv) The group meets the criterion in Section 7(b) at more than a minimal level.

(v) There are internal conflicts which show controversy over valued group goals, properties, policies, processes and/or decisions.

(2) A petitioning group shall be considered to have provided sufficient evidence to demonstrate the exercise of political influence or authority at a given point in time by demonstrating that group leaders and/or other mechanisms exist or existed which:

(i) Allocate group resources such as land, residence rights and the like on a consistent basis.

(ii) Settle disputes between members or subgroups by mediation or other means on a regular basis;

(iii) Exert strong influence on the behavior of individual members, such as the establishment or maintenance of norms and the enforcement of sanctions to direct or control behavior;

(iv) Organize or influence economic subsistence activities among the members, including shared or cooperative labor.

(3) A group that has met the requirements in paragraph 83.7(b)(2) at a given point in time shall be considered to have provided sufficient evidence to meet this criterion at that point in time.

(d) A copy of the group's present governing document including its membership criteria. In the absence of a written document, the petitioner must provide a statement describing in full its membership criteria and current governing procedures.

(e) The petitioner's membership consists of individuals who descend from a historical Indian tribe or from historical Indian tribes which combined and functioned as a single autonomous political entity.

(1) Evidence acceptable to the Secretary which can be used for this purpose includes but is not limited to:

(i) Rolls prepared by the Secretary on a descendancy basis for purposes of distributing claims money, providing allotments, or other purposes;

(ii) State, Federal, or other official records or evidence identifying present members or ancestors of present members as being descendants of a historical tribe or tribes that combined and functioned as a single autonomous political entity.

(iii) Church, school, and other similar enrollment records identifying present members or ancestors of present members as being descendants of a historical tribe or tribes that combined and functioned as a single autonomous political entity.

(iv) Affidavits of recognition by tribal elders, leaders, or the tribal governing body identifying present members or ancestors of present members as being descendants of a historical tribe or tribes that combined and functioned as a single autonomous political entity.

(v) Other records or evidence identifying present members or ancestors of present members as being descendants of a historical tribe or tribes that combined and functioned as a single autonomous political entity.

(2) The petitioner must provide an official membership list, separately certified by the group's governing body, of all known current members of the group. This list must include each member's full name (including maiden name), date of birth, and current residential address. The petitioner must also provide a copy of each available former list of members based on the group's own defined criteria, as well as a statement describing the circumstances surrounding the preparation of the current list and, insofar as possible, the circumstances surrounding the preparation of former lists.

(f) The membership of the petitioning group is composed principally of persons who are not members of any acknowledged North American Indian tribe. However, under certain conditions a petitioning group may be acknowledged even if its membership is composed principally of persons whose names have appeared on rolls of, or who have been otherwise associated with, an acknowledged Indian tribe. The conditions are that the group must establish that it has functioned throughout history until the present as a separate and autonomous Indian tribal entity, that its members do not maintain a bilateral political relationship with the acknowledged tribe, and that its members have provided written confirmation of their membership in the petitioning group.

(g) Neither the petitioner nor its members are the subject of congressional legislation that has expressly terminated or forbidden the Federal relationship.

Section 8. Previous Federal acknowledgment.

(a) Unambiguous previous Federal acknowledgment is acceptable evidence of the tribal character of a petitioner to the date of the last such previous acknowledgment. If a petitioner provides substantial evidence of unambiguous Federal acknowledgment, the petitioner will then only be required to demonstrate that it meets the requirements of Section 7 to the extent required by this section.

(b) A determination of the adequacy of the evidence of previous Federal action acknowledging tribal status shall be made during the technical assistance review of the documented petition conducted pursuant to Section 10(b). If a petition is awaiting active consideration at the time of adoption of these regulations, this review will be conducted while the petition is under active consideration unless the petitioner requests in writing that this review be made in advance.

(c) Evidence to demonstrate previous Federal acknowledgment includes, but is not limited to:

(1) Evidence that the group has had treaty relations with the United States.

(2) Evidence that the group has been denominated a tribe by act of Congress or Executive Order.

(3) Evidence that the group has been treated by the Federal Government as having collective rights in tribal lands or funds.

(d) To be acknowledged, a petitioner that can demonstrate previous Federal acknowledgment must show that:

(1) The group meets the requirements of the criterion in Section 7(a), except that such identification shall be demonstrated since the point of last Federal acknowledgment. The group must further have been identified by such sources as the same tribal entity that was previously acknowledged or as a portion that has evolved from that entity.

(2) The group meets the requirements of the criterion in Section 7(b) to demonstrate that it comprises a distinct community at present. However, it need not provide evidence to demonstrate existence as a community historically.

(3) The group meets the requirements of the criterion in Section 7(c) to demonstrate that political influence or authority is

exercised within the group at present. Sufficient evidence to meet the criterion in Section 7(c) from the point of last Federal acknowledgment to the present may be provided by demonstration of substantially continuous historical identification, by authoritative, knowledgeable external sources, of leaders and/or a governing body who exercise political influence or authority, together with demonstration of one form of evidence listed in Section 7(c).

(4) The group meets the requirements of the criteria in paragraphs 83.7 (d) through (g).

(5) If a petitioner which has demonstrated previous Federal acknowledgment cannot meet the requirements in paragraphs (d) (1) and (3), the petitioner may demonstrate alternatively that it meets the requirements of the criteria in Section 7 (a) through (c) from last Federal acknowledgment until the present.

Section 9. Notice of receipt of a petition.

(a) Within 30 days after receiving a letter of intent, or a documented petition if a letter of intent has not previously been received and noticed, the Assistant Secretary shall acknowledge such receipt in writing and shall have published within 60 days in the Federal Register a notice of such receipt. This notice must include the name, location, and mailing address of the petitioner and such other information as will identify the entity submitting the letter of intent or documented petition and the date it was received. This notice shall also serve to announce the opportunity for interested parties and informed parties to submit factual or legal arguments in support of or in opposition to the petitioner's request for acknowledgment and/or to request to be kept informed of all general actions affecting the petition. The notice shall also indicate where a copy of the letter of intent and the documented petition may be examined.

(b) The Assistant Secretary shall notify, in writing, the governor and attorney general of the state in which a petitioner is located. The Assistant Secretary shall also notify any recognized tribe and any other petitioner which appears to have a historical or present relationship with the petitioner or which may otherwise be considered to have a potential interest in the acknowledgment determination.

(c) The Assistant Secretary shall also publish the notice of receipt of the letter of intent, or documented petition if a letter of intent has not been previously received, in a major newspaper or newspapers of general circulation in the town or city nearest to the petitioner. The notice will include all of the information in paragraph (a) of this section.

Section 10. Processing of the documented petition.

(a) Upon receipt of a documented petition, the Assistant Secretary shall cause a review to be conducted to determine whether the petitioner is entitled to be acknowledged as an Indian tribe. The review shall include consideration of the documented petition and the factual statements contained therein. The Assistant Secretary may also initiate other research for any purpose relative to analyzing the documented petition and obtaining additional information about the petitioner's status. The Assistant Secretary may likewise consider any evidence which may be submitted by interested parties or informed parties.

(b) Prior to active consideration of the documented petition, the Assistant Secretary shall conduct a preliminary review of the petition for purposes of technical assistance.

(1) This technical assistance review does not constitute the Assistant Secretary's review to determine if the petitioner is entitled to be acknowledged as an Indian tribe. It is a preliminary review for the purpose of providing the petitioner an opportunity to supplement or revise the documented petition prior to active consideration. Insofar as possible, technical assistance reviews under this paragraph will be conducted in the order of receipt of documented petitions. However, technical assistance reviews will not have priority over active consideration of documented petitions.

(2) After the technical assistance review, the Assistant Secretary shall notify the petitioner by letter of any obvious deficiencies or significant omissions apparent in the documented petition and provide the petitioner with an opportunity to withdraw the documented petition for further work or to submit additional information and/or clarification.

(3) If a petitioner's documented petition claims previous Federal acknowledgment and/or includes evidence of previous Federal acknowledgment, the technical assistance review will also include a review to determine whether that evidence is sufficient to meet the requirements of previous Federal acknowledgment as defined in Section 1.

(c) Petitioners have the option of responding in part or in full to the technical assistance review letter or of requesting, in writing, that the Assistant Secretary proceed with the active consideration of the documented petition using the materials already submitted.

(1) If the petitioner requests that the materials submitted in response to the technical assistance review letter be again reviewed for adequacy, the Assistant Secretary will provide the additional review. However, this additional review will not be automatic and will be conducted only at the request of the petitioner.

(2) If the assertion of previous Federal acknowledgment under Section 8 cannot be substantiated during the technical assistance review, the petitioner must respond by providing additional evidence. A petitioner claiming previous Federal acknowledgment who fails to respond to a technical assistance review letter under this paragraph, or whose response fails to establish the claim, shall have its documented petition considered on the same basis as documented petitions submitted by groups not claiming previous Federal acknowledgment. Petitioners that fail to demonstrate previous Federal acknowledgment after a review of materials submitted in response to the technical assistance review shall be so notified. Such petitioners may submit additional materials

concerning previous acknowledgment during the course of active consideration.

(d) The order of consideration of documented petitions shall be determined by the date of the Bureau's notification to the petitioner that it considers that the documented petition is ready to be placed on active consideration. The Assistant Secretary shall establish and maintain a numbered register of documented petitions which have been determined ready for active consideration. The Assistant Secretary shall also maintain a numbered register of letters of intent or incomplete petitions based on the original date of filing with the Bureau. In the event that two or more documented petitions are determined ready for active consideration on the same date, the register of letters of intent or incomplete petitions shall determine the order of consideration by the Assistant Secretary.

(e) Prior to active consideration, the Assistant Secretary shall investigate any petitioner whose documented petition and response to the technical assistance review letter indicates that there is little or no evidence that establishes that the group can meet the mandatory criteria in paragraphs (e), (f) or (g) of Section 7.

(1) If this review finds that the evidence clearly establishes that the group does not meet the mandatory criteria in paragraphs (e), (f) or (g) of Section 7, a full consideration of the documented petition under all seven of the mandatory criteria will not be undertaken pursuant to paragraph (a) of this section. Rather, the Assistant Secretary shall instead decline to acknowledge that the petitioner is an Indian tribe and publish a proposed finding to that effect in the Federal Register. The periods for receipt of comments on the proposed finding from petitioners, interested parties and informed parties, for consideration of comments received, and for publication of a final determination regarding the petitioner's status shall follow the timetables established in paragraphs (h) through (l) of this section.

(2) If the review cannot clearly demonstrate that the group does not meet one or more of the mandatory criteria in paragraphs (e), (f) or (g) of Section 7, a full evaluation of the documented petition under all seven of the mandatory criteria shall be undertaken during active consideration of the documented petition pursuant to paragraph (g) of this section.

(f) The petitioner and interested parties shall be notified when the documented petition comes under active consideration.

(1) They shall also be provided with the name, office address, and telephone number of the staff member with primary administrative responsibility for the petition; the names of the researchers conducting the evaluation of the petition; and the name of their supervisor.

(2) The petitioner shall be notified of any substantive comment on its petition received prior to the beginning of active consideration or during the preparation of the proposed finding, and shall be provided an opportunity to respond to such comments.

(g) Once active consideration of the documented petition has begun, the Assistant Secretary shall continue the review and publish proposed findings and a final determination in the Federal Register pursuant to these regulations, notwithstanding any requests by the petitioner or interested parties to cease consideration. The Assistant Secretary has the discretion, however, to suspend active consideration of a documented petition, either conditionally or for a stated period of time, upon a showing to the petitioner that there are technical problems with the documented petition or administrative problems that temporarily preclude continuing active consideration. The Assistant Secretary shall also consider requests by petitioners for suspension of consideration and has the discretion to grant such requests for good cause. Upon resolution of the technical or administrative problems that are the basis for the suspension, the documented petition will have priority on the numbered register of documented petitions insofar as possible. The Assistant Secretary shall notify the petitioner and interested parties when active consideration of the documented petition is resumed. The timetables in succeeding paragraphs shall begin anew upon the resumption of active consideration.

(h) Within one year after notifying the petitioner that active consideration of the documented petition has begun, the Assistant Secretary shall publish proposed findings in the Federal Register. The Assistant Secretary has the discretion to extend that period up to an additional 180 days. The petitioner and interested parties shall be notified of the time extension. In addition to the proposed findings, the Assistant Secretary shall prepare a report summarizing the evidence, reasoning, and analyses that are the basis for the proposed decision. Copies of the report shall be provided to the petitioner, interested parties, and informed parties and made available to others upon written request.

(i) Upon publication of the proposed findings, the petitioner or any individual or organization wishing to challenge or support the proposed findings shall have 180 days to submit arguments and evidence to the Assistant Secretary to rebut or support the proposed finding. The period for comment on a proposed finding may be extended for up to an additional 180 days at the Assistant Secretary's discretion upon a finding of good cause. The petitioner and interested parties shall be notified of the time extension. Interested and informed parties who submit arguments and evidence to the Assistant Secretary must provide copies of their submissions to the petitioner.

(j)(1) During the response period, the Assistant Secretary shall provide technical advice concerning the factual basis for the proposed finding, the reasoning used in preparing it, and suggestions regarding the preparation of materials in response to the proposed finding. The Assistant Secretary shall make available to the petitioner in a timely fashion any records used for the proposed finding not already held by the petitioner, to the extent allowable by Federal law.

(2) In addition, the Assistant Secretary shall, if requested by the petitioner or any interested party, hold a formal meeting for the purpose of inquiring into the reasoning, analyses, and factual bases for the proposed finding. The proceedings of this meeting

shall be on the record. The meeting record shall be available to any participating party and become part of the record considered by the Assistant Secretary in reaching a final determination.

(k) The petitioner shall have a minimum of 60 days to respond to any submissions by interested and informed parties during the response period. This may be extended at the Assistant Secretary's discretion if warranted by the extent and nature of the comments. The petitioner and interested parties shall be notified by letter of any extension. No further comments from interested or informed parties will be accepted after the end of the regular response period.

(l) At the end of the period for comment on a proposed finding, the Assistant Secretary shall consult with the petitioner and interested parties to determine an equitable timeframe for consideration of written arguments and evidence submitted during the response period. The petitioner and interested parties shall be notified of the date such consideration begins.

(1) Unsolicited comments submitted after the close of the response period established in Section 10(i) and Section 10(k), will not be considered in preparation of a final determination. The Assistant Secretary has the discretion during the preparation of the proposed finding, however, to request additional explanations and information from the petitioner or from commenting parties to support or supplement their comments on a proposed finding. The Assistant Secretary may also conduct such additional research as is necessary to evaluate and supplement the record. In either case, the additional materials will become part of the petition record.

(2) After consideration of the written arguments and evidence rebutting or supporting the proposed finding and the petitioner's response to the comments of interested parties and informed parties, the Assistant Secretary shall make a final determination regarding the petitioner's status. A summary of this determination shall be published in the Federal Register within 60 days from the date on which the consideration of the written arguments and evidence rebutting or supporting the proposed finding begins.

(3) The Assistant Secretary has the discretion to extend the period for the preparation of a final determination if warranted by the extent and nature of evidence and arguments received during the response period. The petitioner and interested parties shall be notified of the time extension.

(4) The determination will become effective 90 days from publication unless a request for reconsideration is filed pursuant to Section 11.

(m) The Assistant Secretary shall acknowledge the existence of the petitioner as an Indian tribe when it is determined that the group satisfies all of the criteria in Section 7. The Assistant Secretary shall decline to acknowledge that a petitioner is an Indian tribe if it fails to satisfy any one of the criteria in Section 7.

(n) If the Assistant Secretary declines to acknowledge that a petitioner is an Indian tribe, the petitioner shall be informed of alternatives, if any, to acknowledgment under these procedures.

These alternatives may include other means through which the petitioning group may achieve the status of an acknowledged Indian tribe or through which any of its members may become eligible for services and benefits from the Department as Indians, or become members of an acknowledged Indian tribe.

(o) The determination to decline to acknowledge that the petitioner is an Indian tribe shall be final for the Department.

(p) A petitioner that has petitioned under this part or under the acknowledgment regulations previously effective and that has been denied Federal acknowledgment may not re-petition under this part. The term "petitioner" here includes previously denied petitioners that have reorganized or been renamed or that are wholly or primarily portions of groups that have previously been denied under these or previous acknowledgment regulations.

Section 11. Independent review, reconsideration and final action.

(a)(1) Upon publication of the Assistant Secretary's determination in the Federal Register, the petitioner or any interested party may file a request for reconsideration with the Interior Board of Indian Appeals. Petitioners which choose under Section 3(g) to be considered under previously effective acknowledgment regulations may nonetheless request reconsideration under this section.

(2) A petitioner's or interested party's request for reconsideration must be received by the Board no later than 90 days after the date of publication of the Assistant Secretary's determination in the Federal Register. If no request for reconsideration has been received, the Assistant Secretary's decision shall be final for the Department 90 days after publication of the final determination in the Federal Register.

(b) The petitioner's or interested party's request for reconsideration shall contain a detailed statement of the grounds for the request, and shall include any new evidence to be considered.

(1) The detailed statement of grounds for reconsideration filed by a petitioner or interested parties shall be considered the appellant's opening brief provided for in 43 CFR 4.311(a).

(2) The party or parties requesting the reconsideration shall mail copies of the request to the petitioner and all other interested parties.

(c)(1) The Board shall dismiss a request for reconsideration that is not filed by the deadline specified in paragraph (a) of this section.

(2) If a petitioner's or interested party's request for reconsideration is filed on time, the Board shall determine, within 120 days after publication of the Assistant Secretary's final determination in the Federal Register, whether the request alleges any of the grounds in paragraph (d) of this section and shall notify the petitioner and interested parties of this determination.

(d) The Board shall have the authority to review all requests for reconsideration that are timely and that allege any of the following:

(1) That there is new evidence that could affect the determination; or

(2) That a substantial portion of the evidence relied upon in the Assistant Secretary's determination was unreliable or was of little probative value; or

(3) That petitioner's or the Bureau's research appears inadequate or incomplete in some material respect; or

(4) That there are reasonable alternative interpretations, not previously considered, of the evidence used for the final determination, that would substantially affect the determination that the petitioner meets or does not meet one or more of the criteria in Section 7 (a) through (g).

(e) The Board shall have administrative authority to review determinations of the Assistant Secretary made pursuant to Section 10(m) to the extent authorized by this section.

(1) The regulations at 43 CFR 4.310–4.318 and 4.331–4.340 shall apply to proceedings before the Board except when they are inconsistent with these regulations.

(2) The Board may establish such procedures as it deems appropriate to provide a full and fair evaluation of a request for reconsideration under this section to the extent they are not inconsistent with these regulations.

(3) The Board, at its discretion, may request experts not associated with the Bureau, the petitioner, or interested parties to provide comments, recommendations, or technical advice concerning the determination, the administrative record, or materials filed by the petitioner or interested parties. The Board may also request, at its discretion, comments or technical assistance from the Assistant Secretary concerning the final determination or, pursuant to paragraph (e)(8) of this section, the record used for the determination.

(4) Pursuant to 43 CFR 4.337(a), the Board may require, at its discretion, a hearing conducted by an administrative law judge of the Office of Hearings and Appeals if the Board determines that further inquiry is necessary to resolve a genuine issue of material fact or to otherwise augment the record before it concerning the grounds for reconsideration.

(5) The detailed statement of grounds for reconsideration filed by a petitioner or interested parties pursuant to paragraph (b)(1) of this section shall be considered the appellant's opening brief provided for in 43 CFR 4.311(a).

(6) An appellant's reply to an opposing party's answer brief, provided for in 43 CFR 4.311(b), shall not apply to proceedings under this section, except that a petitioner shall have the opportunity to reply to an answer brief filed by any party that opposes a petitioner's request for reconsideration.

(7) The opportunity for reconsideration of a Board decision provided for in 43 CFR 4.315 shall not apply to proceedings under this section.

(8) For purposes of review by the Board, the administrative record shall consist of all appropriate documents in the Branch of Acknowledgment and Research relevant to the determination involved in the request for reconsideration. The Assistant Secretary shall designate and transmit to the Board copies of critical documents central to the portions of the determination under a request for reconsideration. The Branch of Acknowledgment and Research shall retain custody of the remainder of the administrative record, to which the Board shall have unrestricted access.

(9) The Board shall affirm the Assistant Secretary's determination if the Board finds that the petitioner or interested party has failed to establish, by a preponderance of the evidence, at least one of the grounds under paragraph (d)(1–4) of this section.

(10) The Board shall vacate the Assistant Secretary's determination and remand it to the Assistant Secretary for further work and reconsideration if the Board finds that the petitioner or an interested party has established, by a preponderance of the evidence, one or more of the grounds under paragraph (d)(1–4) of this section.

(f)(1) The Board, in addition to making its determination to affirm or remand, shall describe in its decision any grounds for reconsideration other than those in paragraphs (d)(1–4) of this section alleged by a petitioner's or interested party's request for reconsideration.

(2) If the Board affirms the Assistant Secretary's decision under Section 11(e)(9) but finds that the petitioner or interested parties have alleged other grounds for reconsideration, the Board shall send the requests for reconsideration to the Secretary. The Secretary shall have the discretion to request that the Assistant Secretary reconsider the final determination on those grounds.

(3) The Secretary, in reviewing the Assistant Secretary's decision, may review any information available, whether formally part of the record or not. Where the Secretary's review relies upon information that is not formally part of the record, the Secretary shall insert the information relied upon into the record, together with an identification of its source and nature.

(4) Where the Board has sent the Secretary a request for reconsideration under paragraph (f)(2), the petitioner and interested parties shall have 30 days from receiving notice of the Board's decision to submit comments to the Secretary. Where materials are submitted to the Secretary opposing a petitioner's request for reconsideration, the interested party shall provide copies to the petitioner and the petitioner shall have 15 days from their receipt of the information to file a response with the Secretary.

(5) The Secretary shall make a determination whether to request a reconsideration of the Assistant Secretary's determination within 60 days of receipt of all comments and shall notify all parties of the decision.

(g)(1) The Assistant Secretary shall issue a reconsidered determination within 120 days of receipt of the Board's decision to remand a determination or the Secretary's request for reconsideration.

(2) The Assistant Secretary's reconsideration shall address all grounds determined to be valid grounds for reconsideration in a remand by the Board, other grounds described by the Board pursuant to paragraph (f)(1), and all grounds specified in any Secretarial request. The Assistant Secretary's reconsideration may

address any issues and evidence consistent with the Board's decision or the Secretary's request.

(h)(1) If the Board finds that no petitioner's or interested party's request for reconsideration is timely, the Assistant Secretary's determination shall become effective and final for the Department 120 days from the publication of the final determination in the Federal Register.

(2) If the Secretary declines to request reconsideration under paragraph (f)(2) of this section, the Assistant Secretary's decision shall become effective and final for the Department as of the date of notification to all parties of the Secretary's decision.

(3) If a determination is reconsidered by the Assistant Secretary because of action by the Board remanding a decision or because the Secretary has requested reconsideration, the reconsidered determination shall be final and effective upon publication of the notice of this reconsidered determination in the Federal Register.

Section 12. Implementation of decisions.

(a) Upon final determination that the petitioner exists as an Indian tribe, it shall be considered eligible for the services and benefits from the Federal government that are available to other federally recognized tribes. The newly acknowledged tribe shall be considered a historic tribe and shall be entitled to the privileges and immunities available to other federally recognized historic tribes by virtue of their government-to-government relationship with the United States. It shall also have the responsibilities and obligations of such tribes. Newly acknowledged Indian tribes shall likewise be subject to the same authority of Congress and the United States as are other federally acknowledged tribes.

(b) Upon acknowledgment as an Indian tribe, the list of members submitted as part of the petitioner's documented petition shall be the tribe's complete base roll for purposes of Federal funding and other administrative purposes. For Bureau purposes, any additions made to the roll, other than individuals who are descendants of those on the roll and who meet the tribe's membership criteria, shall be limited to those meeting the requirements of Section 7(e) and maintaining significant social and political ties with the tribe (i.e., maintaining the same relationship with the tribe as those on the list submitted with the group's documented petition).

(c) While the newly acknowledged tribe shall be considered eligible for benefits and services available to federally recognized tribes because of their status as Indian tribes, acknowledgment of tribal existence shall not create immediate access to existing programs. The tribe may participate in existing programs after it meets the specific program requirements, if any, and upon appropriation of funds by Congress. Requests for appropriations shall follow a determination of the needs of the newly acknowledged tribe.

(d) Within six months after acknowledgment, the appropriate Area Office shall consult with the newly acknowledged tribe

and develop, in cooperation with the tribe, a determination of needs and a recommended budget. These shall be forwarded to the Assistant Secretary. The recommended budget will then be considered along with other recommendations by the Assistant Secretary in the usual budget request process.

Section 13. Information collection.

(a) The collections of information contained in Section 7 have been approved by the Office of Management and Budget under 44 U.S.C. 3501 et seq. and assigned clearance number 1076-0104. The information will be used to establish historical existence as a tribe, verify family relationships and the group's claim that its members are Indian and descend from a historical tribe or tribes which combined, that members are not substantially enrolled in other Indian tribes, and that they have not individually or as a group been terminated or otherwise forbidden the Federal relationship. Response is required to obtain a benefit in accordance with 25 U.S.C. 2.

(b) Public reporting burden for this information is estimated to average 1,968 hours per petition, including the time for reviewing instructions, searching existing data sources, gathering and maintaining the data needed, and completing and reviewing the collection of information. Send comments regarding this collection of information, including suggestions for reducing the burden, to both the Information Collection Clearance Officer, Bureau of Indian Affairs, Mail Stop 336-SIB, 1849 C Street, NW., Washington, DC 20240; and to the Office of Information and Regulatory Affairs, Office of Management and Budget, Washington, DC 20503.

Source: 25 CFR Part 83, Procedures for Establishing That an American Indian Group Exists as an Indian Tribe.

167. *United States v. Sioux Nation of Indians*, June 30, 1980 [Excerpts]

Introduction

In the Treaty of Fort Laramie of April 29, 1868, the United States established an extensive reservation in South Dakota for the Sioux and allied tribes. The treaty provided that no further land cessions would be valid without the consent of three-fourths of all adult Sioux males. Just eight years later war with the Sioux broke out, due in no small part to the discovery of gold deposits in the Black Hills. In 1877 the federal government essentially confiscated the Black Hills by forcing on the Sioux a treaty signed by only a small percentage of the tribe. By 1890 the U.S. Army had quashed all Sioux resistance. In the ensuing decades the Sioux fought through the U.S. court system for the return of the Black Hills, arguing that the land was taken in violation of American treaty obligations. The U.S. Court of Claims ruled in 1979 that the 1877 confiscation was illegal and that the Indians were entitled to compensation with interest, an amount of more than $100 million. In this 1980 decision, the U.S. Supreme Court upheld the Court of Claims ruling. However, as of 2011 the Sioux had not accepted the compensation because they would have to finally cede any claim to the return of the Black Hills. With accumulated interest, the unclaimed compensation has grown to about $1 billion.

Primary Source

448 U.S. 371 (1980)
UNITED STATES
v.
SIOUX NATION OF INDIANS ET AL.
No. 79-639.
Supreme Court of United States.
Argued March 24, 1980.
Decided June 30, 1980.
CERTIORARI TO THE UNITED STATES COURT OF CLAIMS.

Deputy Solicitor General Claiborne argued the cause for the United States. With him on the briefs were *Solicitor General McCree, Assistant Attorney General Moorman, William Alsup, Dirk D. Snel,* and *Martin W. Matzen.*

Arthur Lazarus, Jr., argued the cause for respondents. With him on the brief were *Marvin J. Sonosky, Reid P. Chambers, Harry R. Sachse,* and *William Howard Payne.*[*]

MR. JUSTICE BLACKMUN delivered the opinion of the Court.

This case concerns the Black Hills of South Dakota, the Great Sioux Reservation, and a colorful, and in many respects tragic, chapter in the history of the Nation's West. Although the litigation comes down to a claim of interest since 1877 on an award of over $17 million, it is necessary, in order to understand the controversy, to review at some length the chronology of the case and its factual setting.

I

For over a century now the Sioux Nation has claimed that the United States unlawfully abrogated the Fort Laramie Treaty of April 29, 1868, 15 Stat. 635, in Art. II of which the United States pledged that the Great Sioux Reservation, including the Black Hills, would be "set apart for the absolute and undisturbed use and occupation of the Indians herein named." *Id.,* at 636. The Fort Laramie Treaty was concluded at the culmination of the Powder River War of 1866–1867, a series of military engagements in which the Sioux tribes, led by their great chief, Red Cloud, fought to protect the integrity of earlier-recognized treaty lands from the incursion of white settlers.[1]

The Fort Laramie Treaty included several agreements central to the issues presented in this case. First, it established the Great Sioux Reservation, a tract of land bounded on the east by the Missouri River, on the south by the northern border of the State of Nebraska, on the north by the forty-sixth parallel of north latitude, and on the west by the one hundred and fourth meridian of west longitude,[2] in addition to certain reservations already existing east of the Missouri. The United States "solemnly agree[d]" that no unauthorized persons "shall ever be permitted to pass over, settle upon, or reside in [this] territory." *Ibid.*

Second, the United States permitted members of the Sioux tribes to select lands within the reservation for cultivation. *Id.,* at 637. In order to assist the Sioux in becoming civilized farmers, the Government promised to provide them with the necessary services and materials, and with subsistence rations for four years. *Id.,* at 639.[3]

Third, in exchange for the benefits conferred by the treaty, the Sioux agreed to relinquish their rights under the Treaty of September 17, 1851, to occupy territories outside the reservation, while reserving their "right to hunt on any lands north of North Platte, and on the Republican Fork of the Smoky Hill river, so long as the buffalo may range thereon in such numbers as to justify the chase." *Ibid.* The Indians also expressly agreed to withdraw all opposition to the building of railroads that did not pass over their reservation lands, not to engage in attacks on settlers, and to withdraw their opposition to the military posts and roads that had been established south of the North Platte River. *Ibid.*

Fourth, Art. XII of the treaty provided:

"No treaty for the cession of any portion or part of the reservation herein described which may be held in common shall be of any validity or force as against the said Indians, unless executed and signed by at least three fourths of all the adult male Indians, occupying or interested in the same." *Ibid.*[4]

The years following the treaty brought relative peace to the Dakotas, an era of tranquility that was disturbed, however, by renewed speculation that the Black Hills, which were included in the Great Sioux Reservation, contained vast quantities of gold and silver.[5] In 1874 the Army planned and undertook an exploratory expedition into the Hills, both for the purpose of establishing a military outpost from which to control those Sioux who had not accepted the terms of the Fort Laramie Treaty, and for the purpose of investigating "the country about which dreamy stories have been told." D. Jackson, Custer's Gold 14 (1966) (quoting the 1874 annual report of Lieutenant General Philip H. Sheridan, as Commander of the Military Division of the Missouri, to the Secretary of War). Lieutenant Colonel George Armstrong Custer led the expedition of close to 1,000 soldiers and teamsters, and a substantial number of military and civilian aides. Custer's journey began at Fort Abraham Lincoln on the Missouri River on July 2, 1874. By the end of that month they had reached the Black Hills, and by mid-August had confirmed the presence of gold fields in that region. The discovery of gold was widely reported in newspapers across the country.[6] Custer's florid descriptions of the mineral and timber resources of the Black Hills, and the land's suitability for grazing and cultivation, also received wide circulation, and had the effect of creating an intense popular demand for the "opening" of the Hills for settlement.[7] The only obstacle to "progress" was the Fort Laramie Treaty that reserved occupancy of the Hills to the Sioux.

Having promised the Sioux that the Black Hills were reserved to them, the United States Army was placed in the position of having to threaten military force, and occasionally to use it, to prevent prospectors and settlers from trespassing on lands reserved to the Indians. For example, in September 1874, General Sheridan sent instructions to Brigadier General Alfred H. Terry, Commander of the Department of Dakota, at Saint Paul, directing him to use force to prevent companies of prospectors from trespassing on the Sioux Reservation. At the same time, Sheridan let it be known that he would "give a cordial support to the settlement of the Black Hills," should Congress decide to "open up the country for settlement, by extinguishing the treaty rights of the Indians." App. 62–63. Sheridan's instructions were published in local newspapers. See *id.,* at 63.[8]

Eventually, however, the Executive Branch of the Government decided to abandon the Nation's treaty obligation to preserve the integrity of the Sioux territory. In a letter dated November 9, 1875, to Terry, Sheridan reported that he had met with President Grant, the Secretary of the Interior, and the Secretary of War, and that the President had decided that the military should make no further resistance to the occupation of the Black Hills by miners, "it being his belief that such resistance only increased their desire and complicated the troubles." *Id.,* at 59. These orders were to be enforced "quietly," *ibid.,* and the President's decision was to remain "confidential." *Id.,* at 59–60 (letter from Sheridan to Sherman).

With the Army's withdrawal from its role as enforcer of the Fort Laramie Treaty, the influx of settlers into the Black Hills increased. The Government concluded that the only practical course was to secure to the citizens of the United States the right to mine the Black Hills for gold. Toward that end, the Secretary of the Interior, in the spring of 1875, appointed a commission to negotiate with the Sioux. The commission was headed by William B. Allison. The tribal leaders of the Sioux were aware of the mineral value of the Black Hills and refused to sell the land for a price less than $70 million. The commission offered the Indians an annual rental of $400,000, or payment of $6 million for absolute relinquishment of the Black Hills. The negotiations broke down.[9]

In the winter of 1875–1876, many of the Sioux were hunting in the unceded territory north of the North Platte River, reserved to them for that purpose in the Fort Laramie Treaty. On December 6, 1875, for reasons that are not entirely clear, the Commissioner of Indian Affairs sent instructions to the Indian agents on the reservation to notify those hunters that if they did not return to the

reservation agencies by January 31, 1876, they would be treated as "hostiles." Given the severity of the winter, compliance with these instructions was impossible. On February 1, the Secretary of the Interior nonetheless relinquished jurisdiction over all hostile Sioux, including those Indians exercising their treaty-protected hunting rights, to the War Department. The Army's campaign against the "hostiles" led to Sitting Bull's notable victory over Custer's forces at the battle of the Little Big Horn on June 25. That victory, of course, was short-lived, and those Indians who surrendered to the Army were returned to the reservation, and deprived of their weapons and horses, leaving them completely dependent for survival on rations provided them by the Government.[10]

In the meantime, Congress was becoming increasingly dissatisfied with the failure of the Sioux living on the reservation to become self-sufficient.[11] The Sioux' entitlement to subsistence rations under the terms of the Fort Laramie Treaty had expired in 1872. Nonetheless, in each of the two following years, over $1 million was appropriated for feeding the Sioux. In August 1876, Congress enacted an appropriations bill providing that "hereafter there shall be no appropriation made for the subsistence" of the Sioux, unless they first relinquished their rights to the hunting grounds outside the reservation, ceded the Black Hills to the United States, and reached some accommodation with the Government that would be calculated to enable them to become self-supporting. Act of Aug. 15, 1876, 19 Stat. 176, 192.[12] Toward this end, Congress requested the President to appoint another commission to negotiate with the Sioux for the cession of the Black Hills.

This commission, headed by George Manypenny, arrived in the Sioux country in early September and commenced meetings with the head men of the various tribes. The members of the commission impressed upon the Indians that the United States no longer had any obligation to provide them with subsistence rations. The commissioners brought with them the text of a treaty that had been prepared in advance. The principal provisions of this treaty were that the Sioux would relinquish their rights to the Black Hills and other lands west of the one hundred and third meridian, and their rights to hunt in the unceded territories to the north, in exchange for subsistence rations for as long as they would be needed to ensure the Sioux' survival. In setting out to obtain the tribes' agreement to this treaty, the commission ignored the stipulation of the Fort Laramie Treaty that any cession of the lands contained within the Great Sioux Reservation would have to be joined in by three-fourths of the adult males. Instead, the treaty was presented just to Sioux chiefs and their leading men. It was signed by only 10% of the adult male Sioux population.[13]

Congress resolved the impasse by enacting the 1876 "agreement" into law as the Act of Feb. 28, 1877 (1877 Act). 19 Stat. 254. The Act had the effect of abrogating the earlier Fort Laramie Treaty, and of implementing the terms of the Manypenny Commission's "agreement" with the Sioux leaders.[14]

The passage of the 1877 Act legitimized the settlers' invasion of the Black Hills, but throughout the years it has been regarded by the Sioux as a breach of this Nation's solemn obligation to reserve the Hills in perpetuity for occupation by the Indians. One historian of the Sioux Nation commented on Indian reaction to the Act in the following words:

"The Sioux thus affected have not gotten over talking about that treaty yet, and during the last few years they have maintained an organization called the Black Hills Treaty Association, which holds meetings each year at the various agencies for the purpose of studying the treaty with the intention of presenting a claim against the government for additional reimbursements for the territory ceded under it. Some think that Uncle Sam owes them about $9,000,000 on the deal, but it will probably be a hard matter to prove it." F. Fiske, The Taming of the Sioux 132 (1917).

Fiske's words were to prove prophetic.

II

Prior to 1946, Congress had not enacted any mechanism of general applicability by which Indian tribes could litigate treaty claims against the United States.[15] The Sioux, however, after years of lobbying, succeeded in obtaining from Congress the passage of a special jurisdictional Act which provided them a forum for adjudication of all claims against the United States "under any treaties, agreements, or laws of Congress, or for the misappropriation of any of the funds or lands of said tribe or band or bands thereof." Act of June 3, 1920, ch. 222, 41 Stat. 738. Pursuant to this statute, the Sioux, in 1923, filed a petition with the Court of Claims alleging that the Government had taken the Black Hills without just compensation, in violation of the Fifth Amendment. This claim was dismissed by that court in 1942. In a lengthy and unanimous opinion, the court concluded that it was not authorized by the Act of June 3, 1920, to question whether the compensation afforded the Sioux by Congress in 1877 was an adequate price for the Black Hills, and that the Sioux' claim in this regard was a moral claim not protected by the Just Compensation Clause. *Sioux Tribe* v. *United States,* 97 Ct. Cl. 613 (1942), cert. denied, 318 U. S. 789 (1943).

In 1946, Congress passed the Indian Claims Commission Act, 60 Stat. 1049, 25 U. S. C. § 70 *et seq.,* creating a new forum to hear and determine all tribal grievances that had arisen previously. In 1950, counsel for the Sioux resubmitted the Black Hills claim to the Indian Claims Commission. The Commission initially ruled that the Sioux had failed to prove their case. *Sioux Tribe* v. *United States,* 2 Ind. Cl. Comm'n 646 (1954), aff'd, 146 F. Supp. 229 (Ct. Cl. 1956). The Sioux filed a motion with the Court of Claims to vacate its judgment of affirmance, alleging that the Commission's decision had been based on a record that was inadequate, due to the failings of the Sioux' former counsel. This motion was granted and the Court of Claims directed the Commission to consider whether the case should be reopened for the presentation of additional

evidence. On November 19, 1958, the Commission entered an order reopening the case and announcing that it would reconsider its prior judgment on the merits of the Sioux claim. App. 265–266; see *Sioux Tribe* v. *United States,* 182 Ct. Cl. 912 (1968) (summary of proceedings).

Following the Sioux' filing of an amended petition, claiming again that the 1877 Act constituted a taking of the Black Hills for which just compensation had not been paid, there ensued a lengthy period of procedural sparring between the Indians and the Government. Finally, in October 1968, the Commission set down three questions for briefing and determination: (1) What land and rights did the United States acquire from the Sioux by the 1877 Act? (2) What, if any, consideration was given for that land and those rights? And (3) if there was no consideration for the Government's acquisition of the land and rights under the 1877 Act, was there any payment for such acquisition? App. 266.

Six years later, by a 4-to-1 vote, the Commission reached a preliminary decision on these questions. *Sioux Nation* v. *United States,* 33 Ind. Cl. Comm'n 151 (1974). The Commission first held that the 1942 Court of Claims decision did not bar the Sioux' Fifth Amendment taking claim through application of the doctrine of res judicata. The Commission concluded that the Court of Claims had dismissed the earlier suit for lack of jurisdiction, and that it had not determined the merits of the Black Hills claim. The Commission then went on to find that Congress, in 1877, had made no effort to give the Sioux full value for the ceded reservation lands. The only new obligation assumed by the Government in exchange for the Black Hills was its promise to provide the Sioux with subsistence rations, an obligation that was subject to several limiting conditions. See n. 14, *supra.* Under these circumstances, the Commission concluded that the consideration given the Indians in the 1877 Act had no relationship to the value of the property acquired. Moreover, there was no indication in the record that Congress ever attempted to relate the value of the rations to the value of the Black Hills. Applying the principles announced by the Court of Claims in *Three Tribes of Fort Berthold Reservation* v. *United States,* 182 Ct. Cl. 543, 390 F. 2d 686 (1968), the Commission concluded that Congress had acted pursuant to its power of eminent domain when it passed the 1877 Act, rather than as a trustee for the Sioux, and that the Government must pay the Indians just compensation for the taking of the Black Hills.[16]

The Government filed an appeal with the Court of Claims from the Commission's interlocutory order, arguing alternatively that the Sioux' Fifth Amendment claim should have been barred by principles of res judicata and collateral estoppel, or that the 1877 Act did not effect a taking of the Black Hills for which just compensation was due. Without reaching the merits, the Court of Claims held that the Black Hills claim was barred by the res judicata effect of its 1942 decision. *United States* v. *Sioux Nation,* 207 Ct. Cl. 234, 518 F. 2d 1298 (1975). The court's majority recognized that the practical impact of the question presented was limited to a determination of whether or not an award of interest would be available to the Indians. This followed from the Government's failure to appeal the Commission's holding that it had acquired the Black Hills through a course of unfair and dishonorable dealing for which the Sioux were entitled to damages, without interest, under § 2 of the Indian Claims Commission Act, 60 Stat. 1050, 25 U. S. C. § 70a (5). Only if the acquisition of the Black Hills amounted to an unconstitutional taking would the Sioux be entitled to interest. 207 Ct. Cl., at 237, 518 F. 2d, at 1299.[17]

The court affirmed the Commission's holding that a want of fair and honorable dealings in this case was evidenced, and held that the Sioux thus would be entitled to an award of at least $17.5 million for the lands surrendered and for the gold taken by trespassing prospectors prior to passage of the 1877 Act. See n. 16, *supra*. The court also remarked upon President Grant's duplicity in breaching the Government's treaty obligation to keep trespassers out of the Black Hills, and the pattern of duress practiced by the Government on the starving Sioux to get them to agree to the sale of the Black Hills. The court concluded: "A more ripe and rank case of dishonorable dealings will never, in all probability, be found in our history, which is not, taken as a whole, the disgrace it now pleases some persons to believe." 207 Ct. Cl., at 241, 518 F. 2d, at 1302.

Nonetheless, the court held that the merits of the Sioux' taking claim had been reached in 1942, and whether resolved "rightly or wrongly," *id.*, at 249, 518 F. 2d, at 1306, the claim was now barred by res judicata. The court observed that interest could not be awarded the Sioux on judgments obtained pursuant to the Indian Claims Commission Act, and that while Congress could correct this situation, the court could not. *Ibid.*[18] The Sioux petitioned this Court for a writ of certiorari, but that petition was denied. 423 U. S. 1016 (1975).

The case returned to the Indian Claims Commission, where the value of the rights-of-way obtained by the Government through the 1877 Act was determined to be $3,484, and where it was decided that the Government had made no payments to the Sioux that could be considered as offsets. App. 316. The Government then moved the Commission to enter a final award in favor of the Sioux in the amount of $17.5 million, see n. 16, *supra,* but the Commission deferred entry of final judgment in view of legislation then pending in Congress that dealt with the case.

On March 13, 1978, Congress passed a statute providing for Court of Claims review of the merits of the Indian Claims Commission's judgment that the 1877 Act effected a taking of the Black Hills, without regard to the defenses of res judicata and collateral estoppel. The statute authorized the Court of Claims to take new evidence in the case, and to conduct its review of the merits *de novo*. Pub. L. 95-243, 92 Stat. 153, amending § 20 (b) of the Indian Claims Commission Act. See 25 U. S. C. § 70s (b) (1976 ed., Supp. II).

Acting pursuant to that statute, a majority of the Court of Claims, sitting en banc, in an opinion by Chief Judge Friedman, affirmed the Commission's holding that the 1877 Act effected a

taking of the Black Hills and of rights-of-way across the reservation. 220 Ct. Cl. 442, 601 F. 2d 1157 (1979).[19] In doing so, the court applied the test it had earlier articulated in *Fort Berthold,* 182 Ct. Cl., at 553, 390 F. 2d, at 691, asking whether Congress had made "a good faith effort to give the Indians the full value of the land," 220 Ct. Cl., at 452, 601 F. 2d, at 1162, in order to decide whether the 1877 Act had effected a taking or whether it had been a noncompensable act of congressional guardianship over tribal property. The court characterized the Act as a taking, an exercise of Congress' power of eminent domain over Indian property. It distinguished broad statements seemingly leading to a contrary result in *Lone Wolf* v. *Hitchcock,* 187 U. S. 553 (1903), as inapplicable to a case involving a claim for just compensation. 220 Ct. Cl., at 465, 601 F. 2d, at 1170.[20]

The court thus held that the Sioux were entitled to an award of interest, at the annual rate of 5%, on the principal sum of $17.1 million, dating from 1877.[21]

We granted the Government's petition for a writ of certiorari, 444 U. S. 989 (1979), in order to review the important constitutional questions presented by this case, questions not only of long-standing concern to the Sioux, but also of significant economic import to the Government.

III

Having twice denied petitions for certiorari in this litigation, see 318 U. S. 789 (1943); 423 U. S. 1016 (1975), we are confronted with it for a third time as a result of the amendment, above noted, to the Indian Claims Commission Act of 1946, 25 U. S. C. § 70s (b) (1976 ed., Supp. II), which directed the Court of Claims to review the merits of the Black Hills takings claim without regard to the defense of res judicata. The amendment, approved March 13, 1978, provides:

"Notwithstanding any other provision of law, upon application by the claimants within thirty days from the date of the enactment of this sentence, the Court of Claims shall review on the merits, without regard to the defense of res judicata or collateral estoppel, that portion of the determination of the Indian Claims Commission entered February 15, 1974, adjudging that the Act of February 28, 1877 (19 Stat. 254), effected a taking of the Black Hills portion of the Great Sioux Reservation in violation of the fifth amendment, and shall enter judgment accordingly. In conducting such review, the Court shall receive and consider any additional evidence, including oral testimony, that either party may wish to provide on the issue of a fifth amendment taking and shall determine that issue de novo." 92 Stat. 153.

Before turning to the merits of the Court of Claims' conclusion that the 1877 Act effected a taking of the Black Hills, we must consider the question whether Congress, in enacting this 1978 amendment, "has inadvertently passed the limit which separates the legislative from the judicial power." *United States* v. *Klein,* 13 Wall. 128, 147 (1872).

A

There are two objections that might be raised to the constitutionality of this amendment, each framed in terms of the doctrine of separation of powers. The first would be that Congress impermissibly has disturbed the finality of a judicial decree by rendering the Court of Claims' earlier judgments in this case mere advisory opinions. See *Hayburn's Case,* 2 Dall. 409, 410–414 (1792) (setting forth the views of three Circuit Courts, including among their complements Mr. Chief Justice Jay, and Justices Cushing, Wilson, Blair, and Iredell, that the Act of Mar. 23, 1792, 1 Stat. 243, was unconstitutional because it subjected the decisions of the Circuit Courts concerning eligibility for pension benefits to review by the Secretary of War and the Congress). The objection would take the form that Congress, in directing the Court of Claims to reach the merits of the Black Hills claim, effectively reviewed and reversed that court's 1975 judgment that the claim was barred by res judicata, or its 1942 judgment that the claim was not cognizable under the Fifth Amendment. Such legislative review of a judicial decision would interfere with the independent functions of the Judiciary.

The second objection would be that Congress overstepped its bounds by granting the Court of Claims jurisdiction to decide the merits of the Black Hills claim, while prescribing a rule for decision that left the court no adjudicatory function to perform. See *United States* v. *Klein,* 13 Wall., at 146; *Yakus* v. *United States,* 321 U. S. 414, 467–468 (1944) (Rutledge, J., dissenting). Of course, in the context of this amendment, that objection would have to be framed in terms of Congress' removal of a single issue from the Court of Claims' purview, the question whether res judicata or collateral estoppel barred the Sioux' claim. For in passing the amendment, Congress left no doubt that the Court of Claims was free to decide the merits of the takings claim in accordance with the evidence it found and applicable rules of law. See n. 23, *infra.*

These objections to the constitutionality of the amendment were not raised by the Government before the Court of Claims. At oral argument in this Court, counsel for the United States, upon explicit questioning, advanced the position that the amendment was not beyond the limits of legislative power.[22] The question whether the amendment impermissibly interfered with judicial power was debated, however, in the House of Representatives, and that body concluded that the Government's waiver of a "technical legal defense" in order to permit the Court of Claims to reconsider the merits of the Black Hills claim was within Congress' power to enact.[23]

The question debated on the floor of the House is one the answer to which is not immediately apparent. It requires us to examine the proper role of Congress and the courts in recognizing and determining claims against the United States, in light of

more general principles concerning the legislative and judicial roles in our tripartite system of government. Our examination of the amendment's effect, and of this Court's precedents, leads us to conclude that neither of the two separation-of-powers objections described above is presented by this legislation.

B

Our starting point is *Cherokee Nation* v. *United States,* 270 U. S. 476 (1926). That decision concerned the Special Act of Congress, dated March 3, 1919, 40 Stat. 1316, conferring jurisdiction upon the Court of Claims "to hear, consider, and determine the claim of the Cherokee Nation against the United States for interest, in addition to all other interest heretofore allowed and paid, alleged to be owing from the United States to the Cherokee Nation on the funds arising from the judgment of the Court of Claims of May eighteenth, nineteen hundred and five." In the judgment referred to by the Act, the Court of Claims had allowed 5% simple interest on four Cherokee claims, to accrue from the date of liability. *Cherokee Nation* v. *United States,* 40 Ct. Cl. 252 (1905). This Court had affirmed that judgment, including the interest award. *United States* v. *Cherokee Nation,* 202 U. S. 101, 123–126 (1906). Thereafter, and following payment of the judgment, the Cherokee presented to Congress a new claim that they were entitled to compound interest on the lump sum of principal and interest that had accrued up to 1895. It was this claim that prompted Congress, in 1919, to reconfer jurisdiction on the Court of Claims to consider the Cherokee's entitlement to that additional interest.

Ultimately, this Court held that the Cherokee were not entitled to the payment of compound interest on the original judgment awarded by the Court of Claims. 270 U. S., at 487–496. Before turning to the merits of the interest claim, however, the Court considered "the effect of the Act of 1919 in referring the issue in this case to the Court of Claims." *Id.,* at 485–486. The Court's conclusion concerning that question bears close examination:

"The judgment of this Court in the suit by the Cherokee Nation against the United States, in April, 1906 (202 U. S. 101), already referred to, awarded a large amount of interest. The question of interest was considered and decided, and it is quite clear that but for the special Act of 1919, above quoted, the question here mooted would have been foreclosed as *res judicata.* In passing the Act, Congress must have been well advised of this, and the only possible construction therefore to be put upon it is that Congress has therein expressed its desire, so far as the question of interest is concerned, to waive the effect of the judgment as *res judicata,* and to direct the Court of Claims to re-examine it and determine whether the interest therein allowed was all that should have been allowed, or whether it should be found to be as now claimed by the Cherokee Nation. The Solicitor General, representing the Government, properly concedes this to be the correct view. *The power of Congress to waive such an adjudication of course is clear.*" *Id.,* at 486 (last emphasis supplied).

The holding in *Cherokee Nation* that Congress has the power to waive the res judicata effect of a prior judgment entered in the Government's favor on a claim against the United States is dispositive of the question considered here. Moreover, that holding is consistent with a substantial body of precedent affirming the broad constitutional power of Congress to define and "to pay the Debts . . . of the United States." U. S. Const., Art. I, § 8, cl. 1. That precedent speaks directly to the separation-of-powers objections discussed above.

The scope of Congress' power to pay the Nation's debts seems first to have been construed by this Court in *United States* v. *Realty Co.,* 163 U. S. 427 (1896). There, the Court stated:

"The term 'debts' includes those debts or claims which rest upon a merely equitable or honorary obligation, and which would not be recoverable in a court of law if existing against an individual. The nation, speaking broadly, owes a 'debt' to an individual when his claim grows out of general principles of right and justice; when, in other words, it is based upon considerations of a moral or merely honorary nature, such as are binding on the conscience or the honor of an individual, although the debt could obtain no recognition in a court of law. The power of Congress extends at least as far as the recognition and payment of claims against the government which are thus founded." *Id.,* at 440.

Other decisions clearly establish that Congress may recognize its obligation to pay a moral debt not only by direct appropriation, but also by waiving an otherwise valid defense to a legal claim against the United States, as Congress did in this case and in *Cherokee Nation.* Although the Court in *Cherokee Nation* did not expressly tie its conclusion that Congress had the power to waive the res judicata effect of a judgment in favor of the United States to Congress' constitutional power to pay the Nation's debts, the *Cherokee Nation* opinion did rely on the decision in *Nock* v. *United States,* 2 Ct. Cl. 451 (1867). See 270 U. S., at 486.

In *Nock,* the Court of Claims was confronted with the precise question whether Congress invaded judicial power when it enacted a joint resolution, 14 Stat. 608, directing that court to decide a damages claim against the United States "in accordance with the principles of equity and justice," even though the merits of the claim previously had been resolved in the Government's favor. The court rejected the Government's argument that the joint resolution was unconstitutional as an exercise of "judicial powers" because it had the effect of setting aside the court's prior judgment. Rather, the court concluded:

"It is unquestionable that the Constitution has invested Congress with no judicial powers; it cannot be doubted that a

legislative direction to a court to find a judgment in a certain way would be little less than a judgment rendered directly by Congress. But here Congress do not attempt to award judgment, nor to grant a new trial *judicially;* neither have they *reversed* a decree of this court; nor attempted in any way to interfere with the administration of justice. Congress are here to all intents and purposes the defendants, and as such they come into court through this resolution and say that they will not plead the former trial in bar, nor interpose the legal objection which defeated a recovery before." 2 Ct. Cl., at 457–458 (emphases in original).

The *Nock* court thus expressly rejected the applicability of separation-of-powers objections to a congressional decision to waive the res judicata effect of a judgment in the Government's favor.[24]

The principles set forth in *Cherokee Nation* and *Nock* were substantially reaffirmed by this Court in *Pope* v. *United States,* 323 U. S. 1 (1944). There Congress had enacted special legislation conferring jurisdiction upon the Court of Claims, "notwithstanding any prior determination, any statute of limitations, release, or prior acceptance of partial allowance, to hear, determine, and render judgment upon" certain claims against the United States arising out of a construction contract. Special Act of Feb. 27, 1942, § 1, 56 Stat. 1122. The court was also directed to determine Pope's claims and render judgment upon them according to a particular formula for measuring the value of the work that he had performed. The Court of Claims construed the Special Act as deciding the questions of law presented by the case, and leaving it the role merely of computing the amount of the judgment for the claimant according to a mathematical formula. *Pope* v. *United States,* 100 Ct. Cl. 375, 379–380, 53 F. Supp. 570, 571–572 (1944). Based upon that reading of the Act, and this Court's decision in *United States* v. *Klein,* 13 Wall. 128 (1872) (see discussion *infra,* at [1261–1262]), the Court of Claims held that the Act unconstitutionally interfered with judicial independence. 100 Ct. Cl., at 380–382, 53 F. Supp., at 572–573. It distinguished *Cherokee Nation* as a case in which Congress granted a claimant a new trial, without directing the courts how to decide the case. 100 Ct. Cl., at 387, and n. 5, 53 F. Supp., at 575, and n. 5.

This Court reversed the Court of Claims' judgment. In doing so, the Court differed with the Court of Claims' interpretation of the effect of the Special Act. First, the Court held that the Act did not disturb the earlier judgment denying Pope's claim for damages. "While inartistically drawn the Act's purpose and effect seem rather to have been to create a new obligation of the Government to pay petitioner's claims where no obligation existed before." 323 U. S., at 9. Second, the Court held that Congress' recognition of Pope's claim was within its power to pay the Nation's debts, and that its use of the Court of Claims as an instrument for exercising that power did not impermissibly invade the judicial function:

"We perceive no constitutional obstacle to Congress' imposing on the Government a new obligation where there had been none before, for work performed by petitioner which was beneficial to the Government and for which Congress thought he had not been adequately compensated. The power of Congress to provide for the payment of debts, conferred by § 8 of Article I of the Constitution, is not restricted to payment of those obligations which are legally binding on the Government. It extends to the creation of such obligations in recognition of claims which are merely moral or honorary.... *United States* v. *Realty Co.,* 163 U. S. 427.... Congress, by the creation of a legal, in recognition of a moral, obligation to pay petitioner's claims plainly did not encroach upon the judicial function which the Court of Claims had previously exercised in adjudicating that the obligation was not legal. [Footnote citing *Nock* and other cases omitted.] Nor do we think it did so by directing that court to pass upon petitioner's claims in conformity to the particular rule of liability prescribed by the Special Act and to give judgment accordingly.... See *Cherokee Nation* v. *United States,* 270 U. S. 476, 486." *Id.,* at 9–10.

In explaining its holding that the Special Act did not invade the judicial province of the Court of Claims by directing it to reach its judgment with reference to a specified formula, the Court stressed that Pope was required to pursue his claim in the usual manner, that the earlier factual findings made by the Court of Claims were not necessarily rendered conclusive by the Act, and that, even if Congress had stipulated to the facts, it was still a judicial function for the Court of Claims to render judgment on consent. *Id.,* at 10–12.

To be sure, the Court in *Pope* specifically declined to consider "just what application the principles announced in the *Klein* case could rightly be given to a case in which Congress sought, *pendente lite,* to set aside the judgment of the Court of Claims in favor of the Government and to require relitigation of the suit." *Id.,* at 8–9. The case before us might be viewed as presenting that question. We conclude, however, that the separation-of-powers question presented in this case has already been answered in *Cherokee Nation,* and that that answer is completely consistent with the principles articulated in *Klein.*

The decision in *United States* v. *Klein,* 13 Wall. 128 (1872), arose from the following facts: Klein was the administrator of the estate of V. F. Wilson, the deceased owner of property that had been sold by agents of the Government during the War Between the States. Klein sued the United States in the Court of Claims for the proceeds of that sale. His lawsuit was based on the Abandoned and Captured Property Act of March 3, 1863, 12 Stat. 820, which afforded such a cause of action to noncombatant property owners upon proof that they had "never given any aid or comfort to the present rebellion." Following the enactment of this legislation, President Lincoln had issued a proclamation granting "a full pardon" to certain persons engaged "in the existing rebellion" who desired to resume their allegiance to the Government, upon the condition that they take and maintain a prescribed oath. This pardon was to have the effect

of restoring those persons' property rights. See 13 Stat. 737. The Court of Claims held that Wilson's taking of the amnesty oath had cured his participation in "the . . . rebellion," and that his administrator, Klein, was thus entitled to the proceeds of the sale. *Wilson* v. *United States,* 4 Ct. Cl. 559 (1869).

The Court of Claims' decision in Klein's case was consistent with this Court's later decision in a similar case, *United States* v. *Padelford,* 9 Wall. 531 (1870), holding that the Presidential pardon purged a participant "of whatever offence against the laws of the United States he had committed . . . and relieved [him] from any penalty which he might have incurred." *Id.,* at 543. Following the Court's announcement of the judgment in *Padelford,* however, Congress enacted a proviso to the appropriations bill for the Court of Claims. The proviso had three effects: First, no Presidential pardon or amnesty was to be admissible in evidence on behalf of a claimant in the Court of Claims as the proof of loyalty required by the Abandoned and Captured Property Act. Second, the Supreme Court was to dismiss, for want of jurisdiction, any appeal from a judgment of the Court of Claims in favor of a claimant who had established his loyalty through a pardon. Third, the Court of Claims henceforth was to treat a claimant's receipt of a Presidential pardon, without protest, as conclusive evidence that he had given aid and comfort to the rebellion, and to dismiss any lawsuit on his behalf for want of jurisdiction. Act of July 12, 1870, ch. 251, 16 Stat. 230, 235.

The Government's appeal from the judgment in Klein's case was decided by this Court following the enactment of the appropriations proviso. This Court held the proviso unconstitutional notwithstanding Congress' recognized power "to make 'such exceptions from the appellate jurisdiction' [of the Supreme Court] as should seem to it expedient." 13 Wall., at 145. See U. S. Const., Art. III, § 2, cl. 2. This holding followed from the Court's interpretation of the proviso's effect:

"[T]he language of the proviso shows plainly that it does not intend to withhold appellate jurisdiction except as a means to an end. Its great and controlling purpose is to deny to pardons granted by the President the effect which this court had adjudged them to have." 13 Wall., at 145.

Thus construed, the proviso was unconstitutional in two respects: First, it prescribed a rule of decision in a case pending before the courts, and did so in a manner that required the courts to decide a controversy in the Government's favor.

"The court is required to ascertain the existence of certain facts and thereupon to declare that its jurisdiction on appeal has ceased, by dismissing the bill. What is this but to prescribe a rule for the decision of a cause in a particular way? In the case before us, the Court of Claims has rendered judgment for the claimant and an appeal has been taken to this court. We are directed to dismiss the appeal, if we find that the judgment must be affirmed, because of a pardon granted to the intestate of the claimants. Can we do so without allowing one party to the controversy to decide it in its own favor? Can we do so without allowing that the legislature may prescribe rules of decision to the Judicial Department of the government in cases pending before it?

[…]

". . . Can [Congress] prescribe a rule in conformity with which the court must deny to itself the jurisdiction thus conferred, because and only because its decision, in accordance with settled law, must be adverse to the government and favorable to the suitor? This question seems to us to answer itself." *Id.,* at 146–147.

Second, the rule prescribed by the proviso "is also liable to just exception as impairing the effect of a pardon, and thus infringing the constitutional power of the Executive." *Id.,* at 147. The Court held that it would not serve as an instrument toward the legislative end of changing the effect of a Presidential pardon. *Id.,* at 148.

It was, of course, the former constitutional objection held applicable to the legislative proviso in *Klein* that the Court was concerned about in *Pope.* But that objection is not applicable to the case before us for two reasons. First, of obvious importance to the *Klein* holding was the fact that Congress was attempting to decide the controversy at issue in the Government's own favor. Thus, Congress' action could not be grounded upon its broad power to recognize and pay the Nation's debts. Second, and even more important, the proviso at issue in *Klein* had attempted "to prescribe a rule for the decision of a cause in a particular way." 13 Wall., at 146. The amendment at issue in the present case, however, like the Special Act at issue in *Cherokee Nation,* waived the defense of res judicata so that a legal claim could be resolved on the merits. Congress made no effort in either instance to control the Court of Claims' ultimate decision of that claim. See n. 23, *supra.*[25]

C

When Congress enacted the amendment directing the Court of Claims to review the merits of the Black Hills claim, it neither brought into question the finality of that court's earlier judgments, nor interfered with that court's judicial function in deciding the merits of the claim. When the Sioux returned to the Court of Claims following passage of the amendment, they were there in pursuit of judicial enforcement of a new legal right. Congress had not "reversed" the Court of Claims' holding that the claim was barred by res judicata, nor, for that matter, had it reviewed the 1942 decision rejecting the Sioux' claim on the merits. As Congress explicitly recognized, it only was providing a forum so that a new judicial review of the Black Hills claim could take place. This review was to be based on the facts found by the Court of Claims after reviewing all the evidence, and an application of generally controlling legal principles to those facts. For these reasons, Congress was not reviewing the merits of the Court of Claims' decisions, and did not interfere with the finality of its judgments.

Moreover, Congress in no way attempted to prescribe the outcome of the Court of Claims' new review of the merits. That court was left completely free to reaffirm its 1942 judgment that the Black Hills claim was not cognizable under the Fifth Amendment, if upon its review of the facts and law, such a decision was warranted. In this respect, the amendment before us is a far cry from the legislatively enacted "consent judgment" called into question in *Pope,* yet found constitutional as a valid exercise of Congress' broad power to pay the Nation's debts. And, for the same reasons, this amendment clearly is distinguishable from the proviso to this Court's appellate jurisdiction held unconstitutional in *Klein.*

In sum, as this Court implicitly held in *Cherokee Nation,* Congress' mere waiver of the res judicata effect of a prior judicial decision rejecting the validity of a legal claim against the United States does not violate the doctrine of separation of powers.

IV

A

In reaching its conclusion that the 1877 Act effected a taking of the Black Hills for which just compensation was due the Sioux under the Fifth Amendment, the Court of Claims relied upon the "good faith effort" test developed in its earlier decision in *Three Tribes of Fort Berthold Reservation* v. *United States,* 182 Ct. Cl. 543, 390 F. 2d 686 (1968). The *Fort Berthold* test had been designed to reconcile two lines of cases decided by this Court that seemingly were in conflict. The first line, exemplified by *Lone Wolf* v. *Hitchcock,* 187 U. S. 553 (1903), recognizes "that Congress possesse[s] a paramount power over the property of the Indians, by reason of its exercise of guardianship over their interests, and that such authority might be implied, even though opposed to the strict letter of a treaty with the Indians." *Id.,* at 565. The second line, exemplified by the more recent decision in *Shoshone Tribe* v. *United States,* 299 U. S. 476 (1937), concedes Congress' paramount power over Indian property, but holds, nonetheless, that "[t]he power does not extend so far as to enable the Government 'to give the tribal lands to others, or to appropriate them to its own purposes, without rendering, or assuming an obligation to render, just compensation.'" *Id.,* at 497 (quoting *United States* v. *Creek Nation,* 295 U. S. 103, 110 (1935)). In *Shoshone Tribe,* Mr. Justice Cardozo, in speaking for the Court, expressed the distinction between the conflicting principles in a characteristically pithy phrase: "Spoliation is not management." 299 U. S., at 498.

The *Fort Berthold* test distinguishes between cases in which one or the other principle is applicable:

"It is obvious that Congress cannot simultaneously (1) act as trustee for the benefit of the Indians, exercising its plenary powers over the Indians and their property, as it thinks is in their best interests, and (2) exercise its sovereign power of eminent domain, taking the Indians' property within the meaning of the Fifth Amendment to the Constitution. In any given situation in which Congress has acted with regard to Indian people, it must have acted either in one capacity or the other. Congress can own two hats, but it cannot wear them both at the same time.

"Some guideline must be established so that a court can identify in which capacity Congress is acting. The following guideline would best give recognition to the basic distinction between the two types of congressional action: Where Congress makes a good faith effort to give the Indians the full value of the land and thus merely transmutes the property from land to money, there is no taking. This is a mere substitution of assets or change of form and is a traditional function of a trustee." 182 Ct. Cl., at 553, 390 F. 2d, at 691.

Applying the *Fort Berthold* test to the facts of this case, the Court of Claims concluded that, in passing the 1877 Act, Congress had not made a good-faith effort to give the Sioux the full value of the Black Hills. The principal issue presented by this case is whether the legal standard applied by the Court of Claims was erroneous.[26]

B

The Government contends that the Court of Claims erred insofar as its holding that the 1877 Act effected a taking of the Black Hills was based on Congress' failure to indicate affirmatively that the consideration given the Sioux was of equivalent value to the property rights ceded to the Government. It argues that "the true rule is that Congress must be assumed to be acting within its plenary power to manage tribal assets if it reasonably can be concluded that the legislation was intended to promote the welfare of the tribe." Brief for United States 52. The Government derives support for this rule principally from this Court's decision in *Lone Wolf* v. *Hitchcock.*

In *Lone Wolf*, representatives of the Kiowa, Comanche, and Apache Tribes brought an equitable action against the Secretary of the Interior and other governmental officials to enjoin them from enforcing the terms of an Act of Congress that called for the sale of lands held by the Indians pursuant to the Medicine Lodge Treaty of 1867, 15 Stat. 581. That treaty, like the Fort Laramie Treaty of 1868, included a provision that any future cession of reservation lands would be without validity or force "unless executed and signed by at least three fourths of all the adult male Indians occupying the same." *Id.,* at 585. The legislation at issue, Act of June 6, 1900, 31 Stat. 672, was based on an agreement with the Indians

that had not been signed by the requisite number of adult males residing on the reservation.

This Court's principal holding in *Lone Wolf* was that "the legislative power might pass laws in conflict with treaties made with the Indians." 187 U. S., at 566. The Court stated:

"The power exists to abrogate the provisions of an Indian treaty, though presumably such power will be exercised only when circumstances arise which will not only justify the government in disregarding the stipulations of the treaty, but may demand, in the interest of the country and the Indians themselves, that it should do so. When, therefore, treaties were entered into between the United States and a tribe of Indians it was never doubted that the *power* to abrogate existed in Congress, and that in a contingency such power might be availed of from considerations of governmental policy, particularly if consistent with perfect good faith towards the Indians." *Ibid.* (Emphasis in original.)[27]

The Court, therefore, was not required to consider the contentions of the Indians that the agreement ceding their lands had been obtained by fraud, and had not been signed by the requisite number of adult males. "[A]ll these matters, in any event, were solely within the domain of the legislative authority and its action is conclusive upon the courts." *Id.,* at 568.

In the penultimate paragraph of the opinion, however, the Court in *Lone Wolf* went on to make some observations seemingly directed to the question whether the Act at issue might constitute a taking of Indian property without just compensation. The Court there stated:

"The act of June 6, 1900, which is complained of in the bill, was enacted at a time when the tribal relations between the confederated tribes of Kiowas, Comanches and Apaches still existed, and that statute and the statutes supplementary thereto dealt with the disposition of tribal property and purported to give an adequate consideration for the surplus lands not allotted among the Indians or reserved for their benefit. Indeed, the controversy which this case presents is concluded by the decision in *Cherokee Nation* v. *Hitchcock,* 187 U. S. 294, decided at this term, where it was held that full administrative power was possessed by Congress over Indian tribal property. In effect, the action of Congress now complained of was but an exercise of such power, a mere change in the form of investment of Indian tribal property, the property of those who, as we have held, were in substantial effect the wards of the government. *We must presume that Congress acted in perfect good faith in the dealings with the Indians of which complaint is made, and that the legislative branch of the government exercised its best judgment in the premises.* In any event, as Congress possessed full power in the matter, the judiciary cannot question or inquire into the motives which prompted the enactment of this legislation. If injury was occasioned, which we do not wish to be understood as implying, by the use made by Congress of its power, relief must be sought by an appeal to that body for redress and not to the courts. The legislation in question was constitutional." *Ibid.* (Emphasis supplied.)

The Government relies on the italicized sentence in the quotation above to support its view "that Congress must be assumed to be acting within its plenary power to manage tribal assets if it reasonably can be concluded that the legislation was intended to promote the welfare of the tribe." Brief for United States 52. Several adjoining passages in the paragraph, however, lead us to doubt whether the *Lone Wolf* Court meant to state a general rule applicable to cases such as the one before us.

First, *Lone Wolf* presented a situation in which Congress "purported to give an adequate consideration" for the treaty lands taken from the Indians. In fact, the Act at issue set aside for the Indians a sum certain of $2 million for surplus reservation lands surrendered to the United States. 31 Stat. 678; see 187 U. S., at 555. In contrast, the background of the 1877 Act "reveals a situation where Congress did not 'purport' to provide 'adequate consideration,' nor was there any meaningful negotiation or arm's-length bargaining, nor did Congress consider it was paying a fair price." 220 Ct. Cl., at 475, 601 F. 2d, at 1176 (concurring opinion).

Second, given the provisions of the Act at issue in *Lone Wolf,* the Court reasonably was able to conclude that "the action of Congress now complained of was but . . . a mere change in the form of investment of Indian tribal property." Under the Act of June 6, 1900, each head of a family was to be allotted a tract of land within the reservation of not less than 320 acres, an additional 480,000 acres of grazing land were set aside for the use of the tribes in common, and $2 million was paid to the Indians for the remaining surplus. 31 Stat. 677–678. In contrast, the historical background to the opening of the Black Hills for settlement, and the terms of the 1877 Act itself, see Part I, *supra,* would not lead one to conclude that the Act effected "a mere change in the form of investment of Indian tribal property."

Third, it seems significant that the views of the Court in *Lone Wolf* were based, in part, on a holding that "Congress possessed full power in the matter." Earlier in the opinion the Court stated: "Plenary authority over the tribal relations of the Indians has been exercised by Congress from the beginning, and the power has always been deemed a political one, not subject to be controlled by the judicial department of the government." 187 U. S., at 565. Thus, it seems that the Court's conclusive presumption of congressional good faith was based in large measure on the idea that relations between this Nation and the Indian tribes are a political matter, not amenable to judicial review. That view, of course, has long since been discredited in takings cases, and was expressly laid to rest in *Delaware Tribal Business Comm.* v. *Weeks,* 430 U. S. 73, 84 (1977).[28]

Fourth, and following up on the political question holding, the *Lone Wolf* opinion suggests that where the exercise of

congressional power results in injury to Indian rights, "relief must be sought by an appeal to that body for redress and not to the courts." Unlike *Lone Wolf,* this case is one in which the Sioux have sought redress from Congress, and the Legislative Branch has responded by referring the matter to the courts for resolution. See Parts II and III, *supra.* Where Congress waives the Government's sovereign immunity, and expressly directs the courts to resolve a taking claim on the merits, there would appear to be far less reason to apply *Lone Wolf's* principles of deference. See *United States* v. *Tillamooks,* 329 U. S. 40, 46 (1946) (plurality opinion).

The foregoing considerations support our conclusion that the passage from *Lone Wolf* here relied upon by the Government has limited relevance to this case. More significantly, *Lone Wolf's* presumption of congressional good faith has little to commend it as an enduring principle for deciding questions of the kind presented here. In every case where a taking of treaty-protected property is alleged,[29] a reviewing court must recognize that tribal lands are subject to Congress' power to control and manage the tribe's affairs. But the court must also be cognizant that "this power to control and manage [is] not absolute. While extending to all appropriate measures for protecting and advancing the tribe, it [is] subject to limitations inhering in . . . a guardianship and to pertinent constitutional restrictions." *United States* v. *Creek Nation,* 295 U. S., at 109–110. Accord: *Menominee Tribe* v. *United States,* 391 U. S. 404, 413 (1968); *FPC* v. *Tuscarora Indian Nation,* 362 U. S. 99, 122 (1960); *United States* v. *Klamath Indians,* 304 U. S. 119, 123 (1938); *United States* v. *Shoshone Tribe,* 304 U. S. 111, 115–116 (1938); *Shoshone Tribe* v. *United States,* 299 U. S. 476, 497–498 (1937).

As the Court of Claims recognized in its decision below, the question whether a particular measure was appropriate for protecting and advancing the tribe's interests, and therefore not subject to the constitutional command of the Just Compensation Clause, is factual in nature. The answer must be based on a consideration of all the evidence presented. We do not mean to imply that a reviewing court is to second-guess, from the perspective of hindsight, a legislative judgment that a particular measure would serve the best interests of the tribe. We do mean to require courts, in considering whether a particular congressional action was taken in pursuance of Congress' power to manage and control tribal lands for the Indians' welfare, to engage in a thoroughgoing and impartial examination of the historical record. A presumption of congressional good faith cannot serve to advance such an inquiry.

C

We turn to the question whether the Court of Claims' inquiry in this case was guided by an appropriate legal standard. We conclude that it was. In fact, we approve that court's formulation of the inquiry as setting a standard that ought to be emulated by courts faced with resolving future cases presenting the question at issue here:

"In determining whether Congress has made a good faith effort to give the Indians the full value of their lands when the government acquired [them], we therefore look to the objective facts as revealed by Acts of Congress, congressional committee reports, statements submitted to Congress by government officials, reports of special commissions appointed by Congress to treat with the Indians, and similar evidence relating to the acquisition. . . .

"The 'good faith effort' and 'transmutation of property' concepts referred to in *Fort Berthold* are opposite sides of the same coin. They reflect the traditional rule that a trustee may change the form of trust assets as long as he fairly (or in good faith) attempts to provide his ward with property of equivalent value. If he does that, he cannot be faulted if hindsight should demonstrate a lack of precise equivalence. On the other hand, if a trustee (or the government in its dealings with the Indians) does not attempt to give the ward the fair equivalent of what he acquires from him, the trustee to that extent has taken rather than transmuted the property of the ward. In other words, an essential element of the inquiry under the *Fort Berthold* guideline is determining the adequacy of the consideration the government gave for the Indian lands it acquired. That inquiry cannot be avoided by the government's simple assertion that it acted in good faith in its dealings with the Indians." 220 Ct. Cl., at 451, 601 F. 2d, at 1162.[30]

D

We next examine the factual findings made by the Court of Claims, which led it to the conclusion that the 1877 Act effected a taking. First, the Court found that "[t]he only item of 'consideration' that possibly could be viewed as showing an attempt by Congress to give the Sioux the 'full value' of the land the government took from them was the requirement to furnish them with rations until they became self-sufficient." 220 Ct. Cl., at 458, 601 F. 2d, at 1166. This finding is fully supported by the record, and the Government does not seriously contend otherwise.[31]

Second, the court found, after engaging in an exhaustive review of the historical record, that neither the Manypenny Commission, nor the congressional Committees that approved the 1877 Act, nor the individual legislators who spoke on its behalf on the floor of Congress, ever indicated a belief that the Government's obligation to provide the Sioux with rations constituted a fair equivalent for the value of the Black Hills and the additional property rights the Indians were forced to surrender. See *id.*, at 458–462, 601 F. 2d, at 1166–1168. This finding is unchallenged by the Government.

A third finding lending some weight to the Court's legal conclusion was that the conditions placed by the Government on the Sioux' entitlement to rations, see n. 14, *supra*, "further show that the government's undertaking to furnish rations to the Indians until they could support themselves did not reflect a congressional

decision that the value of the rations was the equivalent of the land the Indians were giving up, but instead was an attempt to coerce the Sioux into capitulating to congressional demands." 220 Ct. Cl., at 461, 601 F. 2d, at 1168. We might add only that this finding is fully consistent with similar observations made by this Court nearly a century ago in an analogous case.

In *Choctaw Nation* v. *United States,* 119 U. S. 1, 35 (1886), the Court held, over objections by the Government, that an earlier award made by the Senate on an Indian tribe's treaty claim "was fair, just, and equitable." The treaty at issue had called for the removal of the Choctaw Nation from treaty-protected lands in exchange for payments for the tribe's subsistence for one year, payments for cattle and improvements on the new reservation, an annuity of $20,000 for 20 years commencing upon removal, and the provision of educational and agricultural services. *Id.,* at 38. Some years thereafter the Senate had awarded the Indians a substantial recovery based on the latter treaty's failure to compensate the Choctaw for the lands they had ceded. Congress later enacted a jurisdictional statute which permitted the United States to contest the fairness of the Senate's award as a settlement of the Indian's treaty claim. In rejecting the Government's arguments, and accepting the Senate's award as "furnish[ing] the nearest approximation to the justice and right of the case," *id.,* at 35, this Court observed:

"It is notorious as a historical fact, as it abundantly appears from the record in this case, that great pressure had to be brought to bear upon the Indians to effect their removal, and the whole treaty was evidently and purposely executed, not so much to secure to the Indians the rights for which they had stipulated, as to effectuate the policy of the United States in regard to their removal. The most noticeable thing, upon a careful consideration of the terms of this treaty, is, that no money consideration is promised or paid for a cession of lands, the beneficial ownership of which is assumed to reside in the Choctaw Nation, and computed to amount to over ten millions of acres." *Id.,* at 37–38.

As for the payments that had been made to the Indians in order to induce them to remove themselves from their treaty lands, the Court, in words we find applicable to the 1877 Act, concluded:

"It is nowhere expressed in the treaty that these payments are to be made as the price of the lands ceded; and they are all only such expenditures as the government of the United States could well afford to incur for the mere purpose of executing its policy in reference to the removal of the Indians to their new homes. *As a consideration for the value of the lands ceded by the treaty, they must be regarded as a meagre pittance.*" *Id.,* at 38 (emphasis supplied).

These conclusions, in light of the historical background to the opening of the Black Hills for settlement, see Part I, *supra*, seem fully applicable to Congress' decision to remove the Sioux from that valuable tract of land, and to extinguish their off-reservation hunting rights.

Finally, the Court of Claims rejected the Government's contention that the fact that it subsequently had spent at least $43 million on rations for the Sioux (over the course of three-quarters of a century) established that the 1877 Act was an act of guardianship taken in the Sioux' best interest. The court concluded: "The critical inquiry is what Congress did—and how it viewed the obligation it was assuming—at the time it acquired the land, and not how much it ultimately cost the United States to fulfill the obligation." 220 Ct. Cl., at 462, 601 F. 2d, at 1168. It found no basis for believing that Congress, in 1877, anticipated that it would take the Sioux such a lengthy period of time to become self-sufficient, or that the fulfillment of the Government's obligation to feed the Sioux would entail the large expenditures ultimately made on their behalf. *Ibid.* We find no basis on which to question the legal standard applied by the Court of Claims, or the findings it reached, concerning Congress' decision to provide the Sioux with rations.

E

The aforementioned findings fully support the Court of Claims' conclusion that the 1877 Act appropriated the Black Hills "in circumstances which involved an implied undertaking by [the United States] to make just compensation to the tribe."[32] *United States v. Creek Nation,* 295 U. S., at 111. We make only two additional observations about this case. First, dating at least from the decision in *Cherokee Nation* v. *Southern Kansas R. Co.,* 135 U. S. 641, 657 (1890), this Court has recognized that Indian lands, to which a tribe holds recognized title, "are held subject to the authority of the general government to take them for such objects as are germane to the execution of the powers granted to it; provided only, that they are not taken without just compensation being made to the owner." In the same decision the Court emphasized that the owner of such lands "is entitled to reasonable, certain and adequate provision for obtaining compensation before his occupancy is disturbed." *Id.,* at 659. The Court of Claims gave effect to this principle when it held that the Government's uncertain and indefinite obligation to provide the Sioux with rations until they became self-sufficient did not constitute adequate consideration for the Black Hills.

Second, it seems readily apparent to us that the obligation to provide rations to the Sioux was undertaken in order to ensure them a means of surviving their transition from the nomadic life of the hunt to the agrarian lifestyle Congress had chosen for them. Those who have studied the Government's reservation policy during this period of our Nation's history agree. See n. 11, *supra.* It is important to recognize that the 1877 Act, in addition to removing the Black Hills from the Great Sioux Reservation, also ceded the Sioux' hunting rights in a vast tract of land extending beyond the boundaries of that reservation. See n. 14, *supra.* Under such circumstances, it is reasonable to conclude that Congress' undertaking of an obligation to provide rations for the Sioux was a *quid pro quo* for depriving them of their chosen way of life, and was not intended to compensate them for the taking of the Black Hills.[33]

V

In sum, we conclude that the legal analysis and factual findings of the Court of Claims fully support its conclusion that the terms of the 1877 Act did not effect "a mere change in the form of investment of Indian tribal property." *Lone Wolf* v. *Hitchcock,* 187 U. S., at 568. Rather, the 1877 Act effected a taking of tribal property, property which had been set aside for the exclusive occupation of the Sioux by the Fort Laramie Treaty of 1868. That taking implied an obligation on the part of the Government to make just compensation to the Sioux Nation, and that obligation, including an award of interest, must now, at last, be paid.

The judgment of the Court of Claims is affirmed.

It is so ordered.

MR. JUSTICE WHITE, concurring in part and concurring in the judgment.

I agree that there is no constitutional infirmity in the direction by Congress that the Court of Claims consider this case without regard to the defense of res judicata. I also agree that the Court of Claims correctly decided this case. Accordingly, I concur in Parts III and V of the Court's opinion and in the judgment.

MR. JUSTICE REHNQUIST, dissenting.

In 1942, the Sioux Tribe filed a petition for certiorari requesting this Court to review the Court of Claims' ruling that Congress had not unconstitutionally taken the Black Hills in 1877, but had merely exchanged the Black Hills for rations and grazing lands—an exchange Congress believed to be in the best interests of the Sioux and the Nation. This Court declined to review that judgment. *Sioux Tribe* v. *United States,* 97 Ct. Cl. 613 (1942), cert. denied, 318 U. S. 789 (1943). Yet today the Court permits Congress to reopen that judgment which this Court rendered final upon denying certiorari in 1943, and proceeds to reject the 1942 Court of Claims' factual interpretation of the events in 1877. I am convinced that Congress may not constitutionally require the Court of Claims to reopen this proceeding, that there is no judicial principle justifying the decision to afford the respondents an additional opportunity to litigate the same claim, and that the Court of Claims' first interpretation of the events in 1877 was by all accounts the more realistic one. I therefore dissent.

I

In 1920, Congress enacted a special jurisdictional Act, ch. 222, 41 Stat. 738, authorizing the Sioux Tribe to submit any legal or equitable claim against the United States to the Court of Claims. The Sioux filed suit claiming that the 1877 Act removing the Black Hills from the Sioux territory was an unconstitutional taking. In

Sioux Tribe v. *United States, supra,* the Court of Claims considered the question fully and found that the United States had not taken the Black Hills from the Sioux within the meaning of the Fifth Amendment. It is important to highlight what that court found. It did not decide, as the Court today suggests, that it merely lacked jurisdiction over the claim presented by the Sioux. See *ante,* at [1257]. It found that under the circumstances presented in 1877, Congress attempted to improve the situation of the Sioux and the Nation by exchanging the Black Hills for 900,000 acres of grazing lands and rations for as long as they should be needed. The court found that although the Government attempted to keep white settlers and gold prospectors out of the Black Hills territory, these efforts were unsuccessful. The court concluded that this situation was such that the Government "believed serious conflicts would develop between the settlers and the Government, and between the settlers and the Indians." 97 Ct. Cl., at 659. It was also apparent to Congress that the Indians were still "incapable of supporting themselves." *Ibid.*

The court found that the Government therefore embarked upon a course designed to obtain the Indians' agreement to sell the Black Hills and "endeavored in every way possible during 1875 and 1876 to arrive at a mutual agreement with the Indians for the sale. . . ." *Id.,* at 681. Negotiation having failed, Congress then turned to design terms for the acquisition of the Black Hills which it found to be in the best interest of both the United States and the Sioux. The court found that pursuant to the 1877 agreement, Congress provided the Indians with more than $43 million in rations as well as providing them with 900,000 acres of needed grazing lands. Thus the court concluded that "the record shows that the action taken was pursuant to a policy which the Congress deemed to be for the interest of the Indians and just to both parties." *Id.,* at 668. The court emphasized:

> "[T]he Congress, in an act enacted because of the situation encountered and pursuant to a policy which in its wisdom it deemed to be in the interest and for the benefit and welfare of the . . . Sioux Tribe, as well as for the necessities of the Government, required the Indians to sell or surrender to the Government a portion of their land and hunting rights on other land in return for that which the Congress, in its judgment, deemed to be adequate consideration for what the Indians were required to give up, which consideration the Government was not otherwise under any legal obligation to pay." *Id.,* at 667.

This Court denied certiorari. 318 U. S. 789 (1943).

During the course of further litigation commencing in 1950, the Sioux again resubmitted their claim that the Black Hills were taken unconstitutionally. The Government pleaded res judicata as a defense. The Court of Claims held that res judicata barred relitigation of the question since the original Court of Claims decision had clearly held that the appropriation of the Black Hills was not a taking because Congress in "exercising its plenary power over Indian tribes, took their land without their consent and substituted for it something conceived by Congress to be an equivalent." *United States* v. *Sioux Nation,* 207 Ct. Cl. 234, 243, 518 F. 2d 1298, 1303 (1975). The court found no basis for relieving the Sioux from the bar of res judicata finding that the disability "is not lifted if a later court disagrees with a prior one." *Id.,* at 244, 518 F. 2d, at 1303. The court thus considered the equities entailed by the application of res judicata in this case and held that relitigation was unwarranted. Again, this Court denied certiorari. 423 U. S. 1016 (1975).

Congress then passed another statute authorizing the Sioux to relitigate their taking claim in the Court of Claims. 92 Stat. 153. The statute provided that the Court of Claims "*shall* review on the merits" the Sioux claim that there was a taking and that the Court "*shall determine that issue de novo.*" (Emphasis added.) Neither party submitted additional evidence and the Court of Claims decided the case on the basis of the record generated in the 1942 case and before the Commission. On the basis of that same record, the Court of Claims has now determined that the facts establish that Congress did not act in the best interest of the Sioux, as the 1942 court found, but arbitrarily appropriated the Black Hills without affording just compensation. This Court now embraces this second, latter-day interpretation of the facts in 1877.

II

Although the Court refrains from so boldly characterizing its action, it is obvious from these facts that Congress has reviewed the decisions of the Court of Claims, set aside the judgment that no taking of the Black Hills occurred, set aside the judgment that there is no cognizable reason for relitigating this claim, and ordered a new trial. I am convinced that this is nothing other than an exercise of judicial power reserved to Art. III courts that may not be performed by the Legislative Branch under its Art. I authority.

Article III vests "the judical Power . . . of the United States" in federal courts. Congress is vested by Art. I with *legislative* powers, and may not itself exercise an appellate-type review of judicial judgments in order to alter their terms, or to order new trials of cases already decided. The judges in *Hayburn's Case,* 2 Dall. 409, 413, n. 4 (1792), stated that "no decision of any court of the United States can, under any circumstances, in our opinion, agreeable to the Constitution, be liable to a reversion, or even suspension, by the Legislature itself, in whom no judicial power of any kind appears to be vested." We have interpreted the decision in *United States* v. *Klein,* 13 Wall. 128 (1872), as having "rested upon the ground that . . . Congress was without constitutional authority to control the exercise of . . . judicial power . . . by requiring this Court to set aside the judgment of the Court of Claims" and as holding that Congress may not "require a new trial of the issues . . . which the Court had resolved against [a party]." *Pope* v. *United States,* 323 U. S. 1, 8, 9 (1944).

This principle was again applied in *United States* v. *O'Grady,* 22 Wall. 641, 647 (1875), where the Court refused to legitimize a congressional attempt to revise a final judgment rendered by the Court of Claims finding that such judgments "are beyond all doubt the final determination of the matter in controversy; and it is equally certain that the judgments of the Court of Claims, where no appeal is taken to this court, are, under existing laws, *absolutely conclusive of the rights of the parties, unless a new trial is granted by that court. . . .*" (Emphasis added.) The Court further found that there is only one Supreme Court and "[i]t is quite clear that Congress cannot subject the judgments of the Supreme Court to the re-examination and revision of any other tribunal or any other department of the government." *Id.,* at 648. See also *Chicago & Southern Air Lines, Inc.* v. *Waterman S. S. Corp.,* 333 U. S. 103 (1948). Congress has exceeded the legislative boundaries drawn by these cases and the Constitution and exercised judicial power in a case already decided by effectively ordering a new trial.

The determination of whether this action is an exercise of legislative or judicial power is of course one of characterization. The fact that the judicial process is affected by an Act of Congress is not dispositive since many actions which this Court has clearly held to be legitimate exercises of legislative authority do have an effect on the judiciary and its processes. Congress may legitimately exercise legislative powers in the regulation of judicial jurisdiction; and it may, like other litigants, change the import of a final judgment by establishing new legal rights after the date of judgment, and have an effect on the grounds available for a court's decision by waiving available defenses. But as the Court apparently concedes, Congress may not, in the name of those legitimate actions, review and set aside a final judgment of an Art. III court, and order the courts to rehear an issue previously decided in a particular case.

The Court relies heavily on the fact that Congress was acting pursuant to its power to pay the Nation's debts. No doubt, Congress has broad power to do just that, but it may do so only through the exercise of legislative, not judicial powers. Thus the question must be, not whether Congress was attempting to pay its debts through this Act, but whether it attempted to do so by means of judicial power. The Court suggests that the congressional action in issue is justified as either a permissible regulation of jurisdiction, the creation of a new obligation, or the mere waiver of a litigant's right. These alternative nonjudicial characterizations of the congressional action, however, are simply unpersuasive.

A

The Court first attempts to categorize this action as a permissible regulation of jurisdiction stating that all Congress has done is to "provid[e] a forum so that a new judicial review of the Black Hills claim could take place." But that is the essence of an appellate or trial court decision ordering a new trial. While Congress may *regulate* judicial functions it may not itself *exercise* them. Admittedly, it is not always readily apparent whether a particular action constitutes the assignment or the exercise of a judicial function since the assignment of some functions is inherently

judicial—such as assigning the trial court the task of rehearing a case because of error. The guidelines identified in our opinions, however, indicate that while Congress enjoys broad authority to regulate judicial proceedings in the context of a *class* of cases, *Johannessen* v. *United States,* 225 U. S. 227 (1912), when Congress regulates functions of the judiciary in a *pending* case it walks the line between judicial and legislative authority, and exceeds that line if it sets aside a judgment or orders retrial of a previously adjudicated issue. *United States* v. *Klein, supra; Pope* v. *United States, supra.*

By ordering a *rehearing* in a pending case, Congress does not merely assign a judicial function, it necessarily reviews and sets aside an otherwise final adjudication; actions which this Court concedes Congress cannot permissibly take under the decisions of this Court. . . . The Court concludes that no "review" of the Court of Claims decisions (and our denials of certiorari) has occurred, and that the finality of the judgments has not been disturbed, principally because Congress has not dictated a rule of decision that must govern the ultimate outcome of the adjudication. The fact that Congress did not dictate to the Court of Claims that a particular result be reached does not in any way negate the fact it has sought to exercise judicial power. This Court and other appellate courts often reverse a trial court for error without indicating what the result should be when the claim is heard again.

It is also apparent that Congress must have "reviewed" the merits of the litigation and concluded that for some reason, the Sioux should have a second opportunity to air their claims. The order of a new trial inevitably reflects some measure of dissatisfaction with at least the manner in which the original claim was heard. It certainly seems doubtful that Congress would grant a litigant a new trial if convinced that the litigant had been fairly heard in the first instance. Unless Congress is assuming that there were deficiencies in the prior judicial proceeding, why would it see fit to appropriate public money to have the claim heard once again? It would seem that Congress did not find the opinions of the Court of Claims fully persuasive. But it is not the province of Congress to judge the persuasiveness of the opinions of federal courts—that is the judiciary's province alone. It is equally apparent that Congress has set aside the judgments of the Court of Claims. Previously those judgments were dispositive of the issues litigated in them; Congress now says that they are not. The action of Congress cannot be justified as the regulation of the jurisdiction of the federal courts because it seeks to provide a forum for the purposes of reviewing a previously final judgment in a pending case.

B

The action also cannot be characterized and upheld as merely an exercise of a litigant's power to change the effect of a judgment by agreeing to obligations beyond those required by a particular judgment. This Court has clearly never found that the judicial power is encroached upon because Congress seeks to change the law after a question has been adjudicated. See, *e. g., Pennsylvania* v. *Wheeling & Belmont Bridge Co.,* 18 How. 421 (1856); *Hodges* v. *Snyder,* 261 U. S. 600 (1923). This is a recognition of the right of every litigant to pay his adversary more than the court says is required if he so chooses. Congress, acting under its spending powers, is, like an individual, entitled to enlarge its obligations after the court has adjudicated a question. The decision in *Pope* v. *United States,* 323 U. S. 1 (1944), clearly rests upon this distinction.

But here Congress has made no change in the applicable law. It has not provided, as our opinions make clear it could have, that the Sioux should recover for all interest on the value of the Black Hills. Counsel for respondents in fact stated at oral argument that he could not persuade Congress "to go that far." Congress has not changed the rule of law, it simply directed the judiciary to try again. Congress may not attempt to shift its legislative responsibilities and satisfy its constituents by discarding final judgments and ordering new trials.

C

The Court also suggests that the congressional action is but a "mere waiver" of a defense within a litigant's prerogative. . . . Congress certainly is no different from other litigants in this regard, and if the congressional action in this case could convincingly be construed as having an effect no greater than an ordinary litigant's waiver, I certainly would not object that Congress was exercising judicial power. But it is apparent that the congressional action in issue accomplished far more than a litigant's waiver. Congress clearly required the Court of Claims to hear the case in full, and only if a waiver of res judicata by a litigant would always impose an obligation on a federal court to rehear such a claim, could it be said that Congress has exercised the power of a litigant rather than the power of a legislature.

While res judicata is a defense which can be waived, see Fed. Rule Civ. Proc. 8 (c), if a court is on notice that it has previously decided the issue presented, the court may dismiss the action *sua sponte,* even though the defense has not been raised. See *Hedger Transportation Corp.* v. *Ira S. Bushey & Sons,* 186 F. 2d 236 (CA2 1951); *Evarts* v. *Western Metal Finishing Co.,* 253 F. 2d 637, 639, n. 1 (CA9), cert. denied, 358 U. S. 815 (1958); *Scholla* v. *Scholla,* 92 U. S. App. D. C. 9, 201 F. 2d 211 (1953); *Hicks* v. *Holland,* 235 F. 2d 183 (CA6), cert. denied, 352 U. S. 855 (1956). This result is fully consistent with the policies underlying res judicata: it is not based solely on the defendant's interest in avoiding the burdens of twice defending a suit, but is also based on the avoidance of unnecessary judicial waste. *Commissioner* v. *Sunnen,* 333 U. S. 591, 597 (1948); *Blonder-Tongue Laboratories, Inc.* v. *University of Illinois Foundation,* 402 U. S. 313, 328 (1971); *Parklane Hosiery Co.* v. *Shore,* 439 U. S. 322 (1979). The Court of Claims itself has indicated that it would not engage in reconsideration of an issue previously decided by the Court of Claims without substantial justification:

"It is well to remember that *res judicata* and its offspring, collateral estoppel, are not statutory defenses; they are defenses adopted by the courts in furtherance of prompt and efficient administration of the business that comes before them. They are grounded on the theory that one litigant cannot unduly consume the time of the court at the expense of other litigants, and that, once the court has finally decided an issue, a litigant cannot demand that it be decided again." *Warthen* v. *United States,* 157 Ct. Cl. 798, 800 (1962).

It matters not that the defendant has consented to the relitigation of the claim since the judiciary retains an independent interest in preventing the misallocation of judicial resources and second-guessing prior panels of Art. III judges when the issue has been fully and fairly litigated in a prior proceeding. Since the Court of Claims found in this case that there was no adequate reason for denying res judicata effect after the issue was raised and the respondents were given an opportunity to demonstrate why res judicata should not apply, it is clear that the issue has been heard again only because Congress used its legislative authority to mandate a rehearing. The Court of Claims apparently acknowledged that this in fact was the effect of the legislation, for it did not state that readjudication was the product of a waiver, but rather that through its decision the court "carried out the *obligation imposed upon us* in the 1978 jurisdictional statute." (Emphasis added.)

Nor do I find this Court's decision in *Cherokee Nation* v. *United States,* 270 U. S. 476 (1926), dispositive. Again, in *Cherokee Nation,* the Court was asked to consider and decide a question not previously adjudicated by the Court of Claims. The Court stated that the theory of interest presented in the second adjudication was not "presented either to the Court of Claims or to this Court. It is a new argument not before considered." *Id.,* at 486. Thus even *Cherokee Nation* did not involve congressionally mandated judicial re-examination of a question previously decided by an Art. III court.

Here, in contrast, the issue decided is identical to that decided in 1942. It is quite clear from a comparison of the 1942 decision of the Court of Claims and the opinion of the Court today that the only thing that has changed is an interpretation of the events which occurred in 1877. The Court today concludes that the facts in this case "would not lead one to conclude that the Act effected 'a mere change in the form of investment of Indian tribal property.'" . . . But that is precisely what the Court of Claims found in 1942. . . . There has not even been a change in the law, for the Court today relies on decisions rendered long before the Court of Claims decision in 1942. It is the view of history, and not the law, which has evolved. See *infra,* at [1270]. The decision is thus clearly nothing more than a second interpretation of the precise factual question decided in 1942. As the dissenting judges in the Court of Claims aptly stated: "The facts have not changed. We have been offered no new evidence." 220 Ct. Cl. 442, 489, 601 F. 2d 1157, 1184.

It is therefore apparent that Congress has accomplished more than a private litigant's attempted waiver, more than legislative control over the general jurisdiction of the federal courts, and more than the establishment of a new rule of law for a previously decided case. What Congress has done is uniquely judicial. It has reviewed a prior decision of an Art. III court, eviscerated the finality of that judgment, and ordered a new trial in a pending case.

III

Even if I could countenance the Court's decision to reach the merits of this case, I also think it has erred in rejecting the 1942 court's interpretation of the facts. That court rendered a very persuasive account of the congressional enactment. . . . As the dissenting judges in the Court of Claims opinion under review pointedly stated: "The majority's view that the rations were not consideration for the Black Hills in untenable. What else was the money for?" 220 Ct. Cl., at 487, 601 F. 2d, at 1183.

I think the Court today rejects that conclusion largely on the basis of a view of the settlement of the American West which is not universally shared. There were undoubtedly greed, cupidity, and other less-than-admirable tactics employed by the Government during the Black Hills episode in the settlement of the West, but the Indians did not lack their share of villainy either. It seems to me quite unfair to judge by the light of "revisionist" historians or the mores of another era actions that were taken under pressure of time more than a century ago.

Different historians, not writing for the purpose of having their conclusions or observations inserted in the reports of congressional committees, have taken different positions than those expressed in some of the materials referred to in the Court's opinion. This is not unnatural, since history, no more than law, is not an exact (or for that matter an inexact) science.

But the inferences which the Court itself draws from the letter from General Sheridan to General Sherman reporting on a meeting between the former with President Grant, the Secretary of the Interior, and the Secretary of War, as well as other passages in the Court's opinion, leave a stereotyped and one-sided impression both of the settlement regarding the Black Hills portion of the Great Sioux Reservation and of the gradual expansion of the National Government from the Proclamation Line of King George III in 1763 to the Pacific Ocean.

Ray Billington, a senior research associate at the Huntington Library in San Marino, Cal., since 1963, and a respected student of the settlement of the American West, emphasized in his introduction to the book Soldier and Brave (National Park Service, U.S. Dept. of the Interior, 1963) that the confrontations in the West were the product of a long history, not a conniving Presidential administration:

"Three centuries of bitter Indian warfare reached a tragic climax on the plains and mountains of America's Far West. Since the early seventeenth century, when Chief Opechancanough rallied his Powhatan tribesmen against the Virginia intruders on their lands, each advance of the frontier had been met with stubborn resistance. At times this conflict flamed into open warfare: in King Phillips' rebellion against the Massachusetts Puritans, during the French and Indian Wars of the eighteenth century, in Chief Pontiac's assault on his new British overlords in 1763, in Chief Tecumseh's vain efforts to hold back the advancing pioneers of 1812, and in the Black Hawk War. . . .

". . . In three tragic decades, between 1860 and 1890, the Indians suffered the humiliating defeats that forced them to walk the white man's road toward civilization. Few conquered people in the history of mankind have paid so dearly for their defense of a way of life that the march of progress had outmoded.

"This epic struggle left its landmarks behind, as monuments to the brave men, Indian and white, who fought and died that their manner of living might endure." *Id.,* at xiii–xiv.

Another history highlights the cultural differences which made conflict and brutal warfare inevitable:

"The Plains Indians seldom practiced agriculture or other primitive arts, but they were fine physical specimens; and in warfare, once they had learned the use of the rifle, [were] much more formidable than the Eastern tribes who had slowly yielded to the white man. Tribe warred with tribe, and a highly developed sign language was the only means of intertribal communication. The effective unit was the band or village of a few hundred souls, which might be seen in the course of its wanderings encamped by a watercourse with tipis erected; or pouring over the plain, women and children leading dogs and packhorses with their trailing travois, while gaily dressed braves loped ahead on horseback. They lived only for the day, recognized no rights of property, robbed or killed anyone if they thought they could get away with it, inflicted cruelty without a qualm, and endured torture without flinching." S. Morison, The Oxford History of the American People 539–540 (1965).

That there was tragedy, deception, barbarity, and virtually every other vice known to man in the 300-year history of the expansion of the original 13 Colonies into a Nation which now embraces more than three million square miles and 50 States cannot be denied. But in a court opinion, as a historical and not a legal matter, both settler and Indian are entitled to the benefit of the Biblical adjuration: "Judge not, that ye be not judged."

[*] *Steven M. Tullberg* and *Robert T. Coulter* filed a brief for the Indian Law Resource Center as *amicus curiae.*

[1] The Sioux territory recognized under the Treaty of September 17, 1851, see 11 Stat. 749, included all of the present State

of South Dakota, and parts of what is now Nebraska, Wyoming, North Dakota, and Montana. The Powder River War is described in some detail in D. Robinson, A History of the Dakota or Sioux Indians 356–381 (1904), reprinted in 2 South Dakota Historical Collections (1904). Red Cloud's career as a warrior and statesman of the Sioux is recounted in 2 G. Hebard & E. Brininstool, The Bozeman Trail 175–204 (1922).

[2] The boundaries of the reservation included approximately half the area of what is now the State of South Dakota, including all of that State west of the Missouri River save for a narrow strip in the far western portion. The reservation also included a narrow strip of land west of the Missouri and north of the border between North and South Dakota.

[3] The treaty called for the construction of schools and the provision of teachers for the education of Indian children, the provision of seeds and agricultural instruments to be used in the first four years of planting, and the provision of blacksmiths, carpenters, millers, and engineers to perform work on the reservation. See 15 Stat. 637–638, 640. In addition, the United States agreed to deliver certain articles of clothing to each Indian residing on the reservation, "on or before the first day of August of each year, for thirty years." *Id.,* at 638. An annual stipend of $10 per person was to be appropriated for all those members of the Sioux Nation who continued to engage in hunting; those who settled on the reservation to engage in farming would receive $20. *Ibid.* Subsistence rations of meat and flour (one pound of each per day) were to be provided for a period of four years to those Indians upon the reservation who could not provide for their own needs. *Id.,* at 639.

[4] The Fort Laramie Treaty was considered by some commentators to have been a complete victory for Red Cloud and the Sioux. In 1904 it was described as "the only instance in the history of the United States where the government has gone to war and afterwards negotiated a peace conceding everything demanded by the enemy and exacting nothing in return." Robinson, *supra* n. 1, at 387.

[5] The history of speculation concerning the presence of gold in the Black Hills, which dated from early explorations by prospectors in the 1830's, is capsulized in D. Jackson, Custer's Gold 3–7 (1966).

[6] In 1974, the Center for Western Studies completed a project compiling contemporary newspaper accounts of Custer's expedition. See H. Krause & G. Olson, Prelude to Glory (1974). Several correspondents traveled with Custer on the expedition and their dispatches were published by newspapers both in the Midwest and the East. *Id.,* at 6.

[7] See Robinson, *supra* n. 1, at 408–410; A. Tallent, The Black Hills 130 (1975 reprint of 1899 ed.); J. Vaughn, The Reynolds Campaign on Powder River 3–4 (1961).

The Sioux regarded Custer's expedition in itself to be a violation of the Fort Laramie Treaty. In later negotiations for cession of the Black Hills, Custer's trail through the Hills was referred to by a chief known as Fast Bear as "that thieves' road." Jackson, *supra*

n. 5, at 24. Chroniclers of the expedition, at least to an extent, have agreed. See *id.,* at 120; G. Manypenny, Our Indian Wards xxix, 296–297 (1972 reprint of 1880 ed.).

[8] General William Tecumseh Sherman, Commanding General of the Army, as quoted in the Saint Louis Globe in 1875, described the military's task in keeping prospectors out of the Black Hills as "the same old story, the story of Adam and Eve and the forbidden fruit." Jackson, *supra* n. 5, at 112. In an interview with a correspondent from the Bismarck Tribune, published September 2, 1874, Custer recognized the military's obligation to keep all trespassers off the reservation lands, but stated that he would recommend to Congress "the extinguishment of the Indian title at the earliest moment practicable for military reasons." Krause & Olson, *supra* n. 6, at 233. Given the ambivalence of feeling among the commanding officers of the Army about the practicality and desirability of its treaty obligations, it is perhaps not surprising that one chronicler of Sioux history would describe the Government's efforts to dislodge invading settlers from the Black Hills as "feeble." F. Hans, The Great Sioux Nation 522 (1964 reprint).

[9] The Report of the Allison Commission to the Secretary of the Interior is contained in the Annual Report of the Commissioner of Indian Affairs (1875), App. 146, 158–195. The unsuccessful negotiations are described in some detail in Jackson, *supra* n. 5, at 116–118, and in Robinson, *supra* n. 1, at 416–421.

[10] These events are described by Manypenny, *supra* n. 7, at 294–321, and Robinson, *supra* n. 1, at 422–438.

[11] In Dakota Twilight (1976), a history of the Standing Rock Sioux, Edward A. Milligan states:

"Nearly seven years had elapsed since the signing of the Fort Laramie Treaty and still the Sioux were no closer to a condition of self-support than when the treaty was signed. In the meantime the government had expended nearly thirteen million dollars for their support. The future treatment of the Sioux became a matter of serious moment, even if viewed from no higher standard than that of economics." *Id.,* at 52.

One historian has described the ration provisions of the Fort Laramie Treaty as part of a broader reservation system designed by Congress to convert nomadic tribesmen into farmers. Hagan, The Reservation Policy: Too Little and Too Late, in Indian-White Relations: A Persistent Paradox 157–169 (J. Smith & R. Kvasnicka, eds., 1976). In words applicable to conditions on the Sioux Reservation during the years in question, Professor Hagan stated:

"The idea had been to supplement the food the Indians obtained by hunting until they could subsist completely by farming. Clauses in the treaties permitted hunting outside the strict boundaries of the reservations, but the inevitable clashes between off-reservation hunting parties and whites led this privilege to be first restricted and then eliminated. The Indians became dependent upon government rations more quickly than had been anticipated, while their conversion to agriculture lagged behind schedule.

"The quantity of food supplied by the government was never sufficient for a full ration, and the quality was frequently poor. But in view of the fact that most treaties carried no provision for rations at all, and for others they were limited to four years, the members of Congress tended to look upon rations as a gratuity that should be terminated as quickly as possible. The Indian Service and military personnel generally agreed that it was better to feed than to fight, but to the typical late nineteenth-century member of Congress, not yet exposed to doctrines of social welfare, there was something obscene about grown men and women drawing free rations. Appropriations for subsistence consequently fell below the levels requested by the secretary of the interior.

"That starvation and near-starvation conditions were present on some of the sixty-odd reservations every year for the quarter century after the Civil War is manifest." *Id.,* at 161 (footnotes omitted).

[12] The chronology of the enactment of this bill does not necessarily support the view that it was passed in reaction to Custer's defeat at the Battle of the Little Big Horn on June 25, 1876, although some historians have taken a contrary view. See Jackson, *supra* n. 5, at 119.

[13] The commission's negotiations with the chiefs and head men is described by Robinson, *supra* n. 1, at 439–442. He states:

"As will be readily understood, the making of a treaty was a forced put, so far as the Indians were concerned. Defeated, disarmed, dismounted, they were at the mercy of a superior power and there was no alternative but to accept the conditions imposed upon them. This they did with as good grace as possible under all of the conditions existing." *Id.,* at 442.

Another early chronicler of the Black Hills region wrote of the treaty's provisions in the following chauvinistic terms:

"It will be seen by studying the provisions of this treaty, that by its terms the Indians from a material standpoint lost much, and gained but little. By the first article they lose all rights to the unceded Indian territory in Wyoming from which white settlers had then before been altogether excluded; by the second they relinquish all right to the Black Hills, and the fertile valley of the Belle Fourche in Dakota, without additional material compensation; by the third conceding the right of way over the unceded portions of their reservation; by the fourth they receive such supplies only, as were provided by the treaty of 1868, restricted as to the points for receiving them. The only real gain to the Indians seems to be embodied in the fifth article of the treaty [Government's obligation to provide subsistence rations]. The Indians, doubtless, realized that the Black Hills was destined soon to slip out of their grasp, regardless of their claims, and therefore thought it best to yield to the inevitable, and accept whatever was offered them.

"They were assured of a continuance of their regular daily rations, and certain annuities in clothing each year, guaranteed by the treaty of 1868, and what more could they ask or desire, than that a living be provided for themselves, their wives, their children, and all their relations, including squaw men, indirectly, thus leaving them free to live their wild, careless, unrestrained life, exempt from all the burdens and responsibilities of civilized existence? In view of the fact that there are thousands who are obliged to earn their bread and butter by the sweat of their brows, and that have hard work to keep the wolf from the door, they should be satisfied." Tallent, *supra* n. 7, at 133–134.

[14] The 1877 Act "ratified and confirmed" the agreement reached by the Manypenny Commission with the Sioux tribes. 19 Stat. 254. It altered the boundaries of the Great Sioux Reservation by adding some 900,000 acres of land to the north, while carving out virtually all that portion of the reservation between the one hundred and third and one hundred and fourth meridians, including the Black Hills, an area of well over 7 million acres. The Indians also relinquished their rights to hunt in the unceded lands recognized by the Fort Laramie Treaty, and agreed that three wagon roads could be cut through their reservation. *Id.,* at 255.

In exchange, the Government reaffirmed its obligation to provide all annuities called for by the Fort Laramie Treaty, and "to provide all necessary aid to assist the said Indians in the work of civilization; to furnish to them schools and instruction in mechanical and agricultural arts, as provided for by the treaty of 1868." *Id.,* at 256. In addition, every individual was to receive fixed quantities of beef or bacon and flour, and other foodstuffs, in the discretion of the Commissioner of Indian Affairs, which "shall be continued until the Indians are able to support themselves." *Ibid.* The provision of rations was to be conditioned, however, on the attendance at school by Indian children, and on the labor of those who resided on lands suitable for farming. The Government also promised to assist the Sioux in finding markets for their crops and in obtaining employment in the performance of Government work on the reservation. *Ibid.*

Later congressional actions having the effect of further reducing the domain of the Great Sioux Reservation are described in *Rosebud Sioux Tribe* v. *Kneip,* 430 U. S. 584, 589 (1977).

[15] See § 9 of the Act of Mar. 3, 1863, 12 Stat. 767; § 1 of the Tucker Act of Mar. 3, 1887, 24 Stat. 505.

[16] The Commission determined that the fair market value of the Black Hills as of February 28, 1877, was $17.1 million. In addition, the United States was held liable for gold removed by trespassing prospectors prior to that date, with a fair market value in the ground of $450,000. The Commission determined that the Government should receive a credit for all amounts it had paid to the Indians over the years in compliance with its obligations under the 1877 Act. These amounts were to be credited against the fair market value of the lands and gold taken, and interest as it accrued. The Commission decided that further proceedings would be necessary to compute the amounts to be credited and the value of the rights-of-way across the reservation that the Government also had acquired through the 1877 Act.

Chairman Kuykendall dissented in part from the Commission's judgment, arguing that the Sioux' taking claim was barred by the res judicata effect of the 1942 Court of Claims decision.

[17] See *United States* v. *Tillamooks,* 341 U. S. 48, 49 (1951) (recognizing that the "traditional rule" is that interest is not to be awarded on claims against the United States absent an express statutory provision to the contrary and that the "only exception arises when the taking entitles the claimant to just compensation under the Fifth Amendment"). In *United States* v. *Klamath Indians,* 304 U. S. 119, 123 (1938), the Court stated: "The established rule is that the taking of property by the United States in the exertion of its power of eminent domain implies a promise to pay just compensation, *i. e.,* value at the time of the taking plus an amount sufficient to produce the full equivalent of that value paid contemporaneously with the taking."

The Court of Claims also noted that subsequent to the Indian Claims Commission's judgment, Congress had enacted an amendment to 25 U. S. C. § 70a, providing generally that expenditures made by the Government "for food, rations, or provisions shall not be deemed payments on the claim." Act of Oct. 27, 1974, § 2, 88 Stat. 1499. Thus, the Government would no longer be entitled to an offset from any judgment eventually awarded the Sioux based on its appropriations for subsistence rations in the years following the passage of the 1877 Act. 207 Ct. Cl., at 240, 518 F. 2d, at 1301. See n. 16, *supra.*

[18] Judge Davis dissented with respect to the court's holding on res judicata, arguing that the Sioux had not had the opportunity to present their claim fully in 1942. 207 Ct. Cl., at 249, 518 F. 2d, at 1306.

[19] While affirming the Indian Claims Commission's determination that the acquisition of the Black Hills and the rights-of-way across the reservation constituted takings, the court reversed the Commission's determination that the mining of gold from the Black Hills by prospectors prior to 1877 also constituted a taking. The value of the gold, therefore, could not be considered as part of the principal on which interest would be paid to the Sioux. 220 Ct. Cl., at 466–467, 601 F. 2d, at 1171–1172.

[20] The *Lone Wolf* decision itself involved an action by tribal leaders to enjoin the enforcement of a statute that had the effect of abrogating the provisions of an earlier-enacted treaty with an Indian tribe. See Part IV-B, *infra.*

[21] Judge Nichols concurred in the result, and all of the court's opinion except that portion distinguishing *Lone Wolf.* He would have held *Lone Wolf's* principles inapplicable to this case because Congress had not created a record showing that it had considered the compensation afforded the Sioux under the 1877 Act to be adequate consideration for the Black Hills. He did not believe that *Lone Wolf* could be distinguished on the ground that it involved an action for injunctive relief rather than a claim for just compensation. 220 Ct. Cl., at 474–475, 601 F. 2d, at 1175–1176.

Judge Bennett, joined by Judge Kunzig, dissented. The dissenters would have read *Lone Wolf* broadly to hold that it was within Congress' constitutional power to dispose of tribal property without regard to good faith or the amount of compensation given. "The law we should apply is that once Congress has, through

negotiation or statute, recognized the Indian tribes' rights in the property, has disposed of it, and has given value to the Indians for it, that is the end of the matter." 220 Ct. Cl., at 486, 601 F. 2d, at 1182.

[22] In response to a question from the bench, Government counsel stated:

"I think Congress is entitled to say, 'You may have another opportunity to litigate your lawsuit.'" Tr. of Oral Arg. 20.

[23] Representative Gudger of North Carolina persistently argued the view that the amendment unconstitutionally interfered with the powers of the Judiciary. He dissented from the Committee Report in support of the amendment's enactment, stating:

"I do not feel that when the Federal Judiciary has adjudicated a matter through appellate review and no error has been found by the Supreme Court of the United States in the application by the lower court (in this instance the Court of Claims) of the doctrine of res judicata or collateral estoppel that the Congress of the United States should enact legislation which has the effect of reversing the decision of the Judiciary." H. R. Rep. No. 95-529, p. 17 (1977).

Representative Gudger stated that he could support a bill to grant a special appropriation to the Sioux Nation, acknowledging that it was for the purpose of extinguishing Congress' moral obligation arising from the Black Hills claim, "but I cannot justify in my own mind this exercise of congressional review of a judicial decision which I consider contravenes our exclusively legislative responsibility under the separation of powers doctrine." *Id.,* at 18.

The Congressman, in the House debates, elaborated upon his views on the constitutionality of the amendment. He stated that the amendment would create "a real and serious departure from the separation-of-powers doctrine, which I think should continue to govern us and has governed us in the past." 124 Cong. Rec. 2953 (1978). He continued:

"I submit that this bill has the precise and exact effect of reversing a decision of the Court of Claims which has heretofore been sustained by the Supreme Court of the United States. Thus, it places the Congress of the United States in the position of reviewing and reversing a judicial decision in direct violation of the separation-of-powers doctrine so basic to our tripartite form of government.

"I call to your attention that, in this instance, we are not asked to change the law, applicable uniformly to all cases of like nature throughout the land, but that this bill proposes to change the application of the law with respect to one case only. In doing this, we are not legislating, we are adjudicating. Moreover, we are performing the adjudicatory function with respect to a case on which the Supreme Court of the United States has acted. Thus, in this instance, we propose to reverse the decision of the Supreme Court of our land." *Ibid.*

Representative Gudger's views on the effect of the amendment vis-a-vis the independent powers of the Judiciary were not shared by his colleagues. Representative Roncalio stated:

"I want to emphasize that the bill does not make a congressional determination of whether or not the United States violated the fifth amendment. It does not say that the Sioux are entitled to the interest on the $17,500,000 award. It says that the court will review the facts and law in the case and determine that question." *Id.,* at 2954.

Representative Roncalio also informed the House that Congress in the past had enacted legislation waiving the defense of res judicata in private claims cases, and had done so twice with respect to Indian claims. *Ibid.* He mentioned the Act of Mar. 3, 1881, 21 Stat. 504 (which actually waived the effect of a prior award made to the Choctaw Nation by the Senate), and the Act of Feb. 7, 1925, 43 Stat. 812 (authorizing the Court of Claims and the Supreme Court to consider claims of the Delaware Tribe "de novo, upon a legal and equitable basis, and without regard to any decision, finding, or settlement heretofore had in respect of any such claims"). Both those enactments were also brought to the attention of a Senate Subcommittee in hearings on this amendment conducted during the previous legislative session. See Hearing on S. 2780 before the Subcommittee on Indian Affairs of the Senate Committee on Interior and Insular Affairs, 94th Cong., 2d Sess., 16–17 (1976) (letter from Morris Thompson, Commissioner of Indian Affairs). The enactments referred to by Representative Roncalio were construed, respectively, in *Choctaw Nation* v. *United States,* 119 U. S. 1, 29–32 (1886), and *Delaware Tribe* v. *United States,* 74 Ct. Cl. 368 (1932).

Representative Pressler also responded to Representative Gudger's interpretation of the proposed amendment, arguing that "[w]e are, indeed, here asking for a review and providing the groundwork for a review. I do not believe that we would be reviewing a decision; indeed, the same decision might be reached." 124 Cong. Rec. 2955 (1978). Earlier, Representative Meeds clearly had articulated the prevailing congressional view on the effect of the proposed amendment. After summarizing the history of the Black Hills litigation, he stated:

"I go through that rather complicated history for the purpose of pointing out to the Members that the purpose of this legislation is not to decide the matter on the merits. That is still for the court to do. The purpose of this legislation is only to waive the defense of res judicata and to waive this technical defense, as we have done in a number of other instances in this body, so this most important claim can get before the courts again and can be decided without a technical defense and on the merits." *Id.,* at 2388.

See also S. Rep. No. 95-112, p. 6 (1977) ("The enactment of [the amendment] is needed to waive certain legal prohibitions so that the Sioux tribal claim may be considered on its merits before an appropriate judicial forum"); H. R. Rep. No. 95-529, p. 6 (1977) ("The enactment of [the amendment] is needed to waive certain technical legal defenses so that the Sioux tribal claim may be considered on its merits before an appropriate judicial forum").

[24] The joint resolution at issue in *Nock* also limited the amount of the judgment that the Court of Claims could award Nock to a sum that had been established in a report of the Solicitor of the Treasury to the Senate. See 14 Stat. 608. The court rejected the Government's argument that the Constitution had not vested

in Congress "such discretion to fetter or circumscribe the course of justice." See 2 Ct. Cl., at 455. The court reasoned that this limitation on the amount of the claimant's recovery was a valid exercise of Congress' power to condition waivers of the sovereign immunity of the United States. "[I]t would be enough to say that the defendants cannot be sued except with their own consent; and Congress have the same power to give this consent to a second action as they had to give it to a first." *Id.,* at 458.

Just because we have addressed our attention to the ancient Court of Claims' decision in *Nock,* it should not be inferred that legislative action of the type at issue here is a remnant of the far-distant past. Special jurisdictional Acts waiving affirmative defenses of the United States to legal claims, and directing the Court of Claims to resolve the merits of those claims, are legion. See *Mizokami* v. *United States,* 188 Ct. Cl. 736, 740–741, and nn. 1 and 2, 414 F. 2d 1375, 1377, and nn. 1 and 2 (1969) (collecting cases). A list of cases, in addition to those discussed in the text, that have recognized or acted upon Congress' power to waive the defense of res judicata to claims against the United States follows (the list is not intended to be exhaustive): *United States* v. *Grant,* 110 U. S. 225 (1884); *Lamborn & Co.* v. *United States,* 106 Ct. Cl. 703, 724–728, 65 F. Supp. 569, 576–578 (1946); *Menominee Tribe* v. *United States,* 101 Ct. Cl. 10, 19 (1944); *Richardson* v. *United States,* 81 Ct. Cl. 948, 956–957 (1935); *Delaware Tribe* v. *United States,* 74 Ct. Cl. 368 (1932); *Garrett* v. *United States,* 70 Ct. Cl. 304, 310–312 (1930).

In *Richardson,* the Court of Claims observed:

"The power of Congress by special act to waive any defense, either legal or equitable, which the Government may have to a suit in this court, as it did in the *Nock* and *Cherokee Nation cases,* has never been questioned. The reports of the court are replete with cases where Congress, impressed with the equitable justice of claims which have been rejected by the court on legal grounds, has, by special act, waived defenses of the Government which prevented recovery and conferred jurisdiction on the court to again adjudicate the case. In such instances the court proceeded in conformity with the provisions of the act of reference and in cases, too numerous for citation here, awarded judgments to claimants whose claims had previously been rejected." 81 Ct. Cl., at 957.

Two similar decisions by the United States Court of Appeals for the Eighth Circuit are of interest. Both involved the constitutionality of a joint resolution that set aside dismissals of actions brought under the World War Veterans' Act, 1924, 38 U. S. C. § 445 (1952 ed.), and authorized the reinstatement of those war-risk insurance disability claims. The Court of Appeals found no constitutional prohibition against a congressional waiver of an adjudication in the Government's favor, or against conferring upon claimants against the United States the right to have their cases heard again on the merits. See *James* v. *United States,* 87 F. 2d 897, 898 (1937); *United States* v. *Hossmann,* 84 F. 2d 808, 810 (1936). The court relied, in part, on the holding in *Cherokee Nation,* and the sovereign immunity rationale applied in *Nock.*

[25] Before completing our analysis of this Court's precedents in this area, we turn to the question whether the holdings in *Cherokee Nation, Nock,* and *Pope,* might have been based on views, once held by this Court, that the Court of Claims was not, in all respects, an Art. III court, and that claims against the United States were not within Art. III's extension of "judicial Power" to "Controversies to which the United States shall be a Party." U. S. Const., Art. III, § 2, cl. 1. See *Williams* v. *United States,* 289 U. S. 553 (1933).

Pope itself would seem to dispel any such conclusion. See 323 U. S., at 12–14. Moreover, Mr. Justice Harlan's plurality opinion announcing the judgment of the Court in *Glidden Co.* v. *Zdanok,* 370 U. S. 530 (1962), lays that question to rest. In *Glidden,* the plurality observed that "it is probably true that Congress devotes a more lively attention to the work performed by the Court of Claims, and that it has been more prone to modify the jurisdiction assigned to that court." *Id.,* at 566. But they concluded that that circumstance did not render the decisions of the Court of Claims legislative in character, nor, impliedly, did those instances of "lively attention" constitute impermissible interferences with the Court of Claims' judicial functions.

"Throughout its history the Court of Claims has frequently been given jurisdiction by special act to award recovery for breach of what would have been, on the part of an individual, at most a moral obligation. . . . Congress has waived the benefit of *res judicata, Cherokee Nation v. United States, 270 U. S. 476, 486,* and of defenses based on the passage of time. . . .

"In doing so, as this Court has uniformly held, Congress has enlisted the aid of judicial power whose exercise is amenable to appellate review here. . . . Indeed the Court has held that Congress may for reasons adequate to itself confer bounties upon persons and, by consenting to suit, convert their moral claim into a legal one enforceable by litigation in an undoubted constitutional court. *United States v. Realty Co., 163 U. S. 427.*

"The issue was settled beyond peradventure in *Pope v. United States, 323 U. S. 1.* There the Court held that for Congress to direct the Court of Claims to entertain a claim theretofore barred for any legal reason from recovery—as, for instance, by the statute of limitations, or because the contract had been drafted to exclude such claims—was to invoke the use of judicial power, notwithstanding that the task might involve no more than computation of the sum due. . . . After this decision it cannot be doubted that when Congress transmutes a moral obligation into a legal one by specially consenting to suit, it authorizes the tribunal that hears the case to perform a judicial function." *Id.,* at 566–567.

The Court in *Glidden* held that, at least since 1953, the Court of Claims has been an Art. III court. See *id.,* at 585–589 (opinion concurring in result). In his opinion concurring in the result, Mr. Justice Clark did not take issue with the plurality's view that suits against the United States are "Controversies to which the United States shall be a Party," within the meaning of Art. III. Compare *370 U. S., at 562–565 (plurality opinion),* with *id.,* at 586–587 (opinion concurring in result).

[26] It should be recognized at the outset that the inquiry presented by this case is different from that confronted in the more typical of our recent "taking" decisions. *E. g., Kaiser Aetna* v. *United States,* 444 U. S. 164 (1979); *Penn Central Transp. Co.* v. *New York City,* 438 U. S. 104 (1978). In those cases the Court has sought to "determin[e] when 'justice and fairness' require that economic injuries caused by public action be compensated by the government, rather than remain disproportionately concentrated on a few persons." *Penn Central,* 438 U. S., at 124. Here, there is no doubt that the Black Hills were "taken" from the Sioux in a way that wholly deprived them of their property rights to that land. The question presented is whether Congress was acting under circumstances in which that "taking" implied an obligation to pay just compensation, or whether it was acting pursuant to its unique powers to manage and control tribal property as the guardian of Indian welfare, in which event the Just Compensation Clause would not apply.

[27] This aspect of the *Lone Wolf* holding, often reaffirmed, see, *e. g., Rosebud Sioux Tribe v. Kneip,* 430 U. S. 584, 594 (1977), is not at issue in this case. The Sioux do not claim that Congress was without power to take the Black Hills from them in contravention of the Fort Laramie Treaty of 1868. They claim only that Congress could not do so inconsistently with the command of the Fifth Amendment: "nor shall private property be taken for public use, without just compensation."

[28] For this reason, the Government does not here press *Lone Wolf* to its logical limits, arguing instead that its "strict rule" that the management and disposal of tribal lands is a political question, "has been relaxed in recent years to allow review under the Fifth Amendment rational-basis test." Brief for United States 55, n. 46. The Government relies on *Delaware Tribal Business Comm. v. Weeks,* 430 U. S., at 84–85, and *Morton v. Mancari,* 417 U. S. 535, 555 (1974), as establishing a rational-basis test for determining whether Congress, in a given instance, confiscated Indian property or engaged merely in its power to manage and dispose of tribal lands in the Indians' best interests. But those cases, which establish a standard of review for judging the constitutionality of Indian legislation under the Due Process Clause of the Fifth Amendment, do not provide an apt analogy for resolution of the issue presented here—whether Congress' disposition of tribal property was an exercise of its power of eminent domain or its power of guardianship. As noted earlier, n. 27, *supra,* the Sioux concede the constitutionality of Congress' unilateral abrogation of the Fort Laramie Treaty. They seek only a holding that the Black Hills "were appropriated by the United States in circumstances which involved an implied undertaking by it to make just compensation to the tribe." *United States* v. *Creek Nation,* 295 U. S. 103, 111 (1935). The rational-basis test proffered by the Government would be ill-suited for use in determining whether such circumstances were presented by the events culminating in the passage of the 1877 Act.

[29] Of course, it has long been held that the taking by the United States of "unrecognized" or "aboriginal" Indian title is

not compensable under the Fifth Amendment. *Tee-Hit-Ton Indians* v. *United States,* 348 U. S. 272, 285 (1955). The principles we set forth today are applicable only to instances in which "Congress by treaty or other agreement has declared that thereafter Indians were to hold the lands permanently." *Id.,* at 277. In such instances, "compensation must be paid for subsequent taking." *Id.,* at 277–278.

[30] An examination of this standard reveals that, contrary to the Government's assertion, the Court of Claims in this case did not base its finding of a taking solely on Congress' failure in 1877 to state affirmatively that the "assets" given the Sioux in exchange for the Black Hills were equivalent in value to the land surrendered. Rather, the court left open the possibility that, in an appropriate case, a mere assertion of congressional good faith in setting the terms of a forced surrender of treaty-protected lands could be overcome by objective indicia to the contrary. And, in like fashion, there may be instances in which the consideration provided the Indians for surrendered treaty lands was so patently adequate and fair that Congress' failure to state the obvious would not result in the finding of a compensable taking.

To the extent that the Court of Claims' standard, in this respect, departed from the original formulation of the *Fort Berthold* test, see 220 Ct. Cl., at 486–487, 601 F. 2d, at 1182–1183 (dissenting opinion), such a departure was warranted. The Court of Claims' present formulation of the test, which takes into account the adequacy of the consideration given, does little more than reaffirm the ancient principle that the determination of the measure of just compensation for a taking of private property "is a judicial and not a legislative question." *Monongahela Navigation Co.* v. *United States,* 148 U. S. 312, 327 (1893).

[31] The 1877 Act, see *supra,* at [1256–1257], and n. 14, purported to provide the Sioux with "all necessary aid to assist the said Indians in the work of civilization," and "to furnish to them schools and instruction in mechanical and agricultural arts, as provided for by the treaty of 1868." 19 Stat. 256. The Court of Claims correctly concluded that the first item "was so vague that it cannot be considered as constituting a meaningful or significant element of payment by the United States." 220 Ct. Cl., at 458, 601 F. 2d, at 1166. As for the second, it "gave the Sioux nothing to which they were not already entitled [under the 1868 treaty]." *Ibid.*

The Government has placed some reliance in this Court on the fact that the 1877 Act extended the northern boundaries of the reservation by adding some 900,000 acres of grazing lands. See n. 14, *supra.* In the Court of Claims, however, the Government did "not contend . . . that the transfer of this additional land was a significant element of the consideration the United States gave for the Black Hills." 220 Ct. Cl., at 453, n. 3, 601 F. 2d, at 1163, n. 3. And Congress obviously did not intend the extension of the reservation's northern border to constitute consideration for the property rights surrendered by the Sioux. The extension was effected in that article of the Act redefining the reservation's borders; it was not mentioned in the article which stated the consideration given for

the Sioux' "cession of territory and rights." See 19 Stat. 255–256. Moreover, our characterizing the 900,000 acres as assets given the Sioux in consideration for the property rights they ceded would not lead us to conclude that the terms of the exchange were "so patently adequate and fair" that a compensable taking should not have been found. See n. 30, *supra.*

Finally, we note that the Government does not claim that the Indian Claims Commission and the Court of Claims incorrectly valued the property rights taken by the 1877 Act by failing to consider the extension of the northern border. Rather, the Government argues only that the 900,000 acres should be considered, along with the obligation to provide rations, in determining whether the Act, viewed in its entirety, constituted a goodfaith effort on the part of Congress to promote the Sioux' welfare. See Brief for United States 73, and n. 58.

[32] The dissenting opinion suggests, *post,* at [1270], that the factual findings of the Indian Claims Commission, the Court of Claims, and now this Court, are based upon a "revisionist" view of history. The dissent fails to identify which materials quoted herein or relied upon by the Commission and the Court of Claims fit that description. The dissent's allusion to historians "writing for the purpose of having their conclusions or observations inserted in the reports of congressional committees," *post,* at [1270], is also puzzling because, with respect to this case, we are unaware that any such historian exists.

The primary sources for the story told in this opinion are the factual findings of the Indian Claims Commission and the Court of Claims. A reviewing court generally will not discard such findings because they raise the specter of creeping revisionism, as the dissent would have it, but will do so only when they are clearly erroneous and unsupported by the record. No one, including the Government, has ever suggested that the factual findings of the Indian Claims Commission and the Court of Claims fail to meet that standard of review.

A further word seems to be in order. The dissenting opinion does not identify a single author, nonrevisionist, neorevisionist, or otherwise, who takes the view of the history of the cession of the Black Hills that the dissent prefers to adopt, largely, one assumes, as an article of faith. Rather, the dissent relies on the historical findings contained in the decision rendered by the Court of Claims in 1942. That decision, and those findings, are not before this Court today. Moreover, the holding of the Court of Claims in 1942, to the extent the decision can be read as reaching the merits of the Sioux' taking claim, was based largely on the conclusive presumption of good faith toward the Indians which that court afforded to Congress' actions of 1877. See 97 Ct. Cl., at 669–673, 685. The divergence of results between that decision and the judgment of the Court of Claims affirmed today, which the dissent would attribute to historical revisionism, see *post,* at [1270], is more logically explained by the fact that the former decision was based on an erroneous *legal* interpretation of this Court's opinion in *Lone Wolf.* See Part IV-B, *supra.*

[33] We find further support for this conclusion in Congress' 1974 amendment to § 2 of the Indian Claims Commission Act, 25 U. S. C. § 70a. See n. 17, *supra.* That amendment provided that in determining offsets, "expenditures for food, rations, or provisions shall not be deemed payments on the claim." The Report of the Senate Committee on Interior and Insular Affairs, which accompanied this amendment, made two points that are pertinent here. First, it noted that "[a]lthough couched in general terms, this amendment is directed to one basic objective—expediting the Indian Claims Commission's disposition of the famous Black Hills case." S. Rep. No. 93-863, p. 2 (1974) (incorporating memorandum prepared by the Sioux Tribes). Second, the Committee observed:

"The facts are, as the Commission found, that the United States disarmed the Sioux and denied them their traditional hunting areas in an effort to force the sale of the Black Hills. Having violated the 1868 Treaty and having reduced the Indians to starvation, the United States should not now be in the position of saying that the rations it furnished constituted payment for the land which it took. In short, the Government committed two wrongs: first, it deprived the Sioux of their livelihood; secondly, it deprived the Sioux of their land. What the United States gave back in rations should not be stretched to cover both wrongs." *Id.,* at 4–5.

See also R. Billington, Introduction, in National Park Service, Soldier and Brave xiv (1963) ("The Indians suffered the humiliating defeats that forced them to walk the white man's road toward civilization. Few conquered people in the history of mankind have paid so dearly for their defense of a way of life that the march of progress had outmoded").

Source: *United States v. Sioux Nation,* 448 US 371, U.S. Supreme Court (1980).

Index